JIHADI POI

TORE HAMMING

# Jihadi Politics

## *The Global Jihadi Civil War 2014–2019*

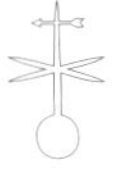

HURST & COMPANY, LONDON

First published in the United Kingdom in 2022 by
C. Hurst & Co. (Publishers) Ltd.,
New Wing, Somerset House, Strand, London, WC2R 1LA



A Cataloguing-in-Publication data record for this book is available from the British Library.

ISBN: 9781787387027

www.hurstpublishers.com

Printed in Great Britain by Bell and Bain Ltd, Glasgow

*Til Bent, min mor & mine piger*
*Ellen og Vera*

# CONTENTS

## PART FOUR
## MOVEMENT FRAGMENTATION, POLARISATION AND INTERNATIONALISATION



## PART FIVE
## BETWEEN PURITY AND PRAGMATISM



## PART SIX
## INTERNALISING FITNA

# TABLES AND FIGURES

*Tables*



*Figures*

# ACKNOWLEDGEMENTS

Since this book builds on my PhD dissertation, it only seems appropriate to begin with an academic acknowledgement to express my deep appreciation for some scholarly work that has been truly important for my academic evolution. This scholarship represents my introduction to the field of radical Islam and the steps I have taken down the ladder of militant Islamist ideology. Stéphane Lacroix's book *Awakening Islam* was my first serious encounter with Salafism and how it relates to both more moderate and more militant ideological expressions. It was his research that first opened my mind to radical Islamic thought and ever since I started as a master student at Sciences Po in 2012, I have owed my academic trajectory and interests to him. It was Thomas Hegghammer's book *Jihad in Saudi Arabia* that opened my mind to militant Islamism. As an aspiring student focusing on Salafism, it was Hegghammer's book that captivated my interest in those actors committed to militancy as a legitimate and necessary methodology to instigate political change. Not only did the book present a convincing argument, but what also intrigued me was the methodology and style Hegghammer applied to study and explain Jihadi actors. Joas Wagemakers' book *A Quietist Jihadi* on Abu Muhammad al-Maqdisi turned my attention to ideology. It inspired me to pursue my inner geek, look for the nitty-gritty details in arguments and understand the importance of individuals vis-à-vis groups and movements. Finally, Nelly Lahoud's book *The Jihadis' Path to Self-Destruction* introduced me to the intricacies of debate and contestation within Jihadism and by doing so it kick-started a fascination that evolved to a deep dive into the much-neglected debates and conflicts that threaten the Jihadi project from the inside. These four books are all scholarly masterpieces and while I have no naive ambitions to produce anything of a resembling quality, I feel obliged to extend my gratitude to the authors as they have been great sources of inspiration and guidance throughout my research. These books thus explain better than anything else my intellectual development from my entrance to Sciences Po in 2012 to the submission of my PhD at the European University Institute in 2020.

This book owes a lot to a much larger group of people, however. Firstly, the process of developing the idea and how it evolved into a finished dissertation has benefitted hugely from the guidance of my two supervisors Olivier Roy and Stéphane Lacroix, two pioneers of research on Islamism and its radical expressions. Besides inspiring through example, Olivier and Stéphane have generously helped with their advice and expertise, just as they have been strong sources of support throughout the process. Due to their vast experience doing fieldwork within related topics, I was lucky to learn a lot on how to identify and cultivate networks and how to approach the specific interviews. This provided me with important comfort to carry out some occasionally challenging work. An equal amount of appreciation goes to Maureen Lechleitner, who has been a tremendous help with all her institutional acumen, alleviating most of the hurdles that a researcher faces in the final part of the writing process. This is no minor feat, and I am deeply grateful for her assistance.

In the end, I would never have been able to do this research if the people I study had been unwilling to discuss the issues with me. For several reasons, interviewing Jihadis is full of challenges such as establishing contact, issues of how to conduct the interview and convincing them to talk to someone that is often portrayed as their enemy. Nonetheless, these discussions—whether in person or through digital platforms—have been essential to the quality of the dissertation, just as they have been a source of light in the otherwise rather gloomy world of researching violence. Hence, I want to thank all the people that agreed to meet and talk with me. Several of them are considered extremists—even terrorists—which places certain security constraints on them, but they always opened their doors and welcomed me into their homes and introduced me to their families, while making me much more knowledgeable about the Sunni Jihadi movement and its internal dynamics. Visiting Sheikh Abu Qatada during Eid al-Fitr greatly expanded my familiarity with Jordanian sweets and my coffee preferences, since I was served delicious and tasteful Arabic coffee. I also appreciate his advice on where to find the best jalabiyya in Zarqa, although it takes more than a piece of clothing for a blond Scandinavian to resemble a local in Jordan. I also extend my gratitude to Abu Qatada's student Abu Mahmoud for his kindness and openness during the many hours spent sipping coffee in West London's coffee shops.

During the PhD research, I have been fortunate to have spent time at incredible academic institutions that not only offered inspiring settings to pursue academic work but also exposed me to communities of truly fascinating professors and researchers. Situated in the picturesque hills between Florence and Fiesole, the European University Institute offered a unique setting to contemplate and devote oneself to research. There I learned tremendously from my supervisor Olivier Roy, along with an incredibly talented cohort of researchers. The evenings spent among the members of the Wine Society were particularly enlightening. I am also grateful for the opportunity to have spent time as a visiting researcher at Sciences Po and Oxford University. Few places offer more stimulating academic environments and smarter people to exchange ideas with. Paris, especially, will always be my academic home, while the pubs in Oxford's winding streets turned out to be surprisingly productive workstations.

For large parts of the research process my closest colleagues were a small group comprised of some of the most talented and knowledgeable researchers and journalists working on Jihadism. It was an incredibly helpful forum in which to exchange ideas and receive feedback from a group of people who were often more knowledgeable about al-Qaida and the Islamic State than the groups themselves. Jazakum allahu khayran to all of you—Pieter van Ostaeyen, Aymenn Jawad al-Tamimi, Wassim Nasr, Aaron Zelin,

Pieter Nanninga, Moustafa Ayad, Guy van Vlierden, Daniele Raineri, Charlie Winter and Amar Amarasingam!

Besides this group, a large group of people—researchers, journalists, professionals, and friends—have contributed one way or another. Some were so kind as to share important material with me, while others helped me with their knowledge, encouragement and support. I am particularly grateful for those who spent their valuable time reading chapter drafts and provided valuable advice and comments, all of which made this research more insightful and concise. This includes Jérôme Drevon, Aymenn Jawad al-Tamimi, Kévin Jackson, Pieter van Ostaeyen, Craig Whiteside, Lars Erslev Andersen, Ibn Nabih and Mona Kanwal Sheikh. I would also like to extend my gratitude to several colleagues including Jérôme Drevon (few were more supportive than you), Cole Bunzel, Felix Kuehn, Charles Lister, Romain Caillet, Thomas Hegghammer, Joas Wagemakers, Maja Greenwood, Jacob Zenn, Shiraz Maher, Will McCants, Sergio Altuna, Paweł Wójcik, Michael Krona, Anne Stenersen, Sam Heller, Mina al-Lami, Nagieb Khaja, Thomas Joscelyn, Laurence Bindner, Adam Hoffman, Jean-Charles Brisard, Colin Clarke, Paul Cruickshank, @Switched, Hetav Rojan, Jennifer Cafarella and Leah Farrall. Special thanks must be given to Cole Bunzel and Aymenn Jawad al-Tamimi for digging up esoteric ideological material and for making it accessible and understandable to mortals.

Also, I benefitted greatly from the assistance and support of my friends. Going back to our first day as students at Sciences Po's master program in International Security, Lahib Higel, you have been a dear friend. Not only did I learn from almost every single conversation with you (not least about Iraq), but your continuous encouragement also often helped me find the spirit to continue the work during those tough periods that all PhD students encounter. Christian Freudlsperger, another companion from the days at Rue Saint-Guillaume, you have similarly been a major source of inspiration and support through your own dedication to academic work and your constant belief in me. Besides being a close friend, Theis Hjalte Thorn Jakobsen, you assisted with your digital expertise. Without your help, this research would be void of illustrations. Finally, Alaa Saad, you helped to arrange my stays at IFPO Amman and to guide me through the city's culinary scene. Over the years, you have become a close friend, and your translation skills have been an invaluable help to decipher the philosophical codes of Jihadi ideologues.

Yet I owe my biggest thanks to Kathrine, Ellen and Vera. This dissertation has not been an ordinary job for the past five years but rather an obsession that rarely fit with a conventional 37-hour working week. This is partly because I never truly managed to impose the necessary restrictions upon myself, and also because following Jihadi media and responding to online conversations with Jihadists occurred around the clock. More than anyone else, you have suffered from this absurd working routine, trips around the world, the occasional mood swings that most PhD students experience, stacks of Jihadi propaganda flooding the home and anashid playing from the speakers—most often tolerating it, but from time to time also pushing me to make changes. Your mere presence made it all easier and enjoyable. Once so unthinkable to me, but eventually it would only take a smile on Ellen and Vera's faces to make Jihadis fade into total insignificance. Thank you.

# ABBREVIATIONS

| | |
|---|---|
| AQAP | Al-Qaida in the Arabian Peninsula |
| AQI | Al-Qaida in Iraq |
| AQIM | Al-Qaida in the Islamic Maghreb |
| AQIS | Al-Qaida in the Indian Subcontinent |
| HTS | Hayat Tahrir al-Sham |
| IMU | Islamic Movement of Uzbekistan |
| ISGS | Islamic State's Greater Sahara Province |
| ISI | Islamic State in Iraq |
| ISIS | Islamic State in Iraq and Sham |
| ISKP | Islamic State's Khorasan Province |
| ISL | Islamic State's Libya Province |
| ISS | Islamic State's Somalia Province |
| ISY | Islamic State's Yemen Province |
| ISWA | Islamic State's West Africa Province |
| JFS | Jabhat Fatah al-Sham |
| MSC | Mujahideen Shura Council |
| SJM | Sunni Jihadi Movement |
| TIP | Turkistan Islamic Party |
| TTP | Tehreek-e-Taliban Pakistan |

# VIGNETTES

## [THE PAST]

*'Ikhwan Muslimin was very far from the fighting in Afghanistan, but in Jalalabad something significant happened. During the Jalalabad fight in 1989 and in 1990, strange comments were coming from Ikhwan Muslimin circles in Peshawar. They were giving warnings to the leaders of al-Qaeda. They said, "We will never let Abu Abdullah [Usama bin Laden] be the leader of the Arabs, or the hero of the Arabs, which he tried to build himself as when he went to Jalalabad."'*[1]

Mustafa Hamid

On July 5–7, 1989 al-Qaida and its militant allies suffered a striking defeat in the battle of Jalalabad in eastern Afghanistan. It was only two years after the imperious victory at Jaji in which Usama Bin Laden's nascent al-Qaida movement located at al-Masadah camp defeated an offensive by Russian special forces. In Jalalabad, however, the militants quickly succumbed to the Afghan army. Although the battle for Jalalabad continued until 1992, it was effectively lost in the three-day period in July 1989, and it turned out to have critical consequences for the future of the Sunni Jihadi movement. The immediate aftermath of the defeat witnessed a leadership vacuum owing to the fate of the two dominant figures within the Sunni Jihadi movement: Abdallah Azzam and Bin Laden (the former was assassinated, while the latter left for Saudi Arabia). Before their 'disappearance', however, both told their followers to retreat from the battlefield. Removed from the ongoing fighting and deprived of two major sources of authority, the Jihadi youth grew increasingly rebellious towards its leadership. These emerging tensions would time and again in the following decades pose a severe threat to the authority of al-Qaida and to the cohesion of the Sunni Jihadi movement. Although Bin Laden did finally emerge as the hero of Muslims with Jihadi inclinations, the broader Jihadi trend has suffered from critical cleavages since its modern re-emergence in the 1960s. On several occasions, and in geographical arenas ranging from the Afghan mountains to the metropolis of London, fault lines between Jihadis have been expressed through debates and infighting. In Algeria, the election of Djamel Zitouni in 1994 as the new amir of the *Groupe Islamique Armé* (GIA) not only signalled the emergence of an increasingly violent campaign against the group's external opponents and the wider Algerian society but also caused hitherto unseen tensions between Jihadi groups. The stance of Zitouni and his successor was that Jihadis not fighting in the ranks of GIA were opponents, irrespective of whether they were actually supportive of the GIA cause. This led the group to start killing both competing militant actors within Algeria and also a larger contingent of Libyan Jihadis sent from Sudan to assist Zitouni's group. Even Bin Laden did not avoid the enmity of the GIA leadership. In an account of a visit by Redouane Makador, GIA's mufti, to Bin Laden in Sudan in late 1995, the mufti said, 'No one is to get involved in Algeria without going through us', and continued, 'This is what will happen if they do', drawing his finger across his throat.[2]

## [THE PRESENT]

> *'And here we are extending our hands to you again, to be the worthy successor to the best predecessor; for the shaykh Usama bin Ladin united the Mujahidin upon one word, while you [Ayman al Zawahiri] disunited them, split them and dispersed them in total dispersion.'*[3]
>
> Abu Muhammad al-Shami al-Adnani

On the February 3, 2014, al-Qaida disowned what was then known as the Islamic State of Iraq and Sham and thereby formalised a direct confrontation and competition between the two groups that had already been ignited months before. Not only was it the first time an al-Qaida affiliate had left the network, it was also the first time a *fitna* (conflict) of this magnitude had occurred within Sunni Jihadism with repercussions for the entire Jihadi movement. With the announcement of the Islamic caliphate on June 29, 2014, Abu Muhammad al-Shami al-Adnani, the late spokesperson of the Islamic State, declared that Abu Bakr al-Husseini al-Qurashi al-Baghdadi

> is the imam and khalifa for Muslims everywhere (…) it is incumbent upon all Muslims to pledge allegiance to the khalifa Ibrahim and support him. The legality of all emirates, groups, states, and organizations, becomes null by the expansion of the khilafa's authority and arrival of its troops to their areas.[4]

Claiming the title of *amir al-mu'iminin* (commander of the faithful), al-Baghdadi directly challenged the dominant position of the al-Qaida network within Sunni Jihadism and the authority of its leader Ayman al-Zawahiri, who had inherited the leadership of the global Jihad movement after the death of Bin Laden. As is well known, the split between al-Qaida and the Islamic State started with a dispute between al-Baghdadi and Abu Muhammad al-Julani, leader of Jabhat al-Nusra, in the context of the Syrian civil war, but it quickly took on a global character. On several occasions, al-Zawahiri stepped in to settle the emerging dispute, but with little success. According to the Islamic State, its caliphate was indeed the promise of Allah, and al-Qaida had so critically deviated from the correct Jihadi *manhaj* (methodology) that it was no longer to be trusted as the vanguard of the Muslim nation. The Islamic State quickly managed to overtake al-Qaida and to establish itself as the premier Sunni Jihadi group, but in 2015, as the international coalition intervened, the caliphate's success began to dwindle while al-Qaida was once again on the rise. The crucial question, however, is how several years of infighting and delegitimizing critique between Jihadi groups affected the broader cohesion of the movement.

## [THE FUTURE]

*'The Kharijites' rigid doctrinal beliefs and the accusations of takfir that they declared against each other and which led to internal in-fighting serve to shed light on the possible fate of modern jihadis. Indeed, the internal in-fighting of the Kharijites was the main factor that led to the destruction of their militant groups, so much so that when the seventh century Governor al-Hajjaj ordered his military commander al-Muhallab to pursue fighting the Kharijites, al-Muhallab calmly responded: I see no point in fighting them since they themselves are fighting each other. If they carry on like this, that is [after all] what we desire, for therein lies their destruction (halak).'*[5]

Nelly Lahoud

Like the historic *Khawarij*, a purist understanding of religion and an emphasis on extreme purity of faith is both the strength of contemporary Jihadis but also their weakness. Khawarij and Jihadis alike have a strong foundation in the concept of *al-wala' wa-l-bara'* (loyalty and separation) that is strongly connected with the praxis of *takfir* (excommunication). This eventually led to the self-destruction of the Khawarij and, as Nelly Lahoud writes, Jihadism is similarly 'plagued with internal differences that have the potential to destroy it from within.' Contemporary Jihadis have continuously contested each other during the previous four decades and are caught up in infighting to the extent that they are now involved in a total war. Paradoxically, they appear stronger than ever before. How can that be, when they, like the Khawarij, should be on the path to self-destruction because of this internal contestation? Is it simply a matter of time? Probably not. The Jihadi movement is afflicted with fragmentation that will affect its cohesion in years to come, but it will survive, having learned to navigate internal conflict strategically and, more generally, to act pragmatically. This is something the Khawarij were incapable of doing. But for the future leaders of the Jihadi current, the great task of promoting unity lies ahead.

## Figure 1: Map of the Territorial Presence of al-Qaida and the Islamic States

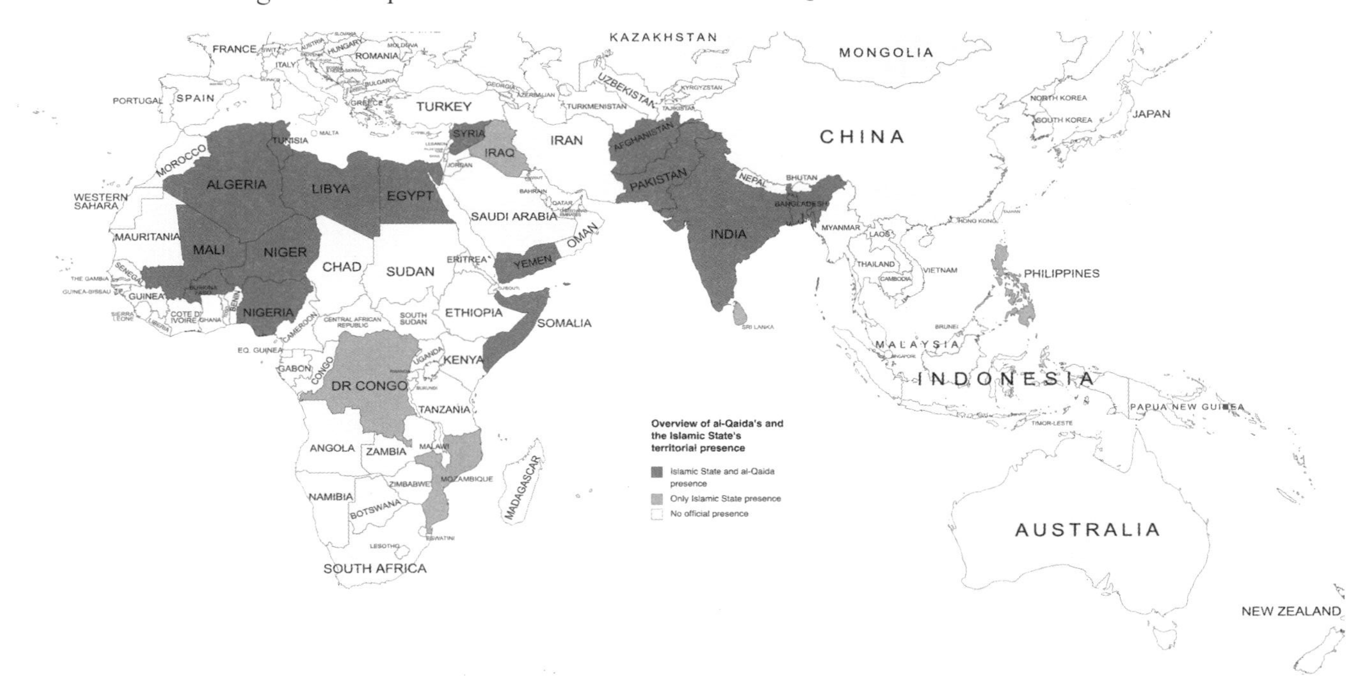

*"For the bearers of new ideas, each preceding period seems no more than a gross deviation from the correct path, an historical aberration, a sum of errors, the result of a fortuitous combination of theoretical mystifications."*

Leon Trotsky
*Our Political Task*, 1904

*"And if two factions among the believers should fight, then make settlement between the two. But if one of them oppresses the other, then fight against the one that oppresses until it returns to the ordinance of Allah. And if it returns, then make settlement between them in justice and act justly. Indeed, Allah loves those who act justly."*

Qur'an 49:9

# INTRODUCTION

*It was late 1988 in Peshawar. Usama Bin Laden was in his car with Abdallah Azzam and Abdallah Anas. The driver was a Syrian named Abu Qutaiba. The four were listening to the radio when the muazzin started to make the adhan. Azzam told Abu Qutaiba to turn off the radio so they could listen to the call, but in a prompt reaction, Bin Laden, who was in the front seat of the car, said: 'Leave the radio on.'*[1]

In the afternoon of February 23, 2014, two armed men approached a base of the Jihadi group Ahrar al-Sham in the al-Halq area of Aleppo on foot, speaking in local dialect.[2] When they reached the checkpoint in front of the base they suddenly opened fire, hurting and killing several of the fighters at the base, who were slow to react. Inside was Mohammed al-Bahaiya, better known as Abu Khalid al-Suri, or, in the Syrian context, Abu Omeir al-Shami, a senior Ahrar al-Sham commander and the target of the operation. Under cover from his comrade, one of the two men managed to enter the base and, after climbing the stairs to the second floor, detonated his suicide vest, blowing himself up. The other was soon killed by Ahrar fighters returning fire. Whether al-Suri died from the explosion or the bullet that had already hit him remains unknown, but the announcement of his death in the very city he was born in sent shockwaves through the Jihadi milieu in Syria and abroad. With his impressive grey beard and imposingly corpulent frame, and a reputation gained from having fought on numerous Jihadi battlefields, it is no surprise that al-Suri had quickly turned into an icon of the Syrian Jihad. Although the Islamic State denied all accusations one week later, there remains little doubt that the two armed men were acting on its behalf.[3]

Because of his pedigree as an Afghan veteran and his close relations with Jihadi legends like Usama Bin Laden and Abu Musab al-Suri, Abu Khalid al-Suri had been trusted by al-Qaida leader Ayman al-Zawahiri to mediate the emerging conflict between Jabhat al-Nusra and the Islamic State. The month before his death he issued a statement, mainly coming across as a criticism, addressing the Islamic State, but no one could imagine the price he would soon pay for his words.[4] In a quick response to al-Suri's death, al-Nusra leader Abu Muhammad al-Julani responded with an ultimatum offering the Islamic State five days to halt all attacks against Syria's Jihadis or face retaliation. But as history shows, the Islamic State was just about to commence.

Bin Laden's innocent overruling of Azzam in Peshawar is an early example of a young and ambitious Jihadi challenging his mentor, and of the potential for rebellion inherent in Jihadism. However, the Islamic State's killing of al-Suri and its disobedience of its superiors in al-Qaida years later represent a critical escalation in the history of internal conflict among Jihadis. While al-Suri's death was a bombshell, it was also a signal of what was to come. The years that followed would see the intra-Jihadi conflict escalate and expand to unprecedented levels, with detrimental impact on the broader Jihadi movement. This escalation and expansion would go on to cause the death of more than 8,000 Jihadis at the hands of other Jihadis.

Despite its almost perpetual presence, immense impact and paradoxical character, internal conflict dynamics within the Jihadi movement have received little academic and analytical attention. Instead, Jihadi groups or the movement as a whole are most often treated as monoliths, mainly judged through the threat they pose. In the words of Kepel and Milelli, since its establishment al-Qaida has fought a 'war at the heart of Islam—a war of references, sources, and authority.'[5] While this war has traditionally been against non-Jihadi *outsiders*, this book tells the story of how this war has also moved inside the Jihadi movement, thus becoming the last stage in a cycle of enemy orientation starting with the armed struggle to depose local 'apostate' governments, moving on to the defence of Muslim lands threatened by non-Muslim invaders, then the offensive against the Western world, and finally the *internal enemy*.

### *Fratricidal Jihadis*

This book should be regarded as a history of intra-Jihadi conflict seen through the Jihadis' own lens. Primarily dealing with the conflict between al-Qaida, the Islamic State,[6] and related Jihadi groups, it covers the intra-group period leading up to the split between al-Qaida and its Iraqi affiliate (1999–2013), the split itself (2014) and the ensuing period of inter-group contestation and infighting (2014–19). The 2014–19 period is particularly important for the study of internal conflict dynamics within the Sunni Jihadi movement (SJM) for several reasons. Besides witnessing the most serious example of Jihadi infighting in modern history, it also involved two episodes of organisational division, an escalation from inter-group contestation to infighting and movement fragmentation and polarisation. This dedicated focus makes this book the first systematic attempt to enhance our shared understanding of intra-Jihadi contestation and fratricide.

The paradox driving the investigation rests on three assumptions. Firstly, on an ideological level, Jihadis share more than what divides them. Secondly, given that they are usually facing a superior enemy, it would seem reasonable to think that Jihadis would (often) gain more from cooperation than from infighting.[7] Thirdly, Jihadis are extremely isolated political actors with few other potential cooperative partners. The negative effects of infighting appear obvious: intra-Jihadi conflict diverts focus from their common enemy; it has a radicalising and polarising impact on the Jihadi movement; it *de*mobilises the Jihadi masses; and it leaves high numbers of their fighters dead. It has even been argued that it is the main reason they lose their wars.[8] So why do Jihadis debate with and fight each other? Would collaboration with likeminded associates against a common enemy not be a wiser strategy?

Asking the simple yet complex question '*Why* do Sunni Jihadi groups fight each other *when* they do?', the intention is to remedy some of the shortcomings in our understanding about why Jihadi groups split and engage in intra-movement competition and conflict, and to what extent such internal conflict affects movement cohesion.

Parallel examples of contestation, fragmentation and infighting within non-state actor movements illustrate that Jihadi infighting is not a unique phenomenon. Similar conflict dynamics have been observed in various other groups and movements: The Russian Communist Party, Algeria's nationalist movement in the 1950s,[9] Sri Lanka's Tamil factions,[10] the IRA,[11] ETA[12] and the Palestinian nationalist movement,[13] Kashmiri groups,[14] Algeria's Islamist factions in the 1990s,[15] and Islamists in Iraq in the 2000s.[16] But given their fear of internal conflict, or fitna, Jihadis should be different, since their loyalty is to their religion and to following the path of Allah rather than temporal political agendas. Why would these servants of God, one might ask, become the victims of counterproductive internal conflict that risks derailing their ambition of reaching a common social, political and religious objective, and one that is shared (apart from minor details)?

Notwithstanding, internal conflict has a long history within Islam and specifically within the SJM. It is inextricably related to the concept of fitna. Fitna is a term that has its origins in early Islamic sources, being mentioned in one form or another sixty times in the Quran with varying meaning ranging from 'trial' to 'insanity'.[17] Although the original meaning of fitna may be 'testing' or 'trial' in relation to the believer's faith, it also signifies sedition, civil strife or conflict within the Muslim community.[18] Fitna, understood as conflict, is generally perceived negatively by Muslims.[19] In normative Islamic theology, the dogma is to discourage rebellion and prohibit infighting while promoting the method of giving *advice* (nasiha).[20] Laying the groundwork for understanding the concept's importance in Islamic thought is the juridic maxim of the famous medieval Islamic theologian ibn Taymiyya, a highly revered figure among Jihadis, that *60 years of tyranny is better than one night of fitna*.

The concept has a long genealogy within Islam. The negative perception of the notion is not just based on the warnings in holy sources, but also on the experience of fitna in Muslim history. The first fitna in Islam, known as the *Great Schism* (al-fitna al-kubra), was provoked by the killing of Uthman, the third caliph after the prophet Muhammad, which led to infighting in the years 656–61.[21] In 656, Uthman's supporters, in an effort to revenge Uthman's death, commenced the *Battle of the Camel* against his successor, Ali ibn Abi Talib, whom they believed did too little to punish those responsible. While Ali left the battle victorious, the following year he would confront Muawiya ibn Abi Sufyan, the Governor of Damascus, in the *Battle of Siffin*. In a famous incident, Muawiya's forces allegedly fixed the Quran to their spears to encourage arbitration. When Ali accepted, a faction of his soldiers rebelled against him. They not only considered Muawiya and his forces apostates because of their rebellion against Ali, but with Ali's acceptance of arbitration, he and the majority of the prophet's companions (sahaba) would also become apostates since they were accepting an authority other than God. This faction would become known as the Khawarij (seceders) and would succeed in assassinating Ali in 661.[22] Soon after, in 680, a second fitna erupted when the sons of Zubayr ibn al-Awam and Ali rebelled against Yazid, the son of the late Muawiya. These early events of rebellion marked the end of political unity within Islam, leaving cleavages that remain to this day. They also crossed an important barrier that would open the door to future conflict.[23]

During the Abbasid and Umayyad caliphates, rebellion against political and religious authority continued and Muslim jurists, in response, developed a *law of rebellion* (ahkam al-bughat) consisting of legal stipulations governing the contexts in which lawful rebellion could be initiated and how rebels should be treated.[24] Because all infighting between Muslims is prohibited and considered fitna, the justification for modern intra-Jihadi conflict is intimately connected to the historical discourse and *law of rebellion*. In his excellent study of normative Islamic theology and the ahkam al-bughat, Khaled Abou el-Fadl outlines the juristic distinction between fighting *apostates* (murtaddin), *bandits* (muhabirun) and *rebels* (bughat)[25] which informs the legality of fighting the actor in question and decisions about the methods to be used.[26] While apostates and bandits can legitimately be killed, the conventional view among jurists is that rebels cannot be either killed or tortured.[27]

The first examples of fitna in Islamic history all took place on a community level, but fitna can also occur within smaller subsets of society and on its margins. In *The Neglected Duty*, Muhammad Abd al-Salam Faraj used the term *fitna* to legitimise attacks against the Egyptian regime.[28] In Afghanistan, it was used by the militant Islamists themselves to describe the civil war that broke out in the 1990s. And most recently, Jihadis have used it as a label to describe the contemporary infighting that erupted in 2013. Applying the concept of fitna to these events is thus partly legitimised by Jihadis' own use of the term to describe current events. While a historical legacy is obviously involved here, it also indicates how seriously Jihadis view the infighting; as God's trial to test their faith through fighting former brothers-in-arms who have deviated from the correct path.

Besides threatening unity and God's commandments,[29] what essentially makes fitna so sensitive is that it involves killing other Muslims *or* declaring others as apostates to legitimise their killing. Jihadis are very explicit about the sanctity of Muslim blood and the sensitivity of the notion of *takfir* (excommunication),[30] which are issues that have preoccupied several Jihadi ideologues.[31] Traditionally, Jihadis have been concerned with the delineation of the Muslim community, but while these discussions mainly focused on non-Jihadis, this debate has now become an internal matter as Jihadis engage more and more in internal definitions of in-groups and out-groups that are critically changing norms and discourses within the movement.

### *The Sunni Jihadi Movement and its Fault Lines*

This book's broader object of analysis is the SJM. The definition of the movement, however, is not as straightforward as it may appear. Classic analyses of Jihad have described its Quranic foundation and militant and philosophical expression,[32] the different currents of thought of its main thinkers,[33] and its modern emergence[34] and ideology.[35] But which groups should be considered part of the SJM is not always clear. One reason for this is that Jihadis themselves constantly engage in efforts to negotiate inclusion and exclusion within the movement.[36]

During my second visit to the outskirts of Zarqa in northern Jordan, to the home of Abu Qatada al-Filastini—one of the most senior living Jihadi ideologues—he emphasised the need to understand the history of Jihad in order to define the movement. This is not a controversial view. Kepel has previously described the SJM as a development of three distinctive *generations*,[37] while Jordanian analyst Abu Hanieh talks about three *schools of Jihadi thought*[38] which capture not just the movement's modern genealogy but also its internal diversity. Even within the SJM, Abu Musab al-Suri, a famous Jihadi strategist, has provided an account of the ideological composition of the movement[39] and its methodological diversity in terms of strategy.[40] From its emergence in the early 1960s, I identify four different Jihadi currents that together show the movement's modern historical evolution and diversity.[41] Together, these currents form the basis of a broad definition of the SJM that is not based on a certain theology or political preference, but on the foundation of Jihad as a legitimate and necessary method in a political and social struggle.

The first current of the modern SJM emerged in the early 1960s (1963 according to al-Suri) in Egypt, with Sayyid Qutb and later Muhammad Abd al-Salam Faraj as the intellectual and organisational pioneers. This current, which can be termed a *nationalist Jihad* with an ideological foundation in the Muslim Brotherhood, viewed local governments as illegitimate since they were not ruling according to God's law—the shari'a. While they did have their disagreements, both Qutb and Faraj considered Jihad a means to achieve a certain objective: toppling *the near enemy* (al-aduw al-qarib) through the struggle of a vanguard movement.

The second current, the *solidarity Jihad*, started in 1979 and lasted until the mid-1990s. Led by Abdallah Azzam, this new current still emphasised the need for a vanguard, but it focused its attention on the anti-Soviet struggle in Afghanistan. Its innovation was Azzam's reframing of Jihad as an *individual duty* (fard al-ayn).[42] Jihad was not a matter of a certain nationality but the concern of the entire umma. It was also around this time that the debate about whether to prioritise the near enemy (un-Islamic Arab governments) or the far enemy (Israel) emerged. Ayman al-Zawahiri, a senior member of

Egyptian Al Jihad at the time, wrote that the liberation of Palestine goes through Cairo,[43] but in the mid-1990s other Jihadis gradually started to doubt such an assertion.

This re-orientation towards the far enemy after the fall of the Soviets initiated the third current. In the West, this is referred to as *global Jihad*. Unlike in the early debates, it was now the US and not Israel that was viewed as the main far enemy, the head of the snake, that had to be defeated to facilitate successful national Jihadi campaigns. There have been different accounts of whether this re-orientation was led by Bin Laden or the Egyptian contingent represented by al-Zawahiri.[44] It appears likely, however, that it occurred due to a combination of, on the one hand, al-Zawahiri's disillusion with the unsuccessful struggle against the Egyptian regime, and, on the other, Bin Laden starting to see the US as the main obstacle to Palestinian liberation and as a transgression against Islam because of its presence in the holy land of Saudi Arabia. The rise to prominence of Abu Musab al-Zarqawi implied a return to prioritising the near enemy and thus does not represent a qualitative shift or evolution in the character of the Jihadi current, despite his extreme sectarian focus. Salafi ideas were already a strong influence within al-Qaida, but they gained even more traction within al-Zarqawi's Iraqi network, especially in terms of the impact of concepts such as *al-wala' wa-l-bara'* and takfir. With the US invasion of Iraq, the ideas of Bin Laden and al-Zarqawi coalesced to some degree, eventually facilitating a union between the two in 2004. For Bin Laden, striking the far enemy in the Middle East region became an acceptable alternative to striking in the far enemy's own countries.

The fourth and most recent current, *statehood Jihadism,* emerged with the Islamic State in 2014. Ideas such as *controlling territory* (tamkin) or establishing an Islamic political entity, whether a caliphate or an emirate, were not new, but were prioritised and taken to new heights by the Islamic State. The group concretised the Jihadis' political project and developed a highly systematised governance structure unlike that of any previous Jihadi project. In addition, the group adopted an unprecedented focus on both the near *and* far enemy, resulting in an extreme level of ideological hybridisation in terms of enemy hierarchies and ambitions.[45] This *glocal* outlook is evident in its campaign of international terrorist attacks and its extensive establishment of provinces around the world.[46]

This evolution, with overlapping stages, illustrates how broadly the SJM can be defined. The Jihadi current has never been as homogenous as it is often portrayed, neither in terms of enemy definition nor of theology.[47] It is true that Jihadism in the past decade has become increasingly dominated by what has been referred to as a Jihadi–Salafi ideational system, but Jihadism continues to be broader than the subcategory of Jihadi–Salafism, which is why we need to embrace a broader definition of the SJM. Jihadis themselves refer to the movement in a variety of ways. Notions such as the 'Jihadi movement' (*al-haraka al-jihadiyya*),[48] the 'Jihadi current' (*al-tayyar al-jihadi*),[49] 'global Jihad' (*al-jihad al-'alamiyy*)[50] and 'Jihadi–Salafism' (*al-salafiyya al-jihadiyya*)[51] are terms regularly employed by Jihadis to describe their movement.[52] Apart from the 'Jihadi–Salafism' description, all these endonyms place emphasis on *Jihad* as the defining characteristic. This illustrates a fault line highlighted by Jihadis (as well as by outsiders) between those who emphasise the action of *Jihad* as the defining characteristic and those who emphasise *Salafism* as the movement's theological foundation.

This book's argument is that the main driver of intra-Jihadi conflict is politics rather than theology, and thus we need a broader definition of the SJM while being careful not to lose the internal solidarity that is integral to the conceptualisation of the movement.[53] Hence, I define the SJM as a movement *comprised of groups and individuals who consider militant Jihad a legitimate and necessary method to realise socio-political change and who reject alternative methods as substitutes.* The main reason for this relatively broad definition is that most of the groups fighting Jihad (with the sword or the tongue) are competing for the same power, authority and recruits, and that they are—to some extent—working towards the same objectives, albeit with differences in their ambitions.

## *Methodology and Sources*

The study's methodological approach takes inspiration from historical sociology. This attempts to explain social phenomena through a focus on processes and the impact from agency and structures, while placing a strong emphasis on chronology and the explanatory power of a detailed narrative providing a nuanced account and explanation of empirical events.[54] This implies that the book's primary contribution will be of hagiographical nature, presenting a 'thick' narrative of events, behaviour, and discourses. The conceptualisation and explanation of intra-Jihadi conflict proposed here is based on a religio-political explanatory framework that captures the idiosyncrasy of Jihadis since the process of intra-Jihadi conflict must necessarily be understood as a complex process where politics and religion are intertwined. While the analysis primarily deals with the relational complexity of conflict dynamics between al-Qaida and the Islamic State, it is not limited to these two groups. This is because the struggle between these two protagonists in the intra-Jihadi conflict must be analysed within the context and structures of the broader movement that they are both a part of.[55] For the same reasons—and due to the expansionist, de-territorialised and global character of the conflict—the analysis is not limited to a specific geographical area, though events in Syria will be the main focus.

The study of Jihadi actors always involves challenges in the collection of material. Groups often operate clandestinely in remote areas of the world and are not easily accessible for various reasons. Previously, their written and recorded material did not circulate widely outside closed circles, whether these were the geographical areas in which they operated or password-protected internet fora. Nowadays, although it still poses several challenges, most obviously security concerns, collecting Jihadi material and arranging interviews has become a lot more feasible, primarily due to the internet and various digital communication platforms.[56] This has facilitated a much more elaborate academic study of Jihadism since both primary and secondary sources are now available in abundance.

The sources used in this book are divided into four types. The main source is primary material produced by the actors under study. Such primary material can be divided into official group-level and individual group member communication, and communication by individuals who are not officially members of any group, mainly represented by 'independent' Jihadi ideologues and supporter networks. These primary sources were collected via two methods. The more formal is through online databases run by scholars, academic institutions, or the Jihadi actors themselves. The less formal method is through media platforms, namely Twitter, Telegram and Rocket.Chat, where Jihadi groups and sympathisers manage accounts.[57] First Twitter (until 2016) and later Telegram have offered Jihadis a unique platform to disseminate their material, to provide their analysis of events and to engage with people outside Jihadi circles. For the researcher, these platforms offer similarly distinctive opportunities to collect material, to adopt the role of a digital anthropologist and, in some cases, to engage with Jihadis themselves.[58]

A second important source is interviews, mainly with current and former Jihadis. Due to the precarious situation in many of the geographical arenas where Jihadis operate, the interviews were conducted either face-to-face during field trips or online through encrypted communication platforms. While some of the interviewees will be mentioned by name, others will be anonymised for reasons of security. All the interviews have been carried out in informal settings such as while strolling around a London mall, while speaking over a Subway sandwich, while picking up the interviewee's children from school, or while enjoying *Eid* sweets while half of the local village drops by. The process of getting access to Jihadis, particularly senior ideologues, is typically long and troublesome, with ups and downs. I have mainly relied on a snowballing approach: lower-ranking Jihadis have been my access point and have helped me to establish contact with more senior figures. On most occasions this approach works well; the lower-ranking figure vouches for you (essentially giving you *tazkiya*), thus reassuring the senior Jihadi. Even so, it is far from foolproof.[59]

A third source is internal letters. Most of these letters come from the cache of documents collected at Usama Bin Laden's Abbottabad residence following his death, which were made public through the US Director of National Intelligence (DNI);[60] others I have acquired myself through online channels or through contact with Jihadis. The fourth source relied on is secondary material, which includes newspaper articles, think tank reports and existing research related to the field of study.

In total, the study is based on a vast literary corpus, audio-visual material, and interviews collected and conducted over a period of six years.[61] The corpus includes speeches, statements, pamphlets, magazines, reports and videos. Some of the material has, of course, been studied before, but as a collective corpus consisting of many thousands of documents it has not been studied in a comprehensive manner—and not with the specific purpose of understanding conflict dynamics *between* Jihadi actors.

## *Organisation of the Book*

The book is structured in six parts comprising thirteen chapters. Part one presents the conceptual framework applied throughout the book and discusses the process, scope and causes of internal conflict within the SJM. It begins by identifying a typical conflict cycle and the discursive narratives employed to legitimise conflict. Afterwards, it presents the book's overall theoretical argument, developing the idea of *Jihadi politics* and discussing the dominant mechanisms driving conflict. Part two proceeds by presenting the historical background for the contemporary conflict; it is setting the stage. It first examines the historical examples and evolution of internal contestation and conflict since the emergence of the modern SJM in the 1960s. It then turns to the empirical precursor to the ongoing fitna within the SJM, tracing the Islamic State's split from al-Qaida and how the latter continuously sought to manage internal rebellion. This analysis of historical events is not only essential to grasping the present situation, but it also illustrates the inherently volatile and multifaceted character of intra-Jihadi dynamics.

Parts three to six analyse the 'global Jihadi civil war' in the period 2014–19. The development of the intra-Jihadi conflict is divided into four stages, with each stage corresponding to a distinctive dynamic: *intensification* (part three), *fragmentation* and *internationalisation* (part four), *radicalisation* (part five) and *internalisation* (part six). Part three explains how the intra-Jihadi conflict intensified and escalated in discourse and in action in 2014, and how al-Qaida responded to the challenge and the struggle for authority playing out between the various groups, their senior members and their supporters. Part four examines how the SJM fragmented as a result of the ongoing conflict and the peculiar logic enforced upon the movement in late 2014 and 2015. It explains the expansion and disappearance of prominent groups and how the fitna spilled over from Syria to other regions, finally producing a global struggle for authority within the movement. Part five takes a deeper look at the ideological differences between the actors, how they frame the conflict and their utilisation of religion as a strategic political tool in the infighting. It pays particular attention to the politicisation of religious concepts in the struggle for authority. Finally, part six looks at how the intra-Jihadi conflict became internalised within the respective groups in 2016–19 as pressure from the inside to 'reform' led to renewed fragmentation and escalation of hostilities.

# PART ONE

# THE POLITICS OF SUNNI JIHADISM

*'If we call for unity, then we must not rebel against our leaders. If we call to listen and obey, then we must set an example for it. If we call to fulfil the covenants and pledges, then we must not break them. If we call to expel the foreign disbeliever occupier from the lands of Muslims, then we must not destroy the jihadi gathering with internal fighting. And if we call for the promotion of virtue and the prohibition of vice, then we must apply it on ourselves.'*[1]

Ayman al-Zawahiri

*'Despite all the events that took place during the recent years, some people are still unaware of the reality of the animosity between the Islamic State and al-Qaida organization. Some of those ignorant people still believe in the lies of the bad 'ulama, stating that the Islamic State kills Muslims and does not disturb idolaters. They invented these lies to justify describing the Islamic State unjustly as Khawarij and therefore, justify fighting it and shedding the blood of its soldiers.'*[2]

The Islamic State

# 1

# FROM CONTESTATION TO INFIGHTING

The questions this book strives to answer are why Jihadis engage in internal conflict when they do and how such conflict impacts the SJM. The point of departure is the logical assumption that as an extremely isolated movement confronted by many enemies, and with few potential allies, internal conflict should largely be absent within the SJM. However, the 2014–19 period is a vivid example of how this is not the case. Ideological fault lines certainly do exist within the movement, but these fault lines, if considered the exclusive parameter, hardly explain examples of internal conflict. The argument proposed in this book is that intra-Jihadi conflict dynamics are the result of an intertwined relationship between religion and politics, but that the ambition for power and hegemony within the Jihadi milieu are the primary drivers.

In the study of religious actors, including religious extremists, there is a general tendency to view the actors as static due to their foundation in religion. Speaking of this misleading perception, Juergensmeyer reports how a Palestinian student explained that unlike secular entities, 'Hamas won't change over time' because it was 'founded on religious principles.'[3] This book's analysis shows how Jihadi groups and individuals do change over time, despite their foundation in religious principles, and how these principles are occasionally secondary to political objectives. We see how conflict between Jihadis is primarily driven by political objectives as part of their struggle for power and survival and should be considered a strategic process rather than the direct result of ideological or theological fault lines. The struggle is, however, framed through religious narratives and specific theological concepts which are strategically instrumentalised to legitimise conflict.

The conceptual distinction and interconnectedness between *groups* and *movements* is important for the book's argument. In terms of movement structure, a distinction is made between a *fragmented* and a *cohesive* movement which are defined based on: (1) the number of groups in the movement; (2) the degree of institutionalisation across groups; and (3) the distribution of power among groups.[4] This implies that a *movement* with a high number of groups, low supra-group institutionalisation and diffuse power distribution is considered *fragmented*, while a movement with a low number of groups, supra-group institutionalisation and centralised power is more *cohesive*. The argument is that fragmented movements are more likely to experience infighting than cohesive movements due to the higher concentration of groups, the lack of institutions to influence inter-group relations, and the relatively equal distribution of power.[5] As the analysis shows, while fragmented movements are more likely to experience infighting, infighting is also likely to result in further fragmentation. We see how the SJM from 2014–19 has wavered between dynamics of fragmentation and cohesion through attempts to facilitate mergers and supra-group institutions while repeatedly experiencing new episodes of contestation and infighting.

In his research on the outcome of nationalist movement campaigns, Krause differentiates between a hegemonic movement on the one hand and a united or fragmented movement on the other. He argues that the structural configuration of a movement is what has a decisive impact on struggle outcome. As I am interested in intra-movement conflict dynamics—which is one of the dual struggles that groups engage in, according to Krause, and which he labels the *war of position*—the focus here slightly differs from his. In my view, inter-group relations and movement structure influence one another reciprocally: some groups fight for a better position within the movement at the same time as movement structure impacts upon each group's chances of success.[6] This conceptualisation of a reciprocal movement-group dynamic is not unique to the SJM but rather a common trait of movements, and it highlights the importance of both agency and structures. The logic is that movement structure places opportunities and limits on its members in terms of inter-group interaction, but at the same time movement structure is also affected by group behaviour and inter-group interaction in a dynamic process that involves macro-, meso- and micro-level developments. Based on the conceptualisation of fragmentation and cohesion, the argument proposed here is that there is a qualitative difference between a cohesive movement and a fragmented movement, both in terms of how prone the movement is to internal conflict and with regard to its potential for reaching its objectives.[7]

### *Conflict Cycle: From Discursive to Military Manifestations*

In terms of conflict variance, it is possible to identify a scale of escalating forms of conflict dynamics ranging from competition to infighting. *Competition* is the least intense form and denotes an environment within a movement that can have a tangible impact on, for example, strategic or tactical competition, also referred to as outbidding. These efforts are mainly geared towards distinguishing one group from another, qualitatively or quantitatively, but do not involve direct interaction between the competing actors. *Discursive contestation* is an escalation from competition, as it involves directly criticising or attacking another group or individual through discourse. It aims at correcting or delegitimising one's rival, or occasionally at priming further escalation in the form of military conflict. The history of internal conflict within the SJM is full of examples of discursive contestation where groups or individuals target an opposing actor or even internal sub-factions and affiliates.[8] For a movement as occupied with defining the correct methodology and delineation of in-group and out-group members, internal criticism is particularly severe as it creates disunity and detrimental confusion within the movement and among its sympathisers. *Non-violent confrontations* are an escalation from discursive contestation, as actors no longer rely on words to attack their rival but engage in direct confrontations such as arrests that nonetheless fall short of military infighting. This represents a critical change in inter-group and intra-group relations, as non-violent confrontations make infighting much more likely compared to discursive contestation. *Infighting* is the most extreme form of internal conflict and is defined as when two or more actors begin using lethal force against one another.

Based on the historical account presented in this book, it is possible to identify a typical pattern of how intra-Jihadi tensions evolve from discursive contestation to military infighting. This pattern involves narratives to legitimise conflict, a general failure to establish supra-group institutions so as to prevent or de-escalate conflict, and a normalisation of violence as a tool for handling intra-Jihadi relations. In her research on political violence, Della Porta discusses the concept of *protest cycles* to explain how the campaigns of various clandestine militant groups evolve over time, both in relation to the state they are opposing and rival groups within their own movement, through the following stages: *expansion through diffusion*, *radicalisation*, *exhaustion* and *restabilisation*. A characteristic feature of these cycles is that they have their own dynamics which make them somehow predictable. A similar conclusion can be made about episodes of intra-Jihadi conflict, which I define as *conflict* cycles. Since 2013, several episodes of intra-Jihadi conflict with a recurring trajectory have taken place. While some of the stages parallel Della Porta's, this chapter also suggests a distinctive pattern for the observed conflict cycles (see figure 2). Initially, tensions emerge either as a result of ideological cleavages, power-related struggles for territory, resources or recruits, or the implementation of a specific model or strategy of Jihad. Tensions are followed by discursive contestation whereby actors begin to criticise one another (comparable to *diffusion*), and—in cases where the conflict escalates—they begin to rhetorically prime legitimations for infighting (*radicalisation* of the relationship). In situations where infighting erupts, it will occasionally be preceded by group factionalisation or splintering. After the eruption of infighting, groups typically attempt to establish supra-group institutions to de-escalate infighting and drive reconciliation. On most occasions, these efforts fail, and tensions re-emerge, launching a new conflict cycle.

Figure 2: Conflict Cycle

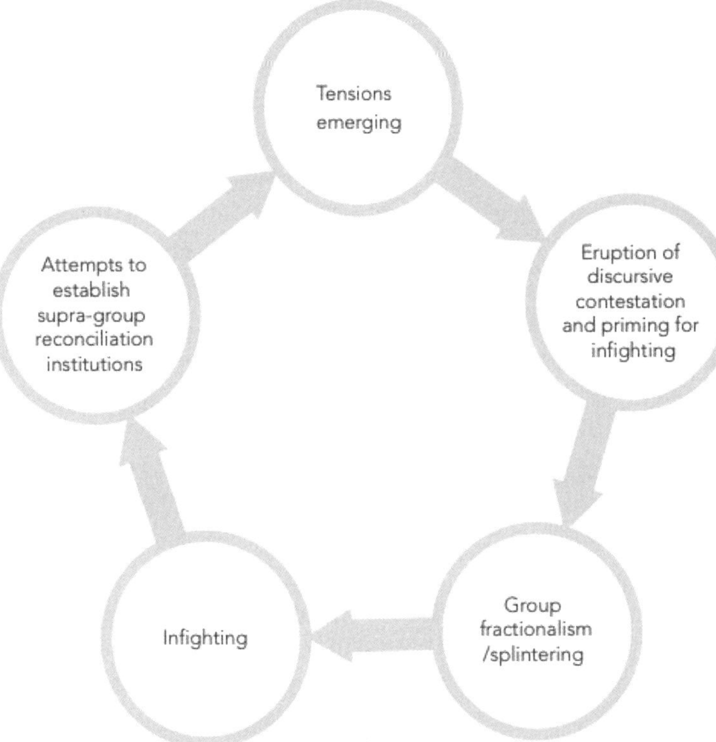


An interesting question is to what extent intra-Jihadi dynamics follow a similar pattern to Della Porta's protest cycles between opposing movements. Della Porta argues that

> diffusion happens at the beginning of a cycle, as the first movements to emerge lower the cost of collective action for other actors (…) During cycles, the repertoires of collective action tend to change. In the initial stages of protest, the most disruptive forms often come to the fore. New actors invent new tactics, as emerging collective identities require radical action.[9]

This suggests that the use of violence is not exclusively a result of strategy but also the product of relational dynamics, and that escalation in violent repertoires of action will tend to occur early in a cycle.[10] The general expectation in such cycles is a spiralling radicalisation in the form of violence. In *Clandestine Political Violence*, Porta describes *competitive escalation* as a causal mechanism that explains 'the radicalization of forms of action during competitive interactions not only with political adversaries but also with potential allies and within the movement family itself.'[11] In the literature on reciprocal radicalisation there is a similar expectation that one group's violence fuels the discourse and actions of the opponent,[12] while in the terrorism literature this phenomenon is referred to as *outbidding*. Interestingly, this was not the case within the SJM, or at least not at the beginning of the conflict cycle. Instead, it appears that the radicalising actions of one group in many instances had a pacifying impact on other groups.

In early 2014, it was evident that al-Qaida and the Islamic State were following opposing strategies and that tensions within the SJM had reached such a level that an escalation of intra-movement military conflict was inevitable. Della Porta notes that 'violence often develops in situations of competition over the control of specific places' and this was precisely the situation in eastern Syria in early 2014.[13] Unsurprisingly, the conflictual and competitive relationship between the two groups resulted in a radicalisation of repertoires of action. However, unlike the typical expectations in the literature, generally it did not affect the repertoires of action of both groups but primarily only that of the Islamic State. Locally, the Islamic State executed brutal massacres, such as the Camp Speicher massacre (June 2014), the Yazidi genocide in Sinjar (August 2014), executions of Coptic Egyptians in Libya (February 2015) and the Palmyra executions (July 2015). In August 2014, the group began to behead foreigners on tape, indicating that its focus was not just local, and this was followed by a string of terrorist attacks outside the Muslim world.[14] Neither Jabhat al-Nusra nor any other al-Qaida affiliate perpetrated similar actions, implying that the spiralling radicalisation of repertoires of action was one sided.[15] Similar observations can be made in terms of the intra-Jihadi violence. Arguably the very logic behind al-Qaida abstaining from similar behaviour is not only to be found in theological differences, but in its desire to qualitatively distinguish itself from the Islamic State and its brutality.

This also answers a question posed by Gartenstein-Ross and Moreng. In April 2015 they wrote,

> The Islamic State's challenge to Al Qaeda's holdings and supremacy over the jihadist movement will certainly cause Al Qaeda to adapt. The question is whether Al Qaeda will replicate ISIL by becoming louder and more overt—a rival would-be caliphate, in effect—or if its adaptation will be more unconventional, a kind of fundamentalist jiujitsu that waits for the Islamic State to overreach and be destroyed thanks to its baleful prominence in the fight against the West.[16]

While it has been argued that the emergence of the Islamic State led al-Nusra to reveal its more hard-line Islamist nature,[17] it seems more appropriate to emphasise that *despite* its hard-line nature, it differed qualitatively from the behaviour of the Islamic State. In terrorism research, outbidding has been the dominant theory used to explain the effect of competition between terrorist groups on their behaviour. The logic of outbidding is to demonstrate a group's capabilities, commitment, and intentions relative to other groups. Bloom showed how both religious and nationalistic Palestinian groups adopted suicide bombing as a tactic to keep up with the popularity of Hamas. In his quantitative examination of how often outbidding occurs, Nemeth argues that religious groups are more likely to engage in outbidding due to their spiritual motivation.[18] But after examining the inter-group behaviour in the 2014–19 period, we can conclude that the conflict dynamics are not characterised by outbidding—either strategically or tactically—but by a dynamic of *diversification*. Walter and Kydd explain that groups in a competitive environment have an incentive to appear strong, and that outbidding is the mechanism to ensure that[19]—but depending on the context, we can see diversification functioning in a similar way as a mechanism of competition.

*Overview of Jihadi Infighting: Assessing Fratricidal Casualties*

The evolution from intra-Jihadi contestation to infighting first occurred in summer 2013 in Syria but intensified in early 2014, before spreading to Afghanistan, Libya, Somalia, Nigeria, Egypt, Yemen and the Sahel. Figure 3 provides an overview of episodes of infighting and non-violent confrontations in the 2014–19 period coded by type (infighting, assassination and arrest campaign) and intensity (intense and low intensity) based on my own data. Not only does the figure illustrate the development over time and the geographical distribution of intra-Jihadi conflict, but also how it became more pervasive as a result of movement fragmentation, the presence of hegemonist rationales and the normalisation of conflict with other Jihadis.

Besides exhibiting the detrimental effects of intra-Jihadi conflict for the SJM, it has been a priority to elucidate the impact of conflict in terms of casualties. This, however, has been extremely challenging for the following reasons:

- Jihadi infighting has taken place within the context of ongoing conflict and reporting from conflicts is always messy.
- Jihadis have occasionally—and particularly in 2014—fought in alliances with non-Jihadi groups, which makes it impossible to determine from news reporting which specific group the casualties stem from.
- Groups' own self-reported communication on infighting is likely biased. They have an incentive to inflate the numbers of fighters they have killed and to lower their own casualty numbers.
- Because of the illegitimate nature of infighting, some groups also refrain from publishing detailed reports on infighting while the other party in the conflict does. Obviously, this results in a skewed account of casualty numbers.
- Most Jihadi reporting on infighting simply states that an attack occurred without mentioning the number of casualties. On other occasions a total number of casualties and wounded is reported, making it impossible to identify the number of deaths.

From the beginning of the infighting, I have tried to count casualties from Jihadi infighting. However, because of the issues

Figure 3: When Jihadis Fight Jihadis
Six years of militant infighting between Jihadi fractions, 2013–20

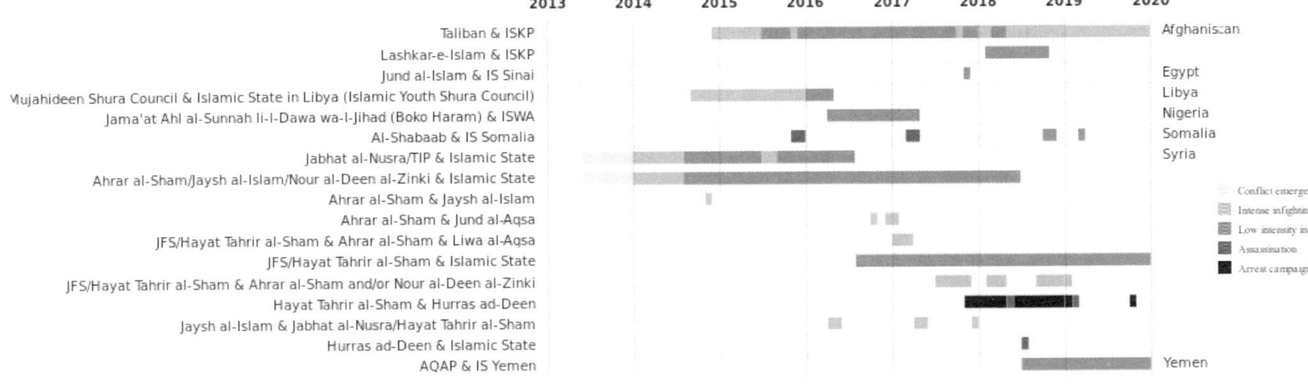

mentioned above this quickly became too challenging. Instead, I have mainly relied on numbers from the Uppsala Conflict Data Program (UCDP) database, which records conflict casualties. The UCDP has faced similar challenges, so rather than perceiving the numbers to be exact, we should consider them the most accurate that we can obtain at this time. As the UCDP data only covers the period 2013–17, I provide two tables. The first (table 1) covers casualty numbers from 2013–17 and is based on UCDP data, while the second (table 2) covers the period 2018–19 and previous Jihadi infighting that is not included in the UCDP database and is based on my own data compilation. Some inter-group conflicts are included in both tables and total casualty numbers from these conflicts, for example the infighting between the Taliban and ISKP, must thus be combined from both tables.

Adding up the figures in the tables, the total number of casualties from intra-Jihadi conflict in the period 2013–19 is more than 8,000. This is probably a conservative estimate because some infighting remains unreported in primary and secondary sources and because of the objection most Jihadi groups have to providing detailed information on infighting. For example, the Taliban and ISKP have

Figure 4: Casualties divided by country

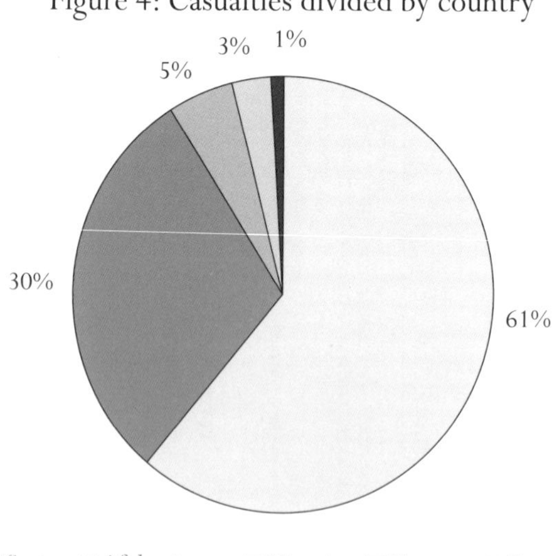

Table 1: Jihadi Infighting Casualty Numbers 2013–17

| Jihadi infighting casualty numbers, 2013–17 | | | | |
|---|---|---|---|---|
| *Groups* | *Period* | *Country* | *Main Areas* | *Total number of casualties* |
| Islamic State vs. HTS | 2017 | Syria | North-East Hama (Oct–Dec/17) | 595 |
| Ahrar al-Sham vs. HTS | 2017 | Syria | Idlib | 183 |
| Ahrar al-Sham vs. Liwa al-Aqsa | 2017 | Syria | Idlib | 40 |
| HTS vs. Jaysh al-Islam | 2017 | Syria | Ghouta | 45 |
| HTS vs. Liwa al-Aqsa | 2017 | Syria | Idlib and Eastern Hama | 346 |
| Islamic State vs. Jaysh al-Islam | 2014–17 | Syria | Daraa | 31 |
| Islamic State vs. Islamic Front (without Jabhat al-Nusra participation) | 2013–17 | Syria | Aleppo countryside | 235 |
| Islamic State vs. Jabhat al-Nusra/JFS | 2013–16 | Syria | Deir ez-Zour, Raqqa and Hasaka | 1121 |
| Islamic State vs. Islamic Front & Jabhat al-Nusra | 2014 | Syria | Eastern Qalamoun | 1197 |
| Taliban vs. Islamic State | 2014–17 | Afghanistan | Achin (2015–18) Khogyani (2015–18) Chaparhar (2015–18) Darzab (2017) | 816 |
| Taliban vs. High Council of Afghanistan | 2015–17 | Afghanistan | Shindand | 446 |
| Taliban vs. Islamic State/Abdul Rauf Khadim | Jan/15 | Afghanistan | Kajaki District | 50 |

Casualty numbers are retrieved from the UCDP database, which can be accessed here: https://ucdp.uu.se

Table 2: Jihadi Infighting Casualty Numbers 2018–19

| Jihadi infighting casualty numbers, 2018–19 | | | | | | | |
|---|---|---|---|---|---|---|---|
| *Group 1* | *Group 2* | *Period* | *Country* | *Main Areas* | *Total number of casualties* | *Group 1 casualties* | *Group 2 casualties* |
| Hurras al-Deen | HTS | 2018–19 | Syria | Aleppo countryside | 2 | 1 | 1 |
| Islamic State | Lashkar al-Islam | 2018 | Afghanistan | Achin and Nazyan | 85 | 53 | 32 |
| Taliban | Islamic State | 2018–19 | Afghanistan | Nangarhar, Jowzjan and Kunar | 340 | 240 | 100 |
| HTS | JTS | Feb–April/2018 & Jan–Feb/2019 | Syria | Idlib | 1094 | 811 | 283 |
| Al-Shabab | Islamic State | 2015–18 | Somalia | Puntland and Middle Juba | 26 | 14 | 12 |
| AQAP | Islamic State | 2018–19 | Yemen | Qifa | 114 | 59 | 55 |
| Hurras al-Deen | Islamic State | Jul/18 | Syria | Idlib | 2 | 1 | 1 |
| HTS | Islamic State | 2018–19 | Syria | Idlib and Aleppo | Numbers unknown, but likely between 100–200 | - | - |

| *Group 1* | *Group 2* | *Period* | *Country* | *Main Areas* | *Total number of casualties* | *Group 1 casualties* | *Group 2 casualties* |
|---|---|---|---|---|---|---|---|
| Boko Haram | Islamic State | 2016–18 | Nigeria | Yobo and Borno states | Reported number is 400 | - | - |
| Jund al-Islam | Islamic State | 2017 | Egypt | - | Numbers unknown, but likely less than 10 | - | - |
| HTS | Nour al-Deen al-Zinki | 2017–19 | Syria | Western Aleppo | Reported number of al-Zinki casualties is 140–150 | - | - |
| Derna Mujahideen Shura Council | Islamic State (Islamic Youth Shura Council) | 2014–16 | Libya | Derna | Numbers unknown | - | - |

Numbers are collected from official group statements and news articles.

consistently fought each other in Afghanistan between late 2014 and the present day, but the Taliban very rarely publishes accounts stating the number of ISKP fighters killed, while ISKP appears eager to publish information on attacks on the Taliban. This trend has continued after the Taliban's takeover of Afghanistan in August 2021 and its renewed crackdown on ISKP. This results in skewed and likely conservative estimates. The data we have nonetheless offers insight into how serious intra-Jihadi conflict is in terms of casualties. Jihadi groups remain attractive only for a small group of people worldwide, so for the SJM to lose more than 8,000 fighters at the hands of other Jihadis is particularly problematic and strategically counterproductive, given that their main enemies are local governments and/or the West.

## *Narratives of Conflict*

In the various episodes of infighting in the 2014–19 period, groups and individuals have relied on three distinctive narratives to justify their behaviour. The first, *cleansing the ranks*, builds on the argument that infighting is necessary to distinguish true Muslims from hypocrites. The second, *eradicating extremism*, argues that extremism is destroying the Jihadi project from within and must be proactively annihilated. And the third, *defending from extremism*, concurs that extremism is a threat but argues for a reactive stance that favours defending against attacks from extremist actors. Below I briefly elaborate on each of these narratives.

### Cleansing the Ranks

The narrative of *cleansing the ranks* is particularly associated with the Islamic State and stems from a speech by Abu Bakr al-Baghdadi in which he says:

> It's from God's tradition and wisdom that the rows of believers and mujahids is mingled with hypocrites. God will not leave this row mixed with those hypocrites and pretenders and therefore creates fitna and trials for them. The row must be melted so that the maliciousness leaves, and be pressured so that the weak

> building blocks crumble and the lights must shine at it exposing the intricacies and inner personalities.[20]

Here, al-Baghdadi claims that the SJM has been weakened by insincere Muslims who have deviated in thought if not in action, and who must be fought in order to ensure a cohesive movement on the correct methodology.

Bearing in mind the timing of the statement—January 2014—there is little doubt that it was directed against rival Jihadis who, in the eyes of al-Baghdadi's group, have deviated from the proper methodology. Issued at the beginning of the Jihadi civil war and at the height of tensions with al-Qaida's leadership, al-Baghdadi's call to cleanse the ranks was intended to justify and rationalise fighting other Jihadis. The ongoing conflict is explained as resulting from the presence of these hypocrites who claim to be Muslims, or even Jihadis, while in fact they should be considered neither. Their true nature must be revealed so that they can be fought, thus leaving the ranks of Muslims fighting for their religion united.

In their modern history, Jihadis have consistently engaged in exercises of delineation of the Muslim community as a method of identifying legitimate enemies. But while the Islamic State's narrative as exampled in al-Baghdadi's speech relies on the same argument, it directs it against other Jihadis, essentially defining an *internal enemy*. The rationale of the argument is that *cleansing the ranks* proactively is necessary to *protect* the Jihadi project, and more generally to protect Islam. Hence, in the view of its proponents it is a *fratricide to create unity*. From 2017, HTS has relied on a similar rationale, framed slightly differently, in its offensive against competitors Ahrar al-Sham and Nour al-Deen al-Zinki. The existence of rival groups was explained as a challenge to the Jihadi project to protect Idlib. But instead of referring to its rivals as *hypocrites*, it used the term *rebels* (bughat) to justify attacking them.

The *cleansing the ranks* narrative is closely associated with the *hegemonist* rationale that will be further explained in the following chapter. In the period under scrutiny, hegemonists have relied on this narrative to justify proactive action against fellow Jihadis in an attempt to overcome the sensitivities associated with fighting other

Muslims. Of the three narratives, this narrative plays a central role in explaining the *process* of conflict eruption, and it is evidently the most damaging for the SJM, as it opens the door to internal conflict both *between* and *within* groups.

## Eradicating Extremism

The narrative of *eradicating extremism* has been used by opponents of the Islamic State. The narrative goes that extremists, generally referred to as *khawarij*, must be fought and annihilated. Similar to the *cleansing the ranks* narrative, *eradicating extremism* has its foundation in religious sources, specifically several hadith that concern the imperative of fighting extremism, and its proponents have claimed that it is a necessary action to protect the SJM and its image. Hence, it is largely a reactive narrative to counter aggressive behaviour from other groups within the movement.

This narrative has mainly been used to justify actions against the Islamic State and sympathetic groups like Jund al-Aqsa. On a group level, examples include Ahrar al-Sham, the Taliban and al-Qaida's affiliates in Somalia and Yemen. On an individual level, Jihadi ideologues such as Hani al-Sibai, Tariq Abdelhaleem and Abu Basir al-Tartusi have supported the narrative. The decisive rationale justifying the assertive posture is either that the opponent represents a serious threat to the future survival of the SJM or that the group itself has hegemonic ambitions. The former includes the majority of groups fighting the Islamic State, while the latter is best exemplified by HTS's campaign to expel the Islamic State from Idlib and the Taliban's campaign against the Islamic State Khorasan Province in Afghanistan.

*Eradicating extremism* has been the default narrative for repelling attacks by the Islamic State and for legitimising fighting the group proactively. Because of the excessive actions of the Islamic State, it was relatively straightforward for groups and ideologues in 2014 to adopt this narrative to fight former brothers-in-arms, enabling them to adopt an assertive stance in the intra-Jihadi conflict.

## Defending from Extremism

In the *defending from extremism* narrative, extremists are viewed as a threat to the SJM. Yet as they are still considered Muslims, the only legitimate course is to defend oneself against their attacks. Generally, this has been the attitude of al-Qaida's leadership and several senior ideologues such as al-Maqdisi and Abu Qatada. At the very beginning of the conflict in 2014, al-Julani also instructed Jabhat al-Nusra fighters only to defend themselves against attacks, but later his group would shift to the *eradicating extremism* narrative.

The proponents of the *defending from extremism* narrative argue that since extremists are still considered Muslims, one should be careful about killing them. Some, like al-Maqdisi, initially made a distinction between the Islamic State *leadership* and its *rank and file*, claiming that only the former should be considered khawarij. This limits the possibility of attacking the alleged extremists and is a key factor in explaining why the infighting between al-Qaida and the Islamic State did not spiral out of control. Over time, however, several proponents of this narrative shifted to a more assertive stance towards the Islamic State when they realised that the group was not willing to halt its attacks against fellow Jihadis and was, in fact, escalating the conflict. Despite labelling the Islamic State *neo-khawarij*, al-Zawahiri has consistently called for unity and instructed his fighters to refrain from fighting fellow Muslims, thus indicating his continued reliance on the *defending from extremism* narrative.

### *Failure of Conflict Mitigation: Inadequate Institutionalisation*

Despite al-Zawahiri's continuous attempts to mitigate conflict, the SJM as a whole has failed to establish effective mechanisms to manage conflict. This is true both at the stage of emerging tensions and in cases where tensions escalate to infighting. The primary reason appears to be a general failure of institutionalisation resulting *not* from an inability to set up institutions to mitigate conflict, but rather from these institutions rarely having the necessary authority to implement their rulings. As may have been expected, *ideology* is not sufficiently powerful as an alternative mitigating mechanism. While ideological overlap does impact the process and scope of conflict through enforcing certain restrictions and limitations, it falls short of preventing it.

A defining feature of the SJM is a general failure of supra-group institutionalisation. Supra-group institutions are important because they can instil trust among groups and function as mechanisms to prevent and de-escalate emerging contestation and conflict. A consequence of this absence of institutions with a mandate to adjudicate is that such tensions have escalated on several occasions. Jihadi groups have been better at establishing *military* alliances such as the *Islamic Front* (al-jabha al-islamiyya), *Army of Conquest* (jaysh al-fatah) and *Incite the Believers* (wa harid al-mu'minin). However, while these alliances have been crucial for strengthening Jihadis' capabilities on the battlefield and for bolstering the level of trust between groups, they have proved insufficient to prevent or manage inter-group conflict.

This failure of institutionalisation on a group or supra-group level is not unique to the conflict period studied here but appears to be a general feature of the SJM. For example, in the context of Egypt's militant environment, the differences in internal institutionalisation within al-Jama'a al-Islamiyya and Al Jihad are instructive in explaining their handling of internal tensions and diversity. Coming from a broad student movement, al-Jama'a al-Islamiyya established strong institutions which helped the group cope with internal differences. In Al Jihad, which was structured as a clandestine vanguard, such institutions were largely absent, and this hampered its ability to settle the internal differences that eventually fractured the group. On a supra-group level, the groups never managed to establish successful institutions to manage inter-group tensions and their various merger attempts.[21]

In the 2014–19 period, the primary failure of Jihadi groups has been their inability to establish effective supra-group institutions to adjudicate and de-escalate tensions. This failure is not for the lack of trying but is predominantly the result of continuous rejection by one or several groups involved in the conflict. On several occasions this failure resulted in an escalation of inter-group tensions, manifesting either as infighting or arrest campaigns. Bacon observes a similar inability within the broader context of terrorism, arguing that one problem that afflicts terrorist groups is that they 'cannot overcome mutual distrust by creating institutions to bind themselves to agreements.'[22] On the occasions when Jihadi groups attempted to establish institutional mechanisms to mitigate or solve conflict, such as shari'a courts or judiciary councils, such attempts have failed.

As mentioned in chapter 4, from late 2013 to October 2014, fifteen calls for arbitration and reconciliation to solve the conflict between the Islamic State and rival groups can be identified; several proposed the establishment of formal supra-group independent institutions to adjudicate. The story was largely the same in 2017–18, first between HTS and Ahrar al-Sham/Nour al-Deen al-Zinki and later between HTS and Hurras al-Deen. On all these occasions, adjudication was suggested or attempted but was consistently rejected or lacked the necessary authority. A similar experience is noticeable inside the respective groups when they attempt to establish judicial institutions to solve intra-group tensions.

Another institutional failure is Jihadis' difficulty in bringing about mergers between groups. Arguably the most decisive examples of failed mergers are Jabhat al-Nusra's rejection of the offer to join the Islamic Front in 2013, the highly anticipated merger between Jabhat al-Nusra/JFS and Ahrar al-Sham in 2016–17 and the establishment of HTS—a situation where, despite the merger being realised, substantial defection resulted. The main causes of these failures are Jihadis' general reluctance to accept diversity along with disagreement about the strategy of the Jihadi project. These causes are prevalent among all political groups and thus not unique to the SJM, but it is nonetheless likely that they are more decisive within a rigidly 'Manichean' movement.

The way groups and individuals perceive themselves is obviously also important for explaining this failure. The caliphate is considered the ultimate authority and is inherently an exclusivist construction in terms of its dealing with other entities. When proponents of the caliphate rejected arbitration as a reconciliation mechanism, they argued that the caliphate could not be treated as a group since its authority was above that of a group. But the rejection of arbitration is more strongly linked to a certain attitude than to a specific religio-political entity. Despite not having declared a caliphate or even an emirate, HTS similarly refused independent arbitration to help solve its conflict with Ahrar al-Sham and Nour al-Deen al-Zinki. These examples show that groups seeking hegemony are generally unwilling to submit to supra-group institutional authority which they cannot control themselves since the delegation of authority is perceived as a threat and incompatible with their hegemonic project. Such a position, however, is particularly damaging to the broader SJM, because it promotes the escalation of tensions at the expense of reconciliation.

Efforts to establish internal institutional mechanisms to manage tensions have similarly been a failure. They have been overly politicised, and driven by a desire to suppress rather than reconcile, and by groups' inability to accept diversity. Within the Islamic State, a political struggle for control of key institutions played out in 2016–18 between competing factions with the intention to suppress the competitor. For instance, the so-called *Office for Methodological Inquiry* (maktab al-tadqiq al-manhaji), also known as the Methodological Committee (al-lajna al-manhajiyya), was intended to identify and punish internal voices of opposition. In HTS, the *Follow-up Committee* (lajnat al-muttaba'a) was created to handle internal quarrels and dissatisfaction in the aftermath of the split from al-Qaida. But in neither of these cases did the institutions manage to unite their respective groups.

In this light, it is interesting to note that some groups have recently shown an increasing interest in establishing internal mechanisms of conflict resolution. For example, the *codes of conduct* released by the Taliban[23] and AQIS[24] in 2017 and by the TTP[25] in 2018 are explicitly addressing the development of mechanisms to manage conflict including their implementation and execution. These are important institutional steps for Jihadi groups to prevent future intra-group conflict, but they will most likely fall short of addressing the more acute challenge linked to establishing institutions on a supra-group level.

### *Group and Counter-Group: Internalisation of Conflict Dynamics*

To better understand conflict dynamics among non-state actors, scholars have dealt thoroughly with conflict between opposing movements—but much less with conflict within movements. However, the study of intra-Jihadi conflict testifies that intra-movement conflict dynamics closely resemble conflict dynamics between a movement and a countermovement. In their work on movements and countermovements, Zald and Useem write that 'much of a movement's activity is aimed at neutralising, confronting, or discrediting its corresponding countermovement. Similarly, the countermovement gains its impetus and grows from showing the harmful effects of the movement. It attacks the movement leaders, bombs its sites of program action, and associates the movement with evil.'[26] Such dynamics are plentiful between nationalist groups with opposing ideologies and in the literature on reciprocal radicalisation. Animosity between movement and countermovement is a logical phenomenon, however, since they have opposing ideologies and generally fight for conflicting objectives (although they occasionally unite against a common enemy). That similar conflict dynamics occur *within* a movement between groups with relatively similar ideologies is a less intuitive finding, and has implications for how we assess the impact of ideology, which is generally viewed as a unifying factor.

Since 2014, actors within the SJM have found themselves in a cooperation–polarisation paradox. Their ideological affinity and military inferiority vis-à-vis their enemies result in natural incentives to cooperate. In reality, however, their actions tend to be more conducive to polarisation than cooperation. Groups and individuals have engaged in vilification campaigns against rival Jihadis to enable their own success. They have ridiculed rivals' ideological programs to undermine them and have refused to share material resources. They call each other degrading names and occasionally they kill each other.

In the terrorism literature on cooperation, ideology is identified as an important component. The argument is not that ideological affinity automatically leads to cooperation, but that it is conducive to it. A competing view, however, is that ideological affinity risks producing a competitive environment because groups sharing the same ideology typically also struggle for the same authority and the same resources. In relation to conflict, we see on the one hand that ideological affinity does not prevent groups and individuals from contesting and fighting one another, but on the other that it does not automatically lead to competition. That said, it is possible to infer that the degree of affinity probably does have an impact on the initial process of conflict. Fighters in Jabhat al-Nusra explained that one of the reasons the group adopted an aggressive attitude towards the Islamic State later than most other groups was because of their closer ideological affinity. But in the end, this did not prevent the group from attacking its former ally.

Historic empirical examples prove that this belligerent group and counter-group dynamic is not unique to the SJM. Several nationalist, revolutionary and Islamist movements have experienced a similar conflict dynamic—for example, in Sri Lanka the Tamil rebellion saw factionalism and infighting as a result of the Tamil Tigers' hegemonist ambitions. The Russian Communist movement and the Irish Republican movement are other examples of how movement and countermovement dynamics internalise within a movement, thus establishing a group and counter-group relationship characterised by name-calling, demonisation, fragmentation and polarisation, and occasionally by military conflict. Groups and individuals stress their own orthodoxy or methodological acumen while declaring their opponents' behaviour deviant, often making accusations of heresy that stress the opponents' purported *extremism* or *dilution*. An especially typical element in these conflicts between radicals is how the actors engage in an exercise of labelling or accusing rivals using an *extreme–moderate* spectrum, placing themselves in the middle. In 2016, this process was internalised within the Islamic State when conflict broke out between competing factions of the group.

The fact that ideological affinity within the SJM contains a religious element would make us expect greater solidarity among groups because of the 'sticky' character of religion as an identity marker. Yet there are reasons to question this assumption in the specific context of the SJM. Their general emphasis on a rigid and literal textual reading of religious texts coupled with a Manichean worldview makes Jihadis sensitive even to small internal ideological differences. One result of this is that Jihadis find it challenging to handle internal diversity both within their own group and within the broader movement. While this has obvious benefits for their enemies (that can be strategically exploited), it has potentially catastrophic consequences for Jihadis themselves.

Hence, an important finding from this book's analysis is that in combination, Jihadis' political ambitions and the distinctive role of ideology produce highly volatile internal relations and a latent risk of internal conflict that easily turns from discursive contestation to infighting. Since 2014, this risk has been continuously triggered by the competitive environment within the SJM, forcing Jihadi groups and individuals to relate to one another in ways that the movement as a whole has been incapable of managing. Furthermore, over the six-year period from 2014 to 2019, Jihadis have time and again proved unable to learn from their mistakes and instead reproduced conflict cycles.

# 2

# EXPLAINING JIHADI FRATRICIDE

Building on the previous chapter, the purpose of this chapter is to suggest an explanation for why Jihadis have fought each other so intensely in the studied period. We know much about why Jihadis cooperate, as there is a fairly good literature on this. In contrast, within research on Islamism and the subfield of Jihadism, the analytical focus has rarely been on describing and understanding conflictual relations and dynamics *between* actors, but rather on studying their relation to the state, their ideology or how they mobilise. In the cooperation literature it is argued that understanding internal relations is key to reaching a nuanced view of Jihadis and the threat they pose.[1] This includes internal conflict relations. One of the reasons such fratricidal dynamics are important is that they occasionally take priority over more long-term ideological objectives. Another is that they affect group survival.[2] Yet factionalism and internecine infighting too often remain neglected, in part because Jihadi groups are usually treated as homogenous terrorist or religious organisations.

In his work to revise and further nuance the various branches of Salafism, Wagemakers acknowledged that Jihadis are 'perhaps the least understood of the three branches of Salafism' and, quoting Hegghammer, 'ill-defined'.[3] Arguably the best researched internal issue is the differences in political preferences and enemy hierarchy.[4]

Hegghammer's typology, in particular, is instructive for grasping important differences in the rationales guiding Jihadis in their strategy and actions, while also stressing that competing rationales exist within groups.[5] More recently, Stenersen introduced another typology that is even more relevant to understand the internal fault lines within the contemporary SJM. She places Jihadi groups on two scales: how they relate to society (integration vs. separation) and whom Jihadis fight for (the nation vs. the umma).[6] This typology represents an important framework that allows for a more fine-grained analysis of the internal divisionary issues within the movement. It also enables a more nuanced understanding of internal diversity, including how this changes over time.

Since 2013, a flood of academic[7] and journalistic articles,[8] reports[9] and book chapters[10] have tackled the conflict between al-Qaida and the Islamic State from different angles, though usually without analysing events and their dynamics in an exhaustive manner. Existing explanations of internal conflict can roughly be divided into three categories: those emphasising ideology; others stressing the struggle for power; and finally some highlighting material and economic concerns. While all explanations have their respective merits, they are insufficient on their own to account for the complexity of internal conflict within the SJM. This book proposes that to understand why groups like the Islamic State and al-Qaida evolve from affiliation to contestation and finally to infighting we must look at processes on a macro-, meso- and micro-level. This involves: the political context facilitating a change in the inter-group relationship; how groups and particularly their senior members develop and disseminate new discourses and change behaviour; and how prominent individuals and virtual supporter networks participate in framing efforts to delegitimise certain forms of behaviour and mobilise for action.[11]

Based on empirical observations in the period 2014–19, this book presents a new typology focusing on how groups approach other Jihadis and how they view their own role within the movement. It suggests three distinctive rationales to describe variations in intra-Jihadi relations (see table 3), namely *hegemonist*, *unitarian* and *isolationist*. The argument is that these rationales impact upon intra-Jihadi collaborative and conflictual dynamics because they inform the strategy groups follow when dealing with other groups as well as their attitudes towards the legitimacy of infighting and ideological diversity.

Table 3: Rationales for Intra-Jihadi Competition and Conflict

| *Typology / rationale* | *Logic behind intra-movement actions* | *Strategy towards other groups* | *Attitude to intra-movement infighting / fitna* |
|---|---|---|---|
| Hegemonist | Seeking to become a movement hegemon | Exclusivism,[12] co-optation & competition | Legitimate and necessary |
| Unitarian | Seeking unity within the movement | Inclusivism[13]/ cooperative | Illegitimate and only to defend |
| Isolationist | Neutrality as a principle | Staying neutral | Illegitimate and only to defend |

These categories are ideal types, and one should expect some degree of gradualism between the categories, not least in different geographical settings. As is evident throughout the book, these rationales operate both on a global and a local level since a group can seek dominance within the movement in its specific area of operations while not necessarily striving to become a global hegemon. The distinctive character of the three rationales is that:

- *Hegemonists'* attitude to intra-Jihadi relations is primarily driven by power ambitions and a desire to dominate the SJM locally, regionally or globally. This is founded on the self-perception that it represents the sole Jihadi authority in its territory of operations. Rivalling Jihadi groups are seen as competitors, if not threats, that potentially need to be fought.
- *Unitarians'* main rationale is to seek unity within the movement. This rationale is founded on a self-perception as a *group* (jama'a) rather than all-encompassing authoritative entities such as a *state* (dawla) or a *caliphate* (khilafa). Unity is sought through an inclusivist attitude that is promoted through alliances and cooperation, while infighting with other Jihadi groups is generally considered illegitimate.

- *Isolationists'* rationale is to entirely isolate itself from Jihadi infighting. They consider themselves as groups among equals and are in favour of unity and intra-Jihadi collaboration, but their reaction to any act of aggression is isolation rather than retaliation. Such abstention comes from the view that infighting is illegitimate, or from a refusal to take sides because of inferiority.

While these typologies aid understanding of the variance in groups' self-perception that informs their attitude to other groups within the same movement and their propensity to engage in fratricide, hegemonic ambitions alone, as Mendelsohn correctly argues, 'cannot account for the timing of the dominant actor's drive for unity' or conflict.[14] Several factors or mechanisms play important roles in enabling, facilitating and instigating intra-Jihadi conflict. Throughout the analysis, four environmental, cognitive and relational mechanisms will be discussed, since they all affect relations among groups within the SJM and help explain variance in conflict level and the timing of infighting.[15] The argument is not that all mechanisms are necessarily at play in every episode of intra-Jihadi conflict. Rather the following mechanisms have been identified as central in either the main case study (al-Qaida versus the Islamic State) or in one of the sub-cases as conflict *enablers* or *triggers*.

The following sections focus on the four factors that I argue have been decisive causes prompting intra-Jihadi conflict. First is the increased competition within the SJM coupled with specific groups' hegemonic ambitions, which proved a particularly explosive combination. Second is the interference of external state actors, whose engagement had an impact on conflict dynamics and exerted strong political pressure on Jihadis and alterations in military balance between groups. Third is the role of ideology both as a factor constraining intra-movement diversity and as a mechanism to legitimise infighting. Fourth is how socialisation to intra-Jihadi conflict is lowering the threshold for future conflict, thus helping to explain the prevalence of fratricide over time.

*Competition and the Struggle for Hegemony*

Quickly after the Syrian civil war broke out, a myriad of new rebel groups were established with the objective of ousting Syrian President Bashar al-Assad. This growing rebellion involved several Jihadi groups that, despite their common aims in terms of removing al-Assad and replacing his government with a religious state of some sort, were competing for the same recruits, territory, funding and (not least) authority. While recognising ideological affinities, Jihadi groups are acutely aware that they compete for the same limited resources, which are essential for their continued survival.[16] Willingly or not, it is implied that Jihadi groups are pitted against one another. At first, this level of increased competition turned out to be manageable and groups like Jabhat al-Nusra, Ahrar al-Sham, Jaysh al-Islam, and the TIP occasionally cooperated, but with the Islamic State's expansion to Syria in April 2013, intra-Jihadi relations changed considerably. Unlike the other Jihadi groups, the Islamic State's ambition was not simply to represent one piece in the rebellion but to subsume other Jihadi groups with the aim of representing the entire Jihadi movement, first in Syria and later in other countries. The declaration of the caliphate was a crucial step to realising this hegemonic vision.

The Islamic State's threat directed against competing Jihadi groups sparked unprecedented tensions within the SJM that over the following months turned increasingly militant until it finally exploded in January 2014—and further intensified when the group targeted several senior figures from rival groups. The assassination of Ahrar al-Sham's Abu Khalid al-Suri was particularly grave and an early indication of what was about to come. From this point on, Jihadi groups started to devote considerable financial, human and military resources to conflict with other Jihadis, in addition to elaborate discursive discrediting. Over the course of 2014, Jihadi infighting only grew in strength and ferocity, to the extent that fratricide would represent a substantial part of Jihadi groups' military activities. As such 2014 was the year *the internal enemy* became an integral part of Jihadis' enemy hierarchy. Hence, when the Islamic State eventually expanded outside of Syria, it turned out to only be a matter of time before infighting erupted in other countries where the group had declared official *provinces*.

The caliphate was essentially a claim for hegemony, since it left no room for competing Jihadi groups. The numerous mediation and reconciliation initiatives from other groups and high-ranking ideologues were consistently rejected through the argument that a state does not negotiate with a group. Faced with attacks from the Islamic State, rival Jihadis would ally as a mechanism to survive, but their response was mainly to defend. Due to its early success in attracting the majority of new recruits and controlling large swaths of territory in Syria, however, the Islamic State felt emboldened to continue its aggression. This involved an intensification in discourse relying on theological discrediting notions to legitimise the otherwise controversial acts of violence. In contrast, al-Qaida's leadership would become the main proponent of a unitarian rationale.

From 2015 infighting between the Islamic State and groups like Jabhat al-Nusra and Ahrar al-Sham would lessen in intensity, mainly as a result of their geographical separation. Simultaneously, however, tensions were building up in other parts of the world, and the first place for infighting to erupt outside of Syria was in Afghanistan, where the Islamic State's hegemonic ambitions would conflict with the Taliban's own objective to represent an exclusive Islamic authority.

Back in Syria, cracks eventually started to emerge among Jihadi groups in Idlib. Jabhat al-Nusra had gone through a rebranding and a merger to establish Hayat Tahrir al-Sham (HTS). In the process, it had abandoned its allegiance to al-Qaida. Previously the victim of the Islamic State's ambitions, HTS would embark on a hegemonic project of its own. On the political side, the group formed a government while it militarily started to suppress any Jihadi competitor including former allies. The group would eventually issue a statement prohibiting the establishment of new groups and severely restricting the actions of already existing groups. In Afghanistan and Somalia, similar rationales would guide local crackdowns against competitors.

The main argument here is that most episodes of Jihadi infighting are driven by one or more actors' claims to local or global hegemony and to represent an exclusive authority. In a competitive environment like the SJM during the studied period, such power ambitions have generally proved stronger than the uniting bond of a shared ideology. The 2000s Jihadi environment in Afghanistan testifies that internal competition does not necessarily lead to conflict. As we have seen in the post-2014 period, it largely depends on the dominant rationales.

### *Interference of External Actors and Changing Military Balances*

Tensions resulting from the growing competition and the Islamic State's (and later HTS's) hegemonist rationale became even more complex due to the interference of external state actors. In chapter 4, I argue that the US' killing of Usama Bin Laden fundamentally changed the structures of authority within the SJM by creating a leadership vacuum that enabled other Jihadi groups to challenge the authority of the al-Qaida–Taliban nexus. The killing of Bin Laden was effectively an act by an external actor that caused this shock to the movement hierarchy and eventually facilitated change. Throughout the 2014–19 period, the political and military interference of external state actors similarly affected inter-group dynamics, including the relative military balance among groups. This not only affected groups' external priorities, but also the likelihood of internal conflict.

External actors became involved in the Syrian conflict shortly after it erupted, both on a political and a military level. At first, it was mainly Arab states and Turkey that offered support to various rebel groups, but over time other states would join too in a bid to defeat the Jihadi insurgency or in support of the Assad regime. On numerous occasions, this interference would have a substantial impact on conflict dynamics and on specific Jihadi groups, thus directly affecting the context Jihadis were operating within and the power balance among them. This was not only the case in Syria but in most of the conflicts witnessing Jihadi infighting, including Nigeria, Mali, Somalia, Yemen and Afghanistan.

At first in Syria, in 2013–14, the Islamic State was largely ignored by state actors. This provided the group with the freedom to strengthen itself and expand its territorial control at the expense of other Syrian rebels, including Jihadis, during the outbreak of the Jihadi civil war. This early trajectory allowed the group to establish its image as the most successful Jihadi group in the Syrian war, something that was instrumental to its future ability to attract and control important resources such as foreign and local fighters and key sources of income. The addition of resources further favoured the Islamic State vis-à-vis its rivals since it made the group comparatively stronger. These dynamics would make confrontations against its competitors more attractive, which the group was not slow to realise.

Later during the war, external actors started to exert enormous military pressure on a few select Jihadi groups but mainly targeting the Islamic State. One change was the tighter border control between Turkey and Syria that hampered the flow of foreign fighters to and from Syria. Yet more importantly, military intervention—first the international US-led coalition, then the Iranian militias and Russia's air campaign, and finally the military offensive launched by Turkey—had a hugely negative impact on the group. It began to lose territory, its military capabilities degraded and its ability to move freely and recruit was limited. It also lost several prominent leadership figures in the process and their deaths had considerable influence on inter- and intra-group dynamics and the power balance among groups. These developments affected the Islamic State's strong dominance of Syria's Jihadi environment and the group scaled down its military aggression against Jihadi competitors in Syria, instead focusing on discrediting rivals through its media productions. There are several examples in Afghanistan, the Sahel and Nigeria of how Jihadis would similarly take advantage of external military interference to confront their local Jihadi rivals.

Another important point is how political interference and cooperation also played its part in affecting how Jihadi groups viewed one another. This would particularly inform the situation in Syria's northwest from 2016, when Ahrar al-Sham (and later HTS) established close relations with Turkey. Jihadis generally consider engagement with states illegitimate, so when the groups started to coordinate and collaborate with Turkey, it prompted substantial defection and strong criticism both from within and from their rivals. Stressing the fluid and evolving context, HTS was the hardest critic of Ahrar al-Sham when it refused to merge and instead moved closer to Turkey. Only a year after, however, HTS would establish cordial relations with Turkey, triggering fierce criticism from al-Qaida loyalists and from the Islamic State. In discussions of the situation in Syria, Yemen and Afghanistan, rumours would also begin to circulate on media platforms that some groups were actively assisting states in the targeting of rivalling Jihadi leaders.

Roy has analysed how participation in political processes has weakened the Islamic movement because it has resulted in increased secularisation and pragmatism.[17] A similar observation can be made for the SJM, which only confirms the warning from hardliners within the movement. Similar to how extremism and the radicalisation of violence are threats to cohesion within the SJM, so is the 'moderation' that comes with engaging in political processes, partly because it leads to tensions with other, more purist, groups. But unlike in nationalist movements where rivals act as spoilers to upset negotiations, Jihadis appear to attack rivals who engage in political collaboration with states to punish them and capitalise on their concessions.[18] The impact of external interference also stresses the extent to which Jihadis' internal dynamics were not exclusively driven by their own ambitions and agency but were adjusting to a constantly evolving military and political context. These developments forced Jihadis to revise their strategies and priorities. This proved challenging to manage and occasionally drove internal conflict.

### *Ideological Constraints and Legitimation*

A third factor is how ideology has played a central role both constraining movement diversity within a constantly changing context and as an enabler of violence. Jihadis generally have a narrow view of the acceptable ideological spectrum. This view leaves little room for change. First in the context of Syria, and later in other battlefields as well, the internal competition led to increased diversification within the movement and a *politicisation of differences* that were occasionally framed as a threat to the entire Jihadi project. The constraining role of ideology was thus a constant source of tension with groups and individuals alike negotiating boundaries of acceptable behaviour. This mainly involved issues related to the establishment of an Islamic state and allegiances with other groups and states.

The main focus on ideology throughout this study, however, has been on the micro level, exploring how individuals, primarily ideologues (or scholars) and supporters (munasirun), have struggled to frame their own group, their rivals and conflict between them in specific ways—to either prohibit or legitimise intra-Jihadi violence—and how these discourses were disseminated. A regular issue within research on Jihadism, and more broadly on Islamism, is assessing the impact of religious figures—referred to in this study as ideologues and scholars—on groups and individuals. Similar conclusions hold true for Jihadi supporters. Hence, the findings here are illustrative not only of ideologues' and supporters' actual impact in terms of the specific phenomenon of conflict, but also of their role more generally within the SJM.[19]

Since 2014, ideologues have played the role of *guides, unifiers* and *troublemakers*. At first, on one hand they were central in the formulation of religious justifications which legitimised or prohibited infighting, and on the other hand proponents of numerous reconciliation initiatives. In the Islamic State, Abu Ali al-Anbari and Turki al-Binali in particular authored several fatwas portraying rival groups and ideologues in a discrediting light and occasionally legitimised attacks against them, which was crucial for Islamic State members to overcome a general opposition to intra-Muslim conflict. In contrast, al-Qaida affiliated scholars issued rulings prohibiting attacks against the Islamic State except in self-defence. Over time, some developed a more conciliatory discourse while others chose a strategy of vilification. Ideologues also played an important role in managing and occasionally escalating tensions *within groups*.

Studying these articulations of micro-level frames has demonstrated their impact on group-level affairs and movement dynamics. Due to their authoritative standing among Jihadi rank and file, ideologues are important to group leaders. Interviews with rank and file and leadership figures from the Syrian Jihad confirm this conclusion.[20] For instance, in the confusing environment of spring 2013, after the expansion of the Islamic State into Syria, rank and file Jihadis, more than anyone else, awaited the rulings of Abu Qatada and al-Maqdisi before deciding on which group to join. Despite their waning influence over time, ideologues' framing of organisational conflict and infighting through fatwas and general statements had an immense impact on the ground. Yet as Lahoud notes, ideological voices are not always obeyed: this depends on their social standing and on how their intervention aligns with group interests.[21] Nonetheless, as the analysis here has illustrated, it is essential to follow the evolution of ideological discourse (see table 4 for an example) and its resonance both on a rank and file level and a leadership level in order to understand *why* and *when* groups engage in certain actions.

Table 4: The Evolution of the Discourses of al-Maqdisi and Abu Qatada 2013–19

| | *Dominant discourse* | *Period* |
|---|---|---|
| Abu Qatada al-Filastini | Strong condemnation of the Islamic State | November 2013–Summer 2015 |
| | Remaining quiet | Summer 2015–November 2016 |
| | Pacification and unification | November 2016–December 2019 |
| Abu Muhammad al-Maqdisi | Controlled condemnation of the Islamic State | November 2013–Summer 2016 |
| | Purifying Jihad | Summer 2016–November 2017 |
| | Vilification | November 2017–December 2019 |

While these ideologues may exert substantial influence on the Jihadi masses and their organisational leaders, the relationship is reciprocal since ideologues are also influenced by groups through institutionalisation and isolation. In the studied period, groups have increasingly attempted to co-opt ideologues to their internal institutions as *instruments of legitimisation*. The Islamic

State and HTS have been particularly successful in recruiting ideological figures and appointing them to senior positions, which has enabled groups to rely on and manipulate their authority and opinions, thus essentially turning them into instrumental sources of authority.[22] The Islamic State initially sought to attract senior ideologues. When that failed, it offered its institutional platform to younger and lesser known ideologues who loyally complied with the group's political and strategic interests, for example in the excommunication of rivals. The logic behind this was to limit the dependence on independent individuals and to gain control over a critically important mechanism that proved especially important in terms of internal conflict.

In contrast, the main role of supporters has not been the *articulation* of frames but their *dissemination*, something which is key to ensuring their resonance. This study has mainly focused on the online dimension of such dissemination by following al-Qaida, Islamic State and HTS supporter accounts and channels on Twitter and Telegram. On these platforms, supporters have been effective distributors of official group material and ideological frames, which has helped to strengthen the message that groups and ideologues want to convey, as well as the global resonance of the message. It is probably fair to argue that no Jihadi group or ideologue would have been as successful in their internal and external communication without the existence of active supporter networks acting as decentralised agents.

The Islamic State has shown how the use of supporter networks is directly related to its media structure, effectively blurring the boundaries between official and unofficial media centres, while al-Qaida has built its media apparatus around semi-independent but supportive disseminators. Even the channels of some Jihadi ideologues are managed by supporters rather than the ideologues themselves. In terms of internal conflict, supporters have disseminated religious rulings, defended the position of their groups, incited infighting and contributed to the polarised environment within the movement. In some periods, supporters' vilification of rivals and ideologues has been as important as reporting on their own group. In addition, supporters have published their own material which aligns with their group's position and attacks rivals more directly than official material typically does. Together this adds up to an ideological textual corpus on internal conflict.

Studying these micro-level frames and discourses and their interaction with macro- and meso-level factors is thus important for grasping the complexity of intra-Jihadi conflict. One of the distinctive features of the SJM is that the justification for conflict, the cautioning against it and attempts at reconciliation have become pervasive on this individual level, which then informs group behaviour.

### *Socialisation to Fratricide*

The final key factor is socialisation to fratricidal practices.[23] Within the studied period, socialisation had a decisive impact on the scope of internal conflict with potentially critical repercussions for the future SJM. Socialising its members to Jihadi infighting has been integral to groups, since infighting represents a distinctive type of violence against fellow Jihadis which is highly sensitive and controversial. As a result, it has been driven by several factors, namely framing of narratives, religious rulings and exposure, which together involved vertical and horizontal dimensions and resulted in three dynamics: *normalisation of infighting, radicalisation of inter-group relations* and *reciprocal distrust*. Literature on the role of socialisation in violence, including specific types of violence, offers support for such a process.[24]

Some of these factors have already been described. Jihadi actors have developed distinctive narratives to frame and legitimise a certain behaviour in terms of infighting. These narratives are central for explaining to rank and file members the justification for, and necessity of, attacking fellow Jihadis, and have played an important role in desensitising fratricide through contextualising it and providing it with a religious basis. This religious basis has been further cemented through the issuing of religious rulings, considered a prerequisite within the SJM, which reinforced the socialisation process.[25] Interviewees and textual accounts indicate the importance of ideologues' input and rulings, specifically in relation to how one should behave towards rival groups. Although framed in a religious terminology, the driving force behind the issuing of many of these religious rulings appear to have been groups' ambitions to increase their own power at the expense of rivals, thus illustrating how Jihadi leaders have systematically politicised ideologues.

The exposure to infighting also had an important impact in various ways. Occasionally, groups would execute members of rival Jihadi groups in public places in front of audiences consisting of young and old alike. In mid-2015, several groups started to issue visual material showing these executions. Later, this would include pictures and recordings of military raids against rivals. On numerous occasions, the Islamic State also issued propaganda material calling for the death of specific high-ranking Jihadi individuals including the al-Qaida leader al-Zawahiri. These factors functioned both vertically and horizontally. Narratives and religious rulings came from the leadership while the experience of witnessing one's peers engaging in Jihadi infighting likely eased one's own acceptance of the phenomenon.

Although we do not know the exact numbers, there are numerous examples of group members objecting and rebelling against fratricidal practices, resulting in them either leaving Jihad altogether or defecting from their specific group to join another. These stories surfaced, especially in interviews with foreign fighters returning to their home countries early in the Syrian conflict. Many mentioned the fight against other Jihadi groups as the primary reason for their disillusionment. Later, there are examples of fighters deciding to leave a group which was engaged in infighting to join another because they considered it an illegitimate fight.

While this micro-level rebellion against fratricidal practices is illustrative of the agency involved in the socialisation process, it nonetheless seems fair to conclude that the vast majority of Jihadis have become more accustomed to (and tolerant of) Jihadi infighting. Hence, what we have witnessed in the 2014–19 period is arguably not merely the outcome of a rational calculation in response to group norms and expectations but a widespread internalisation of fratricidal practices, resulting in a thorough socialisation of group members in the logic of fratricide. One result of this socialisation is the *normalisation of infighting*. Previous sensitivities and objections have largely been deconstructed and replaced by a reconstruction of new narratives legitimising infighting in various ways. Whereas the initial episodes of infighting were highly controversial, later episodes were followed by much less criticism. In their work on children in terrorism, Bloom and Horgan describe similar socialisation processes and note that children are more easily affected. Therefore it seems logical to suggest that the effects of fratricidal socialisation have a greater impact on the younger generation of Jihadis, who are generally more susceptible and whose entire experience of Jihad has involved episodes of internal conflict.[26]

Socialisation and the ensuing normalisation of fratricide have also entailed a *radicalisation of inter-group relations*. Since the emergence of the modern SJM in the 1960s, Jihadis have debated internally, contested one another's authority, creed or methodology, and on rare occasions engaged in infighting. Even so, the escalation of intra-Jihadi conflict in 2014 represents a qualitative change in the way Jihadis relate to one another, increasing the risk of disagreement evolving into military conflict. A third dynamic is a *reciprocal distrust*, which similarly affects inter-group relations and the degree of cohesion within the SJM. Few events, if any, leave scars as deep as those left by war. Having fought each other on several occasions since 2014 and given that the *internal enemy* has periodically been prioritised as the *primary* enemy, these experiences have left a movement where there is little trust among groups and individuals. Jihadis have time and again shown themselves capable of turning against their former brothers-in-arms simply for the sake of power. Initially, this dominated the extent to which groups cooperated, but it is to be expected that mistrust will have a significant impact on future chances of organisational mergers and the ability of the movement to once again become cohesive.

# PART TWO

# SETTING THE STAGE

*'Even if our bodies are far apart, the distance between our hearts is close.'*[1]

Abu Musab al-Zarqawi
Letter to the al-Qaida leadership

*'We do not see ourselves as fit to challenge you, and we have never striven to achieve glory for ourselves.'*[2]

Abu Musab al-Zarqawi
Letter to the al-Qaida leadership

# 3

# THE HISTORY OF JIHADI POLEMICS AND CONFLICT

Internal disagreements, competition and contestation have impacted Sunni Jihadism since its modern inception in the 1960s.[3] Time and again, individuals and groups have engaged in polemical debates and on rare occasions, they have even directed their weapons against one another. In order to foster a better understanding of the contemporary struggle between al-Qaida and the Islamic State, the following two chapters look at the history of intra-Jihadi conflict up until the infighting that erupted in 2014. This chapter traces how Sunni Jihadi individuals and groups have disagreed and competed on several occasions and for different purposes from the 1960s onwards. As will become evident, in some of these examples disagreement led to violent confrontation, while in others the outcome remained on the level of discursive accusations. In some instances, it was both.

## *Jihadism's Emergence as a Heterogenous Movement*

Despite being a relatively unified movement in terms of objectives and ideology, Sunni Jihadism has witnessed its fair share of internal disagreement and conflict. In 1964, the Egyptian Jihadi theorist Sayyid Qutb published his manifesto legitimising Jihad, *ma'alim fi-l-tariq*, commonly known as 'Milestones'. In the widely disseminated book, Qutb criticises Western decadence and the *jahiliyya* (pre-Islamic ignorance) that, in his view, has infested Islamic societies. Set in the context of a severe crackdown on Islamist forces by the Egyptian regime, Qutb's answer to the state of *jahiliyya* was to legitimise rebellion against Muslim rulers and to propagate Jihad exercised through an Islamic vanguard movement. This stance, however, was considered too radical by many in the Muslim Brotherhood, where Qutb was still a leading figure, provoking Hassan al-Hudaybi, the leader of the Muslim Brotherhood, to publish the book *du'at la qudat* ('Preachers, Not Judges') that thoroughly opposed Qutb's suggested solution.[4]

Unlike future Jihadi ideologues, Qutb did not consider Jihad a goal in and of itself, but rather a means to an end to create a more just and Islamic society.[5] He also viewed Jihad as a process consisting of several stages. Before one could be part of the vanguard and participate in the militant Jihad, one would need to go through an inner Jihad (*jihad al-nafs, literally 'Jihad of the soul'*) to obtain the necessary knowledge to 'see the milestones along the road', as Qutb puts it. Obviously, this functioned as a *restriction* on the operationalisation of Jihad.

In 1966, after spending ten very productive years in prison, Qutb was hanged, and martyred in the eyes of his sympathisers, but his vision for an emerging Jihadi movement was about to be brought into being. The first organisation to find inspiration in Qutb's ideas was Jama'at al-Muslimeen, better known as al-Takfir wa-l-Hijra (Excommunication and Withdrawal), led from 1972 by Shukri Mustafa. Mustafa's extreme approach, which involved declaring everyone refusing to join his group an *apostate* (murtadd) and stressing the requirement to isolate in the desert to establish an Islamic state, resulted in the group's own demise.[6] Hence, it was not until the late 1970s, when Muhammad Abd al-Salam Faraj as part of Tanzim al-Jihad (Al-Jihad Group)[7] wrote the manifesto *al-Farida al-Gha'iba* (The Neglected Duty), that Qutb's vision of Jihad took proper organisational shape.

While Faraj's view of Arab governments was clearly influenced by Qutb, he also disagreed with Qutb on several important issues. Like

Qutb, he believed in a vanguard movement to topple the Egyptian government and he prioritised a focus on *the near enemy* (al-aduw al-qarib). However, on the issue of the necessity of education, training and knowledge prior to engaging in Jihad, Faraj implicitly criticised his predecessor, believing that the SJM was in fact ready for action.[8] In 'The Neglected Duty', Faraj writes that:

> There are some who say that at present the true road is the quest for knowledge. 'How can we fight when we have no knowledge [of Islam and its prescripts]? The quest for knowledge is an obligation too.' But we shall not heed the words of someone who permits the neglect of a religious command or one of the duties of Islam for the sake of [the quest for religious] knowledge, certainly not if this duty is the duty of jihad.[9]

While criticism is also directed at the official religious establishment in Egypt, it is hard not to read a critique of Qutb's precautions here, as Faraj continues:

> We find that today jihad is an individual duty of every Muslim. Nevertheless we find that there are those who argue that they need to educate their own souls, and that jihad knows successive phases; and that they are still in the phase of jihad against their own soul.[10]

For Faraj, the objective was to simplify the rules of engagement and the understanding of militant Jihad by removing restrictions. Whereas Qutb sought to *legitimise* Jihad, Faraj wanted to *operationalise* it. Hence, he argued that Jihad was indeed *fard al-ayn* (individual duty), that it was both defensive and offensive, and that training and education were not prerequisites. Modern Jihadi ideology started with Qutb and Faraj; even though the latter criticised several of his predecessors and contemporaries, including Qutb, Shukri Mustafa and the al-Azhar establishment, such criticism did not result in debate between adherents of the two ideological trends at that time. The modern Jihadi movement was still in its infancy, yet the schism between Faraj and Qutb was an early indicator of future debates and disagreement within the movement.

### *Afghanistan's Competitive Militant Environment in the 1980s*

It was in the 1980s, during the fight against the Soviet invasion and the communist Afghan regime, that tensions between organised factions would first emerge. Afghan mujahideen, supported from 1984 onwards by Arab fighters, the so-called Arab–Afghans, united to fight against a common enemy. However, the struggle was not limited to the battle between communists and mujahideen as tensions also arose among the mujahideen. The firsthand accounts by Abdallah Anas[11] and Mustafa Hamid[12] are particularly enlightening about these intra-mujahideen problems, which began simply as matters of access to funding, power and mobilisation of recruits.

The Jihadi scene in Afghanistan was an extremely competitive environment. In their conversational book, Leah Farrall and Mustafa Hamid, the latter a Jihadi journalist close to the Taliban, describe the Jihadi community as 'a melting pot of different Jihadi groups who fought over things like funding, recruits and resources in addition to the favour of the Taliban', while concluding that this internal competition 'destabilized the Jihadi community and caused disunity'.[13] It makes sense to divide the intra- and inter-group competition within Afghanistan's Sunni Jihadi environment into before and after portions, taking as the division point the critical defeat at Jalalabad in 1989. Up until then, debates and competition had in the main not been the result of ideological disagreements. However, this changed with the defeat and the ensuing assassination of Abdallah Azzam, al-Qaida's isolation in its training camps and Bin Laden's departure to Saudi Arabia. These events led to a vacuum that facilitated what Hamid calls the *Jalalabad School*, which ideologically and doctrinally challenged the existing Jihadi groups and organisations during the 1990s.

The real war between Afghan warlords broke out in 1992, after Russian forces had left the country and the Afghan communist regime finally crumbled, but already in the early 1980s the different warlords started to compete against each other for power.[14] Abdul Rasul Sayyaf won the struggle early on and, in January 1980, was elected president of the Ittihad i Islami Tahrir Afghanistan (Islamic Union for the Liberation of Afghanistan),[15] which included all the main parties engaged with the Russians.[16] Although the factions were fighting on the same side against the Russians, they also competed for funding and weapons coming from Pakistan, and later from Saudi Arabia. To address these issues, a meeting was convened in Peshawar in 1981 where Mawlawi Mansur, the leader of Harakat-i-Inqilab (the Revolutionary Movement), complained not only about the corrupt practices of many of the parties but also about the fact that the rivalry resulted in the leaders preventing their followers from collaborating with each other. In a manner characteristic of the competitive nature of the time, Mansur concluded that every attempt of unity ended with the creation of a new party.[17] The rivalry between Afghan commanders eventually cost Mansur his life as he was reportedly killed by the forces of Gulbuddin Hekmatyar, the leader of Hizb-e-Islami, in 1993.[18] It is clear, then, that the fragmentation between Afghan Sunni Jihadi factions did not occur with the fall of Najibullah's communist regime in 1992,[19] but was already critically affecting the struggle against Russian forces from the very beginning in the early 1980s.

Tensions only increased when Arab mujahideen arrived in more substantial numbers from 1984 onwards. In his famous 1979 book *Defence of the Muslim Lands: The First Obligation after Faith*, Azzam concludes that Jihad is *fard al-ayn* (individual duty), thus providing the theological foundation necessary for Arabs to join in greater numbers. Azzam was in Afghanistan in the early 1980s and saw with his own eyes that this was not sufficient, so he created the *Maktab al-Khadamat* (the Services Bureau, MAK) in 1984, which helped facilitate the travel and organisation of Arab foreign fighters to Afghanistan.[20] As problems between Afghan Jihadi warlords were already present in 1984, Azzam also saw the MAK as an opportunity to bring unity and to prevent the negative consequences of a divided opposition. Abdallah Anas, Azzam's son-in-law, was placed in charge of de-escalating any arising tensions.[21] What Azzam probably did not foresee was that such interference would eventually exacerbate internal relations between Jihadi groups and individuals.[22]

The establishment of the Badr Camp by Azzam in 1984 was similarly undertaken with the direct purpose of promoting unity. Unlike other camps, it did not offer military training, but rather stressed the importance of fighters praying and fasting together, while also offering religious courses to them. The idea behind Badr was for diverse groups of fighters to become friends.[23] While Azzam may have succeeded in his endeavour at Badr, this was not the case in other camps. With more and more Arabs arriving, among them many Salafis from the Gulf, doctrinal orientation started to become a problem. At the Qais Camp—which was run by Mawlawi Mansur, a Sufi following the Hanafi school of *fiqh* (jurisprudence)—Salafis were invited to come and train. Although the experiment succeeded in the end, initially the different groups clashed internally, especially regarding how to pray correctly.[24] Another example was the Zhawar Camp in Khost which was run by Haqqani but used by several groups, including the Egyptian Al Jihad. Once again, doctrinal disagreements occurred between rigid Salafis and supporters of Haqqani, who were more traditional and less concerned about rigid doctrinal praxis.[25] Similar problems were to grow more severe in the 1990s.

There still exists some disagreement about the establishment of al-Qaida. Documents reported to be its founding papers are dated August 8 and September 10, 1988; they refer to the facilitation of military training and the establishment of an 'Advisory Council'. Around this time, in the final phase of the war against Russia, Bin Laden and Azzam started to drift apart. Some accounts explain this by emphasising that the Egyptians, led by al-Zawahiri, hijacked Bin Laden's mind, but it is also very likely that the two simply differed regarding future priorities. Vahid Brown and Don Rassler claim the split was a direct result of Bin Laden establishing his Masada camp, as Azzam saw it as a misuse of resources and a direct threat to the MAK.[26] At the time, the MAK ran the Sada training camp, so Bin Laden's Masada camp was considered a competitor.[27] That Azzam perceived Bin Laden's activities as a threat is not so surprising, since Bin Laden had become the most popular Arab–Afghan in 1987, a popularity that endured until his defeat at Jalalabad in 1989. With the establishment of al-Qaida, people started to leave Azzam's MAK to join the new group.[28] As a result, the main purpose of the advisory council was to unify Azzam, Bin Laden and their respective followers.[29]

The final years of the struggle against the Russians turned out to have severe implications for the future SJM, both in Afghanistan and abroad. The great Battle of Jalalabad in the spring of 1989 ended in a devastating defeat for the mujahideen, including the nascent al-Qaida, and was a severe personal blow to Bin Laden. The battle was the first time the Muslim Brotherhood joined the front and they started to criticise Bin Laden, warning against him becoming the leader of the Arabs: 'We will never let Abu Abdullah [Bin Laden] be the leader of the Arabs, or the hero of the Arabs, which he tried to build himself as when he went to Jalalabad.'[30] Around the same time, the so-called *takfiri* (excommunication) trend started to gain prominence on the Afghan scene, and represented the forerunner to what later would be known as the Jalalabad School. It is reported that before being assassinated in November 1989, Azzam said that some mujahideen—referring mainly to al-Zawahiri and the Egyptians—were creating fitna, and that takfir was the real issue.[31] Increasingly extreme religious interpretation, however, was not exclusively an Egyptian phenomenon, but also present among other North Africans such as Libyans and Algerians, who eventually brought it back home, leading to the critical events below.[32]

## *Contestation Turning Ideological*

After the fall of the Najibullah regime, Afghan warlords turned their guns against each other, thus transforming what in the 1980s was mainly inter-group *competition* into actual *infighting* as seen in the civil war waged between 1992 and 1998.[33] But it was another event, in 1989, that would transform the character of intra-Jihadi conflict. The defeat at Jalalabad turned out to be of extreme significance for the Jihadi environment, both in Afghanistan and abroad.[34] Not only did the post-Jalalabad period give rise to a more ideologically founded contestation, but it also witnessed personal power struggles between Bin Laden on one side and prominent Jihadi figures like Mullah Umar, Abu Musab al-Suri and Ibn Khattab on the other.

### The Emergence of the 'Jalalabad Current'

In the late 1980s, a survey was conducted among Egyptian Al Jihad members in Afghanistan on their view of Jihad in the country. In their opinion, 'nothing is to be hoped for from the war in Afghanistan, nor will there arise an Islamic State there, on account of doctrinal/ideological defects among the leaders and the masses.'[35] Perhaps this was an opinion limited to the Egyptians (and maybe to the Algerians and Libyans), but it was a sentiment that was about to become more widespread. In the aftermath of the defeat at Jalalabad, three important events occurred that all helped facilitate the emergence of the Jalalabad School, which is better understood as an ideological trend pertaining to certain ideas in matter of *'aqida* (creed) and *manhaj* (methodology).

After the defeat at Jalalabad, neither Azzam nor Bin Laden supported further Arab involvement in the fighting and focused instead on training. This left some Arab fighters disgruntled, as fighting was the reason they had left their home countries to travel to Afghanistan, and they considered it a religious obligation. As is evident in the account by Abu Jandal (at a later date Bin Laden's bodyguard), some Arabs like himself were men who wanted to be on the front lines.[36] But to fight they would have to find new leaders, and this could be a challenge in a context where Arab mobilisation was still heavily dominated by Azzam and Bin Laden. Hence, when Azzam was assassinated in November 1989 and Bin Laden left for Saudi Arabia in the aftermath of the defeat at Jalalabad, a leadership vacuum emerged. The youth who were originally mobilised to fight found themselves nowhere near the battlefield and suddenly without the presence of their authoritative leaders. It is this opening that facilitated the emergence of the ideology of Jalalabad, which Mustafa Hamid defines as an 'everything goes' approach. Characteristic of the new ideological trend was its obvious lack of experience. Its leaders were mostly in their twenties, they had—according to their critics—limited political and military understanding[37] and they agreed on the weakness of the existing leadership. Observers may compare this to the emergence of the Islamic State in 2013.

The new ideological trend developed in and around the Khaldan Camp located in Khost, Afghanistan. In several accounts, Khaldan has been described as an al-Qaida camp, but it is important to note that this was not the case.[38] In fact, a rumour suggests that Bin Laden was once refused entrance to the camp[39] and it was eventually forced to close in 2000 because al-Qaida and the Taliban opposed its continuing operation.[40] Initially, Khaldan was associated with Azzam and Bin Laden's MAK, but this changed under the new leadership of Ibn Shaikh al-Libi and, from 1994, Abu Zubaydah. The jump to a more rigid focus on doctrine occurred as part of this leadership transition as both leaders were influential in the institutionalisation of a more extreme takfir-oriented ideology.

Khaldan was approximately one and a half football fields, providing mainly basic training in small arms, but its doctrinal influence has proven much greater than its limited size would suggest. Unlike other camps, it was never run by a single organisation, but welcomed recruits from all over, although it was mainly made up of Algerians. Hence, it was perhaps no surprise that Algeria a few years later became the first place to witness an organised expression of the Jalalabad ideology.[41] Under the leadership of Ibn Shaikh al-Libi and Abu Zubaydah, Khaldan became the strongest critic of and competitor to al-Qaida and its alliance with the Taliban.[42] Perhaps the main reason behind this was the presence of the Egyptian Abu Abdullah al-Muhajir (born Muhammad Ibrahim al-Saghir), a critically understudied Egyptian figure who was a fierce opponent of al-Qaida and Bin Laden during his time at Khaldan.[43] Abu Rumman and Abu Hanieh were the first to show the close connection between al-Muhajir and Abu Musab al-Zarqawi, arguing that al-Zarqawi considered al-Muhajir his main ideological mentor. At Khaldan, al-Muhajir became the camp's shari'a official (mas'ul shara'i) in charge of the religious Beliefs Battalion Institute. As in other camps, the religious component was complementary to the military training, and thus al-Muhajir's extreme ideology and hostility towards others who disagreed or whose views simply differed[44] influenced the Arab recruits joining the camp, as it conveyed some level of anti-Taliban and anti-al-Qaida discourse.[45] It has been claimed that 'the students at the al-Muhajir's institute began to expose what they see as deviances from Bin Ladin' and, according to Mustafa Hamid, as quoted by Kévin Jackson, 'the most tolerant of them [the Algerian and Tunisian factions at Khaldan] saw the Taliban as infidels... Their stance was the most easily comprehensible, simple and contrarian; it began with excommunicating [takfir] the Taliban and ended with excommunicating everyone in their vicinity.'[46] The strong focus on an extremely rigid doctrine, and especially the issue of takfir, was corroborated by other Jihadi groups present in Afghanistan at the time. For instance, the Uyghurs from Turkestan were initially training in the camp but quit as the emphasis on takfir became too dominant.[47] A similar account has been offered by the Indonesian Jama'a Islamiyya, who refrained from frequenting Khaldan.[48] The increasing importance and influence of takfir was evident in Algeria in the following years, but there are also examples in Afghanistan pointing to this. Some Arab Salafis, for instance, found it difficult to fight Masoud in the 1997 battle for Kabul as his fighters were nominally Muslims and the Salafis would only continue the fight if the enemy was declared kafir. Thus, in order to keep the fighting on track, al-Qaida eventually excommunicated Masoud's forces. Another example involves fighters from Libya known for their strict creed, which led them to pronounce takfir on the Taliban.[49]

The shift in a more ideologically extreme direction prompted by the emergence of the Jalalabad School was the main source of division within Sunni Jihadism. Struggles were not exclusively ideological, however, as competition for power, scarce resources, recruits and funding[50] continued to play a role—not least in the Afghan civil war. But the post-Jalalabad period certainly did witness a division between pragmatists—or strategists—and doctrinarians (as Brynjar Lia has referred to them)[51] that had immediate repercussions in Algeria, later in Iraq, and finally is now seen in an organised form as part of the Islamic State. This extended to a more general contempt among many Arab Afghans towards the Taliban. As Lia explains, letters and documents found at guesthouses in Afghanistan revealed criticism, especially from Salafis, of the Taliban and its mistaken manhaj. The dividing issue was to what extent the Taliban could be considered a legitimate Islamic emirate and a starting point for a future caliphate.[52] The feeling among many Arab fighters in Afghanistan and senior Jihadi ideologues in London was that this was not the case. It should be noted that the takfiri trend was not exclusive to the hardcore Khaldan trainees—it is also a central notion in Salafi theology and Wahhabi activism. Mustafa Hamid recounts how, during a lecture he and Abu Musab al-Suri delivered at the al-Qaida-run Jihadwal camp, a fierce argument broke out, which eventually led to people proclaiming takfir on others.[53]

The early 1990s Jihadi melting pot in Afghanistan was truly a battlefield. Parties fought not only over the definition of the proper ideological foundation for Jihad but also over its more basic priorities and objectives. In a survey around 1990 of some of the most senior Arab Jihadis in Afghanistan, the question 'what is your position on battle participation in Afghanistan and for what reasons?' produced a wide range of strategic differences and priorities, as displayed vividly in Table 5, below:[54]

Table 5: Summary of Arab Jihadi Perspectives on Fighting in Afghanistan

| | |
|---|---|
| Abdallah Azzam | Token participation for the purpose of raising the Afghans' morale, training the Arabs, and spreading the spirit of Jihad among the Arabs, with the long-term goal being the waging of Jihad against the Jews in Palestine. |
| Usama Bin Laden | Deep participation in the battles in accordance with the political and strategic vision of the leadership in Peshawar, with the long-term goal being the liberation of South Yemen from communism. |
| Egyptian Al Jihad | Participation in battles for the purpose of training personnel in a battlefield environment. Nothing is to be hoped for from the war in Afghanistan, nor will there arise an Islamic state there, on account of doctrinal/ideological defects among the leaders and the masses. Egypt is the heart of the Islamic world, and it is necessary to establish the caliphate there first. |
| Abu Musab al-Suri | Participation for the purpose of training cadres and for forming a Jihadi organisation or coordinated organisations. Fighting in Afghanistan is a religious duty, though it is a lost cause. |
| Mustafa Hamid | Total participation with the Islamic mujahideen forces in Afghanistan for the purpose of achieving a military and political victory for the sake of Islam and for transforming Afghanistan into a base (qa'ida) of support for the Muslim peoples, providing them with military cadres and expertise, and shelter and support for the needy. |

While the 1980s saw a rise in mobilisation to Jihad on an international scale, the 1990s witnessed the most critical changes in the Jihadi environment. Even during the early days of Jihad in Afghanistan, problems within and between groups were present, but it was mainly about access to resources and dominance of certain territories. In the leadership vacuum that emerged after the defeat at Jalalabad when Azzam was killed and Bin Laden left for the Gulf (and later Sudan), a more purist and extreme ideological trend emerged as a result of Salafis from the Gulf and North Africa and the ideological development in Khaldan Camp. Despite internal hostilities, the Jihadi family was still operating on a common base, but the family was slowly becoming a more problematic one. In general, there exists a myth of unity among the Arabs in Afghanistan,[55] but with a closer look it is clear that the field suffered from severe fragmentation. Not only did competing factions—often divided according to their nationalities—fight for influence, resources and recruits, but from the early 1990s onwards, ideological fault lines emerged and became a central source of division. The increasing number of Arabs migrating to Afghanistan around 2000–01 aggravated the already fractured field of Jihadi actors, even adding anti-Shia attitudes to the equation. Hamid explains how such anti-Shia sentiments grew as Arabs, mainly from the Gulf, arrived with the objective of fighting Shi'ites in the north.[56] Similar sentiments were present in al-Qaida but on orders from Bin Laden any such sentiments were curbed within the movement. This trend only grew stronger in al-Zarqawi's Iraq in later years.

## Algeria: The First Manifestation of the 'Jalalabad Ideology'

Far from Afghanistan, in Algeria, was where the first organisational manifestation of these ideological divisions occurred. The reliance on takfir was already dominant in the writings of such early Jihadi ideologues as Qutb and Faraj, although implicitly, and had been instrumental as a tool to legitimise killings of 'moderate' Muslims in Afghanistan.[57] But in Algeria it started to cause problems between Jihadi groups.[58]

The history of the Groupe Islamique Armé (GIA) is already well described.[59] In the years 1994–96 during the terror campaign under the leadership of the thirty-year-old Djamel Zitouni, the GIA's attitude towards other Jihadi groups radicalised.[60] The group had operated since 1992 but was formally established in May 1994 as it merged with a faction from the Front Islamique du Salut (FIS) and the Mouvement de l'État Islamique (MEI). Already in the two years leading up to the merger, the increasing violence of the GIA had forced other Islamist groups to step up their campaigns of violence in order to compete. Camille Tawil reports a steady stream of Arab Afghans returning from Afghanistan who were central to the GIA's establishment, as prominent Afghan veterans like Qari Saïd and Abu Leith al-M'sili were among the founders of the group, while the Bayt al-Mujahideen guesthouse in Peshawar facilitated the transfer and training of GIA fighters.[61] Initially, the GIA's main enemy was the Algerian state and its French patron, and in these efforts the group was supported by al-Qaida and other Jihadi groups.[62] Jihadi authorities like Abu Qatada al-Filastini, Abu Hamza al-Masri and Abu Musab al-Suri either ran the group's weekly magazine Usrat al-Ansar or legitimised the GIA's jihad through *religious rulings* (fatwas). The GIA's hierarchy of enemies and its external support changed, however, when Zitouni took leadership and started a campaign of attacks against everyone less rigid in doctrine than himself.[63] When Zitouni was killed in 1996, Antar Zouabri—a twenty-six-year-old close associate of Zitouni—took over the leadership of the group and continued the escalation of violence.

Although neither Zitouni nor Zouabri themselves spent time in Afghanistan, it seems fair to assume that the relatively high number of Algerians training in Khaldan, and experience from Afghanistan in general, did play a part in the radicalisation of the GIA's stance towards other groups. The same ideological tenets that characterised the Jalalabad School informed the GIA after Zitouni assumed the leadership. This started to cause internal dissent within the GIA in late 1995. The GIA's escalating extremism did not go unnoticed among supporting groups and ideologues, but when it started to launch attacks against fellow mujahideen who did not follow a similarly rigid doctrine, refused to join the GIA or simply disrespected the GIA leadership's view of its own authority, Jihadi groups and ideologues started to oppose it.[64] Tellingly, by June 6, 1996, the Egyptian groups

Al Jihad and al-Jama'a al-Islamiyya, the Libyan Islamic Fighting Group (LIFG) and the two ideologues Abu Qatada and Abu Musab al-Suri had all withdrawn their support,[65] claiming Zitouni was 'guilty of "deviations" in the implementation of the Jihad.'[66] The GIA's extremism reached its high point in September 1997, when Zouabri proclaimed takfir on the whole Algerian population except people fighting in the ranks of his own group, thus ensuring the Algerian Jihadi project lost all popular support.[67]

The direct aggression against Islamists and Jihadis had started earlier, however. In 1994, the FIS merged with the Mouvement Islamique Armé (MIA) to establish the Armée Islamique du Salut (AIS) which, in contrast to the GIA, had a long-term Jihad campaign as its objective. As the AIS was perceived as a competitor, the GIA started to attack the group in 1994[68] and in November 1995, and even targeted allied Jihadis originally from the FIS who had joined the GIA as part of the merger the prior year. When Zouabri took over, this internal purge only intensified. Eventually, senior Jihadi figures like Bin Laden and al-Zawahiri began to consider the GIA a threat to the general Jihadi project. The vision of Algeria as a new base for Jihad slowly crumbled.

One tangible example of the animosity of the GIA towards other Jihadis took place when the LIFG sent several delegations to Algeria to assess the GIA and enquire about the possibilities of setting up camps in the country. In 1994, a delegation of 15 LIFG members travelled to Algeria to fight alongside the GIA against the Algerian army, but as soon as the delegation arrived, all contact with the group ceased. It was later discovered that all the fighters had been killed by the GIA, the group they were sent to aid.[69] Following the disappearance of the fifteen Libyans, a story was reported that the GIA's mufti Redouane Makador paid a visit to Bin Laden in Sudan and directly commanded the al-Qaida leader not to get involved in the Algerian Jihad.[70] In another instance, without consideration for the actual proposals, he rejected recommendations from al-Zawahiri.[71]

The GIA leadership opposed any Jihadi project that differed from or interfered with its own. Similar to the discourse of the Islamic State today, Zitouni claimed that other Jihadi groups were too moderate and had abandoned the true Jihadi methodology. The GIA was the first organisation after Shukri Mustafa's Jama'at al-Muslimeen that focused so rigorously on doctrine that it became directly counterproductive for the broader SJM. This mainly manifested through the use of powerful concepts like takfir and al-wala' wa-l-bara' (loyalty and separation). These concepts are traditionally applied by Jihadis to distinguish between pious Muslims and apostates and to manage the relationship with the latter, but instead the GIA began systematically applying them to delegitimise competing Jihadi actors. During the reign of Zitouni, the GIA was finally accused of being khawarij, but—as is also the case with the Islamic State—such an accusation was fiercely rejected by Zitouni, who claimed that the GIA killed any person with khawariji tendencies they came across.[72]

## *The Struggle for Power*

The contentious nature of intra-Jihadi relations was more than just a matter of ideological divergence. Individuals and groups competed for recruits, funding, control of territory, definition of strategy and likely also for personal fame; in short, it was a struggle for power. This was particularly striking in Afghanistan's militant melting pot in the mid-1990s, and in Egypt, where the two dominant Jihadi groups failed to merge and instead ended up competing.

### Mullah Umar, Abu Musab al-Suri and Ibn Khattab

Back in Afghanistan the competition and fragmentation within the Jihadi environment of the 1990s was not just a result of the emerging ideological division, but also driven by personal power struggles among senior individuals at the time. Bin Laden had extensive leadership ambitions and that put him at odds with other senior and popular Jihadi figures, such as the Taliban's Mullah Umar, Abu Musab al-Suri and his Saudi compatriot Ibn Khattab.

When Bin Laden and the majority of his al-Qaida members relocated back to Afghanistan in May 1996 after spending several years in Sudan, he sought to revive his organisation and to cement his own position as the most authoritative figure within the Sunni Jihadi movement. A challenge to this objective was Mullah Umar, who was heading the Taliban's newly established emirate and who had claimed the authoritative title of amir al-mu'minin (leader of the faithful). The competition with and dislike of Mullah Umar can be divided into two distinct areas: on the one hand, the relationship between Bin Laden and Mullah Umar; and on the other, how Mullah Umar was perceived by the broader Jihadi–Salafi trend.

It seems unlikely, as some sources argue, that Bin Laden initially did not know of the Taliban when he arrived in Afghanistan in 1996.[73] During his exile in Sudan he must have been a keen follower of events in Afghanistan, where he had spent many years and where he still had fighters and camps (although in reduced numbers). To explain the initial friendliness of Mullah Umar to Bin Laden, it is first necessary to understand how the Saudi was perceived by the Taliban regime upon his return. Firstly, he was seen as an Arab mujahideen who fought bravely for Afghanistan in the 1980s. Secondly, and perhaps more importantly, for a new and struggling regime Bin Laden was also a Saudi businessman whom they hoped would help revitalise the Afghan economy and infrastructure. From the insider account of Mustafa Hamid, who was close to both Bin Laden and the Taliban, it is obvious that Bin Laden seemed neither to respect nor to care much about Mullah Umar. This was not so much because Bin Laden as a Salafi had doctrinal issues with Mullah Umar, but more because he simply saw himself as the leader of the SJM and had his eyes fixed on his own activities. The latter became the key issue between the two as Bin Laden saw a strong media presence as central to his project, much to the annoyance of his Afghan host.[74] On several occasions, Bin Laden gave interviews without the permission of Mullah Umar and acted directly against his orders, most provocatively in the 1998 press conference at which Bin Laden announced the 'World Islamic Front for Jihad against the Jews and Crusaders'. These provocations and Bin Laden's global agenda led Mullah Umar to put the Saudi under surveillance and on one occasion he allegedly confiscated Bin Laden's phone.[75] Mullah Umar continuously pleaded for Bin Laden to understand the Taliban's delicate situation and how the Saudi's activities were harmful. Mustafa Hamid narrates from one of the discussions between the two leaders:

> he [Mullah Umar] told Abu Abdullah [Bin Laden], 'Please don't talk. Keep quiet. We are in a dangerous position here now. Everything is against us. We have troubles everywhere, from every place. We have a lot of problems. We have no money … Please wait; we are going to help you and help all the Muslims. But wait.' … he said frankly, 'Look I can't help you now. I am just like this,' and he motioned to how he was crouching. He said, 'I am not sitting and not standing; and this position is a very hard position. Leave things until I stand or sit'.[76]

To end the meeting on a polite note, Mullah Umar concluded, 'You are in your country; you can do whatever you want.'[77] Bin Laden chose to understand this literally, continuing to carry out his Jihadi project. The story shows how Bin Laden clearly had issues with subordinating himself to Mullah Umar. This is also evident from his hesitancy to pledge allegiance to the Taliban leader as was expected of him; when he finally acquiesced, he did so through a proxy.

The criticism from the hard-core Jihadi–Salafi contingent in Afghanistan against Mullah Umar took a more doctrinal focus. At Khaldan, an anti-Taliban rhetoric was espoused from the mid-1990s onwards. Such a stance was not shared by all Arabs in Afghanistan, but in the eyes of purist Salafis, the Taliban's religious practices were a point of criticism and a potential problem when fighting on the same side. Documents captured in Afghanistan containing surveys from 2001 conducted in al-Qaida-run camps show how trainees asked questions about the religious legitimacy of the Taliban and the ruling on fighting next to them.[78] Al-Zawahiri and his fellow Egyptians in Al Jihad were particularly against the idea of pledging allegiance to the Taliban due to their perceived doctrinal faults.[79] Similar objections were widely present among Saudi Jihadis.[80] Perhaps the strongest voice against the Taliban was a coalition of individuals called 'the Peshawar Group' who authored pamphlets criticising the Taliban's political deviance in wanting to join the United Nations and its *polytheist* (shirk) practices, especially grave-worshipping and the mixing of religious and cultural customs. After the bombings of the US embassies in Kenya and Tanzania, and even more so after 9/11, al-Qaida and what was left of the Jihadi–Salafi movement in Afghanistan became more dependent on the Taliban's protection. Ideological disagreement continued as the Taliban was only focused on its nationalist Jihadi project within the geographical confines of Afghanistan, while al-Qaida, now with Al Jihad and al-Zawahiri onboard, were fully committed to a global Jihad project. Nonetheless, the volatile context made the Salafis more lenient towards the Taliban and saw the alliance as a strategic necessity, so much so that even al-Zawahiri started to support the relationship.

A second example of leadership ambitions at fault for intra-Jihadi competition is between al-Qaida and Abu Musab al-Suri.[81] Al-Suri had already found himself in a personal conflict with Abu Qatada al-Filastini during his stay in London in the mid-1990s. As he returned to Afghanistan, Bin Laden came to see him as both a competitor and a direct threat—although the two men initially were close.[82] Al-Suri allegedly left al-Qaida in 1997 and shifted his allegiance to the Taliban, mainly due to his opposition to al-Qaida's strategy of targeting the West, which he was convinced would entail an increased threat to the Taliban's hold in Afghanistan.[83] Time and again, al-Suri criticised Bin Laden for not following the rules of conduct set out by the Taliban after the movement had finally established its Islamic Emirate and agreed to host Bin Laden. Lia reports how the tensions led to a quarrel between the two in 1996, after which Bin Laden suggested that they should 'keep away from one another'.[84] Perhaps the best insight we have on the relationship is a letter from al-Suri and his companion Abu Khalid al-Suri in which they criticise Bin Laden and emphasise the need to respect Mullah Umar's leadership. In the letter the two Syrians also touch on a raw spot by claiming that Bin Laden does not honour shura (consultation) and that senior people close to him, including Abu Hafs al-Masri and al-Zawahiri, hold a similar view.[85]

Brian Fishman has provided an informative account of how stark the competition between al-Qaida and al-Suri really was, arguing that the competition between the two was integral in al-Qaida's decision to support Abu Musab al-Zarqawi when he arrived in Afghanistan.[86] Fishman's account confirms that of Hamid, who writes that 'Abu Musab al-Suri and al-Qaeda were at this time in heavy competition' and that Arab Afghans at odds with Bin Laden sided with al-Suri.[87] Interestingly, the competition between the two was not borne out of ideological disagreement. This is not to say that al-Qaida's leadership did not differ with al-Suri on substantial issues. Firstly, al-Suri was not a Salafi and detested the rigidity and inflexible attitude of Salafis. While al-Qaida was not exclusively Salafi, Salafism was dominant among its senior leadership. Secondly, al-Suri did not agree that there were strategic benefits to attacking the West at this stage; he believed supporting the Taliban's Islamic Emirate should be the main priority. Rather than these differences, however, it was the conflicting ambitions of al-Suri and senior al-Qaida leaders that was the main trigger for their conflict. Al-Suri was in charge of his own organisation in Afghanistan and had permission from the Taliban, as one of six commanders, to set up a camp in Afghanistan.[88] Al-Qaida got the impression that al-Suri was stealing their recruits and thus banned him from entering any al-Qaida guesthouse.

Similarly to al-Suri, Bin Laden's compatriot Samir Saleh Abdullah al-Suwailem, better known as Ibn Khattab, was seen as a threat to al-Qaida's Jihadi project and Bin Laden's own leadership ambitions. Hamid says that 'Khattab was a big threat and he refused many attempts by al-Qaeda to draw him in' in the period covering 1997–98.[89] The young Saudi was among the youth that took advantage of the leadership vacuum after the Jalalabad defeat when he moved to Afghanistan in May 1988. Although he never really became particularly fond of Jihad in Afghanistan, even claiming 'we didn't really do jihad in Afghanistan',[90] he nevertheless spent approximately six years there. During that time, he set up his own very popular camp to train Saudis.[91] From Bin Laden's perspective, this was problematic, as they were competing for the same recruits. Tired of the competitive nature of the work, Khattab travelled to Tajikistan between 1994 and 1995 and then moved on to Chechnya, where he spent the remaining part of his life as the leader of the Islamic Army. It was in Chechnya that he emerged as a revered leader among his fighters and a legend within the SJM. Chechnya was an example of classical Jihad fighting against the invading Russian forces. For this reason, Chechnya became perhaps the most important Jihadi arena in the late 1990s and early 2000s. This was not least the case from a Saudi perspective and thus Bin Laden had an interest in expanding his own project to Chechnya. Against his wishes, however, this was not possible, because soon after Khattab had established himself, he monopolised Arab Jihadi activity in Chechnya, making it impossible for al-Qaida to gain a foothold there.[92]

Unlike al-Qaida, Ibn Khattab never diverted from the classical Jihad of focusing on invading foreign forces in Muslim countries. When Bin Laden started to focus more on 'apostate' Arab governments or the West, Khattab kept his eyes on the Russian forces.[93] This ideological difference between supporting classical Jihad or global Jihad is important, Thomas Hegghammer notes, which was evident within Saudi Arabia's militant milieu where Jihadis were divided between the 'Khattabists' and 'Bin Ladinists'.[94] Another striking difference was how small a role doctrine played for Khattab after he came to Chechnya: he realised most of the Muslims there were Sufis and thus he could not expect people suddenly to adopt a Salafi creed. Studying religion was important, but he expected only the minimum from his recruits, such as praying, fasting and reading the Quran. He acknowledged this himself in his memoirs, noting the challenge of up to 60 to 80 percent of his trainees being Sufis: 'I wanted to leave the issue of disagreement, dispute or extremism about the Madhahib, this is Shafee, or Hanbali, or Hanafi. Although I didn't have knowledge to convince or comprehend much of these matters, I mentioned to them this matter and they agreed to continue in the camp.'[95]

When in Chechnya, the popularity of Ibn Khattab's front exceeded that of Bin Laden's Jihad in Afghanistan, both in the eyes of many young recruits, but also among Saudi clerics and businessmen. The latter group's support was not least the result of Bin Laden's critique of the Saudi regime. This was problematic for Bin Laden since he considered Khattab a competitor not only for authority and leadership but also for Saudi recruits and funding. In a letter from the senior al-Qaida figure 'Abd al-Hadi al-Iraqi, written in 1999 to the al-Qaida leadership, he mentions the competition al-Qaida is facing from Khattab and his Jihad in Chechnya. In the letter, al-Iraqi argues that most of the Jihadi youth in Afghanistan would leave for Chechnya if they were allowed to.[96] However, this was soon to change, not least for practical reasons. Khattab was victorious in the first Chechen war, but when the second Chechen war broke out in 1999 the situation was different. This time Russia wanted to win in Chechnya, and it basically sealed off the country, thus limiting the entrance of new foreign fighters who were eager to join a conflict against the invading unbelievers. What was Ibn Khattab's misfortune turned out to be Bin Laden's luck as many of the recruits looking to join Khattab eventually ended up in Bin Laden's arms in Afghanistan.[97]

## Internal Conflict in the Egyptian Jihadi Movement

In Egypt, two Jihadi groups emerged in the 1970s from the country's contentious Islamist environment that would eventually have an immense impact on the evolution of Sunni Jihadism. Both groups shared an ambition to establish an Islamic state and a rejection of the reformist approach of the Muslim Brotherhood, which had categorically failed in the Jihadis' eyes. Despite their common aim, they differed substantially in theology and in matters of organisation and mobilisation. *Al-Jama'a al-Islamiyya* emerged in university circles in Upper Egypt initially as a loose non-violent student organisation focusing on dawa activities. *Jama'at al-Jihad*, which later became known simply as Al Jihad, started as loosely connected cells in Cairo and in northern Egypt under the ideological tutelage of Abd al-Salam Faraj. Organisationally, one aimed to become a mass movement while the other was a clandestine elitist vanguard that aimed to mobilise members. Al-Jama'a al-Islamiyya's radicalisation to accept violence was partly the result of the closing of political opportunities in Egypt in the 1970s and partly the result of President Anwar Sadat's rapprochement with the USA and Israel; for Al Jihad, the process to violence was led by group leaders framing Jihad as the only successful way to establish an Islamic state.

It was after the operation in October 1981 when the two groups briefly allied under the tutelage of Faraj[98] and Umar Abd al-Rahman[99] to assassinate Sadat that internal divisions between the groups started to emerge. Both groups were severely targeted by mass repression, with many leaders and members imprisoned or forced to operate clandestinely. In prison, tensions between senior figures of the two groups intensified, relating to issues of strategy and leadership (according to the account by Al Jihad member Hani

Sibai).[100] In terms of strategy, al-Jama'a al-Islamiyya's decision to launch the attack against the security directorate in Asyut two days after Sadat's death was considered a critical mistake by Al Jihad leaders since it did not follow a greater plan, but only deteriorated the situation for the Jihadis. In terms of leadership, the groups could not decide between al-Jama'a al-Islamiyya's al-Rahman and Al Jihad's Aboud Zomour. Al-Rahman was theologically respected, while Zomour was militarily savvy, but the former's blindness was considered a serious handicap to his becoming amir of the groups should they merge.

The tensions between the two groups and within Al Jihad only increased in the mid- and late 1980s, when members of the groups fled to Afghanistan and Pakistan after their release from prison. After serving their sentences, al-Jama'a al-Islamiyya came out as a relatively united group, while Al Jihad was plagued by internal division over strategy. The release of second-tier leaders in the mid-1980s was central to this division as many of them travelled to Afghanistan to revive the organisation, which isolated the still-imprisoned traditional leadership. In this period remnants of Al Jihad elected a new amir, Sayyid Imam, better known as Dr Fadl. However, in the eyes of many of the rising stars in the group, Ayman al-Zawahiri was considered the real amir because of his central role in the trials in Egypt.[101] The establishment of a new faction with a new leadership naturally caused fragmentation within Al Jihad, with tensions building up between the imprisoned leadership in Egypt and the new leadership in Afghanistan.

In Peshawar, the groups once again attempted to merge, largely driven by the efforts of Abu Talal al-Qasimi, but again the groups were not able to find common ground, mainly because of differences in their styles of organisation that were considered incompatible. In 1992 al-Jama'a al-Islamiyya rejected the proposal. Around the same time, members of al-Jama'a al-Islamiyya and Al Jihad, like so many other Jihadis, were forced to leave the Afghanistan-Pakistan region and relocated to Sudan. Upon arrival, Al Jihad sought to reinvigorate its campaign of violence in Egypt to keep up with al-Jama'a al-Islamiyya, which was very active in the early 1990s. First in 1993 and again two years later, Al Jihad attempted high-level attacks against senior Egyptian politicians, including President Hosni Mubarak, but the campaign backfired with the tragic death of an innocent girl. This put pressure on Al Jihad to engage in renewed merger talks to survive. In contrast to the previous discussions in Peshawar, Al Jihad was now suffering from severe internal fragmentation, a lack of resources and a dearth of public support, which weakened its position with regard to al-Jama'a al-Islamiyya and ensured that the talks were more serious than before. In particular, the internal tensions proved troublesome as an internal power struggle between different factions within the group played out. Hundreds of Al Jihad's members were on trial in Egypt in the famous 'Vanguard of Conquest' (Tala'al al-Fateh) case. At the same time, rank and file members were calling for authorisation to launch attacks in Egypt. Members of the group called on Sayyid Imam, who was still in Peshawar, to join them in Sudan to resolve the conflict. After he refused, Abu Ubaydah al-Banshiri suggested he resign from his position as amir of Al Jihad, a suggestion to which he agreed. While al-Banshiri himself was a strong candidate to succeed Sayyid Imam, group members eventually elected al-Zawahiri.

Hence, in late 1994 or early 1995, the leading figures of the negotiations were al-Zawahiri for Al Jihad and Abu Yassir for al-Jama'a al-Islamiyya, but once again the obstacles preventing the merging of the two groups proved too great. Somewhat paradoxically, considering how fragmented Al Jihad was at the time, one of the group's points of criticism was the fragmented nature of al-Jama'a al-Islamiyya. The talks ended up dividing Al Jihad in two factions: the hawks, led by Abd al-Hamid, argued that al-Jama'a al-Islamiyya needed to elect an internally accepted shura council before any merger negotiations to ensure the group could speak with one voice. Meanwhile the pro-unity doves, led by al-Zawahiri, argued that a new shura council including members of both groups should be established.[102] This was a minor issue, however, with the real obstacles once again being the leadership of the blind sheikh Umar Abd al-Rahman and the theological question of *excuse of ignorance* (al-'adhir bi-l-jahl) that would later become a major point of contestation within the Islamic State.[103] While al-Jama'a al-Islamiyya accepted ignorance as an excuse (even in matters relating to God's unity) and claimed that one would in fact be an *innovator* (mubtida') if one did not accept it, Al Jihad took the opposite opinion. At the final meeting, al-Jama'a al-Islamiyya was allegedly not willing to compromise on any of the contentious issues and informed Al Jihad that for the merger to go through, it would have to accept all of al-Jama'a al-Islamiyya's demands.[104]

For al-Zawahiri, the failed merger was clearly a disappointment, as was the decision by the al-Jama'a al-Islamiyya's imprisoned leadership in 1997 to launch its *initiative to cease violence* (mubadarat waqf al-unf).[105] Even though al-Zawahiri himself in 1995 announced a ceasefire, it was only a temporary measure and not an abandonment of Jihad. In contrast, al-Jama'a al-Islamiyya's leadership in 2001 published a *'Series for Correcting Ideas'* (silsilat tashih al-mafahim) consisting of four books that on a theological foundation delegitimised the use of violence through a *reality-based jurisprudence* (fiqh al-waqi'). While Jihad was still a legitimate Islamic concept, they argued, in the context of Egypt (and likely elsewhere) it was prohibited because the *harm* (mafsada) of fighting Jihad was greater than the *benefits* (maslaha).

Al-Zawahiri had continuously opposed groups that renounced the importance of Jihad, let alone those accepting a political process not governed by the law of God. In the early 1990s he had already published a raging critique of the Muslim Brotherhood, titled *The Bitter Harvest*, and a decade later, after joining al-Qaida, his criticism was now directed at al-Jama'a al-Islamiyya in the book *Knights under the Prophet's Banner*. He dedicates a substantial portion of the 200-page book to criticising al-Jama'a al-Islamiyya's decision and outlining how the initiative divided the group internally. Al-Zawahiri leaves no doubt that he does not respect the decision of al-Jama'a al-Islamiyya. He narrates the hadith of Abdallah bin al-Zubayr, a companion of the prophet, who went to his mother's house and told her that everyone, even his sons and relatives, was letting him down and joining his enemy, al-Hajjaj, and that his opponents were willing to give him all worldly goods if he abandoned his struggle. Al-Zubayr's mother replied, 'Son, you know yourself better. If you are convinced that you are right and that you are advocating a rightful course of action, then endure.' In response, al-Zubayr kissed his mother's head. Al-Zawahiri continues, quoting Sayyid Qutb saying, 'Brother, push ahead, for your path is soaked in blood. Do not turn your head right or left but look only up to heaven.'[106] This clearly shows the fault line that emerged between Egypt's two major Jihadi groups and how the initiative affected al-Jama'a al-Islamiyya internally. Even al-Jama'a al-Islamiyya's spiritual leader, Umar Abd al-Rahman, withdrew his support for the initiative, which was clearly important for al-Zawahiri as he had tremendous respect for the US-imprisoned sheikh.[107] The late 1990s, with al-Jama'a al-Islamiyya's cessation of violence and Al Jihad's increasing focus on distant enemies, thus represented the final break between the two groups as their paths diverted for good.[108]

## *Strategy, Revisionism and Purges*

From the 2000s, internal debates within the SJM turned increasingly to the issue of strategy. This materialised in discussions about the proper military strategy and if violence was the appropriate strategy at all in the current context. These debates represented a serious threat to the cohesion of Jihadi groups which made it necessary for group leaders to attempt and control the situation either through discursive rebuttals or—as in the case of Somalia's al-Shabab—through a violent crackdown on internal critical voices.

### 9/11 and Debate on the Legitimate Jihadi Ideology

With Al Jihad's campaign failing in Egypt and Bin Laden returning to Afghanistan to revitalise al-Qaida, the leaders of the two faltering groups agreed to steer their focus away from national or regional revolutionary projects to instead focus on the USA and its Western allies. The period between 1996 and 2001 is thus central to understanding a key ideological development within Sunni Jihadism, specifically concerning the political preferences and enemy hierarchy of the SJM, and not least al-Qaida's rise. Although al-Qaida somehow managed to turn the reprioritisation of the Jihadi enemy hierarchy to its advantage and emerge as the primary recruiter of young Jihadis, it was nonetheless an extremely contentious issue that several senior Jihadi figures, even within al-Qaida, initially opposed and contested.

When Bin Laden returned to Afghanistan in the summer of 1996, he sought to revive al-Qaida and expand its influence with the aim of becoming the pioneering Jihadi organisation. In Sudan, Bin Laden had been more of a farmer and entrepreneur than a Jihadist[109] and al-Qaida's organisational infrastructure in Afghanistan had declined during his absence. From 1992 to Bin Laden's return in 1996, it was allegedly only al-Qaida's Jihadwal camp that was still operating, though Bin Laden himself had ordered everything closed when he left Pakistan in 1992.[110] Upon his return to Afghanistan, he authored his first fatwa explicitly identifying the USA and its allies as the main enemy of al-Qaida. Steven Brooke's article 'Jihadist Strategic Debates before 9/11' provides a good chronological overview of the strategic and ideological development of Jihadi groups, from the different expressions of a *revolutionary approach* in Egypt to Azzam, who favoured *classical defensive Jihad* and conquest of former Muslim land, and finally to the *global Jihad* of al-Qaida. The revolutionary trend was already a break with classical defensive Jihad as a communal duty, which Azzam later pronounced as an individual duty, but Bin Laden's redefinition of the enemy hierarchy was of equal if not greater significance. The shift from the 'near enemy' to the 'far enemy' has already been well described by several scholars, but perhaps less attention has been given to the opposition within the Jihadi movement that followed this shift in ideological prioritisation.[111]

In the early 1990s, Bin Laden was under pressure from the Egyptian Jihadi groups to adopt a revolutionary approach—preferably with a focus on Egypt. During his stay in Saudi Arabia between 1989 and 1991, Bin Laden contemplated initiating a campaign in Yemen; yet after the Saudi regime rejected his help to fight Saddam Hussein, his animosity also turned towards his native Saudi Arabia. However, Bin Laden never fully dedicated to the revolutionary fight. Rather he shifted from a defensive Jihad in Afghanistan to a prioritisation of global Jihad. Experience garnered from Saudi Arabia, Bosnia and Somalia was undoubtedly important in this strategic shift as they made him realise that the way to Jerusalem did not go through Cairo (or any other Arab capital), as al-Zawahiri famously argued, but rather through the Western world, by cutting off the 'head of the snake.'[112]

The first step in his turn towards the far enemy was his 1996 fatwa, '*A Declaration of Jihad against the Americans Occupying the Land of the Two Holy Sanctuaries (Expel the Infidels from the Arabian Peninsula).'* Approximately 30 pages long, the fatwa had the task of convincing Jihadis and Muslims in general that the USA was in fact the primary enemy: it had either occupied the Muslim world or through its support ensured the survival of tyrant Muslim rulers. Criticising the Al Saud regime the fatwa justified a defensive Jihad against US forces initially stationed in Saudi Arabia to fight Saddam's Iraq.[113] Two years later, Bin Laden authored a new fatwa entitled '*Jihad Against Jews and Crusaders*', published by a new Jihadi alliance called the *World Islamic Front*. Only two pages long, this fatwa was a much more direct attack against the USA and its allies, proclaiming the killing of both civilians and military personnel from these countries an 'individual duty incumbent on every Muslim in all countries.'[114]

With the two fatwas, the change in enemy hierarchy of al-Qaida and a few other individuals was cemented. At the time, al-Qaida was numerically extremely small, lacked funding and found itself a guest in an Afghanistan controlled by the Taliban. In this context it was particularly surprising that Bin Laden succeeded in changing the discourse around what constituted legitimate Jihad in the face of staunch opposition from fellow Jihadis. The Taliban was not fond of Bin Laden's media offensive during the late 1990s, and it unsuccessfully attempted to govern and limit his activities. But the group was not the only ones disagreeing with al-Qaida's new strategic outlook. The opposition to the shift in political preferences and more specifically to 9/11 can be divided into three groups, depending on the main source of opposition: on strategic grounds, on theological grounds or as a matter of authority. Within al-Qaida were examples of the first two types of opposition, while objections based on authority came mainly from external sources. By the early 2000s, several years after Bin Laden started to focus on the global enemy, he had won over only a fraction of the Jihadis to his cause; the majority still favoured local Jihad.[115] This was even the case within al-Qaida: the decision to strike the USA was one that divided al-Qaida's leadership, as vividly demonstrated by the 9/11 attack. Those in favour of the attack included Bin Laden, al-Zawahiri and some of the youth affiliated with the group, while the remaining part of the senior leadership to a great extent opposed it. It is well known that Saif al-Adl, Abu Hafs al-Mauritani and Abu al-Yazid all disagreed with the attack,[116] but in his 2012 interview with Al Jazeera, al-Mauritani also claimed that Mohammed Atef, al-Qaida's military chief, similarly opposed it even though he had duly supported Bin Laden in the preparations for the operation. The case of Saif al-Adl is particularly interesting, as he served as a high-ranking member of al-Qaida and at the time of the attack was in charge of the group's training operations (and from November 2001 also headed its military committee). While there is no doubt that al-Adl opposed the 9/11 attack,[117] there are even indications that he did not favour foreign attacks against the West at all. In a letter to Khalid Sheikh Muhammad, he pleads with him to stop all foreign activities, as they harm the Jihadi project since people lose faith in al-Qaida. He does this by referring to the difficult conditions al-Qaida is operating in after the 9/11 attacks and states that he did criticise the attack before it took place but that this critique was not widely seen.[118] Despite his opposition, however, he publicly supported al-Qaida and 'the blessed attacks'.[119] For al-Adl, the main objection was not on ideological grounds, but rather strategic. He rightly feared a strong US response that would decimate the Jihadis' position in Afghanistan. A similar line of argument was adopted by Abu Musab al-Suri.

Abu Hafs al-Mauritani, head of al-Qaida's Shari'a Committee, also opposed the attack, but his opposition was based on theological grounds.[120] In a 2012 interview, he explains how he was the strongest opposition to the 9/11 attack as he found the attack religiously illegitimate.[121] His objection allegedly took the form of a letter to Bin Laden prior to the attacks in which he discouraged it. His arguments were that Jihad was not about pointless killing, that the attack would involve things prohibited by Islamic law (civilians would be killed and transgression of the 'treaty of protection' in Islam) and that al-Qaida was a guest of the Taliban who opposed the attack. Al-Mauritani says that, as a result of the attacks going ahead, he decided to resign from all of his positions in al-Qaida.

Opposition to the shift in enemy hierarchy was not only an internal challenge for al-Qaida. In 2000, a meeting was held in Kandahar, in Afghanistan, where representatives from different Jihadi organisations discussed al-Qaida's new strategic outlook. The

LIFG heavily disagreed with al-Qaida and even urged the group to pledge not to attack the USA.[122] Unsurprisingly, the imprisoned leadership of al-Jama'a al-Islamiyya in Egypt also disagreed with the global focus.[123] But the group that would suffer most from al-Qaida's strategy of attacking the West was the Taliban and its Afghan emirate. The Taliban was not necessarily against attacks outside of Afghanistan, but to launch an attack that would risk a forceful retaliation from the USA was not favoured by the group. Time and again al-Qaida overstepped this boundary, first through Bin Laden's statements and then with the attacks against Western targets in East Africa, Yemen and finally on US homeland. Individuals like Mustafa Hamid and Abu Musab al-Suri similarly had objections that were based on al-Qaida overstepping the authority of its host and the repercussions an attack would prompt. By way of example of how controversial the attack actually was, Hegghammer explains how even clerics around Yusuf al-Uyairi—the first leader of al-Qaida in the Arabian Peninsula—doubted the legitimacy of the attack. In contrast, more hard-core Jihad-Salafi ideologues, such as Abu Muhammad al-Maqdisi, Abu Qatada al-Filastini, and the Shuaybi school led by the Saudi Hamoud al-Uqla al-Shuaybi and his prominent students Ali bin Khudair al-Khudair, Sulayman al-Ulwan and Nasr al-Fahd were supportive of the attack.[124]

Despite the opposition, al-Qaida went through with several attacks against Western targets in the period between 1998 and 2001 and, perhaps surprisingly, the effects were arguably positive for the group. Firstly, the attacks, especially 9/11, had the effect of uniting Jihadi groups in Afghanistan that had until then been fragmented and, from time to time, competed and fought each other. Secondly, the attacks and the post-9/11 Jihadi environment finally established al-Qaida as the dominant Jihadi organisation. While the primary objective was the symbolic attack on the USA, important side effects were to satisfy the Jihadi youth and unify the Jihadi movement in support of al-Qaida's war on the West.[125]

### Sayyid Imam's Revisionism and Attack on al-Qaida

In the mid 2000s, al-Qaida had established itself at the top of the Sunni Jihadi movement, but it was about to experience another attack from within. al-Jama'a al-Islamiyya was the first group to embark on a revisionist project to delegitimise violence, but for al-Qaida the arguably more threatening efforts came in 2007 from Imam 'Abd al-Aziz al-Sharif, also known as Sayyid Imam or, more famously, Dr. Fadl. It came as a shock when the former Al Jihad leader, close friend of al-Zawahiri and author of one of the most influential Jihadi tracts issued a condemnation of al-Qaida and its violence. Although many dismissed Sayyid Imam's prison writings as the work of Egyptian intelligence, they nonetheless represent another important example of Jihadi revisionism and of discursive contestation between two of Sunni Jihadism's most senior ideologues; namely Sayyid Imam and al-Zawahiri.

To understand the importance of Sayyid Imam's revisionism, it is first necessary to know a little of his history. Alongside al-Zawahiri, in the late 1960s Sayyid Imam established a group that would later become Al Jihad,[126] which he led for a period, serving as its amir until he resigned in 1993[127] due to disagreement regarding the editing of one of his books and his unwillingness to leave Peshawar for Sudan to settle internal tensions within his group.[128] Despite his resignation he still commanded much respect in Egyptian militant circles and as a result was invited to join his countrymen in Afghanistan in the mid-1990s. He rejected the invitation and instead left for Yemen. Due to an Egyptian arrest order issued in 1999, however, he was finally brought into custody in Yemen in 2001 and extradited to Egypt in 2004. The critique from Sayyid Imam is important and interesting because of his theological credentials within militant circles and his once close relationship to al-Zawahiri, to whom he initially served as a mentor. In his prime, he was considered one of the most important theoreticians of Jihad, and argued meticulously in favour of proper financial and military preparation for Jihad,[129] an argument he explained in his strategic work '*Manual for Planning the Necessary Provisions to Mount Jihad in the Cause of God*' (al-'umda fi-i'dad al-udda li-l-jihad fi sabil allah), published in either 1987 or 1988, which was used by many as a textbook on the laws of Jihad.[130] Together with Faraj, he was the main ideological and strategic mastermind of Al Jihad and, in a similar fashion to his fellow ideologue, he elevated Jihad from a matter of fiqh to a matter of doctrine.

The debate between Sayyid Imam and al-Qaida played out mainly in 2007 and 2008 and took the form of three books: Sayyid Imam's '*Advice Regarding the Conduct of Jihadist Action in Egypt and the World*' (tarshid al-'amal al-jihadi fi misr wa al-'alam, known as the 'Advice' or the 'rationalisation document') from November 2007, al-Zawahiri's response '*The Exoneration: A Letter Exonerating the Ummah of the Pen and Sword from the Unjust Allegation of Feebleness and Weakness*' (tabri`at `a`imat al-qalam wa al-sayef min manqasat tuhmat al-khawar wa al-da'f, known as 'Exoneration') from March 2008, and, finally, a direct answer to al-Zawahiri from Sayyid Imam entitled '*Treatise on Exposing the Exoneration*' (mudhakkirat al-ta'riya li kitab al-tabri'a, known as 'Exposure') and published in November 2008, one year after his first book.

The so-called rationalisation document is a thorough critique of al-Qaida's approach to Jihad, its excessive violence, and what Sayyid Imam calls the distorted religious interpretations of its two leaders. Interestingly, he begins the document by delegitimising himself, declaring that he is not a mujtahid, a person qualified to do ijtihad (religious interpretation), but simply a person transmitting knowledge. Nonetheless, he does not hold back in condemning specific strategies of al-Qaida. The points Sayyid Imam especially focuses on are the decision to strike the far enemy, the practice of using civilians as *human shields* (al-tatarrus), which leads him to a rejection of killing non-combatant civilians in Western countries, and the prohibition of martyrdom operations.[131] Unlike al-Jama'a al-Islamiyya, Sayyid Imam does not delegitimise Jihad as such, maintaining it is a holy duty, but he revises the preconditions for Jihad to the extent that it becomes an impossible endeavour. For example, he argues that only Muslims who have been granted permission by their parents and received religious training can perform Jihad and that Jihad cannot be justified based on the nationality of one's opponent. When the harm (mafsada) is greater than the common good (maslaha), which it is in our era, Sayyid Imam claims, then military Jihad is not legal.[132] Furthermore, he seeks to set limits for when a person can be considered an unbeliever (kafir), exploring under what circumstances the proclamation of takfir is legal.[133] It is important to note, however, that the 'Advice' is not a retraction of

Sayyid Imam's previous works including al-'umda and al-jami', but a distinction between theory and its application in practice. According to Sayyid Imam, the 'Advice' thus simply instructs Jihadis how to behave in the specific context of Egypt at the time of writing.

Al-Zawahiri responded with his 'Exoneration'. He begins the book, which stretches to over 200 pages, by claiming that it has been the most difficult thing he has ever written, but that it was necessary to protect the Jihadi creed.[134] He continues by saying Sayyid Imam's document only serves the interest of the US–Israeli alliance and that it is 'an attempt to sedate their mujahidin enemies, make them doubt their methods, and drive them from the battlefield.'[135] According to al-Zawahiri, the 'Advice' was perhaps authored by Sayyid Imam, but it was orchestrated by US and Egyptian intelligence. He is not surprised by Sayyid Imam's criticism, however. Perhaps influenced by their common history, al-Zawahiri claims the retractions are not new as Sayyid Imam, he says, already withdrew from Jihad in 1994.[136] This assessment clearly stems from the fallout between the two when Sayyid Imam gave up leadership of Al Jihad in 1993 and in the same year directed his anger towards al-Zawahiri, after the latter, without permission, edited Sayyid Imam's encyclopaedia, '*The Compendium in Pursuit of Divine Knowledge*' (al-jami' fi talab al-'ilm al-sharif).[137] Although al-Zawahiri does not consider Sayyid Imam's critical views to be new, he goes on to question the contradictions between arguments in the book and Sayyid Imam's older opinions, focusing, among other things, on whether he still considers supporters of the regime to be unbelievers.[138]

AbuYahya al-Libi, at the time a senior al-Qaida commander, takes a different approach to al-Zawahiri in his criticism of Sayyid Imam.[139] On March 10, 2008, but probably produced as early as January the same year, a video statement by al-Libi entitled 'I Am not a Deceiver Nor Will I Allow Someone to Deceive Me' was posted to a Jihadi forum. In the statement, he defiantly claims that Sayyid Imam's book has been authored by Egyptian intelligence services, concluding no one should give its content any consideration. He gives three reasons why the intelligence service would create it: firstly, to intensify the military battle against the Jihadis; secondly, to 'flood the battlefields of jihad with deviated fatwas', making it illegitimate to join Jihadi groups; and thirdly, to soften the view on Jihad and spread doubt among Muslims about its reasons. In December of the same year al-Libi expands on his criticism in an 85-page-long book entitled '*Eliminating the Falsehood of the Document of Rationalization, Part One*'. He maintains that the document is the work of the intelligence service, but in the book focuses more on the substance of Sayyid Imam's retraction, criticising it for abandoning the Jihadi cause and directly opposing it through religious language.

The final part of the debate came in the form of the 'Exposure', a second book from Sayyid Imam that, in stark contrast to his first book, developed a substantial criticism of al-Qaida's Jihadi ideology and theology. The 'Exposure' was, more than anything, a scathing personal attack to delegitimise al-Zawahiri and Bin Laden. Kamal Habib describes the change from the first to the second book as a move 'from the level of ideas to the level of personalities, from the level of sources and derivations of religious law to the level of slander, accusations of treason, lies and deception.'[140] This change in tone, Habib argues, influenced its reception and the lack of power it had as a counter-narrative to Jihad.[141] Not only is Sayyid Imam slandering the personalities of the two al-Qaida leaders by comparing them to the devil, but he also calls al-Qaida's ideology *criminal* and warns the youth of the temptations of joining.

The authenticity of Sayyid Imam's criticism has been doubted and discussed ever since its publication. People differ on whether it was an orchestrated attempt by the Egyptian intelligence service, probably aided by Western actors, to discredit Jihad, or in fact an attempt from Sayyid Imam to launch a new ideological project for Jihad.[142] Hani Sibai, a former Al Jihad member and close friend of Sayyid Imam, has explained how in mid-2007 he received a phone call from Sayyid Imam's son, Ismail, who had an important message from his father. Ismail warned that Sibai would soon hear news from Sayyid Imam in the media but warned him against believing a word of what would be published.[143] Sayyid Imam's criticism never had the intended effect on al-Qaida and the broader Jihadi movement's legitimacy, but it did initially pose a challenge to the authority of al-Qaida's Jihadi discourse. For the al-Qaida leaders the criticism was not simply a matter of *ikhtilaf* (differences of opinion on religious matters) but an attack against a fundamental part of Islam and therefore the leaders were forced to react. To this day, Sayyid Imam's publications stand out as one of the foremost examples of Jihadi revisionism.[144]

## The Purge Within al-Shabab

In Somalia, talking was not enough. Between 2011 and 2013, al-Shabab went through an internal purge that eventually took on a violent hue. The internal conflict is often portrayed as a purge against foreigners in the ranks of al-Shabab or as tensions between global-oriented and local-oriented Jihadis,[145] but it is in fact better understood as a power struggle between two wings of the movement, represented by Ahmed Abdi Godane (aka Mukhtar Abu Zubayr) and Mukhtar Robow (aka Abu Mansur) respectively, with diverging visions for how Jihad in Somalia should proceed. Tensions go as far back as 2008[146] or 2009[147] when Ethiopian troops pulled out of Somalia, but really blossomed in 2010 and turned violent in 2013 when the leadership initiated a campaign to kill senior opposing voices.

The two wings of the group can with some justification be divided into a hard-line wing and a more moderate wing. Al-Shabab amir Godane represented the hardliners and held an uncompromising view of the implementation of Islamic law in the territory controlled by the group. His opponents differed and argued that some Islamic rulings should wait until the population would be ready for them and that suicide bombings in populated areas should be abandoned. To a great extent, the debate resembles the disagreement between al-Qaida and its Iraqi affiliate in the mid-2000s and an ongoing internal debate within al-Qaida leadership circles. As will be discussed in the following chapter, prior to his death, Bin Laden's main preoccupation was revising his group's strategy to ensure more public support. The Pakistani Taliban (TTP)[148] and the al-Qaida affiliate in North Africa (AQIM)[149] also faced reprimands from the al-Qaida leadership for their hard-line and violent practices, which did not fit into Bin Laden's new vision for the organisation.

In 2010, Godane's internal popularity further suffered, not least because of an unsuccessful Ramadan offensive in Mogadishu, and the amir began to centralise his power and suppress internal dissent. Reacting to the tensions, an internal council was created to solve differences and in mid-2011 it announced a ruling that largely went against Godane and provided him with six months to leave the post as amir of al-Shabab. Godane initially showed willingness to leave the post, but under the radar he worked to cement his internal power base further through firing his two deputies, Robow and Ibrahim al-Afghani, both founding members of al-Shabab with strong clan-relations. It has been claimed that what essentially held al-Shabab together at this point was the widespread respect for Bin Laden, and al-Qaida more generally, and no wing was willing to jeopardise the evolving relationship with al-Qaida of which al-Shabab still was not an official member.[150]

In March 2013, the debate, so far kept internal, went public when Omar al-Hammami, a senior American foreign fighter in al-Shabab, issued a video explaining that differences over Islamic law and strategy were prevalent within the group. Already two months prior, however, he insinuated something was about to happen; on Twitter he wrote that al-Shabab had given him fifteen days to surrender or be killed. Al-Hammami decided to flee but was nonetheless exposed to an assassination attempt in April. In a second video, issued in October but likely filmed in March, he added that tensions existed between globally and locally oriented Jihadis in al-Shabab. Al-Hammami's characterisation of the tensions was likely coloured by his personal experience of being increasingly sidelined within al-Shabab,[151] but his decision to make the internal tensions publicly known escalated the conflict further. In an attempt to defuse the situation, the figures in opposition to Godane (at this point led by al-Afghani, as Robow had effectively left al-Shabab) suggested that al-Qaida should mediate. Al-Afghani wrote at least three letters to al-Zawahiri and in one of the letters he asked al-Qaida to intervene to save the group.[152] Opposing senior figures allegedly also issued a fatwa instructing al-Shabab fighters not to follow the amir due to his transgressions of the Quran.[153] It should be noted that at the time al-Shabab had just become an official affiliate of al-Qaida, eventually accepted into its fold by al-Zawahiri who had taken over the reigns of the group after the death of Bin Laden. However, Godane would not accept al-Qaida's interference, and had previously stated that he would not tolerate members of al-Shabab contacting the al-Qaida leadership without his permission. From that point on, tensions only escalated.

Godane's imminent internal crackdown was facilitated by a supportive Somali-Kenyan ideologue who, during a lecture in Nairobi, legitimised fighting rebellious Jihadis, whom he referred to as *bughat*. The following month, the al-Shabab amir issued a direct threat to his internal opponents, and in June 2013, he authorised the arrest of senior rivals. The first major figure to be assassinated was none other than Ibrahim al-Afghani, a founding member of al-Shabab, its former media chief and the most vocal opponent to Godane's internal authoritarianism. On his way to a mosque for evening prayer, al-Afghani was assaulted by a team of al-Shabab amniyat (intelligence) who shot him in the head from behind while screaming 'munafiq' (hypocrite).[154] In September 2013, Omar al-Hammami met a similar fate.

# 4

# TRACING THE ISLAMIC STATE'S SPLIT FROM AL-QAIDA 1999–2014

In early 2014, the SJM fragmented and an unprecedented internal *conflict* (fitna) broke out, with al-Qaida and the Islamic State as the main protagonists. The conventional story goes that in early February al-Qaida denounced its Iraqi affiliate, then known as the *Islamic State of Iraq and Sham* (ISIS), after its expansion into Syria in April 2013. The Islamic State has consistently presented an alternative version of events, arguing that since its establishment of the *Islamic State of Iraq* (ISI) in October 2006, it has not been bound by a *pledge of allegiance* (bay'a) to al-Qaida, but simply revered the group during the lifetime of Usama Bin Laden. Through a close examination of the relationship between al-Qaida and its 'affiliate' in Iraq, this chapter argues that both accounts have some truth to them, and that this sheds light on the complex nature of the inter-group dynamics which governed the process of splintering—as well as the timing of the split—between the groups.

This is important to understand if only because 'history matters'. The al-Qaida leadership has always prioritised unity within the SJM. In his 2001 book *Knights Under the Prophet's Banner*, Ayman al-Zawahiri warned that 'The Jihad movement must realize that half the road to victory is attained through its unity, rise above trivial matters, gratitude, and glorification of the interests of Islam above personal whims', but despite continuous efforts from senior al-Qaida figures it proved impossible for the group to stay united in 2014. It has been argued that the reason for the split needs to be sought in a difference between being focused on doctrine versus strategy, the latter being more 'willing to present a unified front and avoid airing the dirty laundry of other groups in public.'[1] Such ideological differences are only part of the explanation needed to understand factionalism within the SJM, however.[2] In order to reach a more nuanced understanding of the process we need to consider group dynamics, power ambitions and the political context that groups navigate within.

It was after long consideration and negotiations that Abu Musab al-Zarqawi's group *Jama'at al-Tawhid wa-l-Jihad* finally consented to become al-Qaida's affiliate in Iraq in 2004, but as history has shown, it never became a happy marriage. As the intra-movement conflict broke out in 2014, so did the debate about *when* and *why* the Islamic State rescinded its ties to al-Qaida and if, in fact, the Islamic State left the al-Qaida network or it was kicked out. Morrison has worked extensively on organisational splits in the context of the Irish Republican movement and stresses the importance of tracing tensions that are present prior to a split in order to properly understand it.[3] He offers a useful stage model for understanding why groups split. This model focuses on various dynamics prior to the split, the split itself and its aftermath. Applying this model, we can divide the split between al-Qaida and its Iraqi affiliate into the following six stages:

- Stage 1: origins of conflict (1999)
- Stage 2: factional development (2005–08)
- Stage 3: mutual dissatisfaction and subgroup (AQI/ISI) preparation for the split (2005–13)
- Stage 4: subgroup (ISIS) disobedience and challenges to authority (2013–14)
- Stage 5: organisational split into two separate groups (2014)
- Stage 6: inter-group competition, contestation and infighting (2014–19)

The first part of this chapter will focus on stages 1–3 while the second part will look closer at stages 4–5. Chapters 5–13 concentrate on the final stage—stage 6—and provide a detailed case study of the aftermath of the split.

## *Becoming an al-Qaida Affiliate*

Al-Zarqawi's personal experience with al-Qaida began in late 1999. In March of that year he was released after spending five years in a Jordanian prison and quickly immigrated to Afghanistan for the second time with his two deputies Abu al-Qassam and Abdul Hadi Daghlas.[4] Within, it was mainly Saif al-Adl, the group's future military chief and current third-in-command, that saw great potential in the Jordanian. According to its founding ideals, al-Qaida was interested in supporting other Jihadi actors and al-Zarqawi was no exception. Even if the collaboration did nothing more than curb the ambitions of Bin Laden's rival Abu Musab al-Suri by supporting another Jihadi leader with a Levantine support base, it would nonetheless have been attractive to al-Qaida.[5] In the spring of 2000, al-Suri had established his own organisational setup, *al-Ghuraba Camp*, located at the Kargha military base just outside of Kabul, which would compete with al-Qaida for Arab fighters and align itself more closely with the Taliban.[6] Al-Qaida had never been capable of attracting large numbers of *muhajireen* (foreign fighters) from the Levant, but coming from Syria, al-Suri was expected to attract people from the region. The Jordanian al-Zarqawi would be al-Qaida's way of competing with al-Suri for the sympathy of Levantine Jihadis.[7]

Much of what we know about this initial alliance is from al-Adl's 2005 testimony.[8] At first, al-Qaida did not demand allegiance from al-Zarqawi in the form of a bay'a, but simply proposed 'coordination and cooperation'. Not only was this in the organisational spirit of al-Qaida at the time (it had not yet embarked on its expansion-through-affiliates strategy), but it also provided the group with a 'trial' period for al-Zarqawi. Already at this time, al-Qaida as an organisation and idea involved actors with quite diverse religious and political outlooks. This was also the case with al-Zarqawi, which apparently worried Bin Laden. From al-Adl we know that initially the critical issue between al-Qaida and al-Zarqawi was that the latter was insisting on making takfir on the Saudi regime, something that clearly illustrates the influence of his ideological mentor Abu Muhammad al-Maqdisi. Al-Adl makes a few observations about al-Zarqawi's character and al-Qaida's attitude to the collaboration that are relevant here. About al-Zarqawi, he says that the Jordanian was 'uncompromising' and not willing to change his beliefs. Al-Adl and his superiors in al-Qaida were aware of the doctrinal and ideological differences between al-Zarqawi and the al-Qaida leaders even at this early stage,[9] but as al-Adl recounts 'we listened to him, but we did not argue since we wanted to win him over to our side in the first place.' Going into further detail, he elaborates, 'The reason was the diverse understanding of some aspects of the faith that pertain to al-wala' and the al-bara' and the subsequent issues of takfir.'[10] Not only does this indicate that al-Qaida considered the SJM to be competitive (to say nothing of al-Qaida's desire to monopolise the struggle), but it also illustrates that al-Qaida was willing to accept al-Zarqawi's differences because of its political and strategic ambitions. Even during his time in Herat, al-Zarqawi's character and vision evolved. Al-Adl reports that the Jordanian became more assertive as a leader and clearly had higher ambitions than managing a camp in western Afghanistan. These ambitions would later make it difficult for al-Zarqawi to tolerate the stringent criticism levelled by al-Qaida leaders at his project in Iraq.

It was during his experiences in Afghanistan that al-Zarqawi was influenced by the so-called *Jalalabad current*. This current arose after the defeat at Jalalabad in July 1989 and the ensuing emergence of a leadership vacuum resulting from the death of Abdullah Azzam and Bin Laden's return to Saudi Arabia.[11] It was mainly comprised of rebellious youth who opposed the established Jihadi leadership and wanted to fight on the battlefield despite clear orders to refrain from action. During his first visit to Afghanistan from 1989–93, it is likely that al-Zarqawi was in contact with some of the rebellious youth, but it was during his second visit that he really became familiar with the more radical ideas that were present in the Jihadi community at the time and that had been propagated by—among others—Abu Abdullah al-Muhajir. Al-Muhajir, an Egyptian ideologue, developed into al-Zarqawi's most important ideological mentor during his stay in Afghanistan. His radical ideas, espoused especially in the book *Jurisprudence of Jihad* (fiqh al-jihad, although popularly known as *Jurisprudence of Blood*, fiqh al-dima), came to dominate al-Zarqawi's view on issues such as suicide bombing. In the mid- to late 1990s, al-Muhajir was affiliated to the independent *Khaldan Camp* and was initially critical of al-Qaida, occasionally attacking the group, although he later ended up joining it.[12] It is likely, however, that these experiences influenced al-Zarqawi's view of authority and particularly his view on al-Qaida; as a dominant Jihadi group but not one above criticism.[13]

Already at this point, al-Zarqawi distinguished his group from most others. He did not send fighters to the Taliban frontlines like other groups operating in the country;[14] indeed, he even considered the Taliban and other Jihadi fronts as misguided and as innovators.[15] The 9/11 attacks made it impossible for al-Zarqawi to remain in Afghanistan. Like many other Jihadis, he fled. Passing through Iran, he would eventually settle in Iraqi Kurdistan, from where he continued his organisational activities and evolved into a key actor in the Iraqi insurgency from 2003. It was during the Iraqi insurgency that al-Zarqawi's distinctive vision and sectarian approach would really reveal themselves. On several occasions, he displayed his extreme anti-Shia attitude and his willingness to escalate the level of barbarity in the conflict with the Shias and with government and coalition forces.[16] Vivid examples include the bombing of the Imam Ali shrine in Najaf on August 29, 2003, which killed prominent Shia cleric Mohammad Baqir al-Hakim, and the decapitation of the American Nick Berg on May 7, 2004.

Al-Zarqawi did nothing to keep his ideological conviction and organisational priorities a secret. As part of the negotiating process to become an al-Qaida affiliate, he authored a letter in February 2004 to Bin Laden and his second-in-command Ayman al-Zawahiri. The letter, which was basically al-Zarqawi's *feuille de route*, had two purposes: to set down his view of Jihad in Iraq including his enemy hierarchy, and to inform the al-Qaida leadership about the status of the Iraqi insurgency as a first step towards assessing the possibility of future cooperation in the form of a pledge of allegiance.[17] Concerning the Shia, al-Zarqawi writes that they are the most important enemy, and that his aim is to drag them into a sectarian war in order to rouse the Sunni masses to action. Hence, there could be no doubt among the al-Qaida leadership regarding the priorities of al-Zarqawi when later that year they officially declared al-Zarqawi's group al-Qaida's affiliate in Iraq.[18] Al-Zarqawi finishes his letter,

> If you agree with us on it, if you adopt it as a program and road, and if you are convinced of the idea of fighting the sects of apostasy, we will be your readied soldiers, working under your banner, complying with your orders, and indeed swearing fealty to you publicly (...). If things appear otherwise to you, we are brothers, and the disagreement will not spoil our friendship.

By the time that al-Zarqawi's group officially became an al-Qaida affiliate, the Jordanian's actions and rhetoric should have marked him out as a potential source of trouble to the al-Qaida leadership. Al-Qaida has always played down doctrinal differences and has historically been more interested in working together with a broad range of people. This is arguably what drove al-Qaida to strengthen the relationship by incorporating al-Zarqawi's Iraqi group as an official *affiliate* with a legally binding bay'a. From the perspective of resource mobilisation theory, the alliance did initially make sense for both parties. For al-Zarqawi, the official affiliation with al-Qaida would have provided him with funding and legitimacy; two important factors in his efforts to succeed in the competitive Iraqi insurgency that developed in 2003–04. Being officially associated with Bin Laden supported al-Zarqawi's ambition of making his group the dominant one among local rebel groups just as it made it attractive for other mujahideen to join. For al-Qaida, there were several benefits to accepting al-Zarqawi's pledge. The group was under pressure in Afghanistan, while Iraq was seen as the most important Jihadi battlefield. Al-Zarqawi's group thus ensured al-Qaida remained relevant and extended its project outside of Afghanistan by associating with a successful entrepreneur in a Jihadi hotspot. The two groups were bound together by roughly similar ideologies in terms of religious interpretation and political ambitions; even so, strategic differences existed which illustrate the diversity within the SJM. As Bacon and Moghadam explain in their work on cooperation, such differences can be overcome when the benefits from allying are greater. Once al-Zarqawi was in the fold, al-Qaida hoped that the Jordanian's action and rhetoric could be curbed through internal consultation.[19]

On October 17, 2004, Abu Musab al-Zarqawi's organisation *Jama'at al-Tawhid wa-l-Jihad* merged into al-Qaida and became its Iraqi affiliate popularly known as *al-Qaida in Iraq* (AQI). The official statement was communicated first by al-Zarqawi's group and immediately reprinted by al-Qaida in its online magazine *Mu'askar al-Battar*. One comment in particular from the pledge of allegiance can help us understand the process leading up to the announcement and how the relationship between the two groups—al-Qaida as the central organisation and AQI as its affiliate—should be viewed. The announcement reads,

> Numerous messages were passed between 'Abu Musab' (God protect him) and the al-Qaeda brotherhood over the past eight months, establishing a dialogue between them. No sooner had the calls been cut off than God chose to restore them, and our most generous brothers in al-Qaeda came to understand the strategy of the Tawhid wal-Jihad organization in Iraq, the land of the two rivers and of the Caliphs, and their hearts warmed to its methods and overall mission.[20]

On paper, Al-Zarqawi was al-Qaida's representative in Iraq, but in reality the al-Qaida leaders were in no position to tell him how to behave.

Al-Zarqawi was now finally an official part of al-Qaida, but the initial doubts al-Qaida had about him were quickly becoming a reality, ensuring that the affiliation would become a source of trouble and regret for Bin Laden. Al-Adl was the first to believe in al-Zarqawi and was put in charge of the liaison between the Jordanian and al-Qaida. Appropriately enough, al-Adl also authored the first guidelines for al-Zarqawi. In the final three pages of his biography of al-Zarqawi, he offers four pieces of advice to al-Zarqawi. Al-Adl, in captivity in Iran, has not been in contact with al-Zarqawi for years, but he has heard about his ventures in Iraq and feels it necessary to guide his ally so that the sectarian situation in Iraq will not be exacerbated.

Al-Adl advises that (1) every action should have a clear goal, (2) there should be a clear banner in the form of leadership, (3) there should be a plan guiding all actions from the very beginning, and (4) one should take advantage of available opportunities.[21] Given his emphasis on these four points, it is clear that al-Adl was not satisfied with how al-Zarqawi was managing the Jihad in Iraq. This, however, was already a point that had been raised the previous year by al-Zarqawi's former mentor Abu Muhammad al-Maqdisi and, as the following section shows, a point that would be repeated in numerous letters from high-ranking al-Qaida leaders in the following years.

### *Al-Qaida's Critique of al-Zarqawi and His Dispute with al-Maqdisi*

Ever since his rise to Jihadi stardom, al-Zarqawi had been connected to Abu Muhammad al-Maqdisi.[22] Al-Maqdisi was an intellectual mentor to al-Zarqawi during their time in Jordan, although how intimate the bond between the two was would later be questioned by al-Zarqawi. Nonetheless it came as a blow when al-Maqdisi targeted his criticism against his former student in a July 2004 letter titled *al-zarqawi: munaseha wa munasera* (Al-Zarqawi: Advice and Support).[23] Al-Maqdisi's criticism has been labelled by some as *ideological revisionism* resulting from his time in prison and his alleged subservience by the Jordanian intelligence (similar to the accusation against Dr Fadl). However, as Wagemakers has argued, it is more likely al-Maqdisi simply differed on certain central issues relating to creed and methodology.[24] In the letter, al-Maqdisi points out several major errors that he believes al-Zarqawi committed due to his inexperience and immaturity. He mentions in particular the mistake of leaving for Afghanistan in 1999, the mistake of proclaiming takfir on the Shia as a group, and the strategic failure of attacks carried out by al-Zarqawi's group after relocating to Iraq.[25] The last mistake was caused by al-Zarqawi's careless attitude towards protecting Muslim blood and avoiding civilian casualties. In the eyes of al-Maqdisi, al-Zarqawi was not just incapable of instilling a correct ethical attitude in his followers; crucially he lacked the viable vision and program necessary for a successful Jihad. Although al-Maqdisi probably had personal reasons for his verbal attack, such as reclaiming leadership, the points he made turned out to be valid in the following years.[26] For someone who already considered himself a great leader—popular, and at that moment deeply involved in a successful Jihadi campaign in Iraq—al-Maqdisi's critique would have been difficult if not impossible for al-Zarqawi to accept.

Approximately a year later, on July 5, 2005, al-Maqdisi turned up again with criticism—but this time also with praise of al-Zarqawi. In a taped al-Jazeera interview, al-Maqdisi repeats some of his criticism from the year before. On the same day, however, al-Maqdisi also published a short message to calm the disagreement. Commenting on two articles about him published in Arab newspapers, he claims they are either made up or that they contain important omissions intended to sow conflict between the mujahideen. Although al-Maqdisi stands by his previous critique of al-Qaida in Iraq, he feels the need 'to close the door on any fitna.' Referring to al-Zarqawi as 'our beloved brother the hero of the mujahideen', he claims that despite their disagreements they share the Jihadi struggle.[27] At this point, al-Maqdisi would have had no interest in escalating the conflict more than necessary, partly because al-Zarqawi was enjoying success, but also because his position was that such conflict was illegitimate. Thus his criticism should be seen as an attempt to reclaim some of his lost intellectual leadership within the SJM and to reorient the Jihadi struggle back towards his own vision of the correct methodology, one that employs less extreme tactics and adopts a local focus.[28]

As if the criticism from his former mentor was not enough, al-Zarqawi began to receive warnings from al-Qaida leaders, who were formally his superiors. The critique, which took the form of a series of personal letters, came first from Ayman al-Zawahiri and needs to be seen in the context of mounting dissatisfaction with AQI in the eyes of other Iraqi insurgent groups. It must also be seen in the context of the increasingly brutal sectarian killings that were then occurring.[29] In a letter dated July 9, 2005 and written in a friendly tone, al-Zawahiri explains that al-Zarqawi needs to focus more on winning the support of the Muslim public if the Jihad in Iraq is to be successful. In the words of al-Zawahiri, the 'mujahid movement must avoid any action that the masses do not understand or approve.'[30] At this point, he seems to be driven not by an ambition to re-balance the authority between the two groups but by a desire to correct what he considers to be a problematic strategy that is doomed to fail. Al-Zawahiri's main point is that AQI needs to think more strategically about its military engagement and become more politically conscious. To al-Zawahiri this implies strengthening the bonds of alliance and cooperation throughout the Iraqi Sunni landscape, uniting the mujahideen, gaining the support of the 'ulama and, arguably most importantly, halting the indiscriminate attacks on the Shia.[31] Al-Zawahiri's argument is not that the Shia is not a deviant group or a legitimate target, but that the Muslim masses do not necessarily understand this. Indiscriminate attacks on the Shia and their holy places, he believes, thus risk decreasing popular support for AQI. Al-Zawahiri was clearly aware of the sensitivity of raising these issues, especially given that he was far away from Iraq. While acknowledging this, he also notes that

> monitoring from afar has the advantage of providing the total picture and observing the general line without getting submerged in the details, which might draw attention away from the direction of the target. As the English proverb says, the person who is standing among the leaves of the tree might not see the tree.[32]

At the end of the letter, al-Zawahiri, like al-Maqdisi, implicitly calls for mature and responsible leadership from al-Zarqawi in order to manage the enthusiasm of his supporters, especially the youth. From the perspective of the al-Qaida leadership, however, the years that followed demonstrated that al-Zarqawi and his successors had not been up to the task. Despite some contemporary attempts at historical revisionism, it is clear that AQI did not follow al-Zawahiri's advice that it should change its attitude towards the Shia population.[33] These differences not only show the divergence between AQI and the al-Qaida leadership in terms of their view of reality (*waqi'*) on the ground in Iraq; they also indicate a degree of pragmatism on the part of al-Qaida, one that would turn out to be an important characteristic in the widening division between the two groups in the years to come.

It would take an entire year for al-Zarqawi to respond to al-Maqdisi, but in a letter to al-Maqdisi dated July 12, 2005, he makes no remarks about the criticism he had just received from another insider: al-Zawahiri. Clearly provoked by al-Maqdisi's continued reproach, he felt obliged to respond. Al-Zarqawi does not hide the fact that al-Maqdisi's attack was a surprise, especially since it came from a person he used to hold dear and with whom he shares a creed. He begins the letter by stating that al-Maqdisi's criticism is helping the enemies of Jihad—a similar argument would be made years later by al-Qaida in the context of the Islamic State's aggression. Al-Zarqawi does acknowledge that al-Maqdisi was his mentor, saying that he 'is indeed indebted to Sheikh Abu Muhammad, may Allah preserve him, he was one of those whom I learned details of *Tawhid* (unity of Allah) from, and my position with respect to many issues was similar to his.' But in a clear attempt to delegitimise his mentor, al-Zarqawi claims that their relationship was not a matter of *taqlid* (blind following) but that he believed al-Maqdisi was preaching the correct creed and methodology. Al-Zarqawi continues,

> This does not mean that I have to implement everything Maqdisi says, besides, he does not and should not have a monopoly on knowledge, and not everything he says is correct, especially when it comes to jihad and the current state of affairs of the Umma in view of the crusader's campaign against Islam.

Al-Zarqawi's line of argument clearly illustrates that he took al-Maqdisi's accusations personally and in response he seeks to undermine his former teacher by claiming that he has little knowledge of practical affairs, which al-Zarqawi and his followers value higher than scholarly knowledge. This point is underlined when al-Zarqawi scolds al-Maqdisi, saying 'Allah knows that I keep constant communication with some righteous scholars who are far more knowledgeable than Maqdisi to get their opinion on most of what I am faced with on daily bases.'[34] Provoking al-Maqdisi, al-Zarqawi almost goes as far as to suggest that his senior cares more about his own standing than committing to tawhid, on the grounds that al-Maqdisi, in his letter, speaks of his own *sheikhdom* and the *Manhaj of Abu Muhammad*. On al-Maqdisi's criticism of attacks on the

Shia, al-Zarqawi blasts him for comparing the ordinary Sunni to the ordinary Shia. He recalls that prominent Jihadi scholars including Hammod al-Uqla, Sulayman al-Alwan, Ali al-Khudair, Abu Abdullah al-Muhajir and Sheikh al-Rashoud have all proclaimed the Shia kuffar (unbelievers). In a bold move, he continues his attempt to tarnish al-Maqdisi's standing within the SJM, arguing that al-Maqdisi is in fact disagreeing with the al-Qaida leaders and the aforementioned Jihadi scholars regarding the importance of the Iraqi Jihad. In this way, al-Zarqawi implicitly raises the question of how al-Maqdisi can be correct if all other respected Jihadi leaders and scholars are of another opinion. Al-Zarqawi's supporters joined in with this counterattack on al-Maqdisi, engaging in a struggle to define what counts as authority within the Jihadi movement—scholarly knowledge or practical experience.[35] Al-Zarqawi's supporters promoted the latter. This discussion would eventually extend to the broader Jihadi environment beyond Jordan and Iraq, spreading to other regions, such as the Gulf, where it ignited a sensitive debate that to some extent had existed since the 1980s.

A few months later, al-Zawahiri had not received any response from al-Zarqawi, whose actions showed no signs of moderation (one example of this being the November 2005 Amman hotel bombings). This led two senior al-Qaida lieutenants, *Abu Yahya al-Libi* and *Atiyyah Abd al-Rahman*, to address al-Zarqawi in late 2005. Authored four months after he escaped from prison in Afghanistan, Abu Yahya's message, a twenty-page letter dated November 23, is the more subtle of the two communications.[36] Because Iraq has now overtaken Afghanistan as the most important Jihadi battlefield, following a sound strategy is imperative, he argues. The letter is structured into five points, but they are all framed in a way that makes it difficult to perceive the letter as a direct critique unless one is aware of the context. The first point is that the enemies of Islam seek to provoke schisms between groups from within, and that it is the leader's responsibility to keep his group together and to be open to pragmatic solutions. The second point is the importance of consulting other groups and individuals. The third point was already raised by al-Zawahiri, but Abu Yahya reiterates in much more subtle language: Jihadi groups need to act and communicate in a manner that people understand even if it means abstaining from actions that are correct according to religion. The fourth point is to remain focused on the most important targets and not to expand the struggle to include too many enemies, as this risks putting unnecessary pressure on the movement. Abu Yahya's last point opens a door for al-Zarqawi, pointing out that the mujahideen must have the courage and the determination to backtrack from mistakes. There is no doubt that this is a reference to al-Zarqawi's mistakes in the eyes of the al-Qaida leadership, which the Jordanian had so far proved unwilling to correct.

Less than a month later, al-Zarqawi received another letter, this time authored by Atiyyah Abd al-Rahman, better known as *Atiyyatullah,* who at that time was already an important liaison between the leadership and affiliated groups.[37] Atiyyatullah's letter, which is dated December 11, stands in stark contrast to Abu Yahya's letter in that it is far more explicit in its criticism of al-Zarqawi and in the orders (framed as 'advice and instruction') which it issues to him. A few months earlier, in August 2005, Atiyyatullah authored a shorter letter to al-Zarqawi and his men in which he warns them about their attitude to the population, especially those participating in elections. Already at this time, the leadership saw clear signs of extremism in AQI's application of takfir.[38] In the much longer letter of December, Atiyyatullah begins by congratulating al-Qaida in Iraq for posing the greatest threat to the enemy, but goes on to explain that success of this kind is inevitably followed by a good deal of scrutiny and necessitates mature leadership. In this context, seeking support and advice from the higher leadership is imperative, and in a very straightforward manner he tells al-Zarqawi, 'you need to keep in mind that you are the leader in the field that is under a greater leadership that is more potent and more able to lead the Muslim nation.' Echoing Abu Yahya and al-Zawahiri,[39] he continues: 'Policy must be dominant over militarism.' This comes in a reference to the experience with the GIA in Algeria in the 1990s—Atiyyatullah suggests that he is beginning to see similar signs in Iraq. In Algeria, he claims, the GIA's 'enemy did not defeat them, but rather they defeated themselves'; to prevent this, al-Zarqawi needs to change, or even reform, his group, and to exercise leadership. Clearly annoyed that al-Zarqawi has not yet responded to the al-Qaida leadership or changed his approach, Atiyyatullah toughens his rhetoric and lists nine orders to al-Zarqawi:

- Do not stop your Jihad, but correct your mistakes (he even keeps the door open to the possibility that someone else should take over the leadership of AQI),
- Refrain from making any decision on bigger issues until you have consulted with the al-Qaida leadership,
- Begin consulting with other Jihadi groups in Iraq,
- Begin consulting with non-Jihadi Sunnis in Iraq such as tribes and religious scholars,
- Establish a stronger connection between al-Qaida in Iraq and the al-Qaida central leadership,
- Seek to win the sympathy of the people through behaviour that the Sunni masses understand,
- Start paying attention to the religious scholars of Iraq (he emphasises that one of al-Zarqawi's most important jobs is to bring closer together the people of scholarship and the people of Jihad),
- Educate the people in the organisation 'in good conduct, by providing them with a good model in manners, respect, modesty, the giving of advice, accepting advice, admitting mistakes, respecting others, proficiency in dialogue, politeness with those who disagree, mercy, justice, kindness', and
- Abstain from foreign attacks until you have coordinated with al-Qaida's leadership.

Atiyyatullah's 'advice' is an important illustration of the differences in thinking between al-Qaida's central leadership and AQI, with the former following a much more nuanced political approach in contrast to al-Zarqawi's focus on military success and his inflexibility regarding religious belief. This is captured in Atiyyatullah's recommendation, 'do not act alone and do not be overzealous.' The al-Qaida leaders asked al-Zarqawi for a quick response, even offering instructions in how to contact them through internet fora, but al-Zarqawi's answer came shortly afterwards not in words but in actions—before and after his own death.

Arguably the most effective approach for al-Qaida would have been for Saif al-Adl—who had initially established contact between al-Zarqawi and al-Qaida and who had a good connection with the Jordanian—to be in charge of the communication, but at this time al-Adl was under house arrest in Iran. That Bin Laden made three of his most senior members produce a substantial critique of al-Zarqawi within six months illustrates the seriousness of the affair. Much more than an attempt by al-Maqdisi and the al-Qaida leadership to exercise authority over an affiliate, this critique was primarily intended to safeguard their vision of the Jihadi project and to encourage what they considered a sound strategy for future behaviour. Not only did al-Zarqawi and many of his followers disagree with the al-Qaida leaders' view of the political context and their methodology, but it is also very likely that he was provoked by being told what to do. Unlike many of his seniors, he was not primarily a product of Afghanistan's school of Jihad in the 1980s and 1990s, despite the periods he spent in the country, and was less willing to subordinate himself to others' authority. To a great extent, Al-Zarqawi and his group were the product of a different generation with different priorities—and, in the case of al-Zarqawi himself, with the ambition to lead. He had not been moulded inside a Jihadi organisation or battlefield, but rather on the streets of Zarqa, in prison and by a specific ideological orientation. The exchanges of letters represent the beginning of factionalism that would continue in the following years concurrently with a process leading up to the eventual split. This process, however, was dramatically affected by a changing political environment in Iraq that put AQI on the defensive.

### *Distancing From al-Qaida: The Establishment of a State in 2006*

In his February 2004 letter to Bin Laden, al-Zarqawi wrote, 'We do not see ourselves as fit to challenge you.' This was obviously still the situation in 2006, and after al-Zarqawi's death in June, but by then the relationship between al-Qaida's leaders and the local leadership in Iraq had become so tense that the alliance was no longer desirable in the eyes of the latter. Despite the overwhelming criticism that was levelled at al-Zarqawi by the senior leadership, it is very possible that al-Zarqawi was more annoyed with al-Qaida than the other way around. Years later, in 2016, the Islamic State disclosed that al-Zarqawi 'was very sad about the dealings of some of the leaders of al-Qaeda in Khorasan [Afghanistan–Pakistan] with him and their evil thoughts about him.'[40]

The years 2006–07 were critical for AQI. The group witnessed a string of important internal developments, the implications of which were insufficiently understood until 2014 and to some extent remain misunderstood to this day. In January 2006, AQI established the Mujahideen Shura Council (MSC) together with five smaller Jihadi groups.[41] The MSC did not dissolve the individual groups but acted as a temporary conduit for AQI to monopolise Iraq's Jihadi insurgency under the leadership of Abdallah al-Rashid al-Baghdadi (Abu Ali al-Anbari, real name Abd al-Rahman Mustafa al-Qaduli), until then AQI's deputy amir and the man in charge of the group's shari'a committees in northern Iraq.[42] One explanation is that the establishment of the MSC was in fact al-Zarqawi giving in to al-Qaida pressure.[43] However, although the union was a move towards unity, as the al-Qaida leadership called for, it now appears more likely that it was an attempt by al-Zarqawi to consolidate and expand his authority, and possibly also a first step towards separation from al-Qaida. Some months later, in October 2006, AQI took a second and even more decisive step towards independence. With al-Anbari arrested in April and al-Zarqawi killed in June, AQI and the MSC were under the tutelage of Abu Hamza al-Muhajir (Ayyub al-Masri)[44] when they announced a merger with seven other groups to form the Islamic State of Iraq (ISI).[45] Unlike the MSC, the ISI—importantly—implied the effective dissolution of the individual groups that had come together to establish it.

Back in 2004, when al-Zarqawi announced his pledge of allegiance to al-Qaida, he 'pledged allegiance to the mujahid sheikh Osama bin Laden, to hear and obey' (al-same'a wa-l-ta'a),[46] but in late 2006, ISI was no longer willing to obey. Looking at the communication between ISI and al-Qaida between 2006 and 2014 and the former's actions, it can be argued convincingly that the transformation from the MSC to ISI brought about the rupture with al-Qaida,[47] which later would become a major topic of debate. In this period, the

ISI rhetoric was not very different from Bin Laden's own attitude towards the Taliban in the late 1990s. Officially Bin Laden respected the Taliban and was obedient towards its authority, but his actions rarely followed his words.

AQI probably viewed the SJM in a manner similar to *Bourdieu*: a field of actors broadly united around militant Jihad, but hierarchically ordered and dependent on several relatively volatile sources of authority and legitimacy (capitals in Bourdieu's parlance).[48] Going public with a statement confirming the separation from al-Qaida would risk too much as long as the group could not seriously position themselves as an alternative to al-Qaida and the position it occupied within the SJM. Separating from al-Qaida as a means of challenging al-Qaida would have required an opportune contextual setting and a degree of equilibrium in the status of the two groups that simply did not exist in 2006, when AQI's fortunes were changing in the Iraqi insurgency. Local opinion among Sunnis was increasingly turning against AQI, and this eventually led to the *Sahwa rebellion* of powerful Sunni tribes supported by the US, which had an increasing number of troops in Iraq.[49] Having previously thrived in the fight against the coalition and the Shia community, AQI now faced serious challenges even to remain a potent force on the ground. Its attempt to rely on sectarianism as a mechanism to gain popular support backfired after the February bombing of the Al Askari mosque in Samarra. While the bombing caused a flare up of sectarianism, AQI proved unable to protect the Sunni communities from retribution, leading to further local alienation.[50]

Nonetheless, there are several arguments for viewing the ISI as separate from al-Qaida with the establishment of the state in October 2006. To the disappointment of al-Qaida, ISI did not ask for permission or advice, or even inform al-Qaida's leadership, when it established its state initially, or again four years later when it appointed Abu Bakr al-Baghdadi as its new leader.[51] There is also the evidence offered by the most elaborate document dealing with the ISI's state creation; entitled *Informing the People of the Birth of the Islamic State* (I'lam al-anam bi-milad Dawlat al-Islam), it was written by the group's head of the shari'a committee, Uthman Bin Abdul Rahman al-Tamimi, and released on January 7, 2007. The ninety-one-page document does not once mention any relationship between the newly founded state and al-Qaida, as might be expected if the ISI truly did consider itself part of (and subordinate to) al-Qaida.

Abu Umar al-Baghdadi, until then the chief of staff in the MSC, was elected amir of ISI because of al-Anbari's imprisonment and quickly cast himself as *Commander of the Faithful* (amir al-mu'minin), a title also bestowed on the Taliban's Mullah Umar. In his very first speech Abu Umar announced that 'al-Qaeda is nothing more than a group in the groups of the Islamic State.'[52] This was a small shift from Abu Hamza's statement one month earlier that the soldiers of ISI 'are the army of al-Qaeda.' In December 2007, Abu Umar further explained the hierarchy, saying, 'The amir of Al-Qaeda [Abu Hamza] declared to all that Al-Qaeda would be part of the Islamic State of Iraq, and today, the soldiers of Al-Qaeda are its loyal soldiers and knights.'[53] Although al-Zawahiri himself suggested in his 2005 letter to al-Zarqawi that (as a second stage of the Jihad in Iraq) an Islamic state and later a caliphate should be set up, the way events played out was most likely not how al-Zawahiri had imagined.[54] As already mentioned, al-Zarqawi did not respond directly to the numerous accusations coming from al-Qaida's central leadership in 2005–06, but instead sent an envoy in the form of al-Anbari.[55] From his biography, we learn that al-Anbari travelled for a month and that his task in Pakistan was indeed to discuss the criticism coming from the al-Qaida leadership. While in Pakistan, al-Anbari met with Mustafa al-Yazid, Abu Yahya al-Libi and Atiyyatullah, two of the authors of critical letters addressed to the AQI leadership.[56] Unfortunately, no details exist on how the discussions went.

The ISI's ambitious way of framing the relationship with al-Qaida triggers the important question of *when* the pledge of allegiance was severed. Although this will be dealt with in greater length later in the book, it is necessary to make a few points here. Already in 2005, in a letter to Bin Laden, al-Zarqawi wrote that his group was going to maintain the covenant it had with al-Qaida, but referring to it as *al-ahd* (covenant) and not *bay'a*,[57] the latter having a different legal meaning and thus different obligations. Even more illustrative is that after the establishment of ISI, Abu Hamza pledged allegiance to Abu Umar and declared that al-Qaida in Iraq no longer exists but is a part of ISI.[58] Within al-Qaida it is tradition that when an affiliate appoints a new amir, he renews his pledge of allegiance, but Abu Hamza did not do so when he was elected leader of AQI in mid-2006—unlike, for instance, Qassim al-Rimi when he took over the leadership of AQAP in 2015.[59] Nor did ISI pledge allegiance to al-Zawahiri in July 2011 (as AQIM and AQAP did) after he was announced as the new al-Qaida leader.

It is likely that in 2006 the downsides of allying with al-Qaida had overcome the benefits. The strength of alliances of this type depends on four factors: foundational ideological/theological affinity, strategic benefits, personalities and political context. While the first factor is relatively stable, the remaining three can easily change. Al-Zarqawi's group likely realised that the affiliation with al-Qaida placed restrictions on it that outweighed the gains from the relationship; also, the group's success in the Iraqi insurgency probably instilled in it a belief that it could do without al-Qaida.[60] For al-Qaida, on the other hand, unity was important. It wanted to keep the transnational Jihadi project together and to change it from within. In January 2006 al-Zawahiri sent two letters to the leader of Ansar al-Sunna in Iraq—a group with close ties to al-Qaida but often at odds with al-Zarqawi's group—asking him to unite with AQI. But as this did not happen, al-Qaida took the risk of sending a senior official, Abd al-Hadi al-Iraqi, to Iraq in October of the same year to rein in—or perhaps replace—the Iraqi leadership, showing just how important the matter was.[61] With the evolution of the MSC into ISI, however, the damage was already done. Not only was the declaration of a state contrary to Bin Laden's plans,[62] but it also laid the foundation for an organisational split—the renouncement of the bay'a—that surfaced in 2014.

### *Al-Qaida's Internal Management Challenges*

The years 2007–12 turned out to be a challenging period for al-Qaida internally. While the most urgent and critical issue was how to handle the group in Iraq, with its increasingly rebellious behaviour and its declaration of its Islamic state, other affiliates would also turn out to be troublesome for the leadership. Affiliates in Yemen and the

Maghreb were similarly displaying disobedience or internal tensions that al-Qaida's leadership would need to address, in addition to having to rebuke non-affiliated but related groups in Somalia and Pakistan.

## *Managing a Rebellious 'Affiliate'*

The declaration of ISI took al-Qaida's leadership by surprise, leaving it in a delicate position on how to respond. The first response to the state declaration and the rebellious attitude of ISI came from Atiyyatullah in December 2006. In a statement essentially addressed to the Jihadi masses, he celebrated ISI, but between the lines he also issued a warning to the group. While the general tone of the statement was one of support, he criticised the choice of name, the *Islamic State of Iraq*, and the title of its leader, *Abu Umar al-Baghdadi*, claiming that his self-presentation as 'commander of the faithful' (amir al-mu'minin) was misleading. To counter claims that the new entity is superior to al-Qaida, Atiyyatullah explains that neither of these titles should be taken to indicate that the group or its authority extends beyond the borders of Iraq; they need to be understood simply as choices made by the group. Atiyyatullah finishes his message by cautioning the 'zealous young people' in Iraq who rush to excommunicate other Muslims.[63]

A similar message was directed towards Abu Umar in the form of a private letter from Abu Yahya al-Libi in April 2007, illustrating the reservations al-Qaida had about ISI's state project.[64] The letter came in reaction to a speech by Abu Umar in which he defined a new enemy: people rejecting the payment of *jizya*.[65] Not only does Abu Yahya explain that such a decision is strategically foolish, he also reminds Abu Umar of his responsibility as an amir of a state when publishing statements, and reiterates some of the points made in his letter to al-Zarqawi a year and a half before. Perhaps most interestingly, he chastises Abu Umar for going into details on issues of takfir which are agitating the youth and sowing discord within Iraq's Jihadi environment. Instead, Abu Yahya remarks, 'We should accustom our youth to accept other opinions as long as they are within the framework of accepted difference that is far from poisoning diluted ideas.' He goes on to warn the ISI amir, saying:

'Beware—dear sheikh—for this matter [takfir]. Put its danger as a priority and give it attention. I swear to Allah that the disease of exaggeration has ripped the Jihadi groups, eradicated its entity, and supported its enemy.'[66]

Externally, the situation was different. Bin Laden obliquely commented on the mistakes of ISI in two speeches in late 2007,[67] but otherwise he instructed his senior leaders to publish only positive statements about the group,[68] while placing al-Zawahiri in charge of handling the issue with the Iraqi movement internally.[69] Bin Laden's decision to support Abu Umar and his group discursively clearly reflects his fear of alienating ISI further. In an undated letter to al-Zawahiri, the al-Qaida leader says that in the upcoming phase it is important to 'maintain the support of the truthful Mujahidin in Iraq—beginning with our brothers in the Islamic State of Iraq.'[70] Internally, al-Zawahiri was already working on reining in the group. In what appears to be a letter from al-Zawahiri to Mustafa al-Yazid (the letter is addressed to Adnan Hafiz Sultan),[71] the former writes about the mistakes of Abu Hamza and Abu Umar and how their actions push people away and show their extremist tendencies. Al-Zawahiri wants al-Yazid's help to get senior al-Qaida figures—if possible, even Bin Laden himself—to write directly to ISI to inform members of their mistakes and warn them of the consequences. He mentions specifically that ISI should not rush (this is probably a reference to its state declaration), that they should be open to receiving advice, and that they should not criticise other mujahideen.[72] The best indication of Bin Laden's instructions came in an interview with al-Zawahiri in December 2007, which is arguably the most detailed public al-Qaida statement on Iraq between 2006 and 2012. Al-Zawahiri makes a point of giving support to ISI and praises its methodology, encouraging others to join the group. He also makes a point of emphasising that AQI does not exist anymore but is now part of ISI, which is the pioneer of Jihadi unity in Iraq. Defending ISI against accusations levelled against it, he states that the group is not at fault for everything that is said about it, and that even if it has made mistakes, it is not the only one to have done so.

We now know that the feelings of al-Qaida's leadership towards ISI were not as warm as public statements at the time indicated. In fact, al-Qaida's leaders were growing ever more annoyed with Abu Umar's group, which they had no control over. One problem that really troubled the leadership and revealed its lack of control was the increasing hostility between Jihadi groups in Iraq.[73] As early as January 2006, al-Zawahiri had expressed a desire for Ansar al-Sunna to unite with AQI. Generally, al-Qaida was extremely keen for other groups such as Ansar al-Islam and Ansar al-Sunna to integrate into its Iraqi affiliate.[74] However, in 2007, the intra-Jihadi relations in Iraq became increasingly tense, mainly because of ISI's attitude to other groups—ISI demanded that they pledge allegiance or face being killed.[75] On several occasions, other Jihadi groups reported that ISI had attacked and killed their members. In a letter from Ansar al-Sunna to the ISI leadership, they condemn the latter for not tolerating the fact that other groups do not necessarily want to join them or the fact that theological differences exist. On other occasions, complaints were sent to al-Qaida's leadership. The events showed that ISI at the time already had hegemonic ambition on a local scale which, just like years later, would weaken the movement in Iraq.[76] This whole affair also illustrated that al-Qaida's senior leaders were unable to affect developments within the Jihadi environment in Iraq at the time. It was also another indication of how little attention Abu Umar paid to the directions coming from Khorasan.

A second challenge that emerged for the al-Qaida leadership was when Abu Sulayman al-Utaybi, previously the senior shari'a judge in ISI, fled from Iraq to Khurasan in late 2007 to complain about the ISI leadership.[77] Al-Utaybi had just been removed from his position by ISI, thus casting serious doubts about the accusations he sent in a private letter to the al-Qaida leadership before travelling to see them. His accusations mainly focused on how detached ISI leaders were from the battlefield, and also that they had allowed the rise of 'corrupt people' within the group. In addition, al-Utaybi claimed that Abu Hamza was certain that the *mahdi* was about to return, making the declaration of the state urgent.[78] This created a serious dilemma for Bin Laden and al-Zawahiri; should they believe a recently deposed shari'a judge, or should they have faith in the rebellious Abu Umar and Abu Hamza who continuously disrespected al-Qaida's authority? Judging by the response, it appears al-Qaida chose to downplay the problem, and a few months later al-Utaybi himself was killed in Afghanistan.[79]

The problem was that al-Qaida's leaders had trouble contacting the leadership in Iraq. In a letter found in Iraq written by an unnamed senior AQ representative (most likely Mustafa al-Yazid or Atiyyatullah), it is mentioned that al-Qaida does not have any contact with Abu Umar; the letter even asks Abu Hamza for advice on how to communicate with the ISI amir.[80] In fact, in the post-state-declaration period, and until the death of Bin Laden in May 2011, there was remarkably little communication between the two groups. Abu Ali al-Anbari visited Khorasan in December 2005 to clarify the situation from an Iraqi perspective, but apart from that, the letters in table 6 are the only direct communications that I have been able to identify.[81]

Table 6: Overview of correspondence between al-Qaida's senior leadership and its Iraqi 'affiliate' ISI, between ISI's declaration of a state in October 2006 and the death of Bin Laden in May 2011.

| *From* | *To* | *Date* | *Published* |
|---|---|---|---|
| Abu Hamza al-Muhajir | al-Qaida general command | Unknown (but after state establishment) | No |
| Usama Bin Laden | Abu Hamza al-Muhajir | February 12, 2007 | No |
| Abu Yahya al-Libi | Abu Umar al-Baghdadi | April 5, 2007 | Yes |
| Abu Sulayman al-Utaybi | al-Qaida leaders | Between August 25, 2007 and November 19, 2007 | Yes |
| al-Qaida (Likely Atiyyatullah or Mustafa al-Yazid) | Abu Hamza al-Muhajir | Between November 19, 2007 and January 25, 2008 | Yes |
| al-Qaida (Likely Atiyyatullah or Mustafa al-Yazid) | Abu Hamza al-Muhajir | January 25, 2008 | Yes |

| *From* | *To* | *Date* | *Published* |
|---|---|---|---|
| Abu Hamza al-Muhajir | al-Qaida general command | Likely between January 25, 2008 and March 3, 2008 | No |
| Ayman al-Zawahiri | Abu Umar al-Baghdadi | March 6, 2008 | Yes |
| Anonymous al-Qaida senior member | Abu Hamza al-Muhajir | March 10, 2008 | Yes |
| Ministry of Legal Authorities of the Islamic State of Iraq | al-Qaida general command | Early 2010 | No |
| Atiyyatullah | ISI leadership | April 21, 2010 | No |
| Atiyyatullah | Media Ministry of ISI | September 29, 2010 | No |
| A delegate of the Shura of ISI | Atiyyatullah | October 2010 | No |

In the period 2008–10, al-Qaida leaders grew ever more desperate to influence the situation in Iraq. In one of the letters mentioned above, al-Zawahiri tells Abu Hamza that Bin Laden has advised the Iraqi group to set up an independent committee to rule in disputes, but this appears not to have happened. Undeterred by the arrest of Abd al-Hadi al-Iraqi, Bin Laden also contemplated sending a senior al-Qaida figure to Iraq, but was told by al-Yazid that such a plan was impossible in the current security context.[82] It seems that by 2010 Bin Laden had transferred much of the *Iraqi file* to Atiyyatullah, telling him

> I do remind you to put forward your maximum effort to achieve unity and resolve any conflicts between all of the Jihadi entities in Iraq. In these efforts to achieve unity, there should be a special message directed to our brothers there that stresses the importance of unity and collectiveness and that they maintain a basic foundation of the religion, so it must get precedence over names, titles, or entities if they obstruct the achievement of that great duty.[83]

But when ISI's two senior leaders, Abu Umar and Abu Hamza, were killed in 2010, it once again became obvious that the al-Qaida leaders in Khorasan had nothing to say. A new leader, Abu Bakr al-Baghdadi,[84] was elected, although Atiyyatullah, on the orders of Bin Laden, wrote to ISI telling them to choose an interim command before forwarding candidates for the position of amir to Bin Laden so that he could make the final choice. Once again, Bin Laden was left frustrated, complaining to Atiyyatullah about the lack of communication.[85] The following year, ISI's new spokesperson Abu Muhammed al-Adnani said in his first speech that there had been no problems regarding the choice of a new leader, indirectly taunting al-Qaida.[86]

The transformation of AQI into ISI and the rebellious behaviour of the Iraqi group coincided with al-Qaida finding itself in a difficult period. The group was affected by the elimination several high-ranking figures and from waning operational relevance, making it difficult for the leadership to act firmly in its response to its Iraqi 'affiliate', to say nothing of controlling it.[87] This eventually led its spokesperson, Adam Gadahn, to suggest some serious actions in an internal letter to an unidentified senior al-Qaida member. In the letter, Gadahn criticises ISI for several things: for allowing its enemies to proliferate, for failing to leave space for other Jihadi groups, for its lack of territorial control turning it into a pseudo-state, and for its position on Iraqi Christians (a position he argues contrast with the attitude of Bin Laden, al-Zawahiri, Azzam and al-Maqdisi). Most importantly, he criticises the group (and the TTP) for its attacks on mosques and markets that kill innocent Muslims. He does not find it problematic to criticise ISI publicly for its actions as long as these actions are not based on orders or consultation with al-Qaida; moreover, he believes that criticism alone is insufficient, and he suggests that al-Qaida cut organisational ties with ISI since 'relations between al-Qa'ida organization and (the state) have been practically cut off for a number of years.' Gadahn continues, 'This is the only solution facing al-Qa'ida organization, otherwise its reputation will be damaged more and more as a result of the acts and statements of this group, which is labelled under our organization.'[88] He concludes that while breaking ranks is not a positive move, al-Qaida may be better off doing so. While some within al-Qaida seem to have accepted turning a blind eye to actions considered illegitimate, Gadahn stresses that when it comes to actions that are directly against their religion, such leniency is not acceptable.

## *Al-Qaida's Modified Strategy: Bin Laden's Letter to Atiyyatullah*

It was not just the strategy of targeting public places that was a cause of worry within al-Qaida. For its leaders, particularly Bin Laden, there was a greater problem with the Jihadi project that needed correction. As with any reform process, it turned out to be a challenging issue for al-Qaida that not only put it at odds with ISI but also other Jihadi groups, including its official affiliates in Yemen and North Africa. Later, this would become a central source of tensions between al-Qaida and the Islamic State—at least in terms of how tensions were framed—as the latter claimed al-Qaida under the leadership of al-Zawahiri had deviated from the path of Bin Laden.

Al-Qaida's new strategy is particularly well described in a letter from Bin Laden to Atiyyatullah in 2010. In the letter, Bin Laden appoints Atiyyatullah as his new general manager following the death of Mustafa al-Yazid and instructs him that al-Qaida is 'in a new phase of amendment and development' which 'require[s] an advisory reading and development of our entire policy.'[89] This comes as a reaction to the mistakes made by Jihadis after Jihad was extended across the Islamic world. Bin Laden was always cautious about al-Qaida's expansion because he considered it a risk that could tarnish the image of the SJM and destroy its entire project. At the time of his letter, it was Jihadis in Iraq and in Pakistan that caused Bin Laden particular concern, but shortly after Bin Laden's death, his successor al-Zawahiri would experience further problems with official al-Qaida affiliates in Yemen and North Africa.

The main thrust of Bin Laden's new strategy is to correct the military and media efforts of al-Qaida and related groups. His analysis is that after the 9/11 attacks, Jihadis gained sympathy in the eyes of the Muslim masses, but this sympathy has since disappeared, due in part to the actions of Jihadis themselves. The new strategy is intended to change this dynamic once again, so that the mujahideen can emerge as the vanguard of a struggling umma. One aspect of the new strategy is the use of media. Bin Laden suggests that general guidelines for publications are produced and that each Jihadi group selects a person responsible for, and tasked with coordinating, the group's media productions. This implies that the person should review all media productions, and that they should have the authority to halt any material that contradicts the general guidelines.

On the military side, Bin Laden wants to introduce a general policy for military work, outlining a framework for how future military operations should be planned and conducted. He focuses especially on the issue of *barricading* (tatarrus), i.e. using people as human shields. Reading between the lines, this comes as a critique of the practices of ISI in Iraq and the TTP in Pakistan. Bin Laden insinuates that some in al-Qaida have misused this tactic to negative effect and that it is paramount that no Muslims will be killed by Jihadis 'except when it is absolutely essential.'[90] This shows how important public Muslim sympathy was to Bin Laden. He also warns against targeting apostates in or near mosques[91] as this causes people to lose sympathy.[92] The new military policy should also include a ban on attacks in Islamic countries unless they are under attack, as the focus needs to be exclusively on the far enemy to avoid Muslim casualties. The change in military strategy needs to be viewed in the context of another letter that Atiyyatullah sent to al-Zarqawi in 2006 in which he criticised his violent methods. He explained that military policy was subordinate to political objectives and warned that if al-Zarqawi did not halt this type of violence, he would risk eroding public sympathy for al-Qaida. In a letter to al-Wuhayshi, Bin Laden elaborates on the importance of public support; echoing Mao's theory of revolutionary warfare, he states that 'the people's support for the mujahideen is as important as water for the fish'.[93] The new media and military policies were clearly an attempt by Bin Laden to re-establish the authority of the broader al-Qaida network. The policies would essentially centralise Jihadi media releases[94] and the operational work of regional groups by requiring the leaders of these groups to commit to a memorandum of understanding devised by al-Qaida.

Much of this is not new. Already in 2001, in his book *Knights Under the Prophet's Banner*, al-Zawahiri (probably post-rationalising events in Egypt) had mentioned the importance of having the public's support; four years later, he wrote that in order to achieve success the mujahideen in Iraq need the support of the Muslim masses.[95] In his 2011 eulogy for Bin Laden, he said that al-Qaida should 'encourage the Muslim Umma through a comprehensive popular movement',[96] and two years later, in his *General Guidelines for Jihad,* he emphasised a population-centric approach, arguing that al-Qaida should cooperate with other groups notwithstanding ideological/doctrinal differences.[97] Bin Laden's letter is the first time such a population-centric focus is elaborated in so much detail and referred to as a tangible '*new phase*'. For that reason it deserves to be considered the launch of an internal reform process within al-Qaida instigated by Bin Laden himself. The letter contains two important leads relating to the future struggle with the Islamic State; one regarding the criticism levelled by al-Qaida against the Islamic State's caliphate project and the other regarding an allegation by the Islamic State regarding al-Qaida's alleged change of methodology. Many of the initial accusations by the Islamic State centred around the fact that al-Zawahiri had drifted away from the path (or manhaj) of Bin Laden, but as the letter testifies, it was the al-Qaida founder himself who initiated the change in attitude.[98]

Al-Qaida's management challenges initially continued outside the framework of its official organisation. In Somalia, al-Shabab had still not become an official al-Qaida affiliate, but al-Qaida nevertheless found it necessary to comment on the group's implementation of shari'a punishment in territories they had conquered. In a letter Anwar al-Awlaki advised al-Shabab

> to go by certainty and to leave doubts; to prefer forgiveness over revenge. The masses of the people are suffering from the illnesses of tribalism, ignorance, and a campaign of defamation of shari'a. Therefore, you need to win the hearts and minds of the people and take them back to their fitrah.[99]

In the context of Pakistan, al-Qaida similarly reprimanded the Pakistani Taliban, Tehrik-e-Taliban (known as the TTP), through a letter authored by Abu Yahya and Atiyyatullah in which they highlight 'clear legal and religious mistakes which might result in a negative deviation from the set path of the Jihadi movement'. Taking the same line as the critique that Adam Gadahn would raise the following month,[100] al-Qaida's main issue with the TTP was its use of martyrdom operations in public places that kill ordinary Muslims and their tactic of attacking holy places, be they mosques or churches. They also criticised the TTP leader for making unnecessary takfir and trying to co-opt al-Qaida members. The two senior al-Qaida figures end the letter by writing,

> We stress the fact that real reform is the duty of all, and to succeed we should look for and correct our mistakes and take the advice of others. We hope that you will take the necessary action to correct your actions and avoid these grave mistakes; otherwise we have to take decisive actions from our end.[101]

In 2010–12 more problems emerged inside al-Qaida's official organisation, first with its Yemeni affiliate, AQAP, and later with its group in North Africa, AQIM. In spring 2011, AQAP managed to conquer substantial territory in southern Yemen and eventually declared an emirate in parts of Abyan and Shabwa provinces. However, this attempt to establish something resembling an Islamic state entity crumbled in May 2012 when a regime offensive aided by Yemeni tribes dismantled the emirate. Even though Bin Laden in mid-2010 considered Yemen the country most suited to the establishment of an Islamic state, he remained adamant that even Yemen did not have the fundamental elements needed to establish a state[102] and that therefore certain stages prior to the establishment of a state were necessary.[103] In spring 2010, a senior al-Qaida figure, most likely Bin Laden himself, instructed al-Wuhayshi to focus exclusively on the US, either targeting it in the region or on US soil, while emphasising that establishing the Islamic state can wait; now is not the right time, because the mujahideen will not be able to administrate and protect such a state satisfactorily.[104] A similar message was stressed by Atiyyatullah in March 2011, the same month AQAP proceeded to announce the emirate. Around 2010–11, Bin Laden saw the Jihadi project as consisting of three stages. The first was to focus on the far enemy (the US and its allies). The second redirected the focus to the near enemy (local governments in the

Islamic world) once the far enemy had been 'defeated'. Finally, the third stage was the establishment of the Islamic state.[105] Hence, the declaration of an emirate by al-Wuhayshi's group probably dismayed Bin Laden greatly, since at that moment he was seeking to implement his new strategy that not only involved a change in behaviour but also demanded more obedience to the decisions made by al-Qaida's senior leadership. Despite this incident of disobedience, AQAP would later align more closely with Bin Laden and al-Zawahiri's new strategy. In December 2013, when the Yemeni group attacked the ministry of defence, some of the militants overstepped orders and attacked employees in an attached hospital building. To redress the expected negative effects of this action, senior AQAP member Qassim al-Rimi released a public apology and offered compensation to the families of the victims.[106] In May 2015, when AQAP eventually re-conquered swaths of territory in eastern Yemen, it refrained from declaring an emirate and chose to adopt a very different model than that of 2011–12.

Further west, in the Maghreb and Sahel region, al-Qaida would experience a new management challenge. This is revealed by the 'Timbuktu papers' that were discovered after AQIM and groups allied to it retreated from Mali. The positive takeaway for al-Qaida's central leadership was illustrated in two letters written by AQAP's amir, al-Wuhayshi, to AQIM's amir, Abdelmalek Droukdal, advising AQIM to pursue a gradual approach in the implementation of shari'a in conquered areas (especially regarding hudud punishment) since the local population was not ready for such a radical change. This shows how al-Wuhayshi learned from his own mistakes in Yemen and listened to orders coming from Bin Laden. But the Timbuktu papers also revealed a problem for al-Qaida. Already, in 2010, AQIM had written to al-Qaida's leadership to complain about the difficulty of communicating with the central leadership, and to receive feedback on how they should go about establishing an Islamic state in the future.[107] The real problem, it seemed, was internal and within AQIM. Mokhtar Belmokhtar (Khaled Abu al-Abbas), rebellious Jihadi veteran and leader of a brigade under the formal authority of AQIM, challenged Droukdal's leadership on several occasions. Belmokhtar was unhappy with his own position within the group and with its strategy, eventually suggesting to al-Zawahiri that Belmokhtar himself should establish his own al-Qaida affiliate in the Sahel under the authority of al-Zawahiri, not Droukdal.[108] This would imply a further decentralisation of al-Qaida which conflicted with the new strategy promoted by Bin Laden. How al-Qaida's senior leadership responded to the inquiries from Belmokhtar, and how it handled the internal crisis within AQIM, is unknown. However, since Belmokhtar's plan for a new affiliate was not approved, and since years later there emerged a new entity called Jabhat al-Nusrat al-Islam wa-l-Muslimin that broadly aligned with Droukdal's vision, it seems that al-Zawahiri sided with the AQIM amir.

As in the case of the Irish Republican movement, al-Qaida's leadership was right to insist that public support was a prerequisite for achieving success.[109] According to Ingram, 'Success in modern small wars is largely dependent on winning popular 'support'. But support operates on a spectrum where, at one end, there is 'behavioural' support (compliance with a group's politico-military system) while, on the other, is a deeper 'attitudinal' or 'perceptual' support (adherence to a group's agenda).'[110] With his new policy, Bin Laden sought to obtain perceptual support. Years later, the Islamic State would similarly prioritise winning people's support, but, unlike Bin Laden, it would seek behavioural support to strengthen its claim to a caliphate and to facilitate its own expansion.

### *Jihadi Factionalism: Understanding the Split*

On February 3, 2014, al-Qaida could no longer accept the rebellious action and disobedience of the Iraqi group. In a brief statement, al-Zawahiri expelled the Islamic State of Iraq and Syria (ISIS)—as the group had renamed itself in April 2013—saying that ISIS 'is not a branch of al-Qaida and we [al-Qaida] have no organisational relationship with it. Nor is al-Qaida responsible for its actions and behaviour.'[111] The split was unprecedented in the era of al-Qaida's affiliate system, which was intended to expand, not contract, its global project by adding new local franchises to its global network. But for al-Zawahiri, the Iraqi group's disobedience and its instigation of Jihadi infighting in Syria had become intolerable.

Unlike in most cases of organisational splintering, the split did not lead to the establishment of a new organisation but rather a change for an al-Qaida *affiliate*, which moved from being officially subordinate to independent; in other words, this situation is more about changes to existing hierarchies. But as with traditional organisational splintering, it would turn out to be an enabler of violence. It is important to note that organisational splits are the result of specific internal dynamics whereby one subgroup has become so dissatisfied that it no longer sees a future for itself without organisational changes.[112] In the case of this split, neither the Islamic State (an al-Qaida affiliate/subgroup) nor al-Qaida (the mother organisation) could live with the status quo. The immediate process (stage 4) that led to the official split (stage 5) began when al-Baghdadi in April 2013 ordered his group to expand into Syria in an attempt to establish command over Jabhat al-Nusra, a group set up and financed by al-Baghdadi in either July[113] or August[114] 2011. From December 2012, this group was recognised as al-Qaida's affiliate in Syria. In a message entitled *Give Glad Tidings to the Believers*, Baghdadi explained that al-Nusra was part of ISI and that al-Nusra amir Abu Muhammad al-Julani (Ahmad al-Shara) was one of his soldiers, originally dispatched to Syria to facilitate future expansion of ISI into the neighbouring country. Al-Julani was a veteran of the Iraqi insurgency, having joined ISI early on and then advancing to become its governor in Ninewa. As the context was now suitable for announcing the expansion to Syria, al-Baghdadi proclaimed the cancellation of al-Nusra and the establishment of ISIS.[115] Al-Baghdadi's statement led to a series of actions in the following days. The first move was taken by al-Julani, who pledged allegiance directly to al-Zawahiri. This was followed by al-Baghdadi writing to al-Zawahiri explaining that al-Julani was in fact under his authority.[116] As a temporary response to the matter, al-Zawahiri ordered al-Baghdadi to suspend expansion until the issue had been resolved.[117] Al-Zawahiri had previously sought to get more insights—and probably direct influence—on al-Nusra's project; he had instructed Abu Yahya al-Libi, who at the time was in charge of al-Qaida's Syrian file, to make inquires to al-Julani about his project.[118] On two occasions between August 2011 and June 2012, Abu Yahya messaged al-Julani. He received no response. The al-Nusra version is that al-Julani did respond, but that ISI refused to forward the correspondence. Eventually al-Julani did respond, but the first letter was allegedly heavily edited by the ISI media department. This led the al-Nusra leader to send another letter directly to al-Zawahiri informing him about the group's project.

After consultations with his shura council, al-Zawahiri issued his final ruling in a letter dated May 23, 2013 sent to both al-Baghdadi and al-Julani; he stated that the former should continue as the amir of ISI, confined to Iraqi, while the latter would head al-Nusra, a separate al-Qaida affiliate based in Syria.[119] But as history shows, this was all too late. The Islamic State had already taken advantage of the confusion within the Jihadi environment in Syria to mobilise fighters in its favour. It would take al-Baghdadi three weeks to answer, but on June 14, 2013, he delivered his first criticism of al-Zawahiri in the audio speech entitled 'Remaining in Iraq and the Levant'. As the title indicates, al-Baghdadi rejected al-Zawahiri's ruling, stating instead that his group would remain in Syria. He also officially indicated his concerns over issues relating to shari'a and methodology in al-Qaida, stating that 'As for the message that was attributed to Sheikh Ayman al-Zawahiri, we have found several Shari'a and method-based issues with it', continuing, 'It is a state that Abu Musab al-Zarqawi wanted and that mixed with the blood of our Sheikhs Abu Umar al-Baghdadi and Abu Hamza al-Muhajir, and it will not go away from a spot that it has reached, nor will it become smaller after its growth.'[120] The criticism of al-Zawahiri was taken a step further in a statement by al-Adnani three days later in which the spokesperson identified seven issues with al-Zawahiri's ruling, as follows: the al-Qaida leader is dividing an existing group and thus causing disunity in Jihad; he is acknowledging the borders of Sykes–Picot; he is supporting the 'rebellious defectors' of Jabhat al-Nusra; he is setting a critical precedent by splitting up groups, which will only lead to disunity; he took the decision without consulting the two groups; he is implicitly rewarding the group that made the mistake [al-Nusra]; and finally, he is ordering the Islamic State to stay away from Syria at a time when Muslims are being slaughtered. For al-Adnani there was no doubt: 'Iraq and the Levant will remain one arena, one front, one command, and no borders will separate them!'[121] Despite an effort by al-Zawahiri to promote unity and to rein in the group in his *General Guidelines for Jihad* published in September 2013, it was clearly too late to change the course of events.[122]

ISI's expansion into Syria, its disobedience to al-Zawahiri and aggressive attitude towards other Jihadi groups led to increasing tensions within the Jihadi environment in Syria during the summer and autumn of 2013. These tensions eventually escalated into an intra-Jihadi civil war in December 2013–January 2014.[123] The argument here is that the split and conflict between al-Qaida and its former affiliate in Iraq is not unprecedented in terms of organisational factionalism but rather because of the intensity of the infighting it caused and its repercussions on the entire SJM. The split should thus be seen as an important change in the SJM, with the Islamic State going from being a critical voice within al-Qaida to a counter-group opposed to al-Qaida.[124]

## *The Process of Factionalism and Splintering*

Research on insurgency and movement fragmentation and conflict highlights various causes for group splintering and infighting ranging from extreme ideology, factionalised leadership, centre–periphery discrepancy, competition for resources and political positioning prior to peace negotiations. These cover the most obvious fault lines that cause internal tensions. In his theorisation of factionalism and the fragmentation of non-state actor movements, Kalyvas argues that internal splits occur whenever there is too much discrepancy, or distance, between what he defines as the *centre* and the *periphery* within a movement. 'When local cleavages subvert central ones', he writes, 'factional conflicts emerge within supposedly unified political camps.'[125] While it is easy to identify discrepancies between the al-Qaida leadership and AQI/ISI in terms of strategic priorities, ideology and nationality which certainly led to intra-group tensions, the centre–periphery dichotomy does little to help us understand why the Iraqi group's challenge to al-Qaida and the official split occurred in 2013–14 and not in 2006. More helpful are the four factors Zald and Useem identify as influential in the emergence of countermovements:

1. Movement progress and success (the success, or the potential for success, of a movement leads to the emergence of a countermovement),
2. Appropriate countermovement ideology (definition of an ideology to counter the movement),
3. Availability of resources, and
4. Constraint and opportunity.

While the first factor is specific to movement and countermovement relations, the other three are also useful for explaining the process of factionalism and splintering *within* a movement. Since its founding, al-Zarqawi's Iraqi group had to some extent presented an ideology that was at odds with al-Qaida. This was further developed in 2013, especially in the discourse of al-Adnani and senior ideologue Turki al-Binali, which had the intention of outlining the differences between the two groups and offering Jihadi sympathisers an alternative. In the same period, al-Baghdadi's group had unique access to resources. The conflicts in Iraq and Syria offered access to financial, military, and human resources essential for any political or military challenge against competitors or rivals. With the conflict playing out on its home turf in the Levant, the group was able to take advantage of this opportunity to undermine other Jihadi groups, including its former subordinate al-Nusra, and to strengthen its capabilities and narrative vis-à-vis other groups.

The literature shows that internal conflict dynamics have occurred quite regularly in modern history, even in narrowly defined movements like the SJM. The Russian Communist Party in the early twentieth century is arguably the most famous example of an isolated movement splintering into factions which eventually turned against one another. Comparing the intra-Jihadi conflict to left-wing revolutionary movements is not entirely new. Atran has argued that 'The current rivalry between Al-Qaeda and the Islamic State echoes that between the anarchists and Bolshevists.'[126] I would argue, though, that the Jihadi split may be more accurately compared to the contestation between Bolsheviks and Mensheviks, as this acknowledges that the contestation and conflict is taking place within a relatively cohesive ideological movement. In 1903, when the party split in two factions, the Bolsheviks and the Mensheviks, it was still part of an isolated underground movement with a revolutionary ambition of toppling the regime and fundamentally changing the existing structure of society. The internal conflict developed in stages, and although it emerged from strategic and organisational differences, it resulted in personal feuds between leading figures, with each faction contesting the authority of the other.[127] As in the chapters that follow here on intra-Jihadi conflict, the literature on the Russian Communist Party discusses a movement which, to a great extent, had a coherent ideological vision of how society should be, but was caught up in endless internal conflicts and factionalism. Other examples from the terrorism and civil war literature include the IRA, ETA and the Shining Path: all three groups splintered on several occasions, mainly as the result of disagreements about strategy and the use of violence.[128] While the trajectory of these empirical examples may not precisely fit the development of conflict within the SJM, they still point to important common features in the experience of politically isolated movements in relation to internal factionalism, resulting either from diverging strategic visions or from the personal ambitions of leading individuals.

In 1964, writing on the social and organisational differences within the Russian Social Democratic Party, D.S. Lane wrote that in general 'relatively little is known about the basis of splits within parties, or the composition of illegal parties working underground.'[129] Now, in 2020, a similar argument can be made. The Russian Social Democratic Party split into two factions during the second party congress; in the aftermath of this, these factions competed and contested each other's authority. Although Jihadism split in a far less official setting, the inter-group dynamics are arguably not dissimilar. The sociologist Robert Michels has worked extensively on the internal dynamics within political parties, focusing mainly on the German Social Democratic Party. In his theory of the *iron law of oligarchy*, he argues that parties will eventually turn oligarchic, partly because of the personal ambitions that accompany the wielding of power. Michels divides the reasons for competition between leaders into two. One is when there is substantial disagreement between them (regarding philosophy, strategy, ideology, etc.), and the other is when it is personal. Often a conflict begins over a substantial difference and then evolves over time into a personal conflict. Michels argues, however, that the fact that it is personal will never be acknowledged, meaning that the conflict will always be framed in terms of a substantial difference.[130] A relatively similar pattern characterises the relationship between al-Qaida and its Iraqi 'affiliate'. While *substantial differences* and ideology did matter, focusing exclusively on these issues will not get us far unless we also consider the importance of power ambitions and the political context that Jihadis operate within.

### *The Timing of the Split*

In order to understand the timing of the announcement of the split, it is necessary to consider the configuration of the SJM, its changing structures and the logic of intra-Jihadi relations. Focusing on the diverging theological interpretations or strategic priorities undoubtedly helps us grasp why a schism occurred in the first place and how it was articulated, but an exclusive focus on these matters will not lead to a deeper understanding of the timing of the split or, arguably, the most important reasons for it.[131] Rather, two key events in 2011 affected the structures of the SJM, and also created opportunities for the existing authority structures within the movement to be challenged. These were the death of Usama Bin Laden and the outbreak of the Syrian civil war.

The importance of the leadership vacuum created by Bin Laden's death is often overlooked. In a series of stages starting with Bin Laden's military victory at Jaji in 1987, continuing with his framing of an ideological shift for the SJM in the mid- and late 1990s, and finishing with the 9/11 attacks, Bin Laden had established himself as the authoritative figurehead of Sunni Jihadism. Twenty years before Bin Laden's death, the SJM was affected by the death of Abdullah Azzam, which left a vacuum that enabled other and younger Jihadis to challenge for power.[132] Bin Laden's death offered a similar context.[133] Lahoud writes, via the words of Fadil Harun, that one should be careful about exaggerating the importance of Bin Laden as a person. Rather, it was the ideals he stood for; as long as he was alive, these ideals were hard to challenge and compete with.[134] Even Bin Laden's son, Omar, questioned whether the SJM would stay united if his father should die, comparing the situation to a body attempting to move without a head.[135] Still worse for al-Qaida, Bin Laden's death was followed by that of several other senior figures from 2010–14, most notably Mustafa al-Yazid, Atiyyatullah and Abu Yahya al-Libi. This aggravated the position of the group within the larger SJM.[136] The argument I make here is that this leadership vacuum was of central importance to the challenge posed by the Islamic State in 2013 when it expanded into Syria and directly disobeyed al-Zawahiri's orders. The new al-Qaida leader was not considered an authoritative leader at Bin Laden's level. There were doubts about him from the very beginning since he lacked the charisma of his Saudi predecessor.[137] Contrary to the prediction of some Western analysts, Bin Laden's death did not threaten the Jihadi project, but it did make al-Qaida more vulnerable to internal challenges. As Mustafa Hamid stressed, 'When Abu Abdullah [Bin Laden] was alive nobody could say 'I am the real al-Qaeda' because he was still there.'[138] But soon after challenging al-Qaida, ISIS started to publish videos featuring the late al-Qaida leader in an attempt to appropriate his legacy and supporters.[139]

Reminiscent of Stalin's approach in the mid-1920s, in mid-2012 Abu Bakr al-Baghdadi instigated a process to rule over, and later undermine, the increasingly rebellious Jabhat al-Nusra.[140] The first senior person that al-Baghdadi sent from Iraq to Syria to put pressure on al-Nusra was his spokesperson, Abu Muhammed al-Adnani, who around March 2012 entered Syria and was involuntarily appointed amir of the northern region by al-Julani. A little later, al-Adnani was demoted by al-Julani because he was causing problems; these included the fact that he received pledges of allegiance in the name of ISI rather than al-Nusra, and he was instead appointed amir of borders and incoming fighters. According to an account by a senior al-Nusra member, al-Julani fired al-Adnani shortly afterwards, communicating this in a twenty-five-page letter to al-Baghdadi. After receiving the letter, al-Baghdadi asked for al-Julani to travel to Iraq to see him in person to discuss the matter. Al-Baghdadi's eventual ruling did not please al-Julani since the ISI amir decided to promote al-Adnani to the position of al-Julani's deputy. Furthermore, al-Baghdadi instructed al-Anbari to travel to Syria to investigate a rumour ignited by al-Adnani that al-Julani intended to break away from ISI.[141] Al-Anbari ended up staying for four months. When he returned to Iraq, he wrote a critical report about al-Nusra. Shortly after, al-Anbari returned to Syria to manage the imminent expansion of the Islamic State.[142]

Around the same time in late 2012, Haji Bakr, who allegedly was al-Baghdadi's organisational mastermind, entered northern Syria to prepare for the expansion, independent of al-Julani. Months before, al-Baghdadi had asked al-Julani publicly to announce the group's affiliation to ISI, but al-Julani refused, and when he later ignored al-Baghdadi's orders to kill FSA leaders, the ISI amir began to seriously question al-Julani's loyalty.[143] In early 2013 (most likely in January), al-Baghdadi himself travelled to Syria. The ISI amir and his top theological, organisational and external communication figures—including all members of the group's consultative shura council—were all present to coordinate the challenge the group was about to make public in April 2013, when it announced its expansion into Syria and ordered the dissolution of Jabhat al-Nusra.[144] Al-Julani was warned a final time during meetings on March 10–13, but as the problems were not settled, al-Baghdadi went ahead with his plans.[145] Even prior to the expansion into Syria, al-Baghdadi had initiated a process to recruit fighters from al-Nusra and other groups. In one instance in March, al-Anbari hosted a major meeting in Aleppo to receive pledges of allegiance.[146] A person present at the meeting explained how al-Anbari—who had just been appointed deputy and the *general religious official* (al-shar'i al-'am) of the Islamic State—and his representatives left the Jihadis there at the meeting with the impression that the bay'a was to either al-Baghdadi, al-Zawahiri or even Mullah Umar, depending on the fighter's preference.[147] After the April expansion, a series of secret meetings were held in northern Syria, in Kafr Hamra, between al-Baghdadi and senior Jihadi figures including Amr al-Absi and Abu Umar al-Shishani, where al-Baghdadi received their pledges of allegiance.[148] It seems that al-Baghdadi and his deputies systematically told doubting Jihadis that they were indeed maintaining their allegiance to al-

Zawahiri, but this was most likely a strategy to convince people to join their group.

In an article, Bacon and Arsenault raise the hypothetical question of whether the split would have occurred had Bin Laden still been alive. Based on their analysis of differences in *management attitude* and the *ability* of Bin Laden and al-Zawahiri, they argue that the former would have handled the conflict differently.[149] Although this remains speculative, events might well have transpired as they suggest. Even so, these authors misinterpret Bin Laden vis-à-vis al-Zawahiri. Like Bin Laden before him, for more than a decade al-Zawahiri has emphasised the need for unity between Jihadi groups. There are many vivid examples of this in *Knights Under the Prophet's Banner* and in his letter to al-Zarqawi. As this book illustrates, al-Zawahiri constantly stressed unity in the lead up to the conflict, as it escalated, and even after the split. In fact, Bin Laden arguably had a bigger ego than al-Zawahiri. He certainly worried more about al-Qaida's brand from a strategic organisational perspective.[150] It is obvious that Bin Laden and al-Zawahiri had different qualities in terms of leadership and personality, but more important than these qualities were Bin Laden's authority and status within the SJM, which affected how the conflict evolved and even whether it would have occurred at all.

The eruption of the Syrian civil war was another facilitating factor that offered a suitable context for challenging al-Qaida's authoritative position within the SJM. Up until the civil war, ISI was only operating in Iraq, but the eruption of conflict in Syria provided the group with fertile ground in which to expand its area of operations, to recruit, to gain access to funding and eventually to proclaim a caliphate in Syria and Iraq—the historic sites of the Umayyad and Abbasid caliphates and the area mentioned in hadith as the location of the final battle against the anti-Christ.[151] It only took the ISI leadership a few months to realise the potential of the neighbouring conflict before sending in a group of senior people to establish Jabhat al-Nusra. Together, Bin Laden's death and the eruption of the Syrian civil war are contingent events that help us understand the timing of the split between al-Qaida and the Islamic State. Since 2006, the ISI has not once behaved or spoken in a manner that would indicate that it was al-Qaida's affiliate in Iraq and that it was subordinate to al-Qaida's leadership. In its speeches, the group has referred to the al-Qaida leadership politely, giving the impression that it was a close ally of al-Qaida, but there has been no mention or indication of a relationship between the two in legal (shar'i) terms. With Bin Laden and the authority he embodied out of the picture, and a fertile operational front in Iraq and Syria, the ISI could finally step up its claim for authority through provocative behaviour, forcing al-Qaida's leader to make the split public.

In 2014–15, the status of the pledge of allegiance and the question of when exactly it had been terminated became a point of fierce contention between the two camps, with both leaders and rank and file members providing respective versions to influence the narrative. Al-Qaida's version is that AQI remained loyal to its pledge of allegiance after the establishment of ISI, but that this was made secret to ease pressure on both groups. This led to al-Zawahiri claiming in a 2007 interview that there is no al-Qaida in Iraq. The al-Qaida leader supported this claim by noting that ISI leaders referred to him with veneration between 2006–13, and also with 'textual and verbal proof' relating to Abu Hamza al-Muhajir, an old accomplice of al-Zawahiri's from their time together in Al Jihad.[152] According to al-Zawahiri, Abu Hamza sent him a letter after the creation of ISI reassuring him that he would remain loyal to its alliance with al-Qaida.[153] However, al-Zawahiri contradicted himself in another statement by insinuating that Abu Umar al-Baghdadi lied to Abu Hamza about ISI's loyalty.[154] Allegedly, Abu Hamza made his own pledge of allegiance to Abu Umar conditional on the ISI amir remaining subordinate to Bin Laden, which Abu Hamza communicated (with Abu Umar's permission) to the al-Qaida leadership.[155] Al-Zawahiri offered an even more recent example—a statement by Abu Bakr al-Baghdadi, made in a letter to the al-Qaida leader:

> Our blessed sheikh, we would like to make it clear to you and declare to you that we are part of you and we are from you and for you, and we are indebted to God that you are the guardian of our affairs, and we owe you obedience as long as we are alive, and that your advice and mention are rights we have from you. Your orders are obligatory to us, but some matters

> may require clarification as we live the reality of the events in our battlefield.[156]

But as this letter has never been made public and was most likely destroyed, there is no way of confirming that al-Baghdadi actually wrote these words to al-Zawahiri.

The Islamic State's version is slightly simpler. The break of allegiance occurred with the evolution from AQI to ISI, at which point AQI ceased to exist. From October 2006 on, the Islamic State has never mentioned the pledge of allegiance, either in private or public communication, or acted according to it. The group has usually referred to Abu Umar's first speech as ISI leader, in which he says that 'al-Qaeda is nothing more than a group in the groups of the Islamic State.'[157] The group's subsequent discursive veneration for al-Qaida and its leaders was due to respect for their seniority and dedication to Jihad but was not an indication of organisational linkage. Al-Adnani characterised the situation in this way: 'the amirs of the Islamic State remained addressing Qaedat al-Jihad as soldiers addressing their amirs, as a pupil addressing his professor, and a student to his sheikh, and the young boy addressing his elder.' He continues: 'The State is not a branch that belongs to al-Qaeda, and it never was for a day.'[158] If the word of al-Maqdisi can be trusted on this issue, he supports the Islamic State's narrative, saying the group invalidated ('abtalu) its pledge of allegiance when it established its first state in 2006.[159]

One much-promoted theory to explain the rebelliousness and internal change in behaviour within ISI is that it is the result of a *ba'thification* process in the aftermath of the *de-ba'thification* of the Iraqi state. The argument goes that senior ba'thists from Saddam's regime joined the group after the regime's fall and hijacked the group's leadership to use it as a vehicle to reclaim power in Iraq.[160] The proponents of this argument claim that there was a split between AQI and ISI, and that AQI (led by al-Zarqawi) followed the ideology of al-Qaida, while ISI became a tool of the ex-ba'thist members.[161] While many members of ISI, including some of its leaders, did have a past in the Iraqi army, the theory of a ba'thification of ISI is misleading, as Whiteside[162] and Tønnessen have argued.[163] The mistake which is commonly made is to consider previous membership in the ba'thist regime in opposition to being a convinced Jihadi or Salafi.[164] Saddam himself launched his *Faith Campaign* in the 1990s which resulted in parts of his military becoming increasingly religious and subscribing to conservative viewpoints.[165] The ISI was not slow to realise the potential offered by de-ba'thification, which left thousands of former regime employees without a job and salary. In his first speech, Abu Umar al-Baghdadi even invited high ranking ba'thists to join the group, but he emphasised that they must pass an exam to show that they know their 'aqida.[166] When scholars or opponents of the Islamic State emphasise the group's ba'thist constituency, they seem to forget that people's history within the ba'thist regime does not necessarily imply an opposition to a conservative religious interpretation shared by Jihadi groups. In comparison, several of al-Qaida's senior Egyptian members have a past in the Egyptian army, and this has never raised questions about their devotion to Jihadi ideology.[167] Gerges promotes an alternative argument, saying that the Islamic State does indeed have many ba'thists in its ranks, but that these figures of the former regime have been strategically exploited by group leaders, rather than the other way around as is usually claimed by scholars and analysts.[168] This account, however, still misinterprets the identity of former regime figures by implicitly emphasising their allegiance to a ba'thist ideology over that of a Jihadi ideology.

In 2006–07, the change to a ba'thist-dominated ISI was allegedly the result of an *Iraqisation* of ISI.[169] While it is true that the ISI did go through a process to make the group appear more native, it is misleading to conclude that this Iraqisation led to ba'thification. Arguably, the best example of how nationality mattered is the choice of Abu Umar al-Baghdadi as the new amir of the group in October 2006 at the expense of the more senior—but Egyptian—Abu Hamza al-Muhajir. In 2005–06, many of the senior leaders of AQI-ISI were still foreigners, but this was about to change.[170] Al-Qaida has traditionally been dominated by Saudis and Egyptians, especially within its senior echelons, and the increasing number of Iraqis in the ISI leadership likely aggravated the schism between ISI and al-Qaida. This became an issue especially when al-Zawahiri became the leader of al-Qaida since he, more than anyone else, represented the Egyptian wing of al-Qaida, which has always been a source of contention within the SJM.[171]

In an exercise of post-rationalising the events of the post-2014 period, both groups have presented their version of the trajectory of the split. Despite the contrasting narratives, it may well be that both groups are correct in their reading of the hierarchical relationship, and that these contrasting versions are simply illustrative of long held but seldom discussed differences in perceptions of the relationship between the two groups. However, what began as a leadership split eventually resulted in a conflict between the Jihadi masses. With the ISI's expansion into Syria, the group became a *counter-group* in opposition to most other Jihadi groups, including al-Qaida. Insights from SMS on movement and countermovement relations tells us that

> Counter-movements arise in reaction to the successes obtained by social movements, and the two then develop in symbiotic dependence during the course of mobilisation. (...) Sometimes, however, as was the case in Italy in the 1970s, their interaction resembles far more a battle in which the objective is to annihilate the enemy.[172]

As the following chapters show, a similar observation can be made about group and counter-group dynamics within the SJM.

## *Conclusions*

The two previous chapters offer new empirical knowledge about the historical cohesion of al-Qaida and theoretical insights about intra-movement dynamics within the SJM. As a starting point for understanding the conflict that erupted between al-Qaida and the Islamic State in early 2014, they provided a detailed historical examination of the relationship between the two groups. Concurring with Morrison, who argues that any analysis of an organisational split must include an examination of the period leading up to the splintering,[173] the chapters illustrate the historical roots of the conflict and the necessity of understanding this history to explain ongoing dynamics. Hoffman writes that 'All terrorist movements throughout history have presented themselves as monoliths: united and in agreement over fundamental objectives, aims, strategies, tactics and targets.'[174] This holds true for al-Qaida too, with the group's leadership continuously trying to present a positive relationship with its Iraqi affiliate despite its increasingly fractious nature. Breaking with conventional wisdom, this chapter offered a narrative suggesting that (1) from late 2006, the Iraqi group no longer considered itself subordinate to al-Qaida's leadership, but that (2) the official organisational split could only be made public with the emergence of a certain political context that emerged in the years following 2011, when Bin Laden was killed and the Syrian civil war erupted.

# PART 3

# INTENSIFICATION OF CONFLICT

*'These methods [of the Islamic State] clearly caused the biggest rift in the global Jihad that the umma has ever seen since the fall of the Khilafa.'*[1]

Abu Sulayman al-Muhajir

*'Another adversary for Al-Qaeda appeared but not under the name of knowledge and the Salafi but under the name of jihad itself. It is an adversary that seeks to compete with Al-Qaeda, overrule it and strip it from the characteristics of jihad! It is an adversary that does not want to eliminate the jihad, but wants to steal the whole jihadi project, adapt it to its own aims and policy... The jihad became for the State [Islamic State] the equivalent of fighting the mujahedeen! (...) This State became a jihad that is the opposite of the jihad.'*[2]

Abu al-Mundhir al-Shinqiti

5

# DIVERGING DESIRES

After the official split between al-Qaida and the Islamic State, the SJM was officially fragmenting. An eruption of infighting and an intensification of conflict characterised the initial period of intra-movement conflict, which was largely the result of the Islamic State's hegemonist rationale. In his September 2013 General Guidelines for Jihad, al-Zawahiri sought to prevent the imminent escalation, saying 'Our basic confrontation is with the enemies of Islam and those who hold animosity towards Islam. Therefore, our differences with other Islamic groups should not distract us from confronting the enemies of Islam on the military, propagational, ideological or political fronts.'[3] But this did little to help.

In her research, Della Porta identifies the process of political violence as consisting of three steps: *context*, *organisational process* and *organisation favours diffusion of violence*. A trigger occurs in the period between context and process.[4] The organisational split and the Islamic State's assassinations of senior figures within the other Jihadi groups represent that trigger,[5] which escalated not just intra-Jihadi violence but also the competitive nature of the relationship between al-Qaida and the Islamic State and the latter's challenge for authority through discursive framing efforts. In contrast, al-Qaida's approach was characterised by a unitarian rationale which emphasised reconciliation. However, the challenge from the Islamic State simultaneously led to internal desperation and criticism within al-Zawahiri's group. By contrast, the Islamic State's interests were diametrically opposed to this, and it intended to strengthen the polarisation.

Figure 5: 'The process of political violence', adapted from the work of Donatella Della Porta.

*Source:* Donatella Della Porta, *Social Movements, Political Violence, and the State: A Comparative Analysis of Italy and Germany* (Cambridge: Cambridge University Press, 1995), 83-85.

Initially, when the Islamic State started expanding its area of operations to Syria, the group mainly focused on conquering territory and establishing a state, leaving the fight against the Assad regime as a secondary priority. Despite the Islamic State's aggressive attitude, largely defined by a focus on *taghallub* (overpowering) and *tamkin* (consolidation), other Jihadi groups remained hesitant about opposing it.[6] Their foundational similarities, common objectives and sometimes a history of being brothers-in-arms were pacifying mechanisms. This started to change when the Islamic State began assassinating senior members of other Jihadi groups. The first senior person to be killed was Ahrar al-Sham's head of relief operations, Abu Ubayda al-Binnishi, in September 2013,[7] followed by Abu Sa'd al-Hadrami, Jabhat al-Nusra's amir in Raqqa Province, in late 2013, following months spent in an Islamic State prison.[8] The official explanation was that al-Hadrami was allying with apostate factions in a clear violation of al-wala' wa-l-bara'.[9] In December 2013, Abu Rayyan, Ahrar al-Sham's amir in Tal Abyad, was brutally tortured by the Islamic State; this eventually triggered the Jihadi civil war, and led the Jihadi groups Ahrar al-Sham and Jaysh al-Islam to adopt a much more aggressive stance in opposing the hegemonist attitude of the Islamic State.[10] In late February 2014, arguably the most shocking assassination occurred when Abu Khalid al-Suri, a veteran Jihadist who was also a senior Ahrar al-Sham member with strong ties to al-Qaida, was killed.[11] Although the Islamic State denied killing al-Suri, there remains little doubt that the group was the perpetrator. His death led to a critical escalation in the intra-movement animosity and infighting.[12] Finally, in April 2014, the Islamic State also killed Abu Muhammad al-Fateh, Jabhat al-Nusra's amir in Idlib.

Reading the literature on inter- and intra-movement dynamics we find many similarities between the SJM and other movements in terms of conflict dynamics. Describing inter-movement dynamics, Zald and Useem remark that 'much of a movement's activity is aimed at neutralising, confronting, or discrediting its corresponding countermovement. Similarly, the countermovement gains its impetus and grows from showing the harmful effects of the movement. It attacks the movement leaders, bombs its sites of program action, and associates the movement with evil.'[13] But while the movement countermovement conflict can be explained as an ideological struggle, group and counter-group dynamics of conflict are mainly politically motivated. Despite this difference, groups and counter-groups 'seek to directly damage or destroy the other group, pre-empt or dissuade the other group from mobilizing or recruit the other group's members.'[14] While there is a clear similarity here to movement and countermovement dynamics, we see that in the situation we are concerned with, the logic of intra-movement conflict still had to manifest itself since the groups had diverging desires; the Islamic State adopted an attitude of aggression and polarisation, while al-Qaida favoured reconciliation.

## *The Aftermath of the Split: The Beginning of Infighting*

The infighting in early 2014 emerged as a result of the Islamic State's desire to dominate Syria's Jihadi landscape—not because of any noticeable ideological shifts. It is important to understand that Syria represented an important battlefield for Jihadis at the time. Not only does 'Sham', a term referring to modern-day Syria, carry important connotations within Islamic eschatology,[15] but the country's civil war and increasing sectarianism offered a context ripe for a successful

Jihadi campaign in terms of territorial expansion and mobilisation. When the group expanded from Iraq to Syria, its hegemonist rationale was confronted with the presence of a plethora of other Jihadi groups, which—from the beginning—were considered competitors. The Assad regime initially directed its military crackdown against the Islamic State's competitors, thus providing the group with important time and space to take advantage of the civil war dynamics to expand its territorial control and attract recruits.[16] This enabled the group to win the initial *war of positioning*.[17]

More generally, the local Jihadi landscape in Syria suffered severely from the fragmentation caused by the split between al-Qaida and the Islamic State and the creation of several new Jihadi groups like Ahrar al-Sham and Jaysh al-Islam. The sheer number of groups, the diffusion of power, and the absence of supra-group institutions made for a highly charged situation that was likely to explode. In the civil war literature, it is theorised that social ties across groups reduce the risk of infighting,[18] but despite the fact that many of the fighters had a shared history—within al-Qaida, other militant and/or Islamist networks, or from being imprisoned together—this did not prevent infighting from breaking out, first in Syria's Deir ez-Zour, Raqqa, Aleppo and Idlib provinces, and later in countries including Afghanistan, Libya, Somalia and Yemen. As it turned out, this emerging *logic of reciprocal enmity* would rapidly embed itself in the Syrian context and eventually also on a global scale.[19]

In his study of the Irish Republican movement, Morrison describes the logic at play in the immediate aftermath of an organisational split. These translate well to the period immediately after the split between al-Qaida and the Islamic State. He captures the general dynamics particularly well in this lengthy statement:

> This competition can oftentimes distract the organizations from the pursuit of their purposive objectives with an over proportionate amount of time and energy being spent on competition between two groups who to many external observers may be regarded as indistinguishable in nature. As the conflict intensifies purposive goals are often times displaced by the aspiration to harm and inflict injury on the

> rival organization. This can lead to growing animosity between the two groups, and may lead to a redefinition of 'enemy' in the eyes of some members. No longer are these former allies merely rivals, they can become enemies, irrespective of their closeness in goals. Invariably both groups share a common enemy, be it organizational, governmental or societal. However, they can be distracted by the perceived necessity to undermine former comrades, and therefore may concentrate more on the developing competition.[20]

As this chapter illustrates, the early conflict period is characterised by the Islamic State's dual strategy of projecting strength vis-à-vis rival rebel groups and legitimising infighting.[21] In the confusing and increasingly competitive conflict environment in Syria, the group sought to recruit and mobilise fighters, including those from other Jihadi groups, and to articulate a discourse of justification in order to escalate intra-Jihadi conflict. This was a strategy the group had already employed in Iraq in 2012–13 when it initiated attacks against Ansar al-Islam while attempting to recruit its fighters.[22] Already during the lead up to the split, the group was engaged in a campaign to convince fighters to pledge allegiance. The Islamic State was successful in attracting the majority of incoming foreign fighters in that period, not least because of popular commanders like Amr al-Absi and Abu Umar al-Shishani shifting to the group and bringing along large contingents of their foreign fighters. Simultaneously, the group's most senior ideological figure Abu Ali al-Anbari authored a statement about the Islamic Front, an alliance of seven Islamist groups including Jihadi outfits like Ahrar al-Sham and Jaysh al-Islam, concluding that its leaders were apostates (murtadd)—and, if they did not defect and repent, its fighters were too.[23]

The first rebel groups to begin fighting the Islamic State were the non-Jihadi groups the Syrian Revolutionaries Front and the Mujahideen Army. They were eventually followed by the Islamic Front.[24] At the time, Islamic State started accusing al-Nusra of collaborating with infidels, which forced al-Nusra leaders to deny that any such collaboration took place but that the various groups simply repelled Islamic State attacks simultaneously but *not* in coordination.

Al-Nusra's reluctance to launch attacks against the Islamic State was mainly the result of its ideological affiliation between the two groups, their shared history, and al-Nusra's unitarian rationale. Hence, Jabhat al-Nusra and its fighters awaited the ruling of senior ideological figures—primarily Abu Qatada and al-Maqdisi—before engaging the Islamic State militarily.[25] In March 2014, al-Nusra leader Abu Abdullah al-Shami confirmed that the two Jordanian ideologues had instructed al-Nusra to refrain from proactively confronting the Islamic State and instead restrict its response to repulse the group's attacks.[26] Indicative of the intimacy of the evolving fratricide at this stage is the fact that in spring 2014 in Deir ez-Zour the Islamic State's offensive against other rebels, including Jihadis, was led by Abu Ayman al-Iraqi, while Jabhat al-Nusra's forces were led by Abu Mariya al-Qahtani—a cousin of Abu Ayman.

Jabhat al-Nusra and its senior figures mainly responded to the Islamic State's aggressiveness with strong words of condemnation. Despite the disagreement with its former superiors in Iraq, al-Nusra considered the Jihadi project a unified struggle against a common enemy. The group also emerged from the split with the Islamic State as the smaller group in terms of numbers, which gave it less of an incentive to fight. To compensate for its inferiority, al-Nusra allied with other groups. This enabled it to project some force on the battlefield. For example, in Deir ez-Zour in May 2014, Jabhat al-Nusra established a military alliance called *Mujahideen Shura Council* with several other groups to counter the Islamic State's aggression against them.[27]

## *Early Reconciliation Efforts*

The first public Jihadi criticism of the Islamic State's aggressive behaviour prior to the eruption of infighting came from Ahrar al-Sham's political office shortly after the Islamic State entered Syria in April 2013. Addressing both the Islamic State and al-Nusra, the Ahrar al-Sham statement offers both advice (al-nush) and admonition (al-tadhkir) to the conflicting parties. Illustrative of the group's unitarian rationale, the statement stresses that it is imperative that Jihadis unify against their common enemy, al-Assad, that none of the groups on their own have the ability or authority to claim to represent *al-imama*, and that their dispute is in conflict with the general Jihadi project.[28] Later, in January 2014, Ahrar al-Sham leader Hassan Abboud elaborated on the group's criticism and offered his version of how the escalation to infighting had happened, exclusively blaming the Islamic State as the culprit.[29]

Since the intra-Jihadi conflict erupted and intensified quickly, al-Qaida and affiliated ideologues knew they had to react too. One way al-Qaida's leadership tried to manage the evolving conflict was by dispatching a number of highly respected figures to Syria. Another peacemaking effort came through diplomacy. In conjunction with the intensification of intra-Jihadi tensions in late 2013, and the eruption of a full-blown Jihadi civil war in early 2014, an abundance of mediation and reconciliation initiatives were suggested (see tables 7 and 8). All bar one of these proposals came from al-Qaida or aligned ideologues, while the Islamic State appeared less interested in settling the escalating infighting.

Al-Zawahiri officially designated Abu Khalid al-Suri[30] and amir of AQAP Nasir al-Wuhayshi[31] to oversee the handling of the conflict. Almost nothing is known about al-Suri's diplomacy work in private meetings and his only public statement about the fitna came on January 16, 2014. Al-Suri warned the Islamic State that continued infighting would only benefit the Assad regime, and that Jihadi infighting had destroyed the Jihadi project in Algeria in the 1990s. Al-Suri finally asked Islamic State leaders and fighters to repent and to submit to a shari'a court.[32] Likewise, little is known about the concrete efforts taken by al-Wuhayshi in his attempts to rein in the rebellious Islamic State, but he failed miserably.[33] At some point, al-Wuhayshi wrote a letter to both al-Baghdadi and al-Julani. Only the latter responded.[34] A major issue for al-Wuhayshi was that he was not on the ground in Syria where the fitna first emerged; from Yemen it was difficult to influence opinions. As the efforts of these two men were not producing results, senior figures on the ground in Syria stepped in. The first was Hamad al-Ali, a Kuwaiti associated with the Muslim Brotherhood and that al-Zawahiri allegedly liked. Al-Ali first met with al-Julani to hear his side of the story before meeting with al-Anbari or al-Baghdadi to hear the Islamic State's version.[35] Apparently al-Ali was so convinced by what al-Julani told him that he decided to record his conversation with al-Anbari/al-Baghdadi. According to one al-Qaida source, the Islamic State was afraid that the conversation would be leaked. As a countermeasure, the group initiated its propaganda campaign against al-Qaida, and especially its Syrian affiliate, Jabhat al-Nusra. Another inside source states that al-Baghdadi considered al-Ali a 'spy' after he learned that the conversation was recorded (this is allegedly why al-Ali had to flee the country).[36] On his own initiative, al-Nusra's spokesman Abu Sulayman al-Muhajir took over mediation efforts, interceding between al-Julani and al-Baghdadi in an attempt to find common ground that could de-escalate the conflict and eventually lead to peace.[37] Perhaps because al-Muhajir could never be considered neutral because of his affiliation with al-Nusra, he brought Abu Abd al-Aziz al-Qatari (Muhammed Yusuf Uthman Abd al Salam), the founder of the al-Qaida-aligned but Islamic State-sympathetic Jund al-Aqsa,[38] to one of his meetings with al-Baghdadi. Al-Qatari was an Afghanistan veteran and allegedly had close ties to AQI-ISI leaders Abu Musab al-Zarqawi, Abu Hamza al-Muhajir, Abu Omar al-Baghdadi and Abu Anas al-Shami. However, after meeting with al-Baghdadi, al-Anbari and al-Adnani, he was unable to convince them to stop their aggression before he was killed in January 2014.[39]

Table 7: Overview of Calls to De-escalate the Fitna

| *Calls to end infighting* | *Description* | *Date* |
|---|---|---|
| Iyadh al-Tunisi | Al-Tunisi warns people against judging either of the two groups in the infighting as little is known about what is actually going on. The groups have made mistakes, but this is inevitable. He calls on Jihadi ideologues to issue statements of support to the mujahideen in Syria, including the Islamic State. | January 14, 2014 |
| Abu Bakr al-Baghdadi[40] | Calls for parties to stop fighting while claiming that the Islamic State is only defending itself.[41] | January 19, 2014 |

| *Calls to end infighting* | *Description* | *Date* |
|---|---|---|
| AQAP[42] | A call to stop the infighting as it benefits the enemy and destroys the Jihadi project. Part of al-Wuhayshi's diplomacy efforts. | February 27, 2014 |
| Ayman al-Zawahiri | A call to stop the infighting and for Jihadi groups to unite against the enemy. | May 3, 2014 |
| Hussein ibn Mahmoud | Calls for infighting to stop and the groups to reconcile. The conflict should be kept internal and not debated in public. | May 11, 2014 |

Table 8: Overview of Reconciliation Initiatives

| *Reconciliation initiatives* | *Description* | *Date* |
|---|---|---|
| Abu Muhammed al-Julani | Through al-Qatari, al-Julani proposed to al-Baghdadi that he should cancel both groups and that a new group with the name Tandheem Qaedat al-Jihad fi Bilad al-Sham should be established. Al-Julani suggested two models: (1) a bilateral meeting between himself and al-Baghdadi where they decide on the details of a new group or (2) al-Julani and al-Baghdadi both step down and elect a nominee from each group, with al-Zawahiri deciding between them.[43] This was refused.[44] | Late 2013 |
| Jabhat al-Nusra delegation[45] | A delegation led by Abu Hasan Taftanasi, Abu Firas al-Suri, Abu Hummam al-Shami and Abu 'Ubaidah al-Tunisi.[46] In addition there were representatives from Al-Farouq and from Ajnad al-Aqsa. Abdullah al-Mohaysini was also at the meeting. | December 2013 or January 2014 |
| Hussein ibn Mahmoud | Proposes a 5-point plan: A ceasefire should be implemented, a committee of scholars from the fighting factions and from Syria should be established to arbitrate with all factions abiding by its judgement, joint | January 5, 2014 |

| *Reconciliation initiatives* | *Description* | *Date* |
|---|---|---|
| | operation rooms to promote unity should be established, group members should abstain from discussing conflicts in public, and a joint media room outside Syria should be established. | |
| Abu Muhammed al-Julani[47] | Chastises the Islamic State for being the aggressor and not submitting to a shari'a court. His proposal is to establish a new independent shari'a court with representatives from all factions and to implement a ceasefire. The court's decision should be enforced if any rejects it. | January 7, 2014 |
| Ayman al-Zawahiri[48] | Calls for the factions in Syria to halt the infighting and establish an independent court. | January 15, 2014 |
| Hani al-Sibai and Tariq Abdelhaleem[49] | Came in reaction to al-Baghdadi's call for a ceasefire. They provide seven pieces of advice. The most important are: Establishment of a joint committee to settle any grievances between Jihadi groups. The committee should consist of a judge from the Islamic State, one from the other group and a third independent judge. They call upon the leaders of the Jihadi groups to instil a sense of brotherhood in their fighters. Establishment of a supra-group shura council to facilitate consultation between them regarding jihad and the management of liberated places. And a liberated area should be controlled by the group liberating it and other groups should not interfere. | January 21, 2014 |
| Abdullah al-Muhaysini | Al-Muhaysini's mubadarat al-umma [Initiative of the Umma] proposed a 9-point process to reconcile the warring factions in Syria. | January 24, 2014 |

| *Reconciliation initiatives* | *Description* | *Date* |
|---|---|---|
| Abu Muhammed al-Julani | In the wake of the killing of Abu Khalid al-Suri, al-Julani demands once again that the Islamic State submits to a shari'a court led by Abu Muhammad al-Maqdisi, Abu Qatada al-Filastini and Abu Sulayman al-Ulwan to adjudicate. He gives the group five days to respond. | February 24, 2014 |
| Abu Khalil al-Madani | The establishment of a 'High Shari'a Committee' led by scholars who are present in Syria and members of the involved parties. Their task should be to provide advice and facilitate unity. The committee should preferably work in secret and a security committee should be established under the shari'a committee. | April 9, 2014 |
| Abu Muhammad al-Maqdisi[50] | Calls for a reconciliation process led by a third-party judge to arbitrate in the conflict. | May 26, 2014 |
| Scholarly reconciliation proposal[51] | In the *Initiative and Call for a Truce Between the Factions in Sham*, the scholars call for a ceasefire beginning on October 3, 2014 and ask the involved groups to express their opinion on the initiative within three days of publishing the statement. | September 30, 2014 |
| Omar Khaled al-Khorasani (TTP/Jama'at al-Ahrar) | Offers to send a 'reconciliation delegation' from Pakistan to Syria to mediate between the two groups. | October 4, 2014 |
| Ayman al-Zawahiri | Re-announces an initiative consisting of five parts: Stop the infighting, stop the call to kill those who disagree with you, establishment of an independent shari'a court with authority in Syria and Iraq, a general amnesty and cooperation in every possible way. | October 2015 |

From late 2013 to October 2014, fifteen calls for arbitration and reconciliation can be identified, ten of which involve tangible initiatives to settle the conflict. One year later, al-Zawahiri proposed another reconciliation initiative. This abundance of initiatives clearly illustrates the seriousness of the infighting and how imperative it was from an al-Qaida perspective to reunite the groups. An important thing to notice about these early calls for reconciliation is how the authors emphasise that both al-Nusra and the Islamic State should be considered truthful mujahideen, showing that around the time of the split in February 2014 the ambition was still to keep the factions together and not alienate Islamic State leaders and fighters.

It was especially the initiatives by al-Julani, al-Muhaysini and al-Maqdisi that received attention. Early after the outbreak of the Jihadi civil war in January, al-Muhaysini presented his *initiative of the umma* [mubadarat al-umma], a detailed nine-point reconciliation plan which aimed to settle the conflict and establish the conditions for an arbitration process:

1. Implement an immediate ceasefire throughout Syria,
2. Establishment of a court with independent judges agreed to by all participating parties,
3. All groups present in the area where the initiative is agreed shall guarantee the implementation of the court's ruling,
4. Ten candidates from factions adhering to the correct creed, but who are not involved in the conflict, shall be nominated,
5. Groups have five days to decide if they agree with the initiative,
6. A media centre should be created to communicate matters relating to the reconciliation process,
7. Each party shall choose a representative to negotiate on its behalf,
8. The following period for trials should be limited in time, and
9. The Islamic State, Jabhat al-Nusra and other groups should explicitly express if they agree to the initiative.[52]

The initiative of al-Muhaysini, who was clearly attempting to position himself as the 'Abdallah Azzam of the Syrian Jihad', was based on the logic of *benefitting the umma* (maslaha al-umma) rather than *benefitting the group* (maslaha al-jama'a). Although mubadarat al-umma received prominent backing from ideologues like Iyad al-Qunaybi and al-Maqdisi[53] and commanders like Hassan Abboud[54] and al-Julani,[55] it never succeeded in gaining approval from the Islamic State despite all other parties accepting its conditions. The proposals from al-Julani and al-Maqdisi also involved arbitration—although they slightly differed in their setup. This mattered little to the Islamic State, however, as it generally rejected any efforts at *adjudication* (tahkeem).[56] The reason for the complete rejection of an independent court, as most of the initiatives call for, is, according to al-Adnani, that the SJM has been divided in two camps: one that supports the Islamic State and one that does not. This makes it impossible to elect a neutral candidate to arbitrate.[57] He also bases his argument in hierarchy; the Islamic State is a *state* and thus superior to *group*, and it would not be proper for adjudication to happen between a state and a group. Al-Zawahiri had hinted at something similar in 2009 during a push to unite Jihadi groups in Iraq. Back then he claimed that the ISI was superior to ordinary Jihadi groups and that the latter should join the state.[58] Al-Zawahiri surely did not imagine in 2009 that five years later this argument would be used by the Islamic State against his own group, al-Qaida.

Interestingly, the main figure within the Islamic State to respond to these reconciliation initiatives and the critique that followed was not the group's deputy (na'ib) and general religious official (al-shar'i al-'am) Abu Ali al-Anbari but Turki al-Binali, a young Bahrani scholar who had taken advantage of the organisational platform offered by the Islamic State and the implicit authority attached to this. Al-Binali was far from being a nobody in the SJM. He had studied under al-Maqdisi and had even been awarded a place on al-Maqdisi's Minbar al-Tawhid wa-l-Jihad shari'a council,[59] which publishes fatwas on the most influential Jihadi digital platform. Al-Binali also had experience from the battlefield after having spent time in Yemen with AQAP, and he had visited Iraq as early as 2004, spending time with al-Zarqawi's group.[60] However, al-Binali, being born in 1984, was only twenty-nine or thirty years old in early 2014 and thus still a youngster in comparison to most other Jihadi ideologues. Travelling to Syria twice in 2013, and ending up staying on his second visit, he suddenly found himself the group's in-house scholar tasked with responding to incoming discursive attacks. Between late 2013 and early summer 2014, al-Binali thus condemned prominent Jihadi figures like Abu Basir al-Tartusi,[61] Iyad al-Qunaybi, Abu Qatada, al-Julani and even al-Qaida's leader al-Zawahiri and his own former mentor al-Maqdisi. In several statements, the youngster defended his group's claim to be a state[62] and its rejection of third party arbitration,[63] promoted the qualifications of al-Baghdadi,[64] explained the origins of the infighting[65] and countered the accusations that the Islamic State's members are modern Khawarij.[66]

Although the infighting was intensifying, late 2013 and early 2014 was still characterised by loyalty confusion and the acceptability of collaboration. For instance, in July 2013, the Islamic State in Iraq and Sham offered its condolences following the death of AQAP deputy leader Abu Sufyan al-Azdi, and al-Qaida affiliates continued to applaud the Iraqi group's advances in the spring of 2014. Locally, collaboration between the Islamic State and Jabhat al-Nusra also took place from time to time. Internationally, it took even longer for the *fitna logic* to gain ascendency and become totalitarian, as illustrated by the collaboration between the Kouachi brothers and Coulibaly in their Paris attacks in January 2015. Surprisingly, AQAP also published a pamphlet applauding the attack in Nice in July 2016 claimed by the Islamic State.

In their reconciliation proposals, al-Julani, al-Muhaysini, al-Khorasani and al-Madani all cite the Quranic verse 49:9, saying

> And if two factions among the believers should fight, then make settlement between the two. But if one of them oppresses the other, then fight against the one that oppresses until it returns to the ordinance of Allah. And if it returns, then make settlement between them in justice and act justly. Indeed, Allah loves those who act justly.

But despite the Islamic State's unwillingness to commit to an arbitration process, al-Qaida was not prepared to escalate the conflict through actively attacking its opponent. In early 2014, al-Zawahiri probably realised that he was is no position to manage the challenge posed by the Islamic State on his own or by relying exclusively on in-house al-Qaida officials, and he thus began to mobilise Jihadi ideologues to pacify the escalating conflict. The al-Qaida leader asked the ideologues to insist upon the establishment of the independent shari'a commission, while reassuring them about his position and that of al-Qaida:

> me and my brothers, by the grace of Allah, are still as you knew us, calling for jihad against the enemies of Islam, both inside and outside, and insisting upon the call for being judged by shari'a, and that no rule goes above it, with all that we own and work with. As for those who claim other than this against us, then I ask Allah to forgive him, and to bring us and him together over what He loves and approves of.[67]

Luckily for al-Zawahiri, help was on its way. The early reaction from al-Qaida's leadership, its affiliates and affiliated ideologues was partly the result of al-Qaida's weakened position at the time, which discouraged a more assertive response. More importantly, however, it was driven by an ideal of ensuring unity within the SJM as a measure to protect the movement. For the Islamic State, the situation was different. Although al-Baghdadi himself called for the infighting to end, this was not with the goal of reuniting the movement but to protect the group's own hegemonic project. This clearly illustrates the distinctive rationales of al-Qaida and the Islamic State.

Within the Islamic State, it was mainly Turki al-Binali who responded to the reconciliation proposals. As will become clear in this chapter, more than anyone else al-Binali's writings in the 2013–14 period are instructive in helping us understand the dynamics at play and the necessity for the Islamic State to legitimise its actions while undermining opposing voices. In his responses to Iyad al-Qunaybi and al-Julani,[68] al-Binali emphatically rejected arbitration as a reconciliation mechanism. In response to al-Qunaybi's proposal that the groups should submit to a third party who could arbitrate in the conflict, he raises four issues: (1) the Islamic State is a *state* and cannot be subject to arbitration on the *group* level; (2) the Islamic State's own judiciary follows the rules of God and not organisational interests, and is thus capable of arbitrating in the conflict itself; (3) any such third party tribunal will not be entirely independent; and (4) the tribunal will have no power to enforce its decision.[69] Other scholars like Abu Sa'd al-Amili[70] and Abu Mundhir al-Shinqiti would issue similar statements in support of Islamic State.

Remarkably, over the next five years, Jihadis would time and again attempt to institutionalise reconciliation mechanisms on a supra-group level. However, with detrimental effects for the SJM, these attempts consistently failed. Despite the religious imperative to avoid and settle internal conflict, the political objectives of the groups were obstacles preventing most of these initiatives from succeeding.

### *The Necessity of Fitna, al-Adnani's Attacks, and the Point of No Return*

A clear difference in attitude to intra-movement infighting and contestation is identifiable at a very early stage. Al-Baghdadi's speech from January 2014 proved to be a defining moment in intra-Jihadi relations which critically affected the logic of the movement in the following years. In the speech, al-Baghdadi escalated the conflict by legitimising intra-movement infighting, even calling for its necessity:

> It's from God's tradition and wisdom that the rows of believers and Mujahids is mingled with hypocrites. God will not leave this row mixed with those hypocrites and pretenders and therefore creates Fitna and trials for them. The row must be melted so that the maliciousness leaves and be pressured so that the weak building blocks crumble and the lights must shine at it exposing the intricacies and inner personalities.[71]

This was in stark contrast to al-Qaida's ambitions of reconciliation.

Spring 2014 was one extended military success for the Islamic State, who conquered swaths of territory from the regime and other rebel and Jihadi groups. Such military success along with rises in recruits and funding offered the group a suitable context to intensify the conflict with al-Qaida further. While the dynamics of military infighting were still being negotiated in a constantly changing environment,[72] the discursive contestation was unequivocal in two speeches by the Islamic State's spokesperson al-Adnani, published in April and May respectively. The April speech 'This is not our methodology, and it will not be' is the Islamic State's first official response to al-Zawahiri's decision in February to disown the group. Its main objectives are to discredit al-Qaida and to defend the Islamic State.[73] Al-Adnani touches especially on four issues: the pledge of allegiance to al-Qaida, the exclusivity of the mujahideen, al-Qaida's alleged methodological deviance, and his own group's claim to the authority of Bin Laden. On the issue of the pledge of allegiance from his group to al-Qaida, he provides an account that conflicts with conventional knowledge at the time. Although his narrative certainly serves the interest of the Islamic State, this fact does not automatically disqualify it. According to al-Adnani, the Islamic State ceased to be a part of al-Qaida in October 2006 when it established its state in Iraq.[74] Ever since, there has been a relationship between equals characterised by respect.

On methodology, he acknowledges that differences between the Islamic State and its predecessors on the one hand, and al-Qaida on the other, have existed for a long time; even so, it was not necessary to react to these until al-Qaida's *distorted understanding of religion* (deen a'awaj) and *deviating methodology* (manhaj inharaf) became too critical. Now, he claims,

> the leaders of Al-Qaida deviated from the right manhaj [methodology], we say this as sadness overwhelms us and bitterness fills our hearts. (…) Verily al-Qaida today is no longer the Qaidat al-Jihad, and so it is not the base of Jihad, the one praising it is of the lowest, and the tyrants flirt with it, and the deviants and the misguided attempt to woo it. (…) Verily Al-Qaida today has ceased to be the base of Jihad, rather its leadership has become an axe supporting the destruction of the project of the Islamic State and the coming Khilafah.

Al-Adnani furthermore criticises al-Qaida for destroying the Jihadi movement by broadening the definition of the umma and the mujahideen. Although in practice this does not affect its recruitment policy, the Islamic State officially has a much more exclusive attitude to who should be considered a Muslim and a mujahideen than al-Qaida has. Finally, al-Adnani laid claim to the legacy of Bin Laden, arguing that the Islamic State, not al-Qaida, is the truthful successor to the al-Qaida founder: 'So be assured O soldiers of the Islamic State, for we are by Allah's Will progressing upon the Manhaj of the Imam Shaykh Usama, and the amir of the martyrdom seekers Abu Musab al-Zarqawi, and the founder of the state Abu Umar al-Baghdadi, and its minister of war Abu Hamza al-Muhajir.' He ends his speech by dividing the SJM into two groups, telling the mujahideen to choose 'whose hand are you going to take? And from among whose ranks shall you be?'

The next speech from al-Adnani in May, provocatively titled 'Apologies Amir of al-Qaida', was a direct response to al-Zawahiri, who earlier in the month made his testimony public.[75] In a convincing manner, al-Adnani uses proficient rhetoric to touch upon the same issues as in his April speech, giving his answers with direct reference to the speech of the al-Qaida leader. He reiterates that 'the State is not a branch that belongs to al-Qaida, and it never was for a day', and continues, 'the amirs of the Islamic State remained addressing Qaidat al-Jihad as soldiers addressing their amirs, as a pupil addressing his professor, and a student to his sheikh, and the young boy addressing his elder', but 'it is not correct for an emirate or a state to pledge allegiance to an organisation.' Portraying his own group as the one seeking unity within the SJM, al-Adnani describes the groups' relationship between 2006 and 2014 as amicable but not bound by Islamic law. He says,

> Until very recently we would answer those who were asking us about the relationship of the State with al-Qaida that it is the relationship of a soldier to its amir. However, O doctor, this status was to make the word of global jihad one, and it had no influence inside the State, and it was also not bound to it; rather, it was humbleness, humility, and an act of honour and generosity from us to you.

Providing instances of this nuanced relationship, he uses the example of the Islamic State abstaining from attacking Iran—according to the wishes of al-Qaida—and the fact that the group continued to attack the Shia in Iraq despite several requests from al-Qaida that they stop. In a clever move, the Islamic State spokesman offers the desperate al-Zawahiri a way out in the hope that he will submit his group to al-Baghdadi's authority:

> You put yourself and your al-Qaida before two choices with no escape: either you continue on your mistake, and be stubborn in it, and the split and infighting among the mujahideen in the world continues, or you acknowledge your mistake, and thus correct it and realise it. Here we are extending our hands anew so that you can be a good successor to a good predecessor, for Sheikh Usama brought all the mujahideen on one word, and you separated them and ripped them apart. We extend our hands to you anew, and call you. First: back down from your lethal mistake, and annul the pledge of allegiance of the cunning traitor [al-Julani], and thus you frustrate the disbelievers and please the believers and save the blood of the mujahideen. You were the one who saddened the Muslims and made the enemies be pleased with the hardship of the mujahideen, for you supported the trick of the cunning and supported it, and thus you burned the eyes and bloodied the hearts. You were the one who ignited the sedition, and you will be the one to turn it off if you wish to do so, Allah willing, so correct [tashih] yourself, stand for Allah and reform what you ruined.

Extending his pressure to al-Qaida's global network, al-Adnani rounds off his criticism with a call to all al-Qaida affiliates to declare their position on the Islamic State. As it turned out, however, the Islamic State would not succeed in convincing any official al-Qaida affiliate to abandon its pledge of allegiance to al-Zawahiri.

Al-Baghdadi and al-Adnani were not alone in their criticism of al-Qaida. Several Jihadi ideologues of lower rank—in addition to Abu al-Mundhir al-Shinqiti and al-Binali—published pro-Islamic State articles in late 2013 and early 2014 to support its narrative of breaking allegiance and its claim to be a state.[76] But al-Adnani's speeches nevertheless represent a watershed in intra-Jihadi relations. Arguably, this was the point of no return for al-Qaida in terms of seeking reconciliation with its renegade affiliate.[77]

### *Outsourcing the Fight: Jihadism's Intellectual Guardians to the Rescue of al-Zawahiri*

The early stage of the contestation and infighting was characterised by Islamic State dominance, enabled by the group's success in mobilisation, military expansion and (coupled with its assertive discourse) media dissemination. As an organisation, al-Qaida did not know how to react to the challenge of a counter-group that it considered inherently illegitimate. Since 9/11 the SJM had been relatively cohesive, and although there was a division between locally (revolutionary) and globally focused groups,[78] there was a general acknowledgement that al-Qaida was the pioneer of the movement.[79] Michels explains that when a challenge to established leaders arises, they typically attack the contesting figures as incompetent and corrupt while associating themselves with the will of the constituents.[80] Interestingly, this was not the case with al-Qaida's senior leadership, foremost among them al-Zawahiri. Instead the leadership's the initial passivity led to an involuntary outsourcing of countermeasures against the Islamic State.[81]

Because of the lack of response from the al-Qaida leadership, the Islamic State's narrative remained largely unchallenged. This allowed it to embed itself among the Jihadi masses and gain ground—something that would eventually turn out to be a disaster for its opponents. Al-Qaida was not helped by the Assad regime's decision to focus its anti-revolutionary military efforts on secular groups, relying on the presence of Jihadis, or 'terrorists', to legitimise the regime's crackdown on the opposition. This enabled the Islamic State to continue its military expansion. This would eventually facilitate its creation of a caliphate, and further its challenge—military and discursive—to other Jihadi groups.

At first, al-Qaida tried to respond through its local affiliate Jabhat al-Nusra. Sitting in a lush garden with a Jabhat al-Nusra flag in the background and, symbolically, a pistol and a book lying on the table, the Jordanian shar'i Sami al-Uraydi outlined the creedal and methodological differences between the Islamic State and al-Nusra in an October 2013 video.[82] He particularly emphasised the Islamic State's rejection of Wahhabi scholars such as Ibn Baz and its vague criteria for declaring someone an apostate. A few months later, al-Nusra and another senior figure, Abu Mariya al-Qahtani,[83] published further criticism of their rival. The official statement describes how the Islamic State invaded areas in Deir ez-Zour under the control of al-Nusra, and showing the differences in rationale, the statement ends with a warning to the Islamic State that al-Nusra will be obliged to respond with force if the Islamic State does not halt its attacks on them.[84]

In 2014, al-Zawahiri did address the emerging conflict in several statements, but he generally adopted a reactive and defensive approach. In one statement he laments the ongoing events and calls for a shari'a court to be established to settle the disagreements.[85] A few months later, after the split, he briefly explains that it happened as a result of al-Baghdadi's unwillingness to comply with al-Zawahiri's orders along with general methodological differences between the groups.[86] Eulogising Abu Khalid al-Suri, al-Zawahiri declares that the situation is becoming so critical that Jihadis must state their opposition to the Islamic State's behaviour in public, yet the al-Qaida leader himself remained too cautious. Eventually, In May, he steps up his criticism slightly. In his testimony he calls on the conflict to halt and directly instructs al-Nusra to stop infighting with other Jihadis. Al-Zawahiri continues to defend the historical consistency of al-Qaida's methodology and outlays his version of the historical trajectory of organisational affiliation between the two groups.[87]

Yet illustrative of the situation in early 2014, the main response to the Islamic State did not come from al-Zawahiri but from outside the organisational framework of al-Qaida and through the writings of senior Jihadi ideologues. This resulted in analysts and academics ruling al-Zawahiri and al-Qaida out as also-rans in the struggle for Jihadi supremacy.[88] On several occasions, senior figures such as Abu Basir al-Tartusi[89] and Hani al-Sibai[90] made public requests to al-Zawahiri to get involved and respond to the accusations being made against him and his group. Waiting for a response, another communal statement symbolically entitled 'A Message from the Umma to the Wise Man of the Umma' and signed by Tariq Abdelhaleem, Hani al-Sibai, Iyad al-Qunaybi, Abdullah al-Muhaysini, Muhammad al-Hassam and Sami al-Uraydi, was published.[91] However, despite having witnessed the aggression of the Algerian Groupe Islamique Armé in the 1990s, the internal turmoil within the Egyptian Jihadi movement, and the retractions of his former mentor Dr Fadl, al-Zawahiri appeared unprepared for the task of confronting a countergroup—a situation where he could not employ his usual anti-imperialist rhetoric.

Luckily for al-Zawahiri, the task of countering the Islamic State's narrative was taken up by senior ideologues who either reacted out of their tremendous respect[92] for the al-Qaida leader or in order to protect the Jihadi project.[93] In this they embody the *intellectual guardians* discussed by Wagemakers.[94] The ideologues' opposition had already begun when the Islamic State expanded into Syria,[95] but it intensified in magnitude and ferocity in spring 2014 around the time of al-Adnani's attack. Figures like Abu Qatada al-Filastini, Abu Muhammad al-Maqdisi, Abu Basir al-Tartusi, Iyad al-Qunaybi, Umar Haddouchi, Abu Sulayman Ulwan, Hani al-Sibai and Tariq Abdelhaleem—undoubtedly the most influential Jihadi ideologues not officially affiliated with any group[96]—presented their criticism of the Islamic State. Early on, however, there were qualitative differences in their critiques that reveal the subtleties of intra-Jihadi conflict as well as the specific attitudes of different ideologues. Al-Tartusi, al-Sibai, Abdelhaleem and Abu Qatada were the first ideologues to adopt a strenuously critical stance on the Islamic State. As will be discussed, Al-Maqdisi approached the infighting slightly differently.[97] Because of their major impact on the SJM, I will mainly focus on the evolving attitudes of Abu Qatada and al-Maqdisi in this period.

Between the expansion of the Islamic State into Syria and its declaration of the caliphate, Abu Qatada released three letters dealing with the group, every time escalating his criticism. In the first letter, he takes a fatherly role, offering advice to Islamic State fighters and its leaders from the position of a veteran Jihadi who had experienced the abysmal effects of infighting on several occasions. He does not believe any group is worthy of calling itself a state, and even indicates that one would be adopting Shia practices if one were to take the title of *caliph* or *amir al-muminin* (leader of the believers). Finally, in an attempt to warn younger Jihadi ideologues against lending their support to the Islamic State, he chastises those people as *students who pretend to have knowledge*.[98] In his second letter, he addresses Islamic State members, telling them to join Jabhat al-Nusra while ordering al-Baghdadi to follow the directions of al-Qaida leader al-Zawahiri. Unlike other ideologues like al-Tartusi, al-Sibai and Abdelhaleem, however, he challenges the legitimacy of fighting the Islamic State as they remain Muslims irrespective of their current deviance. Despite not supporting the course of engaging the group military, he has little faith that the conflict can be resolved peacefully since the group continues to refuse all attempts at arbitration and does not listen to the advice it receives in private from Abu Qatada and his like.[99] Abu Qatada's third letter not only escalates his criticism of the Islamic State but is also the most revealing about how challenging he finds the situation. He begins,

> This is a letter that I write with deep sorrow, and if it were not for the covenant that Allah took upon the creation, I would have not rushed to writing this letter. By Allah, I struggled with myself not to release this letter as much as I could. However, I could not do so, fearing that I would conceal the truth that I believe.

He still refuses to label them khawarij, instead calling the group *dogs of hellfire*. By this point, opponents of Abu Qatada and al-Maqdisi had begun to discredit their statements, disregarding them as the veiled messages of Jordanian intelligence (the two men had spent considerable time in prison in 2013–14. In fact, al-Maqdisi was released in June 2014 after serving a five-year sentence).[100] According to Abu Qatada, however, his imprisonment affected only the quantity, not the quality, of his output. Nonetheless, he acknowledges that his imprisonment left the SJM open to the influence of younger scholars: 'I am in a situation that I am not able to release statements every day, like others. For this reason, the field has been left for the minors and the fanatics clinging to the dawla [Islamic State] like the ignorant clings to his tribe without understanding or awareness.'[101]

In the same period, al-Maqdisi released eight statements addressing the Islamic State, but these never reached the same level of criticism as those from Abu Qatada and other ideologues. Like Abu Qatada, he laments the Islamic State's claim to be a state; he argues that statehood is only attained following certain stages and that skipping any of these stages, as the Islamic State has done, is dangerous.[102] He also expresses abhorrence at the group's criticism of al-Zawahiri, whom al-Maqdisi holds in high regard. However, al-Maqdisi uses more moderate language than his peers. In May 2014, he ramps up his criticism, calling on the Islamic State to repent for its actions and explaining that he has not reacted more forcefully until now because he has been engaged in diplomatic efforts to reform the group in private. In one statement he writes that 'I announce, here, that anzim al-dawla fi-l-'iraq wa-l-sham, is a deviant organisation from the path of truth, [they are] aggressors against the mujahideen. They lean towards ghuluw [extremism]. They have become embroiled in the spilling of unlawful blood', and also

> [They have] turned their rifles from the chests of the apostates and those at war [with the Muslims] to the chests of the Mujahideen and the Muslims.'[103] This was followed by another statement later in the month that begins 'their inclination to exaggeration (janahat ilayhi min ghuluw) and shedding the forbidden blood (safk li-l-dima al-muharrama) and abandoning the arbitration with the shari'a of Allah ('i'rad 'an al-tahakom li-shar'i allah).[104]

Al-Maqdisi explains that he has communicated in public and in private with al-Baghdadi and some of his jurists, and that he informed al-Zawahiri about the initiative he was attempting to set up. But after al-Maqdisi realised that the Islamic State had rejected his initiative and lied to him in the process, he decided to publish his condemnation and to include within it documentation of his correspondence with Islamic State figures. At this time he also began to call for members of the Islamic State to abandon the group and pledge allegiance to Jabhat al-Nusra.

Al-Maqdisi has always been fearful of the emergence of a wave of increasing extremism due to what he perceives as a leniency in proclaiming takfir;[105] as such, he probably considers it his duty to guard against any indications of what he identifies as extremism.[106] At the same time, he was also aware that many within the Islamic State held him in high regard; this provided him with leverage that not even Abu Qatada could boast of. Hence, in a statement published in early July, he partially retracted the criticism made in his May statement, refusing to reject either of the two parties (al-Qaida or the Islamic State) and promising to continue communicating with both. Throughout, al-Maqdisi's perception has been that one should distinguish between the leaders of the Islamic State and its rank and file members. He believes that the group's mistakes and its deviance are the responsibility of its leadership, while the ordinary Islamic State supporter is not to be blamed. This distinction is important, he argues, because to describe the group as homogenous would push the rank and file further into the arms of the leadership and thus polarise the SJM even more. Hence, in the spring and early summer of 2014, al-Maqdisi tried to position himself as an unbiased scholar capable of mediating between the two parties.

The intervention of Jihadi ideologues on behalf of al-Zawahiri is illustrative of the important role ideologues have within the SJM and of the state of al-Qaida at the time. It was in this period that Abu Qatada and al-Maqdisi cemented their position as 'al-Qaida's ideologues' par excellence,[107] replacing al-Qaida's in-house ideologues Abu Yahya al-Libi and Atiyyatullah al-Libi, who were killed in 2012 and 2011 respectively. Thus, there was a shift in the ideological power balance from within the group to external figures with sympathies for the group. Increasingly under pressure, the al-Qaida leadership probably saw few alternatives. In the words of Abu Dujana, a senior al-Qaida leader, the umma should be careful of the 'polytheistic democracy' on one side and 'extremism' on the other.[108] This left al-Qaida in a delicate position.

## *Al-Qaida's Internal Problems*

With the challenge from the Islamic State increasing, the conflictual dynamics between the two groups prompted an internal debate within al-Qaida about how to respond. Not only were al-Qaida-sympathetic ideologues pressing al-Zawahiri to get involved, on several occasions asking him to state publicly his position vis-à-vis the Islamic State,[109] but certain al-Qaida figures were openly beginning to argue in favour of the Islamic State's narrative. In late March 2014, nine al-Qaida officials, among them the brother of Abu Muhammad al-Maqdisi, openly declared their allegiance to the Islamic State and advised others to follow suit.[110] It fell to Abu Amir al-Naji, an official in al-Qaida's as-Sahab media foundation, to respond,[111] but although al-Naji answered every accusation raised by the nine (now former) al-Qaida officials, and advised them to remain with the group, he had little luck. A Pandora's box had been opened and al-Zawahiri was feeling the pressure to react to assert his leadership over al-Qaida and to ensure that the number of people jumping ship would remain as low as possible.

## The Role of Jihadi Media

The first place al-Qaida would face internal problems outside of the battlefield was in the Jihadi media landscape. Already in 2013, an important al-Qaida-affiliated media outlet, the forum *Shumukh al-Islam,* raised the issue of how the fitna affected the media centre. The forum administrator complained that supporters of the Islamic State and Jabhat al-Nusra were interfering, suggesting that the administrators should censor or even delete material in support of the opponent group. At the time, Shumukh al-Islam publicised its neutrality in the conflict, but this would soon change.[112] In spring 2014, the forum was slowing shifting sides to the Islamic State. There were stories about how the release of speeches and statements from al-Qaida was delayed, and when al-Zawahiri commented on the death of Abu Khalid al-Suri, the thread treating the topic on the forum was quickly 'buried' in the archive. Eventually, on April 5, 2014, Jabhat al-Nusra released a statement to the administrator of Shumukh al-Islam claiming that it sided with the Islamic State in the intra-Jihadi fitna and that the group would no longer publish its statements through the forum. Losing the sympathy of one of the main Jihadi forums was not as critical as one would imagine, however, as the Jihadi media landscape was undergoing a transformation. It was migrating to new media platforms such as Twitter, and later Telegram, while also beginning to increasingly use file sharing platforms like justpaste.it and achieve.com to upload material.

More problematic for al-Qaida were the difficulties within *Al Fajr Centre*, a Jihadi distribution outlet established in late 2006 that served all al-Qaida affiliates in addition to functioning as a hub for internal communication between affiliates. In early 2014, people in senior positions in Al Fajr similarly decided to support the Islamic State, and as part of the intra-Jihadi fitna, they ensured that al-Qaida statements countering the Islamic State and related correspondence were either delayed or shared with Islamic State leaders prior to publication, allowing the Islamic State to respond pre-emptively. One important example is al-Zawahiri's speech 'The Reality Between the Pain and the Hope', that gives the al-Qaida leader's version of the split between the two groups at a moment when confusion within the SJM was at a maximum. It was intended for release in early April 2014, but it was delayed by Al Fajr until April 18 to ensure that al-Adnani could release his speech 'This is Not Our Methodology, and it Will Not Be' the day before on April 17.[113] Another example is an internal letter sent by the senior al-Qaida member in Syria, Muhsin al-Fadhli, to the amir of AQAP, Nasir al-Wuhayshi, through Al Fajr; initially this was not delivered to al-Wuhayshi, and when it was, the version he received lacked appendices found in the original letter. Not surprisingly, the letter was about the ongoing conflict between al-Qaida and the Islamic State.[114] The result of all this was a change in the use of Jihadi media. AQAP and al-Qaida senior figures stopped using Al Fajr, which shortly afterwards ceased to exist. Instead, al-Zawahiri and his spokesperson, Adam Gadahn, released statements in spring 2014 through private Twitter accounts to avoid the interference of Islamic State-sympathetic distribution centres.

By mid-2014, the *fitna logic* had finally pervaded the Jihadi media. Media outlets were now open about what group they were loyal to, only publishing material supportive of their own group or its broader agenda.[115] As Bunzel has explained, around this time media infighting also evolved: whereas previously it took place within existing media centres, now it was increasingly a struggle between old-time al-Qaida-affiliated platforms and emerging media centres on Twitter (and later Telegram).[116] One example is the conflict between the newly established pro-Islamic State Al Ghuraba Media Foundation and the al-Qaida sympathetic online Jihadi database, Minbar al-Tawhid wal-Jihad, run by Abu Muhammad al-Maqdisi. Ideologues like Turki al-Binali and Abu al-Mundhir al-Shinqiti left the latter to join the former, from which they launched a critique of their former comrades on Minbar al-Tawhid wa-l-Jihad. This represented an important shift not just from the old platform of Jihadi fora to media centres and foundations on Twitter and Telegram, but also from an environment where Jihadi media was neutral and served several groups as distribution units to a much more polarised media environment. Much later, al-Zawahiri would issue a speech calling for the Jihadi media to halt the internal bickering, but again, this was too late.[117]

Time and again Jihadis have emphasised the importance of the media. Al-Zawahiri himself once famously said that half the battle takes place in the media and Abu Qatada similarly acknowledged that media work is essential to the Jihadi project. Al-Qaida had lost the initial battle with the Islamic State in terms of attracting fighters and popularity. Now it was also losing the media battle because the Islamic State was much more strategic, progressive and innovative in its use of modern media technology.[118] In the period 2013–14, the Islamic State established several new official media centres including al-Itisam Media Foundation (March 2013; focused on social and religious activities), the Ajnad Foundation for Media Production (August 2013; specialising in nasheeds and audio content) and Al Hayat Media Center (May 2014; targeting Western audiences through publications in several languages). In early 2015, the group added its radio channel Al Bayan. This media victory of the Islamic State would have a massive impact on the fitna in the coming years. Overall, the initial hijacking of al-Qaida-affiliated media centres was integral to the Islamic State's early advantage.

## Mounting 'Internal' Pressure: Criticism and Desperate Solutions

Although Abu Basir al-Tartusi was one of the first senior Jihadi ideologues to criticise the Islamic State, he did not spare al-Qaida some provoking comments. Al-Tartusi has always been a lone voice within the SJM, sometimes praising and sometimes criticising specific groups and individuals; as such, he does not have any organisational attachment to al-Qaida, despite occasionally sympathising with its ideology.[119] Al-Tartusi's criticism targets both the Islamic State and al-Zawahiri, but it is his critique of the al-Qaida leader that is of most interest. He laments al-Zawahiri's speech 'Testimony to Preserve the Blood of Al-Mujahedeen in the Levant' since he considers it evidence that all the al-Qaida leader is interested in is reuniting his al-Qaida group—his rejection of the Islamic State is not, in the end, motivated by a principled objection to its ideological extremism.

Al-Tartusi himself relocated to Syria early in the conflict and he argues that al-Zawahiri simply does not have the information necessary to manage the intra-Jihadi conflict because he is not fully up to date and he is isolated as a result of being far away.[120] This is not the first time Abu Basir has criticised al-Qaida practices, however. In 2012, he rejected AQAP's use of suicide bombers. This prompted Abu Zubeir Adil al-Abab, an AQAP shar'i, to respond to Abu Basir that not only was his criticism harmful for the Jihadi project, but it also showed his lack of knowledge of the situation on the ground—a similar argument to the one used two years later by al-Tartusi against al-Zawahiri. But for al-Tartusi, the Syrian Jihad had fundamentally changed the SJM and its needs. He ends his critical statement with an obituary for al-Qaida, saying

> I think that the role of al-Qaida has ended. Its damage is dominating its benefit. It considers itself the fate of the umma (…) It is now the time for Al-Qaida, and the many names that resemble it and its work style, to give its banner to the umma so that it runs itself by itself without the guardianship of anyone.[121]

In the coming years, the ideologue would continue his critique of al-Qaida and in particular Jabhat al-Nusra and its successor organisations.

The first true *internal* problem for al-Zawahiri came from Jabhat al-Nusra and thus from inside al-Qaida. In summer 2014, one of its senior figures, Abu Mariya al-Qahtani, penned an open letter in which he criticised the passivity of al-Qaida's leader and his lack of an assertive response to the Islamic State. Addressing al-Zawahiri, al-Qahtani writes,

> The people of the Levant did not see a single clear statement from your part. They believe that either you are receiving information from people who support the Kharijites [the Islamic State] or you know what is happening, yet you are incapable of supporting your brothers and protecting your methodology.[122]

Al-Qahtani questions whether al-Zawahiri has received the letters from al-Nusra or if he simply does not care. As was revealed later, it was difficult for al-Qaida affiliates to communicate with al-Zawahiri because of the internal power struggle within the media centres; even so, al-Qahtani's criticism runs deeper than this, illustrating a more general disappointment from al-Qaida's *periphery* about the level of engagement of its central leadership. Rhetorically he asks

> Why do we need to stay calm and silent? Why do we need to let the exaggerators [Islamic State] play with the religion of Allah meanwhile we pat their shoulders? The Fitna of the exaggerators arrived in Yemen, Somalia, Gaza and everywhere... Those ideas are gaining ground and are received by the ignorant and are received with approval by the unorthodox.

In a desperate call, al-Qahtani asserts that al-Nusra is incapable of opposing the Islamic State alone. Solving the conflict 'cannot be achieved with individual efforts nor with group efforts but we should reconnect to our scholars and put our hands together to bring back the trust of the nation while unifying with the scholars.'

Al-Qahtani joined AQI in 2004 and took up central roles as the group's religious authority in Mosul and later in its religious police, where he was also in charge of managing the group's relations with local Iraqi tribes. After moving to Syria, he became a founding member of Jabhat al-Nusra, and when the conflict arose with the Islamic State in 2013, he sided with the former. Al-Qahtani was initially employed as al-Nusra amir in Deir ez-Zour, but as the group was pushed out of the province by the Islamic State, al-Julani replaced him with Sami al-Uraydi, since he wanted a stronger theological figure to counter the attractions of the Islamic State.[123] At this point, al-Qahtani was already the strongest critic of the Islamic State within al-Nusra and he continued his criticism of the group after relocating to Deraa. During his time in Deir ez-Zour, al-Qahtani saw the rapid rise in popularity of the Islamic State, and this probably influenced his views about the inadequate response of the al-Qaida leadership. Jihadis on the ground in Syria at the time sorely felt the lack of a more assertive stance from al-Zawahiri, which likely affected the mobilisation dynamics in 2013–14. At the time of his critique, al-Qahtani had already become a problematic figure within Jabhat al-Nusra, however, and this may have affected how his criticism was perceived. Not only did he make it clear that he was unhappy about being removed from his position, he later attempted to organise a coup against al-Julani from his base in Deraa, but his attempt failed miserably, leaving him sidelined for long periods.[124]

## Joining the Islamic State? Abu Iyadh al-Tunisi's Trojan Horse

During spring 2014, al-Zawahiri had provided his testimony about what had transpired between al-Qaida and the Islamic State. His conclusion was that the Iraqi group was an al-Qaida affiliate bound by a pledge of allegiance, until he himself expelled it a few months earlier that year. Pressure had mounted on al-Zawahiri to react and he was probably well aware that a single statement outlining his version of events would not be sufficient to settle the conflict. The Islamic State had at this point taken control of much of eastern Syria, expelling Jabhat al-Nusra and other Jihadi groups, while attracting the majority of al-Nusra's fighters, including foreigners. For al-Zawahiri it was no longer simply a matter of losing the control of a rebellious affiliate, but of containing its hostility so that it would not spread and affect the SJM more generally, or even—hypothetically—tilt the power structures of the movement to the Islamic State's advantage. Isolated, most likely in Pakistan, the al-Qaida leader had lost control over events and had seemingly no strategy besides delegating the task of taming the conflict to other senior figures.

In summer 2014, the lack of response led Abu Iyadh al-Tunisi—a senior al-Qaida figure leading Ansar al-Shari'a in Tunisia and a man close to Abu Qatada al-Filastini—to suggest a desperate move to contain the Islamic State. In January Abu Iyadh had tried to calm tensions, appealing to both groups to stop the infighting while stressing that both al-Nusra and the Islamic State should be considered truthful mujahideen. Some months later, he clearly sided with al-Qaida, but he was also acutely aware that the Islamic State was not going to go away. It was not until January 2016 that it became public that Abu Iyadh had proposed a bizarre solution to settle the conflict. In an article entitled 'The Jews of Jihad', which would become a popular text among Islamic State supporters intent on showcasing the evil intentions of al-Qaida, Islamic State media official Abu Maysara al-Shami published excerpts from two letters written by Abu Iyadh in which he suggests that al-Zawahiri infiltrate the Islamic State by joining the group in order to reform it from within.[125] Al-Shami did not circulate the two letters in their entirety, which is why an al-Qaida-sympathetic media house, al-Hedaya, decided to publish both letters to provide readers with the full picture.[126]

Abu Iyadh's first letter, dated July 14, 2014, was a direct reaction to the fitna in Syria as he considered it the responsibility of senior Jihadi leaders to halt the infighting. This was Abu Iyadh's way of saying in private what Hani al-Sibai had said in public: 'do something!' According to Abu Maysara, the advice Abu Iyadh offered al-Zawahiri was to pledge allegiance to al-Baghdadi to reform the movement from within. The immediate reason for doing this is to stop the bloodshed, but it would also be the beginning of a new phase, Abu Iyadh claims. Since the pledge of allegiance to al-Baghdadi would break al-Qaida's bay'a to Mullah Umar, the Taliban leader should be asked for permission, as the intention is not to cause further internal conflict. Abu Iyadh is aware of the seriousness of his advice, and so he suggests that al-Zawahiri discuss it with senior Jihadi figures, namely al-Maqdisi, Abu Qatada, al-Wuhayshi, Shekau in Nigeria and Abu al-Fadel in Mali.[127] As we know, Abu Iyadh's Trojan horse never materialised; part of the reason was that people like Abu Qatada and al-Maqdisi rejected the proposal, as they considered it too late. The Islamic State had become too extreme and it would be impossible to reform from within.[128] Hence, Abu Iyadh wrote to al-Zawahiri a second time just a month after his first letter, offering a revised opinion on the matter. Abu Iyadh now concurs with Abu Qatada and al-Maqdisi that the renegade Islamic State is out of reach.

Abu Iyadh's suggestion that al-Qaida should join the Islamic State is interesting for several reasons. It is revealing about how intra-movement dynamics are treated internally. It also indicates the desperation of al-Qaida in summer 2014 around the time of the caliphate declaration, and the importance of senior—though officially unaffiliated—ideologues within the movement. Furthermore, Abu Iyadh's suggestion turned out to have lasting effects on the fitna environment within the SJM, as it provided Islamic State supporters with ammunition to criticise al-Qaida. It also reinforced a suspicious attitude towards individuals or groups wanting to desert groups or join other ones. Such suspicion would become increasingly evident as the Islamic State lost momentum and as talks of a *grand merger* between al-Qaida and the Islamic State emerged in 2016–17.

## Al-Fadhli's Letter to al-Wuhayshi

Another important letter was Muhsin al-Fadhli's (Abu Asma'a) letter to AQAP amir Nasir al-Wuhayshi that was initially delayed by Al Fajr. When the letter finally arrived to al-Wuhayshi in Yemen, it did not make for pleasant reading.[129] Al-Fadhli, a Jihadi veteran that used to oversee al-Qaida's network in Iran before relocating to Syria, begins the letter relatively innocently with a diagnosis of the SJM, highlighting current mistakes that are placing the movement at risk. Though he does not initially mention the Islamic State by name, his points of criticism are clearly directed against the group and its behaviour in Syria. The SJM must be protected from itself because if *people of ignorance* (ahl al-jahl) obtain positions of power they will eventually destroy the movement. Al-Fadhli writes that 'they would belittle some matters and increase the importance of some other. They would make mistakes. They would plan and speculate so that the field is filled with intellectual chaos, futility and fooling people. The umma will be leaderless.' One of the threats pointed out by al-Fadhli is the Islamic State's arbitrary recruitment policy: lacking patience, they take in people without consideration of their intellectual knowledge or behaviour. This risks affecting the Jihadi group from the inside. Instead, he advises that Jihadi groups should be patient and await an enabling environment where conditions are ripe for Jihad rather than deviating from the struggle against the primary enemy. Otherwise, the group will become a victim of the 'progressive intellectual disease' (al-marad al-fikriu al-mutasa'id) promoted by al-Baghdadi and al-Adnani.

In the final part of the letter, al-Fadhli moves the focus of his criticism towards al-Qaida itself, since he believes that the passivity of the leadership has had a major impact on the rapid rise of the Islamic State and its ability to mobilise the youth.

> Now, the third generation of the mujahedeen is influenced by the ideas of the State. This matter was caused by many reasons such as the power of the media of the State but also because

> of the silence of the leaderships of al-Qaida. The organisation appeared as weak while the State had a louder voice through the speeches of al-Adnani. The silence of the leaders of al-Qaida and the fact of not showing the mistakes in the methodology of the State pushed the youth towards the State. The truth is now lost to the deadly silence of the jihadi movement.

Al-Fadhli concludes his criticism by saying that the mujahideen 'are going to pay a very high price' for this.

Al-Fadhli's attack is arguably more serious for al-Qaida than the ones from al-Qahtani and al-Tartusi since it comes from a very senior figure inside the group. Al-Fadhli's criticism mainly addresses the leadership and their lack of public communication to counter the Islamic State; he specifically mentions speeches being postponed as a problem. Although it was the radio silence from al-Zawahiri from April 11–May 23, 2013 that had the most severe negative impact, in 2014 the al-Qaida leader also did not make his views known sufficiently strongly. This would dramatically change in 2015–17, however. A major issue for al-Zawahiri in responding to the unfolding events in Syria and Iraq in 2014 was—as mentioned above—the internal problems in al-Qaida media centres; there was also his personal security situation, which was probably the reason he designated al-Wuhayshi to manage the conflict in the first place. Al-Fadhli understands this and hence places responsibility for responding to the challenge of the Islamic State in the hands of al-Wuhayshi and his group in Yemen. As it turned out, al-Zawahiri would take on the leading role in a renewed discursive offensive against the Islamic State. Just two months after al-Fadhli's criticism, al-Zawahiri, in a bid to reassert his authority, started publishing a new audio/video series titled 'The Islamic Spring' which explicitly attacked al-Baghdadi and his group while extending his hands to Islamic State fighters. Furthermore, his total media output would quantitatively increase from eight public appearances in 2014 to nine in 2015, eighteen in 2016, and ten in 2017, and qualitatively shift to focus on the deviancy of the Islamic State.

# 6

# DIVERGING ATTITUDES

The internal worries within al-Qaida in the spring and summer of 2014 were not unfounded. It was becoming evident that the Islamic State was rapidly gaining popularity, especially as it was conquering territory. The group's behaviour was clearly related to its ideology, but it is imperative that we also consider its actions from the perspective of the increasingly competitive environment within the SJM. Arguably the most important factor in the Islamic State's initial success in mobilisation was its ability to enact what it said it would. Over the years, al-Qaida had developed a discourse of anti-imperialism and opposition to the impact of the corruption of Western culture, while also suggesting that the final solution for the umma is the establishment of a state or caliphate. But al-Qaida never suggested a tangible process for how this objective should be reached and, in fact, became increasingly hesitant to establish a state-like entity. Around 2013, al-Qaida made a lot of noise via speeches and statements but hardly delivered except through rare terrorist attacks.[1] This mismatch between words and action is not a new issue within al-Qaida.[2] Vahid Brown has described tensions between what he calls 'brand managers' and 'bureaucrats' within the group, with the former focusing on the group's brand while the latter prioritises building an effective organisation. According to Brown, brand managers often won the battle.[3] Indicative of this internal tension are stories that circulated about how AQAP members began to follow al-Zarqawi rather than al-Qaida's senior leadership simply because they considered his strategy more effective.[4]

The Islamic State's behaviour was to a large extent political symbolism based on a conscious strategy and was intended to support its mobilisation and ranking vis-à-vis other Jihadi (and rebel) groups. In 1917, between the February and October revolutions, the Mensheviks and Bolsheviks competed in a similar way; the latter group succeeded in recruiting large numbers of disaffected Mensheviks because it convinced people that it was more likely to defend the government against counter-revolutionary forces.[5] A similar *persuasion process* occurred in 2013–14 to the advantage of the Islamic State, who identified a major mobilisation potential in choosing a strategy which was characterised by tangible action and which involved the establishment of the caliphate, erasing state borders and employing a more violent approach.

### *The Caliphate and Sanctification*

On June 29, 2014, in a speech entitled 'This is the Promise of Allah', the Islamic State spokesperson al-Adnani declared the restoration of the fallen caliphate. This new state was cemented five days later when al-Baghdadi climbed the pulpit of the great al-Nuri mosque in Mosul. This was the culmination of the group's state project that started back in Herat in 1999 with al-Zarqawi's mini society; it is also a clear illustration of the group's level of ambition. One way to view the caliphate is as a religious obligation, but perhaps of equal importance in understanding the state project and its symbolism are its effects in terms of authority and mobilisation. As time has shown, the establishment of the caliphate initially seemed to be a clever political move, playing on Muslim political symbolism[6] and ideas of the sacred.[7] Across the Muslim ideological spectrum, and particularly among Jihadis, the caliphate has an unparalleled status, and any Islamist or Jihadi would argue that it is their ultimate political objective. Claiming to re-enact the caliphate was thus a central way for the Islamic State to enhance its own legitimacy by sanctifying its state project (and the group itself more broadly)—especially since this involved an implicit denunciation of the legitimacy of other groups. It would also enable a certain approach towards other Jihadis that rebelled against the sacred caliphate, and eventually legitimise excommunicating them.[8]

In his speech, al-Adnani refers to the caliphate as the 'forgotten obligation'. This not only refers to how the umma in general has moved further and further away from establishing a state entity comparable to the caliphate, but it also aligns with the Islamic State's critique of al-Qaida never paying enough attention to state creation.[9] On the same day as al-Baghdadi rose to the pulpit, the Islamic State launched its magazine *Dabiq* with the first issue dealing with 'the return of the Khilafah.' In one article, the group explained the tangible process it followed to create the caliphate, consisting of five stages: (1) Hijra, (2) Jama'a (group), (3) Destabilise the taghut (tyrant), (4) Tamkin (consolidation) and (5) Khilafa.[10] By contrast, al-Qaida never offered a similar roadmap outlining how the caliphate, the final objective, would be reached, for the simple reason that it had none. This should not be taken to imply that al-Qaida is less revolutionary or less focused on establishing an Islamic society. Nonetheless it does provide insight into the differences in identity and strategy between the two groups.

Turki al-Binali was—once again—the main voice providing the religious justification for the caliphate declaration and the ideological foundation for al-Adnani's speech. In August 2013, long before the declaration, Binali issued an important booklet entitled *Extend Your Hands to Give Bay'a to al-Baghdadi* (mudd al-ayadi li-bay'at al-baghdadi).[11] The booklet is significant because it describes al-Baghdadi's characteristics in order to justify his future role as a caliph. In it, al-Binali establishes al-Baghdadi's intellectual background, his lineage and the qualifications he has that are prerequisites for leadership.[12] With the growing confusion raging among Jihadis in the Levant at the time, it was important to settle the matter of al-Baghdadi's credentials; this was also a necessary step to legitimise the eventual declaration of the caliphate. A few months before the declaration, al-Binali issued another booklet with a similar objective. This time it addressed the issue of territorial consolidation, with al-Binali arguing that *full consolidation* (al-tamkin al-kamil) was *not* a requirement. With reference to historical political entities in Islam such as the Abbasid caliphate, he stresses that full control over territory is not necessary for the foundation of an Islamic state as this will come over time; he also puts forward a legal argument that al-Baghdadi's group fulfils the requirements to declare a caliphate.[13]

Current academic and intellectual discourse does not subscribe to the idea that the Islamic State is actually a state or caliphate. However, I will argue that taking this idea seriously is necessary for understanding the group, its sources of authority and the logic of its behaviour. The declaration of the caliphate was a major event if only because of the historic connotations at play, but to appreciate fully the significance of the Islamic State's declaration and its effects on the SJM, we must also regard it as an example of sanctification. The importance of the sacred has already been studied implicitly or explicitly by several authors, who have produced different understandings of what it is and what it can tell us. As in the study of terrorism, the sacred can be a more helpful prism to study intra-Jihadi dynamics than religion. Francis defines the sacred as 'a thing, place, time, or concept that is special and non-negotiable, and that is separated or protected from everyday ideas. It is directly and indirectly expressed in ideas and values that are seen to be core or essential to identities and beliefs.'[14] There should be no doubt that the Islamic State considered it a religious obligation to establish the caliphate, but the caliphate remains much more than a political entity as it is first and foremost a powerful political symbol—something sacred and non-negotiable—not just within the SJM but more broadly among the Muslim masses. The establishment of the caliphate thus needs to be viewed as a process to institutionalise power and authority, one which had a critical impact on the intra-SJM power balance and the group's ability to exercise symbolic power, attract funding and mobilise recruits. The practical effect of this becomes evident when looking at the leaked Islamic State foreign fighter files, where a sharp rise in fighters joining the Islamic State can be observed from mid-2014, around the time of the declaration (see figure 6).

Figure 6: Fighter Entries to the Caliphate by Month, January 2011–January 2015

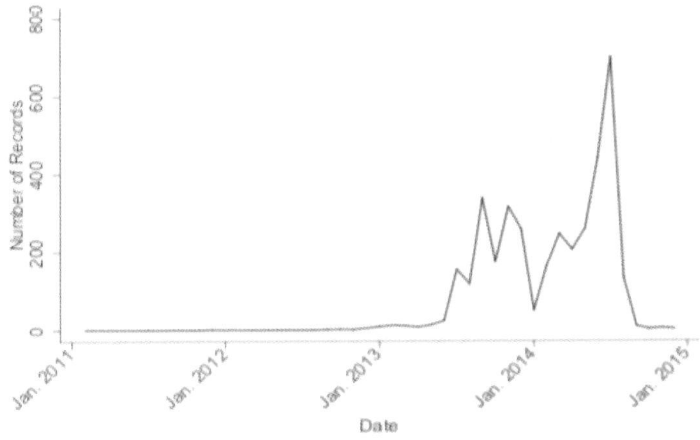


Laying claim to a sacred symbol of this kind offers great potential benefits, as explained by Günther and Kaden. They argue that the Islamic State can be viewed as both 'a sociopolitical movement and a de facto state with different sources of authority and means of power pertaining to each of these two roles.'[15] By purporting to be not just a state but the caliphate, the Islamic State has sought to obtain the authority inherent in the concept and its sacredness. However, success in such an endeavour is always dependent on one's sacred authority being perceived as legitimate.[16]

The Taliban's Mullah Umar claimed the title of *amir al-mu'minin* (commander of the believers) in spring 1996 when he allegedly climbed onto the roof of The Shrine of the Cloak in Kandahar, wrapping himself in the prophet's cloak.[17] Al-Baghdadi acted in a less dramatic way when he ascended the pulpit in the al-Nuri mosque and accepted the title of caliph of the caliphate which had been announced five days earlier. But the idea was the same: to claim authority and sanctify his group. Preparing the way for this declaration, the Islamic State made heavy use of its media apparatus, in addition to official speeches and statements made by senior group members. For example, from August 2013 to March 2014, its al-Itisam Media foundation, which mainly focused on religious matters, ran a series entitled 'A Window Upon the Land of Epic Battles', which provided a view into the soon-to-be caliphate, while in the immediate period after the caliphate declaration, the focus shifted to strengthening the legitimacy of the caliphate and of al-Baghdadi, now Khalifa Ibrahim, framing him as a warrior and a scholar in the image of Bin Laden. In terms of territory, the Islamic State adopted a dual strategy: a tangible focus on conquering, consolidating, and expanding territory, balanced with a more symbolic process of undoing un-Islamic divisions of Muslim land. The Islamic State's desire to capture and control territory is summed up in its infamous slogan *baqiyya wa tatamaddad* (remaining and expanding). Zelin has described the group's approach to territory as a structured process consisting of five phases (intelligence, military, da'wa, hisba and governance) which occur both before territorial control is obtained (pre-territorial) and afterwards (post-territorial).[18]

Focusing on the group's efforts at governance, al-Tamimi has shed light on its comprehensive state apparatus designed to govern the caliphate and its subjects and legitimise its claim to be a state.[19] More symbolically, the Islamic State launched a campaign to erase internationally imposed borders between Syria and Iraq, known as the Sykes–Picot. On the same day that al-Adnani announced the caliphate, the group published two videos entitled 'The End of Sykes–Picot'[20] and 'The Breaking of the Borders'.[21] These showed fighters demolishing the border, with the second video featuring a sequence in which al-Adnani and Umar al-Shishani explain the religious rationale behind the action. Through this idea of transforming territorial borders according to the global nature of the umma, the Islamic State certainly aligned its actions with its ideology. It also played on anti-imperialist symbolism, which held political resonance far outside the SJM.

As has already been mentioned, another important feature of the caliphate is that it implied a challenge to all other Jihadi groups, and it should thus be seen as a clear attempt to monopolise authority within the SJM. In his declaration speech, al-Adnani stipulates that al-Baghdadi 'is the imam and khalifa for the Muslims everywhere (…) it is incumbent upon all Muslims to pledge allegiance to the Khalifa Ibrahim and support him. The legality of all emirates, groups, states, and organisations, becomes null by the expansion of the khilafa's authority and arrival of its troops to their areas.' A similar message is conveyed in its *Dabiq* magazine where the author writes,

> The Islamic State—on account of what Allah has blessed it with of victory, consolidation and establishing the religion—is regarded as an unquestionable imamah. As such, anyone who rebels against its authority inside its territory is considered a renegade, and it is permissible to fight him after establishing the *hujjah* (proof) against him.[22]

These two statements clearly illustrate the importance the Islamic State attached to its caliphate establishment and its hierarchical relationship to other Jihadi groups. The Islamic State argued that the caliphate would have a pacifying influence on the SJM, citing the Qur'an 8:73:

> And those who disbelieve are allies of one another, (and) if you (Muslims of the whole world collectively) do not do so (i.e. become allies, as one united block under one Khalifah to make victorious Allah's religion of Islamic Monotheism), there will be fitnah and oppression on the earth, and a great mischief and corruption (appearance of polytheism).

Yet in fact, the caliphate turned out to have the opposite effect, polarising relations between the groups in the SJM even more.

It is difficult to overestimate the importance of the caliphate declaration for the standing of the Islamic State in the SJM and its impact on the logic of the movement. Along with the conquest of Mosul three weeks before, the caliphate represents the Islamic State's '9/11 moment'—the one that catapulted the group to the top of the Jihadi hierarchy just as had happened to al-Qaida 13 years before. Although the attacks against the US in 2001 were opposed by the majority of the al-Qaida leadership, and most likely by the majority of Jihadis regardless of their group affiliation, the attack placed Bin Laden and his group as the most influential Jihadi group and laid the groundwork for future expansion through affiliations. For many Jihadis and people in search of a revolutionary cause, the caliphate provided a much needed narrative that was less ideologically complex and more tangible and action-oriented than al-Qaida's ideology.[23] Although the Islamic State had already attracted substantial numbers of locals and foreigners to fight under its banner prior to the caliphate declaration, testimonies from the field confirm that the caliphate positively impacted the group's mobilisation.[24] This effectively transformed the SJM from an *intellectual movement* to a *popular movement*.[25]

### *Al-Qaida's Gradualist Approach*

The caliphate posed a direct challenge to all other Jihadi groups and individuals by forcing them either to pledge allegiance or be considered enemies. It appears that most rank and file fighters in Syria were attracted by the newly established caliphate; however, the reaction among Jihadi ideologues and sympathisers, established groups such as al-Qaida, and the wider Muslim world was more sceptical. Ideologues such as Muhammad ibn Saleh al-Muhajir, Abu Muhammad al-Maqdisi, Abu Qatada, Iyad al-Qunaybi, Abdullah al-Muhaysini, Hani al-Sibai, Tariq Abdulhaleem and Ahrar al-Sham's Abu Abdulmalik all published critical articles denouncing not the caliphate *per se* but the Islamic State's *claim* to represent the caliphate. The most substantial of these pieces are those of al-Muhajir[26] and Abu Qatada.[27] Al-Muhajir claimed that the Islamic State's process of establishing the caliphate is illegitimate because it is based on *oppression* (qahr) and *domination* (ghalaba). In his booklet *The Cloak of the Khalifah*, Abu Qatada called it a caliphate based upon *falsehood* (batil) and connected its deviance to the infiltration of ideas from the historical Jama'at al-Khilafa[28] group and to the intellectual impact of extremists and religious newcomers. The caliphate also led al-Maqdisi to escalate his criticism of the group because he believes it is fragmenting rather than uniting the Mujahideen; provocatively, he asks why no knowledgeable scholar has joined it. Al-Zawahiri's own response was to establish a new al-Qaida affiliate in the Indian Subcontinent (AQIS), probably with the dual purpose of signalling strength and as a security measure to protect al-Qaida's network in Southeast Asia should al-Zawahiri himself be killed. In the statement announcing the affiliate he asserts that 'Unity is a blessing and mercy, and discord is a curse and torment (...)The punishment of differences and discord is failure and vanishing of power (...) O mujahideen, unite and reject differences and discord'. In the following months, statements were issued by AQIM, AQAP and the newly created AQIS criticising the Islamic State's caliphate, offering advice on how to settle the conflict and giving their support to al-Zawahiri.[29]

Around the time of the caliphate declaration, the Islamic State escalated its use of violence, both as a mode of governance and to distinguish itself from competing Jihadi groups. In June the group carried out the Camp Speicher massacre, killing more than a thousand Iraqi Shia cadets; this was followed by the Yazidi genocide in August and the group's campaign of beheading Western hostages, resembling the beheadings carried out by al-Zarqawi's AQI. Raqqa's Al-Naeem square was turned into an arena for public executions, one which calls to mind the opening paragraph of Foucault's *Discipline and Punish*.[30] The audiences for these brutal actions are many, not least the media and other Jihadis to whom the Islamic State wanted to send the message that it was the protector of Sunnis. Whether the Islamic State eventually realised the unintended consequences of institutionalising such violence, or simply acted as a means to centralise violence, the group allegedly issued a circular prohibiting its fighters from publishing scenes of extreme brutality without the permission of one of the group's committees.[31] As Girard has noted, however, violence is easier to arouse than to lessen.[32] What initially was a strategic success for the Islamic State in terms of gaining attention would later become one of the main reasons that the group drew opposition from the international community and from other groups within the SJM—something which neatly illustrates the interconnectedness of the macro-, meso- and micro-levels.

The Islamic State's caliphate declaration, its enforcement of shari'a through its elaborate governance structures and its reliance on extreme violence stood in stark contrast to the strategy pursued by al-Qaida. This provided al-Qaida with an opportunity to showcase these differences and effectively change the general perception of the group. In political theory, the *Overton window* refers to the range of ideas that the public is willing to accept.[33] Interestingly, until the emergence of the Islamic State, al-Qaida was generally perceived to be too extreme, but with an even more extreme proponent of indiscriminate violence on the scene, al-Qaida found a platform to realign itself with the ideas introduced by Bin Laden back in 2010; it could now not only win the sympathy of (potential) Jihadis but also influence its public image in the Muslim world and international society.

One should definitely be careful about defining al-Qaida too homogenously in terms of the group's methodology as there are differences across countries.[34] Yet within al-Qaida, Jabhat al-Nusra in particular has received attention because of how its strategy contrasts with that of the Islamic State.[35] In the words of one al-Nusra member, 'Al-Qaeda in Syria has put much of its efforts into gaining local support and integration with the Muslim community of Syria. They rooted themselves into the community instead of alienating and excluding themselves from the Muslim community.'[36] The idea was, in the words of another al-Qaida insider, that 'you are able to get people supporting al-Qaida without them knowing.'[37] Lister has described al-Nusra's strategy as a long game strategy and as showing a development from 'Elitist Jihad' to 'Mass Jihad',[38] while Abu Rumman says al-Nusra represents 'the soft face of al-Qaida' after its transformation in the post-Arab Spring period.[39] Another way to phrase it is that al-Nusra focused on *minding interests and avoiding spoilers* (riayat al-maslaha wa mani' al-mafasid).[40] But as I have discussed in chapter 4, this transformation in fact occurred before the Arab Spring, when al-Qaida started to realise that it was losing the Arab street.

Previous work on al-Qaida has largely seen the group as a terrorist actor and has paid little attention to this strategic shift. Following the Islamic State's caliphate declaration, there has been more of a focus on explaining the strategic differences between the two groups, but this has rarely gone further than concluding that the differences were best understood as representations of the theories of Abu Musab al-Suri and Abu Bakr Naji respectively. The argument goes that al-Qaida follows the strategy laid out by al-Suri in his magnum opus *The Global Islamic Resistance Call*, while the Islamic State focused on controlling territory and state creation, as promoted by Naji in his *Management of Savagery*. This remains a misleading characterisation, however: a closer reading of the two strategists suggests that both groups rely on certain elements in their respective strategies; it is telling, also, that Jihadis themselves reject the claim that this division between al-Suri and Naji reveals much about the strategic differences between al-Qaida and the Islamic State.[41] Al-Qaida-aligned figures have also argued that Naji's strategy is misunderstood if it is aligned with the approach of the Islamic State, since, in the words of an al-Qaida supporter, *Management of Savagery*

> talks about managing the coming stage of savagery, and not creating this stage of savagery. The writer Abu Bakr Naji merely calculates this stage. When, not if, the corrupt (world) powers fall, Islam will replace it gradually. We have seen this many times before in history. Abu Bakr Naji advises the readers on how to prepare for this transition.[42]

Furthermore, al-Suri and Naji's works were developed in a post-9/11 security context which has since changed considerably, making al-Suri's work in particular less relevant as an all-encompassing strategy.

The key difference is in the attitude towards taking territory and governing it. The Islamic State relies on a strategy of *taghallub* (overpowering) and *tamkin* (consolidation) and the immediate implementation of its interpretation of shari'a, while al-Qaida believes in a step-by-step approach that allows for pragmatism and the outsourcing of governance.[43] As anyone familiar with talking to Jihadi ideologues will know, they like talking in metaphors. In a discussion with a Jihadi ideologue closely affiliated with al-Qaida, he stated that Jihadis 'need a strong base to create the caliphate. It is like building a house. You need a solid foundation to support the construction and then you put bricks on it one after the other. Daesh [the Islamic State] is not ensuring a strong foundation.'[44] This image is illustrative of the disconnect between al-Qaida and the Islamic State, with the former prioritising a less imposing and more facilitating approach to ensure the durability of its revolutionary project.

### *Challenging Authority*

Another central dimension of the authority challenge has been a discursive contestation between (senior) members and sympathisers of the two groups. In his analysis, Michels highlights different sources of internal conflict, including fault lines based on generational gaps, nationality, and personal factors, all of which are pertinent to the SJM.[45] But as Michel also notes, fault lines based on these different factors are always framed through more 'legitimate' differences such as ideology, strategy, or tactics. From the beginning the conflict has been framed as a *war between truth and falsehood* (harb been al-haqq wa-l-batil), between *extremism* (ghuluw) and being too *religiously moderate* (the word used is *murjia*), with both groups claiming to adhere to the *prophetic methodology* (al-manhaj al-nubuwwa). This discursive contestation has relied on a diverse range of framing strategies such as *vilification* (demonising competing popular intellectuals), *decredentialling* (raising questions about the expertise of rivals), *exaltation* (praising popular in-group intellectuals) and *credentialling* (emphasising the expertise of the in-group intellectuals)[46] These strategies have been employed to attack the opponent while praising one's own group. Name-calling is also prominent; the Islamic State uses labels such as *murji'a*, *Jabhat al-Julani* (Julani Front), *Tanzim al-Qaida* (the al-Qaida organisation) and *Jabhat al-Riddah* (Apostate Front) to refer to al-Qaida. In the terminology of al-Qaida supporters, the Islamic State are *Kilab al-Narr* (dogs of hellfire), *Tanzim al-Dawla* (the state organisation), *'Usabat al-Baghdadi* (gang of Baghdadi), khawarij and *Jama'at al-Baghdadi* (Baghdadi group). Similarly, Ahrar al-Sham is typically referred to as *Ashrar al-Sham* (the evil ones of al-Sham) by the Islamic State.

### *Al-Mubahala*

One of the first examples of discursive contestation between representatives of al-Qaida and the Islamic State is the curious case of *al-mubahala* (invoking God's curse) between Islamic State spokesperson al-Adnani and senior Jabhat al-Nusra shar'i Abu Abdullah al-Shami. This had the aim of strengthening the authority of one group at the expense of the other. The concept of mubahala derives from the verb to curse (bahala) and has its origin in the Quran and a hadith. The story goes that in year ten after hijra, from Mecca to Yathrib (Medina), the Prophet Muhammed met with a Christian delegation from Najran (Yemen). Disagreeing about the divinity of Jesus Christ, Muhammed allegedly challenged the Christian delegation with a mubahala, leaving it to God to decide whose religion was true. This challenge is mentioned in the Quran 3:61 which states that God's curse will fall upon the liar. The notion's origin in Islamic tradition and holy scripture makes it legitimate and powerful in the eyes of Jihadis. But invoking the mubahala was also a strategic move by al-Adnani because it offered the Islamic State time to prove its project, since God's judgement rarely strikes right away.

The mubahala challenge was issued by al-Adnani in a statement in early March 2014, but it was provoked by a statement from al-Shami a few days earlier.[47] Al-Shami's statement is an elaborate attack on the Islamic State, mentioning the transgressions of the group against other Jihadi groups, its refusal to accept arbitration and its extremism in takfir, which—he argues—makes them similar to the Khawarij. Al-Adnani refuses all these accusations, turning them around by saying that it is in fact the Islamic State that has been the victim of these transgressions carried out by other groups.[48] The mubahala is thus al-Adnani's attempt to reject the idea that the Islamic State refuses arbitration by arguing that only God should be the judge rather than potentially biased people. It took al-Shami more than three months to respond, but in a statement released on 30 June, he hesitantly accepted the mubahala. Such a means to settle a conflict, he says, should only be used in important shar'i matters where no other solutions exist,[49] but as a refusal would be interpreted as a victory for the Islamic State, he had little choice. In a lengthy article in its *Dabiq* magazine, the Islamic State subsequently laid out some of its arguments as to why it is right and the conditions for the challenge, which included a time limit: within one year from the mubahala the result would be known.[50] Judging from the military success of the Islamic State in spring 2015 and its general popularity within the SJM vis-à-vis al-Qaida, there was arguably little doubt about the 'winner' of the challenge, although al-Adnani's death a year later in August 2016 was celebrated by al-Qaida figures as a clear victory and interpreted as God's punishment.

Leaving the matter of the actual 'winner' aside, the mubahala is interesting as one of the early manifestations of the contest for legitimacy and authority that would take centre stage within the SJM in the years to come. The conflict within the movement would eventually develop into a *war of ideas*, but at this stage it was still a *war of narratives*, and the mubahala was essentially geared towards winning legitimacy for one's own version of events in a critically transformative period. The Islamic State's military success undoubtedly helped it win popularity, but the more important dimension from an intra-movement perspective was the struggle to be considered the most correct group in terms of creed and methodology. This struggle would play out both on a meso- and a micro-level, the former referring to group and group leader discourses and the latter referring to group sympathisers and independent ideologues publicising multiple statements criticising the opponent group and its members.

### *The Islamic State as the Modern Khawarij: Teachers Versus Students*

Statements made by al-Qaida-affiliated and Islamic State-affiliated figures in 2014 offer similarly interesting insights into the sources of the conflict and how it is framed, even if these two dimensions are hard to distinguish at times. Especially interesting is how each camp uses certain strategies to delegitimise the other side. Al-Adnani's speeches are one example of such vilification; they focus on the alleged methodological deviance and loss of authority of al-Zawahiri. Two other themes also characterised early discursive contestation: *extremism in creed* and a *generational gap*. The aim of this section is not to analyse the truthfulness of the claims made by the different actors, but to focus on how arguments are used as a means of legitimisation/delegitimisation.

Zald and Useem have described strategies that movements can use to raise the mobilisation cost of countermovements. Among these are to tarnish the opponent's image. Arguably the central issue of discursive contestation between the Islamic State and opposing Jihadi groups surrounds the notion of the al-Khawarij (seceders), with other groups accusing the Islamic State of being a modern manifestation of this historical Islamic sect. This debate is not new and the way labels have been applied as delegitimising markers has been described by several authors, most importantly Wagemakers and Lav.[51] In his work on debates related to the theology of faith, Lav writes that the accusation of kharijism is used as a conscious method 'to portray the radicals as renegade groups who have rebelled against legitimate authority, separated themselves from the religious community, and pronounced takfir on other Muslims.'[52] The meaning of the notion has also been thoroughly described by academic scholars and Muslims, including Jihadis. Al-khawarij, or al-haruriyyah/muhakkima, refers to ancient Islamic sects[53] that initially became infamous for killing Ali, the fourth caliph after the prophet Muhammed, due to Ali's acceptance of arbitration in his conflict with Muawiya.[54] Unsurprisingly, this made the Khawarij hugely unpopular within the Muslim community due to their alleged extremism; this is why, in modern times, it is a term often used to vilify opponents. As such it is not the first time that Jihadis have been accused of being khawarij,[55] and though Lahoud illustrates the obvious differences between the original Khawarij and modern Jihadis, it continues to be applied as a tactic of delegitimisation.[56]

Likely because they have been accused of being khawarij on several occasions, Jihadi scholars have also written extensively about the topic. More elaborate pieces include a 200-page book by Abu Hamza al-Masri authored in 2000, and a fifty-page study by Hussain Ibn Mahmoud in 2014. As Wagemakers has explained, within the Salafi movement a debate between quietists and Jihadis has centred on the labels of al-khawarij and al-murji'a (postponers), with the latter term generally being applied by Jihadis to delegitimise someone for being too *moderate* due to their reliance on *irja* (postponement). According to Wagemakers, postponement is applied

> to the judgement over Muslims' faith, leaving this decision to God instead. The murji'a refrained from labelling sinful acts as kufr, as long as Muslims did not verbally confirm their sinful intention behind such acts, and they even seem to have applied this reasoning to allegedly clear acts of polytheism, such as idol-worshipping.[57]

This trend allegedly emerged as a reaction to the Khawarij; it later fragmented into several factions, with a common factor being their refusal to make takfir (excommunication).[58] Although there is a debate about whether the khawarij and murji'a should be considered Muslims or unbelievers (*kuffar*), the majority position is that neither has fallen into apostasy despite their clear deviance. Hence, applying the labels of khawarij and murji'a is a method to delegitimise a group or an individual or even license fighting against them without the use of takfir.[59] In the early phases of the intra-SJM conflict, it was mainly actors opposed to the Islamic State that instrumentalised the use of vilifying labels as a reaction to the actions and accusations of the group. However, the Islamic State itself would eventually use labels such as murji'a, *sahawat* (literally 'awakening' but referring to government allied groups) and *murtadd* (apostate) to describe opposing groups and individuals.

The first Jihadi ideologues to label the Islamic State as khawarij were Abu Basir al-Tartusi, Hani al-Sibai and Tariq Abdelhaleem in early 2014, followed by Abu Qatada later that year. While the ideologues offer different arguments, their agenda remains fairly similar—to delegitimise the group or, in some cases, to legitimise attacking it. Al-Tartusi wrote in January that the Islamic State has outdone the Khawarij in terms of their extremism, oppression, aggression and spilling of innocent blood. If they do not correct their deviance, they ought to be fought.[60] In a statement made two months later his position had hardened. Comparing the group to the historic Khawarij, he concluded that the Islamic State is worse, and that no one should be allowed to question this characterisation or the necessity of fighting them.[61] For al-Sibai and Abdelhaleem, the tipping point was al-Adnani's speech which

> made it clear beyond any doubt when he declared war against all Jihadi groups and mujahadeen who were not part of their organisation, and their ideology that completely coincides and is in alignment with that of the khawarij in spilling the blood of mujahedeen based on false premises and ridiculous suspicions. Despite the vast differences between ISIS and the Haruriyyah and Khawarij of the past, since the people of ISIS are not a people of courage, knowledge, eloquence nor prowess like Khawarij, yet they matched the Khawarij in their worst characterisation which is legitimising the bloodshed of Muslims.[62]

The two ideologues reject the idea that the characteristics of the Islamic State and the historic Khawarij need to correspond in all respects; the crucial point is that they share an essential 'common principle.'[63] The starting point for Abu Qatada was the Islamic State's caliphate declaration; he based his labelling of the group as khawarij on the argument that it makes takfir on people who simply disagree with them and do not support the caliphate.[64] Other influential ideologues opposed to the Islamic State would eventually follow suit and label the group as khawarij.[65]

One exception was Abu Muhammad al-Maqdisi, who remained more cautious. In June 2015 he explained that the reason he abstained from using the khawarij label is that he only considers the leaders of the groups to be khawarij, while many among the rank and file fighters are not. Labelling the group as khawarij has the purpose of attacking the group and that, he claims, only serves the interest of the mujahideen's enemies. Al-Maqdisi is explicit that he does not criticise other ideologues for applying the label, but since he considers the apostate enemy the greater enemy, he refuses to be pressured into doing so himself.[66] Despite criticism,[67] al-Maqdisi did not change his view, reiterating it the following March when he claimed that unlike the Khawarij, the Islamic State has the good intention of implementing—rather than rebelling against—the law of God; the fact that this implementation may be misguided does not imply that the groups are similar.[68] Al-Maqdisi's position left his entourage in a somewhat awkward situation, with Abu al-Izz al-Najdi, a member of l-Maqdisi's Minbar al-Tawhid wa-l-Jihad's shari'a council, issuing a fatwa on the question whether the Islamic State was in fact khawarij. Al-Najdi referred diplomatically to the opinion of the majority of Jihadi scholars but emphasised that the view of al-Maqdisi has been made public, thus avoiding an actual judgement.[69]

How the khawarij should be characterised remains a topic of debate. In his study, Ibn Mahmoud lists three historical positions. The first is held by Abu al-Hasan al-Ashari and argues that the Khawarij were the ones rebelling against Ali. The second is held by Muhammad al-Shahrastani, who claimed that the khawarij are those who rebel against *any* legitimate ruler. The third position is that of Ibn Hazm, who added additional criteria to the position of al-Shahrastani.

According to Ibn Hazm, the khawarij are those who make takfir based on major sins (*kabira*),[70] who rejected arbitration between Ali and Muawiya, and who accept a non-Qurayshi as imam.[71] This gave the Islamic State some room for manoeuvre in its response, which mainly came from Turki al-Binali. In one piece addressing al-Tartusi's January statement, al-Binali ridiculed the accusations, noting how similar they are to the accusations originally levelled against Muhammed Abd al-Wahhab. In this way he compared the Islamic State's project to that of al-Wahhab who is a revered figure within the SJM.[72] In another statement, al-Binali placed the Islamic State between the *extremism of the Khawarij* (using the term 'ghulat al-mukaffira') and *extremism of the Murji'a* (ghulat al-murjia), indicating that it takes a 'moderate' middle ground position.[73]

The second prominent theme in the initial struggle for authority is an alleged generational gap between al-Qaida and the Islamic State which started to receive attention because young Jihadi ideologues broke with their former mentors. That younger figures rise and challenge their superiors is not uncommon, however. Michels describes this dynamic in the context of non-religious democratic parties,[74] while Marty and Appleby draw a similar conclusion in the context of Islamist movements.[75] Historically, this tendency can also be observed within the SJM. In the 1990s, it was reported that the elements within al-Qaida who applied pressure to execute the 9/11 attacks were younger individuals going against the opinion of established leaders.[76] The rebellious youth of the amirs of GIA, ranging from twenty-six to thirty-two years old at the time of taking charge of the group, is another example.[77]

Since we lack a database on Jihadis covering different time periods and groups, quantitative study of the demography of group members remains challenging. That Islamic State members are, on average, younger than those of al-Qaida is impossible to validate, though it appears likely, not least because the group managed to attract the vast majority of new Jihadis joining the conflict in Syria and Iraq. Many arguably joined because the Islamic State through its military success had positioned itself as the strongest Jihadi brand at the time, but the successful recruitment of the youth was also the result of its propaganda productions that were particularly alluring for the youth due to their high quality and reliance on violence.[78] From the approximately 700 documents uncovered in Iraq in 2007, known as the *Sinjar Documents*, we know that the average age of foreign fighters joining AQI was 24–25 years old.[79] Newer documents coming from the Islamic State, covering the period 2013–14 and referring to 3,581–4,188 individuals, show that the average age of foreign fighters in this period rose to 26–27 years old.[80] But using this data to argue that there is a *generation gap* between the Islamic State and other Jihadi groups, including al-Qaida, is problematic for several reasons, the most important being that we do not have data on other groups to compare it with. Perhaps al-Qaida-affiliated groups have in fact been equally good at recruiting youth despite not receiving the same publicity. Too much attention has been given to the young age of Turki al-Binali when he emerged as one of the main ideological voices within the Islamic State. Al-Binali's age (he was 29 years old in 2013–14) has been used to illustrate the youth of Islamic State leaders, but other senior figures like al-Adnani, al-Baghdadi and al-Anbari were not markedly younger than senior al-Qaida figures.

One way to tackle this issue is to look at how the actors themselves have approached the debate that has been characterised by strategies of vilification and decredentialling opponent ideologues.[81] Younger scholars siding with the Islamic State[82] such as Turki al-Binali, Abu al-Mundhir al-Shinqiti and Umar Mahdi Zaydan immediately sought to legitimise breaking with former mentors, and simultaneously criticised them for not joining the caliphate. All three were connected to al-Maqdisi—the first two because they were members of his shari'a council, and Zaydan through his links to the militant community in Jordan that remains dominated by al-Maqdisi. Breaking from him thus represented a severe fragmentation of scholarly unity. This was legitimised by Zaydan himself in an audio statement where he praises his peers for going against the deviant al-Maqdisi.[83] But it is al-Binali's 2013–14 writings in particular that were integral to this process. From late 2013 to mid-2014, he authored several important statements in response to criticism from Jihadi authorities and rival groups[84] and as a means to affect the Jihadi masses.[85]

Al-Binali's first targets were the ideologues al-Tartusi[86] and al-Qunaybi.[87] While important figures in the SJM, they were not among the most senior, but their opposition nonetheless led al-Binali to issue an audio statement calling for Jihadi 'ulama to come out in support of the Islamic State.[88] This call was most likely intended for Abu Qatada and al-Maqdisi, but as both ideologues shortly afterwards issued increasingly critical statements about the Islamic State, al-Binali eventually directed his anger against them, albeit in slightly different ways. In his response to Abu Qatada, al-Binali underlines the respect he has for him and how he is unwilling to discredit him entirely, arguably leaving open the door for Abu Qatada to shift sides (surely also because the Jordanian would be a powerful enemy). He thus presents two factors mitigating Abu Qatada's recent verbal attacks: that he was coerced by the Jordanian intelligence and that he is unaware of the *reality* (waqi') of the Islamic State due to all the misinformation he has received. As a result, Abu Qatada should be conceived as a *mixed sheikh* (al-sheikh al-mukhtala), meaning that his earlier statements and fatwas should be considered legitimate but that his most recent ones—those criticising the Islamic State—were illustrative of his later deviation.[89]

It was possibly even more sensitive when al-Binali directed his criticism towards his former mentor al-Maqdisi, but in June 2014, briefly before the caliphate declaration, al-Binali issued a long rebuttal of al-Maqdisi's recent proposal for reconciliation. The thirty-seven-page tract entitled *my former sheikh* (sheikhi al-asbaq) begins with al-Binali stressing his own surprise that he is now authoring a response to his former mentor and the person whom he previously praised. Yet according to al-Binali, the break between the two has resulted from al-Maqdisi's deviation and backstabbing. Despite al-Binali's sending three letters to his former mentor to clarify the situation of the Islamic State—and to recruit al-Maqdisi—he was not swayed, and eventually turned against al-Binali and his group.[90] Al-Binali would further develop his criticism of al-Maqdisi in February 2015 in relation to the burning of Jordanian pilot Muadh al-Kasasbeh, falling one step short of labelling al-Maqdisi an unbeliever.[91] Around the same time, al-Binali also reacted to al-Zawahiri's criticism of the Islamic State; he argued that the al-Qaida leader's primary purpose was to prove that al-Baghdadi had a legally binding pledge to al-Qaida, but that he failed to offer any proof.[92] Al-Binali's statements clearly had a decredentialling objective. For instance, he provocatively wrote of Abu Qatada that he does not understand how such an esteemed figure can go against the Islamic State, and the only explanation must be the confusion that comes with getting old.[93] In 2016–17, the Islamic State would return to this topic in its *Rumiyah* magazine: issues one, three and five deal with the issue of scholarly authority and criticise older scholars by denouncing them for not acting based on the knowledge they have.

The older guard siding with al-Qaida responded by chastising the youth for their lack of knowledge and respect while ridiculing them for secretly seeking their help. This aligned with Azzam's argument that extremism and takfir comes from a lack of knowledge, which is typical of the youth.[94] Ideologues such as Abd al-Rahman al-Jaza'iri, Abdallah ibn Ahmad al-Bun al-Husayni, Umar al-Haddouchi, Hani al-Sibai,[95] in addition to al-Maqdisi[96] and Abu Qatada[97] have all issued material commenting one way or the other on their former students, whom they undoubtedly consider their inferiors. Abu Qatada, for instance, has referred to them as *students* and *pretenders of knowledge*. At the same time, the ideologues have supported each other, and especially al-Zawahiri, amidst attacks from the youth. Perhaps this evolution was expected by the established Jihadi authorities. Al-Maqdisi, at least, has long warned about the *zealous young beginners* (al-shabab al-mutahammisin al-mubtadi'in),[98] who

> would go with the wind, exaggerate and fall into disorder. They would exaggerate too much and name things with other names and give them other descriptions (…) The honest and trustworthy were accused of disloyalty and the disloyal was entrusted. We arrived at a time when the ignorant assaulted our dignitaries when idiots insulted our scholar.[99]

### *Al-Munasirun*

Alongside the struggle between ideologues, another group of actors—Jihadi *supporters* (al-munasirun)—entered the discursive battlefield. Supporters of Jihadi groups have always voiced their opinions, but this occurred mainly on Jihadi forums which remained rather exclusive platforms. Due to the clandestine nature of Jihadism, especially in the post-9/11 environment, groups and sympathisers have always shown an impressive level of creativity in their use of communication technology. But with the emergence of new communication platforms the Islamic State and its supporters managed to implement an even more entrepreneurial approach to what may be called *unofficial communication*.[100] In 2014, many of these supporters had migrated to social media platforms like Facebook, Twitter and later Telegram, which offered a much better platform for disseminating their material and opinions. Despite many of the channels and groups on these platforms being managed by supporters who are not part of the Islamic State's *diwan al-'ilam* (media department), it has become apparent that the media department does exercise some level of control over these groups and channels. Not only does the media department push information out to munasirun channels,[101] it also gives directions on their online behaviour[102] and censors their publications.[103]

From the very beginning of the intra-Jihadi conflict, Islamic State supporters were active in promoting the new caliphate. Figures like Hussain Bin Mahmoud,[104] Abu Sa'd al-Najdi, Mustafa al-Iraqi, Abu Abdullah al-Afghani, Gharib al-Sururiyya, Abu Jarir al-Shamali and Abu Hamza al-Rumi published an abundance of statements, either promoting the Islamic State or vilifying al-Qaida and its affiliated ideologues. Although Jihadi fora were still in use at the time and functioned as distributions channels,[105] much of the supporter material was published and promoted by unofficial media foundations like al-Ghuraba,[106] al-Battar,[107] al-Baqiya and al-Wafa'[108] on Twitter and on the websites of Ansar al-Khilafa[109] and Ahl ul-Tawhid.[110] Especially widely disseminated were pieces like Abu Maysara al-Shami's 'Jews of Jihad' and Ibn Mahmoud's 'The Islamic State is a Necessity Of the Era' and 'Upon the Manhaj of Prophecy'. Besides publishing their own material, supporter channels also share official group material; this highlights the connection between the meso- and micro-level. Official group channels usually have a short time span as they are regularly deleted. This increases the importance of supporter channels.

Jihadis siding with al-Qaida were never as good at establishing an unofficial media infrastructure to share material and promote its supporters. Sympathetic media centres like Al Muwahideen Media and Maktab Khayr Umma al-Islamiyyah did exist, but the majority of material sympathetic to al-Qaida continues to be shared on platforms like justpaste.it or through personal Telegram channels which lack the support of an institution. This lack of institutional backing has been highlighted by a prominent al-Qaida supporter as problematic and as a decisive element in the Islamic State's victory in the war of narratives.[111]

This unofficial media infrastructure promoted and assisted by the Islamic State has undoubtedly been important for the spreading and periodical dominance of its narrative, but it remains challenging to assess the impact of the material. We know that statements from ideologues matter, either because they inform group behaviour or the opinion of rank and file fighters. Lacking the authority of ideologues, supporters do not command the same institutional or mobilising influence. Nonetheless, their writings play an important part in the constantly evolving narratives promoted by the different groups. Thus, they help to construct/deconstruct existing Jihadi narratives. We nonetheless need to conceptualise the relationship with munasirun as *double-sided*. On one side, the groups need them, but on the other side, they remain semi-independent voices that can only be partly controlled by the Jihadi groups themselves.

## *Conclusions*

The period from the outbreak of the Jihadi civil war in early 2014 until the end of the year was characterised by the *eruption* and *intensification of* intra-Jihadi contestation and conflict. This intensification was mainly driven by the Islamic State's aggressive military expansion, its refusal to accept arbitration to reconcile the warring parties, and the declaration of its caliphate, which imposed an entirely new (and polarising) logic on the SJM. Jihadi groups, ideologues and supporters were suddenly divided into two factions. The previous two chapters have shown how Jihadi groups from the beginning differed in their attitude to infighting; this was most evident in the diverging approaches of al-Qaida and the Islamic State. From the very beginning al-Qaida followed a unifying rationale, which manifested itself in attempts to de-escalate the conflict and facilitate reconciliation. A similar non-belligerent approach to intra-Jihadi conflict was characteristic of the group back in the 1990s, when it refused to take sides in the Afghan civil war and backed off when threatened by the GIA. For the Islamic State, on the other hand, the objective to overtake al-Qaida as a movement hegemon induced it to adopt a more aggressive posture, to take advantage of an opportune political context, and to exploit al-Qaida's vulnerable situation. The eventual culmination of this was the caliphate.

The Islamic State took advantage of the conflict dynamics in the Syrian conflict to intensify its military campaign and harnessed the extensive confusion that marked the SJM in 2013–14, especially among foreign fighters, to recruit and mobilise fighters. The group also exploited social media platforms, both through official media channels and supporters (munasirun), the latter functioning as semi-independent Jihadi media entrepreneurs. This media dominance greatly helped the group to monopolise the general Jihadi narrative and, especially in a Syrian context, to position itself as the most popular Jihadi outfit.

More generally, the period showcased the importance of individuals in the evolution of internal conflict. Even more influential than media entrepreneurs, Jihadi *ideologues* played a central role in this early stage of the conflict. In the case of the Islamic State, in-house ideological figures, most notably Turki al-Binali and his writings, articulated strong criticism of al-Qaida and senior ideological figures aligned with it; this facilitated a direct challenge to al-Qaida's leading position within the SJM and primed the escalation of conflict. Opposing ideologues, often close to al-Qaida, were not offered the same institutional position to express their criticism of the Islamic State. Acting as the main ideological bulwark against Islamic State criticism, they instead had to rely on their individual authority among the Jihadi masses.

# PART FOUR

# MOVEMENT FRAGMENTATION, POLARISATION AND INTERNATIONALISATION

*'Until now we have been brethren with the same religion and community … if the sword is used … we will be an umma and you will be an umma.'*[1]

A supporter of Hussain ibn Ali ibn Abu Talib
to a supporter of Yazid

*'We are like one body, and we are in one ship.'*[2]

Abu Khalil al-Madani
Late al-Qaida shura council member

# 7

# EXPANDING THE CALIPHATE AND AL-QAIDA'S RESPONSE

The caliphate declaration really changed everything. Analysing underground militant groups, Della Porta writes that 'As violent entrepreneurs, clandestine groups contribute to shaping their environment, as well as being shaped by it.'[3] The caliphate was a game changer that utterly reshaped the internal environment within the SJM. Although Jihadis had always debated and occasionally fought, the logic of the fitna changed entirely when al-Adnani declared al-Baghdadi to be caliph. This instigated dynamics of fragmentation and polarisation; on one side, a desire for diversification, and on the other, a need for Jihadis to place one another in boxes.

The SJM has never been one unified movement—*or* ship, as al-Madani suggests. There have always been differing interpretations of Jihad, and discussions about legitimate warfare, strategy, doctrinal matters and more. However, for the most part these issues have been contained peacefully within the broader movement, partly because of the influence of religious ideals of avoiding conflict. In late 2014, those times were over. Internal tensions and competition had already escalated to infighting, which was now about to expand from Syria to other parts of the world affected by the presence of Jihadis. Lahoud recounts how the early Khawarij reviled Ali and his supporters as

'Enemies of God, you have violated God's command', with Ali's group responding, 'You have rejected our Imam and divided our community.'[4] A similar exchange of accusations was now taking place between the Islamic State and other Jihadis, first and foremost al-Qaida.

A characteristic feature of the internal struggle was that it centred on attracting recruits and group loyalty. Despite its religious extremism, the Islamic State was arguably turning into the closest thing Jihadism has ever had to a mass movement. It managed to transcend the borders of religion and to make its group attractive not only to religious extremists but to broader segments of society.[5] This would also manifest itself in the distinctive recruitment patterns of the Islamic State and al-Qaida, which inevitably affected the evolving identity of the respective groups. In the Islamic State the recipe was quantity over quality. Most interested recruits were accepted; once inside, socialisation and indoctrination would begin. As every student of business knows, if you accept all applicants, you are likely to end up with a bad business. Despite offering immediate gains in terms of high numbers of young men ready to fight, the Islamic State would eventually realise the downside of its recruitment strategy. In contrast, al-Qaida adopted a more rigorous vetting process resulting in a more cohesive group.

The Islamic State's expansion into Syria in April 2013 was only the first step in a larger process of globalising the group's presence and positioning itself as the dominant Jihadi group in the area stretching from West Africa to East Asia. In essence, the group was imitating al-Qaida, its direct rival. The 9/11 attacks ensured al-Qaida's dominance within the SJM;[6] this was followed by the establishment of its affiliate model across North Africa and the Middle East in an effort to globalise its influence.[7] The capture of Mosul and the caliphate declaration was the Islamic State's 9/11 moment. This was swiftly followed by an expansion process outside the Levant region, with groups and individuals adopting its tactics, strategy, narratives and symbols. Al-Qaida's initial response was containment. In promoting Taliban leader Mullah Umar as a counter-caliph, al-Qaida tried to limit the impact of the Islamic State's global challenge while attempting to manage the conflict in the Levant locally by dispatching senior Afghan veterans to Syria.

### *Remaining with the Taliban and Promoting the Counter-Caliph*

While al-Qaida's early approach to the Islamic State was characterised by calls for unity,[8] after the caliphate declaration it slowly became more assertive. At this critical juncture in the lead up to the Islamic State's expansion process it was important for al-Qaida to undermine al-Baghdadi's authority. Because al-Zawahiri could not himself personify a counter-authority, his group instead issued several communications intended to support Mullah Umar's position as the ultimate authority within the SJM. The first effort came nine days after the caliphate declaration, when al-Qaida reissued an old video with footage of Bin Laden.[9] As part of a Q&A session, Bin Laden is asked about his bay'a to Mullah Umar. As noted by Bunzel, Bin Laden answered that he has a *supreme bay'a* (al-bay'a al-'uzma), a reference to the caliphal synonym of *supreme imamate* (al-imama al-'uzma).[10] A second effort came six days later when al-Qaida released the first issue of a new pamphlet entitled *al-Nafir*. The issue begins 'by renewing its bay'a to Amir al-Mu'mineen [commander of the faithful] Mullah Muhammad Umar, the mujahid (may God protect him), and reiterates that al-Qaeda with all its branches are his soldiers working under his victorious banner.'[11] Approximately one and a half months later, a third—and arguably the most important—effort came when al-Zawahiri established a new al-Qaida affiliate in the Indian subcontinent (AQIS).[12] Relevant in this context is that al-Zawahiri reaffirmed his bay'a to Mullah Umar in the video, and how the establishment of an official al-Qaida affiliate partly operating in Afghanistan was intended to strengthen the bond between al-Qaida and the Taliban in this critical period.

Al-Qaida's reaffirming of its pledge of allegiance to Mullah Umar is not in itself controversial, but what is important here is the timing of these statements, which were published in the immediate aftermath of the caliphate declaration. What al-Qaida likely did not know was that Mullah Umar was dead when they began rebranding him as a counter-caliph.[13] The crucial point, however, was the Taliban amir's symbolic status within the SJM. While the complicated relationship between al-Qaida and the Taliban has been the subject of much scholarly research, the important thing to note here is the instrumental or practical nature of al-Qaida's invocation of its allegiance to the Taliban.[14] The first time around it had been to ensure sanctuary in Afghanistan, and this time it was to counter the challenge of the Islamic State.[15] At the time, the Islamic State had already begun to denounce the Taliban, but Mullah Umar nonetheless still commanded substantial respect within the SJM. Just three years earlier, for instance, al-Adnani of the Islamic State leadership had praised Mullah Umar and the Taliban in a speech.[16]

In building the narrative of Mullah Umar as the real caliph, al-Qaida received help from an unexpected source. The Mauritanian, Abu al-Mundhir al-Shinqiti, who since April 2013 had sided with the Islamic State, suddenly reversed his position in reaction to al-Baghdadi's claim to be caliph. In a statement released on July 18, 2014, he rebuked the Islamic State for not consulting Mullah Umar, whom al-Shinqiti considered to be caliph and thus not someone who could be summarily replaced. The Mauritanian ideologue furthermore questioned the Islamic State's motives for declaring the caliphate, arguing that it was intended to trump al-Qaida's Syrian affiliate Jabhat al-Nusra—a motive lacking a legitimate shari'a basis, he argued.[17]

### *Waves of Expansion: Allegiance, Not Cooperation*

Having made its first bid for hegemony with the establishment of its caliphate, in autumn 2014 the Islamic State began to focus on expanding its geographical scope in a bid for global hegemony within the SJM. Capitalising on its momentum and the uncertainty among Jihadi fighters and sympathisers, it successfully managed to sway Jihadis in other countries to pledge allegiance either on a group level or as breakaway factions. From the outset, this was a controversial affair. Jihadis view a pledge of allegiance (bay'a) as a judicially founded, and thus binding, relationship that cannot be broken except in exceptional circumstances. While this only affected Jihadis with an existing bay'a, it nonetheless proved to be a serious obstacle for the Islamic State's expansion strategy. The group tried to circumvent this challenge by declaring all other groups null[18] and arguing that a bay'a can be broken with a legal shari'a basis if a caliphate is established.[19]

From 2013 on, the Islamic State had started to receive pledges of allegiance from individuals and smaller groups around the world, but its formal global expansion process of its province (wilaya) structure did not begin until November 2014. The primary reason for this delay was that expansion depended on the caliphate declaration and on specific criteria relating to the actors pledging allegiance. In the words of the Islamic State,

> This process includes documenting their bay'at, unifying the jama'at who have given bay'ah, holding consultations to nominate a wali [governor] and members for the regional shura assembly, planning a strategy to achieve consolidation [tamkin] in their region for the khilafah so as to implement the shari'a, and presenting all this to the Islamic State leadership for approval.[20]

The first wave of expansion was announced by al-Baghdadi on November 13 when he accepted pledges of allegiance from groups in Saudi Arabia, Yemen, Egypt, Algeria and Libya.[21] The second wave followed soon after. In the first half of 2015 al-Adnani announced—for the first time in January—the establishment of an Islamic State wilaya in Khorasan mainly covering Afghanistan and Pakistan.[22] In March, the group accepted the pledge of allegiance from Boko Haram in Nigeria,[23] and in June it announced the creation of a wilaya in the Caucasus.[24] In the case of both Khorasan and the Caucasus, contact with local sympathisers had been ongoing months prior to the official announcements. In late 2015 and early 2016 new pledges of allegiance were received from Somalia[25] and the Philippines. In the following years, the group would announce new provinces in Central Africa (August 2018), in the Sahara (April 2019) and in Turkey (April 2019), while separating its Khorasan wilaya in order to establish provinces in India and Pakistan (May 2019).

The expansion was helped by macro-structures. Most of the countries where the Islamic State was able to get a foothold (Afghanistan, Libya, Nigeria, Yemen, Somalia and Sinai) were already plagued by domestic conflict; this made it easier to recruit, to mobilise and to find safe havens in which to hide. East Asia is the outlier, but here the Islamic State managed to tap into existing militant and criminal networks and to rely on its momentum to attract followers.

Figure 7: Map of the Islamic State's Territorial Expansion through Official Provinces

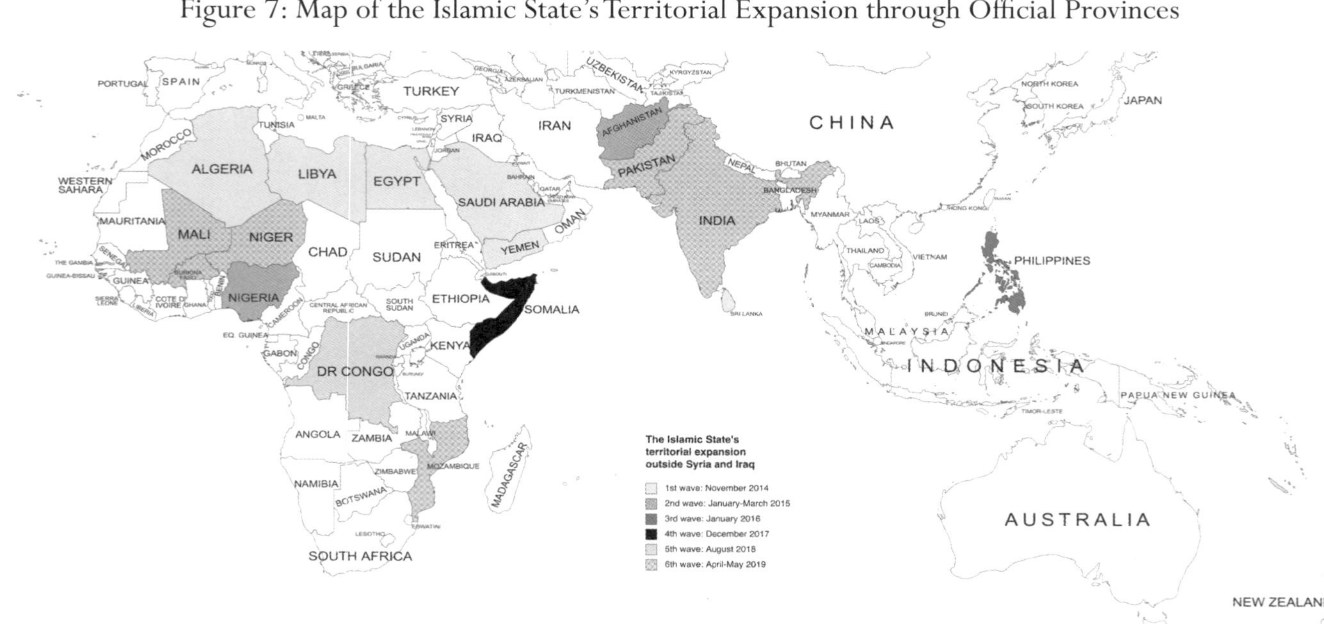


Not included is the Islamic State's declaration of a province in the Caucasus in June 2015.

The group also invested resources in its geographical expansion. In 2013, for example, in a bid to prime its future expansion, the group sent arguably its most important ideologue at the time, Turki al-Binali, to Libya and Tunisia to lecture.[26] Another example is Abu al-Mughirah al-Qahtani (Abu Nabil al-Anbari). Previously a senior figure in Iraq in charge of the Salahuddeen province, in 2014 he was dispatched to Libya where he became wali of the new province.[27] One final illustration of how the Islamic State's central leadership prioritised expansion is Abu Ali al-Anbari, effectively the deputy of the caliph, who was appointed wali of the group's Yemeni affiliate; in the event, however, he was unable to travel, and so the group ended up choosing the Saudi Abu Bilal al-Harbi instead.[28]

The character of the Islamic State's expansion process was closely related to its self-perception. Representing the caliphate, the Islamic State pursued a strategy of allegiance *over* cooperation which placed immense pressure on other Jihadi groups. For al-Qaida it was always different. Established as a vanguard, it always saw itself as one of several groups within the SJM. Even after it initiated its affiliate structure, al-Qaida accepted cooperation rather than exclusively official affiliation.[29] The hesitance to establish formal relations with al-Shabab even shows that al-Qaida did not always favour allegiance. This view is epitomised in the letter from Atiyyatullah to al-Zarqawi, where he writes

> The other matter is to take caution against being zealous about the name 'al-Qa'ida', or any name or organisation. Although all mujahidin are our brothers, the Sunni are our brothers and our friends, as long as they are Muslims, even if they are disobedient, or insolent; whether they come into the organisation with us or not, for they are our brothers, our friends, and our loved ones.[30]

While there are a few examples of cooperation between the Islamic State and non-affiliated groups, its attitude was mainly exclusivist, similar to the GIA in Algeria. Another comparison is the Red Brigades for whom it was a prerequisite when cooperating with other groups that those groups accepted its political and operational program.[31] This form of exclusivism resembles the attitude of the Islamic State, except that the latter took it even further by generally not accepting alliances and demanding allegiance, which effectively implied mergers. One counterexample is Jaysh Khalid ibn al-Waleed, which before its formal affiliation was an Islamic State-linked group in Syria's southwest Deraa province. The group was formed in May 2016 from a merger of three smaller groups[32] but remained operating under the Jaysh Khalid ibn al-Waleed name until June 2018, when it became the Islamic State's Wilayat Houran.

Despite its successful expansion process in 2014–16, it is important to stress that the Islamic State never managed to lure any of al-Qaida's affiliates. Yet there is evidence that it was not for lack of trying. In a series of letters, Abu Ubayda al-Hakim, an Islamic State shura council member, tried to convince AQIM amir, Abdelmalek Droukdal, to shift his allegiance from al-Zawahiri to al-Baghdadi. Rather than relying on defections by rank and file, this charm offensive was meant to dilute horizontal ties on a leadership level in al-Qaida to ease entire the shifting of allegiance of entire groups. In one of the letters, al-Hakim does not simply promote cordial relations between the groups but also instructs the al-Qaida leader to pledge allegiance to the Islamic State since, he argues, this is obligatory according to Islamic law. In particular, the Islamic State would continuously try to entice AQIM and AQAP, but eventually failed due to these al-Qaida affiliates' continuing loyalty to al-Zawahiri.

### *Managing the Chaos: The Misunderstood 'Khorasan Group'*

In the midst of the Islamic State's expansion process in early spring 2015, Jabhat al-Nusra slightly shifted its position in relation to its rival. In May 2014, al-Nusra had issued a statement saying that it followed al-Zawahiri's advice only to defend itself against attacks,[33] but in March the following year the group issued a pamphlet comparing the Islamic State to the Khawarij, thereby reaching the conclusion that it was incumbent on Jihadis to actively fight the group.[34] Meanwhile, al-Zawahiri's strategy was one of containment. Isolated most probably somewhere in the AfPak region, his ability to directly influence events in Syria was limited, as was his communication with Jabhat al-Nusra. As a result, the al-Qaida amir dispatched several senior figures to Syria, first in 2013 and again in

2015, partly to manage the conflict with the Islamic State but also as a mechanism to control al-Nusra.

In 2014, Western media began to report on what it labelled *the Khorasan Group*, claiming it to be a sub-unit within Jabhat al-Nusra mainly comprised of Afghan veterans and with the objective of planning attacks outside of Syria and potentially in the West.[35] This analysis, however, was mistaken. The operationally focused unit referred to in Western media was an elite sniper unit headed by the late Umit Toprak (Abu Yusuf al-Turki), an Afghan veteran, with no ambitions to plan or commit international terrorist attacks. What may be better termed the Khorasan Group is the group of senior figures al-Zawahiri instructed to head to Syria in 2013 and 2015 to manage the Jihad in his absence (see table 9). Many of these figures immediately took senior positions within Jabhat al-Nusra and engaged in reconciliation efforts with the Islamic State, showing that their role was mainly *internal*: to ensure that al-Nusra followed al-Zawahiri's directions, and to navigate the relationship with other Jihadi groups.

Table 9: List of Senior Afghan Veterans Sent by al-Zawahiri to Syria

| *Kunya / Name* | *Date for relocation* | *Prior destination* |
|---|---|---|
| Abd Al-Rahman Muhammad Zafir al-Dubaysi al-Juhani | 2012 or 2013 | Pakistan |
| Abu Hamam al-Suri | Likely 2013 | Lebanon |
| Abu Usama al-Shahabi | Early 2013 | Afghanistan |
| Abu Firas al-Suri | 2013 | Yemen |
| Muhsin al Fadhli | 2013 | Iran |
| Adel Radi Saqr al-Wahabi al-Harbi | 2013 | Iran |
| Sanafi al-Nasr | April 2013 | Iran |
| Abu al-Khayr al-Masri | Autumn 2015 | Iran |
| Abu Abd al-Karim al-Khurasani | Autumn 2015 | Iran |
| Khalid al-Aruri (Qassam) | Autumn 2015 | Iran |
| Abu Khallad al-Muhandis | Autumn 2015 | Iran |

We know from several sources that al-Qaida's leadership proactively dispatched senior figures to Syria, many of them coming from Iran.[36] Several were members of al-Qaida's shura council or senior military commanders; high-ranking figures were probably selected because of the respect they would command within Syria's Jihadi environment. This was especially important from late 2014 onwards, when al-Zawahiri's contact with al-Nusra had allegedly ceased and he would have had few opportunities to guide his Syrian affiliate. With a cadre of Afghan veterans, with whom al-Zawahiri had strong social ties, the al-Qaida leader sought to protect himself and his group the best way that he could in a difficult situation. While these *managers* could not prevent the conflict with the Islamic State from escalating—or al-Nusra from eventually splitting from al-Qaida (see chapters 12 and 13)—it is likely that they still had a critical impact on al-Qaida's trajectory in the Syrian conflict.

### *Fragmentation, Diversification and Evolution*

The Islamic State's geographical expansion and claim for global hegemony within the SJM would instigate dynamics of fragmentation, polarisation and diversification.[37] Bakke et al. have argued that fragmentation is a conduit leading to internal tensions, polarisation and infighting.[38] However, this phenomenon is better described as a reciprocal dynamic that tends to result in a vicious circle which makes internal relations increasingly volatile. In late 2014 and throughout 2015 the SJM effectively fragmented, with a myriad of new groups or networks emerging in response to the Islamic State's call for allegiance; at the same time, a logic of polarisation was becoming entrenched. A similar dynamic was taking place on a personal level: Jihadi scholars, or ideologues, barricaded themselves in their respective camps, showing little willingness to seek common ground. Concurrently, a number of distinct ideological positions were crystalising, mainly represented by Ahrar al-Sham's 'third way' Jihadism and the Islamic State's increasing dedication to terrorist attacks outside its main theatres of operation. Not only did this pose a threat to Western security, but it also challenged existing scholarly conceptualisations of Jihadi actors.

### *Movement Fragmentation and Polarisation*

The caliphate declaration and the Islamic State's expansion project instigated separate but concurrent processes of movement *fragmentation*[39] and *polarisation*. The degree of fragmentation is here defined as (1) the number of groups in the movement, (2) the degree of institutionalisation across groups, and (3) the distribution of power among groups. New Jihadi groups had already been established in Syria as part of the country's civil war, but in late 2014 and 2015, the number of groups within the SJM rose even further on a global scale as a reaction to the caliphate declaration and the Islamic State's call for pledges of allegiance.

Studying the reaction of existing prominent Jihadi groups around the Muslim world, we can distinguish three dynamics:

- Groups that remained *loyal* to their affiliation or linkage with the al-Qaida–Taliban nexus. These groups did suffer defections to the Islamic State, but not on a leadership level.
- Groups that *fragmented*, implying that leadership figures and considerable numbers of rank and file defected to the Islamic State, and
- Groups that *shifted* their allegiance or linkage to the Islamic State.

While most groups and—importantly—all official al-Qaida affiliates remained loyal, several groups splintered or shifted allegiance, helping to boost the Islamic State's global expansion project; at the same time, defections from groups like AQAP and al-Shabab created nascent Islamic State groups in Yemen and Somalia. This increase in the number of groups, and the fact that in many cases there were several groups operating in the same country, was followed by a more diffuse distribution of power, but rarely resulted in the establishment of supra-group institutions to manage inter-group relations.

No single factor can explain the variation in how groups and individuals reacted to the caliphate declaration. Instead, it appears that several factors including opportunism, ideological and/or theological resonance and social ties were determining. The success

Figure 8: Fragmentation of the SJM in Reaction to the Caliphate

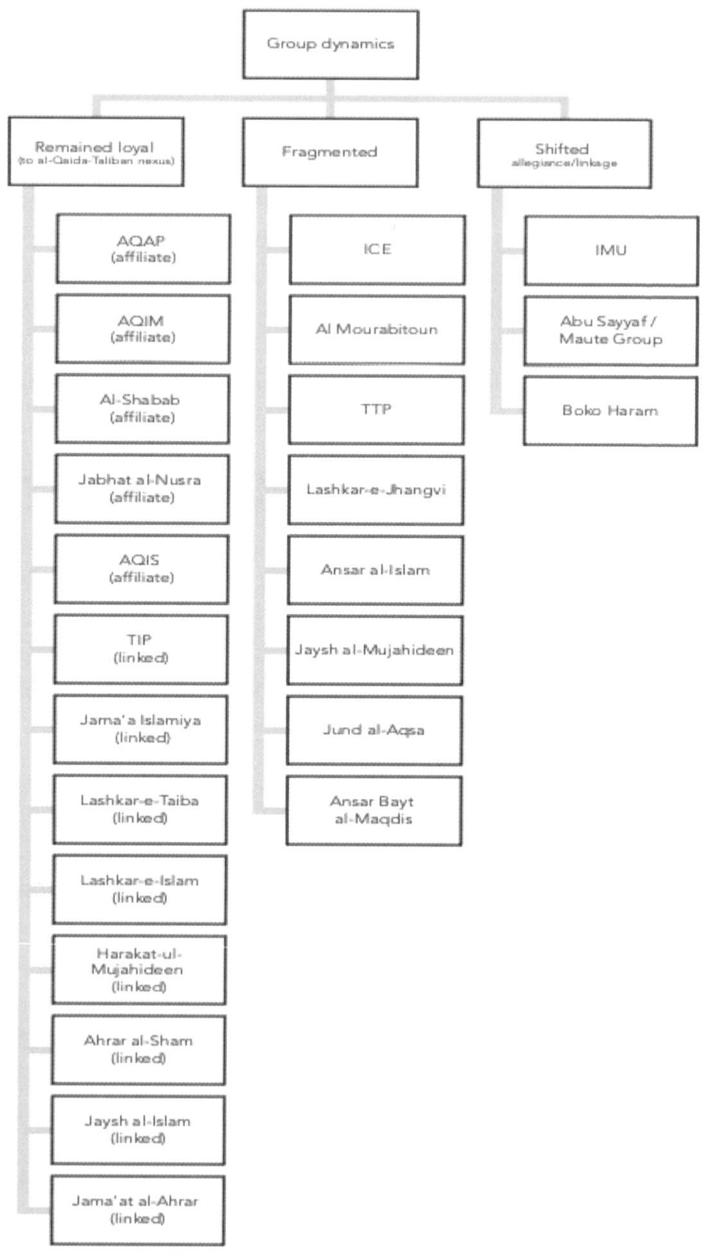


Note: See appendix 3 for details (p. 409).

of the Islamic State in provoking dissidence within other groups and attracting pledges of allegiance was mainly the result of its momentum in 2014–15, the resonance of its religio-political project and the platform it offered new members, individually and on a group level. For instance, many Taliban and TTP commanders and rank and file left their former groups to join the Islamic State because of the personal opportunities it offered them to increase their rank or salary as part of the new *winning* team. Similar dynamics occurred in places like Yemen and Somalia. For some local groups outside of the Levant, shifting their allegiance even offered the opportunity of becoming a *province* within the Islamic State, leading to benefits in terms of economy and/or brand. Others also joined out of fear and to survive, while some considered it an obligation to submit and become part of the Islamic caliphate.

Al-Qaida's ability to remain largely intact organisationally appears to mainly be a result of the longstanding social ties among its global leadership and to a lesser extent among its rank and file. Several affiliate leaders knew al-Zawahiri and other leadership figures from their shared time in Afghanistan, and these relations had been nurtured over a decade. For actors whose existence depends on their ability to operate clandestinely, issues such as trust matter a lot. Ideology is another important factor. Just like the Islamic State managed to attract factions and individuals due to its ideological distinctiveness, so did al-Qaida manage to hold on to segments of its members because they concurred with the group's religio-political project despite the absence of strategic success.

Giugni, McAdam and Tilly argue that the higher the number of groups in a movement, the more likely that movement is to succeed in its overall objective.[40] In contrast, Bakke et al. claim that a high number of groups is likely to make intra-movement relations more volatile, and Krause takes this argument even further in the context of nationalist movements, arguing that a high number of groups is detrimental to success. Adding nuance to this debate, I would argue that it depends on the dominant rationales within the movement and whether the movement is cohesive or competitive, something which is related to power distribution and institutionalisation. In an interesting comparison, Bakke et al. explain how infighting among

Tamil nationalists stopped when power was largely concentrated in one group.[41] Even at the peak of the Islamic State's power in Syria in 2015, however, rival groups did not stop fighting it. This was likely a result of the Islamic State's extremely aggressive attitude to rival Jihadi groups and also because competing groups cooperated in opposing it.

Alongside the process of fragmentation, a powerful logic of polarisation became dominant. This was largely the design of the Islamic State, who consciously eradicated the 'grayzone' as a mechanism to pressure groups to choose a side. One of the achievements of Bin Laden and his group's attack on 9/11 was to elucidate the two camps the world was split into: those with Islam and those against. In an article in its *Dabiq* magazine, the Islamic State explained how this division only lasted a short time and was replaced by a 'grayzone'.[42] But, the group argues, its establishment of the caliphate would represent the final destruction of this grayzone and enforce a binary logic: either you are *with* the Islamic State or you are *against it*. Neutrality or independence would be considered a major sin. Another important factor was the experience of infighting. War and violence always have a polarising impact, as decisions regarding allegiance or sympathy are closely related to death, destruction and submission. Hence, groups not pledging allegiance to the Islamic State, or offering its sympathy, would automatically become rivals, or at the very least competitors. On a global scale, eventually the result would be a strict division of groups: those either part of or sympathetic to the Islamic State, and those either part of or sympathetic to the al-Qaida–Taliban nexus.

### *Scholarly Polarisation*

A similar logic would also dominate the scholarly environment. Jihadi scholars, or ideologues, had generally been fairly united due to the absence of serious inter-group conflict and because of the dominating position of al-Qaida within the SJM. This implied that a certain hierarchy of scholarly authority had developed, largely centred around the Jordanians Abu Qatada and al-Maqdisi and the latter's shari'a council, which was made up of influential ideological figures.[43] But in 2014–15, this unity and hierarchical structure would implode. In general, we can divide ideologues into three categories: those sympathetic to the Islamic State, those sympathetic to al-Qaida and those taking a more independent position. These scholars participated in the debate, praising their respective groups and their senior figures, while at the same time, they ferociously attacked one another, thus establishing a culture of intra-scholarly condemnation.

As already recounted, within the Islamic State it was Turki al-Binali who was the primary voice of disobedience directed at his seniors. His critique of and rebuttals to Iyad al-Qunaybi, al-Tartusi, Abu Qatada and al-Maqdisi set a precedent for further criticism of otherwise respected and authoritative figures within the SJM. Although criticism of senior figures was not entirely unprecedented, the shift represented by al-Binali's writings is important. Furthermore, he even found legitimation for his rebellious writings in the words of Anwar al-Awlaki, a late senior al-Qaida figure, who once wrote in the magazine *Inspire* that

> It is important that we encourage Muslims to respect their scholars. It is to no one's benefit to put down the men of knowledge who represent the religion of Allah. But when some of our scholars—no matter how knowledgeable they are—divert from the straight path, we, the Muslims, need to advise them.[44]

Eventually other Islamic State (or Islamic State-sympathetic) ideologues followed with rebuttals to al-Qaida-aligned scholars.[45] For instance, Abu Abd al-Rahman al-Shami, a senior Islamic State official, authored a 120-page rebuttal of Abu Qatada's *Cloak of the Khalifa*,[46] while the Jamaican Abdullah al-Faisal incited Jihadis to not follow the fatwas and criticism coming from Abu Qatada and al-Maqdisi, since their imprisonment in Jordan rendered their statements invalid.[47] Illustrative of this polarised environment, a personal conversation al-Binali had with a fellow Jihadi in Bahrain after returning from his first visit to Syria in 2013 is most telling:

> when he [al-Binali] returned from Syria, we sat down together, and there was a change in his tone of speech about Jabhat al Nusra and it had become very harsh. And when he was asked

> 'Have you tried to hear from Jabhat un-Nusra when you were in Syria to understand their point of view?' he said 'No, rather the Islamic State and its representatives are trustworthy and they do not lie!'... And so there is no need to hear both sides...![48]

Senior ideologues affiliated with al-Qaida like al-Maqdisi, Abu Qatada, and Umar al-Haddouchi would engage in their own attempt to delegitimise the new Islamic State scholars with criticisms pinpointing their youth, lack of knowledge and naivety. While these ideologues had undoubtedly become the most revered within the SJM, they had problems capturing the youth, who were increasingly fascinated by the Islamic State. As such, it was paramount for al-Maqdisi and his colleagues to delegitimise these rebellious voices as best they could, while also finding ways to attract Islamic State rank and file. The third camp is mainly represented by Abu Basir al-Tartusi. After living for many years in the UK, the Syrian al-Tartusi relocated to his native country after the conflict broke out. At first he aligned himself with Ahrar al-Sham, although all while remaining independent. Al-Tartusi was quick to criticise the Islamic State and its scholars, but he also directed his words against Jabhat al-Nusra and al-Maqdisi. Al-Tartusi's main criticism of the Jordanian is his apparent megalomania and his reluctance to be explicit when discussing the Jihadi groups in Syria and whether he considers them Muslim or not.[49] Al-Maqdisi dismissed al-Tartusi's attack and turns his insinuation that al-Maqdisi has sympathy for the Islamic State into an attack upon al-Tartusi himself, asking why he focuses only on the deviance of the Islamic State and not all the secular factions in the war, whom al-Tartusi allegedly supports. If this is the case, al-Maqdisi asks, 'what purity has remained with you?'[50]

This intra-scholarly vilification would affect not just the relative unity that existed among Jihadi ideologues prior to the conflict but also its hierarchy. Scholars like al-Binali and al-Shinqiti used to be on al-Maqdisi's shari'a council but left when they sided with the Islamic State. Except for a few cases of ideologues like al-Shinqiti[51] and Abu Dharr Azzam, who shifted back and forth between the various camps, their positions became increasingly entrenched, leaving few opportunities for anyone to take up the middle ground. An example of this is al-Maqdisi's attempt to take a more nuanced position on the Islamic State by distinguishing between its leadership and its rank and file. This would eventually lead to so much criticism that he was forced to clarify his stance and apply the *khawarij* label to the group's leadership.

Together, this logic of polarisation, which came to dominate both on the group and individual level, had important implications for the ensuing conflict and a devastating impact on the potential for de-escalation and reconciliation. Groups and scholars were increasingly locked in their respective camps with little interaction between them and no interest in listening to one another.[52] This made it challenging to settle differences or influence the opinions of one's opponent. This was especially the case because the logic of polarisation occurred (particularly among rank and file members and ordinary sympathisers) not just in conflict areas but on a global scale, though it took a little longer to manifest itself outside of conflict zones.[53]

### *Revisionist Jihadism and the Jihadi Continuum*

Besides fragmentation and polarisation, the SJM was also experiencing ideological diversification and evolution, which was putting extra pressure on its ideological cohesion. With groups like the Islamic State and al-Qaida at the more radical end of the spectrum, in the Syrian context the presence and ideological evolution of Ahrar al-Sham would extend the SJM's ideological spectrum in the opposite direction. Because of its idiosyncrasy, the group would put pressure not just on our existing analytical categories relating to Jihadism but also the way other Jihadis related to the group. To some extent Ahrar al-Sham was the elephant in the room, which Heller has referred to as a 'revisionist trend within Islamist militancy' that is 'contesting the nature of the jihadist movement.'[54] It *is*, or *was*, the moderate face of Jihadism.[55]

At its inception in 2011, Ahrar al-Sham was a relatively ideological hard-line group, but over time—and especially after the devastating tragedy in September 2014 where almost the entire leadership of the group was killed in an explosion in Idlib most likely carried out by the Islamic State—it adopted a more pragmatic approach.[56] While the change in leadership did push the group even further in a revisionist direction, this process had already been initiated during the original leadership, largely as a reaction to the experience of, and conflict with, the Islamic State. As Heller has argued, the initial changes in the group's mentality did not imply that Ahrar al-Sham should be excluded from the SJM,[57] though later developments may challenge its inclusion. However, its leaders have consistently been cautious in defining their group as *Jihadi*,[58] instead preferring the term *Islamic mujahid movement* (harakat islamiyya mujahida la harakat jihadiyya).[59] This is partly an indication of the internal tensions within Ahrar al-Sham, but it also illustrates how conscious group leaders were about the symbolic meaning of *Jihad*.

The main point of contestation between Ahrar al-Sham and ideologically more hard-line groups was its approach to al-wala' wa-l-bara'. Initially, in 2014–15, the concern was Ahrar al-Sham's alliances with non-Jihadi and non-Islamist rebel groups, which led to the ruling of apostasy by the Islamic State. Later, in 2016–18, Ahrar would draw criticism from the successor groups of Jabhat al-Nusra and ideologues such as Abu Qatada and al-Maqdisi over its close alliance with Turkey. Despite their ideological differences, al-Nusra and Ahrar collaborated militarily from the early days of the Syrian conflict and, from 2015, through the *Jaysh al-Fatah* military coalition. On several occasions the two groups also co-authored statements on the Islamic State. One such instance occurred in July 2015 when they referred to it as the *renegade sect* (al-firqa al-mariqa). In 2016, however, tensions started to emerge over Ahrar's participation in the Turkey-led Euphrates Shield offensive. Responding to the criticism, Ahrar's deputy at the time, Ali al-Omar, claimed that the group's behaviour was in line with *fiqh al-waqi'* (reality based jurisprudence) and that they understood the Syrian context better than al-Qaida and the Islamic State.[60] Although the leadership attempted to give the impression that Ahrar al-Sham was inclusive and unified, the group would eventually implode in late 2016 when hardliners split to establish Jaysh al-Ahrar before later joining al-Nusra's successor HTS.

Ahrar al-Sham's ambition was to describe an alternative Jihadi vision that was not necessarily defined by Salafi concepts as interpreted by al-Qaida and the Islamic State. Instead, the group sought to define its own Jihadi symbols to create a distinctive group identity which (theoretically at least) was based on theological inclusiveness.[61] Because of its nationally driven political project and its opposition to the rigidity of Salafi concepts like al-wala' wa-l-bara', the group earned comparisons with the Taliban. In fact Ahrar, in a similar way to the Taliban, would on several occasions become a victim of its own identity of inclusiveness, since the group could not contain such a broad range of ideological positions.

Despite its internal challenges, the group's distinctiveness, like that of Jaysh al-Islam, represented an interesting alternative within the SJM that presented two challenges to ideological hardliners within the movement. Firstly, they offered a serious alternative to Jihadis less committed to Salafi theology but still in favour of militant Jihad as the necessary approach; this instantly made Ahrar one of the most popular rebel groups in the Syrian conflict. Secondly, Ahrar forced al-Qaida and the Islamic State to grapple with the question of how to relate to another Jihadi group that to some extent relied on a similar discourse and vision but differed sufficiently in its ideological and theological foundations to foster critical tensions. The Islamic State quickly chose to reject the legitimacy of Ahrar al-Sham entirely; they labelled it an apostate group, thus legitimising military conflict. For al-Qaida, and later HTS, the relationship was more complicated but eventually ended in a breakdown in relations resulting from failed merger attempts.

In her article 'Jihadism after the "Caliphate": towards a new typology', Stenersen divides Jihadi groups according to two parameters: how they relate to society (integration vs. separation) and whom Jihadis fight for (the nation vs. the umma). In contrast with al-Qaida and the Islamic State's focus on the *umma* and various degrees of *separation*, Ahrar al-Sham fought for the nation while striving for integration. This is not unprecedented, but while the history of Jihadism contains examples of groups taking a similar position, the academic discussion remains rather undeveloped in terms of developing clear categories to grasp the internal ideological diversity within the SJM. The distinctiveness of Ahrar and its initial revisionist identity shows that we must understand Jihadi groups through a continuum of positions on the scales suggested by Stenersen, rather than applying labels like Jihadi-Salafi that give an inaccurate impression of a monolithic movement.

### *Evolution of Enemy Hierarchies*

At the other end of the ideological spectrum, the Islamic State would also develop its distinctive ideological outlook, including in terms of its enemy prioritisation. The group's focus had so far been nationally orientated, first on Iraq and, from 2011, on Syria too. In the past its predecessors, AQI and ISI, were linked to terrorist attacks in neighbouring Jordan and in Sweden and France, but its main enemy remained the *near* enemy. From autumn 2014, this would change with a cascade of terrorist attacks outside the group's primary areas of operation, many of them in the West. This essentially transformed the Islamic State into a *hybrid* in terms of its political preferences.[62]

Two issues are often discussed in the debate on the Islamic State's change in behaviour: (1) why it happened and (2) the extent to which the group is responsible for these attacks, which are most often carried out by individuals who have no direct relationship with the group. The launch of terrorist attacks in the West is usually described as retribution for the US-led international military campaign against the Islamic State in Iraq (from August) and Syria (from September). While the Islamic State's new focus on the *far enemy* would overlap with increased interference of external actors in Syria and Iraq concerned with fighting the group—notably the US-led campaign (August–September 2014), the Turkish parliament allowing military operations against the Islamic State (October 2014) and introducing stricter border policies (January 2015), and Russia's military intervention (September 2015)—external interference does not appear to be the original cause. The first attack connected to the Islamic State carried out in the West occurred in May 2014 when Mehdi Nemmouche killed four people at the Jewish Museum in Brussels. The Islamic State never claimed responsibility for Nemmouche's attack, but he did spend time with the group in Syria and subsequently communicated with Abdelhamid Abaaoud, the mastermind of the Paris attack in November 2015 and an Islamic

State external operations planner, thus suggesting that he was *guided* by the Islamic State's external operations unit.[63] Similarly, there are reports indicating that as early as 2013 the Islamic State began establishing structures for external operations. This aligns with al-Baghdadi's speech from January 2014—more than half a year before Western forces got involved in the battle against the Islamic State—where he warned the US:

> Our last message is to the Americans. Know protector of the crusade that this war by proxy in Syria will not help you like it did not in Iraq. Soon we will be in a direct confrontation and the sons of Islam have prepared for such a day. So watch for we are watching you.[64]

In July 2014—again prior to the intervention of external forces—al-Baghdadi would incite attacks against the West.

The discussion about to what extent the Islamic State as a group is responsible for the more than 50 terrorist attacks (see figures 9 and 10) carried out in the West from 2014–19 is equally complicated. The most plausible answer is that the majority of attacks were either *inspired* or *networked*, thus indicating little or no direct interaction between the perpetrators and the Islamic State's external operations unit, while a substantial minority were *organised* or *guided*, implying that the group played a central role in the planning and/or execution.[65] Furthermore, from July 2014 Islamic State leaders began to consistently incite attacks against the West, while its munasirun increasingly circulated similar calls for terrorist operations and issued material with tangible advice on how to plan and execute attacks. So, while direct connection cannot always be established between the group and the perpetrator, the Islamic State was actively pushing the narrative to magnify terrorist attacks committed in its name.

Although retribution certainly played a role, not least to legitimise and mobilise for attacks, it appears more likely that the Islamic State's sudden dedication to focusing on the far enemy, both operationally and discursively, was a natural continuation of its expansionist strategy and hegemonic ambitions. Since 9/11, al-Qaida had been the main Jihadi group associated with international

Figure 9: Islamic State- & al-Qaida-Connected Attacks in the US, Canada, Europe & Australia 2010–19

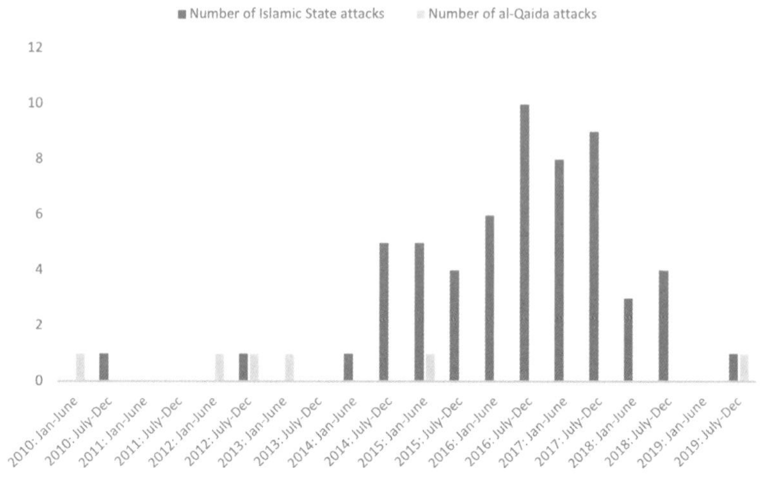


Figure 10: Islamic State Attacks in the US, Canada, Europe & Australia 2013–19 per Year

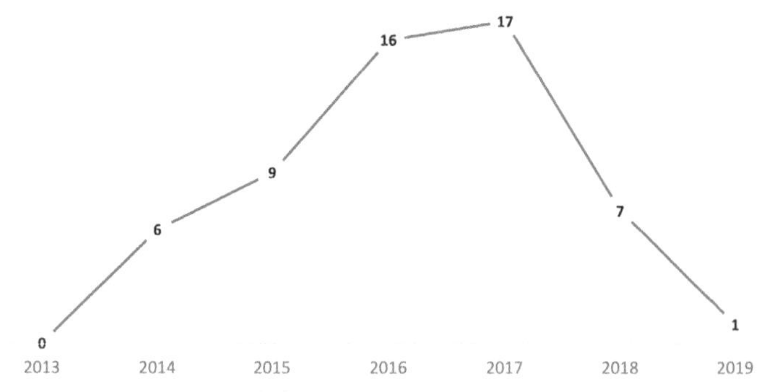


terrorist attacks against the Western world; despite the fact that the group only ever executed a few, these had become its trademark. If the Islamic State wanted to overtake al-Qaida's globally dominant position, it would also have to co-opt this trademark. The motto had to be 'do what al-Qaida does, but do it better'. This underlines the important connection between inter-group dynamics and strategic behaviour. The stark rise in external terrorist attacks is obviously

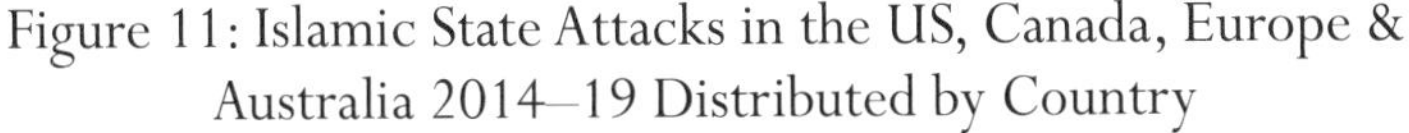

Figure 11: Islamic State Attacks in the US, Canada, Europe & Australia 2014–19 Distributed by Country

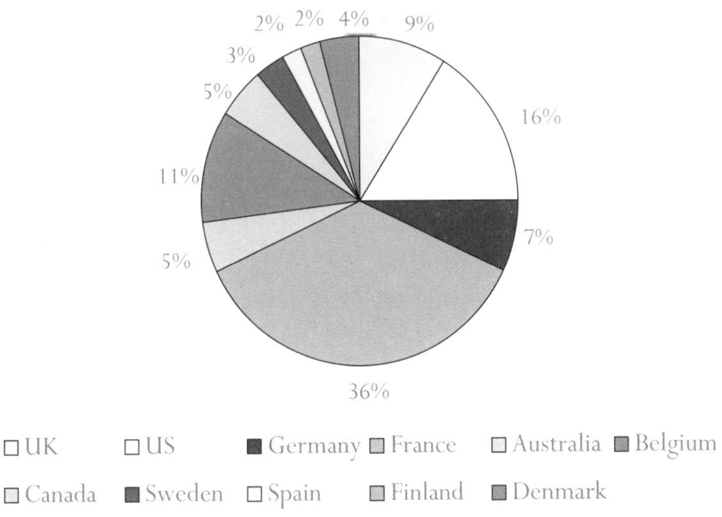


related to the high influx of foreign fighters as well. These foreign fighters helped the Islamic State to recruit and mobilise for external operations and they contributed with knowledge of, networks in and access to their home countries.

At the same time, al-Qaida de-prioritised its operational focus on the far enemy—although the group continued to refer to the West, and especially the US, as its most important enemy. While the former move was probably a strategic choice, the latter was a strategic necessity. Having built its identity partly on representing the foremost Jihadi threat to the West, al-Zawahiri necessarily had to continue a discourse of animosity to the far enemy and incite for attacks. In reality, however, it appears that al-Qaida did not prioritise external attacks in the period 2014–19. Its capacity for executing external attacks must also have been undermined by the death of several senior external operations planners in the 2007–09 period,[66] and the imprisonment of other senior operational figures.[67] Even so, it remains plausible that al-Qaida's priorities changed in the period—to focusing on local conflicts and later distinguishing itself from the Islamic State.

# 8

# OUTSIDE THE LEVANT

With its caliphate declaration, the Islamic State had put pressure on Jihadi groups outside of the Levant, and this would only intensify with its organisational expansion outside the region. Soon tensions and, in some instances, infighting would erupt between Jihadi groups usually affiliated with or linked to al-Qaida in several other countries around the world. This chapter examines the emergence and evolution of these conflict dynamics outside of the Levant, mainly focusing on the 2014–15 period, to show both the global character of inter-Jihadi conflict and its local particularities.

## *Yemen*

The Islamic State's declaration of a province in Yemen occurred as part of its first wave of expansion in November 2014. While the group most likely hoped to persuade the local al-Qaida affiliate AQAP to shift its loyalty and pledge allegiance to al-Baghdadi, it only managed to attract some commanders and rank and file from AQAP on an individual level. However, it was not until March 2015, with the outbreak of the Yemeni civil war, that the Islamic State's province in Yemen (ISY) began to appear on the ground. The civil war offered ISY a platform through which the group could frame its

Figure 12: Map Showing the Geographical Spread of Infighting

struggle with the country's Houthi movement and take advantage of a sectarian narrative to build local support and embed itself in Yemeni society. From its inception, ISY was a rival to AQAP, with both groups seeking to monopolise Yemen's Jihadi scene. Despite the competitive nature of the relationship with the two groups competing for fighters, territory, and operational momentum, they nonetheless managed to exist side by side in a state of controlled tension. The relationship took the form of a discursive rivalry but initially saw none of the infighting that had come to characterise relations between the groups in Syria.

At first, there were doubts about AQAP's reaction to the caliphate. AQAP had always enjoyed close ties with the al-Qaida affiliate in Iraq, but at the same time its leadership was tightly wedded to al-Qaida's leadership in AfPak. For example, Nasir al-Wuhayshi, AQAP's amir until his death in June 2015, was formerly Bin Laden's secretary in Afghanistan, and in 2013, al-Zawahiri elected him to the administrative position of general manager. In contrast to another al-Qaida affiliate, AQIM, it would take AQAP some time to publicise its stance on the caliphate. Immediately after the declaration, two senior AQAP ideologues—Harith bin Ghazi al-Nadhari and Ibrahim al-Rubaish—issued a video, but instead of commenting on the caliphate they focused on the vilification of scholars and the increasing polarisation within the SJM.[1] In November, eight days after al-Baghdadi announced the new province in Yemen, AQAP finally issued a clear criticism of the Islamic State. This came from al-Nadhari, who this time criticised the Islamic State for not meeting the shari'a conditions for establishing a caliphate and for splitting the Jihadi masses. Al-Nadhari emphasised AQAP's pledges of allegiance to al-Zawahiri and Mullah Umar and stated that 'we have not found any reason that necessitates the breaking of the covenant nor the bay'a. Based on this we refuse to heed the calls to split the ranks of the Jihadi groups.'[2] The following month al-Nadhari issued a timely reminder, entitled *Civility of the Dispute Between the Mujahidin*, as part of a running series. In this brief publication he reminds Jihadis that there should be room for diversity, that one should not take a position out of self-interest and that disagreements should be handled in a civil way.[3]

The Islamic State's response came in two articles published in its *Dabiq* magazine. In the first article, Abu Maysara al-Shami, a senior media figure, vilified al-Nadhari and al-Zawahiri. According to al-Shami, both of the al-Qaida leaders have deviated from the correct methodology, especially in terms of al-wala' wa-l-bara'; he elaborates on how this has influenced their reluctance to excommunicate, but at the same time highlights contradictions in their opinions in order to sow confusion in the ranks of al-Qaida.[4] In the second article, an unnamed author focuses on AQAP's handover of Mukalla to the local Hadhrami Domestic Council, which the author claims is partially comprised of apostates. AQAP could have chosen to maintain control of Mukalla and implement shari'a but opted to relinquish control to the council that collaborates with and supports *tyrant governments* (tawaghit). In the eyes of the author this makes AQAP the new *sahwat*—a reference to the movement in Iraq that, in collaboration with the US, fought the ISI. He ends the article,

> If matters carry on as they had in Sham [Syria], the common enemy between the Yemeni Qa'ida and the nationalist resistance will become the khilafa. May Allah guide the soldiers in the ranks of al-Qa'ida out of the ranks of partisanship and into the ranks of jama'a before they follow the footsteps of the apostate Julani front.[5]

Between the two articles, the Islamic State issued a video entitled 'Soldiers of the Caliphate in the Land of Yemen',[6] where the group frames itself as the main enemy of the Houthis and the protector of Sunnis in Yemen. Al-Qaida rebutted this accusation, claiming that ISY's efforts against the Houthis were widely exaggerated, and on another occasion, it described the group as outright lazy in assisting the Jihadi cause on the frontlines.[7] AQAP continued its criticism of ISY's methods. Firstly, the group distanced itself from the ISY's indiscriminate violence, referring to the group's bombings of public places and mosques. This came in an official statement released by al-Qaida in March. Later the same year, Khalid Saeed al-Batarfi—at the time a senior AQAP leader who would later take leadership of the group—issued two other statements about ISY. The first statement reiterated the critique of its indiscriminate bombings; the second, a joint statement on behalf of AQAP and AQIM, rejected the Islamic State spokesman al-Adnani's continuous courting of them, thus ending the Islamic State's last hope of a pledge of allegiance from AQAP.

Two factors are important for understanding why the inter-group dynamics did not initially escalate from discursive attacks to infighting. The first is ISY's obvious inferiority in terms of numbers and military capabilities. Attacking the much stronger and more locally embedded AQAP would have been suicidal. The second reason is the role of the two senior AQAP figures, Mamun Hatem (who died in May 2015) and Nabil al-Dhahab (who died in November 2014). Both appear to have been instrumental in managing the inter-group relationship and functioning as de-escalating intermediaries.[8] From early 2014, Hatem had a foot in both camps. He was officially part of AQAP but openly supported the Islamic State[9] while criticising senior Jabhat al-Nusra leaders. In private he was in contact with the Islamic State in Syria and Iraq. There is evidence of his popularity in both AQAP and ISY circles in the fact that he was eulogised by supporters of both groups. Less is known about al-Dhahab's role, but he was amir of Ansar al-Shari'a (AQAP's front group) in Bayda and was allegedly under Hatem's influence in terms of his views on the Islamic State. Both figures were central in postponing the Islamic State's declaration of its Yemeni province, and Hatem was even in the running to become its first wali.[10] This did not happen, however, and after AQAP's clear declaration of its stance on the caliphate, Hatem turned less vocal in his support.

### *Khorasan*

After establishing itself in the Levant, the Islamic State's most important priority in terms of expansion was arguably the Afghanistan–Pakistan (AfPak) region, referred to as *Khorasan* by the group. There were several reasons for this. Structurally the region had benefits. With conflict ravaging Afghanistan and many Jihadi groups active in the region, there was easy access to recruits. From a Jihadi perspective, the region was particularly important because of the history of Jihadi activity in the area. Finally, the region is the (historical) home of the Islamic State's two most important rivals for global dominance, namely al-Qaida and the Taliban. Hence the project of establishing itself in Khorasan—potentially at the expense of its two major competitors—was integral to the Islamic State's attempt to erode the authoritative position of al-Qaida and the Taliban and to become a movement hegemon.

Of the intra-Jihadi conflicts erupting post-2014, apart from those in the Levant, the conflict between the Taliban and the Islamic State's Khorasan Province (ISKP) remains the most studied. ISKP is generally considered the Islamic State's most successful satellite province. In part, its success was due to the group's creed and methodology. These appealed to disgruntled Jihadis in the region who either felt that the strategy of existing groups had failed or who disagreed with the dominant nationalist focus of militants and their (unofficial) collaboration with government actors. However, it is impossible to understand ISKP's immediate success in attracting pledges of allegiance on both a group and an individual level without emphasising the fact that it presented an attractive organisational platform for Jihadis looking to fulfil their personal ambitions. While ISKP was undoubtedly an attractive destination for Jihadis with Salafi inclinations in Khorasan, it is too simplistic to argue that all Jihadi-Salafis flocked to it, as is sometimes suggested.[11] Even so, having established itself, ISKP did find itself in a position to spread its theological views, narrative and symbols[12] and socialise local constituents.

The objective of the Taliban–al-Qaida nexus was to prevent the Islamic State from getting a strong foothold in Afghanistan and to maintain relations with the region's other militant groups. The Taliban was the main player in curbing ISKP's expansion, while al-Qaida took a more supportive role. Al-Qaida's leadership renewed its bay'a to the Taliban amir, stressed his authority and continuously reminded Jihadis around the world of the Taliban's achievements. In September 2014 al-Zawahiri also announced the establishment of a local al-Qaida affiliate in the Indian subcontinent (AQIS) with its base in Afghanistan. This was probably to ensure al-Qaida's continuing presence in the region in case he died, but it was also a means of strengthening operational relations with the Taliban. In contrast, after a slow start the Taliban was exceptionally active in combatting ISKP on the battlefield while pursuing a more discrete discursive campaign to delegitimise its new rival.[13]

With its expansion to Khorasan, the Islamic State brought with it the logic of polarisation. Jihadis in Khorasan were already quite fragmented: several groups were operating in the region, and organisational splintering was common. The dominant role of the al-Qaida–Taliban nexus nonetheless ensured a degree of stability. On 26 January 2015, Islamic State spokesperson al-Adnani officially announced ISKP. However, the process of its emergence had been ongoing for several months prior to this.[14] While there are reports of fighters from Khorasan pledging allegiance to al-Baghdadi around the time of the caliphate declaration and even before, it was in October 2014 that Hafiz Saeed Khan, a former Taliban member and Tehreek-e-Taliban (TTP) commander in Orakzai agency, pledged allegiance to the Islamic State. When ISKP was announced, Saeed Khan was elected its governor (wali). Saeed Khan was joined by other senior TTP figures including the group's spokesperson Shahidullah Shahid and several district level commanders and officials. Dissatisfied Afghan Taliban members and senior figures like Abdul Rauf Khadim, Mansour Dadullah[15] and Muslim Dost also joined or aligned with ISKP either because they were tempted by the organisational role offered to them or because they opposed Mullah Mansour's election as the Taliban's new amir. In a desperate attempt to halt the defections, the Taliban's leading shura allegedly issued a fatwa making it haram to give bay'a to al-Baghdadi.[16] Defections, however, continued, and even as late as 2017, high level members of the Taliban's Peshawar shura were joining ISKP, with others occasionally returning.

The delay in announcing the wilaya meant that Islamic State sympathisers had plenty of time between the first signs of support in autumn 2014—which came in the form of individual pledges of allegiance and circulation of Islamic State-sympathetic material—and the establishment of the province to network and organise. This ensured that at the time of its establishment ISKP already commanded a substantial force. But to understand ISKP's rapid success in attracting large numbers of Jihadis, it is necessary to grasp how the group tapped into a combination of ideological and organisational frustrations which were common to several groups in the region.

The primary organisational source of new recruits was the TTP and two factors help to explain this. Firstly, ideologically the TTP has always been considered the most radical group in the region, with a strong doctrinal and sectarian focus. As a result there was serious doubt over whether the entire TTP would abandon its loyalty to the Afghan Taliban and pledge allegiance to al-Baghdadi.[17] Secondly, TTP is best understood as an umbrella organisation comprising several factions which regularly compete for internal power. This was certainly the case in 2014–15. In November 2013, the powerful TTP amir Hakimullah Mehsud was killed, leading to internal fragmentation and power struggles. The new amir, Mullah Fazlullah, was not a popular choice among all TTP factions and did not manage to unify the disparate interests. Thus it came as no surprise that large numbers of TTP commanders and fighters, especially from the Orakzai and Bajaur agencies, joined ISKP. Many were appointed to very senior positions.

Similar doubts about loyalty initially surrounded Jama'at ul-Ahrar. In August 2014, the group split from TTP and took a neutral position towards the Islamic State. A few months later, in October, it issued the first edition of its English language magazine *Ihya-e-Khilafat* which began with an explanation of the differences between the group and its parent organization, TTP. One important difference was that Jama'at ul-Ahrar had a wider scope, with one of its aims being the establishment of a global caliphate. Bearing in mind the timing of the magazine, it was probably intended as a first step towards joining al-Baghdadi's caliphate. But in March 2015, Jama'at ul-Ahrar took the surprising step of reintegrating with the TTP.[18]

Another important victory for ISKP was the Islamic Movement of Uzbekistan's (IMU) decision to pledge allegiance and merge into ISKP. The IMU is one of the Jihadi groups with a long and impressive pedigree in Khorasan, and its decade in exile in Afghanistan and later Pakistan meant that it had developed strong relations with both the Afghan and Pakistani Taliban.[19] So it was a surprise in June 2015 when its amir, Uthman Ghazi, made the shift official.[20] One year later, in June 2016, a small faction of IMU in northern Afghanistan rejected the shift in allegiance but this did not include any senior figures,[21] and it is generally understood that the IMU does not exist any longer as an independent group. As will be explained later, after the IMU shifted sides, the Taliban would quickly move to eliminate a substantial part of the former IMU members.

Various other groups would also feel the impact of the Islamic State's expansion. Lashkar-e-Jhangvi, which is known as a sectarian-focused group, did not pledge allegiance to the Islamic State on a group level, but one of its factions—the Lashkar-e-Jhangvi al-Alami—reportedly did join ISKP. Lashkar-e-Jhangvi did cooperate with ISKP more generally, just as other groups such as Lashkar-e-Islam and Jama'at ul-Ahrar have also done.[22] This cooperative nature of ISKP illustrates one of the peculiarities of the Khorasan compared to other regions.

Geographically, ISKP first emerged in Nangarhar, but its presence was also registered in other provinces like Helmand (under the leadership of ISKP deputy Rauf Khadim), Sar-e-Pul and Farah. From mid-2015, it would seek refuge from Taliban attacks in the eastern provinces of Kunar, Paktia and Zabul, in addition to Nangarhar. In 2017 the group experienced a successful but short-lived expansion to the northern province Jowzjan, where it initially managed to expel the Taliban and to conquer and gain control of territory before eventually being ousted by a joint effort from the Taliban and government-supported forces. Showing its ability to penetrate urban centres, ISKP also began to execute attacks in Kabul in 2016. In 2017 this took the form of outbidding with the Taliban, with both groups executing regular attacks in the capital.[23]

For a long time, ISKP's primary enemy was not the Afghan regime or US forces in Afghanistan but the Taliban. There are different accounts of when infighting started between ISKP and the Taliban. One account claims that the first incident occurred in early November 2014 even before ISKP was officially established, and that further incidents followed in Farah, Logar and Kajaki in early 2015.[24] Another account discusses clashes in January 2015 between the Taliban and supporters of Rauf Khadim in northern Helmand.[25] A third account argues that infighting first erupted in early 2015 in Nangarhar's Nazian district when former TTP members ambushed

Taliban fighters, killing two district chiefs. In the aftermath the Taliban retaliated. The two groups would engage in negotiations to manage the escalating conflict, but these failed.[26] There was then further and more intense infighting in late June 2015, mainly in Nangarhar under the ISKP leader Sabir Kochi (known as the 'Butcher of ISIS') when the Taliban changed its attitude from 'passive resistance to head-on confrontation.'[27] At first, ISKP would come out on top, dominating several districts in Nangarhar before the Taliban beat it back in early 2016, forcing ISKP fighters to retreat to Kunar.

Although ISKP allegedly attracted several thousand fighters,[28] the Taliban was still a much stronger fighting force and it increasingly prioritised military confrontation with ISKP. In October 2015, the group established an *elite force* of 1,000 fighters with the aim of combating ISKP fighters. Aided by a fatwa legitimising the fight against ISKP, this elite force was dispatched to several provinces where ISKP had a presence.[29] From mid-2015, in a similar way to how events played out in Syria, the Taliban's newly assertive attitude was strengthened when US forces began their air campaign targeting ISKP and civilians started to oppose ISKP's presence.[30] Nowhere was this assertiveness more evident than in the Zabul Massacre when, in November 2015, the Taliban attacked IMU fighters in the province, killing a high number of its former allies, including the group's leader Uthman Ghazi. One version of what happened comes from an ISKP sympathetic Jihadi's account. He writes that 'What the US and its agents could not do in 14 years, the Taliban did in 24 hours.' Approximately 800 Taliban fighters were deployed to Zabul where they reportedly killed 150 IMU fighters, women, and children. While some IMU fighters had already left Zabul, this still represented the majority of the IMU fighters who had joined ISKP.

Infighting between the Taliban and ISKP continued post-January 2016 in Nangarhar, but at a lower level of intensity. More serious military conflict would erupt further north in Jowzjan Province in October 2017. Already in 2015, Qari Hekmat, a former Taliban shadow governor in Darzab district, had joined ISKP. Hekmat controlled Darzab, but when he attempted to expand into the neighboring district of Qush Tepa, fighting broke out with the Taliban. The infighting for the small Jowzjan enclave can be divided into three periods. The first was in October 2017 when the Taliban launched a counteroffensive to retake lost territory; this was unsuccessful despite the group mobilising fighters from several surrounding provinces. The second period was in January–February 2018 but ended in a similar result. Between the second and third offensive, Hekmat was killed in a US airstrike in April after he appeared in an Islamic State video for the first and only time the month before. With Hekmat out of the picture, the Taliban finally experienced some success in combatting ISKP forces in Jowzjan, not least because of simultaneous attacks from US-Afghan forces. The third offensive in July and August thus represented the end for ISKP in Jowzjan, when the amir following Hekmat surrendered to government forces along with 150 fighters. Finally, from summer 2019 the Taliban launched new offensives against ISKP in Kunar and in Nangarhar that largely decimated the group, killing a large number of ISKP fighters. Once again, the Taliban's crackdown on ISKP was led by the group's special forces, but this time they were assisted by fighters from al-Qaida in the Indian subcontinent (AQIS), which was dispatching a special unit to support the Taliban with expertise in explosives.[31]

Jihadi infighting in Afghanistan did not just involve ISKP and the Taliban, however. The Taliban also cracked down on the High Council of Afghanistan, a faction comprised of former Talibanis, thus emphasising its hegemonist rationale. Mullah Mohammad Rasoul was the former Taliban shadow governor in Nimroz and a close associate of Mullah Umar. Like many other senior Taliban figures, he opposed the election of Mullah Mansour as the new amir, which pushed him to split from the Taliban and establish the High Council of Afghanistan in November 2015.[32] He was joined by Mansour Dadullah, also a former Taliban leader, who briefly flirted with ISKP. Fighting between Rasoul's forces had already broken out in August and lasted until 2017, claiming more than 440 lives. ISKP would also engage another group militarily. From early 2018 until October of the same year, the group turned its aggression towards its former allies in Lashkar-e-Islam. For the most part, the two groups had cooperated, but relations allegedly soured over the issue of control over natural resources, leading to at least eighty-five casualties.[33]

Based on numbers from the UCDP database and my own data (see tables 1 and 2), I estimate that the infighting between ISKP and the Taliban, the Taliban, and the High Council of Afghanistan, and ISKP and Lashkar-e-Islam has led to more than 1500 casualties in total.[34] Estimating casualties is obviously fraught with uncertainty, as will be explained later on, and local observers claim the real number may in fact be double, with ISKP suffering the majority of casualties.[35]

Just as in Syria, the infighting was closely connected with the discursive contestation between the groups involved and their sympathisers. For instance, after an exchange of words between Mullah Mansour and al-Adnani, Taliban-affiliated ʻulama issued a fatwa making it legitimate to fight ISKP in self-defence. This directly initiated the Taliban's change from *passive resistance* to *confrontation*. Studying the rhetoric and the visual productions of the respective groups also offers important insights into their diverging attitudes to infighting.

The Taliban's attitude to discussing ISKP on a religious and political level largely resembled its hesitance to report on military infighting. Its general strategy was to give neither ISKP nor Jihadi infighting unnecessary attention. However, it is useful to consider some exceptions. Shortly before Mullah Umar's death was announced, Mullah Mansour—the soon-to-be new amir of the Taliban—authored a public letter to Abu Bakr al-Baghdadi. This was the moment when infighting was about to start, and Mansour's letter was an attempt to de-escalate tensions and convince al-Baghdadi to abandon his Khorasan expansion. Mansour begins his letter with a historical contextualisation: Jihad in Afghanistan has a history, and that history involves experiences of infighting which have had a devastating impact on its progress. For this reason, he argues, the priority of the Afghan Jihad should be unity. While this might sound like a unitarian rationale, another quotation allows us to see that the Taliban's behaviour is partly driven by ambitions of attaining an organisational monopolisation of Afghanistan's Jihadi environment. Mansour writes,

> By adhering and following the above-mentioned verses from its previous Jihadi experiences and from understanding the

> environment of its society, the Islamic Emirate does not consider the existence of multiple Jihadi groups as beneficial for Jihad or in benefit of the Muslims. Because a characterising feature of the Afghan Jihad is that internal conflicts and disputes always exist and if the leadership is one then this eliminates the chances of disputes and conflict.[36]

He continues by listing nine conditions for operating in Afghanistan; these all centre on the need and obligation to operate under a single banner represented by the Taliban's leadership.

The most comprehensive attempt by the Taliban to delegitimise the Islamic State on a global and local level is Qari Saeed Khosti's document *Daesh from Mosul to Nangarhar*.[37] This 150-page booklet contains an elaborate account of the Islamic State's history, its deviations in creed and methodology and the sins the group has committed from the Taliban's perspective. Khosti's main ambition is to challenge ISKP by delegitimising its foundation in the Levant, largely through the argument that its reliance on takfir supports the accusation that the group is a modern version of the Khawarij. Here Khosti is simply repeating an existing criticism of the Islamic State, but the booklet's real contribution is its empirical content, which outlines the Islamic State's crimes against other Jihadis and civilians in Syria and Iraq. Thus the work is both a theological and an empirical refutation of the Islamic State, one that also links the group's behaviour in the Levant to a future scenario in Khorasan.

The Islamic State's main response would come from its central leadership. Back in 2011, al-Adnani had praised Mullah Umar and the Taliban, but in June 2015, in response to Mullah Mansour's letter, his tone was strikingly different, essentially calling for ISKP fighters to fight anyone who does not pledge allegiance:

> O factions of Khurasan! What will you gain from fighting the Islamic State? Does one of you desire to dig his grave with his own hands, or wish to have his head cut off, or his house demolished? (…) We also call all the mujahidin in Khurasan who truthfully endeavour to implement the Shari'a of Allah to join the ranks of the Khilafah. We call them to abandon discord, the discord of the factions, parties, and groups, for the Khilafah gathers all

> the Muslims (…) And in Khurasan there are those who claim to be mujahidin fi sabilillah while being an ally of the Pakistani intelligence or others. We warn these people and call them to repent. Whoever does not repent and announce his repentance, then he has no one to blame but himself. O mujahidin, do not show these likes any pity nor mercy.[38]

The Islamic State would generally vilify the Taliban and Mullah Mansour in its official publications, criticising the group's alleged relations with the Pakistani intelligence service, its nationalist ideology, and its deviant theology, while also attacking Mansour for keeping Mullah Umar's death a secret.[39] The Islamic State treated the death of Mullah Umar as a means of rending the Taliban's authority and instigating mass defection from the group. In its *Dabiq* magazine released in July 2015—the same month Mullah Umar's death was confirmed—an article appeared dealing with the situation in Afghanistan.[40] The article begins with a question from a 'worried' Taliban member about 'legitimate leadership'. Drawing on a famous hadith which states that 'If bay'a is given to two khulafa, then kill the second of the two', he argues that if Mullah Umar was still alive, al-Baghdadi's claim to be a caliph would not just be invalid but in violation of religious law. However, if Mullah Umar really is dead, then al-Baghdadi would be a legitimate caliph. The answer, taking the form of a fatwa, draws a distinction between a *general shar'i imama* and a *territorial leader*, the latter ruling a specific territory. The fatwa states that establishing a general shar'i imama is a religious obligation, and that such a figure is superior to a territorial leader. Hence, no matter if Mullah Umar is confirmed dead or not, al-Baghdadi's caliphate represents a global Islamic authority, a general shar'i imama, superseding Mullah Umar's imamate.[41] Ending its ruling, the article calls for Taliban fighters to hasten in pledging their allegiance to al-Baghdadi and to join ISKP in accordance with their religious obligations.

Although both groups from mid-2015 adopted confrontational attitudes towards one another as part of their larger ambition of monopolising Afghanistan's Jihadi environment, they differed in their communication about the infighting. From early 2016, ISKP would begin to issue official announcements taking responsibility for attacks on Taliban fighters. Soon after, and even more controversially, the group began to publish photos of assassinations of their Taliban rivals, referring to Taliban fighters as *apostates* (murtaddin). In contrast, the Taliban rarely communicated officially about its infighting with ISKP. Occasionally, it issued formal statements referring to specific offensives against '*daesh*' positions, but it did not generally release visuals from the battles.[42] This divergence is partly down to differences in attitude towards the legitimacy of Jihadi infighting, and is evidence of how the Taliban, like al-Qaida, considered—and continue to consider—the issue much more sensitive than the Islamic State.

The infighting in Khorasan is a vivid example of how conflict dynamics in Syria expanded to other battlefields and transformed local Jihadi environments. When the Islamic State established ISKP, it brought sectarianism,[43] fragmentation and polarisation to the region, and most likely changed its Jihadi landscape for good. These events also show that while conflict dynamics are local in nature, they are also connected to the deeper schism which occurred in Syria, largely evolving through similar processes. A striking difference, however, is the presence of two *hegemonists* in Afghanistan, which led to more intense confrontations and a situation where one Jihadi group—the Taliban—emerged as the most influential actor in curbing the Islamic State's presence in Khorasan.

### *The Maghreb, the Sahel and West Africa*

In contrast with events in Khorasan and what would later erupt in Yemen, the inter-group dynamics in the Maghreb, the Sahel and West Africa, while competitive, did not initially result in infighting. This is most likely because the groups managed to 'divide' the region and thus did not compete for the same areas, and because of the Islamic State's inferiority in the Maghreb and the Sahel.

In the Maghreb and the Sahel, the Islamic State would face the challenge of convincing another al-Qaida affiliate, AQIM, to abandon its loyalty to al-Zawahiri and pledge allegiance to al-Baghdadi. But just as in Yemen, the group ultimately failed to sway the AQIM leadership and only attracted a small AQIM sub-faction, in addition to a small number of rank and file. Furthest to the north, in Algeria, breakaway elements from AQIM led by Abdelmalek Gouri (Khalid Abu Suleiman) pledged allegiance to al-Baghdadi in September 2014 and renewed it in November when the group called Jund al-Khilafa fi ard al-Jaza'ir (Soldiers of the Caliphate in Algeria) was officially declared the Islamic State's new province in Algeria (Wilayat al-Jaza'ir). Gouri explained that his shift from AQIM to the Islamic State was because AQIM no longer followed the correct methodology.[44] But just half a year later, the new wilaya was almost entirely shattered as Algerian security forces killed Gouri and most of his fighters. This is a clear demonstration of how important the local environment/context is, with the Algerian state serving as a useful example. The state left no room for a nascent Islamic State group to operate in and, as a result, it quickly dissolved.

The failure to convince the AQIM leadership to pledge allegiance was not for want of trying. Partly as a charm offensive, partly as an order, Abu Ubayda Abd al-Hakim, a member of the Islamic State's shura council and delegated committee, sent a series of letters to AQIM amir Droukdal in a bid to convince him to abandon his pledge to al-Zawahiri and instead become part of the caliphate. Only one letter in the series has been discovered, but it offers a fascinating glimpse into how the Islamic State attempted to lure away al-Qaida affiliates.[45] At the same time, it reveals how difficult it was for the Islamic State to breach the horizontal ties among al-Qaida leaders, largely founded on shared experiences in Afghanistan or Sudan, or on long-standing cooperative relationships.

Al-Hakim's focus in the letter is on the caliphate's success in Syria and Iraq and its basic legitimacy. He informs Droukdal that the new Islamic state is flourishing, and that Islamic law (shari'a) is implemented across its territory. 'Every single pillar and requirement of the caliphate has been fulfilled', he tells the AQIM amir. It becomes clear from the letter that Droukdal has expressed doubts about this in a previous letter, and al-Hakim invites him to send a delegate to confirm that the caliphate is following the correct methodology. From al-Hakim's letter, we also learn that Droukdal previously raised concerns about three issues: the election of a caliph without the agreement of the *qualified authorities* (ahl al-hall wa-l-aqd), the issue of *consolidation* (tamkin) as a requirement for the caliphate's establishment, and the breaking of bay'a to al-Zawahiri. Sympathetic voices within al Qaida have long suggested that the decision to establish the caliphate was made without consulting the qualified authorities. The Islamic State had claimed it did consult people of authority locally, but time and again it has refused to name them. In response, Droukdal lists six senior ideological figures that he believes should be counted as ahl al-hall wa-l-aqd: Abu Muhammad al-Maqdisi, Abu Qatada al-Filistini, Sulayman al-Alwan, Abu al-Walid al-Ghazi, Ayman al-Zawahiri and Mullah Omar. Al-Hakim clearly took Droukdal's message seriously, as he responds by refuting each of them.[46]

Al-Hakim comments more briefly on the issues of territorial consolidation and the pledge of allegiance. To him, the group's territorial control is clear: not only does it control land, it also rules it according to shari'a. To illustrate its territorial consolidation, he notes that one can travel from Aleppo to Diyala and still be in territory under al-Baghdadi's control. A major issue for individuals and groups loyal to al-Qaida has been the legitimacy of potentially breaking their pledge of allegiance. To address this, al-Hakim turns the argument around, writing 'concerning your argument that the bay'a shall not be broken, we would say that this is valid prior to the caliphate. Now that we have true caliphate without the slightest shari'a fault in itself or its imamate, breaking the bay'a has become mandatory according to the shari'a.' In fact, then, the impermissible act is *not* breaking allegiance to al-Zawahiri so as to extend it to al Baghdadi.

Another argument made by rival Jihadi groups is that the Islamic State has been the aggressor and that the establishment of the caliphate has only exacerbated tensions. Droukdal follows this line of argument, but unsurprisingly al-Hakim objects, claiming that the caliphate is here to unite Muslims. Acknowledging that the ongoing conflict is damaging, however, he invites Droukdal to mediate, writing 'So dear brother, if you wish to mediate for reconciliation and resolution of conflicts amicably and based on compatibility and conciliation between all the mujahedeen unanimous on this imam under this caliph, then you are the right mediator.' Knowing that the Islamic State rejected all reconciliation efforts, this seems a rather empty promise. In a final effort to convince Droukdal and his group to join the Islamic State, al-Hakim writes that

> the defamation and invalidation of its legitimacy by al-Qaida shall not render it [the caliphate] illegitimate without a legal reason based on shari'a. This is the core issue, and we do love you brothers and would love for our mujahedeen brothers and our umma to be united under one word, therefore, the commander of believers has written to you to follow the crowd, overcome the differences, and heal the rift.

AQIM, however, would not be swayed by al-Hakim's offer. At the time, AQIM had already issued a very critical statement in the immediate aftermath of the caliphate declaration, and half a year after the exchange of letters between Droukdal and al-Hakim, a senior AQIM member, Abu Aḥmad Abd al-Karim al-Jazairi, authored a lengthy critique of the Islamic State stressing its illegitimacy.

Further south in the Sahel, the Islamic State fared slightly better. The most likely candidate to defect and pledge allegiance to al-Baghdadi was probably Mukhtar Belmokhtar. Despite Belmokhtar's close relations with al-Zawahiri and most of AQIM, he considered AQIM amir Droukdal a direct rival and on several occasions was disappointed with his treatment by the AQIM leadership. In fact, he had been in the running for Droukdal's position back in 2004 and later expected to become amir of AQIM in the Sahel, but on both occasions he was overlooked. He later split from AQIM to establish his own group, al-Murabitoun. Joining the Islamic State would have offered Belmokhtar the means of finally obtaining the organisational role he had long desired. However, in May 2015, it was not Belmokhtar but another senior al-Murabitoun figure, Abu Walid al-Sahrawi,[47] who announced his pledge of allegiance to al-Baghdadi, taking with him approximately 100 fighters to create the Islamic State's province in the Greater Sahara (ISGS), primarily based in Mali.[48] Later that year, in December, Belmokhtar rejoined AQIM,[49] and in an audio announcement his group al-Murabitoun stated that 'It is not right that the worshipers of the Cross have gathered to fight us, and we, the bearers of the Qur'an, are divided. Dispute is the same as failure.'[50] Al-Qaida's response to the establishment of ISGS would be to unify the ranks of sympathetic Jihadis across the Sahel to establish the Jama'at Nusrat al-Islam wa-l-Muslimin (JNIM) in March 2016. Besides AQIM's Sahel unit (led by Yahya Abu Humman), JNIM consists of Ansar al-Deen (led by Iyad al-Ghali), Macina Liberation Front (led by Amadou Koufa) and Al-Mourabitoun (led by Mukhtar Belmokhtar), all under the regional command of Droukdal and with a pledge of allegiance to al-Zawahiri. Following the trend of al-Qaida, JNIM even extended its pledge to Taliban amir Haibatullah. This shows that while unity had clear operational benefits, the JNIM initiative is best understood from the standpoint of the competitive environment within the SJM in the Sahel. Despite the continuing presence of both AQIM/JNIM and ISGW in Mali, the competitive relationship remained peaceful until 2019 and at the time, in January 2016, Yahya Abu Hummam explained that AQIM even maintained cordial relations with al-Sahrawi's group.[51]

Even further south in Nigeria, the situation was different. The dominant Jihadi group, Boko Haram, was not an al-Qaida affiliate, but for years had enjoyed close relations with AQIM, especially regarding training and ideological development.[52] Boko Haram's leader Abu Bakr Shekau was always seen as too extreme for al-Qaida, which at this point was very much concerned with its brand; thus Boko Haram never became a formal al-Qaida affiliate, despite Shekau's desire for this to happen. In 2015, this meant that the group did not need to revoke a pledge of allegiance to al-Zawahiri but could simply 'join' the Islamic State. This happened on March 7, 2015, and it arguably represents the most important 'victory' in al-Baghdadi's expansion process. Interestingly, Zenn shows that Boko Haram's decision was largely the result of internal power dynamics, highlighting the importance of studying the internal dimensions of Jihadi groups. Internally, Abu Musab al-Barnawi, the group's spokesperson and the son of its founder, Muhammed Yusuf, challenged Shekau for leadership. In 2014–15, Shekau found himself in a catch-22. On the one hand, al-Barnawi saw a pledge to the Islamic State as a way of convincing al-Baghdadi to demote Shekau and thus to become the new amir of Boko Haram himself. On the other hand, Shekau feared an 'internal rebellion or [the] risk [of] sub-commanders making the pledge without him, which they threatened to do.'[53] Again, lines of communication proved to be important. It was some of Shekau's commanders, including al-Barnawi and not Shekau himself, who were in contact with the North Africa based Islamic State intermediaries, which made Shekau nervous.

So, although Shekau did consider al-Baghdadi to be a legitimate caliph, he was aware of the internal dangers of pledging allegiance, and this made him reluctant to do so. In March 2015, Shekau finally relented and offered his bay'a in an audio statement praising al-Baghdadi and his caliphate. But in August 2016, al-Barnawi's own plan came to fruition when the Islamic State announced that al-Barnawi was its new amir. A disgruntled Shekau went back to head a group of loyalists under the Boko Haram name, while continuing to indicate his allegiance to al-Baghdadi and copying the Islamic State's visual identity in his group's digital productions.

### *North and East Africa*

The Islamic State also made inroads in Libya, Egypt and Somalia, along the way engaging in contestation and infighting with existing Jihadi groups. We know least about the situation in Egypt. Early on the Islamic State managed to convince the Sinai-based group Ansar Bait al-Maqdis (ABM) to pledge allegiance and become its Sinai Province. ABM had links but no affiliation to al-Qaida; nonetheless it was an important victory for the Islamic State to claim a province in Egypt. From November 2017 onwards, tensions and infighting were reported between Islamic State fighters and the al-Qaida-linked Jama'at Jund al-Islam. It seemed initially, however, to have been limited to a few incidents. At the time, Jund al-Islam issued a few statements and Telegram posts on the tensions, but the information was extremely limited, thus making it troublesome for outsiders to assess the extent of the conflict. In July 2020, the Islamic State offered its version of events in an account published in its al-Naba newsletter that describes how the conflict already began in May 2017 and was sparked by Jund al-Islam's secret alliance with the Egyptian army. The account explicitly states that the Islamic State in

Sinai only started fighting Jund al-Islam *after* it had established that the group had committed a nullifier of Islam, effectively rendering it an apostate group.[54]

In Libya, an Islamic State province was also announced during the first wave of expansion in November 2014. The month before, the group Majlis Shura Shabab al-Islam (the Islamic Youth Shura Council, MSSI) had declared its allegiance to al-Baghdadi, yet as Zelin explains, MSSI's origins only go back to April 2014, and in June it offered its first support to the Islamic State. The group consisted of a larger contingent of Islamic State fighters dispatched from Syria to Libya as part of the expansion strategy, and it represents the organisational foundation of what eventually became Islamic State's province in Libya (ISL).[55] Unsurprisingly, the appearance of the Islamic State in Libya would cause tensions with existing Jihadi.

Little is known about the intra-Jihadi conflict in Libya, but the epicentre was in the Eastern city of Derna. As early as September 2014, fighting erupted between MSSI and local insurgent groups including some with Jihadi inclinations. With the formal establishment of ISL, the infighting was mainly between the Derna Mujahideen Shura Council (DMSC) and ISL.[56] The DMSC was a military alliance created in December 2014 comprised of several insurgent groups, with the Abu Salim Martyrs Brigade and Ansar al-Shari'a Libya (ASL), another Jihadi group with links to al-Qaida, being the main components.[57] The Abu Salim Martyrs Brigade had lamented the MSSI's pledge to the Islamic State in October while the ISL responded that its opponents were apostates and called for them to repent.[58] The infighting would continue until April 2016 when ISL was forced to flee Derna, but it was already slowing down from late 2015 on.

At the infighting's zenith in June 2015, Abu Qatada al-Filastini issued a fatwa discussing the permissibility of fighting ISL in response to a question from some mujahideen in Libya. The context for the question, as Abu Qatada explains, is that the mujahideen were ambushed by ISL fighters who were then attacked by fighter planes belonging to General Haftar. This led some of the mujahideen to react angrily, crying out that they hoped Haftar's fighters would strike the ISL fighters, but others objected stating such statements equalled unbelief. Abu Qatada's answer builds on an important distinction between a pure legal (fiqh) argument and reality-based jurisprudence (fiqh al-waqi'). 'Only reality can determine the way we look at them [Islamic State]', he writes.

> If the conflict was in general between a disbeliever and a Kharijite, then your wish and prayer in claiming victory to the disbeliever in killing the Kharijite [singular of khawarij] is a criminal act (…) Your duty is to wish for the victory of the Kharijites over the disbeliever (…) However, if the picture conforms to the aforementioned and that the khawarij are assaulting you and suddenly a disbeliever or a true idolater comes and kills a Kharijite, you wish for his death.[59]

This implies that in a situation where the mujahideen are under attack from the khawarij, they are allowed to oppose them. This way of reasoning and, more generally, different actors' perceptions of *reality* play a central role in understanding the disagreement not just between al-Qaida and the Islamic State but also the later contestation between al-Qaida and its Syrian affiliate. Abu Qatada ends his fatwa by stating that he has shared it with Abu Muhammad al-Maqdisi, who agreed with his conclusions. Even so, precisely this distinction between a pure legal (fiqh) argument and reality-based jurisprudence (fiqh al-waqi') would lead to a division between the two ideologues in 2017.

In Somalia, problems emerged in 2015 when the Islamic State managed to attract disgruntled members and ideological hardliners from al-Shabab. At first, the contestation took the form of statements, videos and memos supporting one group over the other, but it eventually escalated into an internal crackdown and military confrontation, first in late 2015, with a second round in 2018. The course of events in Somalia is revealing of both the Islamic State's tendency to capitalise on existing tensions within Jihadi groups to further its global expansion and of how shifting allegiances and infighting are triggered. After the Islamic State's split from al-Qaida and its announcement of the caliphate, two important dynamics typically would occur. Dissatisfied members of a local Jihadi group would identity the Islamic State as an attractive alternative platform on which to build their own powerbase, while the Islamic State or its sympathisers would reach out to these dissatisfied cadres to build up support, offering religious justifications for shifting allegiance. In some cases, local religious authorities would weigh in and offer their support for the Islamic State's caliphate claim, in the process even criticising al-Qaida so as to enable rank and file members to jump ship, or even to legitimise violent confrontation with their former brothers-in-arms. But arguably one atypical aspect of the infighting at this early stage in 2015 is the unidirectional violence by al-Shabab against Islamic State members. Just as in Afghanistan, this was most likely the result of two factors. Firstly, there was an uneven power balance heavily favouring al-Shabab in terms of capabilities, fighters, and local embeddedness.[60] Secondly, al-Shabab, like the Taliban and learning from the experience in Syria, sought to maintain its domestic hegemony and thus quickly moved to suppress challengers.

For the al-Shabab leadership, the objective was to ensure that its group did not splinter. This was particularly challenging because of the recent death of its longstanding leader Ahmed Abdi Godane in September 2014. Godane's leadership was authoritarian and sparked internal opposition and factionalism within al-Shabab, which became particularly evident when the group came to elect a new leader. The context in 2014–15 is important for understanding the dynamics within al-Shabab at the time. While the group was facing operational challenges and internal opposition, the Islamic State in Iraq and Syria was going from one success to another, finally symbolised by the caliphate declaration and the capture of Mosul. Al-Shabab members opposed to Godane used Yemen as a refuge, and it was especially among these dissatisfied cadres that sympathy for the Islamic State grew. They allied with a prominent al-Shabab figure in Somalia, Abd al-Qadir Mumin, who shared their sympathy for pledging allegiance to Abu Bakr al-Baghdadi. Mumin was initially a good ally because of his religious authority as a jurist and his ability to issue fatwas. The problem for these pro-Islamic State sympathisers within al-Shabab was Godane's strong loyalty to al-Qaida. Allegedly, Mumin aired the idea of shifting allegiance to al-Baghdadi among senior al-Shabab leaders, but the majority refused simply because of Godane's staunch support for al-Zawahiri.[61]

The situation changed after Godane's death and the election of Abu Ubayda as the new amir. While Abu Ubayda did try to mend fences with internal critics, he did not have the same relationship and dedication to al-Qaida since he had never spent time in Afghanistan or Pakistan. The leadership change thus opened a window for Islamic State sympathisers in Somalia, with Mumin and Hussein Abdi Gedi being the most prominent figures in the campaign to rouse support for pledging allegiance to al-Baghdadi both internally and among important clans. In early 2015, the Islamic State started to reach out to disgruntled al-Shabab members. In a statement from February entitled 'A Message to our Brothers in Somalia', an Islamic State sympathiser named Hamil al-Bushra lauds Jihadis in Somalia for fighting government forces and implementing shari'a, while also encouraging them to make the final 'required step' and pledge allegiance to the Islamic State to ensure unity among Muslims. Al-Bushra directed his message directly to Abu Ubayda and his shura council, asking them why they have not already offered their allegiance to al-Baghdadi. To pre-empt the expected criticism, al-Bushra made sure to explain to Abu Ubayda that the Islamic State is neither khawarij or murji'a and that it exercises restraint when applying takfir. He ends his message by telling Abu Ubayda how easy it is to pledge allegiance, even instructing him in the procedure on how to do so.[62] In September and October 2015, the Islamic State's official media department and other pro-Islamic State media outlets issued four more articles and five videos directly touching upon the situation in Somalia.[63] The message was clear: al-Qaida is a deviant group which has abandoned the proper creed ('aqida) and it is now a religious obligation to join the Islamic State.[64]

Further aggravating the situation for al-Shabab's leadership was the religious support that al-Baghdadi received from influential voices based in Kenya. In March 2015, Abu Salman, an al-Shabab cleric, issued a statement legitimising pledging allegiance to al-Baghdadi at the expense of the Taliban's Mullah Umar.[65] And six months later, Hassan Husein Adan, a Nairobi-based sheikh who exercised strong influence on al-Shabab members, authored a letter in which he lent support to al-Baghdadi while discrediting al-Qaida's rejection of his caliphate.[66] Importantly, Hassan explains that anyone, including al-

Qaida, who rejects the caliphate should be considered a *rebel* (baghi) who legitimately can be fought.

Pro-Islamic State sentiments were visibly gaining ground within al-Shabab. A tangible indication of this is that Islamic State videos were reportedly screened on al-Shabab members' 'film nights' on Fridays.[67] Although it appeared that al-Shabab leaders would finally give in and pledge allegiance to al-Baghdadi in summer 2015, for reasons that are unknown this did not occur, and in September, the leadership circulated an internal memo cementing its bay'a to al-Zawahiri and enforcing restrictions on any vocal sympathy for the Islamic State. Harun and Joseph explain that the group's spokesperson, Ali Dhere, also made it clear that al-Shabab was the only 'legitimate Islamic authority' in Somalia.[68] Following this memo, an internal purge against pro-Islamic State sympathisers began to cement al-Shabab's Jihadi hegemony in Somalia, critically escalating tensions between al-Shabab and the emerging Islamic State contingent.[69]

On October 22, 2015, Mumin and a group of fighters finally pledged allegiance to al-Baghdadi by issuing a short audio statement. Shortly afterwards this was followed by two further pledges of allegiance. The first was on November 8 when a group of twenty-seven fighters made bay'a to al-Baghdadi in a video. A month later, on December 7, a smaller group of fighters led by Bashir Abu Numan similarly offered their allegiance in a video that was posted online following their assassination by al-Shabab's intelligence unit. An indication of the Islamic State's relative weakness in Somalia, however, is that the group would not refer to its fighters in Somalia as a 'wilaya' (province) before December 24, 2017, effectively creating the Islamic State in Somalia Province (ISS).[70]

The attacks by al-Shabab against Islamic State members and sympathisers started in earnest in November 2015 when Hussein Abdi Gedi and Bashir Abu Numan, two of the highest-ranking al-Shabab defectors, were killed. I have been able to identify at least six episodes of military confrontation in November and December, which left approximately fifteen Islamic State members dead and all but eliminated the group's presence in southern Somalia. According to Harun and Joseph, the confrontations continued during early 2016, with al-Shabab focusing on Mumin and the Islamic State's remaining presence in Puntland. This led an Islamic State media official to claim that targeting Islamic State sympathisers had become al-Shabab's primary concern.[71] In an offensive in March, al-Shabab sent as many as 700 fighters on boats towards Puntland to kill Mumin. Although the operation failed because of the presence of international anti-piracy forces, the sheer number of fighters is revealing of al-Shabab's assertiveness in attempting to destroy domestic rivals.

### *Conclusions*

The previous two chapters have traced the conflict dynamics within the SJM and their repercussions, mainly in the period from 2014–15. It first explained how the distinctive attitudes to the intensifying intra-Jihadi conflict manifested themselves in the diverging strategies adopted by al-Qaida and the Islamic State. While the Islamic State focused on expanding the caliphate outside the Levant, and thus also on exporting internal conflict to other battlefields, al-Qaida's two-pronged strategy was to reinforce the legitimacy of the Taliban amir as a counter-authority and to manage the chaos locally in Syria. These steps led to a global fragmentation within the SJM and an increasingly dominant logic of polarisation that would determine the structure of the movement in the years to come.

Besides movement fragmentation and polarisation, important developments within the SJM took place which not only changed the identity of individual groups but also the diversity of the movement's ideological spectrum, in the process exerting pressure on its ideological cohesion. In particular, Ahrar al-Sham's 'moderation' expanded the ideological orientation of Jihadi groups but simultaneously problematised its relations with more hard-line Jihadi groups. Eventually, this would come to play a key role in the future tensions between former allies in Syria's northwest.

The Islamic State's expansion process and the ensuing infighting in several Jihadi battlefields is evidence of several important dynamics. They indicate how connected, on both the global and local levels, intra-Jihadi dynamics really are. Relations between groups in other countries were affected by the conflict in the Levant, with many of the groups tapping into the same narratives. These dynamics also show the growing normalisation of infighting within the SJM. With conflict ongoing in Syria and justifications for infighting already established, the threshold for the eruption of infighting in other countries was critically lowered. As the following chapters will show, this normalisation process continued as Jihadis were socialised to the legitimacy of fighting their peers.

# PART FIVE

# BETWEEN PURITY AND PRAGMATISM

*'It is a clear methodological conflict between the methodologies of the right monotheism, disbelieving the taghut [tyrant][1] represented by the Islamic state, and between the losing methodology that pledges allegiance to the taghut of the Taliban and stops shari'a on account of the popular environment and accepts the awakening of the unbelievers.'*[2]

Islamic State supporter Gharib al-Sururiyya

*'The fitna does not damage you if you know well your religion. If you are suspicious, then the right and false are tangled and accordingly, you will not know which to follow, then this is fitna.'*[3]

Musannaf Ibn Abi Shaybah

# 9

# FIGHTING OVER THE PROPHETIC METHODOLOGY

This chapter takes a closer look at the *level* of disagreements that drive intra-Jihadi conflict. In his analysis of Jihadi–Salafi ideology, Maher raises an important point, arguing that the SJM is indeed open to divergences in interpretation in certain circumstances and that there is a difference between theory and practice.[4] As we will see, much of the inter- and intra-group conflict within Sunni Jihadism is either based in or framed through this space for interpretation. In research on intra-Salafi tensions, some have argued that such tensions are primarily the result of *methodological*[5] (manhaj) and/or *creedal*[6] ('aqida) disagreements. Adding to this debate, I argue that while intra-Jihadi conflict is a combination of creedal and methodological tensions, it is equally a matter of diverging interpretation and analysis of the contemporary social and political *reality* (waqi') and Jihadis' political interests, which are strategically instrumentalised to provoke and justify military confrontation. From the perspective of the Islamic State, this process was largely driven by an elevation of the importance of *manhaj* in a bid to reorder authority structures, and by a reliance on the principle of *al-wala' wa-l-bara'* (loyalty and separation). For al-Qaida and aligned ideologues, it was a matter of contesting the Islamic State's narrative while also pushing back by labelling it as khawarij.

The use of the term 'manhaj' is relatively new and only became popular among Salafis in Egypt in the 1960s and in Saudi Arabia in the 1970s as a way to oppose Islamists. Hence, from this modern beginning it was used as a conceptual mechanism to include and exclude.[7] The emphasis on methodology as central to the fitna is acknowledged by leaders of both al-Qaida and the Islamic State, with al-Adnani writing that 'The conclusion of the matter is that the conflict between the Islamic State and the leadership of al-Qaeda is one of method, as the amir of al-Qaeda said in his recent interview with al-Sahab. This is the issue.'[8] That said, the argument is not that divergences in creed are absent, or that the conflicting actors do not frame broader disagreements as matters of creed. What my study does illustrate, however, is that tensions, fragmentation and conflict do not neatly correspond to creedal fault lines. Rather, we see that diverging methodologies chiefly derive from diverging interpretations of reality—resulting from a combination of distinctive definitions of theological notions, different sources of empirical information, and political interests—which are then instrumentalised to intensify conflict via a strong emphasis on the example of *prophetic methodology* (al-manhaj al-nubuwwa).

### *A Common Jihadi Creed?*

In the view of most Jihadis, particularly those of a Salafi orientation, *creed* ('aqida) is the most decisive element in religion. An ancient notion, creed comprises belief, doctrine and faith. Creed is central because it represents the foundation of religion, and to many it defines who should be considered a Muslim. Lately, another notion, *methodology* (manhaj), has emerged and become particularly influential among Salafis and Jihadis. Originally, 'aqida and manhaj were considered the same thing due to their strong connection, but in recent decades a separation between them has become increasingly pronounced.[9] While 'aqida is the belief, manhaj is a broader notion that concerns how to apply one's creed.[10] Wagemakers explains how this *application* can be divided into three domains: how to deal with the sources of Islam, the method of *worship* (ibada) and how to deal with politics and society (e.g. whether one should engage in Jihad, da'wa or politics).[11]

As mentioned in the introduction, the SJM is not a homogenous movement in terms of creed, though a *salafised* creed has become dominant in recent years. Comparing the creeds of groups like al-Qaida and the Islamic State on the one side and the Taliban on the other would reveal obvious differences which in the relatively short history of Sunni Jihadism have led to internal conflict on several occasions.[12] However, when studying alliances and conflict within the SJM, we also see that these conflictual dynamics do not always follow creedal fault lines. Confirming this is the fact that several of the conflicting parties adhere to a relatively similar *salafised* creed. Although the devil is often in the detail from a Salafi perspective, the minor divergences that may exist hardly constitute serious fault lines in and of themselves.

Illustrating the centrality of creed, an abundance of written works with titles along the lines of *This is our creed* (hadhihi 'aqidatuna) have been published over the years by groups and individual ideologues. This body of documents not only shows the importance of the notions of creed and methodology but also their authors' urgent desire to delineate the Muslim community. Common themes within these texts include a strong emphasis on *monotheism* (tawhid) and on God's *sovereignty* (hakimiyya), that *loyalty* (wala') should be exclusively to God, and that faith is constituted of intentions, statements and action and is divisible (i.e. it can increase and decrease).[13] While these documents show a remarkable homogeneity in terms of the actors' foundational beliefs and faith, the authors still contest and fight one another while simultaneously establishing alliances with Jihadi groups that evidently adhere to a different creed.

The reason why it is valuable to make an analytical distinction between creed and methodology is not only because the actors in question do this themselves, but primarily to identify the domains in which the conflicting parties disagree. In relation to the study of intra-Jihadi conflict, the distinction is especially important. This is because it is exclusively deviations in creed that can constitute *unbelief* (kufr), while differences in methodology and jurisprudence have largely been tolerated and have not justified *excommunication* (takfir). As will be shown, however, Jihadis find it hard to agree on these matters: the Islamic State relies on the concept of *al-wala' wa-*

*l-bara'* to excommunicate its rivals based on their alliances, while its rivals consider alliances a matter of methodological flexibility. This has led several ideologues to warn against framing the conflict in terms of creed, arguing that this is a theological debate which should take place away from the battlefield. For instance, in my interview with Abu Qatada he defined the fitna as organisational and characterised it as being about the methodology for establishing the caliphate. What distinguishes it from previous disputes, he said, is that 'tanzim al-dawla [the Islamic State] also made it about 'aqida and this is where it gets dangerous. This is something that should be kept in the mosque.'[14] In another statement, the Jordanian claimed that 'those people [Islamic State] turned this jurisprudential dispute—the subject of the caliphate—into a creed-related conflict.'[15] Echoing his mentor, Abu Mahmoud al-Filastini told me 'in the battlefield, it is Muslims versus kafir (unbelievers). Arguments about 'aqida are for the mosque.'[16]

While Wiktorowicz might have overestimated the creedal homogeneity within the Salafi movement, he was right in arguing that differences in the actors' interpretation of *reality* (waqi'), and how this translates into diverging methodologies (manhaj, pl. manahij), is the dominant source of contestation.[17] This even holds true given that the SJM is undoubtedly a more heterogenous creedal landscape than the Salafi movement. Unlike the intra-Salafi debate, however, Jihadis agree on *Jihad* as the method of pursuing social and political change in society. On a more tangible level, however, they disagree about issues relating to governance, the establishment of religio-political institutions and jurisprudential technicalities. In other words, they disagree about strategy and its foundational religious justifications. These differences are framed within the context of following the *prophetic methodology*, while accusations of deviation from this prophetic methodology have become the dominant point of contestation.

### *Diverging Realities and Methodologies*

Much of the disagreement and methodological divergence between the Islamic State on the one hand and most other Jihadi groups on the other results from differences in their interpretation of *reality* (waqi')—meaning, largely, how they understand the social and political context in which they operate. The concept of *fiqh al-waqi'* (reality-based jurisprudence, or reasoning based on reality) builds on the principle that the correct legal course depends on the social and political reality that one finds oneself in. For instance, the transformations of the former Jihadi group al-Jama'a al-Islamiyya resulted from a new reading of the political context in Egypt that necessitated a different response than the violence that the group had previously supported.[18] And in Saudi Arabia's Salafi milieu, awareness of the political context was a key point of contestation, with political Salafis castigating their quietist rivals for neglecting or being ignorant of this, while quietists often responded that fiqh al-waqi'—if taken too far—can turn into an illegitimate engagement in politics and a means of criticising Muslim rulers.[19] A famous example is that when the late Salafi jurist and hadith scholar Muhammad Nasir al-Deen al-Albani issued a fatwa calling for Palestinians to leave their land in order to practice their religion, he was attacked for neglecting the political context his fatwa related to. Islamic State supporters attempted to discredit al-Maqdisi and Abu Qatada on similar grounds: when the two ideologues spoke out against the group, Islamic State supporters responded that they were imprisoned and did not know the reality of the Islamic State's situation; as a result, their fatwas were based on misinformation. A few years later, HTS voices would direct similar criticism towards al-Zawahiri, comparing his hideout to imprisonment.

The increasing tensions between al-Qaida's leadership and al-Zarqawi's Iraqi group, described in chapter 4, were grounded in diverging views of the Iraqi context in addition to jurisprudential disagreements. Al-Zarqawi identified the Shia as the most dangerous opponent to his Islamic project, while Bin Laden and al-Zawahiri considered this threat secondary to the US. The issue was not whether it was justifiable to fight the Shia, but a matter of prioritisation informed by contextual analysis. That said, the groups did differ on the scope of excommunication of Shias. Al-Zarqawi's group declared all Shias apostates and legitimate targets, while the al-Qaida leadership argued that while the Shia as a group is certainly an apostate sect, this did not imply that any individual is an unbeliever.[20]

Bin Laden's modified strategy prior to his death, which emphasised restraint in terms of establishing political entities and opening new battlefields, would eventually escalate the methodological clash with the Islamic State in Iraq years later. In 2014 the Islamic State, which at the time already considered itself *superior* to a mere military group, established the caliphate because it believed that the group fulfilled certain fundamental requirements, namely *territorial consolidation* (tamkin) and the procedurally correct election of a caliph.[21] The Islamic State was of the opinion that its founding and representation of the caliphate should have a direct impact on the global Jihadi hierarchy; as the ultimate religio-political authority, it was not obliged to submit to third-party arbitration. Moreover, within the Islamic State, demanding *allegiance* (bay'a) from other groups, including those with an existing pledge of allegiance that would have to be revoked, was considered in accordance with shari'a.

The opposing view taken by rival groups—one that was eventually delivered by al-Zawahiri in his Islamic Spring series—contested the Islamic State's reading of the situation. In their view, the Islamic State was not in absolute control over territory, and its caliph (and the process of electing him) was also critically flawed. Al-Baghdadi's power was thus the result of an illegitimate *overpowering* (taghallub), one not in accord with the prophetic methodology of how to establish the caliphate. Al-Qaida and aligned ideologues also stressed that the situation was not suitable for the Islamic State's focus on doctrinal and creedal perfection. Instead, the focus should be on winning the wars Jihadi groups were engaged in, which necessitated some level of pragmatism. These opposing views of the political context determined how the groups subsequently reacted to each other and how they framed their opponents' transgressions.[22]

These divergences in interpretation naturally resulted in varied methodological approaches. Despite the agreement that *Jihad* is a legitimate and necessary method for realising political change, this period illustrates that it makes little sense to talk about a common *Jihadi* methodology, or even a common *Salafi–Jihadi* methodology.[23] In fact, even *within* transnational groups like al-Qaida, it is problematic to talk about *one* methodology, as they are typically heterogenous in terms of their approach. Abu Sulayman al-Muhajir, a former high-ranking official in Jabhat al-Nusra, explained that 'it is important to note that AQ [al-Qaida] is not one whole, solid body with the same methodology. AQC [al-Qaida Central] is very different to AQIM.'[24] Even so, we see Jihadis emphasising—in the singular—the prophetic methodology (manhaj al-nubuwwa) as a way of giving legitimacy to their own project while delegitimising rivals.

In 2014–16, the Islamic State issued an abundance of publications and videos asserting themselves as the true followers of the prophetic methodology.[25] Among other things, this involved breaking non-Islamic borders, establishing the caliphate, implementing *hudud* (shari'a based punishment) and introducing the gold dinar. In a speech, Adnani also stressed the importance of following the prophetic example while ridiculing al-Qaida, saying that

> If we knew that any of the righteous predecessors surrendered a hand span of land to the kuffar [unbelievers], using the claim of popular support or to save buildings from being destroyed or to prevent bloodshed, or any other alleged interest, we would have done the same as the Qa'ida of the Fool [al-Qaida] of the so-called Umma.[26]

Unsurprisingly, the Islamic State's rivals would contest its claims to follow the prophetic methodology,[27] and al-Qaida supporters would take it upon themselves to prove that al-Qaida, and not the Islamic State, had the correct methodology. In a statement entitled 'Methodological Difference Between ISIS and Al Qaida: Who are the Ones That Deviated?', the al-Qaida sympathiser Ahmed al-Hamdan lists ten points of disagreement between the two groups. Touching upon what he considers to be the contentious methodological issues dividing the two groups, he highlights the deviance and hypocrisy of the Islamic State while defending his own group against the accusation that al-Qaida changed after the death of Bin Laden.

Later, the concept of fiqh al-waqi' would be the source of further tensions between Jihadi groups isolated in Syria's Idlib enclave, thus proving how contentious a principle it is. While most Jihadis are supportive of politically informed action—just think of Bin Laden's definition of the US as the head of the snake—the most dogmatic Jihadis remain cautious about reasoning based on reality since, in their eyes, it risks *diluting* core Islamic principles. According to its proponents, fiqh al-waqi' is related to the *outcome* of a given behaviour since it should *benefit* (maslaha) rather than *harm* (mafsada), and a correct understanding of reality is needed to grasp the impact of any action. As chapters 12 and 13 show, in the 2016–19 period intra-Jihadi contestation shifted from being centred on opposition to the Islamic State to conflict between groups that previously stood side by side *against* the Islamic State. These groups were mainly Ahrar al-Sham, Nour al-Deen al-Zinki, Hay'at Tahrir al-Sham, al-Qaida's new Syrian franchise and affiliated ideologues. Setting the stage in a videotaped presentation in June 2016, Ahrar al-Sham's deputy leader Ali al-Omar (Abu Ammar) highlighted how his group had acted in accordance with fiqh al-waqi'. He would argue that more than any other group, including al-Qaida and the Islamic State, his own group understood the Syrian reality, which necessitated a pragmatic, gradualist and inclusive approach.[28]

## *The Caliphate and the Caliph*

Arguably the most debated aspect of the methodological disagreement, and one that to some extent represents the true substance of the intra-Jihadi conflict, is the question of the caliphate, the caliph and their requisites. While the Islamic State and al-Qaida always differed in their attitude towards establishing a political entity, the former's declaration of the caliphate critically escalated the inter-group relationship and put pressure on other Jihadi groups, including al-Qaida, to discuss the broader political project of Jihadism in more detail. This created great unease and revealed the lack of depth in many of the political programs within Jihadi ideology.

Al-Zawahiri's *Islamic Spring* series, launched in 2015, represented the al-Qaida leader's first serious rebuke to the caliphate declaration. While there should be no doubt that the disagreement was founded in real differences of interpretation, the debate was also an example of what Michels, in the context of *leadership feuds*, describes as a 'recourse to artifice',[29] understood as a method of strengthening one's own position through rhetorical strategies. This was evident in al-Binali's writings prior to the caliphate declaration, but also in al-Zawahiri's long-awaited response when the veteran leader attempted to delegitimise his opponent while portraying himself and his group as the protector of the Jihadi project.

### *Al-Zawahiri's Islamic Spring*

In 2013–14, al-Zawahiri had tried to manage the conflict but with little success. Although he issued several statements, guidelines and testimonies in this period, his difficulties with communication and weak injunctions were not up the task of handling the challenge to his authority or providing a clear message to doubting Jihadis about how to react to the Islamic State. His 'Testimony to Preserve the Blood of the Mujahideen in Sham' from May 2014 did give al-Zawahiri's first account of the organisational split and the history leading up to it. However, not only did it come too late to halt the building tensions, but it also lacked the necessary scope and ferocity. Though again too late, a more adequate response was his series *The Islamic Spring*. This ran over ten episodes, with the first episodes being published in autumn 2015 and the last in 2018. Indicative of al-Zawahiri's troubles with communicating and responding to current events, the first episodes were recorded back in March and April but not released for several months.

Al-Zawahiri's renewed engagement with the situation was provoked by Abu al-Mundhir al-Shinqiti, the al-Qaida-sympathetic ideologue who briefly sided with the Islamic State until its caliphate declaration. In a statement entitled 'Sheikh Ayman al-Zawahiri: Man of the Umma', al-Shinqiti called for respect for al-Zawahiri and his role in uniting the movement. He explains that

> During these circumstances in which we are living from the fierce struggle of the enemies, the ongoing attacks and the different plots, the umma needs to gather all its powers and unify its efforts… The umma needs every soldier of its soldiers … every scholar of its scholars … any intelligent man with a right opinion.

He then goes on to ask, 'if this is its status, how does it not need its great leaders and esteemed dignitaries?'[30] His more general argument is that al-Zawahiri has the necessary knowledge and experience compared to the youth who are trying to take over his position, and that the SJM should gather around the al-Qaida amir since he can unite the movement.

According to Michels, in times of competition, an older leader must put himself on the level of the masses and 'obey' them.[31] But while al-Zawahiri adopts the posture of promoting the well-being of the broader SJM, he does this by guiding and reprimanding the majority of the Jihadi masses, who are siding with the Islamic State. As a prelude to his series, the al-Qaida amir urged Jihadis to 'compete in achieving this good, rather than competing in accusing each other of being disbelievers and attacking our brothers, excelling in their accusations to justify the shedding of their blood. I pray God to unite the mujahidin.'[32] Around the time that the first episodes of the series were released, al-Qaida also issued a video series entitled *The False Dawn* to prepare audiences for the content of al-Zawahiri's forthcoming statements. The two episodes built on a prophetic saying about the coming of a false dawn and contain clips showing Islamic State transgressions and deviations while sound clips of al-Maqdisi and Abu Qatada are playing. Intended as a warning to Islamic State sympathisers, these videos tell viewers that despite the group's claim to represent the caliphate, it is in fact *a false dawn*, as was prophesised.[33]

After realising that the fitna is not going to stop by itself, al-Zawahiri produced his series to counter the accusations of the Islamic State, acquit al-Qaida and re-establish the Jihadi hierarchy with himself at the top. More tangibly, he had several agendas in the series:

- He clarifies the historical origin of the organisational tensions,
- Establishes his view of the illegitimacy of the caliph, the caliphate and the process leading to it,
- Presents what he considers the correct prophetic methodology in relation to the issues raised by the Islamic State, but does so acknowledging that *differences* in terms of these issues do not justify conflict,

- Stresses the necessity of intra-Jihadi unity and cohesion and presents a final reconciliation initiative to rebuild reciprocal trust and confidence among Jihadis, and
- Describes the impact of intra Jihadi conflict and broadens its impact to a global scale.

In terms of its content, the series can be divided into three parts. Episodes one and two are a comprehensive but general rebuke of the Islamic State's claim to have established a caliphate and to be following the prophetic methodology. They also contain discourse on reconciliation, unity and individual responsibility. Episodes three to five zoom in on the Islamic caliphate, discuss its early genealogy and address the potential concerns of Islamic State sympathisers. Episodes six to ten zoom out and focus on the Jihadi struggle from a global perspective, addressing Jihadi battlefields outside of Syria and relating them to the ongoing struggle between Jihadis. Parts one and three are discussed below, while the second part, which goes into more depth about the characteristics of the caliphate and the caliph, is treated in the next section.

The first part—episodes one and two—deals with the context and the process for the establishment of the caliphate and the election of the caliph, along with al-Zawahiri's judgement on these matters and his proposed solution. To frame his response, he apologises for releasing the series, but states that he felt pressured by the actions of al-Baghdadi. He writes

> We have endured much abuse and harm at the hands of Abu Bakr al-Baghdadi and his supporters. We chose to respond in the least harmful manner possible in order to smother the flames of fitna and pave the way to action from well-doers and reformers amongst the mujahidin. However, Baghdadi and his supporters left us no choice.[34]

Al-Zawahiri relies on statements by Bin Laden to contextualise the Islamic State's caliphate declaration and to say that the situation was not ready for a caliphate, even though this is the long-term objective. Jihadis were under heavy pressure, not least in Syria, and should focus on this military struggle rather than the establishment of political entities. Adding to his criticism, the al-Qaida amir once again points out that a hierarchy already existed within the SJM at the time, with Mullah Umar being the *commander of the believers* (amir al-mu'minin).

In relation to the process, al-Zawahiri stresses two factors in particular. The first is that the caliphate deviates from the prophetic methodology because it was created through *illegitimate overpowering* (taghallub) against the public's will and a *takeover without consultation* (istila' bila shura). The Islamic State's caliphate, he believes, was erected at the expense of Muslim blood, and thus bears comparison to the behaviour of the historic figures Abu Hajjaj[35] and Abu Muslim al-Khorasani.[36] The second factor is that the identity of the *people of authority* (ahl al-hall wa-l-aqd), who legitimised the caliphate's establishment, remains unknown—ever since the declaration, the Islamic State has been unwilling to number and name them. While there are various accounts of the number of ahl al-hall wa-l-aqd required to elect a caliph, allowing for some flexibility, it is considered problematic if their identity is not known since it makes it impossible for outsiders to know the character of these 'people of authority'. Al-Zawahiri writes that

> How can he who rebelled and broke the covenant and went against the pledge and disobeyed his amir clearly give himself the right for three or four unknown people to declare him Caliph, then he demands those who preceded him in jihad by decades to dissolve themselves? Is this reform or corruption? Is this unifying the word or separating it? And is this justice or injustice?[37]

He continues in episode two by saying that the caliphate is the result of an 'unknown minority declaring a caliphate for a caliph not supported either by the majority of the mujahideen or the Muslims.'[38] The al-Qaida amir's final objection in this part of the series is that the proper prophetic methodology for establishing the caliphate does not involve excommunicating the general Muslim masses based on suspicion.[39] The caliphate is intended to be an inclusive and not exclusive entity that seeks to embrace the entire umma. His criticism is that the Islamic State is declaring anyone who disagrees with its project or ideology an apostate, as a strategy to turn its own creed and methodology into a monopoly.

Given these procedural inadequacies and methodological deviations, al-Zawahiri judges that al-Baghdadi is *not* a caliph and that his caliphate is *not* a truthful caliphate founded on the prophetic methodology. 'We do not acknowledge this Caliphate', he says, 'and we do not see it a Caliphate on the prophetic method; instead, it is an emirate of taking over without consultation, and the Muslims are not obligated to pledge allegiance to it, and we do not see Abu Bakr al-Baghdadi as one worthy of the Caliphate.'[40] In his view, al-Baghdadi committed an *illegitimate rebellion* that is detrimental to the SJM, which is already under heavy pressure. According to al-Zawahiri, a caliph should be *uniting* rather than *splitting* the ranks of Jihadis. He writes, 'They called them to jump from one allegiance to another as if it is clothing to be taken off or an offer to be purchased and sold',[41] and questions why al-Baghdadi generally does not offer supportive words for suffering Muslims around the world but instead focuses on calling for pledges of allegiance from existing Jihadi groups to cement his own power. Attempting to deprive al-Baghdadi of all legitimacy, he concludes his judgement by saying that it is a caliphate reached 'by force with explosions and car bombs.'[42]

In al-Zawahiri's view, the obvious solution is intra-Jihadi reconciliation, unity and the establishment of *a solid structure* (bunyanan marsusan) to fight the enemy. Taking into consideration that infighting has been ongoing for more than a year and that the Islamic State had killed high-ranking Jihadi figures like Abu Khalid al-Suri (a personal friend of al-Zawahiri), the al-Qaida amir takes a surprisingly pragmatic approach to the situation, presenting a new reconciliation initiative *and* calling for cooperation with the Islamic State. The illegitimacy of the caliphate should not obstruct cooperation between Jihadis, he says, 'Because the matter is bigger than not acknowledging the legitimacy of their State or their claim of establishing a Caliphate.'[43] Al-Zawahiri frames reconciliation as a strategic necessity, something which reveals a lot about his view of methodological diversity. To foster renewed unity, he suggests a peace initiative consisting of five parts:

1. Stop the infighting,
2. Stop the call to kill those who disagree with you,

3. Establishment of a shari'a court with authority in Syria over all Jihadis,
4. Pursuit of a general amnesty to 'start a new page of cooperation and turn the page on the past and its despicable fitna', and
5. Cooperation in every possible field.[44]

Because of the recent history of conflict, al-Zawahiri is aware that collaboration will be difficult. As a result, he considers it essential to include procedures to rebuild trust and confidence among Jihadis. Just as al-Maqdisi had done previously, the al-Qaida amir attempts to distinguish between the rank and file and the leadership of the Islamic State, challenging the authority of the latter while placing responsibility on each individual. Impermissible actions like shedding Muslim blood, he says, are great sins, even if one is following the orders of one's leader. Citing the Quranic verse 4:93—'But whoever kills a believer intentionally—his recompense is Hell, wherein he will abide eternally, and Allah has become angry with him and has cursed him and has prepared for him a great punishment'—al-Zawahiri calls for individual restraint, which will undermine the leadership. Finally, he endeavours to break with the emerging trend of *revenge* and *retaliation*. Commenting on a video in which a Jihadist exclaims that he wants to avenge an attack against a religious committee carried out by a rivalling Jihadi group, al-Zawahiri pronounces that even if one is the injured party, one should seek arbitration and forgiveness rather than revenge.

The third part—episodes six to ten—are the least interesting in the series. Touching upon the situation for Muslims in Yemen, East Asia (he uses the designation *Nusantara*), East Turkistan (Xinjiang) and Somalia, and praising the Jihadi struggle in these regions, al-Zawahiri attempts to connect with the revolutionary Muslim masses around the globe while articulating the global dimension of the Jihadi struggle and, consequently, the global impact of sedition. He attempts to instil al-Qaida's vision of Jihad, defined by a search for unity among Jihadis while fighting the West and local apostate governments and promoting the proper prophetic methodology. The caliphate is the goal, he asserts, but it should be achieved through *consultation* (shura) and not through violence and bombings. Hence, he says that 'we [al-Qaida] repudiate the actions of Baghdadi and those with him, and we are not like them or of them, and truly this was not our method and it will never be.' Instead, al-Zawahiri mentions the Taliban as a counterexample to the Islamic State, suggesting Mullah Umar's emirate has been a *model of Jihadi unity*.[45] In episode six, the al-Qaida amir highlights contradictions in the Islamic State's behaviour. He questions how Islamic State spokesman al-Adnani could once have praised Mullah Umar and the al-Qaida leadership while now rebuking them, or, in the case of the Taliban, even deriding them as apostates. He also stresses the centrality of Syria as a Jihadi battlefield, but warns that intra-Jihadi conflict is what is destroying this battlefront. The opposition facing the mujahedeen is too powerful for Jihadis to get caught up in infighting, he writes. 'It is a crusader war which we [the Jihadis] are facing, while we make takfir on one and other, and destroy one and other, and kill one and other.'[46]

Overlapping with the *Islamic Spring* series was another series entitled *Brief Messages to a Supported Umma*. This series, however, was much less directly concerned with the Islamic State and instead focused on al-Zawahiri's guidance on how the SJM should evolve.

### *Establishing the Khilafa and Electing the Khalifa*

From the foregoing discussion of the first and third part of al-Zawahiri's *Islamic Spring* series, it is clear that the issues of establishing the caliphate and electing the caliph are a matter of both *context* and *process*. It is about to what extent the current context (or *reality*) is ripe for the establishment of the caliphate and, if so, what a legitimate process should look like. The second part—episodes three to five—goes into more depth on these specific issues.

According to al-Zawahiri, the process of establishing the caliphate and electing the caliph must follow the precedent of the first four caliphs in order to be considered to be founded on the prophetic methodology. Relying on the work of renowned Abbasid jurist Abu al-Hassan al-Mawardi (who died in 1058), the al-Qaida amir explains that there are certain preconditions for the caliphate's establishment and for the election of the caliph. He divides these preconditions into two, concluding that neither the Islamic State nor its leader al-Baghdadi lived up to them. The first is the issue of the *people of authority*. This is a group of scholars and knowledgeable people who act as representatives of the umma in electing a caliph on its behalf. The Islamic State has claimed that it did consult the people of authority locally in Iraq when it founded its state in 2006, but it has been unwilling to declare the identity and number of the people consulted. This receives strong criticism from al-Zawahiri since, he claims, there are certain requirements which relate to the people of authority. While the prophetic tradition does not mention a specific number of people necessary to elect a caliph, the group should nonetheless include the most knowledgeable people alive, and their identities should be known. Consensus among these people is not necessary, but it must be a majority decision. Al-Zawahiri concludes that in the case of the Islamic State, it was an *unknown minority* of people of authority in Iraq who legitimised the state and later the election of al-Baghdadi. Listing a *Who's Who* of al-Qaida sympathetic scholars (including himself and the Taliban's Mullah Umar), al-Zawahiri argues that these people should have been included in any such decision—something that did not happen. Probably teasing the Islamic State, he refers to a debate between Ibn Taymiyyah and the Shia theologian Jamal al-Deen al-Hilli in which the latter supported the view of a legitimate minority. This leads the al-Qaida amir to refer to the Islamic State as the *tyranny of the minority*.

The second issue is the *duties* of the caliph, a role al-Baghdadi does not live up to. The duties of the caliph must first be implemented *in reality* to create a suitable context for the caliphate. Since this did not happen, the caliphate declaration was *premature*.[47] Relying on the authority and continued sway of the deceased figures of Bin Laden, al-Zarqawi and Abu Hamza al-Muhajir, the al-Qaida amir argues that Bin Laden shared his opinion that the context was not ripe for a caliphate, while the two leaders of al-Qaida in Iraq declared their trust in him. The Islamic State and its sympathisers have great veneration for all three figures, something which al-Zawahiri uses strategically here to argue that the current methodology of the group goes against the views of its early leaders.[48]

Well aware of how intriguing and convincing the caliphate declaration was to many seasoned Jihadis, and even more so to newcomers, al-Zawahiri dedicates an entire episode of the series to a Q&A session dealing with questions anyone intrigued by the Islamic State's project might have. The fictive questions are mainly related to the already-discussed issue of the religious legitimacy of the Islamic State's methodology in establishing the caliphate. Al-Zawahiri also discusses the legitimacy of taking a critical posture towards the caliphate, including abstaining from pledging allegiance, postponing the struggle to establish a caliphate and the necessity of having a caliph. For Jihadis lacking religious knowledge, these were indeed relevant questions. Al-Zawahiri probably hoped to offer a religiously legitimate alternative for Islamic State sympathisers, or anyone still confused about how to react to the increasingly polarised environment. Most passionately of all, he discusses how a caliph should be legitimately chosen according to shari'a. His answer is that it should either be through *selection* or *succession*, while *overpowering*, which al-Baghdadi relied on, is a crime.[49]

During the previous decade there has been much debate within al-Qaida about the establishment of a state-like entity, whether an emirate or a caliphate. On several occasions the al-Qaida leadership instructed affiliates to be patient despite their desire to declare a state. But with the challenge from the Islamic State and al-Zawahiri's dedication to following the line of Bin Laden, al-Qaida and its affiliates have managed to reach a unitary position. This was evident in an exchange of letters between the amir of AQIM, Abdelmalik Droukdal and a shura council member of the Islamic State, Abu Ubayda Abd al-Hakim, in which al-Hakim attempted to lure Droukdal into pledging allegiance to al-Baghdadi. Although we only have one letter from the correspondence—a letter from al-Hakim—it is possible to understand the position of Droukdal and his objections in previous letters. Al-Hakim explains to Droukdal that *every single pillar and requirement of the caliphate has been fulfilled* (lam yabq 'amr min muqtadayat al-khilafa 'ila wa tahaqiq) and if al-Qaida fails to see this, it is because *it lives in another realm* (antum fi 'alam akhar). In case Droukdal does not believe him, al-Hakim invites him to send a delegate to see for himself. Aligning himself with his superior, al-Zawahiri, Droukdal stresses the same points of criticism: the election of a caliph without the agreement of the people of authority, the validity of establishing the caliphate without *territorial consolidation* (tamkin), and the issue of breaking its allegiance.[50]

While a pro-Islamic State argument was mainly promoted by al-Binali, Abu 'Abd al-Rahman al-Shami, its official magazines and munasirun,[51] there are countless examples of al-Qaida-aligned ideologues and senior figures publishing criticism similar to al-Zawahiri's.[52] In the debate, both groups attempted to promote their distinctive view of the proper *prophetic methodology* relating to the caliphate and the caliph, and to make their narrative dominant within the SJM. Set against the claims of the two groups to represent and follow the one true prophetic methodology, the prophetic tradition—in terms of both statehood and leadership—is much more diffuse *and* flexible than either the Islamic State or al-Qaida would have us believe; moreover, historic sources indicate a degree of flexibility in these matters precisely because there is no *single* prophetic methodology. Firstly, there is no real mention of the *state* or *government* in the Quran or Hadith, as these are both relatively recent concepts. While the caliphate is mentioned, this refers specifically to the *caliph's office*. Hence, the Islamic state (al-dawla al-islamiyya) does not have any specific normative existence on the basis of early Islamic writings.[53] This diversity of interpretation is also evident in the works of prominent historical jurists like al-Mawardi (who died in 1058), Abu al-Malik al-Juwayni (who died in 1085) and Abu Hamid Muhammad ibn Muhammad al-Tusi al-Ghazali (who died in 1111), all of whom authored political theories of the Islamic state and its leader but differed widely on what actually constituted prophetic tradition. These differences were largely the result of the changing realities of their era and the interests of the ruling political elite.[54] Ibn Taymiyyah, perhaps the most authoritative Islamic jurist from a Jihadi perspective and one whom the Islamic State claims to take inspiration from, abandoned the concept of the caliphate altogether, instead preferring *shari'a politics* (siyasa shar'iyya).[55] Secondly, there is no single process of choosing the political leader, the caliph. The first four caliphs were all elected in different ways, ranging from selection to succession, and with different numbers of people of authority electing the caliph. Talking about a *singular* prophetic methodology thus makes little sense.

To an extent, the Islamic State anticipated the current situation in its justification for the state declaration back in 2006. In the lengthy document issued the following year, Uthman ibn 'Abd al-Rahman al-Tamimi described the various opinions that exist regarding the people of authority necessary to elect a caliph. He explained the Islamic State's own position in vague terms, saying that the election necessitates 'a majority' decision. While this is similar to al-Zawahiri's position, the current debate also encompasses who the people of authority should be and whether their identity needs to be made known. On the question of overpowering (taghallub), Tamimi adds that in certain contexts this can be a legitimate alternative to the pledge of the people of authority and succession.[56]

The discussion between the Islamic State and al-Qaida on the matter of the caliphate and the caliph is illustrative of a general pattern within the SJM, which is for groups to try to turn their distinctive view of a methodological practice into a monopoly on the truth. While this has been a general characteristic of Jihadis in their opposition to less extreme actors, the way it has played out between Jihadis is nonetheless remarkable, not least because it has entailed a critical politicisation of the idea of a prophetic methodology.

10

# STRUGGLING FOR AUTHORITY

Radical Islamic movements, Wiktorowicz writes, 'are collective endeavours to establish networks of shared meaning and religious interpretation—efforts to persuade others to accept a particular understanding of Islam.'[1] But as this study shows, such competitive endeavours also take place *within* movements. *Authority* is a key concept for understanding the conflict within the SJM since it is both an objective and an important resource, not least because authority, especially in a competitive environment, is needed to define a dominant understanding of the proper methodology.

The contest for religious and sacred authority occurs broadly within the Islamic world.[2] Islamists and Salafis have long contested the authority of institutions and individuals, promoting a segregation between religion and politics while at the same time competing internally.[3] From its inception, the SJM also engaged in this endeavour, but its main opposition was directed against *imams of unbelief* (a'immat al-kufr); this usually referred to the Saudi and Egyptian religious establishments, but generally included any religious authority not sympathetic to Jihadi ideology. This study shows how extensive such contestation is within the SJM as well. The following chapter takes a closer look at the volatile subculture of authority within the movement and illustrates some of the most important efforts Jihadis have engaged in to build their own authority while shattering their opponent's. As will become evident, these efforts largely rely on framing exercises involving artifices of exaltation/credentialling and vilification/decredentialling, executed with the aim of appearing more authoritative than one's competitor.[4]

## *The Volatile Culture of Authority Within Jihadism*

The structure and sources of authority within Sunni Islam are distinctive compared to other religions and even other sects within Islam. In Sunnism there is an absence of a central authority comparable to the pope within Catholicism or the marja e-taqlid in Shiism. Since the early days of Islam, after the Prophet passed away, religious authority within Sunnism has been characterised by some level of fragmentation and decentralisation. Political authority most often remained in the hands of the caliph, while religious authority was delegated to the 'ulama, a group of scholars specialising in various religious sciences;[5] this group served as a partial mechanism to centralise issues of faith. Learning, knowledge and seniority were central sources of religious authority in this formal system and were also pathways to entry into the 'ulama. Ever since, however, the 'ulama's authority and its success in institutionalising authority has fluctuated, and in recent times its monopoly has come under increasing pressure due to changing structures.

As several scholars have noted, traditional sources of Islamic authority have changed dramatically over the previous centuries.[6] One explanation is that the intellectual and institutional superstructures of early Islamic history that cherished and regulated religious knowledge were undermined by the effects of European power in the region, which caused religious institutions to become increasingly politicised.[7] Zaman, on the other hand, argues that it was due to a number of factors: changed conditions of ijtihad (specifically, a situation in which there is no longer scope for 'absolute ijtihad', but only 'limited ijtihad', meaning expanding the boundaries of a school of law in accordance with the principles of that school); modern communications; mass higher education; and the spread of liberal thought.[8] These factors, he claims, have led to a challenge to the 'ulama's privileged access to authoritative religious knowledge.[9] This change, however, should not be considered a structural break with previous practices but rather an 'intensification of a tendency towards decentralised authority'[10] that has fostered the emergence of a new group of 'Islamist intellectuals'.[11] The result is that religious authority is now less dependent on knowledge and formal education, while becoming more *individualised* and dependent on practice and piety.[12] Nowhere is this more the case than within the SJM.

The demise of intellectual superstructures, the changing role of religious interpretation and the widespread access to religious material have thus facilitated an alternative platform from which those who were previously outsiders can now challenge, and participate in, the religio-political construction of Islam. Islamists, Salafis and Jihadis have been at the forefront of those taking advantage of these new opportunities. While the latter two groups share an individualistic view of religion, they are divided regarding the emphasis they place on education: Salafis just like Islamists have traditionally emphasised the importance of education,[13] but Jihadis such as al-Maqdisi did not merely claim that education was unnecessary but even discouraged it.[14]

Over the years, and through their challenge to established structures of authority, Jihadis have developed their own distinctive *subculture* of authority, which is characterised by a convergence of religion and politics along with a devaluation and redefinition of the sources of authority. These traits are not exclusive to Jihadis; it is their combination and intensity in Jihadism which is notable. Abandoning traditional sources of authority while stressing alternative sources, Jihadis manage to engage in the construction of religious meaning and the linkage and overlap between religion and politics. Despite this only resonating with a small minority, it nonetheless represents a serious challenge to the broader Islamic environment and a security concern.

Besides their powerful albeit simplistic message, Jihadis' relation to religion aligns well with the changing character of authority structures, and should be considered a key reason for their ability to gain authority in the eyes of supporters. They define their loyalty exclusively to God and are prepared to follow anyone they consider to hold the correct creed and methodology. This is crystallised in the words of the late al-Qaida ideologue Anwar al-Awlaki, who said

> It is important that we encourage Muslims to respect their scholars. It is to no one's benefit to put down the men of knowledge who represent the religion of Allah. But when some of our scholars—no matter how knowledgeable they are—divert from the straight path, we the Muslims need to advise them.

Another example telling of this attitude is the statement by Uthman bin Abd al-Rahman al-Tamimi, a former official of the Shari'a Committee in the Islamic State of Iraq, concerning a hadith in al-Bukhari: 'If an Ethiopian slave with a cut off nose and ear were appointed as your ruler, you would have to listen to and obey his orders as long as he rules in accordance with the Book of Allah.'[15]

While a few senior Jihadi figures, one example being Azzam, did have a solid educational background, this is more the exception than the rule.[16] People like Bin Laden, al-Zawahiri, Abu Yahya al-Libi, Atiyyatullah, al-Adnani, al-Anbari and al-Julani had little formal religious education, but managed to acquire authority through other sources, such as *piety*, *sacrifice* and *dedication*, or by representing the *fighter-scholar* ideal that is idiosyncratic to militant movements. On several occasions, leaders like Bin Laden, Abu Yahya and al-Julani have appeared in videos dressed in military fatigues (symbolising their military experience) while discussing the religious dimension of the struggle. Even Abu Bakr al-Baghdadi, who like Azzam is an anomaly in terms of his extensive religious education, appeared in military-esque uniform in his April 2019 video. In contrast to his Abbasid-inspired attire in the al-Nuri mosque in 2014, this new look was obviously an attempt to come across as trustworthy at a time when Islamic State fighters were under heavy *military* pressure. In Wiktorowicz' study of al-Muhajiroun, he describes how the knowledge and personal characteristics of Omar Bakri, and later Anjem Choudary, were essential to their ability to recruit and mobilise British Muslims. However, as the examples above show us, knowledge is not always a criterion of authority within the SJM; other traits are able to replace it. Even the ideological elite within the movement, who are supposed to represent the highest religious authority, includes few people with extensive formal religious training. Many of them appear to have some level of formal or informal training, but they tend to be self-trained and owe their authority to how they combine their knowledge with personal piety, sacrifice and an ability to relate religion to an actionable analysis of the contemporary political reality.

The changing culture of authority within Islam and the emergence of a distinctive subculture within the SJM has generally benefitted Jihadis in their attempts to contest established authority and build a platform of their own to recruit and mobilise. However, as the rise of the Islamic State illustrates, it has also enabled volatile internal dynamics to contest existing hierarchies of authority. The evolving relationship of al-Zarqawi and al-Maqdisi is a telling example. While al-Maqdisi was initially the mentor of al-Zarqawi, in 2004 the relationship soured due to al-Zarqawi's popularity and his reputation as a *man of action*, which meant he could legitimately challenge the more senior al-Maqdisi.[17] Juergensmeyer writes that 'Both violence and religion have emerged at times when authority is in question, since they are both ways of challenging and replacing authority. One gains its power from force and the other from its claims to ultimate order.'[18] In 2013–14, when the intra-Jihad conflict erupted in Syria, *violence* and *religion* were both integral to the group's challenge to the authority of al-Qaida and aligned ideologues. The Islamic State would pinpoint the religious deviation of its rivals while promoting an even more rigid and doctrinal interpretation of Islam—and showing itself willing to act upon it. This was the case even when it involved violence against other Jihadis and challenging former mentors and senior colleagues. As the following sections describe in detail, two mechanisms the Islamic State relied on were *undermining rivalling ideologues* to rearrange the hierarchical order within the movement and *claiming the ideological lineage* of past Jihadi pioneers.

Interestingly, Jihadi groups have sought to safeguard their authority in various ways. In al-Qaida, the group has always sought to maintain that authority not embedded in a person but in the ideals the group stands for. Leaders give orders; however, these are not binding because they are given by an al-Qaida leader, but because one believes in the underlying principle—or at least that's how the story goes.[19] The truth is more complicated. Although al-Qaida may have encouraged individual Jihadis to take ownership of their personal interpretation of faith and the actions it would entail, the group—being a highly ideologically devoted military organisation—has also cherished its ability to influence and rule its members, not least through the establishment of hierarchical structures and the authority embedded in specific leadership figures. But with the Islamic State, this dynamic is intensified further through an institutionalisation of authority as part of its caliphate and the implementation of an internal code of *listen and obey*.[20] The intention was that authority should become embedded in the caliphate's various institutions—most importantly the caliph, the diwans (departments) and the spokesperson—through bureaucratisation and symbolism, which would eventually function as a mechanism to undermine the very structures that enabled its rise.

### *Truthful and Misleading 'Ulama*

Another thing al-Qaida and the Islamic State differed on is their attitude towards Jihadi scholars or ideologues. While both agreed on opposing non-Jihadi scholars—though not on how they should be treated[21]—since 2014 they have adopted vastly different rationales in their approach to the scholarly environment and their treatment of Jihadi scholars.

It is usually acknowledged within the movement that gaining the support of scholars is a criterion for group success.[22] Well aware of this fact, the Islamic State initially sought to attract established scholars but largely failed, as only mid-level figures and young, unknown scholars joined the group. Scholars like Abu Qatada and al-Maqdisi were both contacted early on by Islamic State representatives, but neither of them sided with the group; later they would become some of its fiercest critics.[23] To remedy this failure, the Islamic State attempted to establish its own scholarly support base while attacking opposing scholars. Debate had occurred among scholars in the past, yet the vilification and decredentialling campaign the group launched in 2015–16 (mainly in its official magazines) represented a critical escalation and a break with the tradition of scholarly respect within the movement.[24] The endeavour was essentially an exercise in rearranging the scholarly hierarchy in a short period of time. Assisted by the group's general popularity, battlefield success and scholarly institutionalisation, the Islamic State partly succeeded.

At first, when the Islamic State's attempt to attract the movement's leading ideological figures failed, one could detect a clear inferiority complex and frustration. Group supporters and lower-ranking scholars were eager to challenge this developing narrative and issued lists of scholars who allegedly sympathised with the group. The problem was, though, that the majority of the scholars were relatively unknown and that some did not support the Islamic State but simply remained passive in terms of choosing sides.[25] As the group established its own scholarly base characterised by a high degree of institutionalisation, it shifted its focus to vilifying scholarly opponents and attacking their credentials. This occurred at a point when the influence of leading Jihadi scholars was already waning, and the Islamic State could convert its popularity and military might to political and religious authority through its organisation.

In a series of articles in its *Rumiyah* magazine, the group discussed the *wicked* and *evil* scholars.[26] The characteristic of these articles is an emphasis on the relationship between *knowledge* and *action*. The first article states: 'The scholars whom Allah praised and called "those with knowledge" are those who act upon their knowledge and convey it to others'; this resonates well with the subculture of authority within the SJM. Those not acting upon their knowledge, the article says, should not be considered *scholars*. This inaction is mainly related to refraining from confronting apostate leaders in the Muslim world and concealing the truth from the Muslim masses about the obligation to fight. Based on this argument, the article concludes that senior 'ulama, including several Salafis, such as Ibn Baz, Ibn Uthaymin, Saleh al-Fawzan and Yusuf al-Qaradawi are not to be considered scholars; even more controversially, it also includes al-Maqdisi, Abu Qatada and al-Haddoushi in the list. Due to their inaction, these figures are '*"imams" of misguidance and "scholars" of taghut*'; eventually the Islamic State would ban their books within the geographical borders of the caliphate.[27] In a later article, the Islamic

State detached knowledge and seniority entirely from authority as long as it is not followed by action, stating: 'It is clear by the shar'i texts that the "scholars" of evil and deviance can never be counted among the scholars no matter how much they memorise and pen and no matter how famous they become.'[28] The Islamic State considers it its role to be to expose the deviance of these scholars, be they pro-Jihad or not, based on the concept of *advice* (nasiha) and prophetic tradition.[29] Moreover, referencing the example of Sayyid Imam (Dr Fadl)—who published several *ideological retractions* in the 2000s after having once been considered one of the preeminent theorists of the SJM—they argue that even if these Jihadi scholars were previously on the right path, this does not imply that they cannot eventually deviate from it.[30]

In 2017, the Islamic State further escalated its position on opposing scholars.[31] In a longer article from April, it identified three types of scholars: the *scholar of the sect* who should be respected and his position acknowledged, the *scholar of the sultan* who is a puppet of the regime, and the *scholar of the people* who conforms to the desires of the majority in his judgement. Scholars of the sultan and of the people are considered evil scholars who legitimately can be killed, it states.[32] A similar message had already been propagated months before by the group's official spokesperson, Abu al-Hassan al-Muhajir:

> O zealous soldiers of tawhid everywhere, dedicate yourselves to killing those evil scholars and callers of fitna everywhere who harm the religion of Allah and His allies. If one of you finds one of them, he should not let his shadow separate from the evil one's shadow until he kills him. Let him attack him—even in the evil scholar's home while he is amongst his family. Begin with those who publicised their enmity and called for the killing of the mujahidin or accused them of atheism or abandonment of the religion.[33]

Despite its differences with Salafi but non-Jihadi scholars, al-Qaida reacted to Muhajir's call. In an article in AQAP's newspaper *Al Masra*, it denounced targeting scholars, saying 'even if we differ from them, we don't make takfir on them or make their blood halal like the new Khawarij.'[34]

In general, al-Qaida's view of Jihadi scholars has always stood in contrast to the Islamic State's exclusivist approach. Scholars are regarded as an important resource and as guides who should be consulted and respected.[35] This includes Jihadi scholars not necessarily aligned with the group. Back in 2014, two senior AQAP officials, Harith bin Ghazi al-Nadhari and Ibrahim al-Rubeish, warned in a video against slandering scholars and experienced jihadi figures, instead encouraging piety and manners.[36] Regarding Jihadi scholars, al-Zawahiri says: 'Those people are our capital, our money, our ammunition, and our precious treasure in this era. So for whose interest do we disrepute them and allege against them and show disrespect?'[37] In another statement, building on a previous proposal of Bin Laden, he suggests the establishment of a supra-group institution of scholars intended to advise Jihadis, both on settling internal disagreement and on setting the guidelines for future behaviour.[38]

### *Following the Path of the Shuyukh*

In extension of the struggle for scholarly support, the groups would also compete to claim the lineage of late Jihadi leaders. In *Beware of Imitators*, Lahoud recounts an interesting story by Fadil Harun, a late senior al-Qaida official who worked as the group's secretary. When Harun arrived in Somalia in the 2000s, he wanted to educate some of the youth (who showed signs of having extreme ideological opinions) in the pragmatism of al-Qaida and Usama Bin Laden. But the only response he got from them was criticism that Harun himself was not following the path of Bin Laden.[39] A similar debate, or competition, has emerged in the conflict between al-Qaida and the Islamic State. Both groups have claimed to adhere to the methodology of several historic important figures, with the contestation mainly focusing on who can legitimately claim to represent the legacy of Bin Laden and Abu Musab al-Zarqawi.[40] The logic behind this still ongoing struggle is to capitalise on the authority that both Jihadi leaders continue to command within the SJM years after their death. Implicit in this logic is that the opponent group would have deviated from the methodology of these Jihadi pioneers.

Al-Qaida's argument goes that Ayman al-Zawahiri continued the methodology and strategy of Bin Laden and that al-Zarqawi—despite occasional dissatisfaction with his actions—held with the methodology of al-Qaida. The Islamic State has opposed this version, claiming instead that al-Zawahiri's al-Qaida strayed from Bin Laden's methodology, and as such represents a deviation from both Bin Laden and al-Zarqawi. Both groups are partly right and partly mistaken, leaving little doubt that their respective efforts to claim the legacy of historic leaders is, at least in part, a conscious strategy to benefit from their standing within the SJM.

Ever since Bin Laden's death in May 2011, the al-Qaida organisation has regularly paid homage to its founder, the *imam al-mujaddid* (the renewing imam) as al-Qaida leaders usually refer to him. But in the wake of the Islamic State's caliphate declaration, al-Qaida intensified its celebration of Bin Laden and its efforts to cement the linkage between the past and the current leadership. For instance, just after the caliphate was established, al-Qaida's al-Sahab Media Foundation issued a link on Twitter to an old Bin Laden video in which he stressed that according to the prophetic tradition, specific pillars were requisites for establishing an Islamic state. Another example is the *Days With the Imam* (ayam ma' al-imam) series, in which al-Zawahiri, over the course of eight episodes, recounts anecdotes about Bin Laden and remembers his qualities.[41] Finally, the introduction of Hamza Bin Laden, Usama's son, as a public figure in al-Qaida in August 2015 was partly to cement the lineage from Usama to the current leadership.[42]

The Islamic State's argument that al-Qaida deviated from the methodology of Bin Laden since al-Zawahiri took charge is about the *actions* of Zawahiri's al-Qaida. Yet on most issues, al-Zawahiri has continued the methodology and strategy laid out during the late leadership of Bin Laden. The emphasis on winning public support,[43] the strong ties to the Taliban, the inclusivist attitude in terms of religious creed and organisational affiliation, the view of the Shia[44] and the critical stance on the establishment of the Islamic caliphate[45] were all integral parts of Bin Laden's al-Qaida. One point where critics can legitimately point to a difference is in Bin Laden's and al-Zawahiri's diverging *strategy of affiliation*.

Interestingly, however, this has never been pointed out by the Islamic State.

In addition to the struggle for the legacy of Bin Laden, al-Qaida has also made a case that al-Zarqawi should be considered *a product of al-Qaida* and not the ideological source of the contemporary Islamic State.[46] Having already discussed the relationship between the al-Qaida leadership and al-Zarqawi (see chapter 4), this is perhaps more surprising, and must be considered a conscious strategy rather than one founded on warm feelings for the late Jordanian. Since 2014, several al-Qaida or al-Qaida-aligned scholars have issued remarks about al-Zarqawi's ideological *home*. Abu Qatada commented that al-Zarqawi was on the correct Jihadi-Salafi manhaj, Abu Abdullah al-Shami claimed that the Islamic State does not follow al-Zarqawi,[47] and according to Abu Sulayman al-Muhajir there are important differences between the Islamic State and al-Zarqawi:

> Ex-communication of a vast majority of Muslims, that is a massive difference. Zarqawi was willing to work with many Muslims in Iraq, sufis included. He did not consider them to be non-Muslims that needed to be killed. IS [Islamic State] have a much tighter circle. You could say that Zarqawi had better PR and was more willing to accommodate to differences within sunni islam.[48]

Abu Qatada adds that while the Islamic State is linked to al-Zarqawi, they do not follow his ideology. In fact, the Jordanian says, it is not possible to divide the methodology of al-Zarqawi and that of Bin Laden.[49] Even al-Maqdisi—al-Zarqawi's former mentor who had a feud with his mentee—rejects the ideological connection between al-Zarqawi and the Islamic State.[50] Al-Maqdisi elaborates using the example of Abu Anas al-Shami, another Jordanian Jihadi of the al-Zarqawi era, whose legacy the Islamic State also claims. Al-Maqdisi says that while Abu Anas might have been a teacher of al-Adnani, this was only briefly. Nevertheless, the Islamic State tried to hijack the authority of these highly esteemed martyrs, who cannot respond because they are dead.[51] From the perspective of Abu Sulayman, al-Qaida's strategy is clear: 'al-Qaida try to win over the younger crowd with Zarqawi, the older crowd with UBL [Bin Laden], but, yes ... legitimacy is key', he explains.[52]

For the Islamic State, the strategy was probably similar, and its efforts to frame itself as a representative of the methodology of al-Zarqawi, the group's founding father, are self-evident and largely correct. It even tried to frame itself as the true inheritor of al-Qaida. In one of his writings, Turki al-Binali makes a distinction between the *legitimate al-Qaida* (tanzim al-qa'ida al-shar'i) and the *popular al-Qaida* (tanzim al-qa'ida al-sha'bi). The former, he explains, refers to the old al-Qaida that followed shari'a and held to the correct methodology while the latter, corrupted through an extensive focus on fiqh al-waqi', deviated and eventually started criticising the Islamic State.[53] Abu Maysara al-Shami, a late American official in the Islamic State's media apparatus, issued a tract criticising al-Zawahiri's deviance from Bin Laden immediately after the latter's death. In the piece, he labels al-Zawahiri as a *murji'a*.[54]

### *Institutionalising Infighting*

Along with the debate over methodology and the struggle for authority, the conflict also involved matters of creed. The Islamic State started to rely on the concept of *al-wala' wa-l-bara'* to proclaim takfir on its rivals, who on the contrary justified fighting the Islamic State by labelling it as khawarij. As we will see, the Islamic State's attitude to other rebel groups, including other Jihadis, evolved incrementally. Initially, the group cooperated with various opposition groups in Syria, including FSA groups, to attract followers and gain ground militarily. But over time it began to declare rivals as apostates, first on a leadership level and later an individual level.[55] In response, opponents of the Islamic State would issue justifications to defend against the group's attacks and in some instances actively fight back. Characteristic of this dual process is that it is elite driven, emanating from group leaders or affiliated ideologues in the form of instructions to cadres; as such, it resembles elites' manipulation of *identity* in civil wars, with a view to building alliances and legitimising infighting.[56]

### *Excommunicating Fellow Jihadis Emphasising Al-wala' wa-l-bara'*

The Islamic State's military conflict with rivalling Jihadis has been accompanied by a discursive process to justify infighting through theological concepts and categories. These accusations against rivals have centred on how rivals relate to the state, their religious orientation, and their alliances with non-Jihadis. The argument made here is that the Islamic State relied primarily on al-wala' wa-l-bara' to discredit its Jihadi rivals, and that by connecting this to belief and faith it justified excommunicating them from Islam. Al-wala' wa-l-bara' like takfir, is founded on a Manichean worldview which divides *truth and falsehood* (haqq wa batil) and *faith and disbelief* (iman wa kufr),[57] yet—as will be shown—the way it has been applied has been largely driven by strategic interests. Al-wala' wa-l-bara' is, then, an extremely powerful notion for distinguishing an *in-group* from an *out-group,* and it was instrumentalised in exactly this fashion by the Islamic State in relation to other Jihadis to justify escalation from discursive contestation to military infighting.[58]

Wagemakers has shown that al-wala' wa-l-bara' does not have a solid foundation in prophetic tradition but is more easily traceable to early Wahhabi ideology, especially the work of Sulayman ibn Muhammad ibn 'Abd al-Wahhab and later Hamad ibn 'Atiq.[59] These authors' focus was on demanding the population's loyalty to the state in confrontations with non-Muslims. Later, the notion was developed to accommodate contemporary challenges.[60] The major change between the Wahhabi conceptualisation and modern reformulations was the shift in focus from allying to a *state* to allying with non-state actors *against* a state. Bin Laden and Saudi political Salafis used al-wala' wa-l-bara' to delegitimise the Saudi state's call for US support in the Gulf War by framing it as a matter of *taking help from non-Muslims* (isti'ana bi-l-kuffar).[61] In the 1980s Afghan war, Jihadis used it to deter Muslims from assisting non-Muslims (i.e. the Russians) against the mujahideen. The most epoch-making reformulation of al-wala' wa-l-bara' was introduced in the writings of al-Maqdisi, however. Relying heavily on the notion in his book *Millat Ibrahim,* al-Maqdisi used it to justify rebellion against regimes that do not implement Islamic law properly and thus violate God's *supremacy* (hakimiyya). Furthermore, Al-Maqdisi gave the notion a much more aggressive dimension by making it dependent on 'affirmative acts' (what Shiraz Maher refers to as a '*doctrine of active dissent and rebellion*'), thus implying that it is incumbent on all Muslims to react *with force* against un-Islamic rulers.[62]

Another key transformation of al-wala' wa-l-bara' was the linking of it with creed and thus, in effect, belief and excommunication. Ibn Taymiyyah had applied the notion to fight *innovation* (bid'a) in Islam, but he never made it a matter of creed. This linkage was born in its Wahhabi interpretation, which represented a clear escalation in the importance of al-wala' wa-l-bara'.[63] Modern ideologues like al-Maqdisi, al-Zawahiri and followers of the *Shuaybi-school*[64] would build on this connection by establishing a linkage between al-wala' wa-l-bara', *tawhid* and takfir, which implied that failing to properly adhere to al-wala' wa-l-bara' would risk placing one outside Islam.[65] For al-Maqdisi, the key is not so much the believer's willingness to engage in Jihad, but to show 'enmity towards those who shirk their duty and to declare them to be unbelievers (takfir man fa'alahu).'[66] Al-Zawahiri's take on al-wala' wa-l-bara' has always been slightly different. As Lahoud explains: 'Whereas al-Zawahiri is interested in emphasizing to fellow jihadis the sound ways of association (wala), al-Maqdisi is more interested in the craft of disassociation (bara).'[67] That said, al-Zawahiri still coupled the notion with unbelief, writing that 'Allah, the Almighty forbade us to take the infidels as guardians and to support them over the Muslims. He who has done so is an infidel like them.'[68]

Obviously, takfir is a highly controversial endeavour, as it concerns *expelling* someone from the religious community.[69] This is not least because, as a famous hadith puts it, 'if a person says to his brother, oh unbeliever! Then surely one of them is such.'[70] Islamic scholars of various orientations have over time warned against engaging in takfir, but Jihadis have generally been less restrictive. Even purists like al-Maqdisi, however, have stressed the caution with which Muslims must approach the issue of takfir, and have warned against transgression and extremism.[71] Nonetheless, the discussion below illustrates how the Islamic State's position on al-wala' wa-l-bara' is related to al-Maqdisi's emphasis on disassociation and the obligation to show enmity to those with creedal shortcomings, which in some instances may constitute unbelief. In fact, the way the Islamic State applies al-wala' wa-l-bara' in relation to other Jihadis is a combination of previous conceptualisations of the notion. In its writings, the group uses the notion to prohibit alliances with apostates (against Muslims) and to call for support for its state (the caliphate), while also making it dependent on affirmative acts. From 2014 on, the Islamic State adopted a similar rationalisation of the linkage between al-wala' wa-l-bara', tawhid and takfir, though it materialised in a manner al-Maqdisi most likely never intended. While al-Maqdisi used al-wala' wa-l-bara' to denounce political leaders in the Muslim world, the Islamic State expanded the notion's remit, using it to denounce fellow Jihadis as well.[72] The discussion below thus exemplifies how al-wala' wa-l-bara' has evolved from a principle mainly used to encourage dissent against political rulers into a tool for managing relations within the SJM and delineating the movement's boundaries.[73]

In January 2014, when infighting between the Islamic State and rival rebel groups (including Jihadis) broke out, the group would emphasise al-wala' wa-l-bara', its linkage to belief and faith and its foundation in the prophetic methodology.[74] We know from the biography of Abu Ali al-Anbari, arguably the most senior religious figure in the Islamic State, that just as the infighting started, he began to write a statement on the *Islamic Front,* which included Jaysh al-Islam and Ahrar al-Sham, concluding that its leaders were apostates because of their groups' alliances with the Free Syrian Army. This judgement, he explained, would include their fighters if they did not leave their groups.[75] Documents obtained by Aymenn Jawad al-Tamimi show that al-Anbari's judgement had already been implemented later in January; in a *conditions for repentance* document issued for the al-Bab region, the Islamic State officially proclaimed *disassociation* from the Islamic Front.[76] This, coupled with a call for repentance, indicates that the Islamic State considered the assemblage of groups to be apostates.

At the same time, al-Baghdadi outlined his group's position towards other groups, including rival Jihadis, in an audio statement, symbolising a shift in intra-Jihadi conflict dynamics. Describing fitna as a necessity to *cleanse the ranks* of the believers, he stated:

> It's from God's tradition and wisdom that the rows of believers and Mujahids is mingled with hypocrites. God will not leave this row mixed with those hypocrites and pretenders and therefore creates Fitna and trials for them. The row must be melted so that the maliciousness leaves, and be pressured so that the weak building blocks crumble and the lights must shine at it exposing the intricacies and inner personalities.[77]

Interestingly, Faraj similarly stressed this 'cleansing the ranks' narrative in his *Neglected Duty*,[78] though to my knowledge the Islamic State has never referenced Faraj on this point. Al-Baghdadi's spokesperson al-Adnani would later contribute to this justification. In direct reference to al-Qaida, he remarks:

> We will divide the groups and break the ranks of the organisations. Yes, because there is no place for groups after the revival of the Jama'a (the Khilafa). So away with the organisations. We will fight the movements, assemblies, and fronts. We will tear apart the battalions, the brigades, and armies, until, by Allah's permission, we bring an end to the factions, for nothing weakens the Muslims and delays victory except the factions (...) Many of you fight us despite claiming to want implementation of the law of Allah. But they have deviated and not found the correct path.

Giving their Jihadi rivals one last chance, al-Adnani continues: 'Whoever throws his weapons aside and repents is safe. Whoever sits in the masjid and repents is safe. Whoever enters his home, closes his door, and repents, is safe. Whoever from the factions and brigades abandons the war against us and repents is safe.'[79]

While the Islamic State was quick to proclaim takfir on more 'moderate' Jihadis like Ahrar al-Sham, Jaysh al-Islam and the Taliban,[80] the process with Jabhat al-Nusra—a group made up of former brothers-in-arms and friends—was more complicated and evolved in *stages*. Documents obtained by al-Tamimi reveal that as early as January 2015 the Islamic State's Wilayat al-Furat invited al-Nusra fighters to *repent*, indicating that on a local level the group considered al-Nusra fighters to have committed kufr.[81] But generally in its public communication, the stance of the Islamic State on Jabhat al-Nusra was more ambiguous and developed over time through a particular emphasis on al-wala' wa-l-bara' and its relation to creed. In an article series entitled 'The Allies of Al-Qa'idah in Sham', which appeared in five editions of its *Dabiq* magazine, the group focused on various allies of Jabhat al-Nusra to show how it *associated* (wala') with allegedly apostate groups in its fight *against* the Islamic State. The general theme of the series is al-Nusra's alliances with groups which the Islamic State considers to be apostates and which it broadly refers to as *Sahwa* (awakening), either because of their nationalist tendencies or their relations with foreign states. In the first article in the series, it is stated that

> Although the game is clear to those with a sound understanding of iman [faith] and waqi' (current affairs), it was unclear to the jihad claimants of Sham (the Julani front) [Jabhat al-Nusra]. These deviants instead fought against the Islamic State alongside the Sahwah factions that later formed the Shamiyyah Front while claiming these factions were battalions of sincere mujahidin.[82]

In a later article in the series, it says that 'there is no such thing as wala' and bara' in the creed of these factions, which is the reality of all the nationalist "Islamic" factions allied to the Julani front.'[83] This leads the author to ask,

> As for the Julani front, will they now repent from their treachery and apostasy and distance themselves from their nationalist 'Islamic' allies whom they allied together with against the Islamic State despite knowing very well of the nationalist apostasy within these factions? Will they wage war against them and return to the ranks of the Islamic State?[84]

Obviously, a central point here is whether these 'allies' are apostates, as the Islamic State claims. Jabhat al-Nusra does consider groups like Jaysh al-Islam and Ahrar al-Sham to have theological shortcomings, but it does not recognise the Islamic State's claim that they are apostates. Defending this position, an al-Nusra leader stressed their more intimate knowledge of these groups, saying 'we are more aware of their condition than the Dawla group [Islamic State] because of our closeness to them.'[85] In the *Dabiq* publication which concluded the article series, the Islamic State included another article focusing on the alliances of al-Qaida's group in Yemen to show how AQAP, just like Jabhat al-Nusra, violates al-wala' wa-l-bara'. The article says, 'These relationships in addition to the irja' and hizbiyyah of al-Qa'idah's leadership are the crucial driving force in converting al-Qa'ida branches from parties resisting the American-led crusades into hardcore sahwat.'[86] Commenting on AQAP's decision to hand over control of Mukalla to a local tribal council named the Hadhrami Domestic Council after seizing it from the Yemeni state, the article elaborates, 'After expelling a taghut [tyrant] in power, al-Qa'idah refused to take control of the land and rule it by Shari'ah themselves and instead handed it over to a selection of Ikhwan, Saudi supporters, grave worshippers, and former parliament, military, and security officials!'

While the first four parts of the article series on al-Nusra were intended to show how the group did not adhere to al-wala' wa-l-bara', they never mentioned the Islamic State's ruling on al-Nusra itself. But in the fifth and final article published in November 2015, it is explained that al-Nusra had committed apostasy after fighting the Islamic State and allying with apostates. This message was communicated even more clearly on June 1, 2016, in an unambiguous internal ruling on Jabhat al-Nusra, which declared it and its allies '*groups forcefully resisting the implementation of the Shari'a of Allah*' (tawaif mumtani'a bi-shawka 'an tahkim shar' allah) who assist apostates in establishing a state of unbelief rather than 'declare their disassociation from them and from their kufr.' These groups, the ruling reads, have committed several *nullifiers* of Islam (nawaqid); well aware of the delicacy of this matter, it requires all individual members of the Islamic State to proclaim takfir on Jabhat al-Nusra. Refusing to do so would place one at risk of being declared an apostate too.[87] A few days later, an Islamic State member named Ibn 'Ata al-Muhajir elaborated on the matter, explaining that

> each member of Jabhat al-Julani [al-Nusra], whether or not he fought against the Islamic State, is required to undergo an istitabah [asking for repentance] course, which means he must repent from the kufr in which he was engaged. Part of that

> course is his personal admission that he was indeed an apostate. The soldiers of Jabhat al-Julani are kuffar [unbelievers]. They are munafiqin [hypocrites] who have blatantly committed kufr [unbelief], so their ruling is that of the murtaddin [apostates].[88]

The Islamic State would later transfer this type of ruling to Jabhat al-Nusra's successor HTS, and to the new Syrian al-Qaida affiliate *Hurras al-Deen* (Guardians of Religion), referring to the latter as *Hurras al-Shirk* (Guardians of Polytheism) and as a *Group of Apostates* (majmu'a min al-murtaddin).[89] The tendency observed since 2014 is thus one of constant expansion: the Islamic State proclaims takfir on *X*. *Y* is then obliged to disassociate from *X* and if *Y* does not do this, then *Y* risks being considered an unbeliever too.

Building on their narrative of the apostasy of these groups, in mid-2015, the Islamic State began issuing visual productions showing violent aggression against their Jihadi rivals. Such publication of violent acts has been a key feature of the group's method of creating and forming narratives, and expanding their range by placing essentially local events on a global scale. In what is probably the first case of this type of communication, in June 2015, the group published a video showing the execution of captured Jabhat al-Nusra and Jaysh al-Islam fighters.[90] Later this became a standard procedure for the Islamic State, and it was followed by photosets and videos depicting killings, including beheadings, of Jihadis in Afghanistan. Moreover, in December 2016, Islamic State supporters offered a bounty for the killing of the al-Qaida-linked ideologue Abdullah al-Muhaysini.[91] In this way, the group contributed to the normalisation and expansion of the practice of intra-Jihadi violence.

As mentioned, al-Qaida's and al-Zawahiri's view of al-wala' wa-l-bara' has always differed. In his 2002 booklet *al-Wala' wa-l-Bara'*, al-Zawahiri's objective is to offer Jihadis a way to identify the necessary criteria for membership in the Muslim community. To him militancy, or Jihad, is what defines the Muslim community, and this inevitably results in entirely different intra-Jihadi dynamics compared to the Islamic State's approach. When applied to the SJM and to factions outside the movement who nonetheless oppose the regime military, al-Zawahiri thus shows a similar inclination to focus on militant solidarity and on what unites their struggle. Agreeing that acts violating the proper creed and constituting unbelief should lead to disassociation, al-Qaida's attitude is nonetheless much more pragmatic in terms of which actors it cooperates with. This is not least because they take the view that divergence of *interpretation* (ijtihad) should not be an obstacle to cooperation when facing a common *apostate* enemy. Both Bin Laden and al-Zawahiri have spoken at length about Jihadi coalitions and the importance of working with locals.[92] Exemplifying this pragmatism is AQAP's collaborative relationship with Yemeni tribes. AQAP amir Khalid al-Batarfi (Abu al-Miqdad al-Kindi) also issued an audio recording in 2016 when he functioned as the group's spokesperson, telling Jihadis in Syria to 'open their hearts to Muslims who differ'.[93] In the context of Syria, Jabhat al-Nusra definitely agreed with the Islamic State that many of the rebel factions did deviate in terms of creed and methodology, but in their view several of these factions were not considered unbelievers. Even if some were outright unbelievers, collaboration could be justified on the principle of *maslaha* (benefit) for the Jihadi project, that is greater than the *mafsada* (harm) involved. And while the Islamic State viewed al-Nusra's alliances as violations of tawhid, al-Nusra considered this a methodological question, one where flexibility could and should be exercised.[94]

The analysis here certainly confirms Lahoud's argument about how al-wala' wa-l-bara' complicates matters 'for jihadis in achieving a unified objective.' However, as will be discussed later, my position stops short of her conclusion that the notion is 'undermining Jihadism from within.'[95] This diverging conclusion is partly the result of my different perspective on Jihadis' application of al-wala' wa-l-bara' compared to Lahoud, one that stresses its strategic and instrumental aspect and does not view it exclusively as a matter of doctrine and a search for purity. The analysis also shows the 'banality' of concepts like al-wala' wa-l-bara' and takfir by illustrating, on the one hand, Jihadis' instrumentalisation of these concepts and, on the other, how common these dynamics are in other religions and political ideologies as tools of contestation and competition. On July 16, 1054, Humbert Of Mournoutiers, cardinal of Silva Candida and chief secretary to the Roman Pope Leo IX, entered Hagia Sophia in Constantinople and left a letter on the altar excommunicating the patriarch Cerularius, famously instigating a great schism within Christianity. The Reformation would later entail similar processes of exclusion and delineation within the religious community. Reflecting on the experiences of the Russian communist movement, Trotsky hit the head of the nail, writing that 'Every group representing a new trend excommunicates its predecessors. To those who come with new ideas the previous period seems to have been but a crude deviation from the correct road, an historical misunderstanding....'[96] Devoted believers and revolutionaries have consistently engaged in exercises to define themselves in contrast to the surrounding society or rivals, including those coming from their own movement, to strengthen their own project. Framed differently, this process involves disassociation from opponents while giving exclusive loyalty to one's own. In that regard, there is nothing particularly distinctive about Jihadis' use of takfir and al-wala' wa-l-bara', apart from terminology and, arguably, the ferocity with which they apply these notions. There should be no doubt that the Islamic State's extensive emphasis on doctrinal purity has had an immense impact on how it views less 'pure' actors, but viewing the group's utilisation of al-wala' wa-l-bara' and takfir exclusively in a theological context misses the dominant strategic dimension of how they rely on these powerful notions as mechanisms to politicise intra-movement relations.[97]

*The Delicate Issue of Disassociating from al-Zawahiri*

The Islamic State's attitude to the status of al-Zawahiri, and al-Qaida more generally, has taken a different route that consciously involves more ambiguity. While al-Zawahiri has been described as the one in charge of the deviance of al-Qaida, official Islamic State publications have stopped short of declaring him an apostate, despite making this type of pronouncement about al-Qaida affiliates in Syria and Yemen, and al-Zawahiri's close ally, the Taliban. Talking to Islamic State sympathisers online, this confusion is evident: characterisations of the status of al-Zawahiri differ between apostasy and deviance. For instance, one Islamic State sympathiser said that 'When Dr Zawahiri praised the apostate ex-president of Egypt, Muhammad

Morsi, it was the RIP for al-Qaeda!! Its branches in Syria (Nusra) and Yemen is a living example of how deviant AQ has become. Allying and cooperating with nationalists, secularists and receiving aid from GCC states.'[98] Another example is a long piece by Islamic State member Abu Sa'd al-Najdi. Despite his support for the Islamic State and criticism of al-Zawahiri's condemnation of the group, he addressed the al-Qaida leader with respect, using the title *sheikh al-jihad*. He finishes his piece calling on Jabhat al-Nusra fighters to disobey al-Julani and join the Islamic State.[99]

At the opposite end of the spectrum, in August 2015, Islamic State supporters in Libya initiated a campaign of publishing *Wanted Dead* posters of rival Jihadis and Islamists in Libya, to legitimise and mobilise for its conflict with local rivals. Surprisingly, this included a poster of al-Zawahiri calling for his death. Summarising the confusion, in a post on the Islamic State-supportive Telegram group *Al Anfaal* on September 26, 2018, a supporter wrote the following in response to a message stating that the Islamic State made takfir on al-Qaida when it was described as *apostate sahwa of al-Zawahiri* in the Dabiq magazine:

> Firstly, I don't think 'apostate Sahwat of Zawhiri' *[sic]* is referring to AQ2.0 [al-Qaida during the reign of al-Zawahiri] (...) if I am wrong in that understanding then to make it clear we should try to find some fatwa by the official scholars of the Islamic State. If there is any such fatwa that AQ2.0 as whole are apostates then it would be better to take THAT as official stance of Islamic State on AQ2.0. Secondly, if there is any such fatwa then I would like to see the scholarly argument that was given by the scholars for making Takfeer *[sic]* on AQ2.0 as whole. As far as my knowledge of it is concerned I don't know them making Takfeer on all of AQ2.0 from the east to the West.

In fact, it would later be revealed that the supporter was right in doubting the claim made about the Islamic State's takfir on al-Zawahiri. A leaked internal report authored by the Islamic State's Public Security Department in November 2015 states that 'as a result this generation of extremists [within the Islamic State] asserted the takfir [excommunication] of leaders of the Dawla [Islamic State] because they did not declare takfir on Ayman al-Zawahiri.'[100]

Nonetheless, the tone regarding the al-Qaida leader did change over time. Three short publications by Islamic State members and supporters are illustrative of the increasing effort to discredit the al-Qaida leader and instigate Jihadis' disavowal of him. The first piece is a testimony by a former member of al-Qaida from Waziristan named Abu Jarir al-Shamali. Al-Shamali told his story in the sixth edition of *Dabiq* magazine, where he explains how, as an al-Qaida member, he and his colleagues wanted clarification from al-Zawahiri on a number of points: the group's stance on the Shia, al-Zawahiri's praise for Muhammad Morsi,[101] his accusation of the Islamic State being khawarij and the change of methodology from militant Jihad to peaceful demonstration and a focus on winning popular support. After allegedly not receiving any response, al-Shamali annulled his bay'a to Mullah Umar and al-Zawahiri—he claims they nullified the conditions of the pledge of allegiance through their behaviour—and pledged loyalty to al-Baghdadi. Eventually, he says al-Qaida entered alliances with non-Jihadis 'in a desperate attempt to save a drowning entity struggling to breathe in deep water as it is exhausted and fatigued by tiredness.'[102] While the Islamic State may not have declared al-Qaida an apostate group in its entirety, al-Shamali writes that he and his colleagues embarked on a war against al-Qaida by *exposing its deviation*.

In 2016, however, after Zawahiri launched his Islamic Spring lecture series, there was a tendency to attack him more directly. The second piece is authored under the pseudonym *Gharib al-Sururiyya*. The name refers to a prominent Islamic State contributor who regularly published through the al-Battar and al-Wafa media foundations, especially just after al-Nusra announced its rebranding as Jabhat Fath al-Sham and effectively left al-Qaida. Ridiculing al-Qaida and al-Zawahiri for their alleged failure after losing yet another affiliate, the author rejects al-Zawahiri's methodology, referring to him as a *dog* and an *apostate*. In his words, 'the Jabhat of infidelity and shame [Jabhat al-Nusra], along with it al-Qaida of corruption and misguidance, had the methodology of taking into consideration the feelings of infidels and unbelievers', leading to its downfall.[103]

Two months later another author, *Ahlam al-Nasr*, popularly known as the poetess of the Islamic State, issued a short publication entitled *Zawahiri: The Old Ball*. Treating the same topic of al-Nusra's de-affiliation from al-Qaida, al-Nasr compares al-Zawahiri to a used football being kicked around at one's pleasure. Al-Nasr's point is that other Jihadis like Jabhat al-Nusra have simply used al-Zawahiri and his organisation for their own benefit, only to dispose of him when he is no longer useful. She writes,

> [Y]ou are a poor old man who is tricked so easily with a praise. You are blinded with your own name and the name of Qaida on the reality of status and consequence. You became like a ball with which a footballer falls in love and dabs gently. He may also whisper some cheerful words even though after a while he will kick it and exhaust it. Afterwards, he will not care about it when he achieves his personal win, he will even not care if he substitutes it with another ball to achieve another new win! Look in what position you put yourself in! Look at what mop you have made al-Qaeda![104]

### *Legitimising the Fight Against the Islamic State*

By declaring its Jihadi rivals apostates, the Islamic State enabled the institutionalisation of infighting. The idea of attacking rivals became theologically justified, framed as a strategic necessity and disseminated through media publications. In Syria, groups like Jaysh al-Islam and Ahrar al-Sham were quick to respond with accusations against the Islamic State, stating that it represented modern-day khawarij and should be fought. As we will see, for al-Qaida and affiliated ideologues, this process proved much more contentious and complicated.[105]

Early on in 2014, some ideologues like Abu Basir al-Tartusi, Tariq Abdelhaleem and Hani al-Sibai labelled the Islamic State *khawarij* and called for attacks against the group.[106] While criticism of the group was already prevalent at the time, explicitly calling for attacks represented a serious escalation that ideologues like al-Maqdisi and Abu Qatada were not ready for. Explaining his opinion at the time, al-Maqdisi wrote that what makes the Islamic State differ from the Khawarij is that the group has good ideas and intentions, but that they are pursuing them in the wrong way. The Khawarij, on the other hand, had bad intentions when they were killing Muslims.[107]

Facing the aggression of the Islamic State, Jabhat al-Nusra had a particular desire to protect itself locally on the ground. In January 2015, when fighting between the two groups in Daraa was ongoing, Abu Mariya al-Qahtani, a former religious figure in the Islamic State and a founding member of al-Nusra, published a strong condemnation of his former group from his new refuge in Daraa after being expelled from Deir ez-Zour, where he was al-Nusra's leading commander. Known as a fierce critic of the Islamic State, al-Qahtani called for al-Nusra fighters and allies to follow the example of Ali ibn Abi Talib who fought against the rebellious khawarij during the first fitna.[108] Afterwards al-Nusra circulated a pamphlet treating the transgression of the Islamic State, and the group also issued an official ruling on the Islamic State, proclaiming that it should be fought. This represented a clear change in attitude on the part of al-Nusra: al-Julani had previously instructed his soldiers not to fight the Islamic State—if al-Nusra fighters were attacked, they should retreat. This was followed by a united statement by al-Nusra and Ahrar al-Sham after the Islamic State attacked them in the city of Sawran, north of Hama, an act which allegedly halted their offensive against the Assad regime. While this statement represented a united *local* position against the Islamic State, it still lacked the support of influential ideologues outside of Syria.

In June 2015, just as the military fortunes of the Islamic State in Syria were changing and it was beginning to lose control over the Syrian-Turkish border, ideologues opposing the group finally managed to establish a united front. For the first time, a larger group of al-Qaida affiliated ideologues issued a religious ruling (fatwa) making it permissible to *repel* attacks from the Islamic State. Signed by al-Maqdisi, Abu Qatada, al-Uraydi, al-Muhaysini and several others, the fatwa was just like the al-Nusra-Ahrar statement provoked by Islamic State attacks against Jihadi rivals in Sawran. Referring to the Islamic State as *the Baghdadi-ists* (al-Baghdadiyyin), the fatwa states:

> we issue the verdict that it is *compulsory* (wajib) to repel their aggression and defend the lands of the Muslims and that it is

> impermissible to hand over the land of Sham [Syria] to them for it has become clear the corrupted beliefs they hold. Their aggression, oppression and aggressiveness has become clear to whoever has some insight.[109]

While the fatwa only makes it permissible to *repel* attacks and not to engage proactively in attacks against the Islamic State, it nonetheless still represents an escalation in the opposition to al-Baghdadi's group. The fact that it was signed by most of the senior Jihadi ideologues also implies that it established a broader and more united ideological justification for fighting the group. Unsurprisingly, early critics of the Islamic State like al-Sibai and Abdelhaleem felt that the fatwa was too lenient. In Facebook postings, the two Egyptian ideologues argued that simply making it legitimate to *defend* oneself against Islamic State aggression was not enough as this would only foster more aggression. The only solution, they argued, was for Jihadis to actively fight the group.[110]

In summer 2015, the context that Jihadis' conflict dynamics in Syria played out within remained relatively simple and was largely defined by the struggle against the *tyrannical* Assad regime and the *atheist* Kurds. This would change when first Russia (in September 2015) and later Turkey (in August 2016) intervened militarily, complicating the political and military context substantially. Despite the problems with the Islamic State, ideologues like al-Maqdisi and Abu Qatada still acknowledged the renegade group's overall contribution to Jihadis' military project in the country. When I met Abu Qatada for the first time, before even being asked a question he told me that he did not want to criticise *tanzim al-dawla* (the Islamic State) as long as they are in a *military situation* (halat al-'askariyya) because now was not the right time for *division* (inqisam). Attacking the group would only help its enemies, he argued.[111] When I sat in his house a year and a half later, his criticism of the group had become much more vocal.

That said, the exact stance of figures like al-Maqdisi and Abu Qatada in 2015–16 remained slightly ambiguous. This was because they were navigating an increasingly complex situation, managing opposing sentiments and attempting to appease all sides. Later in

June 2015, after issuing the fatwa, Abu Qatada authored another religious ruling that al-Maqdisi endorsed. Jihadis in Libya fighting against the local Islamic State affiliate were facing a problem: after having been confronted by their Islamic State rivals and losing many fighters, the Islamic State itself was attacked by General Haftar's *Libyan National Army*. Following this, one of the Jihadis exclaimed: 'May Allah help them shoot and target the right aim.' This led to fierce internal debate between the Libyan Jihadis: some argued that anyone who hoped that Haftar's forces would succeed against the Islamic State had committed an act of unbelief; others claimed that this was haram and constituted a sin; and a third group considered it acceptable. Now they wanted Abu Qatada's judgement. Declaring the Islamic State to be khawarij, the Jordanian ideologue explained that they are nonetheless preferable to unbelievers and to Shias. 'Your duty is to wish for the victory of the Kharijites over the unbeliever', he writes, but also continues: 'However, if the pictures conform to the aforementioned and that the Kharijites are assaulting you and suddenly an unbeliever or a true idolater comes and kills a Kharijite, you can wish for his death.'[112] Adding further criticism of the Islamic State, he made sure to stress that in talking about the *khawarij*, he is only referring to the group's leaders and commander.

Around the same, al-Maqdisi published a statement expressing the same conclusion but also distinguishing his position from that of Abu Qatada. Having received strong criticism from segments within the SJM for his refusal to label the Islamic State as khawarij, al-Maqdisi defends himself by saying that he does consider the group's leaders to be khawarij but not its ordinary members. Hence, he disagrees with the broad categorisation of the group as khawarij which some colleagues have argued for. Touching upon his own influence within the SJM, al-Maqdisi mentions that some fighters have refrained from fighting *jama'at al-dawla* (Islamic State) simply because he himself has not labelled it khawarij. But he fears that if he categorises the entire group, this will lead to further infighting, which only serves the interests of the Jihadis' enemies.[113] Earlier in the month, however, al-Maqdisi had expanded on the fatwa permitting defensive attacks against the Islamic State. In his view, it was not just permissible to repel tangible attacks from the group but also to attack *if* attacks were imminent.[114] Adding further confusion about his actual position on the Islamic State, some months later he would provocatively tweet that his position on the group was not written in stone and that he might reassess his stance on the group entirely and suddenly support it.

As explained previously, labelling the Islamic State as khawarij was no small thing, since it justified fighting the group. The majority position in Islam is that the khawarij are *ahl al-bida'* (people of innovation) who have departed from the *ahl al-sunna* (people of prophetic tradition) *but* who remain within the fold of Islam (a minority position is that they have left Islam). Despite still being considered Muslims, it is obligatory to fight them based on an authentic prophetic hadith that deserves to be quoted in full:

> Jabir b. Abdullah reported that a person came to the Messenger of Allah at Ja'rana on his way back from Hunain, and there was in the clothes of Bilal some silver. The Messenger of Allah took a handful out of that and bestowed it upon the people. He (the person who had met the Prophet at Ja'rana) said to him: Muhammad, do justice. He (the Holy Prophet) said: Woe be upon thee, who would do justice if I do not do justice, and you would be very unfortunate and a loser if I do not do justice. Upon this Umar b. Khattab (Allah be pleased with him) said: Permit me to kill this hypocrite. Upon this he (the Holy Prophet) said: May there be protection of Allah! People would say that I kill my companions. This man and his companions would recite the Qur'an but it would not go beyond their throat, and they swerve from it just as the arrow goes through the prey.[115]
>
> A person among the people then sought permission (from the Holy Prophet) for his murder. According to some, it was Khalid b. Walid who sought the permission. Upon this the Messenger of Allah, said: From this very person's posterity there would arise people who would recite the Qur'an, but it would not go beyond their throat; they would kill the followers of Islam and would spare the idol-worshippers. They would glance through the teachings of Islam so hurriedly just as the arrow passes through the prey. If I were to ever find them I would kill them like 'Ad.[116]

> Adding to this, Ibn Taymiyyah has written that: 'The Khawaarij who deviated, whom the Prophet (blessings and peace of Allah be upon him) enjoined us to fight, and whom Ameer al-Mu'mineen 'Ali (may Allah be pleased with him), one of the Rightly-Guided Caliphs fought, and whom the leading scholars of Islam among the Sahaabah, Taabi'een and those who came after them were unanimously agreed upon fighting, were not described as disbelievers by 'Ali ibn Abi Taalib, Sa'd ibn Abi Waqqaas and others among the Sahaabah; rather they regarded them as Muslims even though they fought them, and 'Ali did not fight them until they shed blood unlawfully and raided the property of the Muslims; then he fought them in order to ward off their wrongdoing and aggression, not because they were disbelievers. Hence he did not take their womenfolk captive and he did not seize their wealth as booty.'[117]

Applying the khawarij label is thus a direct legitimization of fighting someone. Thus, at the beginning of 2016, it is very notable that al-Zawahiri was alone in not describing al-Baghdadi's group as khawarij: but that was about to change.[118] In several speeches made during the first six months of the year, the al-Qaida leader escalated his rhetoric. In January he referred to the Islamic State as *extremist takfiris* (al-ghulat al-takfiriyyin) before explaining how he sees the difference between the Khawarij and the Islamic State: The Khawarij were honest about killing Ali, while the Islamic State lied about killing Abu Khalid al-Suri. For the Khawarij, lying was considered an act of unbelief, while for the Islamic State it is acceptable. For the Khawarij breaking the pledge of allegiance was an act of unbelief, while this was not the case for the Islamic State. And for the Khawarij excommunication was ideological, but for the Islamic State it is political.[119] Just five months later, al-Zawahiri would take matters one step further, calling the Islamic State *the new extremist takfiri khawarij* (al-khawarij al-ghulat al-takfiriyyin al-jadid) and *neo-khawarij* (al-khawarij al-jadid). Outlining a future scenario, he stated: 'The issue of unity today is a matter of life and death for you. Either you unite to live as Muslims in honour, or you will differ and be disunited and be eaten one by one.'[120] At the same time, the al-Qaida-produced pamphlet series *al-Nafir* initiated an anti-Islamic State campaign, calling on al-Baghdadi specifically to offer proof of al-Qaida's alleged apostasy.[121]

## *Conclusions*

Jihadis' political project has always been rather diffuse, but with the Islamic State's caliphate declaration it suddenly took on a more tangible form. Opponents of the group did not disagree with its ambition of establishing a religio-political entity; rather, the crucial issue was the methodology that should be used to do this and their analysis of the contemporary context. The previous two chapters have illustrated how *methodology* and not *creed* is at the centre of the contestation, and how methodology is politicised in this process as a mechanism to facilitate conflict between otherwise relatively likeminded actors.

Breaking his initial reluctance, or inability, to respond in force to the Islamic State, al-Zawahiri would finally come out with an elaborate critique of al-Baghdadi and his group in an attempt to make himself relevant once again. Questioning the Islamic State's claim to follow the correct *prophetic methodology*, he offered an alternative explanation and route for those in disagreement with the caliphate. The two groups continued their internal contestation for authority by nurturing distinctive structural models of authority. This involved discursive processes aimed at crediting or discrediting sections of the scholarly community depending on their loyalty, as well as competition for the legacy of historical figures like Bin Laden and al-Zarqawi. Eventually, the result was a radicalisation of intra-Jihadi relations, as infighting was justified through the use of theological categories that institutionalised military escalation.

# PART SIX

# INTERNALISING FITNA

*'The fitna can deviate him [the Jihadi] from the straight path or can keep him busy from the great aim for which he is striving in this era. The person walking the path of support of religion and ruling with shari'a should avoid all the obstacles that might affect his way of ruling and using the shari'a. Among the most dangerous of those obstacles is the fitna.'*[1]

Sami al-Uraydi

*'When will we vilify the one who opposes the Shari'a and Sunnah and not the one who opposes our methodology only (...) the problem is that our adversaries used to oppose us in issues of faith (imaan) in the past, but now the problem is inside the current itself.'*[2]

Abu Mahmoud al-Filastini

# 11

# THE ISLAMIC STATE

The dominant internal conflict dynamic in 2013–15 was *between* groups, but from 2016 on this was complemented and to some extent replaced with conflict *within* groups. This dynamic initiated a new conflict cycle reminiscent of previous events. In 2016, creedal tensions started to dominate internal affairs within the Islamic State, resulting in factionalisation and the establishment of two distinctive camps within the group. What began as dissatisfaction among fringe elements back in 2014 became a dominating feature of the group's internal well-being and would involve a power struggle for institutional control that eventually turned violent. Within al-Qaida, the group would experience its second organisational de-affiliation when Jabhat al-Nusra rebranded itself first as Jabhat Fatah al-Sham (JFS) and later as Hayat Tahrir al-Sham (HTS). These dynamics were predominantly the result of two factors. The first factor was the changing operational and political context in Syria and Iraq, resulting from state actors' growing assertiveness. Turkey intensified its military and political engagement in Syria, Russia remained strongly committed to its alliance with Bashar al-Assad, and the Iraqi military launched its offensive against the Islamic State while Syrian and Iraqi Kurds took the lead in battling the group. These events drastically changed conflict dynamics on the ground and exerted heavy pressure on the Islamic

State and Jabhat al-Nusra. The second factor was the groups' internal ideological heterogeneity, resulting from their desire to become mass movements. In their pursuit of success, both groups accepted new members with little consideration of their ideological orientation. While this internal diversity was manageable in a specific context characterised by military success, it turned into a serious challenge that would eventually lead to Jihadi fratricide within groups, which—once again—severely affected the power balance within the SJM.

Internal cracks within the Islamic State quickly emerged after the group's divorce from al-Qaida in early 2014. Initially this was mainly a fringe group phenomenon, although in reality, tensions were far more critical than the issues dividing the Islamic State from al-Qaida. The reason that this internal split should be considered more *critical*—at least from a theological perspective—is that it mirrored two distinctive positions on issues pertaining to creed. These differences crystallised as two identifiable factions: one referred to as *extremist* (ghulat) or *Hazimis* (al-hazimiyya or al-hazimiyyun) by its opponents, and the other known as the *Binalis* (al-binaliyyah or al-binaliyyun) or *reformers* (muslehin).

In 2014, the *extremist faction* was still too weak to seriously challenge the existing structures within the group and was suppressed by the group's security establishment. This would change in 2016 when internal competition re-emerged and seriously threatened internal cohesion. That the extremists eventually managed to emerge as a serious contender for institutional power was largely the result of the Islamic State's evolving operational and political context. The group was now under serious military pressure in large parts of Syria and Iraq. Its senior figures, many of whom had functioned as stabilising forces between the competing factions, had been killed, and its internal institutions were rapidly dissolving, leaving a power vacuum. As illustrated by leadership speeches from the period, the group was in crisis.

### *Emerging Factionalism: Al-Hazimiyya and Doctrinal Extremism*

Early 2014 was a tremendously successful period for the Islamic State. The group took swaths of territory in the northern and eastern parts of Syria, and this military success eventually facilitated the caliphate declaration. Around the same time, the group started to face internal divisions, partly because of its 'liberal' recruitment policy and its own theological extremism. Determining exactly *when* these problems emerged is impossible to say, but they must already have been brewing in spring 2014, since in May of that year the Islamic State ideologue Turki al-Binali tweeted a public denouncement of Saudi religious scholar Ahmad ibn Umar al-Hazimi and his views on *excommunication* (takfir).[3] The problems quickly escalated and became increasingly public, with news articles reporting that the Islamic State was imprisoning and executing its own members.

The first to be rounded up was a group of six foreign second-rank leaders and rank and file, who were arrested and killed in August 2014 after being accused of excessive takfir: Abu Ja'far al-Hattab, Abu Musab al-Tunisi, Abu Asid al-Maghribi, Abu al-Hawra al-Jaza'iri, Abu Khalid al-Sharqi and Abu Abdullah al-Maghribi.[4] The most prominent were al-Hattab and al-Tunisi. Al-Hattab, a former member of the Shari'a Committee of the Tunisian Ansar al-Shari'a group, had released an audio recording declaring his view on takfir, including his rejection of ignorance as an excuse for excommunicating other Muslims. Some supporters of Jabhat al-Nusra and the Islamic State even accused al-Hattab of issuing a fatwa stating that all opponents of the Islamic State are infidels, much like the GIA fatwa that proclaimed takfir on the entire Algerian population.[5] Al-Tunisi was amir in Deir ez-Zour, but became unpopular within Islamic State ranks when he allegedly declared the Taliban and Bin Laden infidels. He also pronounced takfir on AQIM and Ansar al-Shari'a in Tunisia.

At the heart of the conflict between the leadership position within the Islamic State and these rebellious figures was a theological question relating to the regulations of excommunication. This can be divided into two parts that are intrinsically connected:

1. Whether *ignorance* (jahl) is acceptable as an *excuse* ('udhr) when committing acts of unbelief (excuse out of ignorance: 'udhr bi-l-jahl).[6] The question is whether somebody committing shirk (polytheism) or in another way breaking Islamic law due to ignorance should be considered an apostate or not.

2. Whether the one excusing the unbeliever should be proclaimed an unbeliever as well (excommunication of the excuser: takfir al-'adhir). The question here is whether one should excommunicate the one who refrains from or rejects excommunicating the one who commits shirk out of ignorance.

These questions are related to the *nullifiers of Islam* (nawaqid al-islam), the ten principles Muhammad Abd al-Wahhab defined to delineate the boundaries of the Islamic faith, which are generally accepted among Salafis. The transgression of any one of these ten nullifiers would automatically expel one from Islam. The questions of *'udhr bi-l-jahl* and especially *takfir al-'adhir* are specifically connected to the *third nullifier* that reads: 'Whoso does not excommunicate the polytheists, or is doubtful about their unbelief, or affirms the validity of their doctrine, he is an unbeliever by consensus.' This 'requirement that Muslims excommunicate not only those guilty of polytheism, but also those who fail or hesitate to excommunicate them' is what Michael Crawford calls *secondary takfir*. Cole Bunzel explains how this was particularly important to al-Wahhab as a mechanism for dividing the community into Muslims and non-Muslims.[7]

According to Ahmad al-Hazimi *ignorance* is not a legitimate excuse, and he considers the one *excusing* the unbeliever to be an unbeliever himself. Even within Jihadi circles, this is a highly controversial opinion only supported by a small, extreme minority. Al-Hazimi himself is not affiliated with the Islamic State. In fact, he is not even considered a Jihadi scholar, though he has been imprisoned since 2015 despite his general loyalty to the Saudi monarchy. His focus is entirely theological and never related to political issues; as such, he has simply provided the interpretations, or tools, for his followers to apply. Another example of such 'facilitation', well-tuned to the logic of the SJM, is al-Hazimi's argument that everyone can proclaim takfir and that it is not a privilege of religious scholars.[8] Before his imprisonment he made trips to Egypt and Tunisia, where he gave lectures on the radical interpretation of the third nullifier and, as Bunzel has noted, elaborated on his doctrine of takfir al-'adhir in 2013.[9] As highlighted by Zelin, this is likely a key reason to explain the extremism within Tunisian Jihadi circles.[10] So, despite not being part of the SJM himself, his interpretation of takfir nevertheless influenced substantial numbers of Jihadis who either were or became members of the Islamic State—hence the eponym *Hazimis*. The dominant faction at the time within the Islamic State would become known as the *Binalis* after Turki al-Binali, who was heading the opposition to the doctrine of takfir al-'adhir and the endless *chain of excommunication* (al-takfir bi-l-tasalsul) it risks resulting in.[11]

Radicalisation often happens at the fringes of a group, and this was also the case in the Islamic State. The rebellious voices were initially a small minority within the group and their view of takfir was considered extreme even by Islamic State standards. In the principle of takfir of the excuser lies the potential for 'chain takfir', which the Islamic State leaders quickly realised would eventually involve excommunication of themselves. In the eyes of some Hazimis, al-Zawahiri is an infidel because of his refusal to excommunicate the Shia as a group and his pledge of allegiance to the Taliban; as a result, al-Baghdadi would become an infidel because of his refusal to excommunicate al-Zawahiri. However, the marginal support the Hazimis enjoyed within the group at this early stage implied that the internal rebellion of this doctrinally extreme faction was manageable for the Islamic State, despite it spreading among rank and file, particularly among foreign fighters and the Russian-speaking contingent.[12]

The Hazimis' main platforms for airing their frustrations about the official Islamic State stance was initially Facebook and Twitter, where they debated the requirements for excommunication. However, some more elaborate primary accounts telling the story from a Hazimi perspective do exist. One of them was written by an Abu Ja'far al-Shami, who—probably in late August 2014—published a strong condemnation of the Islamic State, which he refers to as the *State of al-Baghdadi* (dawlat al-baghdadi).[13] Although he does not mention the name of Ahmad al-Hazimi, he clearly sympathises with known Hazimi figures like Abu Musab al-Tunisi. Al-Shami's article rebukes the Islamic State for refraining from making takfir of the one who excuses greater shirk (idolatry) and for excusing the ignorant. He suggests this is because al-Baghdadi and his loyalists are not sufficiently devoted to theology, but more focused on power and strategy. Interestingly, to illustrate this he uses the example of al-Qaida, explaining that al-Qaida never changed in the period after Bin Laden's death (in al-Shami's view, al-Qaida was always an apostate group) in contrast to the official Islamic State narrative. Instead, it was the Islamic State that changed its view of al-Qaida because of the strategic interest it had in doing so.

In September 2014, the Islamic State executed another of its Shari'a judges, Abu Umar al-Kuwaiti (Husain Rida Lare), under mysterious circumstances. Originally from Kuwait, Abu Umar allegedly entered Syria in 2012, where he established the Soldiers of the Caliphate Battalion, which developed into Jama'at al-Muslimin before finally pledging allegiance to the Islamic State. Even before joining the Islamic State, the vocal Abu Umar became infamous for his takfiri inclination when he pronounced takfir on Jabhat al-Nusra. As a judge within the Islamic State, Abu Umar also argued in favour of excommunicating al-Zawahiri and eventually also al-Baghdadi. Unsurprisingly, this cost him his life.

The Islamic State's hope at this early stage was to suppress the extremist faction, and thus the leadership did not comment officially on the Hazimis. Instead, in late 2014, its General Supervisory Committee[14] (al-lajna al-amma al-mushrifa) issued a general instruction on the 'Precision of the Base of Excommunication on the Dismaying Issues of the Excuse Out of Ignorance' (ihkam al-takfir al-mabniyya ala masail mutfazza'ah 'an al-'adhir bi-l-jahl), forbidding members to discuss matters of excuse out of ignorance and threatening to prosecute members sharing material on this issue. Around the same time, Abu Maysara al-Shami, the American media official, issued a condemnation entitled 'al-Hazimi Between the Great Sin of Abstention and the Error of the Jamiah', in which he discredits Ahmad al-Hazimi, explaining that he is not truly a Jihadi and in fact is part of al-jamiah, who are loyal to the Saudi monarchy.[15] Al-Shami denounced al-Hazimi, stressing his exclusively 'theoretical' approach (which is devoid of any connection to reality) and his decision not to emigrate to the Levant despite being encouraged to do so by his supporters.[16] The Saudi's view of takfir, he claims, is an innovation that resembles the early Khawarij and necessarily results in endless excommunication. Ending his article, al-Shami writes: 'To the "Hazimites" I say: disbelieve your sheikh or shut up. I swear by Allah that you are living in contradiction (…) O Allah reveal the disappointment of Al-Hazimi, reveal his secrets and make him an example to those who might learn.'[17]

The most exhaustive account available about the internal factionalism in 2014–15 comes from an internal report from November 2015 leaked in 2018 and published by al-Tamimi. Authored by the 'public security department' (diwan al-amn al-amm), the report explains the internal challenge that the extremists pose, how they are structured, the substance of the disagreement and how the Islamic State as an institution should deal with them. Firstly, the report dates the eruption of factionalism to spring 2014; this was after the Islamic State ousted other opposition groups from large parts of Northern and Eastern Syria and the group consolidated its control of the territory. Naming several of the Hazimis' early leaders, many of whom occupied senior organisational positions within the Islamic State, the report identifies Abu al-Hawra al-Jaza'iri and Abu Khalid al-Sharqi as central figures in spreading the Hazimis' ideology by giving courses in creed to Islamic State imams and ordinary members in Raqqa. The group's security department responded in various ways to this first phase of Hazimi assertiveness: members suspected of sympathising with extreme views were reported to the security department, arrested, and questioned. Eventually, some were released after retracting their views. Leaders of the faction, however, were mainly executed after being labelled as khawarij.[18] The report explains that the crackdown did not solve the internal problems but it did change how the Hazimis operated in 2015. While initially they had aired their criticisms publicly, they now began to work clandestinely and to organise in secret cells led by Alfir al-Azeri, Abu Huraira al-Shishani, Abu Abdullah al-Tunisi, Abu Suhail al-Masri and Abu Ayub al-Tunisi. In this period, they generally blended in within the Islamic State or, in some instances, left the group in order to publish their criticism.

2014 and 2015 thus witnessed the first two phases of Hazimi rebellion within the Islamic State. This period is characterised by a distinctive operational modus whereby a minority that had once publicly aired their criticism began to operate in clandestine cells.

In 2016, a third phase emerged when the Hazimis managed to take advantage of the Islamic State's changing fortunes in Syria, where it had come under military (and thus also political) pressure.

### *Internal Criticism*

Just as the problems with the Hazimis in Syria appeared to be diminishing, a new *type* of internal criticism emerged within the Islamic State. This time, however, it did not concern creedal issues but was mainly a matter of 'strategy, tactics, and conduct',[19] thus falling into the category of methodological issues. Documents revealing at least two episodes of intra-group methodological criticism exist. The first example concerns the Islamic State's province in Yemen (ISY). In December 2015, two letters, signed by a total of 101 members (including several high-ranking figures) were sent from Yemen to the leadership in the Levant. These declared that the signatories disavowed the ISY wali (governor) that al-Baghdadi had elected, owing to his alleged methodological deviations. Among the examples, they mention:[20]

- Unfairly expelling ISY fighters,
- Failed military strategy during an attack where ISY fighters were killed due to a lack of basic provisions and assistance, and
- Unwillingness to correct a local governor who refused to refer a case of apostasy to the shari'a court.

The frustrated signatories, who declare loyalty to al-Baghdadi, mention that they have already informed the Islamic State leadership, but that these methodological deviations nonetheless continued. After a few days, Abu Ubayda Abd al-Hakim—the same shura council member who tried, in 2014, to convince AQIM amir Droukdal to shift allegiance—responded to the ISY members. He acknowledged receiving their complaint but rejected it outright. Al-Hakim informs the disgruntled members that the Islamic State does not tolerate dissent that risks 'splitting the ranks', and that it is mandatory to listen to and obey elected leaders. Refusing to do so will be met with expulsion. In two separate responses, the *dissenters* reiterate their unambiguous loyalty to al-Baghdadi but remain firm that they will not accept the methodological deviations. Rebuking al-Hakim's threat of expulsion, they respond that remaining on what they consider to be the correct methodology is more important than obeying any leader in shar'i violations. Arguably more interesting than the substance of the dissenters' criticism is the Islamic State's final response to the affair. In a declaration issued by its Administration for Distant Provinces (idarat al-wilayat al-ba'ida), the Islamic State announced that seven named ringleaders of the dissent within ISY have been expelled from the Islamic State, while giving the remaining dissenters a last opportunity to repent. About a month later, in early February 2016, another official statement was issued by the administration, this time stating that the expelled ringleaders no longer have a connection to the Islamic State despite their continuing claims to represent the group. The statement also notes that several of the remaining dissenters failed to repent.

The second example comes from Syria and the pen of a high-ranking Egyptian Islamic State member named Abu al-Faruq al-Masri. He criticises the Islamic State's strategy and conduct from 2014–15 in a statement entitled 'Message on the Manhaj' (risala fi-l-manhaj).[21] At the time of writing, al-Masri was already considered a rebellious figure in the Islamic State, with a history of imprisonment for his outspoken critiques. In the booklet, the author's main points are:

- Aleppo and not Raqqa should have been chosen as the group's 'capital' because of its inhabitants and its industrial development,
- It was a mistake to publicly accept pledges of allegiance from groups around the Muslim world and announce them as new Islamic State *provinces* since the necessary conditions for statehood were not fulfilled in most of these places. Instead, such pledges should have been accepted in secret,
- As the infighting with rivalling opposition groups began in early 2014, the Islamic State should have quickly destroyed its main Jihadi rival, Jabhat al-Nusra, as this would have led to large number of rebels joining al-Baghdadi's group, and

- The rapid expansion of operational activities to include the entire world was a strategic mistake which overstretched the Islamic State and created unnecessary pressure.

Al-Masri's criticism exemplifies the strategic debate that was on the rise within the Islamic State in response to its retreat on the battlefield. Raising several relevant points in order to provoke a process of reflection and self-examination within the group, his ideas stress the pervasive strategic dimension in Jihadism and should be analysed as part of the *jihadi strategic studies* genre.[22] At the same time, the booklet and its reception is indicative of how sensitive it was to air criticism of the Islamic State: al-Masri was allegedly arrested once again after making his challenge to the group's strategy known in public. From a normative perspective, the criticism from the Yemeni Islamic State fighters and from al-Masri is *less critical* than the Hazimis' dissent because it essentially deals with issues pertaining to methodology and not creed. Nonetheless, in both instances the Islamic State reacted with force through arresting and/or assassinating those who challenged the official group position, thus confirming Crenshaw's argument that terrorist groups are generally more averse to internal dissent.[23]

### *Cutting Out the Tumour*

Another place the Islamic State would experience internal problems was Nigeria. Though the origin of the tensions predated the Islamic State's expansion into Nigeria, the Islamic State's problems escalated after the establishment of the group's West Africa province (ISWA). These problems resembled the combined experiences from Syria and Libya insofar as they involved tensions on both a creedal and methodological level, but they differed in their outcome: what started as an intra-group conflict eventually turned into an organisational splinter, leading to conflict between two rival groups. Very few sources exist on the internal problems within Boko Haram (then ISWA) and then between the two groups. What we know mainly comes from a few internal documents and the work of analysts like Jacob Zenn.

The key episode is the Islamic State leadership's decision on August 2, 2016, to remove Abu Bakr Shekau as governor of ISWA and replace him with Abu Musab al-Barnawi. Prior to this, however, internal tensions existed within Boko Haram as early as 2010–11, when Shekau started to introduce increasingly extreme practices. Our best source for the entire period is arguably a 124-page book allegedly authored by two sons of the Boko Haram founder Muhammad Yusuf, most likely Abu Musab al-Barnawi and his brother Abba al-Barnawi: *Cutting Out the Tumor of Shekau's Khawarij Through Pledging Allegiance to the People of Benevolence* (khadh' al-waram min al-khawarij al-shikawiyya bi-bay'a ahl al-karam).[24] As the alleged authors were principal rivals of Shekau, there is an obvious risk that their narration is biased, but the book remains useful for understanding how the Barnawi-wing within Boko Haram and later within ISWA viewed Shekau's rule, and for their points of criticism. From the perspective of this study, the most important points mentioned against Shekau are the following:

- He does not accept excuse out of ignorance ('udhr bi-l-jahl) and makes takfir on the excuser (takfir al-adhir),
- Makes takfir based on major sins (although not consequently),
- Engages in chain takfir (takfir musalsal),
- Considers most people to be unbelievers,
- Individual takfir (takfir ayan) of people residing in the abode of unbelief unless they resist,
- Changed dawa practices,
- Rebellion against al-Baghdadi,
- Believes in the permissibility of multiple imams,
- Aversion to knowledge,
- Tyrannical behaviour and unfair treatment of group members, and
- Carrying out massacres.

In the book, these points are framed by the suggestion that Shekau resembles the Khawarij and the Mu'tazilite. Skimming the list, one notices how several of the points relate to removing obstacles to just killings. This behaviour did not go unnoticed within the SJM and, providing some credence to the Barnawi sons' criticism, in October

2011 AQIM issued a written advice to senior Boko Haram dissidents that largely corresponds with the above-mentioned points.[25]

Shekau's *extremism* evolved incrementally, but already in 2011–12 Boko Haram had fractured into three groups: Shekau and his supporters, the *contrarians* (mukhalifin) who opposed him and a third group abandoning Jihad entirely. Shekau responded to the internal factionalism by killing some of the contrarians, which caused some of them to officially split from Shekau's group. With the support of AQIM, they established Ansar al-Muslimin fi Bilad al-Sudan (The Supporters of the Muslims in the Lands of the Blacks, popularly known as *Ansaru*), whose second leader, Abu Usama al-Ansari, was eventually killed by Shekau's forces.[26] In relation to Ansaru, it is interesting to note that the Barnawi brothers criticised them for being too lax on the issue of excuse out of ignorance while criticising Shekau of being too extreme, thus placing themselves in a middle position.

The contrarians remaining within Boko Haram (who included the Barnawi brothers) were persecuted, with Shekau especially targeting the religious scholars among them. Around the time of joining the Islamic State, Shekau instigated an internal purge against vocal or threatening opposition within his group, killing senior military commanders such as Mustafa al-Chadi, Kaka al-Hajj,[27] Abu Anisa al-Ghambawi,[28] Abu Hanifa[29] and Malim Umar,[30] and the religious scholars Abd al-Malik Kaduna and Abu al-'Abbas Binkuwa. In the process, the Barnawi brothers were also removed from their position in charge of communication with the Islamic State and their media responsibilities, and engaged in a failed attempt to flee to Libya. For those in opposition to Shekau, al-Baghdadi's caliphate declaration thus offered a much needed opportunity to exert pressure on Shekau to change his behaviour through subordination to the caliph's authority. As part of the process of pledging allegiance to the Islamic State, the contrarians contacted the Islamic State with a series of questions directly touching upon some of the transgressions of Shekau. Known as the *Nigerian Questions*, the answers from the Islamic State sheikh Abu Malik a-Tamimi almost exclusively ruled against Shekau's interpretations.[31]

From the perspective of the contrarians, however, being placed under the caliph's authority did not have the desired moderating effect on Shekau. The Barnawi brothers thus sought to distance themselves from Shekau, while planning how they could undermine his leadership. This led them to ally with the powerful commander Abu Fatima, and together they contacted the Islamic State's central leadership to inform them about Shekau's transgressions.[32] Surprisingly, this led to the Islamic State demoting Shekau and appointing Abu Musab al-Barnawi—one of the brothers—as his replacement.

The announcement about Abu Musab al-Barnawi was made in an interview in the Islamic State's weekly newspaper *al-Naba* on August 2, 2016, where he was presented as the wali (governor) of ISWA. There was no mention of what happened to Shekau.[33] The election of al-Barnawi was both the result of intra-ISWA efforts on behalf of Shekau's critics and the interest of the Islamic State's central leadership in managing internal stability and imposing a certain creed and methodology.[34] In the interview, the new leader is asked if bombings in public places like markets and mosques are part of the group's modus operandi, which gave al-Barnawi the opportunity to distance his group from one of the practices for which Shekau had been challenged. Shekau responded immediately through an audio statement the following day. Now presenting himself as imam of Jama'at Ahl al-Sunna li-l-Da'wa wa-l-Jihad (the original name of Boko Haram), Shekau addressed al-Baghdadi directly, asking about why he was replaced with al-Barnawi and announcing his opposition to his successor.[35] Shekau outlines some theological differences between himself and al-Barnawi, insinuating that his rival commits acts of kufr. He alleges that he sent al-Baghdadi as many as eight letters outlining al-Barnawi's transgressions but without receiving a response—something that reveals his difficulties in communicating with the Islamic State leadership.[36] In the speech, and in a later pamphlet describing his ideology, Shekau refers to his 'new group' as the Islamic State in West Africa. It is uncertain whether this represents a claim to be the Islamic State's official province in West Africa or, more likely, that it is an attempt to claim that his group is the only legitimate Jihadi group in the country.[37]

In the immediate aftermath of the split, there were real fears within ISWA that Shekau—as a survival mechanism—would inaugurate a high-intensity conflict with al-Barnawi's group. Occasional skirmishes allegedly killing several hundred fighters did take place, but a military escalation was for once successfully prevented through several de-escalation meetings between the two groups.[38] After the government's new military campaign *Deep Punch* was launched in April 2017, Shekau and al-Barnawi's groups even managed low-level cooperation to repel government attacks, though still criticising one another and trying to recruit one another's members.[39]

The split and the military confrontations also changed how ISWA categorised Shekau. Dedicating forty-five pages of the book to this, the authors explain how at first, they described Shekau and his supporters as *resembling khawarij*—but after the split, they have been justified in declaring them khawarij. Shekau, on the other hand, proclaimed takfir on ISWA.[40] Despite classifying Shekau's Boko Haram as khawarij, the Barnawi brothers' account explains that this only allowed ISWA fighters to *repel* attacks and not proactively to fight Boko Haram. This is similar to the June 2015 fatwa issued by al-Qaida affiliated ideologues that legitimised fighters to *repel* attacks from the Islamic State in the context of Syria.

Al-Barnawi's reign as ISWA governor would entail a change of behaviour, with the group prioritising a 'hearts and minds' approach, which contrasted with Shekau's indiscriminate violence.[41] However, the ousting of Shekau did not solve all the internal problems within ISWA, as there were still ongoing power struggles between *moderates* and *hardliners* within the group. In August and September 2018, ISWA assassinated two of its own senior figures: a commander, Ali Gaga, and al-Barnawi's long-time associate Mamman Nur. The latter was allegedly killed on the orders of the Islamic State's central leadership as the result of accusations that he was too *moderate*.[42] Al-Barnawi himself is considered to belong to the moderate faction within ISWA, which suffered another critical blow to its position on February 28, 2019 when he was replaced with the hardliner Abu Abdullahi Ibn Umar al-Barnawi.[43] This was an obvious victory for ISWA hardliners and arguably for Shekau as well. At the time, there were already rumours of negotiations between ISWA hardliners and Shekau, indicating that closer collaboration was a future possibility.[44]

### *The Internal Power Struggle: Al-Hazimiyya and al-Binaliyya*

Back in Syria and Iraq, the power struggles within the Islamic State were even fiercer. This had critical ramifications for the group's internal cohesion. During 2015, the extremists within the group kept a low profile, operating clandestinely without challenging the internal power balance, but in 2016, tensions between Hazimis and Binalis broke out once again. While the dominant issues in 2014–15 were *excuse out of ignorance* and *takfir of the excuser*, in 2016–19 the debate centred on whether excommunication is a *foundation of religion* (takfir min asl al-deen) or not.[45]

In the first half of 2016, the Binalis continued to be the strongest faction within the Islamic State, with the leadership supporting its position on excommunication while cracking down on the Hazimis. Characterising this situation, one Islamic State supporter told me that 'al-Hazimi manhaj ideology is forbidden within Dawla [the Islamic State] due to its extremism and wrong understanding of the 3rd nullifier of Islam.'[46] And in July, the group's Delegated Committee (al-lajna al-mufawwada, previously known as lajnat al-'amma al-mushrifa) issued a circular with a warrant for an Islamic State member named Muhammad Yahya Qirtas (Abu Muhammad al-Jaza'iri al-'Assimi) on accusation that he pronounced takfir on the group's leadership.[47] Further illustrating the inferiority of the Hazimis, there are stories that hours before his death, al-Adnani, answered a question from a Hazimi named Abu al-Mahi by saying: 'The fronts take precedence over these matters you speak of. Go see how your brothers are sacrificing their lives for the sake of Allah while you discuss these matters. I don't have time to talk to discuss these issues with stupid people.'[48]

In 2017, the situation changed dramatically. Correlating with the group's extensive loss of previously-held territories, Turkey's military intervention (August 2016) and the offensive against Mosul (October 2016–July 2017), the Hazimis evolved from a fringe phenomenon to an increasingly imposing faction able to exert real pressure on the group leadership.[49] The mounting pressure made the group more susceptible to factionalism and division, with the leadership being incapable of either inhibiting the growing strength of the Hazimis or balancing the opposing factions. The situation only became worse when especially al-Adnani but also Abu Muhammad al-Furqan—two senior *centrist* leaders who functioned as barriers against the Hazimis—died within a span of eight days in mid-2016. This ignited a struggle between some of the caliphate's powerful institutions. The Binalis dominated the Office of Research and Studies (maktab al-buhuth wa-l-dirasat) while the Hazimis had extensive control within the Central Media Department (Diwan al-I'lam al-Markazi) and the Security Department (Diwan al-Amn al-Aam). Both factions were competing for the sympathy of (or better, control over) the Delegated Committee, the Islamic State's most powerful institution except for the caliph's office. The rival factions have published and leaked a substantial amount of material in the past two years about this internal conflict, which allows for a comprehensive understanding of events. The analysis relies on these primary sources and existing work done by Cole Bunzel, Aymenn Jawad al-Tamimi and me.

The re-emergence of tensions became clear in two letters from al-Binali addressing the Delegated Committee. In the first letter, written in November 2015, al-Binali complains that he has been accused of *permitting polytheism* and asked to repent, and that the person behind the accusation is Abu Muhammad al-Furqan, the head of the Central Media Department.[50] In the second letter, of February 2016, al-Binali warns against the Hazimis' attitude to takfir while explaining how ignorance is a legitimate obstruction to takfir in some situations. The main point of this letter is that the new position of the Hazimis is to argue that takfir is part of the *foundation of religion* (asl al-deen), and anyone who argues that it is merely a *requirement* (wajib) is murji'a or jamiya. Al-Binali explains how the Hazimis even managed to insert a phrase asserting this in a book published by the group's Al Himmah Library. Stressing how serious this matter is, he begs the Delegated Committee to respond.[51] A few months later, and in relation to the document proclaiming takfir on Jabhat al-Nusra, the Islamic State circulated an internal ruling which was clearly aligned with al-Binali's position, but which nonetheless attempted to reach out to the Hazimis in a diplomatic manner. The document, which was authored by al-Furqan but also had input from al-Binali, established that excuse is invalid on the level of the foundation of religion, but not on the level of *requirements* (wajibat) of religion, while *proof* (hujjah) must be presented to the excuser.[52] In addition, the document prohibits the use of certain terms such as 'takfir of the excuser'.[53] Despite the group's official policy aligning with al-Binali, the Bahrani scholar was becoming increasingly uneasy with how the Hazimis were being accommodated institutionally. Describing it as a *theory of balance*, which he finds *false in theory and in reality* (nazriyan batelah wa waqi'an), he criticises the leadership's appointment of Hazimi figures to positions of power as a means of easing the increasing pressure; this, he argues, provides the faction with additional legitimacy, status and authority. Threatening the leadership to choose sides, al-Binali recounts a story of a lecture given by a Hazimi in a mosque in Tabqa:

> Days ago one of them arose in one of the mosques of al-Tabqa (may God protect it), arose and spoke to the crowd. And among the things he (may God mute his mouth) said: 'And this idolatrous tyrant Abu Bakr al-Baghdadi,' with all boldness and insolence, while the enemy are at the peripheries of al-Tabqa [a town in Raqqa province in northern Syria].[54]

The rivalling groups were competing for the support of al-Baghdadi and for control of the Delegated Committee. The Committee, which oversees all other institutions in the caliphate apart from the caliph, was first headed by al-Adnani. Under his leadership, it managed to find a balance between the Binalis and Hazimis, to the extent that neither faction gained the upper hand. When al-Adnani was killed on August 30, 2016, Abu Muhammad al-Furqan, the head of the Central Media Department and the Central Office for Overseeing the Shari'a Departments (al-maktab al-markazi li-mutaba'a al-dawawin al-shar'iyya), allegedly headed the committee for a week himself before he was killed. The establishment of the Central Office for Overseeing in February 2016 was essentially the first institutional concession to the Hazimis, as it limited the power of the Islamic State's scholars.[55] The situation became worse still for the Binalis when Hajji Abd al-Nasir took charge of the Delegated Committee and established the Office for Methodological Inquiry (maktab al-tadqiq al-manhaji) as a successor to the Central Office for Overseeing, with a mandate to investigate Islamic State scholars and to ensure their creed and methodology was correct. Confirming the fears of al-Binali, the Hazimis did now exercise serious control over the Delegated Committee, while several high-ranking Hazimis like Abu Maram al-Jaza'iri, Abu Ahmed al-Firansi,[56] Abu Anisa and Abu Daoud al-Maghribi had a seat in the Office for Methodological Inquiry. The Office was likely headed by Abu Hafs al-Jazrawi (Abu Hafs al-Wadani),[57] with Abu Asma al-Tunisi as another central figure (see appendix 5).

During this period of Hazimi institutional dominance, two important developments took place. The first was a process of investigating religious scholars, or jurists, within the Islamic State, which eventually developed into a persecution campaign against Binali scholars. We know most about the work of the Central Office for Overseeing when it was under the direction of Abu Muhammad al-Furqan, Abu Maysara al-Shami and Abu Khabbab al-Masri: several reports from the Office have been leaked, including a status report assessing the Office's work after its first four months. The report describes the reasons for the Office's establishment and its early work, which included interviews with twenty-nine jurists of the Islamic State who were either known to have controversial opinions or were under suspicion. While the results of these interviews are only briefly described in the status report, they all led to more exhaustive reports on the individual jurists, of which at least three have been leaked. Originally, the Office was focused on investigating the Hazimis within the Islamic State, whose resurgence al-Binali had warned about in the month before its establishment. However, according to al-Masri, it quickly became apparent that the main problem among the jurists was not their extremism but their adherence to the principle of *postponement* (irja') associated with the Binalis.[58]

The report's conclusion indicates that the Hazimis were able to exert massive pressure on al-Furqan and his colleagues as early as mid-2016.[59] Later on, the Central Office would also question Abu Bakr al-Qahtani, a member of the Delegated Committee. Among Binali scholars, al-Qahtani is renowned for taking the theological debate to the Hazimis early on.[60] Now al-Qahtani would find himself as the one being questioned on matters of takfir of the excuser, and the conclusion reached at the meeting was that his opinions deviated from the methodology of al-Zarqawi and were closer to 'the murjiah of jihad represented by al-Maqdisi and his companions'. He would eventually be asked to repent.[61] On the work of al-Wadani's Office for Methodological Inquiry, we only know of its investigation, led by Abu Maram al-Jazairi, into Abu Abd al-Rahman al-Shami al-Zarqawi.[62] The Hazimis' control finally led the Delegated Committee to issue an exceedingly controversial seven-page memorandum in May 2017, which defined takfir of the idolaters as a foundation of religion. This implied that takfir should be considered mandatory for everyone, thus prohibiting any excuses—like ignorance—for refusing to proclaim another person an apostate. The Hazimis had thus managed to turn their primary objection into official Islamic State ideology, gaining a first—but major—victory.

### *Fluctuating Balances*

Since the caliphate was declared, the scholarly institution within the Islamic State headed by al-Binali had been demoted several times: first from a *department* to a *committee*, and finally to an *office*.[63] Further undermining its impact, other institutions like Al Himmah Library were no longer printing its material; moreover, Abu Muhammad al-Furqan had been appointed an 'advisor' to oversee al-Binali and his colleagues' work.[64] This meant that when the Delegated Committee issued its seven-page memorandum, the Binalis were bereft of much of their institutional power, leaving many scholars as mere spectators. Trying to counter the new official theological line of the caliphate, several of the most senior Binalis authored internal letters to the leadership. Just two days after the memorandum was issued, al-Binali sent a letter to the Delegated Committee condemning the process leading to the memorandum and its impact. The drafting process was too quick and without scholarly oversight, he wrote, and the decision removed many obstacles to takfir.[65]

The letter was followed by several critiques from al-Binali's colleagues, two being particularly condemnatory. The first is a 'public letter' written by Abu Muhammad al-Husayni al-Hashimi which is framed as an *advice* (nasiha); this stands out for its critical and direct tone in addressing the caliph, which somewhat resembles the discourse al-Qaida leaders raised against the Islamic State in 2014–15. Joining the Islamic State's predecessor in 2006, al-Hashimi was a veteran within the group and thus his words did not come from the group's periphery. Indicating that the Islamic State has recently changed, he says, 'it is not my state that I pledged allegiance to' and asks 'why has the flag deviated and the manhaj changed?' (Limadha inharafti al-ra'ia wa taghyara al-manhaj). Although the 'war against the students of knowledge' (harbu talibati al-ilmi) is executed by the Office for Methodological Inquiry, the responsibility, in al-Hashimi's view, is ultimately with the caliph who all along has been aware of the situation. Concluding in an al-Qaida-esque fashion, he declares that the reason the caliphate has ended up in this situation is because its leaders lack knowledge; this has resulted in a caliphate deviating from the prophetic methodology.[66] The second piece is by Abu Abd al-Malik al-Shami, who portrays al-Baghdadi as absent and urges the caliph to intervene to save the group as he is the only one capable of doing so. He argues that the Hazimi-dominated media department is manipulating the news stream, thus misleading the caliph, while Binalis like Abu Yaqub are sent to the frontlines to fight (and get killed). The solution, he concludes, is institutional reform. He argues that al-Baghdadi should step up and manage the situation, and that the Delegated Committee should be dissolved. Eventually, prominent figures like al-Binali and al-Qahtani were killed in coalition bombings, with Binalis drawing a link between these peoples' opposition to the Hazimis and their deaths.

Whether in response to the Binalis or not, al-Baghdadi finally stepped in and arranged a meeting to solve the mounting tensions. Abu Hafs al-Wadani and Abu Zeid al-Iraqi represented the Hazimis, and Abu Muhammed al-Masri, Abu Yaqub al-Maqdisi and Abu Muslim al-Masri represented the Binalis. At the meeting, the caliph decided not only to *retract* the controversial memo, but he also disbanded the Delegated Committee and reconstituted it in a smaller form, appointing Abu Muhammad al-Masri and Abu Abd al-Rahman al-Shami to the committee while imprisoning al-Wadani and Abu Zaid Al-Iraqi.[67] The retraction of the memorandum was officially announced on September 15, 2017, in an internal circular issued by the Delegated Committee; the explanation given was that it contained *knowledge-related errors* and *imprecise phrases* that could easily be misinterpreted. This represented a major and unexpected victory for the Binalis.

Briefly after the retraction, an audio series in six episodes entitled *Knowledge Series Clarifying Matters of Methodology* (silsila 'ilmiyya fi bayan masa'il manhajiyya) was publicised.[68] The author of the series was Abu Abd al-Rahman al-Shami, and it was important because it provided a general explanation of the Islamic State's attitude to excommunication.[69] Of particular relevance here is three central conclusions that it established:

- Acknowledges the principle of *excuse out of ignorance* ('udhr bi-l-jahl) as long as it is not in matters of the *foundation of religion* (asl al-deen),
- *Takfir of the excuser* (takfir al-'adhir) is dependent on the *level* (martabah) of the act and that *proof* (hujjah) is presented to the excuser, and
- Takfir is not part of the *foundation of religion* (asl al-deen) but simply a *requirement of religion* (wajibat al-deen). This is extremely central, because it implies that the one refraining from proclaiming takfir does not necessarily commit an act of unbelief, thus becoming an unbeliever himself. As such, it prevents chain takfir.

Despite this obvious victory for the Binalis, the internal situation remained volatile. Almost a year after the series' release, it was revealed that it originally consisted of nine episodes that al-Baghdadi had cleared. However, three of them were prohibited by Hajji Abdallah (Muhammad Said Abd al-Rahman al-Mawla), the head of the Delegated Committee (and later, the caliph), who feared that they represented a dangerous provocation to the Hazimis. This shows that the leadership really tried to manage the struggle between the two contesting factions. After just forty days in prison, al-Wadani was released in late October. In early December, he sent a letter to al-Baghdadi complaining about his decision to retract the memorandum and the ongoing oppression of the Hazimis. Blaming al-Baghdadi for the situation, he accuses the caliph of being absent and not in control, which leaves his fighters without trust in him. To correct the situation, he writes, al-Baghdadi must assert himself as a leader in control and undo his mistake. Despite the fact that the Hazimis were about to regain control, al-Wadani's letter made him a wanted man, and on June 27, 2018, he was executed by the Islamic State's security department.[70]

Once again illustrating the importance of the media, in the aftermath of the retraction tensions between the two factions became increasingly public through the work of media institutions and Telegram channels siding with or run by one of the two. These institutions and channels began to publish unauthorised material and to leak incriminating internal documents and testimonies. On the side of the Binalis, the main institutions were *Mu'assasat al-Turath al-Ilmi, Mu'assasat al-Wafa, al-Nasiha* and *Ahl al-Tawhid*, while the Hazimis' primary outlets were the Telegram channels *Nadhir al-Uryan* and *Wa Harridh al-Mu'mineen* along with munasirun accounts like *Tarjuman al-Asawarti*. The latter's control of the Islamic State's Central Media Department also meant that to some extent it could control official communication and publications.[71] For instance, in spring 2017, it prevented the publication of a book authored by Abu Yaqub al-Maqdisi on the third nullifier, which was later published through a Binali-loyal institution. A leaked account by Binali loyalists in the subunit of the Central Media Department recounts how the internal tensions within the department even led to the official 'Amaq News Agency closing down for a short period. Intended to counter unauthorised publications from the Binalis, in July 2018 the media department issued a prohibition against publishing any written, audio or visual material through unofficial channels, and clarified that any such material did not represent the Islamic State. This did little to help, however, and the following month *Ahlut Tawhid* released a booklet entitled *Refutation of al-Hazimi and the Misconceptions of al-Ghulah al-Hazimiyyah*, describing al-Hazimi as an *innovator* (mubtadi') and his theology as following the *mu'tazila*.[72]

The Binalis' triumph was short-lived, however. In December 2017, the Hazimis seem to have retaken control of the new

Delegated Committee, and they initiated a crackdown against Binali-scholars. Senior rivals like al-Binali and al-Qahtani were dead, and so were al-Adnani and al-Furqan, who had both attempted to contain the Hazimis to some extent (though there remains some debate on the precise role of the latter). Furthermore, the Islamic State's territorial crisis was escalating by the day, with Mosul, Raqqa and Mayadeen being lost. This led to a change in military strategy back to insurgency.

Judging from a recently discovered series of letters by the Binalis, it appears the faction tried to do its best to oppose this development.[73] In a letter directly addressed to al-Baghdadi, they ask for a meeting with the caliph. While it is very unlikely that such a meeting ever materialised, it forms part of the critique in several of the other letters. One of the main points they raise is that the caliph's 'disappearance' is against the prophetic methodology and that he should be available. Drawing on hadith of the prophet's presence during war, they say that he never fled, and so al-Baghdadi's absence is not justified, as it prevents him from knowing the reality of the situation. Another point is that the current military and religious leaders in the Islamic State are unqualified for the job. As a remedy, the Binalis suggest reforming the system by implementing a committee consisting of three scholars to assess the leaders. A third point is that the group's practice of shura (consultation) is no longer on the prophetic methodology, since the leaders only seek advice from likeminded people. According to Abu Yaqub al-Maqdisi—al-Binali's successor as head of the Office of Research and Studies[74]—the internal struggle against the Hazimis is now the most important challenge to the group. He writes that 'Indeed regulation of the principles of the shar'i manhaj that the Islamic State adopts represents the highest grades of priority, in order to protect its sound manhaj, and for cohesion of its group.' In his view, the solution is to raise the level of knowledge of its leaders, to provide the scholars with more influence and to strengthen their oversight mechanism.[75]

Comparable to the dynamics of conflict between rival groups, the conflict between the two factions similarly involved the application of discrediting names and labels to their opponents. The Binalis generally referred to the Hazimis as *extremists* (ghulat), *innovators* (mubtadi') or the *new mu'tazila*. In 2018 they also described the Islamic State's Hazimi-dominated security department as the *bureau of the oppressive people who wage war against the friends of Allah (diwan al-zalimin al-muhabirin li-awliya' allah)*. In comparison, the Hazimis used slightly more aggressive terms, referring to their rivals as *postponers* (murji'a), *apostates* (murtadd), *the suspect ones* (al-mashbuhin) and *khawarij jahmiyya*. More creatively, they also used phrases like *followers of al-Qaeda within the state* (atba' tanzim al-qa'ida dakhil al-dawla) and *the current of jahmism and postponement* (tayyar al-tajahhum wa-l-irja').

Functioning as mechanisms to legitimise action, these terms justified a tough crackdown on Binali scholars after the Hazimis regained control of key institutions. Beginning in December 2017, Abu Muhammad al-Masri and Abu Yaqub were arrested; although both were released after a week, they would be imprisoned again later.[76] In April 2018, Abu Abd al-Rahman al-Shami was imprisoned on the direct order of Hajji Abdullah, head of the Delegated Committee.[77] As the Binalis feared for al-Shami's life, they asked al-Baghdadi to intervene. Around the same time, Abu Yaqub was also arrested again and, as with al-Shami, there were rumours that he too would be executed.[78] In an attempt to prevent the security department killing him, several Binali scholars authored a defence of Abu Yaqub countering the various accusations against him.[79] In November, it was reported for the first time that three Binalis—Abu Hafs al-Hamdani, Abu Musab al-Sahrawi and Abu Usama al-Gharib—had died following coalition bombing of the building where they were imprisoned. The next month, Abu Muhammad al-Masri and Abu Yaqub al-Maqdisi faced a similar fate.[80] In the words of the Binalis, they were 'killed, imprisoned, removed and hunted.' Even so, they remained loyal to the Islamic State for some time longer, despite addressing al-Baghdadi as *imam*, not *caliph*.[81]

So far, the Hazimis have been described as a homogenous faction. The truth is, however, that the Hazimis are divided in their views about the legitimacy of al-Baghdadi and the caliphate. While the Hazimi actors discussed so far accept al-Baghdadi's claim to be a caliph and his group's claim to constitute a caliphate, others take a more extreme view, describing al-Baghdadi as an apostate and his caliphate as un-Islamic. These differences obviously have an impact on how different actors relate to the caliphate and whether they find it acceptable to reform it from within in line with their ideas, or else disassociate themselves from it entirely. The latter group no longer consider themselves part of the Islamic State but prefers to criticise it from the outside. One such example of this rebellious current is Abu Mu'adh al-Assimi, who authored several articles excommunicating al-Baghdadi, describing him as a *tyrant* and an *apostate*. Compared to the Hazimis, who remained within the Islamic State, the rebellious Hazimis took an even more extreme position on the question of takfir of the excuser and takfir as a religious foundation. They believed that al-Baghdadi committed apostasy in two ways: firstly, he changed the religion of God by declaring takfir as a *requirement* (wajibat) but not *foundation* (asl) of religion, and secondly, he failed to proclaim takfir on apostates such as al-Zawahiri.[82] Similar accusations of the Islamic State being a *state of idols* (dawlat al-asnam) have also been made by other rebellious Hazimis, who implicated al-Adnani in the deviance of the caliphate.[83]

Up until 2019, the Binalis remained loyal to the Islamic State and to al-Baghdadi's authority, despite their discontent with the group and the oppression they had suffered. This, however, would slowly change. Civil war theory indicates that groups fracture during periods of military losses and internal factionalism.[84] The reason why this did not happen until 2019 is probably because both factions felt they stood a chance of winning the internal power struggle, and because neither had an organisational alternative. Instead, they tried to tilt the internal power balance in their favour.

However, from around 2019, these dynamics started to change. The Binalis—or at least some of their leading figures—decided to split from the Islamic State, which they now referred to as the *state of khawarij* (dawlat al-khawarij) and the *khawarij of al-Baghdadi* (khawarij al-baghdadi). Ending their relationship with the Islamic State, they issued a book of more than 200 pages calling for supporters to revoke their pledge of allegiance. In March 2019, a similar dynamic was seen with the Hazimis after the fall of Baghouz, when a group of approximately 350 individuals demanded that al-Baghdadi step down and allow for the election of a new caliph. Since this did not happen, the group announced their intention to fight the Islamic State—but according to reports, they were immediately crushed by an internal security unit.[85]

12

# AL-QAIDA AND THE SYRIAN JIHAD

Like the Islamic State, al-Qaida would witness severe internal tensions when in late July, 2016, its Syrian affiliate Jabhat al-Nusra rebranded itself as Jabhat Fatah al-Sham (JFS) and stated that it had no relations with external actors. At first few believed that the rebranding truly represented a break with al-Qaida, but during the autumn the authenticity of the statement became increasingly clear to close observers of the SJM. This culminated in January 2017 with the merger establishing HTS.

Jabhat al-Nusra's delinking was on one side driven by Turkey's growing assertiveness in the region and a desire to avoid Western military attention, and on the other side by the ambition of reforming the group's Jihadi project. It was only the second time in al-Qaida's more than thirty-year history that an affiliate had left; just like the first time, this presented the group's leadership with renewed challenges in uniting the broader movement and ensuring the group's relevance in a highly important theatre of war.

Interestingly, the delinking would replicate several of the same dynamics witnessed in the conflict between al-Qaida and the Islamic State and would sow further tensions within the SJM. Many al-Qaida loyalists in Syria left al-Nusra or its organisational successors to establish a new group pledging loyalty to al-Zawahiri, but they would become the victim of HTS's hegemonic ambitions in Syria's northwestern region, which eventually developed into a crackdown. Tensions would similarly expand to involve ideologues and supporters of the groups. These actors generally sided with one group while criticising the other, thus exacerbating movement fragmentation and polarisation.

### *From Merger to Fragmentation: HTS and the Split from al-Qaida*

Jabhat al-Nusra's delinking from al-Qaida has been shrouded in mystery, especially within political and analyst circles, where confusion about organisational relations and authoritative hierarchy has been dominant. Central to understanding al-Nusra's decision to revoke its pledge of allegiance to al-Zawahiri and give up its membership of the global al-Qaida network is the evolving political context in Syria in 2016, which left al-Nusra under increasing pressure but also presented the group with alternative routes. As such, it represents an interesting case of how a Jihadi group turns local in contrast to the well-established narrative of the internationalisation of Jihad.

At the time, the Assad government, with strong backing from its Iranian and Russian allies, was taking back territory in and around Aleppo, and with the Islamic State's changing fortunes on the battlefield, the regime's focus was turning more and more towards Idlib. At the same time, Turkey's engagement in Syria was rapidly changing, with a policy shift vis-à-vis the Assad regime in the summer of 2016 and the Euphrates Shield military intervention in August. Simultaneously, the international diplomatic track intensified, which involved attempts to implement nationwide ceasefires. Finally, the US government was slowly expanding its campaign in Syria to target al-Qaida fighters. Together, these changes created a political context that increased the pressure on Jabhat al-Nusra and other rebel groups in Idlib and forced al-Julani to make difficult choices.

To counter these developments, Jabhat al-Nusra engaged in merger talks with other rebel groups—mainly focusing on Ahrar al-Sham—to create a strong and unified opposition under al-Julani's leadership. Negotiations started as early as January 2016, but initially failed because Ahrar required that al-Nusra cease its relations with al-Qaida, something al-Julani was not willing to do at the time. The idea of splitting from al-Qaida was not entirely new, however. In March 2015, Abu Mariya al-Qahtani, a senior al-Nusra commander and shura council member, entertained the idea in a series of tweets when commenting on rumours that al-Nusra would split in order to receive funding from the Gulf.[1] At the time, Ahrar was internally divided and struggling to find its identity, with regular changes in senior positions only making an agreement more difficult.

Despite negotiations continuing during spring 2016, no solution was reached. Instead, on July 28, 2016, Jabhat al-Nusra announced a rebranding of its group that included a change of name to Jabhat Fath al-Sham (JFS). At the press conference, al-Julani with Abu Abdullah al-Shami and Abu al-Faraj al-Masri sitting next to him began by thanking the al-Qaida leaders for their decision to prioritise the 'interests of the people of al-Sham and their jihad' over the interests of any group. Allegedly with the al-Qaida leadership's blessing, al-Julani announced 'the complete cancellation of all operations under the name of Jabhat al-Nusra, and the formation of a new group operating under the name Jabhat Fath al-Sham, noting that this new organisation has no affiliation to any external entity.' This change, he explained, was to ease the pressure on his group but would not compromise its dedication to remaining committed to its religious principles. The split from al-Qaida, referred to as *fakk al-irtibat* (literally 'the untying of ties'), was authorised by al-Zawahiri's Syria-based deputy Abu al-Khayr al-Masri, who prior to the announcement issued an audio statement legitimising the decision.[2] In the days following the announcement, JFS spokesman Abu Sulayman al-Muhajir promoted the break in relations to the Western media. However, the dominant perception among most people was that the creation of JFS was a ruse to trick the international political system, and that al-Julani was still under al-Qaida's authority.

Negotiations continued in the autumn and winter of 2016 to bring about a merger between JFS, Ahrar al-Sham and other Islamist rebel groups. In January 2017, however, negotiations failed once again when Ahrar refused to join. During the autumn, Ahrar moved closer to Turkey with a fatwa legitimising collaboration and participation in Euphrates Shield, and the group did not entirely reject possible participation in the international Astana diplomatic process.[3] The infighting between Ahrar al-Sham and Jund al-Aqsa from September 2016–January 2017 complicated merger talks further. Although Jund al-Aqsa merged into JFS in October to de-escalate tensions, the group was still considered by Ahrar al-Sham to be too extreme and too close to the Islamic State.[4] Nonetheless, it was eventually reported in December 2016 that Ahrar's leader Ali al-Omar had signed an agreement to merge with JFS and other groups. But the deal fell through when the majority of Ahrar's leadership rejected it due to fear of losing Turkey's support. This time, JFS proceeded to announce a merger, proclaiming the establishment of HTS with four other groups (Harakat Nour al-Deen al-Zinki, Liwa al-Haqq, Jabhat Ansar al-Deen and Jaysh al-Sunna)—but without Ahrar al-Sham. Despite this success in unifying several groups, the absence of Ahrar meant that it was not the expected *grand merger* that 2016 had centred around.

The first doubts about the true nature of the organisational relationship between JFS/HTS and al-Qaida were raised in an answer from al-Maqdisi on November 26, 2016, and posted on his Telegram channel. Al-Maqdisi declared that the fakk al-irtibat had not succeeded in either facilitating a merger or de-escalating bombings targeting al-Qaida leaders. Instead, it had only led to a dilution of religious principles. A few months later, in the immediate wake of HTS's establishment, al-Maqdisi started raising doubts about its methodology. In a series of statements on his Telegram channel in late January he questioned the group, warning about its 'dilution' while still recommending to Jihadis in Idlib that they should join it. In early February, however, he demanded that HTS clarify its position on Turkey and the Astana process. Suspicions grew when al-Maqdisi and Sami al-Uraydi, the latter having defected from HTS in February 2017, intensified their criticism of the group in early 2017, and the authenticity of the split was finally confirmed by an al-Qaida insider Ahmad al-Hamdan in April.[5] Months later, between October and December, several high ranking figures including al-Zawahiri, al-Uraydi and Abu Abdullah al-Shami issued their comment on or testimony about these events in an attempt to control the narrative about what had actually happened. Based on interviews and the abundance of information now available, it is possible to trace the sequence of events that led to the split between al-Nusra and al-Qaida, which in turn can allow us to understand the logic behind al-Julani's decision to leave al-Qaida.

Prior to the rebranding from al-Nusra to JFS, the group was divided between 'doves'—those preferring a split (such as Abu Mariya al-Qahtani and Abu Abdullah al-Shami)—and 'hawks', who were against it (these included Sami al-Uraydi, Abu Julaybib, Sari Shihab and Abu Hummam al-Shami). Within al-Nusra a so-called *follow-up committee* (lajnat al-muttaba'a) under the leadership of Abu al-Faraj al-Masri—an Egyptian veteran and al-Zawahiri loyalist with a history in Afghanistan and Azerbaijan—had been established to handle the internal quarrels that erupted during the process.[6] The crucial problem was communication with al-Zawahiri was impossible, as he had been out of reach for several years. Hence, in 2015, after several senior al-Qaida leaders had arrived in Syria from Iran, a consultative council was established consisting of Abu al-Khayr, Abd al-Karim al-Khorasani and Abu al-Qassam, all of whom were on al-Qaida's global shura council. This also implied that Syria had turned into an important hub for al-Qaida's global leadership—at least for some years.

In periods of al-Zawahiri's absence, his three deputies Abu al-Khayr, Saif al-Adl and Muhammad al-Masri (the latter two still in Iran) were left to govern. Al-Khayr, as the first deputy, had the highest level of authority, but any binding decision was based on a majority decision. Hence, two months prior to the creation of JFS, senior al-Nusra members reached out to al-Adl, al-Masri and several Jihadi scholars like al-Maqdisi to get their blessing. Unlike al-Khayr who approved of the split, the two other al-Qaida deputies rejected it.[7] This most likely led al-Nusra to suggest that al-Zawahiri's deputies should only have an advisory role, while binding decisions could be made by Abu al-Khayr, Abu Faraj al-Masri and al-Nusra's amir and deputy.[8] This suggestion was rejected, but al-Nusra amir Abu Muhammad al-Julani decided to continue consulting leaders in Syria. Hence, in another meeting prior to the announcement of JFS, and with the participation of al-Julani and several shura council members (Abu al-Faraj al-Masri, Abu al-Khayr, and Abd al-Karim al-

Khorasani), it was suggested to rebrand al-Nusra as JFS but continue with a secret pledge of allegiance to al-Zawahiri, facilitating a grand merger of rebel groups in Syria. When that happened, the breaking of relations would become real. Al-Adl, al-Masri, and another al-Qaida leader, Abu al-Qassam, continued to oppose the proposal.

In the month following JFS's creation, several high-ranking leadership figures such as Abu Hummam al-Shami, Abu Julaybib and Bilal Khuraysat all defected from the group.[9] But the real problem for al-Julani occurred in September 2016, when he received his first letter from al-Zawahiri since November 2013: a gap of two years and ten months. In the letter, the al-Qaida leader rejects the creation of JFS and the split—no matter how superficial it may be—and explains that the matter is down to an al-Qaida shura decision. Aligning himself with al-Zawahiri's ruling, Abu al-Khayr also began to oppose the project. Al-Julani responded to al-Zawahiri, giving further information on the JFS project and explaining that twenty-three of al-Nusra's twenty-five shura council members voted in favour of continuing with it. In a meeting on October 3, 2016, in the city of Jisr al-Shughour, al-Julani and his deputy Abu Abdullah al-Shami attempted to convince sceptic al-Nusra members about the legitimacy of the project. After leaving the meeting, Abu al-Faraj al-Masri was killed in a drone strike. While al-Masri sat next to al-Julani during the press conference announcing JFS, he is believed to have supported al-Zawahiri's decision. Thus he was a critical 'obstacle' for al-Julani. Al-Zawahiri eventually sent a second letter saying he did not accept secret pledges of allegiance, allegedly calling such an action a 'sin' and an 'act of disobedience.'[10] While JFS was created with a secret pledge of allegiance valid until the creation of a broader organisational merger, the pledge was effectively broken at this stage when al-Julani refused to follow the orders of al-Zawahiri and his three deputies, who were all opposing JFS and ordering it to return to being an official al-Qaida affiliate.[11] The establishment of HTS officially severed the organisational relationship between al-Julani's group and al-Qaida. Shortly afterwards, Sami al-Uraydi and Abu Hajar al-Shami left the group to join the growing faction of al-Qaida loyalists defecting from al-Julani,[12] while Abu al-Khayr was killed in a US airstrike in late February 2017.[13]

The aftermath of the split was dominated by a struggle to control the narrative of events, with HTS circulating a sixty-page book locally in Idlib telling their side of the story.[14] The main points of contestation were the exact authority of Abu al-Khayr, whether the decision should be reverted if al-Zawahiri rejected it, if JFS's secret pledge was honest or a trick and the stance of Abu al-Khayr on JFS after the intervention of al-Zawahiri. Another issue was the religious legitimacy of breaking a pledge of allegiance. Al-Uraydi argued it was a *bay'a shari'yya* and thus could not be broken unless certain conditions were fulfilled. Al-Shami, in contrast, distinguished between a *bay'a qital wa jihad* (fighting pledge) and a *bay'a uzma* (general pledge). Al-Nusra only had a fighting pledge, which can legitimately be broken if it serves the interests of the group. Interestingly, he tried to appeal to al-Zawahiri's bad conscience, claiming that the al-Qaida leader's absence back in 2013 during the emerging fitna between al-Nusra and the Islamic State harmed al-Nusra enormously—but just as they excused him then, he should excuse them now, since they were acting with good intentions.[15]

When al-Zawahiri finally discussed the break publicly, he touched upon many of the same issues: stressing the imperative of unity for the success of the SJM, he claims that HTS's break from al-Qaida is both theologically illegitimate and counterproductive strategically. Comparing the situation to the Taliban's protection of Bin Laden when the US demanded that he be handed over, al-Zawahiri believes that HTS is giving up on al-Qaida because of US interests.[16] On the bay'a, he stated: 'we believe that the pledge of allegiance is a shar'i undertaking; binding in its nature, its violation forbidden.'[17] And in a clear comment on HTS, he continued:

> We fear for these tremendous sacrifices you [mujahideen in general] have rendered and the pure blood you have offered, lest it be wasted in political games and ruses. (…) We have seen how sacrifices were wasted earlier when the leadership sunk into the swamp of political balancing acts and prioritised its own narrow self-interests.[18]

The strongest response was delivered in November 2017 in the speech 'Let Us Fight Them as One Solid Structure', where he offered a scathing critique of HTS:

> I remind my brothers in Sham [Syria] that Qaedat al-Jihad has repeated many times that it is willing to give up its organisational association with the Jabhat al-Nusra if two things are achieved: First, the unification of the mujahideen in Sham. Second, the establishment of an Islamic government in Sham and the people of Sham choosing a leader for themselves. Then and only then, and not before that happens, will we relinquish our organisational association (...) Did you not attack al-Badri [al-Baghdadi] and his gang that they had no legitimacy because they broke their pledge of allegiance to al-Qaeda? So then why do you allow for yourselves what you forbid for others?

Despite his dissatisfaction with al-Julani, he nevertheless calls for al-Qaida loyalists in Syria to unite and cooperate with other Jihadi groups: 'I ask my brothers, the soldiers of Qaedat al-Jihad in Syria, to cooperate with all the honest mujahideen, and to work hard to reunite the troops and mend the rift.'[19]

Kalyvas' theoretical conceptualisation of the *centre* and the *periphery* to explain organisational cleavages and disjunction can be adjusted to help us understand the dynamics at play here.[20] At the centre, al-Qaida's leadership has a defined modus operandi, strategy and organisational hierarchy. Al-Zawahiri and his shura council are the ultimate authority defining the group's overall strategy and controlling the balance between the pursuit of political interests and adherence to religious principles. For al-Nusra, at the periphery, the local political context exerted huge pressure on the group to adapt to its reality, which it eventually did based on its local political interests. However, what was inherently a *political decision* had to be framed and defended using *religious terminology*. This also tells an important story of a Jihadi group turning to a more local focus and in the process largely discarding the global Jihadi project. In the case of al-Nusra, the evolving conflict dynamics in Syria and the political context were determining factors that eventually came to dominate ideology. This should help us to get a better grasp of the ideological priorisation of Jihadi groups in the future and abandon the perception that exists (to some extent) that modern Jihadi groups are inherently global in their focus.

After Abu Muhammad al-Maqdisi's initial criticism of HTS immediately after its establishment, Abu Abdullah al-Shami responded in a long essay. As the head of HTS's shari'a council and a member of its shura council, al-Shami possessed the religious pedigree to respond to a figure of al-Maqdisi's status. The rebuttal can be divided into four points. In a point that would surely have resonated badly in the ears of al-Maqdisi, al-Shami lambasts the Jordanian ideologue for his approach. Such criticism, al-Shami claims, should never come publicly but remain private in order not to damage the SJM. To al-Shami's great disappointment, he allegedly tried on several occasions to communicate with al-Maqdisi to air his concerns but never heard back. Secondly, he points out that al-Maqdisi receives his information from sources that feed him incorrect information due to their animosity towards HTS. The people that al-Shami refers to are the defectors from Jabhat al-Nusra and JFS who stand close to al-Maqdisi. Al-Shami's third point is to lament the Jordanian's use of a term like *mumayyi'a* (diluter) as it does not have any foundation in Islamic jurisprudence and thus is entirely open to interpretation. As it is impossible to point to conditions in shari'a that define who is a diluter, every individual will reach different conclusions, and this, al-Shami points out, is dangerous for the movement's cohesion. In an extension of this criticism, the HTS official decries al-Maqdisi's distinction between diluters and people of shari'a as a way of differentiating between the true mujahideen and those who threaten the Jihadi project.

In a final point, al-Shami asks al-Maqdisi to be explicit about who the diluters and the people of shari'a are. In a final attempt to delegitimise the Jordanian sheikh, al-Shami informs him that those he considers to be people of shari'a are in fact like the Islamic State. Well aware of its history, al-Shami mentions Liwa al-Aqsa—a breakaway group from Jund al-Aqsa broadly considered to harbour sympathies for the Islamic State—as an example of a group that al-Maqdisi considers people of shari'a. Al-Shami's final point is that HTS is the same as al-Nusra. Mentioning the example of Turkey, he explains that there is no scholarly unity on the status of Turkey, and thus al-Maqdisi's judgement cannot be black and white. Cleverly, al-Shami says that 'Sheikh Usama cannot be accused of not disbelieving the government of his country during the first years of jihad. Today, it is not necessarily the case that those who do not consider Erdogan a disbeliever to be diluters.'[21] Abu Fath al-Farghali, a colleague of al-Shami, later added in a television program hosted by al-Muhaysini that this public debate was having a real impact on the ground, with fighters discussing it, asking questions and getting confused.[22] Al-Maqdisi, however, was just getting started despite his friend and colleague Abu Qatada who was attempting to calm things down.[23]

### *The Crusade Against al-Mumayyi'a: Jihad al-Umma or Jihad al-Nukhba*

Al-Julani's split from al-Qaida and the behaviour of HTS resulted in a stream of critical statements from al-Maqdisi and al-Uraydi in 2017–18. No strangers to intra-Jihadi polemics, the two Jordanians launched a crusade against the *dilution* (tamiyy'a) of HTS's ideology in an attempt both to correct the group's ideological deviation and to mobilise its members to defect.[24] Framing themselves as protectors of Jihad and tawhid, they attack *those who dilute* (mumayyi'a) tawhid mainly through establishing alliances with apostates or prioritising political interests over religious principles.[25]

The debate is really about the balance between *doctrinal purity* and *adaption to the political reality*. To some extent, al-Maqdisi has always considered it his role—in fact even a *duty*—to captain the SJM in order to ensure its adherence to the proper theology. This was part of the reason why in 2009 he established his Minbar al-Tawhid wa-l-Jihad database and its shari'a council.[26] However, as Lav has explained, al-Maqdisi has previously stressed the importance of balancing purity with the application of theological principles to real-world situations. In the context of the fidelity of the Taliban, Lav quotes al-Maqdisi at length:

> What we desire, what keeps us awake at night, what we call for and strive for, what we educate the youth on and what we prepare them for, is a jihad that is of godly method and leadership, with a clear banner and a clear path. We do not allow ourselves to urge, encourage, or call the youth to anything but this. However,

> until Allah opens the gates for us and grants us the opportunity for this kind of jihad, it is impermissible for us to stand as an obstacle, through short-sighted fatwas or rulings that weakly fail to comprehend the shari'a and the reality of the Muslims.[27]

In the case of the Syrian Jihad, however, al-Maqdisi has been less indulgent. In early 2018, after Ahrar al-Sham moved closer to Turkey, Abu Basir al-Tartusi, who from the beginning had supported the group, criticised the group's decision. Al-Maqdisi used the opportunity to target al-Tartusi for corrupting the Syrian Jihad. He characterised the development of Ahrar al-Sham as a consequence of al-Tartusi's lack of emphasis on the importance of tawhid in his advice to the group. Al-Maqdisi's—and especially al-Uraydi's—close history with HTS and its predecessor Jabhat al-Nusra made al-Julani's break of allegiance and the group's ensuing behavioural change even more controversial. What started as criticism of HTS's split from al-Qaida and its alliance with Turkey later developed into a broader debate about the nature of the contemporary Jihad in Syria and the means necessary to succeed, with the two Jordanians arguing for *jihad al-nukhba* (Jihad of the elite) while HTS and supportive ideologues stressed the need for *jihad al-umma* (Jihad of the nation).[28]

Breaking the pledge of allegiance to al-Qaida was the first major point of criticism. Al-Uraydi would later issue a series of five testimonies to expose al-Julani and al-Shami's role in the process. Even in the immediate aftermath of the creation of HTS, he attempted to delegitimise the group. He described the pledge of allegiance as a covenant with a shar'i foundation and an illustration of faith that cannot be broken except under particular conditions. Breaking allegiance without legitimate justification is 'a door to evil and division.'[29] He argues that the pledge of allegiance to al-Qaida was in fact what prevented the Syrian Jihad from collapsing. Hence, HTS are framed as the *gamblers of jihad* (muqamirun al-jihad) 'rushing into the *world of politics* (al-'alam al-siyasiyya) without *precept* (dawabit) or *religious legitimisation* (ta'silat shar'iyya). They wage Jihad in the *political markets* (aswaq al-siyasiyya) in a cloak of mystery and concealment.'[30]

Central to al-Julani's plan to split from the authority of al-Zawahiri and avoid the label of al-Qaida was a desire to give his group more flexibility for political manoeuvring as a means of protecting it from the increasing pressure it was under in Idlib. Engaging with Turkey was thus seen as integral to the group's continued existence. The controversy that attached to such collaboration within the SJM was already evident during Turkey's Euphrates Shield military campaign, and intensified after HTS's deal in October 2017 to assist Turkish convoys into Idlib—at which point al-Maqdisi in particular started to post criticism of HTS on his Telegram channel. Al-Maqdisi expanded this criticism to include senior scholars within the group as he launched a severe attack against al-Muhaysini disguised as advice.[31] Al-Maqdisi believes Muhaysini and his colleagues in HTS's shari'a council are preoccupied with small side issues that will never solve the fitna, while they themselves have become a major source of internal tension through their (deficient) statements and position on foreign assistance. Al-Maqdisi lists five points of critique, which can be summarised as a lack of clarity of the shari'a council regarding the legitimacy of supporting secular forces against Muslims (no matter how deviated they may be). On several occasions, both al-Maqdisi and Abu Qatada have argued that deviated Muslims, including the Islamic State, are to be preferred over non-Muslims like the Turkish army, meaning that participation in Euphrates Shield was illegitimate. While Abu Qatada initially agreed that 'anyone who fights under the banner of the apostate Turkish army carries a judgment of apostasy and unbelief', he would later leave it open to HTS to decide on whether it ought to cooperate with Turkey.[32]

Obviously, the criticism was not received well within the HTS camp. In one response, Anas Hassan Khattab, a senior HTS figure and a founding member of Jabhat al-Nusra, complained about al-Maqdisi's and al-Uraydi's use of discrediting terms to describe HTS, arguing that terms such as 'diluter' are not religiously sound and can thus easily be misused.[33] Arguably more important was that the introduction to the article was authored by none other than Abu Qatada, who endorsed its message. HTS members could now point to the support of Abu Qatada when countering attacks from al-Maqdisi; this was one of the first indications of an emerging disagreement between these long-time companions regarding their view of what constitutes legitimate Jihad. Al-Maqdisi responded, defending his use of *dilution*. Explaining that it is connected to tawhid, and is thus a matter of creed, he argued that the term is useful because it indicates a *grading* in situations where religious principles are watered down. He sees HTS's creed as diluted, but not nullified, which represents a difference between deviation and apostasy.[34] Later, al-Uraydi responded to Abu Qatada, criticising his broadening of terms like *extremists* since they could be similarly misused against people like al-Uraydi himself. He added that Abu Qatada's use of 'semi-extremist' to describe al-Qaida loyalists was helping HTS in its crackdown on al-Uraydi and other former HTS members.[35]

The whole discussion soon became part of a larger debate on the nature of the SJM and how it should develop. Bunzel is correct in saying that this started with a reflection from Abu Qatada—published in March 2017—on the historic failure of the movement and its future, in which he argues that the obsession with theological purity had isolated the movement from the Muslim masses, especially the younger generation. To make itself relevant again, the SJM would thus have to abandon this elite-driven and theologically rigid focus and open itself up to differences to become a mass struggle.[36] One solution, he later proposes, is the establishment of a *Syrian Taliban*.

Unsurprisingly, al-Maqdisi and al-Uraydi disagreed, arguing in favour of an elite-driven Jihad to ensure adherence to the proper creed and methodology. Al-Uraydi was the first to describe this in an article where he argued that nationally focused groups 'isolate themselves from the movements of global Sunni jihad', which inevitably brings deviation into one's creed and methodology because one becomes part of local dynamics.[37] The idea is further developed by al-Maqdisi and al-Uraydi in the co-authored booklet *Jihad al-Umma wa Jama'at al-Umma*, where al-Maqdisi argues for its importance in relation to 'the rivalry between us and the sects who want to dilute the Jihad.' He describes two types of Jihad: (1) the fight in the true path of Allah and to implement tawhid, and (2) to defend against and repel aggression. While the first type of Jihad is preferable, the second type of Jihad is legitimate if it is conducted under sound leadership. In his part of the booklet, al-

Uraydi elaborates on al-Maqdisi's ideas. *Jihad al-umma*, he says, is a term used by groups to help them mobilise because no one disagrees in term of its slogans. But 'the conflict arises when it comes to understanding their meanings and the procedure of applying them.' In his view, one of the obligations of Jihad is to place it in the hands of people with expertise. Some Jihadi leaders mistakenly prioritise personal interests over the general cause, becoming so absorbed in their own interests that they do not see their mistakes. Al-Uraydi uses the example of Sayyaf in Afghanistan to warn (implicitly) against al-Julani. The problem is, he argues, that many people want to lead but lack the necessary qualifications. Hence, it is the responsibility of the people of expertise to ensure that the SJM is not infected by deviated ideas.

The ideas promoted in the booklet are important because they challenge HTS and al-Julani, and are an attempt by al-Maqdisi and his supporters to reinstate authority in the hands of the scholarly elite.[38] Al-Uraydi develops his criticism of the current of jihad al-umma in several other articles. His main argument is that the current's nationalist focus inevitably dilutes the religious aspect of Jihad because its overemphasis on fiqh al-waqi' makes adherence to religious principles impossible. 'Either the jihad follows the pillar of this religion or it is a massacre filled with killings and fitna', he writes.[39] Calling HTS and similar groups a modern expression of *jahiliyya* (ignorance), a term employed by Sayyid Qutb to compare the political situation in nominal Muslim states in the 1960s with the ignorance of pre-Islamic society, he states: 'Any movement raising its soldiers on conflict and fighting with a national and regional meaning will find that its soldiers will give up on it if they found solutions that can protect their countries and soils for which they are fighting even if the way was through their enemies.' Defending this view, he says 'The movement that raises and pledges its soldiers on the concept of defending against the assaults of the enemy [a global jihad based on constants], establishing religion and supporting Muslims will never absolve this concept before achieving it in real life even if this aim took many different phases and many generations.'[40] HTS's emphasis on jihad al-umma and fiqh al-waqi' implies a pursuit of gradual change, but al-Uraydi warns about such *jurisprudence of gradual advance* (fiqh al-tadarruj) in the application of shari'a, because it risks becoming a *jurisprudence of attraction* (fiqh al-istidraj) and *concessions* (fiqh al-tanazulat).[41]

### *Abu Mahmoud al-Filastini: Defending Jihad al-Umma*

Arguably the strongest defender of jihad al-umma and the most active opponent of al-Maqdisi and al-Uraydi on this issue has been Abu Mahmoud al-Filastini (Ismail Kalam), a London-based ideologue and close associate of Abu Qatada.[42] Despite his veneration for al-Zawahiri, Abu Mahmoud concurs that the Jihadi project has failed and must evolve, and he sees the transformation of Jabhat al-Nusra to HTS as representing this necessary change to a jihad al-umma. In his view, the reason why the SJM never managed to successfully take the Jihadi project to the next level of establishing Islamic states is that it failed to become a mass movement and remained politically immature. The merger to establish HTS and its ensuing political pragmatism was thus a step in the right direction. He acknowledges that with the merger people with a deviated creed became part of the group, but these people should be educated rather than driven out.[43] In contrast to this view, al-Maqdisi and al-Uraydi saw the inclusion of members from Ahrar al-Sham, Nour al-Deen al-Zinki and other groups as risking the dilution of the group's ideology.

In an article entitled 'The Jihadi Movement Between the *Jurisprudence of Balances* (fiqh al-muwazanat) and the *Jurisprudence of Comparisons* (fiqh al-muqaranat)', Abu Mahmoud breaks with the idea of focusing too much on specific groups and the comparison between groups, as it prevents a unified structure.[44] The present times are too unstable for Jihadi groups to be compared, he writes. Instead, one should consider the *interests* (maslaha) and *mischiefs* (mafsada) for the Jihadi project and strike a balance. In Abu Mahmoud's view, the best solution is a politically savvy compromise to support HTS, which represents a jurisprudence of balances.[45] Calling for a de-escalation of tensions and unity centred around HTS, he writes:

> I think that it is time for all the Islamic movements to stand with itself and to consider the whole experience and to correct the

> mistakes and to be more open and to leave the scientific school conflicts aside in mosques and in books. It should not be carried in the fields of fighting.[46]

Continuing this line of argument in another post, he asks:

> When will we vilify the one who opposes the shari'a and sunna and not the one who opposes our methodology only (...) the problem is that our adversaries used to oppose us in issues of faith (iman) in the past, but now the problem is inside the current itself.[47]

From the beginning of the merger which established HTS, the group and its leading ideologues defended its decision to break allegiance and cooperation with Turkey.[48] In a statement, HTS's shari'a council gave the legal justifications for the group's choices:

> first, that the context of the war forced HTS to compromise some of its creed in order to protect its jihad, creating the legal conditions of compulsion (Idtirar) and necessity (Darura). Second, the concept of Shariah governance (siyasa Shari'a) allows HTS leadership to apply altered judgements which fit this new context. The Council argues that the capability to properly implement a legal judgement (ahkam) is situationally dependent, and when changes to a previously accepted judgement are made, it is only to protect the group's consistent principles within this context. It explains that its 'reference to Shariah is a constant, and the principle of jihad is a constant, but the capability on which rulings are dependent is variable.'[49]

These explanations, however, did little to calm al-Maqdisi and his entourage, who referred to HTS's religious establishment (shar'iyyun) as liars and compared the group's increasingly aggressive behaviour to Macchiavelli.[50] That said, al-Maqdisi stopped short of declaring takfir on HTS. Its dilution implied a watered-down creed and faith, but not its actual nullification.

### *HTS's Hegemonic Project in North-Western Syria*

The delinking from al-Qaida and failed merger efforts led HTS to adopt increasingly aggressive behaviour and escalate its pressure on local rivals. Pursuing its political interests, HTS had split from al-Qaida and engaged in collaboration with Turkey; what was now needed was to suppress its local rivals and become a local hegemon in Syria's north-west. This involved both military and political actions geared towards dominating and controlling rival Jihadi groups' ability to act freely, through a process that calls to mind the Islamic State's behaviour in 2014. HTS's primary tool in suppressing Jihadi rivals was military confrontation. In the 2017–19 period, it attacked Ahrar al-Sham and Nour al-Deen al-Zinki on several occasions, while simultaneously directing campaigns against Islamic State cells and al-Qaida loyalists.

Beginning in January 2017, and continuing over the following two years, HTS would engage in six larger military confrontations with Ahrar al-Sham, al-Zinki or both. The first three rounds, taking place in January, March and July 2017, were clear attempts by HTS to pressure Ahrar into merging with it.[51] While substantial numbers of Ahrar members and leaders had joined HTS immediately after its creation, al-Julani still pursued full assimilation of Ahrar under his command. While HTS succeeded in gaining territory, it lost a lot of its legitimacy. On several occasions, 'doves' within the group such as Abdullah al-Muhaysini and Abu Mariya al-Qahtani tried to halt the infighting while mediation teams comprised of 'independent' scholars intervened. It was all without success: HTS refused arbitration. The first to defect from HTS on March 6 was the scholar Abd al-Razzaq al-Mahdi, directly citing HTS's aggression against Ahrar as the reason. He was followed by Nour al-Deen al-Zinki—a founding member of HTS—on July 20, and two months later on August 13 by Jaysh al-Ahrar, the faction of Ahrar al-Sham members that joined HTS. Arguably the most critical blow to HTS was when al-Muhaysini announced his defection on September 12 after the publication of a series of leaks under the hashtag #HTSleaks. In the leaked audios, HTS leaders discuss how to handle al-Muhaysini, who is clearly opposed to the infighting with Ahrar and who, they fear, will discourage the youth of HTS from taking part. In one audio statement, the suggestion is made of arresting al-Muhaysini, while in another audio leaders even discuss the possibility of killing him. In his resignation statement, however, al-Muhaysini explained that his decision was mainly driven by the fact that the recommendations of the HTS shari'a committee, of which he was a member, were not followed.

In the words of Abu Sulayman al-Muhajir, the former Jabhat al-Nusra spokesperson who left the group after it rebranded as JFS, it was now a *total war* between HTS and Ahrar: neither party was willing to accept the other's project and HTS was unwilling to settle for anything less than a full merger.[52] In a Twitter debate, al-Muhajir elaborated on this, saying 'I don't see any room for an arbitration. If HTS stops now, they will most likely be setting themselves up for elimination. It's do or die.'[53] At this time, HTS was also increasingly beginning to define rivals like Ahrar and al-Zinki as *hypocrites* (munafiqun) and *partisans* (hizbis) in a bid to delegitimise them.[54] But as HTS was perceived to be the main aggressor, most opposition groups sided against it, while others like Ajnad al-Kavkaz (Jund al-Sham) remained neutral.

In February 2018, to prepare for future confrontations, Ahrar and al-Zinki established a new military formation: the Syrian Liberation Front (Jabhat Tahrir Souriyya, JTS). A few weeks later, the worst round of military confrontations with HTS erupted, lasting for more than two months. Despite several scholar-led reconciliation initiatives, like al-Muhaysini and al-Ulayni's Unified Popular Initiative, the infighting continued to escalate, with HTS now referring to JTS as *rebels* (bughat)—an instrumentalisation designed to convince its fighters of the legitimacy of fighting the group.[55] The last round of high-intensity infighting erupted on January 1, 2019, after al-Zinki members killed four HTS members on December 28. HTS once again rejected arbitration and instead took advantage of the situation. Over ten days in January it largely defeated Ahrar and al-Zinki, which were now organised in the Turkey-supported National Front for Liberation (jabhat al-wataniyya lil-tahrir, NFL) together with Faylaq al-Sham.[56] On the other side of the ideological spectrum, HTS also targeted Islamic State cells in Idlib and Hama from summer 2017 on. The group had no established presence in Syria's north-west, but HTS would not even tolerate smaller cells operating in territory under its control (hence it is unlikely that HTS later had any idea that Islamic State leaders, including al-

Baghdadi, were present in Idlib). Especially from summer 2018, HTS's crackdown intensified, and both sides started to issue visuals showing the execution of opponent fighters.

The dominant rationale driving the military confrontations was HTS's hegemonic ambitions in Idlib. But Kydd and Walter's point that negotiations with the state risk causing conflict between 'moderates' and 'radicals' within opposition movements is central too. HTS viewed Ahrar's increasing engagement with Turkey (which included participation in the Euphrates Shield and its later inclusion in the NFL alliance) as a threat to its Jihadi project. A similar point can be made about al-Qaida loyalists' criticism of HTS. Thus, we see that a discourse about the *legitimacy of politics* has become much more prominent within the SJM than it was prior to 2017. Defending its own position, HTS explained in a statement entitled 'Jihad and Shari'a Politics Between Constants and Alternations' that political engagement is a balancing act, with the group trying to order its priorities and neutralise its opponents without compromising its principles. The group claims that its basis in shari'a is a fixed constant and can never be changed, but acknowledges that 'Islamic politics is a part of Jihad.'[57]

HTS's political mission was driven forward by its National Salvation Government (hukuma al-inqadhi wasat), which was established on November 2, 2017, with a view to taking total control over Idlib and western Aleppo. Heavily criticised for not tolerating rival political entities and for implementing contested policies, the Salvation Government came to be viewed as an exclusivist political project. Examples include banning the books of al-Maqdisi,[58] restricting communication within areas under its control[59] and, from December 2018, banning Islamic education unless it was under the Salvation Government's authority. Prior to its establishment, however, HTS had already made several declarations intended to control the political environment and discipline its own members. First it prohibited its preachers and ordinary members from proclaiming takfir without an official fatwa from the shari'a council,[60] then it prohibited its members from watching Islamic State videos and, most controversially of all, it forbade the establishment of any new factions in its territory.[61] While some of these things may appear ridiculous, they are illustrative of HTS's desire to control and dominate.

By the end of 2017, the dynamics between HTS and al-Qaida loyalists were changing, with HTS responding to the discursive criticism with a military crackdown. Tensions were brewing over the autumn and in a bid to de-escalate the situation a group of senior scholars, including al-Maqdisi, Abu Qatada and the Moroccan Umar al-Haddouchi, launched a new peace initiative on October 25. Immediately receiving strong support from both HTS members and al-Qaida loyalists, it was seen as a serious effort to establish a new structural arrangement within Idlib to facilitate both groups. However, after only two days, al-Maqdisi and Abu Qatada were forced to withdraw from the initiative due to pressure from the Jordanian intelligence service.[62] While the initiative at first continued (albeit weakened) it was effectively dismantled when HTS refused to endorse it officially, arguing that it was already in contact with the other side trying to find a solution. This clearly did not happen and, on November 27, the situation escalated when HTS arrested several al-Qaida loyalists, including the senior figures Abu al-Qassam, Sami al-Uraydi, Abu Julaybib, Abu Khallad, Bilal Khuraysat and Umar Abd al-Rahman. Al-Uraydi claims that when he was arrested, more than twenty guns were pointed at him and HTS confiscated a lot of material from his home.[63] HTS's official justification for the arrests was that the al-Qaida loyalists had caused corruption and spread fitna and lies against HTS. Its military shar'i, al-Zubayr al-Ghazi, added that al-Qaida loyalists even proclaimed takfir on HTS or referred to the group in terms that led less knowledgeable people to reach the conclusion of its unbelief.[64]

Arresting al-Qaida loyalists was an extremely risky move for HTS because many fighters with sympathy for al-Qaida remained in HTS. After the arrest, a large number of them went public, demanding that the prisoners be released within twenty-four hours or they would defect from HTS. This was followed by another strong criticism from al-Maqdisi which referred to HTS as the *head of sedition* (ra's al-fitna)—a term HTS had previously used about al-Qaida loyalists—and from Hani al-Sibai. In an hour-long audio statement, al-Sibai called on HTS to release the prisoners, scolding the group for not supporting the scholarly peace initiative and comparing their behaviour to that of al-Baghdadi.[65] This criticism made HTS supporters turn their focus particularly on al-Maqdisi, claiming that he was the mastermind behind all the problems. In order to solve the crisis, a settlement committee (lajna al-fasl) was established on December 2 under the leadership of Abu Abd al-Karim al-Khorasani, an al-Qaida shura council member.[66] HTS announced that it, together with al-Khorasani, had negotiated over the release of the prisoners—but in its statement it also took the opportunity to warn any potentially dissatisfied HTS members: 'There is no excuse for any of the soldiers of HTS to leave Jihad today knowing that HTS is the only one defending the heated fronts of the Muslims in the liberated territories; and this is a shari'a obligation encompassing all of them.'[67] On the same day, HTS circulated an internal document justifying the arrest of Abu al-Qassam, Sami al-Uraydi, Abu Julaybib and Bilal Khuraysat. Rejecting the idea that it had anything to do with their allegiance to al-Qaida, the document stressed that the charges centred on the individuals' online incitement to fitna and their attempts to undermine HTS:

> What we would like to clarify is that our conflict with those brothers was not founded on the fact that they were following al-Qaida. Our conflict with them is not related to al-Qaida at all. Every single one of them has a problem with al-Jabha when it was al-Qaida. They gathered on the existent project to split the lines of al-hay'a [HTS].[68]

The eventual release of al-Qaida loyalists in December did not solve the problems, although there were serious efforts to reach an agreement to neutralise an emerging conflict. Acting as the head of al-Qaida loyalists in Syria, Abu Hummam al-Shami managed to conclude a draft agreement with HTS in January 2018, again under the auspices of a commission led by al-Khorasani consisting of sixteen points. The main conclusions were that:

- All property including weapons should remain with HTS,
- Al-Qaida loyalists are not allowed to establish any areas of control but will be able to operate in HTS-secured areas,

- Al-Qaida loyalists may not engage in action weakening HTS,
- A new al-Qaida group will not accept members from Liwa al-Aqsa, Jund al-Aqsa or the Islamic State, who are all considered enemies of HTS,
- Any future organisational conflicts are handled by the committee president (that is al-Khorasani),
- HTS members may not join a new al-Qaida group except with written permission,
- HTS is obliged to arm al-Qaida loyalists fighting under HTS control,
- Al-Qaida loyalists are prohibited from operating in Deraa in southern Syria,
- Both groups are obliged to follow the rulings of the Islamic courts in their areas of operations, and
- Al-Qaida loyalists must halt their public criticism of HTS.

Al-Qaida loyalists Abu Khallad and Abu Julaybib immediately rejected the deal, using the hashtag #closing_the_doors_of_Shaytan (#saddan_al-bawab_al-shaytan) to indicate their dissatisfaction. This compelled Abu Hummam al-Shami to negotiate a new deal which eventually failed. Two issues in particular continued to cause problems between HTS and al-Qaida loyalists: firstly, the ownership of weapons, and secondly, fighting under the banner of HTS. On the weapons issue, HTS demanded that all weapons and materials were returned because the defectors used to be members of HTS. The defecting al-Qaida loyalists, on the other hand, argued that the weapons used to belong to al-Qaida and since they now represented al-Qaida, they should remain in their possession. The other issue concerned both the legitimacy of fighting under HTS's authority despite being loyal to al-Qaida, and HTS's coercion of fighters to remain in its group. Here the scholars generally agreed that it was legitimate to remain in HTS, since its dilution did not equal disappearance of faith. Scholars like al-Maqdisi, however, questioned HTS's opposition to letting fighters join the Jihad unless they would fight under al-Julani's authority.[69]

HTS's behaviour against other Jihadi groups led to accusations that it had adopted the same attitude as the Islamic State. Rival groups started to refer to it as *hitish*, an acronym comparable to *da'esh*, and applied the term *da'eshni* to describe someone acting like al-Baghdadi's group. In a similar way to the Islamic State, HTS criminalised the creation of new groups and adopted an extremely aggressive posture towards rivals, while consistently rejecting efforts of arbitration in its conflicts with Ahrar, al-Zinki and al-Qaida loyalists, because it was unwilling to transfer any authority to outsiders out of fear of compromising its political interests.[70] This eventually led Abu Qatada to issue a warning that attacking other Muslims on the pretext of unity is a sin.[71] From HTS's perspective, this type of behaviour was considered a necessity to take the Jihadi project further and was thus in the *public interest* (al-maslaha al-mursala). A conversation with a mid-level HTS member illustrates this well: asked about the possibility of a new al-Qaida group in Syria, he answered: 'No, that would be a step back. The natural course is heading towards the formation of one united body of revolutionaries in one trench and sell-outs in another.'[72] From 2017 onwards, that was the new reality HTS was living in.

# 13

# RENEWED COHESION OR CONTINUED POLARISATION?

In 2018–19, the SJM was at a crossroads. The demise of the Islamic State, the internal splintering and factionalism within the Islamic State and al-Qaida, and the evolving, distinctive ideological visions separating al-Qaida and HTS implied that intra-group conflict had to some extent replaced inter-group conflict. Yet the question is to what extent this context could nurture renewed cohesion within the movement, or if intra-group tensions would inevitably complicate any such development. The discussion within terrorism analyst circles of an organisational merger between al-Qaida and the Islamic State, and the general confusion about the relation between HTS and al-Qaida, has been either utopian or simply mistaken. Nonetheless, there was arguably a platform to promote sentiments of movement cohesion and to leave behind the group-centric logic. This opportunity, however, was missed, largely due to three developments: the establishment of a new al-Qaida group in Syria, HTS's continued hegemonist rationale and the sudden outbreak of infighting in Yemen, Somalia and the Sahel.

*Peacemakers and Troublemakers*

For the second time in just a few years, tensions between Jihadi groups in Syria's Idlib province result in a fractured and polarised scholarly environment. Just as when the fitna emerged between the Islamic State and rival Jihadi groups in 2014, ideologues in 2018 would collaborate repeatedly in a bid to de-escalate tensions.[1] Otherwise, however, they would generally align with one organisational camp and follow diverging rationales, either acting as *peacemakers* or *troublemakers.*

In the 2017–19 period, ideologues divided into three camps: pro-HTS, pro-al-Qaida and those unwilling to choose a side. These positions mostly resulted from a clash between organisational logics and doctrinal purity on the one hand, and from a clash between an emphasis on methodology and creed on the other. Al-Maqdisi's pro-al-Qaida position and emphasis on doctrinal purity has already been dealt with. Tariq Abdelhaleem—a strange bedfellow for al-Maqdisi, considering their previous confrontation—would adopt a similar position to al-Maqdisi, issuing strong criticism of HTS's deviation. In the opposing camp, Abu Mahmoud al-Filastini and Abu Qatada were supportive of HTS, though the latter attempted to position himself as a unifier without any organisational preference. In the last camp, Hani al-Sibai largely tried to refrain from taking a partisan position by expressing understanding for both camps and, as in 2014, calling on al-Zawahiri to step in and settle the conflict.[2]

As we have seen, the partisan or rigid positions adopted by al-Maqdisi, Abdelhaleem and Abu Mahmoud have generally contributed to escalating the existing problems between al-Qaida loyalists and HTS. In contrast with this behaviour, Abu Qatada has attempted to adopt the role of peacemaker to de-escalate tensions. While Abu Qatada appears to support the political project of HTS, his criticism has targeted both al-Qaida loyalists and HTS. He laments al-Qaida loyalists' destructive emphasis on doctrinal purity and their lack of understanding of the political and military situation surrounding the Jihadi enclave of Idlib. Simultaneously, Abu Qatada has warned HTS supporters about their hegemonic behaviour that leaves little room for other actors and risks causing infighting with other Muslims, which only obstructs the larger fight against the real enemy. Furthermore, in statements and commentary on his Telegram channel in the period 2017–19, Abu Qatada attempted two things: firstly, to remove matters of creed from the debate and make it a matter of methodology, and secondly, to instruct ideologues how to behave. While some groups may be 'purer' than HTS, Abu Qatada finds it counterproductive to establish new groups because the situation in Idlib calls for a strong opposition, which is best represented by HTS. While HTS may have methodological shortcomings, these should not prohibit Jihadis from fighting in its ranks.[3]

From the perspective of Abu Qatada, the scholars carry a huge responsibility for the current situation of competition and rivalry. In a string of statements that can hardly be understood as anything but a criticism of al-Maqdisi, he laments how every time there is disagreement, people cling to their own biases and start shouting. Abu Qatada notes that if everyone does this, how will we ever solve the issue? Everyone says 'I am right, everyone else is wrong.'[4] Instead, Abu Qatada recommends that scholars give advice privately to help avoid differences between groups becoming public, writing that 'the duty of the scholars is to always call for reconciliation, and not to differ, not to exaggerate the conflict, and put it in the framework of evil and slander.'[5] Continuing his criticism, Abu Qatada writes in another post that unknowledgeable scholars speak too much, while being unwilling to listen or take in new ideas. This kind of talk, he says, should remain in the mosque, because Jihadis on the ground are fragmenting because of the scholarly debate.[6] Hence, through directing criticism against all groups, and promoting de-escalation and the acceptance of diversity, and defining the responsibility of scholars in inter-group conflict, Abu Qatada has attempted to play the role of peacemaker.

Al-Qaida leader al-Zawahiri adopted a similar role, albeit from another underlying basis. Having now witnessed two former affiliates split from his group and move in opposite ideological directions, al-Zawahiri found himself in a complicated situation navigating between rival groups, one more moderate and the other more extreme, while promoting a unifying narrative.[7] In an action illustrative of this complex situation, in early 2018 al-Qaida shared two old documents through its affiliated Telegram channels. The first document, issued in February and authored by the late al-Qaida veteran Abu Yahya al-Libi, was entitled *Fresh Resource to Explain the Rule of Recourse to Infidels in War*.[8] Given the new front cover depicting Erdogan and a Turkish flag, this was obviously directed at HTS and JTS and their alliance with Turkey. The other document, also authored by Abu Yahya and entitled *A Message from Sheikh Abu Yahya to One of the Groups' Amirs* was shared the following month.[9] In this document, Abu Yahya warns against relying on group logic and issues a reminder of the impermissibility of shedding Muslim blood. The re-issuing of these two documents in particular was an attempt by al-Qaida to guide groups and their supporters within both the moderate and the extremist strand, and to take the opportunity to promote a unifying rationale in contrast to polarising, group-centric logic.

Al-Zawahiri's position was summed up in a statement released on October 4, 2017. Talking about other Jihadis, he says: 'Our stance regarding you is dictated neither by politics nor by emotions; it is a principled shar'i stance grounded in faith.' Addressing HTS more directly, he continues:

> We fear for these tremendous sacrifices you [the mujahideen in general] have rendered and the pure blood you have offered, lest it be wasted in political games and ruses. (…) We have seen how sacrifices were wasted earlier when the leadership sunk into the swamp of political balancing acts and prioritised its own narrow self-interests.

Yet disclosing his opinion on HTS breaking its allegiance, he concludes: 'As for us, we believe that the oath of allegiance is a shar'i undertaking; binding in its nature, its violation being forbidden.'[10]

Al-Zawahiri's main problem was that he was physically detached from the situation in Syria and thus was unable to communicate regularly. This led to criticism from a senior HTS member and former associate of al-Zawahiri in Al Jihad, Abu al-Harith al-Masri, who described the al-Qaida leader as the *hidden amir* (al-amir al-musardib) and one isolated from reality—factors that made him incapable of issuing criticism let alone rulings.[11] This attack on al-Zawahiri would quickly put al-Masri in conflict with al-Qaida loyalists such as Abu Ja'far al-Iraqi and Abu al-Qarnayn al-Khorasani, who rejected the categorisation of al-Zawahiri as absent. More importantly, Abu Qatada also came to the defence of al-Zawahiri, claiming that if al-Masri considered him to be hidden it was because he was blind.[12]

Isolated or not, al-Zawahiri's objective was to emphasise the importance of unity and to warn HTS in diplomatic terms of its methodological deviance. The first point comes across in a number of statements in 2017–19. In one he says that

> If the umma condemns the efforts of breaking unity, dividing ranks, violating sanctities, and spilling blood unlawfully, the perpetrators of these crimes will think a thousand times before committing them. Therefore, a broad consensus must be established in all segments of the umma against those who commit these crimes so that the umma's general opinion stands in the way of their evil designs.[13]

In another official publication entitled *Lapses of the Islamic Pens: An Open Letter of Advice to Jihadi Youths*, an al-Qaida official named Awwab bin Hassan al-Hasani promotes a higher ethic for the youth's online behaviour. Focusing on Jihadis' use of Twitter and Telegram, he gives the advice that *before* tweeting: *take an extra look at your tweet before sending it out. Think for a while. And then make it public if you still think it is decent.*[14] While al-Zawahiri acknowledges the methodological differences between groups, his discourse on unity is tightly linked to loyalty and authority. Unity is dependent on obeying leaders, remaining loyal to pledges of allegiance and abstaining from infighting. This, he says, is what Jihadis always call for—yet he insinuates that in recent history they have failed to live up to this in practice.[15]

Extending this criticism to HTS—without mentioning its name—the al-Qaida leader warns about its collaboration with Turkey and its general inclination to follow a political rationale. In two separate statements he says: 'Many groups associated with Islamic work have engaged in the swamp of political activity in accordance with the rules and provisions of secular constitutions and laws. So what was the result? Disaster and loss everywhere';[16] and

'Among the causes of failure is rushing behind the secularists and the henchmen of the West, and to ally with them and derive strength from them, and to be under their leadership and concede to them what contradicts shari'a.'[17] His conclusion is that this behaviour not only contradicts al-wala' wa-l-bara' but also leads to the failure of the Jihadis' political project.

Perhaps the strongest call for unity came in the form of an official al-Qaida statement in August 2019. Calling for the establishment of a broad inter-Jihadi military alliance similar to Jaysh al-Fatah, it reads:

> 'O brothers, bury the differences in this difficult time, and dispense with the propaganda through which we curse each other, as it will not end until it breaks the bonds of our entities and our jihadi gatherings, and then it leaves a fire of enmity, which will not be extinguished by sea water, and scars of grudges and hatred, which will not be erased by the passage of days and then years (...) Let us spend all our money on jihad in the cause of Allah. Let us open our weapons depots to all the mujahideen without looking for a party or organisational affiliation. Let us open the battles on all the fronts to disperse the capabilities of the enemy and cause its exhaustion and attrition.'[18]

## *Al-Qaida's Re-Emergence in Syria*

During 2017, and especially because of the arrest of several high-ranking al-Qaida loyalists by HTS, tensions were constantly escalating between the two camps. Yet this was still a conflict between a settled group and various loosely connected individuals who remained outside any organisational setup. Rumours of a new al-Qaida group began to circulate on Telegram as early as late November 2016 when it was still believed that the rebranded JFS was loyal to al-Zawahiri. At the time, it was argued that the al-Qaida leadership was disappointed that al-Julani had not managed to secure a merger between Jihadi rebel groups, and al-Qaida supporters speculated that figures like Abu Julaybib and Sami al-Uraydi—sanctioned by al-Zawahiri—would initiate a coup against al-Julani. This coup would establish a new group that would facilitate the assimilation of disillusioned Islamic State members. While nothing materialised at the time, new rumours emerged a year later in October 2017, when a group called Ansar al-Furqan fi Balad al-Sham was announced on Twitter. Jihadis on the ground in Syria discarded the rumours as false, and none of the well known al-Qaida loyalists commented on it.[19] The following month, there were new and more trustworthy indications of a new al-Qaida group. A Telegram channel called Supporters of al-Qaida in Sham (ansar qa'idat al-jihad fi balad al-sham) was created on November 29. The following day, a renowned al-Qaida supporter published a message calling on fighters in HTS that still considered themselves to have allegiance to al-Qaida to remain loyal to the pledge, to gather together and to prepare for a new formation under a new leader 'soon'.[20]

These rumours took on a more concrete form in December 2017 and January 2018 as the contours of an organisational structure slowly began to emerge. Two HTS factions—Jaysh al-Badiyya[21] and Jaysh al-Malahim[22]—defected and immediately began to frame themselves as sympathetic to al-Qaida.[23] New indications that something was underway came in late January and early February when several groups and military factions, including the HTS founding member Jabhat Ansar al-Deen (January 26), a faction of HTS fighters in Binnish (February 4) and Jaysh al-Sahel (February 10) defected from HTS, and a new group emerged under the name Jund al-Shariah (February 2). Interestingly, Abu Abdullah al-Shami, the leader of Jabhat Ansar al-Deen, explained that his decision to leave HTS was not because of theological disagreement but rather discontent with the group's administration and political priorities, thus hinting at a separation between theology and politics.[24]

On February 27, 2018, it was finally announced that a new al-Qaida group in Syria named Guardians of Religion (Hurras al-Deen) was to be established through a merger between six groups and factions.[25] The new group was led by al-Qaida and HTS veteran Abu Hummam al-Suri and included several high-ranking AQ loyalists with a history in HTS's leadership.[26] From the outset, HTS exercised strong pressure on Hurras al-Deen, which was massively inferior in terms of numbers and military capability. While Hurras al-Deen had approximately 3,000 fighters,[27] HTS commanded around 15,000 fighters.[28] To counter the disequilibrium, and as a measure to protect itself, on April 29 a military alliance named Hilf Nusrat al-Islam (The Alliance of Supporting Islam) was announced between Hurras al-Deen and Ansar al-Tawhid, a new group composed of remnants of Jund al-Aqsa and al-Qaida loyalists.[29] As expected, HTS supporters saw this alliance as evidence of the extremist character of Hurras al-Deen, which it used to fend off some of the theological criticism al-Qaida loyalists directed against the group. Despite its fight against the Assad regime on the southern Idlib and northern Hama battlefronts, Hurras al-Deen was also targeted by both wings within the SJM. In its *al-Naba* magazine the Islamic State proclaimed takfir on the group, referring to it as *guardians of polytheism* (hurras al-shirk) and a *group of apostates* (majmu'a min al-murtaden).[30] The article explains that just because the group left al-Julani does not make them true followers of monotheism since they oppose the Islamic State. A few days before, the Islamic State spokesman Abu al-Hassan al-Muhajir had told his group's followers to 'Split the heads of all the murtaddin who harm the muwahhid slaves of Allah, even if they were at one point part of the caravan of the mujahidin, and accept the repentance of those who repent before they are subdued.'[31] On July 11, 2018, the first (and so far only) clash between the Islamic State and Hurras al-Deen took place, with both groups reporting that they killed one fighter from the rival group.

It would be the contestation and conflict with HTS that would dominate Hurras al-Deen's early history, however. HTS was opposed to the establishment of a new al-Qaida and was generally disgruntled with the criticism from al-Qaida loyalists. The group had already arrested several high-ranking al-Qaida loyalists, but tensions worsened when HTS killed Abu Uqba al-Kurdi, a Hurras al-Deen shar'i, at a checkpoint in the Aleppo countryside on May 5. A senior HTS shar'i named Abu Malik al-Shami was quick to issue an official statement explaining that the killing was an accident, that the shooter had already been arrested and that Hurras al-Deen and HTS would find a solution to settle the issue.[32] HTS's reaction showed that despite its opposition to Hurras al-Deen, the group was not necessarily interested in escalating the conflict with the group, but rather wanted to subdue its activities in northwestern Syria. In the remaining part of 2018, there were no other casualties, but HTS would occasionally arrest Hurras al-Deen members or sympathisers despite a standing agreement between the groups stipulating that any arrests had to be made known to the leadership prior to being enacted.[33] Simultaneously, Hurras al-Deen would see several factions and individuals, including muhajireen, join after defecting from HTS, which only exacerbated the inter-group relationship.[34]

### *Understanding Realities*

Tensions between HTS and al-Qaida loyalists were the product of several factors. The most concrete sources of this tension were the decision to break the pledge of allegiance to al-Zawahiri and HTS's ruling that all weapons and equipment of former HTS fighters joining Hurras al-Deen must be handed back.[35] But the issue driving tensions between HTS and al-Qaida in 2018–19 was the divergence of their visions of the Jihadi project and specifically the level of engagement with Turkey, something which only intensified as the Assad regime drew up its plan to invade Idlib. In particular, the agreement reached in September 2018 in Sochi between Turkey, Russia and Iran to establish four demilitarised zones across Syria became a problem: the agreement facilitated increased collaboration between HTS and Turkey, which in turn complicated HTS's relations with al-Qaida loyalists. The issue would also provoke tensions between previously allied ideologues, most notably al-Maqdisi and Abu Qatada, who were divided by their support of opposing Jihadi groups in Syria for the first time.

According to Abu Mahmoud al-Filastini, the tensions were grounded in contrasting perceptions of the political reality on the ground, which resulted in disparate analyses of how to continue the Jihadi project.[36] HTS viewed the Syrian Jihad as a nationally focused Jihad (jihad al-umma) under intense pressure, partly due to the interference of external actors. The group's objective is to protect its enclave in Idlib and, in the longer term, control and govern as much territory as possible in Syria. This objective informs the legitimate actions of the group in accordance with the principle of fiqh al-waqi' and whether a certain action is considered a *benefit* (maslaha) or *harmful* (mafsada). It is in this context that HTS's engagement with Turkey must be viewed.

Within HTS, these views were particularly promoted by Abu Abdullah al-Shami, head of its shura council, Abu Fath Farghali,[37] an Egyptian member of the shura council and the group's fatwa council and al-Zubayr al-Ghazi, shar'i in HTS's military committee. Externally, HTS received ideological support from Abu Mahmoud and more indirectly from Abu Qatada. Abu Qatada's ruling on the permissibility of collaborating with Turkey has been particularly important to HTS. Firstly, he issued a fatwa ruling that everyone fighting under the command of Turkey in the Euphrates Shield operation is considered an infidel, but in a later Q&A session he nuanced his view, explaining that any alliance must necessarily be governed by shari'a, and must be a benefit to the Jihadi group and not the apostate.[38] To ensure that such conditions are upheld, he explains that an alliance must be accepted by the group's jurists and not only by its leaders.[39] According to HTS, Abu Qatada's ruling permitted the group to opt for an alliance with Turkey as they are more familiar with the context than he is. This essentially opens a space to follow one's own political interests, potentially at the expense of creedal purity.

Abu Qatada's student Abu Mahmoud has been more explicit about the necessity and legitimacy of following political interests at the present stage of the Jihad in Syria. Framing the alliance with Turkey as a necessity and not a desire, he says that 'we [the Jihadis] have to do politics and fight in all fields to keep the Jihad existing. We cannot afford to lose more countries. We have to keep our existence and make it impossible to our enemies to eliminate us.'[40] Abu Mahmoud argues that the current stage is the time of politics. He asks: 'Why should we fight Turkey? It is not in the Jihadis' interest. We disagree with Turkey, but we should not make them an enemy. It is a mistake to make everything a matter of 'aqida. This does not work in politics. Politics is something that brings you interests.' In a series of messages on Telegram in June 2018, he elaborated on the *legitimate policy* (al-siyasa al-shari'ayya) of the SJM, saying that the movement is *politically in the nursery stage* (siyasiyan ma zilna fi marhalat al-hadana) and lacks a *political jurisprudence* (fiqh al-siyasi). Hence, when HTS began discussing these political issues, it entered a minefield. In an interview with al-Jazeera, HTS's Head of Political

Affairs Yusuf al-Hajar commented on the alliance with Turkey and was afterwards heavily criticised within Jihadi circles for being overly positive about the role of Turkey. However, Abu Mahmoud defends al-Hajar, saying

> He was not successful in clarifying the matter politically that the relationship with the Turks in all its cases is evil, and that between the greatest evil and the lowest evil there are loopholes in which al-hay'a [HTS] tries to work to achieve interests and push away the harms. Those acts can help preserving the gains and protecting the continuity of jihad.

Drawing a comparison to the situation of Ahrar al-Sham, whom HTS itself has criticised for its alliance with Turkey, Abu Mahmoud explains that the decisive difference is that HTS has implemented control mechanisms to ensure that it does not deviate while engaging in politics.[41]

This is where HTS and al-Qaida loyalists in Syria differ. The latter support a more global and purist Jihad in the sense of viewing Syria as simply one piece in the global Jihadi struggle which must be governed at all times and through stricter religious checks and balances to ensure that the methodology does not deviate. This essentially demotes the importance of political interests vis-à-vis adherence to religious principles. During the negotiations of the Sochi agreement between Turkey, Russia and Iran in September 2018, which established the demilitarised zones in Syria, Hurras al-Deen figures responded with a public question to Jihadi ideologues to declare their stance on the legitimacy of a Turkish presence in Idlib, not least as a way of putting pressure on Abu Qatada. The following month, Hurras al-Deen, in alliance with Jabhat Ansar al-Deen and Ansar al-Islam, created the Incite the Believers Operations Room (wa harid al-mu'minin) to strengthen its position against both internal and external enemies.[42]

Unsurprisingly, al-Maqdisi was the first to react to the question, writing on his Telegram channel that he had always opposed assisting the entry of the Turks, whom he considered the same as any other apostate occupier.[43] Al-Maqdisi's ideological criticism generally reiterates the same points al-Uraydi had already raised, but he also comments on organisational aspects. Despite his explicit attacks on HTS, he is careful to emphasise that the group's deviations do not justify attacks against it and that it is certainly better than JTS. His support for Hurras al-Deen leads him to attempt to establish certain rules to govern Idlib's Jihadi environment that will ensure tolerable coexistence. Differences of *interpretation* (ijtihad) among Jihadi groups are acceptable and should not be the cause of infighting, but at the same time it is important that HTS leaves a space for Hurras al-Deen and abandons its desire to control that group. In al-Maqdisi's view, it is HTS's hegemonic project that obstructs coexistence among Jihadi groups rather than al-Qaida's alleged insistence on a certain creed. To explain his willingness to promote intra-Jihadi unity, al-Maqdisi distinguishes between *merging* with a group on a deviant methodology and *coordinating* with it. The problem is, he writes, that he promotes coordination while HTS demands a merger.[44]

The conflict between al-Qaida and HTS would eventually pit Jihadi ideologues previously united in their opposition to the Islamic State against one another in new constellations. This resulted in an even more fragmented ideological environment. Al-Maqdisi and al-Uraydi's steady stream of critical *public* statements on HTS and its deviated methodology were also implicit attacks against ideologues who supported HTS, like Abu Qatada, al-Maqdisi's long-time friend and brother-in-words against the Islamic State. The two Jordanian ideologues had never held entirely similar ideas, but the mounting schism would be the first time they were on opposing sides in an organisational, and political, struggle.[45] As Bunzel explains,

> This has led to mutual recriminations. Al-Maqdisi and his allies routinely accuse Abu Qatada and his followers of 'fusionism' (talfiq), that is, of attempting to fuse jihadi ideology with mainstream Islamism, including its tolerance of democracy and ideological diversity. The so-called 'fusionists' (mulaffiqa), in turn, have cast al-Maqdisi and his friends as purveyors of 'extremism' (ghuluww), that is, as being too inclined to engage in the excommunication (takfir) of fellow Muslims.[46]

### *The Growing Schism Among Ideologues*

Abu Mahmoud would beat Abu Qatada in the race to publicly object to al-Maqdisi's approach. According to Abu Mahmoud in his article 'al-Maqdisi and the Free Fall', the Jordanian ideologue is destroying himself through his attempts to claim a monopoly on the truth and on monotheism, which constantly lead him into confrontations. Abu Mahmoud even insinuates that al-Maqdisi is following the practice of the Islamic State in dividing right and wrong in a Manichean fashion instead of allowing for the existence of a methodological continuum. The problem is, he writes, that al-Maqdisi will end up making the Islamic State the more acceptable group in terms of creed.[47]

In a manner typical of Abu Qatada, his response to al-Maqdisi was more subtle while also leaving no doubt about who and what he was referring to. Beginning in December 2017, Abu Qatada wrote that whenever there is disagreement, people cling to their own position and start shouting, but, he asks, how is this ever going to solve anything?[48] In August 2018, discussing the role of the scholars, he argues that their main role in periods of conflict is to offer private advice to help prevent differences between groups becoming public in a way that may aggravate these differences.[49] In October, Abu Qatada's rebuttal escalated further. In a series of messages, he attacks Jihadis' propensity to engage in irrelevant internal debates and distances himself from this tendency. He argues that Jihadis are fragmenting because of scholarly debates that should in fact take place in the mosque, while the real battle is going on around them.[50] In arguably the strongest provocation directed against al-Maqdisi, Abu Qatada writes about himself that he 'is neither a Salafi, nor a Jihadi'—two concepts which Abu Qatada epitomises. His point is that he does not follow al-Maqdisi's view of a narrow SJM defined by a specific creed but prefers a more inclusive Jihadi movement that broadens the Jihadis' traditional focus on Salafi theology.[51]

Al-Uraydi would not leave Abu Qatada with the last word, however, and in response issued a direct message to his Jordanian colleague. Aware of the authority Abu Qatada commands, al-Uraydi is careful to address him with some rhetorical respect, while placing him at fault for the way HTS is treating Hurras al-Deen, including al-Uraydi himself. He insinuates that Abu Qatada facilitated HTS's crackdown on al-Qaida loyalists by broadening the definition of *extremism*. Al-Uraydi highlights that the proper use of this term is critical because some have used it to justify fighting al-Qaida loyalists.[52]

Taking a position in the middle of the ideological camps, Hani al-Sibai had all along been hesitant to choose sides between HTS and al-Qaida and between Abu Qatada and al-Maqdisi. While he had issued criticism of HTS on several occasions in 2017–18, it was never as fierce as that of al-Maqdisi. And on two occasions in 2018, he discussed the question of whether it is permissible for Jihadis to leave HTS to join another group despite HTS being the strongest Jihadi formation. Like Abu Qatada, al-Sibai argues that in the present Syrian context, the important thing is to fight as part of an Islamic group and not necessarily the group with the purest creed. Instead, one must expect that groups make mistakes, al-Sibai says, but in a remark implicitly addressed to HTS he warns that the red line is if a group begins to attack other Jihadis. In such a scenario, one must leave the group and join another.[53]

By the end of 2018, infighting among Jihadis in Syria had largely died out. There were still occasional confrontations between HTS and Islamic State cells in Idlib, and in the period December 2018–January 2019 hostilities broke out between HTS and Nour al-Deen al-Zinki which were eventually settled in a negotiated ceasefire. This lull in infighting did not imply that tensions had ceased to exist between groups. HTS amir al-Julani was evidently still annoyed with rival factions in Idlib, namely Hurras al-Deen and the JTS consisting of Ahrar al-Sham and al-Zinki, which later became part of the National Front for the Liberation of Syria (Jabhat wataniyya lil-tahrir souriyya). In a November 2018 video, he complained that

> In any work for the Islamic project, be it da'wa or jihad, people can be divided in three groups. The first group is the enemy. The second group are those confronting the enemy. And in this group are people who are within the ranks of the mujahideen or are working for Islam, but they assume a role, the role of de-moralization, the role of inaction, the role of an alarmist who abandons the people and attempts to terrorise them by the

> strength of the enemy and the weakness of the Muslims. They always try to make them doubt in the intentions of this battle or in the intentions of these services provided by those excellent people in service of Islam. So you see them doubting in this battle or saying that this is a political battle.

A major challenge for al-Julani was that the criticism of HTS's political focus did not come simply from figures outside his group. On February 1, 2019, Abu al-Yaqzan al-Masri, a senior religious official representing the hardliners with the group, announced his defection as a direct response to al-Julani declaring his support of Turkey's planned operations against the Kurds in northeast Syria.[54] Al-Masri had long been a critical voice within HTS and had previously said in a videotaped sermon in Idlib that Turkey's battle against the Kurdish YPG is 'between a secular army and a secular, atheist party; a battle that is one episode in a long struggle between Turkish and Kurdish nationalists, in which Islam has no stake, and God's word has no part.'[55] The immediate reaction from HTS was ambiguous. Al-Zubayr al-Ghazi called on al-Masri to remain in HTS despite his differences, saying that 'the brotherhood of faith is greater than the brotherhood of groups and organizations' (fa-ukhuwwat al-iman a'zam min ukhuwwat al-jama'at wa-l-tanzimat). Yet for the group, it was important to send a signal that going against the party line would not be tolerated. Hence, on the same day as al-Masri's resignation, HTS published a ruling stating that no one is allowed to publish fatwas before they have been approved by the shari'a council. Two days later, Abu Abdullah al-Shami sought to defend his group against al-Masri's criticism, writing that it is not HTS that is changing its position, as the critics claim, but rather the strategic context that is evolving, and that this requires the group to navigate the changing environment.

An even more embarrassing development for HTS occurred more than a year later in September 2019 when another veteran, Abu al-Abd Ashida, a senior military commander, head of Aleppo City and administrator of the group's Umar bin Khattab army, published a video lambasting HTS's leadership for corrupting the group militarily, methodologically and financially.[56] The leadership, he states, has turned the group into their personal kingdoms focused on power and money. Ashida surely knew the consequences that issuing the video would lead to, and indeed the reaction to it is illustrative of HTS's desire to exert complete control over the Jihadi environment in Idlib. He was dismissed from his position and arrested, along with a journalist who had shared the video. An interesting point raised in the video is that HTS has begun to increase its internal monitoring of 'critical voices' in opposition to the leadership, much like the extremists within the Islamic State. When HTS shura council member Abu Fath al-Farghali responded, he defended his group against the accusations while belittling Ashida for speaking publicly about such issues when the Jihadis are under severe pressure.[57]

Around the same time as al-Masri defected, the old tensions between HTS and Hurras al-Deen flared up again in relation to the rightful ownership of weapons, as well as issues related to creed and methodology. Abu Hummam al-Shami and al-Uraydi suggested establishing a group of 'independent' ideologues, namely Abu Muhammad al-Maqdisi, Abu Qatada al-Filastini, Nail bin Ghazi, Tariq Abdelhaleem, Hani al-Sibai and Sadiq al-Hashemi, to review the case and issue a judgment. Al-Maqdisi argued that adjudication was impossible, saying 'I won't judge because al-hay'a (HTS) has become like the state group [the Islamic State]. They don't accept judgement unless it satisfies them. And when it goes against them, they don't accept it from me or from Abu Qatada. And not from others.'[58] Abu Qatada was more diplomatic in his response, saying 'I won't adjudicate until I have been accepted by both parties. Perhaps I will talk but my condition does not permit ruling.'[59] In statements on their Telegram channels, Abdelhaleem and al-Sibai offered similar arguments. Abdelhaleem wrote that ruling in this case is impossible because it would require both parties to accept the ruling which could not be enforced. Afterwards al-Maqdisi, al-Sibai, Abdelhaleem, al-Hashemi and Nail bin Ghazi all agreed to mediate in the situation subject to acceptance by HTS. Abu Qatada never responded directly to the invitation but—confirming his general efforts in the last two years to promote reconciliation rather than provoke conflict—he wrote an ambiguous statement stressing that people should focus on good things rather than be sources of enmity.[60]

With the failure of yet another nascent reconciliation initiative, Abu Abdullah al-Shami and al-Uraydi would once again begin debating each other publicly through Telegram. In his response entitled 'Six Issues', al-Shami comments on the unresolved issue of weapons ownership by invoking a ruling by the late al-Qaida deputy Abu al-Khayr, concluding that the weapons are the property of HTS and under no circumstance must they be handed over to Hurras al-Deen. Al-Shami concludes that the weapons issue has been settled from a legal perspective, and thus HTS will not accept arbitration. In a parallel to the Islamic State's attitude in 2014, he nonetheless suggests that arbitration by the Salvation Government, the HTS-dominated government in Idlib, is a possibility. This comparison is picked up by al-Uraydi who claims that Hurras al-Deen has proof that Abu al-Khayr did not in fact rule in favour of HTS. But to satisfy al-Shami's demand, he suggests a combined council of independent ideologues and members of the Salvation Government to settle the conflict. In the end, no council was ever established, but senior al-Qaida figures continued to urge both groups not to fight each other and to resolve their differences through *legal judicial procedures* (tariq al-qada' al-shar'i).[61]

In the end the groups managed to forge a relationship which, despite the continued tensions, was tolerable to both parties. When an HTS fighter in February 2019 died from wounds resulting from an episode of infighting with Hurras al-Deen fighters in the Aleppo countryside, Hurras al-Deen quickly published its condolences and established a court to determine the fate of those responsible. Just a few days later, the two groups reached a deal concerning six issues to de-escalate the conflict. The agreement stipulated that provocations in the media should be halted and that the issue of personnel and weaponry going from one group to the other should be settled. A committee to supervise the implementation of the agreement was created, the statement notes, though the names of its members are not given.[62] The peace lasted until June 2020, when infighting really broke out between the two groups.

Yet the scholarly environment was not equally successful in finding peaceful ground. In late 2019, another round of debate took form—this time dealing with the issue of how to approach the Islamic State, or more precisely the Binali current within the Islamic State. Most likely as an attempt to attract followers of the Binali current, al-Maqdisi began issuing supportive statements on the late al-Binali and his colleagues in the Islamic State for their opposition to the more extreme current within the group. Unsurprisingly, this would lead Abu Qatada and several of his followers including Abu Mahmoud to launch attacks against al-Maqdisi, pointing out that al-Maqdisi was at fault for al-Binali's ideological extremism and speculating that al-Maqdisi was in the process of forming a new Jihadi group in the Levant consisting of hard-line al-Qaida members and 'moderate' remnants from the Islamic State.[63]

### *Renewed Tensions Outside the Levant*

Outside Syria the situation in 2018–19 was evolving slightly differently. Conflicting with al-Zawahiri's call for unity, al-Qaida affiliates in Yemen and in Somalia played a central role in reigniting conflict with local Islamic State affiliates. These developments largely resulted from changing context and inter-group dynamics that triggered a more assertive approach from al-Qaida affiliates. These events also illustrate how group rationales vary within a group in various geographical locations. So, while al-Zawahiri promoted a unitarian rationale, local al-Qaida affiliates would increasingly begin to follow hegemonic rationales.

In Yemen, prior to 2018, local al-Qaida and Islamic State groups had managed to work out a functioning Cold War relationship, coexisting peacefully while criticising one another in their publications. In this competitive environment, AQAP and ISY attempted to position their respective groups favourably at the expense of their opponents. On several occasions, ISY would criticise AQAP for its alleged relations to the Yemeni army and its unwillingness to implement shari'a legislation despite controlling territory.[64] Back in 2015, AQAP ideologue Khalid Saeed Batarfi had responded to some of this criticism while hitting back at ISY. A similar dynamic continued from late 2015 until 2017. Adopting an internal perspective, AQAP released an hour-long video entitled 'Guardians of the Shari'a' (hurras al-shari'a) featuring clips with iconic Jihadi figures like Bin Laden, Anwar al-Awlaki and Nasir al-Wuhayshi. The video discussed the group's strategy including its long term objectives and its dedication to implementing shari'a.[65] This was later complemented by an explicit focus on its rival, which took the form of several publications that sought to ridicule ISY and its struggle against the Houthis.[66] In response, ISY would eventually issue its own video elaborating on the methodology of the group in Yemen.[67]

In mid-2018, the inter-group relationship escalated from controlled tensions to military confrontations.[68] In early July, an al-Qaida-supportive channel on Telegram reported that ISY had killed thirteen fighters from AQAP, who then retaliated by killing twenty-five ISY fighters. Three days later, AQAP would again strike ISY positions in Qayfa which, along with al-Humayda, turned into an epicentre of infighting between the two groups. Tensions between ISY and AQAP had already begun to rise a week earlier when an alleged ISY defector provided his testimony about the wrongdoings and extremist tendencies of his former comrades, not least their extensive reliance on takfir. Soon after these initial military confrontations, the conflict would take a new turn and become more public when, on July 15, the Islamic State's Amaq News Agency uploaded a video showing thirteen AQAP fighters who had been arrested after an incident at an ISY controlled checkpoint.[69] In this video and another published soon after, the imprisoned fighters explain from what appears to be a cave that it was in fact their fellow AQAP fighters who provoked the skirmish.[70] In the second video, one of the imprisoned fighters even claims that his group's leadership authorised fighting ISY the previous year, indicating that AQAP was the aggressor in the conflict. Five days later, the Islamic State publicised an account of an alleged al-Qaida defector, Abu Muslim al-Hashimi, who scorned his former group for cooperating with the Yemeni army.

While these media publications added a new dimension to the conflict in Yemen, they were also an attempt to manipulate the conflict narrative. For instance, AQAP's version of events differed radically from that of the imprisoned fighters. Al-Qaida responded with a statement emphasising that the two groups have so far agreed to let one another's fighters pass through checkpoints—an unusual agreement considering the ongoing conflict between the groups in most other battlefields—but that on this occasion, ISY fighters violated the agreement and arrested its members. Furthermore, AQAP claims that contrary to its competitor's version of events it tried to negotiate the release of the prisoners but that the Islamic State refused any such negotiations.

On August 8, AQAP would escalate the conflict further when the group published a video showing four captured ISY fighters. This acted as a form of retaliation and leverage. As in the ISY videos, the AQAP production includes clips of the four imprisoned fighters 'calmly' telling the 'truth' about their own group: that ISY's leadership proclaims takfir on AQAP, that it does not care about local Yemeni tribes and that fighting AQAP is in fact the group's main priority. Later in August, AQAP would issue another statement linking the behaviour of ISY to that of the Islamic State in other battlefields like Syria and Iraq, stressing its deviated methodology and emphasising how it has raised its sword against other Muslims. Throughout the remainder of 2018–19, such discursive retaliations became a regular phenomenon with each group attempting to ridicule and delegitimise the opponent or influence the narrative of the conflict.[71] At the same time, military confrontations escalated to the point where AQAP became the primary victim of ISY operational activity,[72] and from August–September 2019 AQAP similarly stepped up its military attacks against ISY. Recalling events in Syria in 2016, ISY would also begin to publish photos and videos of military operations against AQAP and of assassinations.

In late 2018, military confrontations also erupted across the Gulf of Aden in Somalia in a second round of fighting following the 2015 purge of Somali Islamic State-sympathetic elements by al-Shabab's internal security forces. Infighting between the two groups in Somalia largely died out in 2016–17 with only a few incidents reported. This lull in infighting allegedly gave way to small-scale cooperation between the groups despite ISS managing to expand its geographical presence and operational activity, which was inherently at odds with al-Shabab's desire to maintain a domestic Jihadi monopoly.[73] As noted by Weiss, the re-eruption of inter-group hostilities probably resulted from the ISS's increased assertiveness and strengthened power base, which involved competition for control of taxation.[74] A further novelty of the second round of infighting is how publicly it was communicated compared to the 2015 hostilities. Illustrating developments seen in other theatres, both al-Shabab and ISS openly discussed the infighting, and on one occasion ISS issued a communique claiming responsibility for an attack against al-Shabab.

In their weekly *al-Naba* newspaper, the Islamic State accused al-Shabab of initiating the second crackdown on its members approximately three years after the first campaign came to an end. The article explains how al-Shabab is killing and arresting everyone suspected of sympathising with ISS or simply for possessing Islamic State videos on their computers. It also claims that ISS supporters already had been assassinated in Mogadishu and Bosasom.[75] The primary purpose of the article thus appears to have been to justify ISS launching retaliations against al-Shabab fighters. These took place just a month later.

While the killings appear to have begun in October—al-Shabab is suspected of assassinating ISS deputy leader Mahad Maalin in that month—the conflict escalated further in mid-December when al-Shabab fighters attacked unprepared ISS members in the Cal Miskaad mountains east of Bosaso, killing three and capturing one. On the following day, ISS fighters, in an attempt to reclaim lost territory, retaliated and managed to kill fourteen al-Shabab fighters. When ISS claimed the attack on December 16, it was the first time that one of the two groups publicly took responsibility for an attack against its rival.[76] The attack took place in Bir Mirali, southwest of Qandala in Puntland, ISS's domestic stronghold. It was initiated by ISS fighters, but, as the statement suggests, it was made to frustrate al-Shabab's preparations for an upcoming attack.

While military confrontations continued into 2019, it was al-Shabab's written reaction to the events that is most interesting. On December 20, 2018, the group's general command (al-qiyada al-amma) issued a lengthy statement expounding on the wrongdoings of ISS and instructing its fighters in how to deal with the rival. The statement accuses ISS of 'igniting the fire of sedition' (yaqtadihu nar al-fitna) and thus diverting focus away from the war against the crusaders and the Somali state. The al-Shabab leadership feels that it is obliged to be explicit about the true nature of the conflict between the Jihadis of al-Shabab and ISS because it is a distinction between *truth* (haqq) and *falsehood* (batil). The statement then proceeds to list nine *infections* (afsad) of ISS: (1) discouraging Muslims from fighting the enemy and encouraging them to leave Jihad, (2) the shedding of impermissible blood, (3) seizing money from Muslims and appropriating their property, (4) takfir on the fighting sects (al-tawaif al-mujahada), (5) lying and breaking covenants, (6) broadcasting *fake news* (arajif) to their sympathisers, (7) harbouring *hypocrites* (munafiqun) and establishing dubious relationships with infidel regimes, (8) fanaticism which has led the group to introduce innovations into religion such as making takfir on people who refused to give bay'a to al-Baghdadi, and (9) wasting their efforts fighting the wrong enemy. The general command ends the statement by calling ISS *people of hypocrisy and corruption and injustice and immorality* (ahl al-nifaq wa fisq wa zalam wa fajur) and instructs al-Shabab fighters to treat this *disease* (da') with *effective medicine* (al-dawa' al-naji') and to confront it with *force* (quwwah) and *wisdom* (hikma). The following day, al-Shabab spokesman Ali Mohamud Rage announced a new military offensive through the group's Al-Andalus radio channel. The offensive, named 'Eradication of the Disease', was intended to target all ISS members in Somalia. Mentioning the statement by the general command, Rage says that the leadership had instructed al-Shabab fighters to 'eliminate the "disease" of IS [ISS] and uproot the tree that would be used to undermine the fruits of the Jihad.'[77]

The question is how the behaviour of al-Shabab and AQAP corresponds to the guidelines of al-Zawahiri. Ever since the fitna broke out, the al-Qaida leader has promoted a de-escalating and unifying discourse, and we know that in the context of Syria and Somalia he directly informed local al-Qaida affiliate leaders to abstain from confrontations.[78] In 2018, tensions between al-Qaida and the Islamic State were arguably at a historic low since their emergence in 2014 since both groups were preoccupied with internal affairs. The shift in strategic behaviour from peaceful coexistence to infighting in Yemen and Somalia thus illustrates the importance of local dynamics for understanding inter-group relations in civil wars and insurgencies. Unlike the hostile nature of the relationship between al-Qaida and the Islamic State in Syria, their affiliates in Yemen and Somalia initially found it more convenient to strike deals to prevent an escalation of their relationship while challenging one another in their media releases. In the Yemeni case, ISY saw its territorial presence continuously limited, and the group failed to embed itself sufficiently into local communities despite the favourable conditions offered by the ongoing war and its sectarian element. 'Desperation' and 'fighting to survive' are thus key concepts for understanding the group's rationale for more assertive action at the time. In Somalia, the situation was slightly different, with 2018 being ISS's most active year in terms of operational activity.[79] Nonetheless, the group remained a peripheral actor compared to al-Shabab. So, it is arguably more instructive to focus on the al-Qaida affiliates. The specific triggers of infighting remain challenging to identify and are most likely of local origin, but a conducive context for a more aggressive posture towards the Islamic State had emerged: the Islamic State was generally considered to be in crisis and over the previous few years a well-supported theological basis for attacking the group had been established. Both AQAP and al-Shabab considered themselves local hegemons and neither of them were interested in leaving space for competing Jihadi groups. Hence, with al-Baghdadi's organisation suffering, it was time for the al-Qaida affiliates to reclaim their local hegemony as quietly as possible.

### *Conclusions*

In a similar way to non-religious groups and movements, the SJM's vulnerability is connected to its internal heterogeneity and to external pressures. The changing political situation on the ground in Syria and other places in 2016 intensified the internal tensions within both the Islamic State and al-Qaida's Syrian affiliate Jabhat al-Nusra. This led to an internalisation of conflict dynamics that were previously dominated by inter-group conflict. This shift was partly the result of changes in groups' external environment and the political interests and agency of key individuals within the groups. The result was increasing factionalism within the Islamic State and al-Qaida, which eventually led to group splinters and renewed intergroup tensions.

To some extent this represents the ending of one conflict cycle and the beginning of a new one, which follows patterns witnessed in the early stage of the conflict in 2013–14. This is interesting and helpful because it confirms the analyses of patterns, or conditions, that characterise intra-Jihadi conflict: tensions emerge, possibly within a group which then splits, and are followed by a discursive process to frame the rival through certain theological terms that legitimate a specific reaction. Attempts to manage escalating conflict dynamics through de-escalation and reconciliation initiatives are most often unsuccessful, allowing the conflict to continue.

These events led to a changed conflict environment in 2018–19 compared to 2013–14. Inter-group conflict is still occurring but is secondary to intra-group conflict, which is likely to become the main driving force of intra-Jihadi evolution in the coming years. Such main drivers include:

- A factionalised Islamic State trying to manage a transition period under the leadership of the new caliph,
- HTS hoping to ensure that its increasingly pragmatic approach will not repel more ideologically rigid members,
- Al-Qaida attempting to navigate in an SJM where it is surrounded by more moderate and more extreme groups,
- The Taliban continuing to interact with an international political system that is highly contentious internally, and
- JNIM potentially getting involved in negotiations with the Malian government.

However, this chapter also cements how inter-group conflict remains detrimental to the SJM and continues to spread outside of the Levant, largely determined by local dynamics but aligning with global narratives. Such parallel dynamics are likely to continue locally as long a hegemonic rationale remains dominant.

# EPILOGUE

When Abu Khalid al-Suri was killed by an Islamic State suicide bomber in late February 2014, it sent shockwaves through the SJM. Al-Suri's Jihadi pedigree as an Afghan veteran, a senior Ahrar al-Sham commander, a personal friend of Bin Laden and al-Zawahiri and a figure in charge of mediation between the Islamic State and Jabhat al-Nusra meant that his death was a critical escalation of the already brewing tensions within Syria's Jihadi environment. The following months and years would reveal that al-Suri's assassination was only the beginning of what would turn into the worst episode of fitna, or internal conflict, in the SJM's approximately-sixty-year history, seriously threatening it from the inside. The conflict that emerged in the ensuing years would come in discursive and militant manifestations and spread from its point of origin in Syria to most other active Jihadi battlefields including Afghanistan, Yemen, Somalia, Libya, Egypt, Nigeria and Mali. Former brothers-in-arms would suddenly turn their rifles and bombs against one another, killing several thousand fellow Jihadis, while ideologues drafted one publication after another vilifying their new rivals and legitimising attacks on them.

Jihadis are acutely aware that fitna is highly controversial and strategically counterproductive. They continuously warn about the negative impact of fratricide, bickering and allegations that divert focus from the primary enemy and deprive them of precious resources. This frustration is clear in the words of a senior al-Qaida leader in June 2019:

> May Allah not give the Kuffar [unbelievers] opportunity to laugh here [Khorasan] like in Iraq and Levant. May Allah instead give victory to ahl al-sunnah wa-l-Jamaah in Iraq and Levant and end this ISIS [Islamic State] fitna forever which has stabbed Jihad and the caliphate in the back. Surely this is the most difficult and deadly fitna for the Jihad and the mujahidin during these forty years of Jihad. Even Qadiani [Ahmadiyya] did not spoil the face of Jihad as much as this fitna has done.[1]

During the first two years of the conflict, academics and analysts concluded unanimously that al-Zawahiri had lost the authority he inherited from Bin Laden and that under the Egyptian's rule, al-Qaida was losing the internal war. The gravity of the situation for the al-Qaida leader is well captured in a quotation from a Jihadi forum in which a user sharply questions al-Zawahiri's authority, concluding 'Jihad was orphaned after you [Zawahiri] departed [from Bin Laden], and we [the Jihadis have all become] orphans!!'[2] Over the years, however, al-Qaida somehow managed to cope with the challenges and rebuild its position within the SJM to ensure that it remains a potent actor in several battlefields around the world while commanding respect from its cadres.

This book's main argument is that Jihadis are both *ordinary* and *idiosyncratic* in terms of their internal conflict processes. In much of the literature on Jihadism, ideological and theological cleavages are seen as the main drivers of conflict, yet this study illustrates that intra-Jihadi conflict is primarily a politically-driven process striving for power and authority, informed by ideological divisions and justified through a religious terminology. In this way Jihadis resemble other types of movements (be they insurgents, nationalist, secular or non-militant movements) in that political power struggles are the primary driving force leading to infighting. At the same time, they stand out for the substantial influence of religion in informing the normative order of the SJM, which influences not only *why* internal conflict occurs but also the process of *how* it occurs, via specific mechanisms that promote violence or peace.

This is generally confirmed, to varying degrees, in the various episodes of internal conflict covered in this book, with groups following a hegemonic rationale with an ambition to dominate the Jihadi movement locally, regionally or even globally. Simultaneously, in some examples the conflict process has been mitigated through the coexistence of a unitarian rationale emphasising de escalation. Yet while such rationales inform how groups view one another and their respective role within the broader movement, they are insufficient to account for the complexity of the process of conflict eruption. We see how various mechanisms on a macro-, meso- and micro-level of analysis impact the context groups operate within, the relative balance of power, the discourse of conflict, and the movement's normative order. Understanding these features enables a more nuanced analysis of both the behaviour of Jihadi groups and the dynamics of the broader movement in the future.

## *Replay of Events*

Now, with the door to Jihadi fratricide wide open, the pressing question is how Jihadis will attempt to manage internal tensions and rivalry and to ensure that conflict does not spiral out of control to the extent that it destroys the Jihadi project—all while groups still manage to fulfil their respective ambitions. The analysis in this book covers the period 2014–19, yet events in the following years illustrate a replay of events, underlining that internal conflict is likely to continue. The year 2020 had only just started when the situation in the Sahel exploded, thus finally ending the *Sahelian exception*. Here, the local Islamic State and al-Qaida affiliates—ISGS and JNIM—had, until mid-2019, managed to work out a balanced coexistence that occasionally involved strategic cooperation.[3] In the latter part of 2019, however, tensions came to dominate interpersonal ties and strategic considerations. The main drivers were ISGS's formal incorporation into the ISWA province in March 2019, which implied an increasing pressure from the Islamic State on its Saharan province to confront JNIM, and internal dissatisfaction within JNIM that resulted from issues of how to divide war spoils and the implementation of shari'a. This internal turmoil enabled ISGS to convince segments of JNIM fighters to shift side, which had an instrumental impact on the inter-group power balance.

While rumours started to emerge of infighting between the two groups in late 2019, it was not until early January 2020 that these tensions regularly started to manifest themselves in militant skirmishes.[4] At first, both groups remained silent, but in a lengthy May 2020 article featured in its *al-Naba* magazine, the Islamic State finally explained the growing tensions over the previous months, arguing that JNIM exploited the Takuba military campaign against ISGS forces that largely excluded targeting the al-Qaida affiliate.[5] Later that same month, the new Islamic State spokesman Abu Hamza al-Qurayshi further explained the escalation. Labelling JNIM as *apostates of al-Qaida*, he said that the group is fighting the war of Western militaries in return for inclusion in political negotiations. This only added fuel to the rumours of upcoming negotiations between the Malian government and JNIM after the latter had issued a statement on March 8, 2020 accepting negotiations with the regime *if* French/MINUSMA forces pull out. In the words of Abu Hamza 'the soldiers of the caliphate had postponed fighting them [JNIM] and persevered against their harm for many years. They call their followers to righteousness with kindness and argue with their commanders and students of knowledge with kindness.' In return, he explains, JNIM accuses ISGS of being khawarij. In a final warning, the spokesman threatens that ISGS' response will be tough: 'Only iron fights iron. When they return to fighting us, we fight them again.'[6] Over the summer, the credibility of the threat was confirmed with several military skirmishes between the two groups, and in early August, ISGS officially claimed an attack against JNIM for the first time in one of the Islamic State's traditional communiques. Now, the Sahel had joined the global Jihadi civil war.

In Syria, where it all started, the military crises and geographical division of both the Islamic State and al-Qaida implied that the groups were no longer prioritising the targeting of one another. Both groups, however, were still facing several challenges to their internal cohesion while suffering from pressure from HTS. Especially in Idlib, tensions between HTS and Hurras al-Deen started to intensify once again in June. The spark was the establishment on June 12, 2020 of a new operation room comprised of Hurras al-Deen and four other Jihadi groups, including several recent defectors from HTS.

Within the following ten days, HTS moved to arrest two former senior commanders, Abu Salah al-Uzbeki and Abu Malik al-Tali, who had joined the new operation room, and on the night of June 22, the first military confrontation occurred in the village of Arab Saeed. Over the following days, HTS would dismantle checkpoints and headquarters controlled by members of the operation room, cementing the group's hegemonic position in Idlib. Although it only took five days before the conflict was settled through several local ceasefire negotiations and the interference of yet another scholarly peace initiative, the events gave rise to new reflections from the opposing parties. From the perspective of HTS, it was clear that the group would no longer tolerate any behaviour from rivalling Jihadi groups that went against its own agenda. Yet even more interesting was an article by Abu Muhammad al-Maqdisi offering a dramatically honest analysis of the Jihadi environment in Syria. HTS, he argued, had finally killed the Syrian Jihad and the group's dominance in Idlib only left two options for Syria's 'true Jihadis': either *hijack and transform* HTS from within or *disband and wait* for the group's eventual demise.[7]

In a further testament to its hegemonic ambitions, in summer 2021 HTS turned its attention to Junud al-Sham, the group of Chechen fighters under the command of Muslim al-Shishani who for years had fought side by side with HTS and its predecessor. In a public statement, HTS ordered al-Shishani to either join HTS or leave HTS-controlled territory around the Jabal al-Turkman area. Although al-Shishani and his fighters did relocate after mediation from TIP, skirmishes were later reported.

In Nigeria, the already tense situation between ISWA and Boko Haram would similarly escalate in 2021. Confrontations between the two groups had already taken place in the past, but now they began to target leadership figures. In May, ISWA fighters managed to track down the hideout of Abu Bakr Shekau, the amir of Boko Haram, killing his comrades before offering Shekau the opportunity to repent. Shekau, however, showed no interest in repenting and allegedly detonated his suicide vest. Three months later, in August, Boko Haram fighters took revenge, killing ISWA amir Abu Musab al-Barnawi in suspicious circumstances. Now, the fratricide was not only causing the death of rank and file but also claiming the lives of the most senior leaders who had been wanted figures for years.

Finally, in Afghanistan, after the Taliban's surprising takeover of the country in August 2021, infighting between the group and its rival ISKP flared up once again. Throughout 2019, the Taliban had decimated ISKP both in the northern and eastern part of the country, but the Islamic State affiliate managed to recover and rebuild, posing a challenge to the Taliban's governance. Between August and December 2021, ISKP claimed more than eighty attacks against the Taliban, while its leaders issued a string of publications targeting the Taliban's alleged nationalist ideology. In the meantime, the Taliban remained largely quiet about its crackdown on ISKP members, yet several thousands of Taliban fighters were deployed to the eastern provinces where they were instructed to hunt down ISKP fighters.

### *Fratricide: The Jihadis' Swan Song?*

Since 2014, the SJM has expanded to new battlefields, it has grown ideologically more diverse, and it has imploded. This begs the question: how do internal conflicts impact the SJM more broadly? Writing in 2015, Mustafa Hamid compared the evolving conflict within the SJM in Syria to the situation in Afghanistan in the early 1990s:

> Returning to the aftermath of Jalalabad, what is striking is that every group seems to have had a desire for immediate action, and operated under their own programme, with their own understanding of Jihad and preparation of the Umma, and a strong belief that everyone else should follow them. I think we can see now with events in Syria and the competition and infighting among the Salafi jihadi groups that history is repeating; it is like Jalalabad all over again.[8]

While Hamid was correct in identifying similarities between the contemporary intra-Jihadi conflict and historical precedents—Afghanistan and Algeria being just two examples—there is an important difference in terms of *scale*. Undoubtedly, today's fitna is the worst internal crisis the modern SJM has ever experienced.

The intra-Jihadi conflict between 2014 and 2019 represents a major crisis for the SJM, one that has threatened its internal cohesion and proved to be a serious obstacle for its constituent groups in reaching their (relatively) common objectives. This should come as no surprise. Scholars of terrorism and political violence have consistently emphasised the negative impact of movement fragmentation and infighting on reaching strategic goals.[9] Even Jihadis themselves have noted the historical and contemporary destructive impact of fitna on the movement's strategic objectives.[10] Some scholars, however, have noted the potentially positive impact of the competitive environment within the SJM. For instance, Clint Watts distinguishes between *destructive* and *escalating* competition: the former refers to a situation where groups split and begin to attack each other, and the latter to a situation when groups separate geographically and attempt to outpace one another, leading to an increase in resources and a positive impact on both groups' image. Watts' argument is that up until the caliphate declaration, the relationship between al-Qaida and the Islamic State was defined by *destructive competition*, but that afterwards it changed to *escalating competition*.[11] While it is true that direct military confrontation did cool off between the two groups in the later part of 2014 due to geographical separation, this book shows that Watts' description is not only incorrect but much too simplistic, since it omits the destructive impact of non-military aspects of the intra-Jihadi conflict.

The intention here is not to rule out any potential positive impact of internal conflict. In theory, competition between groups within a movement can make them 'better', either by strengthening the 'quality' of their actions or diversifying their portfolio so that they can attract new supporters. Rather the argument presented here is that when competition arrives in the form of discursive contestation or infighting, its impact is largely detrimental to the movement as a whole. Based on the empirical analysis, six negative effects of internal conflict can be identified: *fratricidal killings, diversion from the main objective, fragmentation and polarisation, fratricidal socialisation, demobilisation* and *radicalisation.*

- *Fratricidal killings:* The most obvious direct negative consequence of internecine Jihadi conflict is that it results in Jihadis being killed. Numbers are difficult to determine precisely. Nonetheless, the conservative estimate presented in this book is that more than 8,000 Jihadis have died in Syria, Afghanistan, Somalia, Yemen, Egypt, Libya and Nigeria from the bullets (or bombs) of fellow—but rival—Jihadis. While the numbers are relatively low in Egypt and Nigeria, they are more significant in Somalia and Yemen, while in Syria and Afghanistan the numbers exceed one thousand in each country. Fratricidal killings are problematic for any movement but this is particularly the case for the SJM. Despite Jihadis' recent success in attracting large numbers of sympathisers, the militancy of Jihadism still only appeals to a very small number of people around the globe. Bearing in mind the superiority of their common enemy, groups need all possible resources. Killing off one another's most precious resource—dedicated fighters—thus leaves the movement as a whole worse off.
- *Diversion from the main objective:* While Jihadis traditionally have been divided between groups that prioritise the near enemy (local Arab regimes) and the far enemy (Israel and the West), such a distinction makes little sense in battlefields like Syria, Afghanistan, the Sahel and Somalia, where both the near enemy and the far enemy are present and (occasionally) fight on the same side. When Jihadis direct their guns against one another, this depletes critical resources and deflects the strategic focus away from their fight against their primary enemies. Time and again, Jihadis have warned about the danger of strategic blunders which eventually distort their greater ambitions. In his work on the Irish Republican movement, Morrison writes about the aftermath of an organisational split: the ensuing 'competition can often times distract the organisations from the pursuit of their purposive objectives with an over proportionate amount of time and energy being spent on competition between two groups who to many external observers may be regarded as indistinguishable in nature.' A similar conclusion is valid for the SJM. Usama Bin Laden

stressed the danger of opening too many battlefronts, while al-Zawahiri consistently pointed to the detrimental impact of infighting in his attempts to steer the movement back to its main objective. Hafez has gone as far as to argue that rebel infighting is in fact the main reason why rebels—including Jihadis—lose their wars. While such an assertion is probably too charitable to Jihadis, the impact of strategic blunders resulting from infighting is undeniable.

- *Fragmentation and polarisation:* Never since its modern resurgence in the 1960s has the SJM been as fractured and polarised as now, both on a group level and an individual level. As this book shows, fratricide has led to intra/inter-group tensions, groups splintering and the establishment of new groups. The act of killing people ideologically close to oneself, some even being former brothers-in-arms, inevitably gives rise to some level of communal distrust which is hard to heal. Jihadi groups are military organisations and, as any soldier would acknowledge, trust in the person standing next to you is essential. The split between al-Qaida and the Islamic State in 2014 forced an unprecedented polarisation on the broader SJM that only worsened in the aftermath of HTS's split from al-Qaida. The Islamic State required other Jihadi groups to choose sides based on the idea that you are either with us or against us. In theory, neutrality was not tolerated. This Manichean logic later infected the entire movement, even outside the Middle East region, with supporters of one group isolating themselves from rival groups' supporters.
- *Socialisation:* As already highlighted, the act of killing another Muslim or excommunicating someone from Islam is a highly sensitive and controversial issue. Yet Jihadis' justification for and execution of fratricide since 2014 has pushed the view that internecine infighting is an occasionally necessary and acceptable practice. In other words, and as described above, Jihadis have become socialised to fratricide. Della Porta writes that 'Socialization to violence happened in action'[12] and that 'Socialization into a cultural narrative of revenge and martyrdom has been said to be conducive to new waves of

terrorism.'[13] Hence, we can expect that the contemporary cultural narratives of internecine violence will breed new episodes of infighting in the future—especially among the younger generation of Jihadis, whose professional Jihadi experience has involved fighting other Jihadis almost to the same extent as fighting the primary enemy. Religious justifications for infighting are now readily available, and future Jihadis will grow up accustomed to the normality of criticising and attacking other Jihadis. While Jihadism has always been prone to internal conflict, this will likely be even more the case in the future after such an intense period of socialisation. This leaves the question of whether internecine conflict will become the new norm.

- *Radicalisation:* Jihadis are generally considered radicals, but the intensive, internal competitive environment has arguably led to a further radicalisation of ideas and behaviour. Competition and infighting has forced Jihadi groups to evolve and distinguish themselves from competitors through a process of diversification. While this dynamic can produce moderating effects, it also involves more extreme behaviour. Take the example of the use of violence: the predecessors of the Islamic State always employed extreme violence, but in its new iteration, the group has relied even more on violence in the form of regular (filmed) mass beheadings, burnings and sectarian massacres. On an ideational level, similar processes of radicalisation have occurred, partly to legitimise the group's political objectives. For instance, in order to enable attacks against fellow Jihadis, the Islamic State politicised the concept of excommunication to fit its operational needs. Needless to say, such politicisation is a slippery slope which has resulted in a vast broadening of internal conflict, and which has eventually become a problem *within* the group.
- *Demobilisation:* For some, however, fratricide and the dynamics of radicalisation are intolerable. They rebel against these—in their eyes—illegitimate practices by abandoning the Jihadi cause. Back in 2014, there were lots of stories of returning foreign fighters who were disillusioned with Jihad. One

> reason they offered was that they joined the Jihadi struggle to fight the Assad regime but ended up fighting other Muslims.[14] This demobilisation proved to be a problem in previous Jihadi battlefields such as Afghanistan in the 1990s, with Hegghammer pointing out the difficulties of mobilising against an internal enemy.[15] Other movements, as the example of Northern Ireland shows, have experienced similar problems.[16] Jihadis put major efforts into mobilisation, so it is highly counterproductive when their own actions have demobilising effects. While some groups do give attention to this problem, those driving internal conflict appear to consider it a necessary evil that is unavoidable while they are pursuing certain strategic objectives.

### *On the Path to Self-Destruction?*

Following the conclusion that the negative impact of internal conflict for the SJM is obvious, a relevant question to ask is whether internal conflict is in fact such a critical threat to the movement that it risks leading to self-destruction. This is the conclusion of Lahoud's eminent book *The Jihadis' Path to Self-Destruction*. Lahoud's argument is that—in a similar way to the historic Khawarij, whose extreme dedication to doctrinal rigidity and peculiar view of authority led to perpetual excommunication and eventually the movement's demise—modern-day Jihadis are on the path to self-destruction. She contends that while there are many differences between the Khawarij and Jihadis, the Jihadis' similar focus on doctrinal rigidity (expressed, in their conceptual framework, through a focus on al-wala' wa-l-bara') means that they will experience the same fate. She writes: 'As the seventh century military commander al-Muhallab said of the Kharijites [Khawarij], 'if they carry on like this…therein lies their destruction (halak),' a statement that is just as applicable to the jihadis today as it was to the Kharijites then.'[17] A similar albeit less religious argument, that *internal factors* are central to the demise of terrorist groups, has been presented by other scholars as well.[18]

The period from 2014–19 is a useful case study for assessing this argument. This time saw the fiercest internal conflict in the history of the SJM. Arguably the movement became more ideologically diverse in this era than ever before. For a movement that is supposed to have difficulties handling internal diversity, this period should be expected to lead to a movement seriously struggling for its existence. This argument gains strength from Davenport's work on how social movements die. He argues that organisational death depends on a combination of external factors (resource deprivation, problem depletion and state repression) and internal factors (among others, factionalisation and polarisation) and how they are handled and countered by the actors.[19] Inserting the SJM from 2014–19 into his framework, one could make a strong case for its imminent death.

This book, however, tells another story. While the impact of internal conflict is almost exclusively negative in relation to movement cohesion and attempts to reach strategic objectives, it did not result in an uncontrollable spiral of internal violence. The reason for this is that while intra-Jihadi relations may pose the biggest threat to the movement's demise, they also represent its greatest strength in the form of a pervasive level of religiously and strategically founded internal solidarity. During the period under scrutiny, conflict dynamics have been influenced as much by actors wanting to de-escalate tensions and unite the movement as by those attempting to escalate tensions and enable infighting.

Several actors have promoted the desire to reconcile and unite the movement. In particular, al-Qaida's leadership and some of the group's affiliates have consistently identified fitna as the biggest threat to the Jihadi project and pushed for a resolution to internal problems. This discourse comes from its leader al-Zawahiri, its official media productions, and its affiliate leaders. One recent example is:

> O brothers, bury the differences in this difficult time, and dispense with the propaganda through which we curse each other, as it will not end until it breaks the bonds of our entities and our jihadi gatherings, and then it leaves a fire of enmity, which will not be extinguished by sea water, and scars of grudges and hatred, which will not be erased by the passage of days and years.[20]

This *unitarian* rationale, which is characteristic of al-Qaida's leadership and some other groups and ideologues, has not been able to prevent conflict or reconcile conflicting parties on a larger scale. However, it has functioned as an essential counter-dynamic to the *hegemonist* rationale.

While these diverging rationales create a struggle between escalating and de-escalating dynamics, there is no doubt that the recent years of internal conflict have led to serious reciprocal distrust within the SJM, which will be an obstacle to intra-Jihadi cooperation in years to come. Trust—so essential to cooperation within military and clandestine organisations—has been severely eroded after years of infighting and discursive vilification. Al-Zawahiri was aware of this effect early on, writing:

> This painful history may hinder cooperation, because of the bitter trials that took place between the mujahideen, and which could make some of them fear to let forces or equipment of another party enter their areas. Therefore, it is necessary to take urgent procedures to restore confidence among the mujahideen, so that they can have a chance to achieve full cooperation in waging jihad against the Crusader-Safavid-secularist campaign on Iraq and Sham.[21]

Such distrust has already proved a problem when fighters from one group want to join another group. One example is how Islamic State fighters abandoning the group to join a rival have only been allowed to make the move after completing socialisation programmes to acclimatise themselves to the new group.[22]

## *Exploiting Fitna*

In light of fitna's detrimental impact, the instigation of and interference in internal conflict becomes an attractive option for state actors wishing to combat Jihadi groups. Strategic exploitation is not only effective but cost-efficient as a contribution to states' objective of weakening Jihadis. If successful, it could cause the SJM a high number of casualties, diverge focus away from state actors, hamper alliances and generally contribute to tensions, hence negatively affecting the degree of cohesion within the movement. The following three strategies are particularly well suited for external actors wanting to exploit internal conflict; *political involvement*, *military involvement* and the *spread of disinformation* (PsyOps). These efforts, outlined below, offer ways external actors can attempt to take advantage of the ongoing conflictual dynamics within the SJM and further exacerbate their impact.

Over recent years, state actors have successfully taken advantage of Jihadis' political interests to exploit their ideological weakness. The primary way that this happens is through cultivation of relations with Jihadi groups, which rivals perceive critically as a deviation from the proper methodology. The historical case of the Taliban is illustrative; over the years, the Taliban has stepped up its involvement in diplomatic processes and political peace negotiations. For al-Qaida, who maintained a close relationship to the Taliban and an affiliation to the group through a pledge of allegiance, this diplomatic relationship between the Taliban and the West was highly problematic. Inside the Taliban, hardliners also opposed political engagement. When the Islamic State expanded to Afghanistan, one of its main points of criticism of the Taliban was the group's alleged subservience to Western interests. In Syria, Turkey managed to establish close relations first with Ahrar al-Sham and subsequently with HTS. This evolved into a major point of contestation first between Ahrar al-Sham and HTS, and later within HTS and between the group and al-Qaida loyalists. Most recently, JNIM in the Sahel announced that the group would be willing to engage in negotiations with the Malian government, which placed further pressure on the group's relationship with ISGS.[23] By their very existence, these cordial relations between Jihadi groups and state actors are difficult to accept within the SJM and as a result they exercise strong pressure on the movement's ideological continuum. These sentiments have grown in strength because of numerous rumours that groups collaborate with states against other Jihadis. For example, in Idlib al-Qaida loyalists have time and again accused HTS of leaking information to Turkey and the US that was used to target al-Qaida leaders.[24] Similar accusations were made by the Binali faction within the Islamic State against their Hazimi rivals.

External actors can also affect intra-Jihadi conflict dynamics through military engagement. The most direct method is through *strategic targeting*. We know that specific individuals have been crucial as conflict mitigators managing the relationship between rivalling Jihadi groups, and their deaths were key to understanding how tensions escalated to infighting. In Yemen, AQAP commanders Mamun Hatem and Nabil al-Dhahab early on negotiated the relationship with the emerging Islamic State faction in Yemen. After they were killed in drone strikes in May 2015 and November 2014 respectively, the relationship between the groups became more volatile. In the Sahel, senior AQIM leaders Abu 'Iyadh al-Tunisi and Yahya Abu Hummam were similarly central figures managing the relationship with ISGS. When they were killed in February 2019 by French forces, tensions started to escalate, and the so-called 'Sahel-exception' was soon a thing of the past.[25] It is not known whether the intention of the killings was to destabilise inter-group relations or simply to weaken a specific group by taking out its senior figures. Yet the past years have shown the efficiency of strategic targeting in provoking intra-Jihadi tensions. These considerations are also relevant as a method of weakening one group or faction in a competitive relationship and as such affecting the inter/intra-group power dynamics. One example is the assassination of high-ranking al-Qaida leaders in Syria in 2019–20 and another is the killings of Binali figures.

Finally, the spread of disinformation is another way to sow division among Jihadi groups and individuals. Since 2014, there have been numerous examples of fake statements circulating online in the name of a specific group or individual. These efforts often aim at attacking opponents or portray the group in question in a controversial way to provoke tensions and sow confusion. While the authenticity of these statements is often called into doubt, the spread of disinformation remains a particularly cost-effective strategy to alter internal dynamics from a distance. Jihadis' reliance on digital media platforms to communicate and disseminate their material makes it relatively easy to push disinformation. This is shared through fake accounts disseminated across platforms to enhance its credibility and circulation.

### *(Re-)Defining the Jihadi Project*

Ernest May was right in pinpointing our general inability to *think in time*. Projecting the future evolution of the SJM is a particularly challenging endeavour, with the movement currently at a crossroads due to several developments: the caliphate's rise and fall, the movement's all-consuming internal conflict and polarisation, and the diversification of Jihadi ideology. Staying true to this book's methodological argument, forecasting future development is all the more complex because it does not exclusively depend on group strategy but also on the macro- and micro-environments that it operates within.

Many of the SJM's leading figures acknowledge the necessity of change for Jihadi actors in order to adjust to the evolving political and social environment. They all concur on the importance of broad popular support, but the challenges arise when this is combined with the necessity of aligning such support with religious principles and strategic and political interests. When the Islamic State's first caliph Abu Bakr al-Baghdadi was killed on October 26, 2019, it took the group five days to elect a new *caliph*: Abu Ibrahim al-Hashimi al-Qurayshi al-Hussaini. This suggests that the group will continue to pursue an exclusivist project, viewing itself as a *caliphate* among illegitimate *groups*. Despite its continued hegemonic ambitions, the group is likely to prioritise a process of rebuilding and internal consolidation in the short term. This will probably decrease—though not terminate—internal tensions within the movement on a global level. The new caliph's most pressing tasks will be to solve the internal issues of factionalism and the group's general loss of appeal, which is key to ensuring the continued loyalty of Islamic State provinces outside Syria and Iraq.

Al-Qaida's strategic reform process started more than a decade back and is likely to carry on. The group will continue to follow a pragmatic and gradualist strategy that focuses on building durable military, social and religious campaigns which accommodate local populations while following a hybridised ideology and adhering to Al-Qaida's religious principles. The leadership's focus continues to be a de-escalation of tensions within the SJM and the rebuilding of a unified structure under the tutelage of the al-Qaida–Taliban nexus.

While this involves a much more inclusivist approach than the Islamic State, it still considers the leadership, or at least the guidance, of an al-Qaida dominated vanguard as paramount for ensuring that the movement does not stray from the correct Jihadi methodology.

In comparison to the expectation of continuation by al-Qaida and the Islamic State, other Jihadis stress the necessity of structurally redefining the Jihadi project. This idea is mainly promoted by Abu Qatada and Abu Mahmoud al-Filastini through the discourse of *jihad al-umma* that both have expanded on in numerous publications since 2017 and in interviews. In their view, recent years have shown that the current strategy and identity of the SJM is not only an obstacle to success but also fails to align with the younger generation of Jihadis. They argue that nothing less than a major transformation of the SJM is sufficient, which will involve less focus on religious rigidity and a much looser structure devoid of exclusivist groups. Similar revision or redefinition processes have occurred in nationalist and revolutionary movements in their attempts to adjust to a changing political climate or because of their lack of success in terms of mobilisation and political objectives.

According to Abu Qatada and Abu Mahmoud, the problem is that the current group logic counters common movement objectives. In the new structure, which they envision, groups like al-Qaida and the Islamic State are superfluous and should be replaced by supra-group institutional frameworks to manage military campaigns. At first HTS and its attempt to merge Jihadi groups in Syria's northwest was considered a venue for realising this new structure locally, but as it turned out, the group would become embroiled in the same detrimental, polarising logics that it was intended to replace. Essentially, the vision they propose for the SJM is a movement that is primarily politically and militarily driven at the expense of religious rigidity. In the eyes of their critics, the risk of all this is a movement that is no longer loyal to the religious foundation that qualifies it be considered *Jihadi*. Or, summarised in the diagnostic words of Abu Qatada:

> 'The youth loves champions! They rather attend the *School of Rambo* than listen to me. If I tell them in a khutba that people

are not allowed to watch Barcelona versus Real Madrid, then no one listens. But *tanzim al-dawla* [Islamic State] was a bubble from the beginning. It was like a Viagra pill. It goes up fast, but also fast down. The problem is that the Jihadi movement has not gone forward since Afghanistan. Jihadists cannot take over immediately, we have to fight slowly.'[26]

# APPENDIX 1
## TIMELINE

| *Intra-Jihadi conflict events* | | *Political and military events* |
|---|---|---|
| | 2003 | |
| | March | Beginning of the Iraq War |
| | 2004 | |
| Al-Maqdisi criticises al-Zarqawi in a letter | July | |
| Abu Musab al-Zarqawi's group accepts to become al-Qaida in Iraq | October | |
| | 2005 | |
| Al-Zawahiri sends letter to al-Zarqawi | July | |
| Al-Zarqawi responds to al-Maqdisi's criticism | | |
| Abu Yahya al-Libi sends letter to al-Zarqawi | November | |
| Atiyyah sends letter to al-Zarqawi | December | |
| Abu Ali al-Anbari visits Waziristan | | |

| *Intra-Jihadi conflict events* | | *Political and military events* |
|---|---|---|
| | 2006 | |
| | January | Establishment of the Mujahideen Shura Council |
| | June | Al-Zarqawi is killed by US forces |
| | October | Establishment of the Islamic State of Iraq |
| Abu Umar al-Baghdadi declares that al-Qaida is nothing more than one group within the Islamic State of Iraq | December | |
| | 2007 | |
| Abu Yahya al-Libi sends letter to Abu Umar | April | |
| | 2011 | |
| | May | Usama Bin Laden is killed in a raid by US Special Forces in Abbottabad |
| Al-Baghdadi establishes Jabhat al-Nusra | Summer | |
| | August | Atiyyah killed in a drone strike |
| | 2012 | |
| | June | Abu Yahya al-Libi killed in a drone strike |
| | | Beginning of the diplomatic peace talks process in Geneva |
| | 2013 | |
| The Islamic State expands to Syria | April | |

| *Intra-Jihadi conflict events* | | *Political and military events* |
|---|---|---|
| Al-Zawahiri sends his ruling on the controversy between the Islamic State and Jabhat al-Nusra | May | |
| Al-Zawahiri publishes his guidelines | September | |
| Ahrar al-Sham's head of relief operations, Abu Ubayda al-Binnishi, killed by the Islamic State | | |
| Kidnapping and killing of Abu Sa'd al-Hadrami, the leader of Jabhat al-Nusra in the Raqqa | December | |
| Abu Rayyan, Ahrar al-Sham's amir in Tal Abyad, killed by the Islamic State | | |
| | 2014 | |
| The eruption of the Jihadi civil war | January | The Islamic State takes full control over Raqqa from other rebel groups |
| Al-Anbari makes takfir on the Islamic Front | | |
| Al-Zawahiri calls for reconciliation | | |
| Al-Qaida announces that the Islamic State is no longer part of the group | February | |
| The Islamic State kills Abu Khalid al-Suri | | |
| The Islamic State kills Jabhat al-Nusra's leader in Idlib, Abu Muhammad al-Fateh | April | |
| Al-Adnani's first speech attacking al-Qaida | | |

| *Intra-Jihadi conflict events* | | *Political and military events* |
|---|---|---|
| Al-Zawahiri publishes his testimony and calls for non-aggression against the Islamic State | May | First terror attack in the West connected to the Islamic State |
| Al-Adnani's second speech attacking al-Qaida | | |
| | June | The Islamic State captures Mosul |
| | | Establishment of the caliphate |
| | August - November | Beheading of Western hostages |
| | August | The Islamic State commits Yazidi massacre in Sinjar |
| | | US-led air campaign begins in Iraq |
| Infighting begins betwee Derna Mujahideen Shura Council and the Islamic State in Libya | September | US-led air campaign begins in Syria |
| | | Creation of AQIS |
| | October | Turkish parliament allows for military operations against the Islamic State |
| | November | The Islamic State announces its expansion to five countries: Yemen, Saudi Arabia, Egypt, Algeria and Libya |
| First episode of infighting between the Taliban and the Islamic State | December | |
| | 2015 | |
| The Islamic State's Wilayat al-Furat invites Jabhat al-Nusra fighters to repent | January | The Islamic State announces its province in Khorasan |

| *Intra-Jihadi conflict events* | | *Political and military events* |
|---|---|---|
| | | Turkey introduces stricter border policies |
| The Islamic State declares the distinction of the 'grayzone' | February | |
| Al-Zawahiri begins his *Islamic-Spring* series | March | Boko Haram pledges allegiance to the Islamic State |
| | | Establishment of Jaysh al-Fath |
| Ideologues issue fatwa making it legitimate to repel Islamic State attacks | June | The Islamic State announces its province in the Caucasus |
| | | AQAP amir al-Wuhayshi killed |
| | July | Taliban announces Mullah Umar's death |
| | September | Russia intervenes in Syria |
| | October | The Islamic State emerges in Somalia |
| The Islamic State declares Jabhat al-Nusra an apostate group | November | |
| Infighting begins in Somalia between al-Shabab and Islamic State loyalists | | |
| The Taliban's Zabul-massacre of the IMU | | |
| | December | Riyadh conference |
| | 2016 | |
| Al-Julani starts secret discussions about grand merger in Syria | January | The Islamic State announces its province in the Philippines |
| | March | Abu Ali al-Anbari killed |

| *Intra-Jihadi conflict events* | | *Political and military events* |
|---|---|---|
| First rounds of infighting between Jabhat al-Nusra and Jaysh al-Islam | April | |
| The Islamic State issues an internal ruling that al-Nusra is an apostate group | June | |
| Jabhat al-Nusra splits from AQ and establishes JFS | July | |
| Occasional infighting between ISWA and Boko Haram | August | Turkey intervenes in Syria |
| | | Al-Adnani killed in an airstrike |
| | September | Obama gives permission to target JFS |
| | | Russia–US negotiated ceasefire |
| Ahrar al-Sham and Jund al-Aqsa starts to fight | October | Beginning of Mosul offensive |
| | | Abu Faraj al-Masri killed in a drone strike |
| Second round of infighting between Ahrar al-Sham and Jund al-Aqsa | December | The Assad regime recaptures Aleppo |
| | | Astana peace talks begin |
| | 2017 | |
| Third round of infighting between Ahrar al-Sham and Jund al-Aqsa | January | Establishment of Hayat Tahrir al-Sham |
| First round of infighting between Ahrar al-Sham and JFS/HTS | | |
| Jund al-Aqsa splits in three groups | February | |
| Sami al-Uraydi defects from HTS | | |

| *Intra-Jihadi conflict events* | | *Political and military events* |
|---|---|---|
| | | Abu Khayr al-Masri is killed in a US drone strike |
| | March | Establishment of JNIM |
| HTS - al-Qaida split becomes public | April | MOAB bomb blast in Afghanistan |
| | | Iraqi vice president Allawi says there are talks between AQ and the Islamic State about a merger |
| | May | Turki al-Binali killed in a US air strike |
| HTS begins to target Islamic State cells in Idlib | June | Raqqa offensive begins |
| | July | Mosul recaptured |
| HTS and Nour al-Deen al-Zinki begin to fight | August | |
| Jaysh al-Ahrar leaves HTS | September | Al-Muhaysini and al-Ulayni defect from HTS |
| | October | Turkey announces it is ready to launch major offensive against HTS in Idlib |
| | | Raqqa recaptured |
| | | The Islamic State's *al-Naba* newspaper called on its followers to switch to an insurgency |
| HTS arrest al-Qaida loyalists | November | HTS establishes its National Salvation Government |
| Infighting begins between Jund al-Islam and the Islamic State in Egypt | | |

| *Intra-Jihadi conflict events* | | *Political and military events* |
|---|---|---|
| | December | The Islamic State begins referring to its group in Somalia as a province |
| | 2018 | |
| | January | Turkey intervenes in Afrin. HTS is criticised for assisting Turkey's convoys. |
| First episode of infighting between Lashkar-e-Islam and the Islamic State in Afghanistan | February | |
| The Islamic State makes takfir on Hurras al-Deen | April | |
| HTS kills a member of Hurras al-Deen | May | |
| Infighting begins in Yemen between AQAP and the Islamic State | July | |
| Hurras al-Deen and the Islamic State kill one fighter each from the other group | | |
| | August | Turkey lists HTS as a terrorist organisation |
| | | The Islamic State announces group in Central Africa |
| Second round of infighting between al-Shabab and the Islamic State | October | |
| | 2019 | |
| Hurras al-Deen kills a member of HTS | February | |
| | April | SDF declares the Islamic State eliminated after taking Baghouz |

| *Intra-Jihadi conflict events* | | *Political and military events* |
|---|---|---|
| | May | The Islamic State officially accepts the pledge of allegiance from its group in the Sahel and announces a province in Turkey |
| | | The Islamic State splits its province in Khorasan to create new provinces in Pakistan and India as well as Afghanistan |

# APPENDIX 2

## LIST OF INDIVIDUALS

**Abdelmalik Droukdal:** Droukdal, or Abu Musab al-Wadud, was an Algerian veteran Jihadi. He was the amir of AQIM and had long-standing relations with al-Zawahiri. He was killed by French forces in June 2020 in Mali.

**Abdullah al-Muhaysini:** A Saudi scholar who studied under Sulayman al-Ulwan before migrating to Syria in 2013. During his time in Syria, he has mainly been working independently of any group except for a brief period where he joined HTS. Between 2014 and 2018, he was one of the most popular clerics among Jihadis in Syria.

**Abu Julaybib:** Also known as Abu Iyad al-Tubasi, he was a veteran al-Qaida member, a founding member of al-Nusra and a close companion of Abu Musab al-Zarqawi, whose sister he was married to. Abu Julaybib was initially a senior al-Nusra commander in Deraa, but he was later forced to locate to Idlib. He eventually left al-Nusra when the group split from al-Qaida and was a central figure in the establishment of Hurras al-Deen. Abu Julaybib was killed in December 2018.

**Abu Khadija al-Urduni:** Born Bilal Khuraysat, he was a Jordanian commander and shura council member of Hurras al-Deen. He was previously a high-ranking member of Jabhat al-Nusra.

**Abu Khallad al-Muhandis:** Born Sari Shihab, he was a Jordanian senior al-Qaida veteran with extensive experience from Afghanistan who was imprisoned in Iran between 2002 and 2015. He was the brother-in-law of Sayf al-Adl. Abu Khallad left for Syria together with Abu al-Qassam and turned into a prominent figure among the al-Qaida loyalists, who established Hurras al-Deen in 2018. He was briefly arrested by HTS in November–December 2017 and was eventually killed by an IED placed under his car in Idlib on August 22, 2019.

**Abu Abd al-Karim al-Khorasani:** Little is known about al-Khorasani other than he is an Egyptian high-ranking shura council member of al-Qaida and currently residing in Syria. He is an Afghan veteran and a former member of al-Jama'a al-Islamiyya. He likely spent time in prison in Iran and joined Abu al-Khayr in Syria in 2015. Since then al-Khorasani has headed several arbitration initiatives.

**Abu Abdullah al-Shami:** Real name Abd al-Rahim Atoun, he is the head of HTS's shura and shari'a councils. He is the group's highest ranking religious official and as such he serves as the group's primary bulwark against accusations of religious dilution.

**Abu Abdallah al-Muhajir:** An Egyptian ideologue and an Afghan veteran who taught in several military camps in Afghanistan. He was an influential mentor to Abu Musab al-Zarqawi.

**Abu Ali al-Anbari:** Born Abd al-Rahman Mustafa al-Qaduli, al-Anbari was a veteran leader in the Islamic State and its most senior theologian, who authored several important books and lectures on creed. It is assumed that prior to his death in March 2016, he was the second in the group's hierarchy after Abu Bakr al-Baghdadi.

**Anas Hasan Khattab:** Khattab is from Syria and is a founding member and shura council member of Jabhat al-Nusra. Now a high-ranking administrative leader in HTS, Anas Khattab has been actively engaged in the debate between HTS and al-Qaida loyalists in Syria.

**Abu al-Khayr al-Masri:** A former member of al-Zawahiri's Al Jihad who joined al-Qaida in 2001. Since then, he acted as a senior leader in the group despite his imprisonment in Iran. Sometime between 2011 and 2012 he became al-Qaida's second-in-command, which he remained until his death in Syria in February 2017.

**Abu al-Qassam al-Urduni:** Born Khalid Mustafa Khalifa al-Aruri, al-Qassam grew up in Zarqa with Abu Musab al-Zarqawi whom he accompanied to Afghanistan in 1989. He worked as a facilitator for al-Zarqawi in Iran, but at some point he was imprisoned. After his release in 2015, he travelled to Syria (now as a senior al-Qaida leader) and was instrumental in the schism between al-Nusra and al-Qaida loyalists. Al-Qassam was married to al-Zarqawi's sister. He was killed by a US drone strike in 2020.

**Abu Bakr al-Baghdadi**: Born Ibrahim al-Badri, al-Baghdadi was the caliph of the Islamic State between 2014 and 2019 and amir of the group since 2010. He was killed in an American operation in Idlib in November 2019.

**Abu Bakr al-Qahtani:** A senior religious official in the Islamic State who was a member of its shari'a council and Delegated Committee. Originally from Saudi Arabia, al-Qahtani was influential in convincing al-Nusra members to shift allegiance to al-Baghdadi. He was later a staunch ally of Turki al-Binali and is highlighted as the main internal opposition to the Hazimis.

**Abu Basir al-Tartusi:** Born Abd al-Munim Mustafa Halima in Tartus, Syria, he left for Peshawar in 1981 and later went to Zarqa in Jordan. After being expelled from Jordan, and a brief period in Yemen, al-Tartusi settled in London, where he became one of the most important ideologues within the city's radical environment. After the Syrian war broke out, al-Tartusi joined the rebellion on the side of Ahrar al-Sham and is now believed to be living in Istanbul.

**Abu Fath al-Farghali:** An Egyptian senior religious official in HTS. He migrated to Syria in 2012 to join Ahrar al-Sham, but in 2017 he shifted to HTS where he became a member of its shura council and fatwa committee. From 2002–2011 he was imprisoned in Aqrab prison.

**Abu Firas al-Suri:** Born Radwan Nammous, he was a Jihadi veteran from the 1980s in Syria and later in Afghanistan where he became one of the most important Arab trainers in the training camps. He migrated to Yemen in 2003, staying there until he moved back to Syria in 2013. Once in Syria he joined al-Nusra and became one of the group's most senior religious officials and its spokesperson until his death in 2016.

**Abu Hamza al-Muhajir:** Also known as Abu Ayyub al-Masri, al-Muhajir was a former Al Jihad member and the second amir of AQI after al-Zarqawi's death. He was killed in 2010 in an operation along with Abu Umar al-Baghdadi.

**Abu Hummam al-Suri:** Born Samir Hijazi, al-Suri is an Afghan veteran with a long history in al-Qaida. He graduated from Al-Farouq training camp as the second best student. After 9/11, he fled to Iraq, where he worked as a facilitator for al-Qaida until becoming a senior official in Jabhat al-Nusra. He is currently amir of Hurras al-Deen.

**Abu Khalid al-Suri:** Born Mohamed Bahaiah, al-Suri was a veteran Jihadi with experience from several battlefields. He was a close companion of Abu Musab al-Suri and the al-Qaida leadership. In Syria, he became a senior member of Ahrar al-Sham but was appointed by al-Zawahiri to head the reconciliation between al-Nusra and the Islamic State. In February 2014, Islamic State operatives killed him in Aleppo.

**Abu Mahmoud al-Filastini:** Born Ismail Kalam and living in London, Abu Mahmoud is a former student of Abu Qatada al-Filastini. He is close to HTS and a prominent writer on various social media platforms.

**Abu Mariya al-Qahtani:** Born Maysar Ben Ali Al-Jabouri, he is a senior member of HTS and a founding member of Jabhat al-Nusra. Previously a police officer, he joined AQI in 2003 or 2004. In 2011, al-Qahtani joined al-Julani's team of ISI leaders in Syria to establish al-Nusra, where he became the group's first amir in Deir ez-Zour. Despite being a highly controversial figure within the group, he has remained a member of its shura council. He previously studied under Umar al-Haddouchi.

**Abu Muhammad al-Adnani:** Born Taha Falaha in Syria's Idlib province, al-Adnani was the spokesperson of the Islamic State and the person announcing the caliphate in 2014. In addition to Turki al-Binali, he was the main voice within the Islamic State vilifying al-Qaida and its leaders.

**Abu Muhammad al-Furqan:** Born Wael Adel Salman al-Fayad al-Furqan, who is from Iraq, headed the Islamic State's Media Department and served as a member on its Delegated Committee. He was killed in September 2016.

**Abu Muhammad al-Julani:** Born Ahmad al-Shara, al-Julani is the amir of HTS. Born and raised in Syria, al-Julani joined the Iraqi insurgency in 2003 and rose in the ranks of al-Qaida in Iraq to become its governor in Ninawa. In 2011, he was chosen by al-Baghdadi to establish a front group in Syria that would become known as Jabhat al-Nusra, which al-Julani led until the merger that created HTS.

**Abu Muhammad al-Maqdisi:** Born Abu Muhammad 'Asim al-Barqawi, the Jordanian al-Maqdisi is considered one of the most influential ideologues within the SJM and is a respected figure within al-Qaida circles. He is the mentor of Abu Musab al-Zarqawi and Turki al-Binali. Since 2017, al-Maqdisi has been extremely critical of HTS.

**Abu Muhammad al-Masri:** Born Abdullah Ahmed Abdullah, he was an Egyptian senior operative and veteran al-Qaida leader with a seat on the group's shura council. Between 2017 and 2020, he was Ayman al-Zawahiri's second-in-command. Al-Masri was imprisoned in Iran from 2002 to 2015 and was killed in Tehran in 2020.

**Abu Musab al-Zarqawi:** The founder of Jama'at al-Tawhid wa-l-Jihad which later became al-Qaida in Iraq and finally the Islamic State. Mentee of Abu Abdallah al-Muhajir and Abu Muhammad al-Maqdisi.

**Abu Qatada al-Filastini:** Born Umar ibn Mahmud Abu Umar, he is a senior Jihadi ideologue who returned to Jordan in 2012 after living for many years in London. He is close to al-Qaida's amir Ayman al-Zawahiri and considered the preeminent Jihadi authority alive. From 2017, he started moving closer to HTS.

**Abu Sulayman al-Muhajir:** Born Mostafa Mahamed, al-Muhajir is an Egyptian–Australian Jihadi who migrated to Syria to become one of the spokespersons for al-Nusra and later Jabhat Fath al-Sham. He also participated in the reconciliation process between al-Nusra and the Islamic State in 2014. He left Jabhat Fath al-Sham in autumn of the same year.

**Abu Ubayda Abd-al-Hakim:** An Islamic State shura council member who oversaw outreach outside of Syria and Iraq. He attempted to lure AQIM to pledge allegiance to the Islamic State and was later in charge of reprimanding Islamic State dissidents in Yemen.

**Abu Umar al-Baghdadi:** Born in Iraq as Hamid al-Zawi, Abu Umar was the first amir of ISI. He was previously chief of staff in the Mujahideen Shura Council. He was killed in April 2010 together with Abu Hamza al-Muhajir.

**Abu Yahya al-Libi:** Born Mohamed Hassan Qaid. Al-Libi was a charismatic and theologically strong senior al-Qaida leader and former member of the Libyan Islamic Fighting Group. In 2005, he reprimanded Abu Musab al-Zarqawi and from 2011 he was in made in charge of al-Qaida's Syrian file. He was killed in June 2012 in a drone strike.

**Abu Yaqub al-Maqdisi:** Born Yusuf ibn Ahmad Simrin, the Jordanian al-Maqdisi was part of the Binali wing within the Islamic State and took over as Head of the Office of Research and Studies after Turki al-Binali's death. He was likely killed by the Islamic State in November or December 2018.

**Al-Zubayr al-Ghazi:** Al-Ghazi is from Gaza, where he graduated from the Islamic University's shari'a college. After migrating to Syria, al-Ghazi spent time with Abu Mariya al-Qahtani in Deir ez-Zour. He then became a shar'i in HTS's military department before eventually leaving the group.

**Atiyya Abd al-Rahman:** Better known simply as Atiyyah, he was a Libyan senior al-Qaida member and the group's general manager in 2010–11 with responsibility for affairs in Iraq. He was killed in an American drone strike in August 2011.

**Ayman al-Zawahiri:** Amir of al-Qaida since 2011. A medical doctor by training, al-Zawahiri is an it merged Jihadi veteran who once headed the Al Jihad group before merging with Bin Laden's al-Qaida in 2001. After Bin Laden's death, al-Zawahiri has remained committed to al-Qaida's pledge of allegiance to the Taliban.

**Hani al-Sibai:** An Egyptian ideologue and former Al Jihad member who now lives in London. Al-Sibai is a fierce critic of the Islamic State and highly supportive of Ayman al-Zawahiri.

**Nasir al-Wuhayshi:** Also known as Abu Basir, al-Wuhayshi was the amir of AQAP and prior to his death in a drone strike in June 2015 he was fourth in the al-Qaida hierarchy. In 2014, al-Zawahiri made him in charge of the Syria file responsible for settling the conflict between al-Nusra and the Islamic State.

**Sami al-Uraydi:** Born in Amman in 1973, al-Uraydi earned degrees in religious studies from the University of Jordan. A close companion of Abu Muhammad al-Maqdisi, he migrated to Syria after the civil war erupted where he joined Jabhat al-Nusra. Al-Uraydi became one of the group's most senior religious authorities and a member of its shura and shari'a councils. In 2017 he broke away from al-Nusra and is now a senior figure in the al-Qaida-linked group Hurras al-Deen.

**Sayf al-Adl:** His birth name is Mohammed Salah al-Din Zaidan. Al-Adl is an Egyptian senior al-Qaida leader and former colonel in the Egyptian special forces. Since summer 2002 he has been in Iran, held in house arrest until March 2015 and since released but prohibited from leaving the country. Al-Adl is currently an al-Qaida shura council member and Ayman al-Zawahiri's deputy.

**Tariq Abdelhaleem:** An Egyptian ideologue living in Canada. Together with Hani al-Sibai, he has authored several booklets targeting the Islamic State. He later sided with al-Qaida against HTS.

**Turki al-Binali:** A young Bahrani scholar who became the Islamic State's main voice of ideological opposition against al-Qaida. Later, he represented the 'moderate' wing of the Islamic State in the internal conflict between moderates and extremists. Al-Binali was killed in a US air strike in May 2016.

**Usama Bin Laden:** The founder and first amir of al-Qaida. Bin Laden led the group until May 2011 when he was killed in a US raid on his compound in Abbottabad, Pakistan. Until then, he was considered the symbol of the SJM.

# APPENDIX 3

## MOVEMENT FRAGMENTATION

Explanation of categories

- Loyal: Groups that remained *loyal* to their affiliation or linkage with the al-Qaida–Taliban nexus. These groups did suffer defections to the Islamic State, but not on a leadership level
- Fragmented: Groups that *fragmented* implying that leadership figures and considerable numbers of rank and file defected to the Islamic State, and
- Shifting allegiance: When entire groups *shifted* allegiance or linkage to the Islamic State

| *Group* | *AQ connection* | *Dynamic* | *Date* | *Category* |
|---|---|---|---|---|
| AQAP | AQ affiliate | Lost members but not on a leadership level. Dissidents comprised the majority of what became the Islamic State in Yemen. | - | Loyal |
| AQIM | AQ affiliate | Lost members but not on a leadership level. | - | Loyal |

| *Group* | *AQ connection* | *Dynamic* | *Date* | *Category* |
|---|---|---|---|---|
| Al-Shabab | AQ affiliate | Lost members but not on a leadership level. Dissidents comprised the majority of what became the Islamic State in Somalia. | - | Loyal |
| Jabhat al-Nusra | AQ affiliate | Lost a lot of members to the Islamic State in 2013, but mainly rank and file and foreign fighters. Later split from al-Qaida in July 2016. | - | Loyal |
| Boko Haram | AQ linked | The group was never an official al-Qaida affiliate but had close links. In March 2015 it became the Islamic State's province in West Africa. | March 2015 | Shifted allegiance |
| Turkestan Islamic Party | AQ–Taliban linked | Lost members but not on a leadership level. | - | Loyal |
| Jamaat-ul-Ahrar | AQ–Taliban linked | Split away from TTP in August 2014 and took a neutral position vis-à-vis the Islamic State, but in March 2015 the group merged with TTP. | September 2014 (neutral position) → March 2015 (merging with TTP) | Neutral/Loyal |

| *Group* | *AQ connection* | *Dynamic* | *Date* | *Category* |
|---|---|---|---|---|
| Islamic Movement of Uzbekistan | AQ–Taliban linked | The vast majority of the group (including its leadership) pledged allegiance to the Islamic State in June 2015. One year later, in June 2016, a small faction of the IMU that did not include any senior figures rejected the shift in allegiance. Already in September 2014, IMU leader Uthman Ghazi showed support for the Islamic State. | June 2015 and June 2016 | Shifted allegiance |
| Lashkar-e-Taiba | AQ–Taliban linked | Lost members but not on a leadership level. Dissidents joined the Islamic State's Khorasan Province. | - | Loyal |
| Lashkar-e-Jhangvi (LeJ) | AQ–Taliban linked | While LeJ did not pledge allegiance to the Islamic State, one of its factions—the LeJ al-Alami—regularly cooperated with the group. | - | Fragmented |

| *Group* | *AQ connection* | *Dynamic* | *Date* | *Category* |
|---|---|---|---|---|
| Ansar Bayt al-Maqdis | AQ linked | The group pledged allegiance to the Islamic State in November 2014 and became one of the first new Islamic State provinces outside Syria and Iraq when it changed name to the Islamic State Province in Sinai. Part of the group remained loyal to AQ, however, and established Al Murabitoon under the leadership of Hisham Ali Ashmawi. | November 2014 | Fragmented |
| Jemaah Islamiyya | AQ–Taliban linked | Abu Bashir, spiritual leader of JI, pledged allegiance to the Islamic State, but the remainder of the group's senior figures remained within JI. Some rank and file also joined the Islamic State. | - | Fragmented/ Loyal |
| Maute Group | AQ linked | The group pledged allegiance to the Islamic State and became part of its province in East Asia that was accepted in January 2016, but not publicly referred to before August 2018. | April 2015 | Shifted allegiance |

| *Group* | *AQ connection* | *Dynamic* | *Date* | *Category* |
|---|---|---|---|---|
| Abu Sayyaf | AQ linked | The vast majority of Abu Sayyaf fighters shifted allegiance to the Islamic State in July 2014 and became part of its province in East Asia that was accepted in January 2016, but not publicly referred to before August 2018. | July 2014 (Reiterated the pledge in Jan 2016) | Shifted allegiance |
| ICE | AQ linked | Pledges of allegiance from rank and file and senior figures from Chechnya and Dagestate were given in late 2014 and early 2015. In June 2015, much of the leadership of the group gave bay'a to the Islamic State and became the Islamic State in the Caucasus. | June 2015 | Fragmented |
| Jund al-Aqsa | AQ linked | Despite the group being closely related to Jabhat al-Nusra and being effectively considered a front group, it took a neutral approach to the Islamic State and rejected fighting it. Eventually, when Jund al-Aqsa dissolved in 2018, one faction joined the Islamic State. | 2018 | Neutral/ Fragmented |
| Harakat ul-Mujahideen | AQ–Taliban linked | Lost members but not on a leadership level. | - | Loyal |

| *Group* | *AQ connection* | *Dynamic* | *Date* | *Category* |
|---|---|---|---|---|
| al-Mourabitoun | Part of AQ affiliate | In May 2015, Abu Walid Sahraoui pledged allegiance to the Islamic State. The overall leader of al-Mourabitoun, Mokhtar Belmokhtar, rejected Sahraoui's pledge. | May 2015 | Fragmented |
| TTP | AQ–Taliban linked | A high number of members including senior level commanders and high-ranking figures joined the Islamic State. | 2014–15 | Fragmented |
| Ansar al-Islam | AQ linked | In August 2014, the vast majority of Ansar al-Islam's Iraqi faction pledged allegiance to the Islamic State, while confusion remains about the January 2015 pledge from its Syrian faction. | August 2014 and January 2015 | Fragmented |
| Jaysh al-Mujahideen | AQ linked | Umar al-Shishani, the leader of the group, joined the Islamic State in November 2013 with the majority of the group's fighters. | November 2013 | Fragmented |
| Minor groups | | | | |
| Mujahideen of East Timor (MIT) | AQ linked | Pledged allegiance to al-Baghdadi right after the caliphate was declared in 2014. | June 2014 | Shifted allegiance |

| *Group* | *AQ connection* | *Dynamic* | *Date* | *Category* |
|---|---|---|---|---|
| al-Ansar Battle Brigade (Mu'arakat al-Ansar) | AQ linked | Pledged allegiance to the Islamic State in July 2014 | July 2014 | Shifted allegiance |
| Al muhajiroun (pro al-Shabab) | AQ linked | Staying loyal to al-Shabab and al-Qaida despite defections. | - | Loyal |
| Mujahidin Shura Council in the Environs of Jerusalem (MSC) | AQ linked | Initially gave bay'a to al-Zawahiri, but in February 2014 it publicised its sympathy to the Islamic State (although there remains doubt about its allegiance). | February 2014 | Shifted allegiance |

# APPENDIX 4
## OVERVIEW OF SUPPORTER NETWORKS

| *Islamic State (sympathetic)* | *al-Qaida (sympathetic)* | *Hayat Tahrir al-Sham (sympathetic)* |
|---|---|---|
| | Supporters | |
| Gharib al-Sururiyya | al-Maqalaat | al-Maqalaat |
| Hussein ibn Mahmoud | Ahmed Hamdan | Abu Tamim al-Muhajir |
| Ahlam al-Nasr | Ibn al-Qaida | al-Dhahabi |
| Abu al-Harith al-Sami | Shaybat al-Hukama | Abu Muhammad Al-Shimali |
| Abu Azzam Tamimi | Zamray al-Umawi | |
| Abu Khattab al-Qurayshi | Shibl al-'Aqida | |
| Khabab al-Jazrawi | al-Ansari al-Barqawi | |
| Abu Haydara al-Shami | Hussein ibn Mahmoud | |
| Abu Mohamed Zakaria | Adnan Hadid | |
| Abu Juwairiya al-Shami | al-Manahija | |
| Abu Azzam al-Najdi | Abu Hamza | |
| Abu Osama Sinan Ghazi | Al-Tawhid Talab al-'Ilm | |
| Abu Ubayda al-Shinqiti | | |
| Abu Salama al-Shinqiti | | |
| Zakaria Abu Gharara | | |

| | | |
|---|---|---|
| Abu Musab al-Athari | | |
| Ubayda al-Athbaji | | |
| Abu Khabab al-'Iraqi | | |
| Musa'id ibn Bashir | | |
| Mustafa al-Iraqi | | |
| Abu Bara' al-Sayf | | |
| Abu al-Zubayr al-Lubnani | | |
| Yamani wa-aftakhir bi-Islami | | |
| Tamau'n | | |
| Supporter channels | | |
| Ahl al-Tawhid | GIMF | The Banner |
| Al Turath | Muwahideen | Al-Qalam |
| Abd al-Faqir Media Foundation | Fighting Journalists | Shamana Foundation |
| Al-Battar | Al-Bayyan Media Foundation | |
| Halummu | Al Hijrah Media | |
| Al-Wafa | Al-Thabat | |
| Khattab Media Foundation | | |
| Al-Ghuraba | | |
| Infos an-Nur | | |
| Ashhad Media | | |
| Asedaa Foundation | | |
| Constancy | | |
| Yaqeen Media | | |
| Remah | | |
| Muntasir Media | | |
| Al-Muhajireen Foundation | | |

| Turjuman Asawirti | | |
|---|---|---|
| Sawt al-Zarqawi | | |
| Al Irbad media foundation. | | |
| Al-Muntasir Media | | |
| Caliphate Cyber Shield | | |
| United Cyber Caliphate | | |
| Al Azm Media | | |
| Moata | | |
| al-Ma'arij | | |
| Ash-Shaff Media Foundation | | |
| Greenb1rd | | |
| Al-Mutarjim Foundation | | |
| Al-Saqri Foundation | | |
| Aafaq (Horizons) Electronic Foundation | | |
| Akhbar al-Khilafa 24 | | |

# APPENDIX 5

## OVERVIEW OF HAZIMIYYA AND BINALIYYA INDIVIDUALS

*Hazimiyya*

| *Name* | *Position* | *Phase* | *Nationality* | *Dead?* |
|---|---|---|---|---|
| Abu Jafar al-Hattab | Senior figure Official of the Diwan al-Ta'aleem | First phase | Tunisian | Dead |
| Abu Musab al-Tunisi | Senior figure Shar'i of Deir ez-Zour | First phase | Tunisian | Dead |
| Abu Asid al-Maghribi | - | First phase | Moroccan | Dead |
| Abu al-Hawra' al-Jaza'iri | Senior figure Awqaf official in Wilayat al-Raqqa | First phase | Algerian | Dead |
| Abu Khalid al-Sharqi | Senior figure Shar'i of Wilayat al-Raqqa and qadi of the security officials | First phase | UAE | Dead |
| Abu Abdullah al-Maghribi | - | First phase | Moroccan | Dead |
| Abu Muhammad al-Tunisi | Shar'i of Hasakah | First phase | Tunisian | - |

| *Name* | *Position* | *Phase* | *Nationality* | *Dead?* |
|---|---|---|---|---|
| Abu Usama al-Iraqi | Wali of Hasakah | First phase | Iraqi | - |
| Abu Umar al-Kuwaiti | Senior figure Shar'i | First phase | Kuwaiti | Dead |
| Abu Anisa al-Daghestani | - | First phase | Dagestani | - |
| Abu al-Bara' al-Madani | Senior figure | First phase | - | - |
| Abu Hajer al-Jazrawi | Senior figure | First phase | Saudi | - |
| Abu Suhaib al-Tunisi | Senior figure | First phase | Tunisian | - |
| Abu Ahmad al-Daghestani | Senior figure | First phase | Dagestani | - |
| Khattab al-Azeri | Senior figure Military commander | First phase | Azerbaijani | - |
| Umair al-Azeri | Senior figure | First phase | Azerbaijani | - |
| Alfir al-Azeri | Cell leader | Second phase | Azerbaijani | - |
| Abu Huraira al-Shishani | Cell leader | Second phase | Chechen | - |
| Abu Abdullah al-Tunisi | Cell leader | Second phase | Tunisian | - |
| Abu Suhail al-Masri | Cell leader | Second phase | Egyptian | - |
| Abu Ayub al-Tunisi | Cell leader | Second phase | Tunisian | - |
| Abu Muath al-Jazairi / Abu Muath al-Asimi | Senior figure | Third phase | Algerian | - |
| Abu Khaled al-Tunisi | - | Third phase | Tunisian | - |

| *Name* | *Position* | *Phase* | *Nationality* | *Dead?* |
|---|---|---|---|---|
| Abu Daoud al-Maghribi | - | Third phase | Moroccan | - |
| Abu Hafs al-Wad'ani / Jazrawi | Head of the Office for Methodological Inquiry and member of the Delegated Committee | Third phase | Saudi | - |
| Abu Hafs al-Masri | Amir in Jarablus, then amir of emigration and finally amir of Damascus | Third phase | Egyptian | - |
| Abu al-Dahdah al-Tunisi | Amir of fighters | Third phase | Tunisian | Dead |
| Abu Dajana al-Masri | Official in Media Department | Third phase | Egyptian | Dead |
| Abu Maram al-Jaza'iri | Official in Office for Methodological Inquiry | Third phase | Algerian | - |
| Abu Ahmed al-Faransi | - | Third phase | French | - |
| Talha Mulla Hussein | - | Third phase | - | - |
| Abu Hudhaifa al-Tunisi | Qadi Wilayat Aleppo | Third phase | Tunisian | - |
| Abu Zayd al-Iraqi | - | Third phase | Iraqi | - |
| Abu Hakim al-Urduni | Head of the Central Media Department | Third phase | Jordanian | - |
| Abu Saleh al-Iraqi | - | Third phase | Iraqi | - |
| Abu Abdullah al-Australi | Head of Central Media Department after Abu Hakim al-Urduni | Third phase | Australian | - |

| *Name* | *Position* | *Phase* | *Nationality* | *Dead?* |
|---|---|---|---|---|
| Abu Ishaq al-Iraqi | Deputy to al-Furqan in the Central Media Department | Third phase | Iraqi | - |
| Abu Muslim al-Masri | Head of Egyptian Hazimiyya faction | Third phase | Egyptian | - |
| Abu al-Mahi al-Muhajir | - | Third phase | Turkish | - |
| Abu Zayd al-Tunisi | - | Third phase | Tunisian | - |
| Abu Bakr al-Gharib | Member of the Media Tracking Committee | Third phase | Jordanian | Dead |
| Abu Majid al-Falastini (Abu Amer) | Assistant to Hajji 'Abd al-Nasir | Third phase | - | - |
| Abdel Nasser al-Turkmani | - | Third phase | Turkman | - |
| Abu Asma al-Tunisi | - | Third phase | Tunisian | - |
| Abu al-Yaman al-Tunisi | - | Third phase | Tunisian | - |
| Abu Abd al-Rahman al-Libi | - | Third phase | Libyan | - |
| Abu al-Mu'atasem al-Tunisi | - | Third phase | Tunisian | - |
| Jahabdha al-Tunisi | - | Third phase | Tunisian | - |
| Abou Shuaib al-Hadrami (Abu Turab al-Yemeni and Abou Hassan al-Sanaai) | Member of Shari'a council | Third phase | Yemeni | - |
| Abu Saad al-Atibi | - | Third phase | - | - |
| Abu al-Rabab al-Tunisi | Shar'i | Third phase | Tunisian | - |

| *Name* | *Position* | *Phase* | *Nationality* | *Dead?* |
|---|---|---|---|---|
| Abu al-Adham | Shar'i | Third phase | - | - |
| Abu al-Najem | Shar'i | Third phase | | - |
| Abu Maysara al-Tunisi | Shar'i | Third phase | Tunisian | - |
| Abu Ubada al-Tunisi | Shar'i | Third phase | Tunisian | - |
| Abu Talha al-Hijazi | Shar'i in the committee of the governor of Aleppo | Third phase | Saudi | - |
| Abu Omar al-Masri | Qadi of Damascus and Homs | Third phase | Egyptian | - |
| Abu al-Fidaa al-Tunisi | Department of Education in Al-Khayr | Third phase | Tunisian | - |

| *Binaliyya* | | | |
|---|---|---|---|
| *Name* | *Position* | *Nationality* | *Dead?* |
| Turki al-Binali | Amir of Office of Research and Studies | Bahraini | Dead |
| Khabbab al-Jazrawi | - | Saudi | Dead |
| Abu Sarraq al-Hashimi | - | - | - |
| Abu Abd al-Barr al-Salihi al-Kuwaiti | - | Kuwaiti | Dead |
| Abu Muhammad al-Husseini al-Hashimi | Office of Research and Studies | Saudi of Syrian origin | - |
| Abu Muslim al-Masri | - | Egyptian | - |
| Abu Bakr al-Qahtani | Member of Delegated Committee | Saudi | Dead |
| Abu 'Uthman al-Najdi | - | Saudi | Dead |

| *Name* | *Position* | *Nationality* | *Dead?* |
|---|---|---|---|
| Abu Yaqub al-Maqdisi | Amir of Office of Research and Studies after Turki al-Binali | Jordanian | Dead |
| Abu al-Mundhir al-Harbi al-Madani | Office of Research and Studies | Saudi | - |
| Abu Uthman al-Jazrawi | - | Saudi | - |
| Abu Musallam al-Masri | Amir of Grievances Department | Egyptian | Dead |
| Ghassan al-Jazrawi | - | Saudi | Dead |
| Abu Ahmad al-Iraqi | - | Iraqi | - |
| Abu Jandal al-Haili | - | - | - |
| Abu Abdul Rahman al-Shami al-Zarqawi | Member of Delegated Committee | Jordanian-Palestinian | Dead |
| Abu Mohammad al-Masri | Deputy of Turki al-Binali Member of delegated committee | Egyptian | Dead |
| Abu Hafs al-Hamdani al-Yemeni | Amir of the Shar'i Office of Soldiers and amir of the 'Ilm Council | Yemeni | Dead |
| Abu Abdul Rahman al-Gharib | - | - | Dead |
| Abu Eisa al-Masri | Imam | Egyptian | - |
| Abu 'Ubayda al-Shami | Qadi in Wilayat al-Baraka | Syrian | - |
| Bilal al-Shawashi | - | - | - |
| Abu Marwan al-Masri | Qadi in Diwan al-Jund | Egyptian | - |
| Abu Musab al-Sahrawi | - | - | Dead |
| Ibn Jubayr | | - | - |
| Abu al-Hasan al-Filistini (al-Jarrah) | Amir in the Diwan al-Da'wa wa al-Masajid | Palestinian | - |

| *Name* | *Position* | *Nationality* | *Dead?* |
|---|---|---|---|
| Abu Saif al-Urduni al-Hashimi | - | Jordanian | - |
| Abu Umar al-Yemeni | - | Yemeni | - |
| Abu Abd al-Rahman al-Sultan | - | - | - |
| Abu Muhammed al-Jawasi | - | - | - |
| Abu al-Abbas al-Jazrawi | Shar'i | Saudi | - |
| Muhammed al-Tamimi | Deputy Amir in the Diwan al-Qada wa al-Madhlim | - | - |
| Maysara al-Jazrawi | Qadi in Wilayat al-Furat | Saudi | - |
| Abu Yahya al-Hijazi al-Tunisi | Military shar'i | Tunisian | - |
| Abu Aya al-Tunisi | Qadi in Wilayat al-Khayr | Tunisian | - |
| Abu Hammam al-Tunisi | - | Tunisian | - |
| Abu Ali al-Harbi | - | - | - |
| Abu Jandal al-Hanbali | - | - | - |
| Abu al-Bara' al-Jazrawi | - | Saudi | Dead |

# NOTES

## VIGNETTES

1. Mustafa Hamid and Leah Farrall, *The Arabs at War in Afghanistan* (London: Hurst & Company, 2015), 162.
2. Camille Tawil, *Brothers in Arms. The Story of Al-Qaida and the Arab Jihadists* (London, London: SAQI, 2010), 96.
3. Abu Muhammed Al-'Adnani, ''udhran amir al-qai'da [Apologies, Amir of Al-Qaida],' *Al-Furqan Media Foundation*, May 11, 2014.
4. Abu Muhammed Al-'Adnani, 'hadha wa'd allah [This Is the Promise of Allah],' *The Islamic State, Al-'Itisam Media*, June 29, 2014.
5. Nelly Lahoud, *The Jihadis' Path to Self-Destruction* (London: C. Hurst & Co, 2010), 26.

## INTRODUCTION

1. Author's interview with Abdallah Anas, April 14, 2018 (London).
2. Some accounts state that there were five armed men approaching the base, but the above version of the events has been verified by several actors with intimate knowledge of the operation.
3. Islamic State, 'bayan mauqif al-dawlat al-Islamiyya min maqalat al-muftirin [Statement on the Position of the Islamic State to the Article of the Slanderers],' *Al-Itisam Media Foundation*, March 1, 2014.
4. Abu Khalid al-Suri, 'Untitled Statement,' January 16, 2014.
5. Gilles Kepel and Jean-Pierre Milelli, eds., *Al Qaeda in Its Own Words* (Boston: Harvard University Press, 2008), 6.
6. A chronology of the names of the group is as follows: Jama'at al-Tawhid wa-l-Jihad (1999–2004), al-Qaeda in Iraq (2004–06), Mujahideen Shura Council (January 15–October 12, 2006), Islamic State of Iraq or ISI (October 12, 2006–13), Islamic State of Iraq and Sham or ISIS/ISIL (2013–June 29, 2014), and now the Islamic State (June 29, 2014–).
7. Tricia Bacon, 'Alliance Hubs: Focal Points in the International Terrorist Landscape,' *Perspectives on Terrorism* 8, no. 4 (2014): 4–26. Zald and McCarthy also stress that with similar objectives, you would expect Jihadis to cooperate, see Mayer N Zald and John

D. McCarthy, 'Social Movement Industries: Competition and Cooperation Among Movement Organizations,' *CRSO Working Paper 201*, 1979, 1–32.

8. Hafez, 'Fratricidal Rebels: Ideological Extremity and Warring Factionalism in Civil Wars.'
9. Peter Krause, *Rebel Power: Why National Movements Compete, Fight, and Win* (New York: Cornell University Press, 2017).
10. Mia Bloom, *Dying to Kill: The Allure of Suicide Terror* (New York: Columbia University Press, 2005); Amarnath Amarasingam, *Pain, Pride, and Politics: Social Movement Activism and the Sri Lankan Tamil Diaspora in Canada* (London: University of Georgia Press, 2015); Paul Staniland, 'Between a Rock and a Hard Place: Insurgent Fratricide, Ethnic Defection, and the Rise of Pro-State Paramilitaries,' *Journal of Conflict Resolution* 56, no. 1 (2012): 16–40.
11. John Morrison, *Origins and Rise of Dissident Irish Republicanism: The Role and Impact of Organizational Splits* (London: Bloomsbury, 2013); Krause, *Rebel Power: Why National Movements Compete, Fight, and Win*.
12. Cyrus Ernesto Zirakzadeh, 'From Revolutionary Dreams to Organizational Fragmentation: Disputes over Violence within ETA and Sendero Luminoso,' *Terrorism and Political Violence* 14, no. 4 (2002): 66–92.
13. Krause, *Rebel Power: Why National Movements Compete, Fight, and Win*; Bloom, *Dying to Kill : The Allure of Suicide Terror*.
14. Staniland, 'Between a Rock and a Hard Place: Insurgent Fratricide, Ethnic Defection, and the Rise of pro-State Paramilitaries.'
15. Gilles Kepel, *Jihad: The Trail of Political Islam* (London: I.B. Tauris, 2006).
16. Hafez, 'Fratricidal Rebels: Ideological Extremity and Warring Factionalism in Civil Wars.'
17. See Quran Dictionary for the root *f-t-n*: http://corpus.quran.com/qurandictionary.jsp?q=ftn
18. See 'Fitna' in Brill's Encyclopedia of Islam, 2nd Edition, written by Louis Gardet. See also 'Civil war' in Gerhard Bowering et al., eds., *The Princeton Encyclopedia of Islamic Political Thought* (Princeton: Princeton University Press, 2013), 99–101.
19. For a thorough explanation of the term fitna, see Muhammad Ismail Al-Muqaddam, *basair fi fitna [Insights into Fitna]* (Alexandria: Dar al-Tawhid, 2009). A typical Salafi interpretation of the concept can be found here: https://islamqa.info/en/22899.
20. Shiraz Maher, *Salafi–Jihadism: The History of an Idea* (London: Hurst & Company, 2016), 75.
21. Abu Jafar Muhammed bin Jarir al-Tabari, *The History of al-Tabari: The First Civil War*, translation by G.R. Hawting, Volume XVI, 1996; Maher, *Salafi–Jihadism: The History of an Idea*, 77.
22. Al-Khawarij, or al-Haruriyyah/Muhakkima, refers to ancient Islamic sects that initially became infamous for killing Uthman and Ali. Unsurprisingly, this made the Khawarij hugely unpopular within the Muslim community due to their alleged extremism, which has made it a term applied in modern times to vilify one's opponent. There are discussions about how many sects the Khawarij divided into, but Crone mentions the four best known which are the Ibadiyya (only Khariji sect to survive today), Najdiyya (originally from Basra, but mainly active in Arabia and was suppressed in 693, but managed to survive a few centuries), Azariqa (originally from Basra but fled to Iran where they disappeared after suppression in 699) and Sufriyya (active in North Africa until 10th century). These four sects were divided in their view of the

status of non-khariji Muslims and the legality regarding living under kufr rule (some believed one should emigrate and establish their own polity, while others believed it was acceptable to live in kufr territory as long as one did not follow their rules). For more on the Khawarij, see Patricia Crone, *God's Rule: Government and Islam* (New York: Columbia University Press, 2004); T. Kenney, Jeffrey, *Muslim Rebels: Kharijites and the Politics of Extremism in Egypt* (Oxford: Oxford University Press, 2006). The notion of khawarij is also discussed by classical Islamic figures. Ibn Taymiyya discusses the sect in his majmu' al-fatawa and al-Tabari in his 40-volume *tarikh al-Tabari*.

23. Maher, *Salafi–Jihadism: The History of an Idea*, 76–78.
24. See Khaled Abou El Fadl, *Rebellion and Violence in Islamic Law* (New York: Cambridge University Press, 2001).
25. Jurists have debated to what extent the khawarij qualify for the legal status of rebels or bandits. Obviously the was an important issue for the jurists to resolve as it determined the approach and punishment of such people. Another category is 'sectarian groups' (ahl al ahwa') which typically includes mu'tazila, murji'a, shia and khawarij. Again, jurists have not agreed on how sectarian groups should be treated, if they're rebels or outright apostates. See Abou El Fadl, 246–49 and 252–53.
26. Abou El Fadl, 32. While judicial positions on rebellion were revised over time, two general trends can be identified, namely a traditionalist and a revisionist trend. Jurists of the traditionalist trend argued on one side that rulers must be obeyed but stressed that while rebels should be repelled, it was not allowed to execute them. This was only the case, however, if the rebels acted based on an interpretation (ta'wil) or a cause, which essentially distinguishes a rebel from a bandit. The revisionist trend in contrast argued that rebels were not to be considered bandits despite lacking an interpretation or cause.
27. Abou El Fadl, *Rebellion and Violence in Islamic Law*. The Quranic foundation for the negative view of rebels stems from Q49:9–10. While the verses legitimise fighting rebels, they do not define what a rebel is thus leaving it open for interpretation. As a result, accusations of being a rebel were frequently applied by supporters and opponents of the fourth caliph Ali ibn Abi Talib.
28. Muhammad Abd al-Salam Faraj, 'al-farida al-gha'iba [The Neglected Duty]' (Translated by Johannes J. G. Jansen, n.d.), para. 27.
29. The prophet predicted discord (fitna) to erupt among Muslims but warned the pious of his followers not to get involved. See Abou El Fadl, *Rebellion and Violence in Islamic Law*, 117. Another source is the Quranic verse 2:217 which says that 'Fitna is greater [meaning more severe] than killing'. Interestingly, this quote is used by the Islamic State in its English language *Rumiyah* magazine issue 6.
30. See Abu Muhammad al-Maqdisi, 'al-risala al-thalathiniyya fi al-tahdhir min al-ghulu fi al-takfir [Thirteen Messages of Warning of Extremism in Takfir],' 1998. See also Muhammed Hafez, 'Tactics, Takfir, and Anti-Muslim Violence,' in *Self Inflicted Wounds: Debates and Divisions within Al Qa'ida and Its Periphery*, ed. Assaf Moghadam and Brian Fishman (West Point: CTC Harmony Project, 2010), 19–44.
31. For instance Atiyyatullah authored a statement titled 'The Importance of the Sanctity of Muslim Blood,' 2011. See also Christopher Anzalone, 'Revisiting Shaykh Atiyyatullah's Works on Takfir and Mass Violence,' *CTC Sentinel* 5, no. 4 (2012); Abu Muhammad al-Maqdisi, *hadhihi aqidatuna [This Is Our Aqida]*, 1997, 62, where he says that 'The mistake in leaving one thousand kuffar is easier [better] than the mistake of shedding the blood of one Muslim.'

32. David Cook, *Understanding Jihad* (London: University of California Press, 2005); Crone, *God's Rule: Government and Islam*, chap. 21.
33. Rudolph Peters, *Jihad: A History in Documents* (Princeton: Markus Wiener Publishers, 2016).
34. Kepel, *Jihad: The Trail of Political Islam*; Thomas Hegghammer, *Jihad in Saudi Arabia: Violence and Pan-Islamism since 1979* (Cambridge: Cambridge University Press, 2010); Jeevan Deol and Zaheer Kazmi, eds., *Contextualising Jihadi Thought* (London: C. Hurst & Co., 2012).
35. Lahoud, *The Jihadis' Path to Self-Destruction*.
36. For example, Labib Nahhas made it clear to me during my interview with him that he is not a Jihadi and should not be considered part of the movement despite previously occupying an important political role for Ahrar al-Sham, a prominent Jihadi group operating in Syria. Another example is the issue of Hamas, which al-Maqdisi does not consider part of the Jihadi movement while Abu Qatada does.
37. Cécile Daumas, 'Gilles Kepel: 'Il Faut Écouter Les Prêches Du Vendredi',' *Libération*, April 14, 2016.
38. Author's interview with Hassan Abu Hanieh, June 18, 2018, Amman. See also Hassan Abu Hanieh and Mohammad Abu Rumman, *The Jihadi Salafist Movement in Jordan after Zarqawi: Identity, Leadership Crisis and Obscured Vision* (Amman: Friedrich-Ebert-Stiftung, 2009), 117–19.
39. Brynjar Lia, 'Jihadi Strategists and Doctrinarians,' in *Self Inflicted Wounds: Debates and Divisions within Al Qa'ida and Its Periphery*, ed. Assaf Moghadam and Brian Fishman (Combating Terrorism Center at West Point, 2010), 108.
40. See Chapter 8 section 4 in Abu Musab al-Suri, 'The Global Islamic Resistance Call,' December 2004.
41. Choosing the 1960s as the beginning of the modern SJM entails that I do not include the Jihadi campaigns of the 19th and early 20th century figures like Abdelkader and Umar Mukhtar.
42. Azzam Abdullah, 'al-qaida al-sulba [The Solid Base],' *Al Jihad* 41 (April 1988).
43. Hassan Abu Hanieh explains how leftist groups in Jordan said even before al-Zawahiri that liberation of Palestine goes through Amman, which shows a clear inspiration.
44. In general, there seems confusion about the authoritative relationship between Bin Laden and al-Zawahiri with some arguing that the latter was in fact the real thinker of al-Qaida while Bin Laden was its poster boy. For instance Gilles Kepel calls al-Zawahiri for Bin Laden's *mentor*, see Gilles Kepel, *Fitna: Guerre Au Cœur de l'islam* (Paris: Gallimard, 2004), 13.
45. Thomas Hegghammer, 'The Hybridization of Jihadi Groups,' *Current Trends in Islamist Ideology* 9 (2009): 26–45.
46. The historical development of the SJM is exemplified by Aimen Dean's comment that he cannot recognise the Jihadis he fought alongside in Afghanistan and Bosnia in what he sees in the Islamic State, see Aimen Dean, Paul Cruickshank, and Tim Lister, *Nine Lives: My Time as MI6's Top Spy Inside Al-Qaeda* (London: Oneworld Publications, 2018).
47. Anne Stenersen, 'Jihadism after the "Caliphate": Towards a New Typology,' *British Journal of Middle Eastern Studies* 47, no. 5 (2018), 1–20.
48. Regularly used by Abu Mahmoud al-Filastini in his statements on Telegram.
49. Abu Qatada al-Filastini, 'al-tahawwulat al-mutawaqqa'a an tahadatha fi al-tayyar al-jihadi [the Expected Transformations to Happen in the Jihadi Movement],' March 3, 2017.

50. Al-Adnani, 'Apologies, Amir of Al-Qaida.' Another label used is harakat al-jihad al-sunni al-'alamiyy (the global sunni jihadi movement), see Sami al-Uraydi, 'rasail manhajiyya min al-thughur al-shamiyya [Methodological Messages from the Syrian Front],' May 2017.
51. Regularly used by Abu Muhammad al-Maqdisi and Abu Qatada al-Filastini.
52. See also Cole Bunzel, 'Jihadism on Its Own Terms' (Hoover Institution, 2017).
53. I agree with Lahoud that it is incredibly difficult to suggest a fitting definition of Jihadism as it certainly risks simplifying a complex phenomenon, see Lahoud, *The Jihadis' Path to Self-Destruction*.
54. Dennis Smith, *The Rise of Historical Sociology* (Philadelphia: Temple University Press, 1991); Philip Abrams, *Historical Sociology* (Ithaca: Cornell University Press, 1982); Charles Tilly, *As Sociology Meets History* (New York: Academic Press, 1981); Maher, *Salafi–Jihadism: The History of an Idea*; Richard English, *Does Terrorism Work?* (Oxford: Oxford University Press, 2016), 19–21.
55. I consider a movement to be an abstract construction describing a collective behaviour and ideational identity composed of groups and individuals. Movements are thus characterised by the shared beliefs and common goals of their actors and, contrary to some conceptualisations of social movements, are hierarchically structured. In contrast, groups, or organisations, are tangible actors that constitute the movement in question. They are formal entities with an internal structure and a defined leadership. Groups (often) consider themselves part of a movement which they are connected to on the basis of ideology, identity, political priorities and/or solidarity with other groups within the same movement. The SJM is based on groups' self-identification with the movement, a shared ideological umbrella, relatively similar political priorities, and a certain view of other actors within the movement—in other words, a collective identity.
56. Now the challenge for researchers working on Jihadism is the abundance of primary material available if one knows where to look. Following, screening, capturing, cataloguing, and examining this pool of primary data is challenging and time-consuming, and necessitates a systematic approach.
57. Either material is shared directly on the platforms or through links to sites on filesharing platforms such as *justpaste.it* and *archive.org*
58. I have tracked profiles and channels of Jihadi groups, individuals, sympathisers, and ideologues for six years in order to collect the material they disseminate and study their internal discussions as a form of *netnography*. While this is no easy task, it provides a fascinating window into Jihadis' inner debates and contrasting views, and their attempts to assert or reinforce certain narratives over others. On netnography see Robert V Kozinets, *Netnography: Doing Ethnographic Research Online* (London: Sage Publications, 2010). For Jihadis' use of online platforms and the importance hereof for researchers, see Nico Prucha, 'IS and the Jihadist Information Highway – Projecting Influence and Religious Identity via Telegram,' *Perspectives on Terrorism* 10, no. 6 (2016): 48–58. Many of the Twitter profiles and Telegram channels that are referred to throughout this book have since been deleted. However, the author has saved screenshots of all the material found on these platforms that have been used as a source in the book.
59. One example is the Egyptian Jihadi ideologue Hani al-Sibai who continuously refused to meet despite my being referred by other Jihadis.
60. For Bin Laden's Bookshelf access: https://www.dni.gov/index.php/resources/bin-laden-bookshelf?start=1. The most recent batch of documents from the Abbottabad

raid, released in November 2017, have not been included as the timing and enormous quantity of the release made any systematic examination of the material impossible.

61. The author started collecting material in early 2013 and later systematised and organised the material in a personal database.

## CHAPTER 1. FROM CONTESTATION TO INFIGHTING

1. Al-Zawahiri, 'Editorial.'
2. Islamic State, 'Editorial,' *Al-Naba No. 182*, May 15, 2019.
3. Juergensmeyer, *Terror in the Mind of God: The Global Rise of Religious Violence*.
4. Bakke, Cunningham, and Seymour, 'A Plague of Initials: Fragmentation, Cohesion, and Infighting in Civil Wars.'
5. This aligns with Hirchman's theory of voice and exit noting that unity, or cohesion, is 'more challenging to preserve when there are rivals,' see Martha Crenshaw, 'The Causes of Terrorism,' *Comparative Politics* 13, no. 4 (1981): 82.
6. To some extent, my structural view of a movement compares to Pierre Bourdieu's analytical category of the field as hierarchically ordered and dynamic, where actors can shift positions over time, see Pierre Bourdieu, 'Genesis and Structure of the Religious Field,' *Comparative Social Research* Vol. 13 (1991): 1–44; Bourdieu, *Outline of a Theory of Practice*.
7. In Krause's view united movements are still preoccupied with internal wars of position and unlikely to reach its objective unless it is hegemonic, see Krause, *Rebel Power: Why National Movements Compete, Fight, and Win*, 27.
8. Hamming, 'Polemical and Fratricidal Jihadists: A Historical Examination of Debates, Contestation and Infighting Within the Sunni Jihadi Movement.'
9. Della Porta, *Clandestine Political Violence*, 75.
10. Such a relational perspective is also used by Eitan Y. Alimi, Lorenzo Bosi, and Chares Demetriou, *The Dynamics of Radicalization: A Relational and Comparative Perspective* (Oxford: Oxford University Press, 2015); Eitan Y. Alimi, 'Relational Dynamics in Factional Adoption of Terrorist Tactics: A Comparative Perspective,' *Theory and Society* 40, no. 1 (2011): 95–118.
11. Della Porta, *Clandestine Political Violence*, 71.
12. See for instance Graham Macklin and Joel Busher, 'The Missing Spirals of Violence: Four Waves of Movement – Countermovement Contest in Post-War Britain,' *Behavioral Sciences of Terrorism and Political Aggression* 7, no. 1 (2015): 1–16.
13. Della Porta, *Clandestine Political Violence*, 71.
14. Hamming, 'Jihadi Competition and Political Preferences.'
15. There are examples of Jabhat al-Nusra massacres, like in the civilian Druze population in the village of Qalb Lawze, but generally al-Nusra has been much more hesitant to execute massacres similar to those of the Islamic State.
16. Daveed Gartenstein-Ross and Bridget Moreng, 'Al Qaeda Is Beating the Islamic State,' *Politico*, April 2015.
17. Lister, 'The Dawn of Mass Jihad: Success in Syria Fuels Al-Qai'da's Evolution.'
18. Hamming, 'The Al Qaeda–Islamic State Rivalry: Competition Yes, but No Competitive Escalation.'
19. Andrew H. Kydd and Barbara F. Walter, 'The Strategies of Terrorism,' *International Security* 31, no. 1 (2006): 49–80.

20. Al-Baghdadi, 'wa allah ya'lam wa antum la ta'lamun [God Knows and You Do Not Know].'
21. Jerome Nicolas Drevon, 'Theorising Militant Groups' Meso-Level Evolution: A Comparative Study of the Egyptian Islamic and Jihad Groups' (PhD dissertation, Durham University, 2015).
22. Bacon, 'Alliance Hubs: Focal Points in the International Terrorist Landscape,' 8.
23. Haibatullah Akhundzada, 'Guidance to the Mujahideen,' *Taliban's Commission for Cultural Affairs*, May 2017.
24. AQIS, 'Code of Conduct,' *As-Sahab Media*, June 2017.
25. Tehreek-e-Taliban, 'Operation Manual for Mujahideen of Tehreek-e-Taliban Pakistan,' *Umar Media*, September 2018.
26. Zald and Useem, 'Movement and Countermovement: Loosely Coupled Conflict,' 2.

## CHAPTER 2. EXPLAINING JIHADI FRATRICIDE

1. Assaf Moghadam, *Nexus of Global Jihad: Understanding Cooperation among Terrorist Actors* (New York: Columbia University Press, 2017), 10.
2. Jerome Drevon, 'The Jihadi Social Movement (JSM): Between Factional Hegemonic Drive, National Realities and Transnational Ambitions,' *Perspectives on Terrorism* 11, no. 6 (2017): 56.
3. Joas Wagemakers, 'Revisiting Wiktorowicz,' in *Salafism After the Arab Awakening*, ed. Francesco Cavatorta and Fabio Merone (London: Oxford University Press, 2017), 18.
4. Fawaz A. Gerges, *The Far Enemy: Why Jihad Went Global* (Cambridge: Cambridge University Press, 2005); Fawaz A. Gerges, *Journey of the Jihadist: Inside Muslim Militancy* (Orlando, Florida: Harcourt Inc., 2007).
5. Hegghammer, *Jihad in Saudi Arabia: Violence and Pan-Islamism since 1979*; Hegghammer, 'The Hybridization of Jihadi Groups.'
6. Stenersen, 'Jihadism after the "Caliphate": Towards a New Typology.'
7. John Turner, 'Strategic Differences: Al Qaeda's Split with the Islamic State of Iraq and Al-Sham,' *Small Wars and Insurgencies* (Taylor & Francis, 2015); Novenario, 'Differentiating Al Qaeda and the Islamic State Through Strategies Publicized in Jihadist Magazines'; Joas Wagemakers, 'What Should an Islamic State Look Like? Jihadi–Salafi Debates on the War in Syria,' *The Muslim World* 106, no. July (2016): 501–22; Joas Wagemakers, 'Jihadi–Salafism in Jordan and the Syrian Conflict: Divisions Overcome Unity,' *Studies in Conflict & Terrorism*, 2017, 1–22; Niamatullah Ibrahimi and Shahram Akbarzadeh, 'Intra-Jihadist Conflict and Cooperation: Islamic State–Khorasan Province and the Taliban in Afghanistan,' *Studies in Conflict & Terrorism*, 2019; Tricia Bacon and Elizabeth Grimm Arsenault, 'Al Qaeda and the Islamic State's Break: Strategic Strife or Lackluster Leadership?,' *Studies in Conflict and Terrorism* 42, no. 3 (2019): 229–63; Tore Refslund Hamming, 'The Al Qaeda–Islamic State Rivalry: Competition Yes, but No Competitive Escalation,' *Terrorism and Political Violence*, 2017, 1–18; Tore Refslund Hamming, 'Jihadi Competition and Political Preferences,' *Perspectives on Terrorism* 11, no. 6 (2017): 63–88.
8. Bruce Hoffman, 'ISIL Is Winning,' *Politico Magazine*, September 2015; 'How Zawahiri Lost Al Qaeda,' n.d.; Nelly Lahoud and Muhammad Al-'Ubaydi Ubaydi, 'The War of Jihadists against Jihadists in Syria,' *CTC Sentinel* 7, no. 3 (2014): 1–6; J.M. Berger, 'The Islamic State vs. Al Qaeda,' *Foreign Policy*, September 2014; Jenan Moussa

and Harald Doornbos, 'The Greatest Divorce in the Jihadi World,' *Foreign Policy*, August 2016; Crenshaw, 'There Is No Global Jihadist "Movement"'; Clint Watts, 'Deciphering Competition Between Al-Qa'ida and the Islamic State,' *CTC Sentinel* 9, no. 7 (2016): 1–6; Geoff Porter, 'Terrorist Outbidding: The In Amenas Attack,' *CTC Sentinel* 8, no. 5 (2015): 14–17; Hassan Hassan, 'Two Houses Divided: How Conflict in Syria Shaped the Future of Jihadism,' *CTC Sentinel* 11, no. 9 (2018); Cole Bunzel, 'The Islamic State of Disunity: Jihadism Divided,' *Jihadica*, January 2014.

9. Aaron Y. Zelin, 'The War between ISIS and Al-Qaeda for Supremacy of the Global Jihadist Movement,' *Washington Institute for Near East Policy*, June 2014; Charles Lister, 'Jihadi Rivalry: The Islamic State Challenges Al-Qaida' (Brookings Doha Center, 2016); Daveed Gartenstein Ross, Jason Fritz, and Bridget Moreng, 'Islamic State vs. Al-Qaeda: Strategic Dimensions of a Patricidal Conflict,' 2015; Charles Lister, 'Al-Qaeda versus ISIS: Competing Jihadist Brands in the Middle East,' *Middle East Institute*, November 2017; Asaad Almohammad, 'Seven Years of Terror: Jihadi Organisations' Strategies and Future Directions,' *ICCT*, August 2019.
10. Jessica Stern and J.M. Berger, *ISIS: The State of Terror* (London: William Collins, 2015), chap. 8; Barak Mendelsohn, *Jihadism Constrained: The Limits of Transnational Jihadism and What It Means for Counterterrorism* (London: Rowman & Littlefield Publishers, Inc, 2018), chap. 4.
11. The importance of ideologues and supporter networks stems from their individual capacity to influence perceptions and to mobilise within the SJM, either through the authority they possess or through their role as online entrepreneurs. Hence the impact of these two groups of actors can be categorised in four ways: (1) Defining and supporting a specific religio-political project in contrast to opposing projects; (2) Discrediting opponents within the movement; (3) Legitimising specific behaviour towards opponents within the movement (either legitimising or preventing conflict); and (4) Mobilisation for such specific behaviour. Ideologues play an important role within the SJM as sources of ideological legitimation whereas supporter networks are important not because of their authority but because of the amount of output they produce and because of their entrepreneurial use of IT platforms, which enables them to reach a vast audience.
12. Exclusivism is when groups consider alliances and cooperation with other Jihadi groups less attractive or even illegitimate while preferring that other groups join.
13. Inclusivism is when groups consider alliances and cooperation between Jihadi groups attractive and legitimate.
14. Barak Mendelsohn, 'The Battle for Algeria: Explaining Fratricide among Armed Nonstate Actors,' *Studies in Conflict and Terrorism*, 2019, 6.
15. Tulia G. Falleti and Julia F. Lynch, 'Context and Causal Mechanisms in Political Analysis,' *Comparative Political Studies* 42, no. 9 (2009): 1143–66; Charles Tilly, 'Mechanisms in Political Processes,' *Annual Review of Political Science* 4 (2001): 21–41. I follow Tilly's definition of mechanisms as a 'delimited class of events that change relations among specified sets of elements in identical or closely similar ways over a variety of situations.' Mechanisms, he notes, can be divided between environmental, cognitive and relational.
16. See for instance Harun Maruf, 'In Somalia, Businesses Face "Taxation" by Militants,' *VOA News*, December 3, 2018.
17. Olivier Roy, *Globalized Islam: The Search for a New Ummah* (New York: Columbia University Press, 2004), 61.

18. Krause, *Rebel Power: Why National Movements Compete, Fight, and Win*.
19. Ideologues have always played a major role, see Wagemakers, *A Quietist Jihadi: The Ideology and Influence of Abu Muhammad al-Maqdisi*; Abdullah bin Khaled al-Saud, 'The Spiritual Teacher and His Truants: The Influence and Relevance of Abu Mohammad Al-Maqdisi,' *Studies in Conflict and Terrorism* 41, no. 9 (2018): 736–51; Lav, *Radical Islam and the Revival of Medieval Theology*.
20. Author's interviews with Labib Nahhas, April 15, 2018 (London); Abu Sulayman al-Muhajir, June 2017; Danish foreign fighters present in Syria in 2013, conducted in 2018.
21. Lahoud, *The Jihadis' Path to Self-Destruction*, 245.
22. Author's interviews with Labib Nahhas, April 15, 2018 (London); Abu Sulayman al-Muhajir, June 2017; Abdallah Anas, April 14, 2018 (London). In my interview with Labib Nahhas, he tells me how HTS amir al-Julani instructed Abu Yaqzan al-Masri, one of the group's high-ranking ideologues, to issue a fatwa legitimising the attacking of Ahrar al-Sham fighters.
23. I define socialisation as the outcome of 'means through which individual actors adopt particular norms, rules, and practices associated with membership of a given group', see Dennis Rodgers, 'Bróderes in Arms: Gangs and the Socialization of Violence in Nicaragua,' *Journal of Peace Research* 54, no. 5 (2017): 648–60.
24. Jeffrey T. Checkel, 'Socialization and Violence: Introduction and Framework,' *Journal of Peace Research* 54, no. 5 (2017): 592–605; Elisabeth Jean Wood, 'Rape as a Practice of War: Toward a Typology of Political Violence,' *Politics & Society*, 2018, 1–25.
25. Girard, *Violence and the Sacred*.
26. Mia Bloom and John Horgan, *Small Arms: Children and Terrorism* (London: Cornell University Press, 2019); Checkel, 'Socialization and Violence: Introduction and Framework.'

## CHAPTER 3. THE HISTORY OF JIHADI POLEMICS AND CONFLICT

1. Abu Musab al-Zarqawi, 'Untitled Letter,' January 2004, https://2001-2009.state.gov/p/nea/rls/31694.htm. The letter was published by the US State Department in February 2004.
2. Ibid.
3. This chapter is a slightly revised version of the report by Tore Refslund Hamming, 'Polemical and Fratricidal Jihadists: A Historical Examination of Debates, Contestation and Infighting Within the Sunni Jihadi Movement,' *International Centre for the Study of Radicalisation*, August 2019.
4. Kepel has argued that Hudaybi's book was a direct response, see Kepel, *Jihad: The Trail of Political Islam*.
5. Sayyid Qutb, *Milestones*, 1964.
6. Jeffrey B. Cozzens, 'Al-Takfir Wa'l Hijra: Unpacking an Enigma,' *Studies in Conflict & Terrorism* 32, no. 6 (2009): 489–510; Gilles Kepel, *Muslim Extremism in Egypt: The Prophet and Pharaoh* (Berkeley: University of California Press, 1985), 74.
7. Al Jihad consisted of several smaller groups, but Hani al-Sibai narrates that it was established in 1968 through the formation of a small group, counting Ayman al-Zawahiri and Sayyid Imam among the founders. See Hani Al-Sibai, *qissah jama'at al-jzihad [The Story of Al Jihad Group]* (Minbar al-Tawhid wa-l-Jihad, 2002).

8. Aaron Y. Zelin, 'Al-Farida Al-Gha'iba and Al-Sadat's Assassination, a 30 Year Retrospective,' *International Journal for Arab Studies* 3, no. 2 (2012).
9. Faraj, 'Al-Farida Al-Gha'iba [The Neglected Duty],' 188 (§63).
10. Ibid.: 200 (§88).
11. Abdullah Anas and Tam Hussein, *To the Mountains: My Life in Jihad, from Algeria to Afghanistan* (London: Hurst Publishers, 2019).
12. Hamid and Farrall, *The Arabs at War in Afghanistan*.
13. Ibid.: 4.
14. Fotini Christia, *Alliance Formation in Civil Wars* (Cambridge: Cambridge University Press, 2012), 116–21.
15. This union was later replaced by another initiative to unify the Afghan Jihadi factions known as Ittihad i Islami Mujahideen Afghanistan, for which Sayyaf continued as president.
16. The other main warlords or commmanders in Afghanistan were Gulbuddin Hekmatyar (leader of Hizb-e-Islami), Younis Khalis (a prominent Paktia commander), Jalaluddin Haqqani (closely allied to Khalis and probably the most prominent field commander in Paktia Province), Sibghatullah Mujaddidi (leader of Afghanistan National Liberation Front), Burhanuddin Rabbani (leader of Jamiat-e-Islami), and Ahmed Shah Massoud (an ethnic Tajik, he was the most influential commander in the north and close with Rabbani, and was assassinated in two days before 9/11 by al-Qaida). Hekmatyar, Khalis and Haqqani were arguably the most religiously conservative compared to the more moderate Al Azhar-educated Rabbani and Mujaddidi.
17. Hamid and Farrall, *The Arabs at War in Afghanistan*, 50–56.
18. Ibid.: 60.
19. This is argued in Hassan Abbas, *The Taliban Revival* (New Haven: Yale University Press, 2014).
20. Hamid and Farrall point out that facilitation was only one part of the reason why Azzam established the MAK. Probably of greater importance, they argue, was the problem of corruption within the Afghan Jihadi groups, which the MAK was supposed to prevent. Against the conventional wisdom that Azzam was the main source of facilitation of the mobilisation of Arab fighters to Afghanistan, Brown and Rassler argue that Jalaluddin Haqqani was in fact the first to promote and facilitate such mobilization, see Vahid Brown and Don Rassler, *Fountainhead of Jihad: The Haqqani Nexus, 1973-2010* (London: Hurst & Company, 2013).
21. Anas and Hussein, *To the Mountains: My Life in Jihad, from Algeria to Afghanistan*.
22. Hamid and Farrall, *The Arabs at War in Afghanistan*, 80.
23. Ibid.: 81–82.
24. Ibid.: 75.
25. Ibid.: 113.
26. Azzam was not the only one opposed to the Masada camp; most people around Bin Laden tried to talk him out of it as the location of the camp was not suitable for guerrilla warfare.
27. Brown and Rassler, *Fountainhead of Jihad: The Haqqani Nexus, 1973-2010*, 75.
28. Hamid and Farrall, *The Arabs at War in Afghanistan*, 296.
29. Ibid.: 123.
30. Ibid.: 162.
31. Lawrence Wright, *The Looming Tower: Al Qaeda and the Road to 9/11* (New York: Vintage Books, 2006), 140.

32. Author's interview with Ahmed al-Hamdan, November 19, 2016: http://www.jihadica.com/the-increasing-extremism-within-the-islamic-state/
33. In this period, Christia describes seven shifts in alliances in the struggle for power in Afghanistan between mujahideen forces. See Christia, *Alliance Formation in Civil Wars*.
34. Tore Refslund Hamming, 'The Hardline Stream of Global Jihad: Revisiting the Ideological Origin of the Islamic State,' *CTC Sentinel* 12, no. 1 (2019).
35. Paul Cruickshank, 'Al-Qaeda's New Course Examining Ayman Al-Zawahiri's Strategic Direction,' *IHS Defense, Risk and Security Consulting* May (2012).
36. Interview with Abu Jandal in Al-Quds al-Arabi, August 2004.
37. Hamid and Farrall, *The Arabs at War in Afghanistan*.
38. Senate Select Committee on Intelligence, 'Committee Study of the Central Intelligence Agency's Detention and Interrogation Program,' 2014, Appendix 1.
39. Hamid and Farrall, *The Arabs at War in Afghanistan*, 230.
40. 'Statement of Noor Uthman Muhammed,' *Military Commissions Trial Judiciary Guantanamo Bay*, February 17, 2011, 2. This is backed up by Gitmo file on Abu Zubaydah published through Wikileaks.
41. Hamid and Farrall, *The Arabs at War in Afghanistan*, 167.
42. Ibid.: 259.
43. Kévin Jackson, 'Abu Mus'ab Al Zarqawi under Influence: One Mentor?,' May 15, 2012. As will be described later, al-Muhajir later changed his views, coming much closer to al-Qaida and eventually joined Bin Laden. See also Hamming, 'The Hardline Stream of Global Jihad: Revisiting the Ideological Origin of the Islamic State.'
44. Hassan Abu Hanieh and Mohammad Abu Rumman, *The 'Islamic State' Organization: The Sunni Crisis and the Struggle of Global Jihadism* (Amman: Friedrich-Ebert-Stiftung, 2015), 141.
45. Hamid and Farrall, *The Arabs at War in Afghanistan*, 229–30; Brynjar Lia, *Architect of Global Jihad: The Life of Al Qaeda Strategist Abu Musab Al-Suri* (London: Hurst & Company, 2008), 242–43.
46. Jackson, 'Abu Mus'ab Al Zarqawi under Influence: One Mentor?'
47. See articles by Abdullah Mansour in TIP's *Voice of Islam* magazine issues 3 and 4.
48. Hamid and Farrall, *The Arabs at War in Afghanistan*, 166.
49. Ibid.: 228–29.
50. Farrall says that competition between the two groups was exacerbated because of competition for resources and financing, see Ibid.: 231.
51. Lia, 'Jihadi Strategists and Doctrinarians.'
52. Lia, *Architect of Global Jihad: The Life of Al Qaeda Strategist Abu Musab Al-Suri*, 239–44.
53. Mustafa Hamid, 'The Airport 1990,' *Document ID AFGP-2002-600090*, n.d.
54. CTC Harmony Project, 'Cracks in the Foundation: Leadership Schisms in Al-Qaida from 1989–2006 Combating Terrorism Center at West Point,' 2007, 8–9.
55. Hamid and Farrall, *The Arabs at War in Afghanistan*, 262.
56. Ibid.: 270–71.
57. Ibid.: 140.
58. Hafez, 'Fratricidal Rebels: Ideological Extremity and Warring Factionalism in Civil Wars.'
59. Kepel, *Jihad: The Trail of Political Islam*; Tawil, *Brothers in Arms. The Story of Al-Qaida and the Arab Jihadists*; Lia, *Architect of Global Jihad: The Life of Al Qaeda Strategist Abu Musab Al-Suri*, 111–31. For more on the Algerian War, see Luis Martinez, *The Algerian Civil War* (New York: Columbia University Press, 2000).

60. Two aspects in particular characterise the GIA, especially from 1994 onwards. The first is the young age of its senior leadership. The age of the GIA emirs the year they took charge of the group ranged between 26 and 32. The second is the vivid lack of religious training and knowledge among its leaders.
61. Tawil, *Brothers in Arms. The Story of Al-Qaida and the Arab Jihadists*, 67–75.
62. Hegghammer explains how in 1996 Ayman al-Zawahiri praised the GIA for its Jihadi–Salafi methodology in an article titled 'al-kalima al-munawa'a: hiwar al-shaykh al-zawahiri ma' jaridat al-hayat – 1417 [Quality Speech: Sheikh al- Zawahiri's Conversation with al-Hayat in 1996]', see Thomas Hegghammer, 'Violent Islamism in Saudi Arabia, 1979-2006: The Power and Perils of Pan-Islamic Nationalism' (PhD thesis, Institut d'Etudes Politiques de Paris - Ecole Doctorale de Sciences Po, 2007), 62.
63. Tawil, *Brothers in Arms. The Story of Al-Qaida and the Arab Jihadists*, 86.
64. Lia, *Architect of Global Jihad: The Life of Al Qaeda Strategist Abu Musab Al-Suri*, 128.
65. Tawil, *Brothers in Arms. The Story of Al-Qaida and the Arab Jihadists*, 120.
66. Kepel, *Jihad: The Trail of Political Islam*, 270–71. Abu Hamza stayed supportive of Zouabri until late September 1997 when he finally withdrew his support after Zouabri declared the entire Algerian society apostate.
67. Ibid.
68. Ibid.: 265.
69. Tawil, *Brothers in Arms. The Story of Al-Qaida and the Arab Jihadists*.
70. Ibid.: 96; Lia, *Architect of Global Jihad: The Life of Al Qaeda Strategist Abu Musab Al-Suri*, 128.
71. Ibid.
72. Kepel, *Jihad: The Trail of Political Islam*, 269.
73. Assaf Moghadam and Brian Fishman, eds., *Self Inflicted Wounds: Debates and Divisions within Al Qa'ida and Its Periphery* (West Point: CTC Harmony Project, 2010), 140.
74. Ibid.: 140–46; Anne Stenersen, *Al-Qaida in Afghanistan* (Cambridge: Cambridge University Press, 2018).
75. Moghadam and Fishman, *Self Inflicted Wounds: Debates and Divisions within Al Qa'ida and Its Periphery*, 142. Once Mullah Umar even dispatched a helicopter to bring Bin Laden to Kandahar to speak to him although Bin Laden allegedly was convinced that he would be killed by the Taliban, see Hamid and Farrall, *The Arabs at War in Afghanistan*, 1.
76. Ibid.: 221.
77. Ibid.: 222.
78. 'Various Admin Documents and Questions,' *AFGP-2002-801138*, 2000.
79. Tore Refslund Hamming and Olivier Roy, 'Al-Zawahiri's Bay'a to Mullah Mansoor: A Bitter Pill but a Bountiful Harvest,' *CTC Sentinel* 9, no. 5 (2016).
80. Hegghammer, 'Violent Islamism in Saudi Arabia, 1979–2006: The Power and Perils of Pan-Islamic Nationalism.'
81. Hamid and Farrall, *The Arabs at War in Afghanistan*, 256.
82. Ibid.: 254; Dean, Cruickshank, and Lister, *Nine Lives: My Time as MI6's Top Spy inside Al-Qaeda*.
83. Lia, *Architect of Global Jihad: The Life of Al Qaeda Strategist Abu Musab Al-Suri*, 240.
84. Ibid.: 281–82.
85. Ibid.: 284–90.
86. Brian Fishman, 'Revising the History of Al-Qa'ida's Original Meeting with Abu Musab Al-Zarqawi,' *CTC Sentinel* 9, no. 10 (2016).

87. Hamid and Farrall, *The Arabs at War in Afghanistan*, 274.
88. Arab Liaison Committee of the Islamic Emirate, 'Untitled,' *AFGP-2002-0001000-0003*, n.d.
89. Hamid and Farrall, *The Arabs at War in Afghanistan*, 169. His popularity is emphasised by a survey on the Jihadist forum Shumukh al-Islam in 2011 on the reasons why forum members 'loved Jihad'. Ibn Khattab came in second only to 'religious upbringing' and thus above Bin Laden, see Muhammad Al-'Ubaydi, 'Khattab - Jihadi Bios Project,' *Combating Terrorism Center at West Point*, 2015, 1.
90. Samir Saleh Al-Suwailem, 'Memories of Amir Khattab: The Experience of the Arab Ansar in Chechnya, Afghanistan and Tajikistan,' n.d., 6.
91. When Khattab's own camp was closed, his recruits for Chechnya were trained at Khaldan, see Hamid and Farrall, *The Arabs at War in Afghanistan*, 200.
92. Al-'Ubaydi, 'Khattab - Jihadi Bios Project,' 23.
93. Ibid.: 4.
94. Hegghammer, *Jihad in Saudi Arabia: Violence and Pan-Islamism since 1979*, 57.
95. Al-Suwailem, 'Memories of Amir Khattab: The Experience of the Arab Ansar in Chechnya, Afghanistan and Tajikistan.'
96. Abd al-Hadi Al-Iraqi, 'Notes from 'Abd Al-Hadi,' *Document ID AFGP-2002-000091*, 1999.
97. Hegghammer, *Jihad in Saudi Arabia: Violence and Pan-Islamism since 1979*, 56–57.
98. Al-Sibai, *Qissah Jama'at Al-Jihad [The Story of Al Jihad Group]*.
99. Kepel and Milelli, *Al Qaeda in Its Own Words*, 151.
100. Al-Sibai, *Qissah Jama'at Al-Jihad [The Story of Al Jihad Group]*; Tawil, *Brothers in Arms. The Story of Al-Qaida and the Arab Jihadists*, 109.
101. Ibid.: 100.
102. Al-Sibai, *Qissah Jama'at Al-Jihad [The Story of Al Jihad Group]*.
103. Al-'adhir bi-l-jahl concerns the issue if a person who commits shirk or in another way breaks Islamic law due to ignorance should be considered an apostate.
104. Tawil, *Brothers in Arms. The Story of Al-Qaida and the Arab Jihadists*, 103–06.
105. Jérôme Drevon, 'Assessing Islamist Armed Groups' De-Radicalization in Egypt,' *Peace Review: A Journal of Social Justice* 27, no. 3 (2015): 296–303; Sherman A. Jackson, *Initiative to Stop the Violence (Mubadarat Waqf Al-Unf): Sadat's Assassins and the Renunciation of Political Violence* (New Haven: Yale University Press, 2015); Amr Hamzawy and Sarah Grebowski, 'From Violence to Moderation: Al-Jama' Al-Islamiya and Al-Jihad,' *Carnegie Middle East Center*, 2010; Paul Kamolnick, 'The Egyptian Islamic Group's Critique of Al-Qaeda's Interpretation of Jihad,' *Perspectives on Terrorism* 7, no. 5 (2013): 93–110. In 2000, however, Umar Abd al-Rahman—the spiritual guide of al-Jama'a al-Islamiyya—withdrew his support for the initiative.
106. Ayman Al-Zawahiri, *Knights Under the Prophet's Banner* (Translation by Laura Mansfield, 2006), 136–37.
107. In 2002, al-Zawahiri continued with his criticism in the publication 'Loyalty and Separation' (al-wala' wa-l-bara') that, through the concept of al-wala' wa-l-bara', attempted to discredit groups theologically that did not support their Muslim brethren and instead took unbelievers as allies. As Lacroix points out, the latter text was of extreme importance because it underlined how al-Zawahiri had gone from being an Egyptian Jihadist focusing on hakimiyya (the sovereignty of God) and overthrowing the near enemy to a global Jihadist mainly aiming at the far enemy through a focus on al-wala' wa-l-bara', see Kepel and Milelli, *Al Qaeda in Its Own Words*, 166–67.

108. Ibid.: 159.
109. Anas and Hussein, *To the Mountains: My Life in Jihad, from Algeria to Afghanistan*.
110. Hamid and Farrall, *The Arabs at War in Afghanistan*, 196.
111. See for example Gerges, *Journey of the Jihadist: Inside Muslim Militancy*.
112. Mark Fineman and Steven Braun, 'Life inside Al Qaeda: A Destructive Devotion,' *Los Angeles Times*, September 24, 2001.
113. Steven Brooke, 'Jihadist Strategic Debates before 9/11,' *Studies in Conflict & Terrorism* 31, no. 3 (2008): 214.
114. 1998 fatwa entitled 'World Islamic Front for Jihad Against Jews and Crusaders,' can be accessed here: https://fas.org/irp/world/para/docs/980223-fatwa.htm
115. Tawil, *Brothers in Arms. The Story of Al-Qaida and the Arab Jihadists*, 170–71.
116. CTC Harmony Project, 'Cracks in the Foundation: Leadership Schisms in Al-Qaida from 1989-2006 Combating Terrorism Center at West Point,' 18; Hamid and Farrall, *The Arabs at War in Afghanistan*, 281; 'The 9/11 Commission Report,' 2004, 250–52.
117. Ari Weisfuse, 'Negotiating Oblivion. Sayf Al 'Adl: Al Qaeda's Top Operative' (Brandeis University, 2014), 59; 'The 9/11 Commission Report,' 251.
118. Saif al-Adl, 'Untitled Letter to Mukhtar,' *Combating Terrorism Center*, n.d., https://www.ctc.usma.edu/harmony-program/al-adl-letter-original-language-2/.
119. For example, see 'Message to our people in Iraq and the Gulf specifically, and to our Islamic ummah in general', which can be accessed here: https://intelcenter.com/Qaeda-Guerrilla-Iraq-v1-0.pdf.
120. In November 2010 Sulayman Abu Graith, the former spokesperson of al-Qaida, published a 121-page-long book entitled *20 Commandments on the Path of Jihad* with a foreword by Abu Hafs al-Mauritani. The book, which was written while Abu Graith was still under house arrest in Iran, was intended to educate Muslims generally and Jihadis specifically in order to correct mistakes that had been made. As such, the book should be viewed as a critique of Bin Laden's re-focusing of the West through terrorist attacks.
121. See first part of the Al Jazeera 'Special Encounters' interview here: https://www.youtube.com/ watch?v=CPXsiu96QqI and second part here: https://www.youtube.com/watch?v=IbfH92LT2ow [Accessed February 2, 2017]. A transcript of part of the interview concerning the 9/11 events can be found here: http://www.biyokulule.com/view_content.php?articleid=5302.
122. CTC Harmony Project, 'Cracks in the Foundation: Leadership Schisms in Al-Qaida from 1989-2006 Combating Terrorism Center at West Point,' 18.
123. Diaa Rashwan, 'Struggle within the Ranks,' *Al Ahram Weekly*, November 1998.
124. Hegghammer, *Jihad in Saudi Arabia: Violence and Pan-Islamism since 1979*, 148.
125. Hamid and Farrall, *The Arabs at War in Afghanistan*, 286.
126. Lahoud, *The Jihadis' Path to Self-Destruction*, 132.
127. When Sayyid Imam resigned, Ayman al-Zawahiri took over the leadership of Al Jihad.
128. Not only did al-Zawahiri remove portions critical of Al Jihad and al-Jama'a al-Islamiyya, but he even changed the title of the book.
129. This is a main point dividing Sayyid Imam and Faraj, the latter not believing preparation was necessary.
130. For more on Sayyid Imam and al-'Umda, see Ibid.: 131–37.
131. Sayyid Imam, 'Tarshid al-'amal al-jihadi fi misr wa al-'alam' [Advice Regarding the Conduct of Jihadist Action in Egypt and the World],' November 2007.
132. This last point is similar to the revisionist argument of al-Jama'a al-Islamiyya.

133. Marwan Shehada, 'Weakening Al-Qaeda: Literature Review Challenges Its Authority,' *Arab Insights* 2, no. 6 (2009): 30–31.
134. He mentions how it was even more challenging than a letter he wrote to Hamas.
135. Ayman Al-Zawahiri, 'The Exoneration: A Letter Exonerating the Umma of the Pen and Sword from the Unjust Allegation of Feebleness and Weakness,' English translation, 2008, 1.
136. Lahoud, *The Jihadis' Path to Self-Destruction*, 236–37.
137. According to Wright, in 1995 al-Zawahiri allegedly travelled to Yemen and appealed to Sayyid Imam for forgiveness, but Sayyid Imam refused to see him, saying, 'I do not know anyone in the history of Islam prior to Ayman al-Zawahiri who engaged in such lying, cheating, forgery, and betrayal of trust by transgressing against someone else's book.' See Lawrence Wright, 'The Rebellion Within,' *The New Yorker*, May 23, 2008.
138. For elaboration of the debate, see Lahoud, *The Jihadis' Path to Self-Destruction*, 232–39. In total al-Zawahiri formulates 35 questions to Sayyid Imam for which he wants answers.
139. For other reactions to Sayyid Imam's revisions, see Daniel J. Law, 'Jihadists and Jurispredents: The "Revisions" Literature of Sayyid Imam and Al-Gama'a Al-Islamiyya,' in *Political Islam from Muhammad to Ahmadinejad: Defenders, Detractors, and Definitions*, ed. Joseph Morrison Skelly (Santa Barbara: Praeger, 2009), 105–46; Abd-al-Hakim Al-Afghani, 'Our Honorable Shaykh,' *Abbottabad Documents Batch 2*, February 12, 2008.
140. Kamal Habib, 'Another Wave of Jihadist Adjustment: Internal Debates of the Movement,' *Arab Insights* 2, no. 6 (2009): 38. That the personal attack on al-Zawahiri is central in the book is evident from the titles of its four chapters: 1. 'Exposing the lies and slanders of Zawahiri,' 2. 'Exposing the errors in religious law made by Zawahiri,' 3. 'Exposing Zawahiri's obfuscation of the issues for the reader,' and 4. 'Exposing Zawahiri as a seeker of fame and stardom.'
141. Kamal Habib explains the change in tone from a psychological point of view saying it is 'a response to the psychological wound inflicted on him by Zawahiri's "Exoneration",' Ibid.: 42–43.
142. Marwan Shehada is an example of the latter; see Shehada, 'Weakening Al-Qaeda: Literature Review Challenges Its Authority.'
143. For more on the legitimacy of Sayyid Imam's words and especially the view of Hani Sibai, see Lahoud, *The Jihadis' Path to Self-Destruction*, 232–39.
144. Sayyid Imam was not the only senior Jihadi criticising his former colleagues with other examples including Noman Benotman and Abu Hafs al-Mauritani.
145. Bill Roggio, 'Omar Hammami's Personal Dispute with Shabaab,' *Long War Journal*, January 6, 2013; Jeremy Scahill, 'The Purge: How Somalia's Al Shabaab Turned Against Its Own Foreign Fighters,' *The Intercept*, May 19, 2015. It has been claimed that foreign fighters in particular were targeted, but most of these were in fact killed in drone strikes, while some argue that information about their location was passed on by rival al-Shabaab members, see Raffaello Pantucci and A.R. Sayyid, 'Foreign Fighters in Somalia and Al-Shabaab's Internal Purge,' *Terrorism Monitor* 11, no. 22 (2013).
146. Christopher Anzalone, 'The Life and Death of Al-Shabab Leader Ahmed Godane,' *CTC Sentinel* 7, no. 9 (2014).
147. Harun Maruf and Dan Joseph, *Inside Al-Shabaab: The Secret History of Al-Qaeda's Most Powerful Ally* (Bloomington: Indiana University Press, 2018).

148. See Abbottabad letter, 'SOCOM-2012-0000007,' December 3, 2010 from Abu Yahya al-Libi and Atiyyah to TTP leader Hakimullah.
149. See two letters written by AQAP's emir, Nasir al-Wuhayshi, to AQIM's emir, Abdelmalek Droukdel, advising AQIM to pursue a gradual approach in the implementation of shari'a, especially mentioning hudud punishment, in conquered areas as the local population was not ready for such radical changes. The letters can be found as part of the so-called Timbuktu Papers.
150. Maruf and Joseph, *Inside Al-Shabaab: The Secret History of Al-Qaeda's Most Powerful Ally*.
151. Roggio, 'Omar Hammami's Personal Dispute with Shabaab.'
152. Pantucci and Sayyid, 'Foreign Fighters in Somalia and Al-Shabaab's Internal Purge.'
153. Stig Jarle Hansen, 'An In-Depth Look at Al-Shabab's Internal Divisions,' *CTC Sentinel* 7, no. 2 (2014).
154. Maruf and Joseph, *Inside Al-Shabaab: The Secret History of Al-Qaeda's Most Powerful Ally*.

## CHAPTER 4. TRACING THE ISLAMIC STATE'S SPLIT FROM AL-QAIDA 1999–2014

1. Lahoud and al-'Ubaydi, 'The War of Jihadists against Jihadists in Syria.'
2. Most accounts offer a much too simplistic explanation of the the relationship between al-Qaida and its Iraqi affiliate. One example is Andrew Phillips, 'How Al Qaeda Lost Iraq,' *Australian Journal of International Affairs* 63, no. 1 (2009): 64–84. It should be mentioned that part of this is due to the absence of sources at the time of writing.
3. Morrison, *Origins and Rise of Dissident Irish Republicanism: The Role and Impact of Organizational Splits*.
4. Al-Zarqawi's first experience in Afghanistan was from 1989 to 1993 where he also met Abu Muhammad al-Maqdisi for the first time. His deputy Abu al-Qassam would later become a central figure in the intra-Jihadi tensions in Syria. After release from Iranian house arrest in 2015, he joined al-Qaida deputy Abu al-Khayr and went to Syria where he was a staunch opponent of Jabhat al-Nusra's disassociation from al-Qaida.
5. Fishman, 'Revising the History of Al-Qu'aida's Original Meeting with Abu Musab Al-Zarqawi'; Hamming, 'Polemical and Fratricidal Jihadists: A Historical Examination of Debates, Contestation and Infighting Within the Sunni Jihadi Movement.'
6. Lia, *Architect of Global Jihad: The Life of Al Qaeda Strategist Abu Musab Al-Suri*, 250–55.
7. Fishman, 'Revising the History of Al-Qu'aida's Original Meeting with Abu Musab Al-Zarqawi.'
8. In 2005, Saif al-Adl published a history of al-Qaida's encounter with al-Zarqawi. Although it was later rejected as a fake by Bin Laden in a letter to Atiyyatullah on 26 October 2010, Bin Laden's argument was rather unconvincing, and it appears likely that al-Adl did indeed author it from his Iranian house arrest.
9. See also Fu'ad Husayn, 'Al-Zarqawi: The Second Generation of Al-Qa'ida,' June 2006 on the initial disagreement between al-Zarqawi and Bin Laden.
10. Saif al-Adl, 'Jihadist Biography of the Slaughtering Leader Abu Mus'ab al-Zarqawi,' *Global Islamic Media Front*, 2005.
11. Hamid and Farrall, *The Arabs at War in Afghanistan*; Hamming, 'Polemical and Fratricidal Jihadists: A Historical Examination of Debates, Contestation and Infighting Within the Sunni Jihadi Movement.'
12. Abu Hanieh and Abu Rumman, *The 'Islamic State' Organization: The Sunni Crisis and the Struggle of Global Jihadism*; Kévin Jackson, 'Abu Mus'ab Al Zarqawi under Influence:

One Mentor?,' May 2012; Tore Refslund Hamming, 'The Hardline Stream of Global Jihad: Revisiting the Ideological Origin of the Islamic State,' *CTC Sentinel* 12, no. 1 (2019); Hamming, 'Polemical and Fratricidal Jihadists: A Historical Examination of Debates, Contestation and Infighting Within the Sunni Jihadi Movement.'

13. Hamid and Farrall, *The Arabs at War in Afghanistan*, 258.
14. Stenersen, *Al-Qaida in Afghanistan*.
15. Captured Document, 'Status of Jihad,' AFGP-2002-601693, July 26, 2002.
16. At this early point, Abd al-Hadi al-Iraqi, a senior al-Qaida official now held at Guantanamo, was informed through Hassan Ghul, a courier of Bin Laden, about al-Zarqawi's desire to focus his attacks on the Shia in Iraq. Opposed to such sectarian focus, al-Hadi allegedly advised al-Zarqawi against it. See Senate Select Committee on Intelligence, 'Committee Study of the Central Intelligence Agency's Detention and Interrogation Program,' *United States Senate*, December 13, 2012.
17. Abu Musab al-Zarqawi, 'risala min abu musab al-zarqawi ila al-sheikh usama bin laden [Letter from Abu Musab al-Zarqawi to Sheikh Usama Bin Laden],' February 15, 2004. See also Abu Musab al-Zarqawi, 'risala min jundi ila amirihi [Letter from a Soldier to His Prince],' May 2005.
18. In *The Exile* it is claimed that five times during 2000–01 Bin Laden invited al-Zarqawi to Kandahar to give his bay'a but on ever occasion the Jordanian had refused, see Cathy Scott-Clark and Adrian Levy, *The Exile: The Stunning Inside Story of Osama Bin Laden and Al Qaeda in Flight* (New York: Bloomsbury, 2017), 241.
19. Bacon, 'Alliance Hubs: Focal Points in the International Terrorist Landscape'; Moghadam, *Nexus of Global Jihad : Understanding Cooperation among Terrorist Actors*.
20. Jeffrey Pool, 'Zarqawi's Pledge of Allegiance to Al-Qaeda: From Mu'askar Al-Battar, Issue 21,' *Jamestown Terrorism Monitor* 2, no. 24 (December 16, 2004).
21. Al-Adl, 'Jihadist Biography of the Slaughtering Leader Abu Mus'ab al-Zarqawi.'
22. Abu Muhammad al-Maqdisi, born Abu Muhammad 'Asim ibn Muhammad ibn Tahir al-Barqawi in the Palestinian village of Barqa in 1959, is one of the most influential Jihadi ideologues alive. In the early 1960s he moved to Kuwait with his family but after the Gulf war he left for Pakistan after a brief stint in Saudi Arabia. He would eventually settle in the city of Zarqa in Jordan. Ideologically, al-Maqdisi has evolved from a Qutbist to arguably the most preeminent Jihadi–Salafi scholar. Since his stay in Pakistan, he has enjoined huge influence among Jihadis, mainly Arabic speakers, and is often mentioned as the mentor of several influential Jihadis including Abu Musab al-Zarqawi, Abu Anas al-Shami and Turki al-Binali. While it would be a mistake to label al-Maqdisi as an 'al-Qaida ideologue', he is definitely close to the group and its leadership, which also considers him a central source of theological authority. Hence, he is considered an 'al-Qaida affiliated ideologue' throughout this research. For more on al-Maqdisi, Joas Wagemakers, *A Quietist Jihadi: The Ideology and Influence of Abu Muhammad Al-Maqdisi* (Cambridge: Cambridge University Press, 2012).
23. Abu Muhammad al-Maqdisi, 'al-zarqawi: munasaha wa munasara (Al-Zarqawi: Advice and Support),' July 2004. Al-Maqdisi wrote the text while imprisoned in Qafqafa prison.
24. The ideological revisionism argument is made by Shehada, 'Weakening Al-Qaeda: Literature Review Challenges Its Authority.' See also Joas Wagemakers, 'Contesting Religious Authority in Jordanian Salafi Networks,' *Perseverance of Terrorism: Focus on Leaders* 117 (2014): 111–25.

25. In 1998, al-Maqdisi wrote al-risala al-thalathiniyya fi al-tahdhir min al-ghulu fi al-takfir, which deals with 33 separate issues in the proclamation of takfir and shows that he already at this point saw a tendency of too loosely applying the concept.
26. For a thorough examination of the feud between al-Maqdisi and al-Zarqawi, especially in the context of Jordan, see Abu Hanieh and Abu Rumman, *The Jihadi Salafist Movement in Jordan after Zarqawi: Identity, Leadership Crisis and Obscured Vision*; Nibras Kazimi, 'A Virulent Ideology in Mutation: Zarqawi Upstages Maqdisi,' *Current Trends in Islamist Ideology* 2 (2005): 59–73; Joas Wagemakers, 'Reclaiming Scholarly Authority: Abu Muhammad Al-Maqdisi's Critique of Jihadi Practices,' *Studies in Conflict & Terrorism* 34, no. 7 (2011): 523–39; Eli Alshech, 'The Doctrinal Crisis within the Salafi-Jihadi Ranks and the Emergence of Neo-Takfirism,' *Islamic Law and Society* 21 (2014): 419–52.
27. Abu Muhammad Al-Maqdisi, 'Untitled Statement,' July 5, 2005.
28. For a thorough examination of Abu Muhammad al-Maqdisi's texts and ideology, see Wagemakers, *A Quietist Jihadi: The Ideology and Influence of Abu Muhammad Al-Maqdisi*.
29. Lia, 'Jihadi Strategists and Doctrinarians.'
30. Ayman al-Zawahiri, 'Untitled Letter to Al-Zarqawi,' July 9, 2005. The letter was made public in October 2005 by US authorities.
31. See for example Moghadam and Fishman, *Self Inflicted Wounds: Debates and Divisions within Al Qa'ida and Its Periphery*.
32. Al-Zawahiri, 'Untitled Letter to Al-Zarqawi.'
33. Abu Hamza al-Muhajir, al-Zarqawi's successor as AQI leader and with close bonds to the al-Qaida leadership, said in his first speech as new leader in reference to Iraq's Shia: 'You who partnered with the Lord of the two worlds, attacked the honour of the best of messengers, and insulted the honourable companions. You spent your efforts serving the Crusaders… We will apply the same rules of Abu Bakr al-Sadiq with you when he fought the converters. We will continue what Sheikh Abu Musab—may Allah forgive him—started with you. We will fight you so that the Tawhid word will prevail and your devil's word will descend.' See Abu Hamza al-Muhajir, 'sa-yuhzamu al-jam'u wa-yuwalluna al-dubra' [All Will Be Defeated and Flee],' June 2006.
34. Al-Zarqawi says that these scholars are currently imprisoned and therefore he cannot disclose their names.
35. Wagemakers, 'Contesting Religious Authority in Jordanian Salafi Networks.'
36. Abu Yahya al-Libi, 'A Letter to Mujahid Commander Abu Musab Al-Zarqawi from Abu Yahya Yunes Al-Sahrawi,' November 23, 2005.
37. Atiyyatullah al-Libi, 'Untitled Letter to Al-Zarqawi,' December 11, 2005. The letter was published by US authorities in 2006. Atiyyatullah also sent a letter to the mujahideen in Iraq a few months earlier on 24 August 2005. In the first letter he warned the mujahideen in Iraq about being too hard on the Muslim population who voted in elections. Atiyyatullah stressed that people voting should not by default be considered apostates as the intention behind the voting differs from person to person. Hence, it was an early call for Zarqawi and his group to relax their rigid assessment of the general population.
38. Atiyyatullah al-Libi, 'ila ikhwanana al-mujahideen fi al-'iraq: tahiya wa nasah [To the Mujahideen Brothers in Iraq: Greeting and Advice],' August 2005. Thanks to Kévin Jackson for informing me about this understudied letter by Atiyyatullah.
39. He also confirms that al-Zawahiri's letter, that was published by the US, is authentic and that it represents the feeling of the al-Qaida leadership.

40. Abu Abdullah al-Anbari, 'al-waqfu al-dari fi tarjamati al-sheikh al-anbari [Knowledgeable Study on the Biography of Sheikh Al-Anbari],' *Mu'assasat Al-Turath Al-'Ilmi*, 2018.
41. Besides AQI, the groups were Jaysh al-Taifa al-Mansoura, Katibat Ansar al-Tawhid wal Sunna, Saraya al-Jihad Group, al-Ghuraba Brigades and al-Ahwal Brigades.
42. Although AQI was officially just a part of the MSC and its official leader was Abdullah Ibn Rashid al-Baghdadi (al-Anbari), the hierarchy should not be confused. Al-Zarqawi was de facto leader of MSC. The Islamic State writes in al-Naba issue 41 that al-Zarqawi sent his deputy (al-Anbari) to Pakistan to talk with the al-Qaida leaders at a time when the MSC had been established and al-Anbari in reality would be higher in ranking than al-Zarqawi.
43. This is the argument in Brian Fishman, 'The Man Who Could Have Stopped the Islamic State,' *Foreign Policy*, November 23, 2016.
44. Abu Hamza al-Muhajir was from al-Zawahiri's Al Jihad group and it could thus have been expected that he would move AQI closer to the al-Qaida leadership. But Harun was not surprised this did not happen as he considered Abu Hamza to be rigid in his thinking in terms of religion, see Nelly Lahoud, 'Beware of the Imitator: Al-Qa'ida through the Lens of Its Confidential Secretary,' *Combating Terrorism Center*, 2012, 77.
45. The establishment of a state was a natural continuation of al-Zarqawi's ambition to build a social structure (mujtama' mutakamil), see Simon Staffell and Akil N. Awan, eds., *Jihadism Transformed : Al-Qaeda and Islamic State's Global Battle of Ideas* (London: Hurst & Company, 2016), 23–24.
46. Pool, 'Zarqawi's Pledge of Allegiance to Al-Qaeda: From Mu'askar Al-Battar, Issue 21.'
47. Staffell and Awan, *Jihadism Transformed : Al-Qaeda and Islamic State's Global Battle of Ideas*, 26.
48. Pierre Bourdieu, 'The Forms of Capital,' in *Knowledge Vol. 3*, ed. Nico Stehr and Reiner Grundmann (London: Taylor and Francis, 2005), 93–111; Pierre Bourdieu, *Outline of a Theory of Practice* (Cambridge: Cambridge University Press, 1977).
49. For more on how AQI/ISI approached the Sahwa, see Craig Whiteside, 'Nine Bullets for the Traitors, One for the Enemy: The Slogans and Strategy behind the Islamic State's Campaign to Defeat the Sunni Awakening (2006-2017),' *ICCT Research Paper*, September 2018. For the US support of the Sahwa and an analysis of why it worked to degrade ISI, see Stephen Biddle et al., 'Testing the Surge' 37, no. 1 (2012): 7–40; International Crisis Group, 'Iraq after the Surge I: The New Sunni Landscape,' *Middle East Report No. 74*, April 30, 2008.
50. Phillips, 'How Al Qaeda Lost Iraq.'
51. Ayman al-Zawahiri, 'Testimony to Preserve the Blood of the Mujahideen in Sham,' *As-Sahab Media*, May 2, 2014.
52. Abu Umar al-Baghdadi, 'wa qul ja'a al-haqqu wa zahaqa al-batil [Truth Has Come and Falsehood Has Vanished],' *Al-Furqan Media Foundation*, December 22, 2006.
53. Abu Umar al-Baghdadi, 'fa amma al-zabad fa yathhab jafa [As for the Foam It Passes Away as Scum],' *Al-Furqan Media Foundation*, December 3, 2007.
54. Al-Zawahiri says that 'The signs of the caliphate has started to loom in the horizon' in Ayman al-Zawahiri, 'Interview: A Review of Events,' *As-Sahab Media*, December 16, 2007. See also Abu al-Walid al-Ansari, 'risala nasiha li-abu umar al-baghdadi min al-sheikh abu al-walid al-ansari [Letter of Advice to Abu Umar al-Baghdadi from the Sheikh Abu al-Walid al-Ansari],' 2007.

55. Al-Anbari, 'al-waqfu al-dari fi tarjamati al-sheikh al-anbari [Knowledgeable Study on the Biography of Sheikh Al-Anbari].'
56. Ibid.
57. Al-Zarqawi, 'risala min jundi ila amirihi [Letter from a Soldier to His Prince].'
58. Abu Hamza al-Muhajir, 'inna al-hukm illa illaha [the Judgement Is for None but Allah],' November 12, 2006.
59. According to al-Zawahiri, Abu Hamza al-Muhajir sent a letter to al-Qaida's central leadership sometime after the creation of the ISI in which he said that ISI continued on its pledge of allegiance to al-Qaida, but this letter has never been made public. See Al-Zawahiri, 'Testimony to Preserve the Blood of the Mujahideen in Sham.'
60. ISI clearly sought to monopolise the Iraqi insurgency in 2006–07. In his speech from March 2007, Abu Umar al-Baghdadi says that 'we consider the members of other Jihadi groups in Iraq as our brothers and we don't accuse them in disbelief or immorality, but they are disobedient because they didn't do today's duty (of working under one flag),' see Abu Umar al-Baghdadi, 'Say: I Am Aware of My God,' *Al-Furqan Media Foundation*, March 13, 2007.
61. Fishman, 'The Man Who Could Have Stopped the Islamic State.'
62. Nelly Lahoud, 'The 'Islamic State' and Al-Qaeda,' in *Jihadism Transformed : Al-Qaeda and Islamic State's Global Battle of Ideas*, ed. Simon Staffell and Akil N. Awan (London: Hurst & Company, 2016), 21–34. Bin Laden was against state creation both in the context of Yemen, see Abbottabad letter, 'SOCOM-2012-0000019,' May 2010; and in Somalia, see Abbottabad letter, 'SOCOM-2012-0000005,' July 8, 2010.
63. Atiyyatullah elaborates on the character of an Islamic state in Atiyyatullah al-Libi, 'Untitled Article,' January 5, 2007.
64. It seems it is a second letter from Abu Yahya to Abu Umar and that the Libyan never received a response to the first letter.
65. Al-Baghdadi, 'Say: I Am Aware of My God.'
66. Abu Yahya al-Libi, 'risala khassa min fadila al-sheikh al-mujahid abu yahya al-libi ila sheikh al-mujahid abu umar al-baghdadi [Private Letter from the Virtous Mujahid Sheikh Abu Yahya al-Libi to the Mujahid Sheikh Abu Umar al-Baghdadi],' April 4, 2007.
67. In the speeches, Bin Laden also stresses the importance of unity among the mujahideen in Iraq.
68. Just like eulogies for al-Zarqawi by Bin Laden, al-Zawahiri and Abu Yahya were all framed positively despite the internal criticism. Another example is al-Zawahiri's speech 'from Tora Bora to Iraq' from August 2006 in which he says that he has only seen good things from al-Zarqawi although he the year before sent an extremely critical letter to al-Zarqawi. A later example is al-Zawahiri's interview with as-Sahab titled 'The True Facts of Jihad and the Lies of Hypocrisy.'
69. Abbottabad letter, 'Letter to Shaykh Abu Muhammad,' *Batch 2*, August 17, 2007.
70. Abbottabad letter, 'Letter to the Generous Brother Shaykh Abu Muhammad,' *Batch 2*, n.d.
71. Thanks to Kévin Jackson for identifying Sultan as Mustafa al-Yazid.
72. There are actually two letters in SOCOM 11 and the second is from March 2007, but the first one is from before. Al-Zawahiri is specifically referring to a speech by Abu Umar in which he says some obvious mistakes (most likely to the speech 'Truth has Come and Falsehood has Vanished' from December 2006).

73. In fact, we know that other jihadi groups in Iraq had complained to al-Qaida leaders since 2004 about AQI's behaviour towards them, see Abbottabad letter, 'Jihad and Reform Front,' *Batch 1*, May 22, 2007.
74. On al-Qaida's interest in unity, see Abbottabad letter, 'Letter Dtd 07 August 2010,' *Batch 1*, August 7, 2010; Abbottabad letter, 'In the Name of God, the Merciful,' *Batch 2*, 2010.
75. Brian Fishman, 'Ansar Al-Sunnah Threatens Al-Qa'ida in Iraq,' *Combating Terrorism Center*, February 26, 2007; Aymenn Jawad Al-Tamimi, 'A Complete History of Jamaat Ansar Al-Islam,' December 15, 2015; Brian Fishman, 'Dysfunction and Decline : Lessons Learned from Inside Al Qa'ida in Iraq,' *Combating Terrorism Center*, 2009.
76. International Crisis Group, 'Iraq after the Surge I: The New Sunni Landscape.'
77. A copy of al-Utaybi's letter can be accessed here: https://justpaste.it/fhsu [accessed 14 November 2019].
78. Abu Sulayman al-Utaybi, 'risala al-sheikh abu sulaiman al-utaybi li-qiyada fi khorasan [Letter from Sheikh Abu Sulaiman Al-Utaybi to the Leadership in Khorasan],' 2007 (published on November 23, 2013 on https://justpaste.it/do3r [Accessed 12 August 2018]).
79. Brian Fishman, 'The First Defector: Abu Sulayman Al-Utaybi, the Islamic State, and Al-Qa'ida,' *CTC Sentinel* 8, no. 10 (2015). For a discussion of the validity of Abu Sulayman al-Utaybi's criticism, see Whiteside, 'Nine Bullets for the Traitors, One for the Enemy: The Slogans and Strategy behind the Islamic State's Campaign to Defeat the Sunni Awakening (2006-2017).'
80. Bill Roggio, Daveed Gartenstein-Ross, and Tony Badran, 'Intercepted Letters from Al-Qaeda Leaders Shed Light on State of Network in Iraq,' *Long War Journal*, September 12, 2008.
81. See al-Anbari, 'al-waqfu al-dari fi tarjamati al-sheikh al-anbari [Knowledgeable Study on the Biography of Sheikh Al-Anbari].' Before his imprisonment in April 2006, Anbari functioned as an emissary to al-Qaida's leadership. Not only was he a senior member of AQI - he was in fact chosen as amir of MSC - but he was also close to Mustafa al-Yazid, whom he greatly admired for his piety, which could explain why he was chosen as emissary, author's interview with Abu Sulayman al-Muhajir, June 2017.
82. Abbottabad letter, 'Dear Honorable Brother Shaykh Azmaray,' *Batch 2*, March 5, 2008.
83. Abbottabad letter, 'SOCOM-2012-0000019.'
84. It is quite telling, that in a May 2010 letter to Atiyyatullah, Bin Laden asked him to seek information about al-Baghdadi and his new deputy as he knew little about them and he also instructed Atiyyatullah to get information through Ansar al-Islam to ensure that they would receive something but also that the information would be 'objective'.
85. Abbottabad letter, 'SOCOM-2012-0000010,' April 26, 2011.
86. The most comprehensive biography of al-Adnani was authored by Turki al-Binali titled 'al-lafz al-sani fi tarjamat al-adnani [clear words in the understanding of al-Adnani],' May 26, 2014.
87. In the author's interview with Abu Mahmoud al-Filastini, this weakness of al-Qaida's central leadership is mentioned as one of the main reasons why the leadership approached the Iraqi group as leniently as it did.
88. Abbottabad letter, 'SOCOM-2012-0000004,' January 2011.
89. Abbottabad letter, 'SOCOM-2012-0000019.'

90. Ibid.: 4.
91. In letter Abbottabad letter, 'To Our Honorable Emir the Emir of All Believers,' *Batch 2*, 2011, Bin Laden also discredits attacks against mosques and public places.
92. The Islamic State has several times targeted mosques, especially in Saudi Arabia, Yemen and Afghanistan.
93. Abbottabad letter, 'SOCOM-2012-0000016,' 2010. For an elaborate discussion of the similarity to Mao's theory, see Ross, Fritz, and Moreng, 'Islamic State vs. Al-Qaeda: Strategic Dimensions of a Patricidal Conflict.'
94. For instance in Abbottabad letter, 'SOCOM-2012-0000003,' August 27, 2010. SOCOM03 Bin Laden instructs Atiyyatullah to tell AQAP that its leader Nasir al-Wuhayshi should be the only one appearing in media releases in contrast to the ongoing practice within AQAP at the time.
95. Al-Zawahiri, 'Untitled Letter to Al-Zarqawi'; Al-Zawahiri, *Knights Under the Prophet's Banner*.
96. Ayman al-Zawahiri, 'And the Noble Knights Dismount,' June 8, 2011.
97. Ayman al-Zawahiri, 'General Guidelines for Jihad,' *As-Sahab Media*, September 2013.
98. In fact, Abu Bakr Naji also wrote about the importance of the masses, see Abu Bakr Naji, *The Management of Savagery* ([Translation by Will McCants 2006], 2004), 21. The suggested name change of al-Qaida was also with the objective of winning the support of the Muslim masses, see Abbottabad letter, 'SOCOM-2012-0000009,' n.d.
99. Anwar al-Awlaki, 'Salutations To Al-Shabaab Of Somalia,' n.d.
100. Abbottabad letter, 'SOCOM-2012-0000004.'
101. Abbottabad letter, 'SOCOM-2012-0000007.'
102. Abbottabad letter, 'SOCOM-2012-0000019.'
103. Abbottabad letter, 'Give the Tribes More than They Can Handle,' *Batch 2*, n.d.
104. Abbottabad letter, 'SOCOM-2012-0000016.' A senior al-Qaida figure similarly outlines al-Qaida's strategy in Yemen (and other places) to al-Wuhayshi in Abbottabad letter, 'Letter to Abu Basir,' *Batch 2*, n.d.
105. Abbottabad letter, 'Three Stages Letter,' *Batch 3*, n.d.
106. Adam Simpson, 'The 'Islamic State' Challenges Al-Qaeda in Yemen,' *International Institute for Middle East and Balkan Studies*, December 18, 2016.
107. Abbottabad letter, 'Letter about the Matter of the Islamic Maghreb,' *Batch 2*, March 5, 2010.
108. Mathieu Guidère, 'The Timbuktu Letters: New Insights about AQIM,' *Res Militaris*, 2014.
109. Morrison, *Origins and Rise of Dissident Irish Republicanism: The Role and Impact of Organizational Splits*, 42.
110. Haroro J. Ingram, 'How ISIS Survives Defeat: Propaganda and Decisive Minorities,' *Oxford Research Group*, September 26, 2016.
111. Al-Qaida, 'bayan bishan 'alaqa jama'a qa'idat al-jihad bi-jama'a al-dawla al-islamiyya fi al-'iraq wa-l-sham [Statement about the Relations of Al-Qaida with the Islamic State in Iraq and Sham],' February 3, 2014.
112. Morrison, *Origins and Rise of Dissident Irish Republicanism: The Role and Impact of Organizational Splits*, 19.
113. Abu Hanieh and Abu Rumman, *The 'Islamic State' Organization: The Sunni Crisis and the Struggle of Global Jihadism*; Hassan, 'Two Houses Divided: How Conflict in Syria Shaped the Future of Jihadism.'

114. For more on the establishment of Jabhat al-Nusra see Charles Lister, *The Syrian Jihad: Al-Qaeda, the Islamic State and the Evolution of an Insurgency* (London: Hurst Publishers, 2015); Abu Abdullah al-Shami, 'The Establishment of Jabhat al-Nusra and the Events of Al Sham from the Beginning of the Disagreement to the Announcement of Dawlah,' *Biladal-Sham Media*, November 20, 2016.
115. Abu Bakr al-Baghdadi, 'Give Glad Tidings to the Believers,' *Al-Furqan Media Foundation*, April 8, 2013. Al-Julani confirmed al-Baghdadi's account in Abu Muhammad al-Julani, 'About the Fields of Al-Sham,' *Al-Manara al-Bayda Media Foundationa Media Foundation*, April 10, 2013.
116. Al-Zawahiri, 'Testimony to Preserve the Blood of the Mujahideen in Sham.'
117. This letter has never been made public, but in Ayman al-Zawahiri, 'Answers to the Esteemed Shaykhs,' *As-Sahab Media*, May 2, 2014, al-Zawahiri says he wrote a letter in April 2013
118. Abu Yahya's role in charge of the Syrian file was allegedly taken over by Abu Ubayda al-Maqdisi after the Libyan's death.
119. Ayman al-Zawahiri, 'Untitled Letter to al-Julani and al-Baghdadi,' May 23, 2013. It was later revealed that the letter was leaked by Jabhat al-Nusra.
120. Abu Bakr al-Baghdadi, 'Remaining in Iraq and the Levant,' *Al-Furqan Media Foundation*, June 14, 2013.
121. Abu Muhammed al-Adnani, 'So Leave Them Alone with Their Fabrications,' June 18, 2013.
122. Al-Zawahiri sent a long detailed message to ISIS on September 4, 2013 in which he confirms that his judgement (from May) was that of an amir to a problem between his soldiers, see al-Zawahiri, 'Testimony to Preserve the Blood of the Mujahideen in Sham.'
123. The Islamic State identified the start of military confrontations as summer 2013 in its statement where it takes responsibility for killing al-Hadrami.
124. Mayer N Zald and Bert Useem, 'Movement and Countermovement: Loosely Coupled Conflict,' *CRSO Working Paper 302*, 1983, 1–31; Zald and McCarthy, 'Social Movement Industries: Competition and Cooperation Among Movement Organizations.'
125. Stathis N. Kalyvas, 'The Ontology of "Political Violence": Action and Identity in Civil Wars,' *Perspectives on Politics* 1, no. 3 (2003): 481.
126. Scott Atran, 'ISIS is a revolution', AEON, 15 December 2015: https://aeon.co/essays/why-isis-has-the-potential-to-be-a-world-altering-revolution. Kalyvas also makes the comparison to Marxist rebel groups because just like Marxism, Jihadism is a revolutionary and transnational movement. See Kalyvas 'Jihadi Rebels in Civil War.'
127. Yuri Felshtinsky, 'Lenin, Trotsky, Stalin and the Left Opposition in the USSR, 1918–1928,' *Cahiers Du Monde Russe* 31, no. 4 (1990): 569–78.
128. Morrison, *Origins and Rise of Dissident Irish Republicanism: The Role and Impact of Organizational Splits*; Zirakzadeh, 'From Revolutionary Dreams to Organizational Fragmentation: Disputes over Violence within ETA and Sendero Luminoso.'
129. D. S. Lane, 'Social and Organizational Differences between the Bolsheviks and Mensheviks, 1903 to 1907,' *Discussion Paper,* May (1964): 1.
130. Robert Michels, *Political Parties: A Sociological Study of the Oligarchical Tendencies of Modern Democracy* (New York: Hearst's International Library Co., 1915).
131. Lahoud, *The Jihadis' Path to Self-Destruction*, 141–43.
132. Hamid and Farrall, *The Arabs at War in Afghanistan*, 172.

133. Several Jihadis have written testimonies of Bin Laden documenting his life and importance as a Jihadi leader. One example is Abu Mundhir al-Shinqiti. See also Staffell and Awan, *Jihadism Transformed :Al-Qaeda and Islamic State's Global Battle of Ideas*, 12.
134. Lahoud, 'Beware of the Imitator: Al-Qa'ida through the Lens of Its Confidential Secretary.'
135. Scott-Clark and Levy, *The Exile: The Stunning Inside Story of Osama Bin Laden and Al Qaeda in Flight*.
136. Senior figures killed include: Mustafa al-Yazid (2010), Atiyyatullah al-Libi (2011), Abu Yahya al-Libi (2012), Abu Zaid al-Kuwaiti (2012) and Abu Dujana al-Basha (2014).
137. Internally, he received *criticism*, see Saif al-Adl, 'al-khamsa al-shidadd: maqalat jadida min abir sabil [The Five Tough Ones: New Articles from the Wayfarer],' March 23, 2011; and *advice*, see Hussein Ibn Mahmoud, 'A Message to Emir al-Zawahiri,' June 16, 2011.
138. Hamid and Farrall, *The Arabs at War in Afghanistan*, 300.
139. For example in December 2013, the Islamic State circulated a video clip of Bin Laden promoting the Islamic State.
140. In 1924, after the death of Lenin, a leadership vacuum emerged that Stalin capitalised on to the great disappointment of Trotsky. In the years leading up to Lenin's death, Stalin clashed with Lenin in an attempt to position himself for future leadership. This involved a clandestine process of undermining the existing leadership and winning loyalty among party cadres, something his rival, the more elitist Trotsky, could not compete with.
141. Al-Shami, 'The Establishment of Jabhat Al-Nusra and the Events of Al Sham from the Beginning of the Disagreement to the Announcement of Dawlah.'
142. Al-Anbari, 'al-waqfu al-dari fi tarjamati al-sheikh al-anbari [Knowledgeable Study on the Biography of Sheikh Al-Anbari].'
143. Lister, *The Syrian Jihad: Al-Qaeda, the Islamic State and the Evolution of an Insurgency*; Christoph Reuter, 'The Terror Strategist: Secret Files Reveal the Structure of Islamic State,' *Der Spiegel*, April 18, 2015.
144. Aymenn Jawad al-Tamimi, 'The Life of Abu Muhammad al-Furqan: Head of the Media Department of the Islamic State (Part Two),' May 20, 2021.
145. On the last day of the meetings, al-Julani renewed his bay'a to al-Baghdadi according to al-Julani's senior shar'i Abu Abdullah al-Shami.
146. In the beginning, after its expansion to Syria, ISIS was active in the Aleppo area where it early on attracted a lot of foreign fighters, who were particularly present in Aleppo at this time. In Aleppo, ISIS and al-Nusra were separate entities already in summer 2013, see Aymenn Jawad al-Tamimi, 'Jabhat al-Nusra and the Islamic State of Iraq and Ash-Sham: Aleppo Area,' June 13, 2013. As a counter-measure Jabhat al-Nusra established Jund al-Aqsa in early 2013 to prevent fighters from joining the Islamic State.
147. Author's interview with Danish foreign fighter, June 28, 2017 (Copenhagen).
148. Jenan Moussa and Harald Doornbos, 'Present at the Creation,' *Foreign Policy*, August 16, 2016.
149. Bacon and Arsenault, 'Al Qaeda and the Islamic State's Break: Strategic Strife or Lackluster Leadership?'
150. This was clear from Bin Laden's hesitance to accept al-Shabab into the fold of al-Qaida, while al-Zawahiri shortly after assuming leadership of al-Qaida accepted the

Somali group as an official affiliate. The authors also point out that Bin Laden was more diplomatic than al-Zawahiri, but again this seems mistaken at least considered that al-Zawahiri was effectively managing much of the relations with other groups including the relationship with AQI during the reign of al-Zarqawi.

151. William F. McCants, *The ISIS Apocalypse: The History, Strategy, and Doomsday Vision of the Islamic State* (New York: St. Martin's Press, 2015).
152. According to al-Zawahiri, him and Abu Hamza al-Muhajir were extremely close, not just from their time in Egypt but also in Afghanistan, where Abu Hamza allegedly also pledged allegiance to Bin Laden. For al-Zawahiri this makes it unthinkable that Abu Hamza should have agreed to break his pledge of allegiance to al-Qaida, see Ayman a-Zawahiri, 'Islamic Spring Part 5,' *As-Sahab Media*, October 2015.
153. Al-Zawahiri, 'Testimony to Preserve the Blood of the Mujahideen in Sham.'
154. Ayman al-Zawahiri, 'Islamic Spring Part 2,' *As-Sahab Media*, April 2015, 4.
155. Ayman al-Zawahiri, 'Islamic Spring Part 3: A Talk on the Khilafa That Follows the Prophetic Path,' *As-Sahab Media*, April 2015. Al-Zawahiri also claims that an envoy of al-Zarqawi, most likely referring to al-Anbari's 2005 visit, reassured al-Qaida leaders in Khorasan that al-Zarqawi was devoted to his pledge of allegiance, see Al-Zawahiri, 'Islamic Spring Part 5.'
156. Al-Zawahiri, 'Islamic Spring Part 2.'
157. Al-Baghdadi, 'wa qul ja'a al-haqqu wa zahaqa al-batil [Truth Has Come and Falsehood Has Vanished].'
158. Al-Adnani, 'Apologies, Amir of Al-Qaida.'
159. Abu Muhammad al-Maqdisi, 'And be not like her who undoes the thread which she has spun, after it has become strong,' *Minbar Al-Tawhid Wa-l-Jihad*, July 10, 2014.
160. These are examples of works mentioning Ba'thist influence: Reuter, 'The Terror Strategist: Secret Files Reveal the Structure of Islamic State'; Michael Weiss and Hassan Hassan, *ISIS: Inside the Army of Terror* (New York: Regan Arts., 2015); Liz Sly, 'The Hidden Hand behind the Islamic State Militants? Saddam Hussein's,' *The Washington Post*, April 5, 2015; Samuel Helfont and Michael Brill, 'Saddam's ISIS?,' *Foreign Affairs*, January 12, 2016; Stern and Berger, *ISIS: The State of Terror*.
161. This is a typical argument from al-Qaida figures. For instance, in an interview with Abu Mahmoud al-Filastini, he explains how the ISI was overtaken by ba'thists in 2007–08. Another claim by opponents of the Islamic State is that the group is infiltrated by Israeli intelligence. See for instance the letter Abdullah bin Muhammad, 'The Reality of the Penetration of the Islamic State of Iraq's Leadership,' February 17, 2013.
162. Craig Whiteside, 'A Pedigree of Terror: The Myth of the Ba'athist Influence in the Islamic State Movement,' *Perspectives on Terrorism* 11, no. 3 (2017).
163. Truls Hallberg Tonnessen, 'Heirs of Zarqawi or Saddam? The Relationship between Al-Qaida in Iraq and the Islamic State,' *Perspectives on Terrorism* 9, no. 4 (2015): 48–60.
164. Kyle Orton, 'How Saddam Hussein Gave Us ISIS,' *The New York Times*, December 23, 2015.
165. The argument is countered by Joseph Sassoon, *Saddam Hussein's Ba'th Party: Inside an Authoritarian Regime* (New York: Cambridge University Press, 2012).
166. Al-Baghdadi, 'wa qul ja'a al-haqqu wa zahaqa al-batil [Truth Has Come and Falsehood Has Vanished].'
167. For example, al-Qaida's first three heads of its military council (the group's most important institution) Abu Ubayda al-Banshiri, Abu Hafs al-Masri and Saif al-Adl

had all served in the Egyptian army. Another senior figure, Abd al-Hadi al-Iraqi also served in the Iraqi army before joining al-Qaida.

168. Fawaz Gerges, *ISIS: A History* (Princeton: Princeton University Press, 2016).
169. Author's interview with Muhammed Abu Rumman, December 8, 2016 (Amman).
170. Senior non-Iraqi leaders still alive in 2006 include: al-Zarqawi (Jordanian, killed in June 2006), Abu Hamza al-Muhajir (Egyptian, killed in 2010), Abu Usama al-Tunisi (Tunisian, killed in 2007), Abu Ibrahim al-Ansari (Moroccan, killed in 2011). Mustafa Ramadan Darwish (Abu Muhammad al-Lubnani) from Lebanon was killed in 2005 just as Suleiman Khalid Darwish from Syria.
171. Ali Soufan, 'Next in Line to Lead Al-Qa'ida: A Profile of Abu Muhammad Al-Masri,' *CTC Sentinel* 12, no. 10 (2019).
172. Donatella Della Porta and Mario Diani, *Social Movements: An Introduction*, second edition (Oxford: Blackwell Publishing, 2006), 211.
173. Morrison, *Origins and Rise of Dissident Irish Republicanism: The Role and Impact of Organizational Splits*.
174. Moghadam and Fishman, *Self Inflicted Wounds: Debates and Divisions within Al Qa'ida and Its Periphery*, 3–4.

## CHAPTER 5. DIVERGING DESIRES

1. Jabhat al-Nusra, 'Interview with Abu Sulayman al-Muhajir,' *Al Basira Media*, April 2014.
2. Abu al-Mundhir al-Shinqiti, 'yuriduna da'ishnat al-jihad [We Want Daish's Jihad],' December 5, 2015.
3. Al-Zawahiri, 'General Guidelines for Jihad.'
4. Donatella Della Porta, *Social Movements, Political Violence, and the State: A Comparative Analysis of Italy and Germany* (Cambridge: Cambridge University Press, 1995), 83.
5. Guido Steinberg, 'Ahrar Al-Sham: The "Syrian Taliban",' *SWP Comments*, May 27, 2016.
6. For instance, after expanding into Syria in April 2013 the Islamic State allegedly invaded the headquarters of Jabhat al-Nusra and seized ammunition caches and weapons stores.
7. Aaron Y. Zelin, 'The Islamic State's Territorial Methodology,' *The Washington Institute for Near East Policy, Research Note No. 29*, January 2016.
8. Lahoud writes al-Hadrami was killed in December 2013, see Lahoud, 'The "Islamic State" and Al-Qaeda.'
9. Islamic State, 'Irja' – The Most Dangerous Bid'ah,' *Dabiq 8*, March 2015.
10. Aron Lund, 'Pushing Back Against the Islamic State of Iraq and the Levant: The Islamic Front,' *Carnegie Middle East Center*, January 8, 2014.
11. It has been claimed Abu Khalid al-Suri's assassination was retaliation for split but this seems unlikely as ISIS did not regard the split as problematic, see Lahoud, 'The "Islamic State" and Al-Qaeda.'
12. In a message published on March 1, 2014 through its al-Itisam Media, the Islamic State denied killing al-Suri.
13. Zald and Useem, 'Movement and Countermovement: Loosely Coupled Conflict,' 2.
14. Ibid.: 12.
15. William McCants, *The ISIS Apocalypse: The History, Strategy, and Doomsday Vision of the Islamic State* (New York: St. Martin's Press, 2015).

16. Some have made the argument that the Islamic State and the Assad regime agreed not to target one another in this period, however this remains mere speculation. See for instance Anne Speckhard and Ahmet S. Yayla, 'The ISIS Emni: Origins and Inner Workings of ISIS's Intelligence Apparatus,' *Perspectives on Terrorism* 11, no. 1 (2017).
17. Krause, *Rebel Power: Why National Movements Compete, Fight, and Win*.
18. Hanne Fjelde and Desirée Nilsson, 'Rebels against Rebels: Explaining Violence between Rebel Groups,' *Journal of Conflict Resolution* 56, no. 4 (2012): 608.
19. The January 2015 terrorist attacks in Paris committed by the Kouachi brothers and Amedy Coulibaly, respectively, are illustrative of this time lag in institutionalisation of a logic of reciprocal enmity. While the Kouachi brothers were carrying out their attack in the name of al-Qaida and had close ties to AQAP, Coulibaly dedicated his attack to the Islamic State. Despite their differences in allegiance the actors nonetheless coordinated prior to the attacks. See Rukmini Callimachi and Andrew Higgins, 'Video Shows a Paris Gunman Declaring His Loyalty to the Islamic State,' *New York Times*, January 11, 2015.
20. Morrison, *Origins and Rise of Dissident Irish Republicanism: The Role and Impact of Organizational Splits*, 28.
21. Ibid.: 30.
22. Ansar al-Islam, 'Untitled Statement,' June 30, 2014.
23. Al-Anbari, 'al-waqfu al-dari fi tarjamati al-sheikh al-anbari [Knowledgeable Study on the Biography of Sheikh Al-Anbari].'
24. Lund, 'Pushing Back Against the Islamic State of Iraq and the Levant: The Islamic Front.'
25. Author's interview with Danish foreign fighter, June 28, 2017 (Copenhagen). In his eulogy for al-Suri, al-Julani refers the question to al-Maqdisi, Abu Qatada and al-Ulwan; allegedly two of the three rejected the legitimacy of fighting the Islamic State.
26. Abu Abdullah Al-Shami, 'Untitled Statement,' June 30, 2014.
27. 'BREAKING: Mujahideen Shura Council Has Been Formed in Deir Ez-Zor,' May 25, 2014.
28. Ahrar al-Sham, 'No Title,' May 4, 2013.
29. Hassan Abboud, 'kalimat sawtiyya li-l-sheikh abu abdullah al-hamawi 'an ahdath al-sham al-akhira [Audio Message from Sheikh Abu Abdullah Al-Hamawi on the Recent Events in Sham],' January 27, 2014.
30. Al-Zawahiri, 'Untitled Letter to al-Julani and al-Baghdadi.'
31. Ayman al-Zawahiri, 'Islamic Spring Part 1,' *As-Sahab Media*, March 2015.
32. al-Suri, 'Untitled Statement.' Al-Suri also wrote al-Zawahiri a letter in January 2014 which included a report with the claims made by Jabhat al-Nusra and the Islamic State, respectively.
33. Al-Zawahiri, 'Islamic Spring Part 1.'
34. Author's interview with Jihadi media official based in Syria, November 24, 2017.
35. Conflicting accounts exists. One author interview with a Jabhat al-Nusra media official indicates that al-Ali met with al-Anbari, while a senior al-Nusra member told this author that it in fact was al-Baghdadi he met.
36. Author's interview with Abu Sulayman al-Muhajir, June 2017.
37. Abu Firas al-Suri, an al-Qaida veteran, migrated from Yemen to Syria in 2013 to join Jabhat al-Nusra and mediate in the conflict with the Islamic State. Al-Suri was

an experienced mediator after having negotiated between warring Afghan and Arab forces in Afghanistan in the 1990s. Not a lot is known about al-Suri's concrete mediation efforts in Syria though.

38. Al-Qatari was born in Iraq but a Jordanian citizen. Al-Qatari has changed his name on numerous occasions in accordance to his location. He was reportedly a longtime al-Qaida associate, collaborating with al-Qaida in Afghanistan where he met Bin Laden, al-Zawahiri, and Azzam. He is also reported to have fought in Chechnya and afterwards assisting al-Zarqawi establishing Jama'at al-Tawhid wa-l-Jihad in Iraq. After al-Zarqawi's death he remained close to serve in ISI.
39. See 'limadha qatala al-sheikh abu abd al-aziz al-qatari/al-iraqi/al-urduni/al-filastini [Why Did the Sheikh Abu Abd Al-Azaz Al-Qatari/Al-Iraqi/Al-Urduni/Al-Filastini Die],' March 26, 2014.
40. Abu Bakr al-Baghdadi, 'wa allah ya'lam wa antum la ta'lamun [God Knows and You Do Not Know],' *Al Furqan Media Foundation*, January 19, 2014.
41. A similar argument is made in Abu Muhammed al-Adnani, 'May Allah Be With You, O Oppressed State,' *Al-Furqan Media Foundation*, September 30, 2013.
42. AQAP, 'risala ila al-mujahideen fi-l-sham [Message to the Mujahideen in Sham],' *Al-Malahem Media Foundation*, February 27, 2014.
43. Abu Abdullah al-Shami, 'No Title', June 30, 2014.
44. Mentioned Jabhat al-Nusra, 'Interview with Abu Sulayman al-Muhajir'; Al-Shami, 'Untitled Statement.'
45. Abu Firas al-Suri, 'shahadat qabil intiha' muhlat al-mubahala: shahada al-sheikh abu firas al-suri [Testimonies before the Ending of the Mubahala: Testimony of Sheikh Abu Firas Al-Suri],' *Al Basira Media*, March 18, 2014.
46. Al-Tunisi was at the time a shar'i in the military office of Jabhat al-Nusra.
47. Abu Muhammad al-Julani, 'Allah, Allah, in the Field of Al-Sham,' *Al-Manara Al-Bayda Media Foundation*, January 7, 2014.
48. Ayman al-Zawahiri, 'nida' 'ajilun li-ahluna fi-l-sham [An Urgent Call to Our People in Al-Sham],' *As-Sahab Media*, January 15, 2014.
49. Hani al-Sibai and Tariq Abdelhaleem, 'da'wa li-l-sulh wa-l-safh been al-mujahideen fi-l-sham li-l-dawla wa jabhat al-nusra wa ahrar al-sham wa ghayruhum min kata'ib [A call for reconciliation and forgiveness among the Mujahideen in the Levant, call to the state, Jabhat al-Nusra, Ahrar al-Sham and other battalions],' *Minbar Al-Tawhid Wa-l-Jihad*, January 21, 2014.
50. Abu Muhammad al-Maqdisi, 'bayan sadir fi bayan hal 'al-dawla al-islamiyya fi-l-iraq wa-l-sham' wa-l-mawqif al-wajib tujahaha [A Comdemning Statement on the Status of the Islamic State in Iraq and Sham and the Necessary Position against It],' *Minbar Al-Tawhid Wa-l-Jihad*, May 26, 2014.
51. Posted on al-Maqdisi's Minbar al-Tawhid wa-l-Jihad website. The most prominent among the signatories were Abu Muhammad al-Maqdisi, Abu Qatada al-Filistini, Hani al-Sibai, Tariq Abdulhaleem, Omar al-Haddouchi, Abdullah al-Muhaysini, and Abu Muhammad al-Dagestani.
52. Abdullah al-Muhaysini, 'mubadarat al-umma [Initiative of the Umma],' *Telegram Channel*, January 22, 2014.
53. 'al-maqdisi wa al-tahawi yud'aman mubadarat al-umma li-da'iyyat sa'udi [Al-Maqdisi and al-Tahawi Support the Initiative of the Umma by a Saudi Preacher],' *Al-Quds Al-Arabi*, January 26, 2014.

54. Abboud, 'kalimat sawtiyya li-l-sheikh abu abdullah al-hamawi 'an ahdath al-sham al-akhira [Audio Message from Sheikh Abu Abdullah al-Hamawi on the Recent Events in Sham].'
55. Abu Muhammad al-Julani, 'A Message of Support and Acceptance for the "Initiative of the Umma",' January 24, 2014.
56. In late 2013, the Jordanian Jihadi ideologue Iyad al-Qunaybi issued a criticism of the Islamic State for not accepting arbitration, see Iyad al-Qunaybi, 'al-waquf ma "al-dawla" ala muftaraq turuq [Standing with 'the Islamic State' at a Crossroad],' 2013.
57. After the Islamic State's response to al-Muhaysini's arbitration initiative, Iyad al-Qunaybi issued an audio statement titled 'Discussion of the State's response to the Initiative of the Umma' which ran as a critique of the Islamic State's rejection to the initiative, see Iyad al-Qunaybi, 'munaqasha li-radd al-dawla 'ala mubadarat al-umma [Discussion of the State's Response to the Initiative of the Umma],' February 3, 2014.
58. Cole Bunzel, 'The Islamic State of Disobedience: Al-Baghdadi Triumphant,' *Jihadica*, October 5, 2015.
59. For more on al-Maqdisi's shari'a council, see J Wagemakers, 'Protecting Jihad: The Sharia Council of the Minbar Al-Tawhid Wa-l-Jihad,' *Middle East Policy* CVIII, no. 2 (2011): 148–62.
60. Binali was born in September 1984 in Bahrain. At some point he moved to Dubai to study, but he was arrested and deported for his jihadi sympathies. He would then continue his studies in Beirut and in Bahrain, occasionally interrupted by detentions. Al-Binali has studied under several scholars, most notably Umar al-Haddouchi and al-Maqdisi. Al-Binali also travelled to Iraq and later Syria on several occasions. From early on he was particularly sympathetic to al-Zarqawi's group in Iraq. In an interview with a childhood friend of al-Binali, I was told of a conversation in which—after Abu Yahya al-Libi suggested that ISI and Ansar al-Islam should merge—al-Binali said 'The group Al Ansar has rejected this offer to join under the banner of the Islamic State of Iraq, and so I have sworn not to watch any videos or any statement released by them.'
61. Abu Basir al-Tartusi, whose real name is Abd al-Munim Mustafa Halima, was born in the Syrian city of Tartus in 1959. In 1981 he migrated to Peshawar where he met several historical Jihadi figures. He would then move to the Jordanian city of Zarqa where he would live close to Abu Musab al-Zarqawi. At some point al-Tartusi was expelled from Jordan which led him to go to Yemen, where he was also expelled. In then end he settled in the United Kingdom, where he became a central figure in 'Londonistan's' radical environment. After the Syrian war broke out, al-Tartusi join the rebellion on the side of Ahrar al-Sham and is now believed to be living in Istanbul.
62. Turki al-Binali, 'al-qiyafa fi 'adam ishtirat al-tamkin al-kamil li-l-khilafa [the Pursuit of the Caliphate Does Not Depend on Full Consolidation],' April 30, 2014.
63. Turki al-Binali, 'khatt al-midad fi-l-radd 'ala al-duktur iyad [Sufficient Answer to Respond to Doctor Iyad],' December 15, 2013.
64. Turki al-Binali, 'mudd al-ayadi li-bay'at al-baghdadi [Extend Your Hands to Give Bay'a to Al-Baghdadi],' August 5, 2013.
65. Turki al-Binali, 'al-thamar al-dani fi 'l-radd 'ala khitab al-julani [The Low Hanging Fruit in Responding to the Speech of Al-Julani],' January 8, 2014.
66. Turki al-Binali, 'tabsir al-mahajij bi-l-farq bayn rijal al-dawla al-islamiyya wa-l-khawarij [Enlightening Arguments on the Differences between the Men of the Islamic State and the Khawarij),' *Al-Ghuraba Media*, January 19, 2014.

67. Al-Zawahiri, 'Answers to the Esteemed Shaykhs.'
68. Al-Binali, 'al-thamar al-dani fi 'l-radd 'ala khitab al-julani [the Low Hanging Fruit in Responding to the Speech of Al-Julani].'
69. Al-Binali, 'khatt al-midad fi-l-radd 'ala al-duktur iyad [Sufficient Answer to Respond to Doctor Iyad].'
70. For al-Amili's critique, see http://archive.org/detail/bayan_2013 (accessed 26 March 2014).
71. Al-Baghdadi, 'wa allah ya'lam wa antum la ta'lamun [God Knows and You Do Not Know].' In a speech in July 2013, al-Adnani has already indicated future infighting with Muslims groups saying 'the Islamic State in Iraq and the Levant faces the fiercest wars, and it has in this field three foes: the disbelievers with all their trumpets and media; the apostates from among us with all their sects and bad scholars; and the people of desires and false innovations, and those Muslims who follow deviant methodologies, and not only that, but even from some of those who are counted from among the mujahideen,' see Abu Muhammed al-Adnani, 'They Will Do You No Harm, Barring a Trifling Annoyance,' *Al-Furqan Media Foundation*, July 2013.
72. In a report on Belgian foreign fighters, the authors state that the opposite parties (al-Nusra and the Islamic State) tolerated each other immediately after the split and could cooperate locally but by May 2014 relations were getting increasingly hostile, see Pieter Van Ostaeyen and Guy Van Vlierden, 'The Role of Belgian Fighters in the Jihadification of the Syrian War: From Plotting Early in 2011 to the Paris and Brussels Attacks,' 2017.
73. Abu Muhammed al-Adnani, 'This Was Not Our Methodology, and It Will Not Be,' *Chabab Tawhid Media*, April 17, 2014. Citations below are from this speech unless other is stated.
74. Al-Adnani says 'The Amir of the State and the minister al-Muhajir, may Allah have mercy on them both, announced the dissolution of Al-Qa'ida in Mesopotamia (Iraq), thus ceasing to exist.'
75. Al-Adnani, 'Apologies, Amir of Al-Qaida.' Citations below are from this speech unless other is stated.
76. The list of ideologues publishing pro-the Islamic State statements include: Turki al-Binali, Abu Mundhir al-Shinqiti, Umar Mahdi Zaydan, Abu al-Hassan al-Azdi, Abu Jafar al-Hattab and Abu Humam al-Athari. In February 2014 a statement by a group of ideologues, including al-Shintiqi, al-Athari and al-Zaydan, also published a statement calling for support and allegiance to the Islamic State and saying it is illegal to be neutral, see Group of scholars, 'Statement of the Brotherhood of Iman for the Support of the State of Islam: Statement of Scholars, Students of Knowledge and Shuyukh to Support the Joined Firmly Structure,' *Al-Ghuraba Media*, September 30, 2014.
77. In the author's interview with the former senior Jabhat al-Nusra member, Abu Sulayman al-Muhajir, the speeches are referred to as a point of no return, indicating this was how the situation was perceived internally within al-Qaida.
78. Hegghammer, *Jihad in Saudi Arabia: Violence and Pan-Islamism since 1979*.
79. Bacon, 'Alliance Hubs: Focal Points in the International Terrorist Landscape.'
80. Michels, *Political Parties: A Sociological Study of the Oligarchical Tendencies of Modern Democracy*, 172.
81. In an interview with al-Qaida insider Ahmed al-Hamdan, he explains al-Zawahiri's passivity with the state of affairs within al-Qaida characterised by internal chaos with

shifting sympathies and defections. The logic seemed to be that before going public to comment on the intra-Jihadi conflict, he should get things settled internally within al-Qaida first.

82. Jabhat al-Nusra, 'manhajina wa aqidatuna: muqabila ma' al-duktur sami al-uraydi [Our Methodology and Creed: Interview with Doctor Sami Al-Uraydi],' *Al-Manara al-Bayda Media Foundation*, October 21, 2013.
83. Abu Mariya al-Qahtani, 'Humiliating Proofs Regarding The Ignorance Of The Extremists,' *Al Muwahideen*, February 24, 2014; Abu Mariya al-Qahtani, 'risala ila ahluna fi al-sharqiyya [Message to Our People in Al-Sharqiyya],' August 3, 2014.
84. Jabhat al-Nusra, 'wa qad a'thara man anthar [He Who Issues a Warning Is Relieved of Responsibility],' *Al-Manara Al-Bayda Media Foundation*, February 7, 2014.
85. Al-Zawahiri, 'nida' 'ajilun li-ahluna fi-l-sham [an Urgent Call to Our People in Al-Sham].'
86. Ayman al-Zawahiri, 'The Reality Between the Pain and the Hope,' *As-Sahab Media*, April 18, 2014.
87. Al-Zawahiri, 'Testimony to Preserve the Blood of the Mujahideen in Sham.'
88. McCants, 'How Zawahiri Lost Al Qaeda'; Hoffman, 'ISIL Is Winning.'
89. Al-Tartusi was the first to directly request al-Zawahiri to respond to the Islamic State in the statement Abu Basir Al-Tartusi, 'A Declaration Regarding the Fighting Between the ISIS and the Mujahedeen of Al-Sham,' January 14, 2014.
90. Al-Sibai addressed al-Zawahiri directly in his radio show on his Maqreze radio channel on March 26, 2014.
91. 'A Message from the Umma to the Wise Man of the Umma,' April 11, 2014.
92. An anecdote told to this author by Abu Mahmoud al-Filastini goes that Abu Qatada al-Filastini once said that if all the people on earth went in one direction and Ayman al-Zawahiri went in the other direction, Abu Qatada would follow the Egyptian.
93. Although Abu Basir al-Tartusi has had links to al-Qaida he is certainly no man of the organisation and his contribution should rather be seen as anti-Islamic State than pro-al-Qaida.
94. Wagemakers, 'What Should an Islamic State Look Like? Jihadi–Salafi Debates on the War in Syria.'
95. In April 2013, Abu Walid al-Filastini sent out 50 tweets questioning the legitimacy of the Islamic State and rebuked it for disregarding the mandatory principle of shura (consultation).
96. Another very influential ideologue among English speaking audiences is Ahmed Musa Jibril who was not as clear in his position although he does appear to be sympathetic to the Islamic State.
97. In an interview with the TV channel al-Ru'ya, al-Maqdisi explained that he initially tried to use soft words in his criticism of the Islamic State, to the extent that some people claimed he had compassion towards the group, but he did this because he knew the youth joining it was sincere and that he didn't want to push them away.
98. Abu Qatada al-Filastini, 'risala li-ahl al-jihad bi-sham [Message to the People of Jihad in Sham],' November 2013.
99. Abu Qatada al-Filastini, 'A Message from the Sheikh Abu Qatada to the Mujahideen Brothers,' January 2014.
100. Abu Qatada was released from prison on 24 September 2014 while al-Maqdisi was released in June but rearrested on 27 October 2014. He was finally released in early 2015.

101. Abu Qatada al-Filastini, 'A Letter to the People of Jihad and Those Who Love It,' April 28, 2014.
102. Abu Bakr Naji has a similar observation about statehood depending on certain stages.
103. Abu Muhammad al-Maqdisi, 'A Call to the Umma and Mujahideen,' May 2014.
104. Al-Maqdisi, 'bayan sadir fi bayan hal 'al-dawla al-islamiyya fi-l-'iraq wa-l-sham' wa-l-mawqif al-wajib tujahaha [A Comdemning Statement on the Status of 'the Islamic State in Iraq and Sham' and the Necessary Position against It].'
105. See Abu Hanieh and Abu Rumman, *The Jihadi Salafist Movement in Jordan after Zarqawi: Identity, Leadership Crisis and Obscured Vision*; Al-Maqdisi, 'al-risala al-thalathiniyya fi-l-tahdhir min al-ghulu fi-l-takfir [Thirteen Messages of Warning of Extremism in Takfir].'
106. It should be said that al-Maqdisi is generally considered the most 'extreme' Jihadi ideologue in terms of protecting tawhid and practicing al-wala' wa-l-bara'.
107. Already in his book *The Exoneration* Zawahiri writes that al-Maqdisi and Abu Qatada are considered as points of reference for al-Qaida, see Ayman al-Zawahiri, 'The Exoneration: A Letter Exonerating the Umma of the Pen and Sword from the Unjust Allegation of Feebleness and Weakness,' English translation, 2008.
108. Abu Dujana al-Basha, 'This Is Our Message,' September 26, 2014.
109. Al-Zawahiri, 'Answers to the Esteemed Shaykhs'; Al-Zawahiri, 'Testimony to Preserve the Blood of the Mujahideen in Sham.'
110. The statement titled 'Except those who repent and do righteous deeds, and openly declare' was distributed on March 31, 2014, on jihadi forums and Twitter, including the account of al-Battar Media Foundation.
111. Abu 'Amir al-Naji's response 'Comment on the Statement "Except those who repent and do righteous deeds, and openly declare"' was posted on jihadi fora on May 28, 2014.
112. Bunzel, 'The Islamic State of Disobedience: Al-Baghdadi Triumphant.'
113. Author's interview with Ahmad al-Hamdan, September 13, 2016.
114. Muhsin al-Fadhli, 'Untitled Letter to Nasir al-Wuhayshi,' January 1, 2015.
115. Cole Bunzel, 'A Jihadi Civil War of Words: The Ghuraba' Media Foundation and Minbar Al-Tawhid Wa'l-Jihad,' *Jihadica*, October 21, 2014.
116. Ibid.
117. Ayman al-Zawahiri, 'Days with the Imam no. 7', *As-Sahab Media*, August 15, 2015 [video].
118. Ahmed al-Hamdan recounts how an al-Qaida deserter joined the Islamic State and published his testimony in the group's official newsletter *al-Naba*. A former fellow fighter who remained in al-Qaida authored a counter-testinomy, but this was released on justpaste.it and not through an official al-Qaida outlet, which affected its distribution and legitimacy greatly.
119. Joas Wagemakers, 'Between Purity and Pragmatism? Abu Basir Al-Tartusi's Nuanced Radicalism,' in *Jihadism and Terrorism: Jihadi Thought and Ideology*, ed. Rüdiger Lohlker and Tamara Abu-Hamdeh (Berlin: Logos Verlag, 2014), 16–36. From the outset of the revolution, al-Tartusi was supporting the Free Syrian Army and he relocated to Syria in 2012.
120. Abu Basir al-Tartusi, 'Stance on the Words of Sheikh Ayman al-Zawahiri 'Testimony to Preserve the Blood of Al-Mujahedeen in Al-Sham',' March 3, 2014.
121. Ibid.

122. Abu Mariya al-Qahtani, 'risala jadida min al-sheikh abu mariya al-qahtani li-l-sheikh al-zawahiri yakshifu fiha haqaiq jadida [Message from Sheikh Abu Mariya al-Qahtani to Sheikh al-Zawahiri Revealing New Truth],' August 17, 2014. Another example is Abu Mariya al-Qahtani, 'risala Ila ahluna fi al-sharqiyya [Message to our people in al-Sharqiyya]', August 3, 2014.
123. Author's interview with Abu Mahmoud al-Filastini, April 15, 2018 (London)
124. Author's interview with Abu Sulayman al-Muhajir, June 2017.
125. The title of al-Shami's article refers to a hadith about how Jews in the time of the Prophet would enter Medina claiming to have converted to Islam only to leave in the night, passing on the secrets they had learned about the emerging Islamic community in order to defeat it.
126. Al-Hedaya Media Foundation mentions in its introduction to the two letters that it got permission from Abu Iyadh al-Tunisi to publish them.
127. Abu Iyadh al-Tunisi, 'Untitled Letter to Al-Zawahiri,' July 14, 2014 (letter one) and August 17, 2014 (letter two).
128. Author's interview with Abu Qatada al-Filastini, June 17, 2018 (Zarqa).
129. The letter was from Muhsin al-Fadhli was authored January 1, 2015, but it remains unknown when exactly it was received by Nasir al-Wuhayshi due to the internal problems al-Qaida experiences in terms of communication. The below citations are from this letter, which the author has gained access to.

## CHAPTER 6. DIVERGING ATTITUDES

1. The article Hamming, 'Jihadi Competition and Political Preferences' discusses how this can become problematic
2. Moghadam and Fishman, *Self Inflicted Wounds: Debates and Divisions within Al Qa'ida and Its Periphery*: Introduction.
3. Ibid.: 15.
4. Abu Hanieh and Abu Rumman, *The 'Islamic State' Organization: The Sunni Crisis and the Struggle of Global Jihadism*, 49.
5. Zald and Useem, 'Movement and Countermovement: Loosely Coupled Conflict.'
6. Dale F. Eickelman and James Piscatori, *Muslim Politics* (Princeton: Princeton University Press, 1996).
7. Matthew D. M. Francis, 'Why the "Sacred" Is a Better Resource Than "Religion" for Understanding Terrorism,' *Terrorism and Political Violence* 28, no. 5 (2016): 912–27.
8. In Dabiq no. 7 the Islamic State mentions how it is not allowed to rebel against the ruler (meaning legitimate ruler) as this is unlawful rebellion.
9. Staffell and Awan, *Jihadism Transformed: Al-Qaeda and Islamic State's Global Battle of Ideas*, 16.
10. Islamic State, '*Dabiq no. 1*,' July 2014, 38.
11. Al-Binali, 'mudd al-ayadi li-bay'at al-baghdadi [Extend Your Hands to Give Bay'a to Al-Baghdadi].'
12. These are: that he is a male, free (not a slave), has reached the age of puberty, sane, a Muslim, is just, brave, from Qurayshi lineage, a scholar, and politically savvy.
13. Al-Binali, 'al-qiyafa fi 'adam ishtirat al-tamkin al-kamil li-l-khilafa [the Pursuit of the Caliphate Does Not Depend on Full Consolidation].'
14. Francis, 'Why the "Sacred" Is a Better Resource Than "Religion" for Understanding Terrorism.'

15. Christoph Günther and Tom Kaden, 'The Authority of the Islamic State,' *Max Planck Institute for Social Anthropology Working Paper no. 169* (2016).
16. Eickelman and Piscatori, *Muslim Politics*, 57–58.
17. Steve Coll, *Ghost Wars: The Secret History of the CIA, Afghanistan, and Bin Laden, from the Soviet Invasion to September 10, 2001* (New York: Penguin Press, 2005), 328.
18. Zelin, 'The Islamic State's Territorial Methodology.'
19. See for instance Aymenn Jawad Al-Tamimi, 'The Evolution in Islamic State Administration: The Documentary Evidence,' *Perspectives on Terrorism* 9, no. 4 (2015): 117–29.
20. Islamic State, 'The End of Sykes–Picot', al-Hayat, June 29, 2014 [video].
21. Islamic State, 'kasr al-hudud [The Breaking of the Borders]', *al-Itisam Media*, June 29, 2014 [video].
22. Islamic State, '*Dabiq* no. 1,' July 2014: 27.
23. Staffell and Awan, *Jihadism Transformed :Al-Qaeda and Islamic State's Global Battle of Ideas*, 15.
24. Author's interview with Danish foreign fighters, 2016 and 2017.
25. Author's interview with Muhammed Abu Rumman, December 8, 2016 (Amman).
26. Muhammad ibn Saleh al-Muhajir, 'Conclusion in the Caliphate Declaration Discussion,' *Minbar Al-Tawhid Wa-l-Jihad*, 2014.
27. Abu Qatada al-Filastini, 'Cloak of the Khalifah,' *Al Muwahideen Media*, 2014.
28. This is a reference to a group based in London (previously in Peshawar), which appointed Abu Eesa al-Rifaa'i as caliph and claimed to be a caliphate.
29. In its statement, AQIM suggests a grand Jihadi summit including figures like Abu Muhammad al-Maqdisi, Abu al-Walid al-Ghazi, Abu Bakr al-Baghdadi, Mullah Muhammad Omar, Ayman al-Zawahiri, Nasir al-Wuhayshi, Abu al-Zubeir, Abu Muhammad al-Julani to settle the conflict, see AQIM, 'Year of the Group... Hope of the Umma,' *Al-Andalus Media Foundation*, July 4, 2014.
30. Michel Foucault, *Discipline and Punish: The Birth of the Prison* (Harmondsworth: Penguin Books, 1991).
31. Abdallah Suleiman Ali, 'IS Disciplines Some Emirs to Avoid Losing Base,' *Al Monitor*, September 2, 2014.
32. René Girard, *Violence and the Sacred* (Baltimore: John Hopkins University Press, 1977).
33. Interestingly, the concept has received renewed interest after the election of Donald Trump as President.
34. This is the argument of Abu Sulayman al-Muhajir, the former spokesperson of Jabhat al-Nusra. He divides his argument in two: Generally, he says that he has 'come to believe that there isn't a real manhaj as such, they [al-Qaida] are much more pragmatic than people think.' Also, on a global level there are striking differences between al-Qaida's approach in say the maghreb compared to Afghanistan. Author's interview with Abu Sulayman al-Muhajir, June 2017.
35. In July 2014 an audio was leaked in which al-Nusra amir, al-Julani, allegedly unveil a plan to establish an emirate (not a state or a caliphate) in northern Syria. This plan was afterwards dismissed, however.
36. Author's interview JFS Media operative, August 6, 2016.
37. Author's interview with Ahmad al-Hamdan, October 9, 2016.
38. Charles Lister, 'The Dawn of Mass Jihad: Success in Syria Fuels Al-Qai'da's Evolution,' *CTC Sentinel* 9, no. 9 (2016); Charles Lister, 'Al-Qa'ida Plays a Long Game in Syria,' *CTC Sentinel* 8, no. 9 (2015).

39. Author's interview with Muhammed Abu Rumman, December 8, 2016 (Amman).
40. Yasir Abbas, 'Al-Nusra's Quest to Establish an Islamic Emirate in the Levant,' *Current Trends in Islamist Ideology* 20 (2016).
41. In the Islamic State's *Dabiq* no. 12 in the article 'The revival of jihad in Bengal' it says that the Islamic State neither followed Abu Musab al-Suri nor Abu Bakr Naji. The articles ridicule al-Suri's book as 'unnecessarily long' and about Naji it states that when al-Zarqawi read it, it was as if the author knew al-Zarqawi's plan although he did not follow the book.
42. Author's interview with JFS Media Operative, November 25, 2016.
43. Author's interview with Hassan Abu Hanieh, June 18, 2018 (Amman).
44. Author's interview with Abu Mahmoud al-Filastini, April 15, 2018 (London).
45. Michels, *Political Parties: A Sociological Study of the Oligarchical Tendencies of Modern Democracy*, 167–68.
46. Quintan Wiktorowicz, 'Framing Jihad: Intramovement Framing Contests and Al-Qaeda's Struggle for Sacred Authority,' *International Review of Social History* 49, no. S12 (December 2004): 159–77.
47. Abu Muhammed al-Adnani, 'la'natullahi 'alan kadhibin' [May the curse of Allah be Upon the Liars]', March 7, 2014.
48. Al-Shami, 'Untitled Statement.'
49. Ibid.
50. Islamic State, '*Dabiq no. 2*', July 2014.
51. In Wagemakers, '"Seceders" and "Postponers"? An Analysis of the "Khawarij"' and 'Murji'a' Labels in Polemical Debates between Quietist and Jihadi–Salafis,' the author shows how quietist Salafis and Jihadi–Salafis have used the labels of khawarij and murji'a to delegitimise one another. See also Wagemakers, 'What Should an Islamic State Look Like? Jihadi–Salafi Debates on the War in Syria'; Joas Wagemakers, *Salafism in Jordan: Political Islam in a Quietist Community* (New York: Cambridge University Press, 2016); Lahoud, *The Jihadis' Path to Self-Destruction*. In *Radical Islam and the Revival of Medieval Theology*, 130, Lav mentions how the Saudi regime labelled Juhyaman and his entourage 'khawarij', while Abou El Fadl, *Rebellion and Violence in Islamic Law*, 333 explains how it was used to describe the wahhabi rebellion against the ottoman state in the 1830s.
52. Lav, *Radical Islam and the Revival of Medieval Theology*.
53. There are discussions about how many sects the Khawarij divided into, but Crone mentions the four best known which are the Ibadiyya (only Khariji sect to survive today), Najdiyya (originally from Basra, but mainly active in Arabia and was suppressed in 693, but managed to survive a few centuries), Azariqa (originally from Basra but fled to Iran where they disappeared after suppression in 699) and Sufriyya (active in North Africa until 10th century). These four sects were divided in relation to the status of non-khariji Muslims and the legality regarding living under kufr rule (some believed one should emigrate and establish their own polity, while others believed it was acceptable to live in kufr territory as long as one did not follow their rules).
54. For more on the Khawarij, see Crone, *God's Rule: Government and Islam*; Kenney, Jeffrey, *Muslim Rebels: Kharijites and the Politics of Extremism in Egypt*.
55. See for instance Wagemakers, *Salafism in Jordan: Political Islam in a Quietist Community*, 196–98.
56. Examples of how the khawarij label is used by non-Jihadis to delegitimise them see Mohamed Bin Ali, 'Labelling IS Fighters: Khawarij, Not Jihadi–Salafis', *RSIS*

*Commentary*, April 4, 2018; Mohamed al-Daameh, 'Jordanian King: We Will Fight "Khawarij" Without Mercy', *Asharq al-Awsat*, August 13, 2018. The general accusations against the Islamic State is that it proclaims takfir for actions that should not be considered unbelief which involves kufr duna kufr (unbelief less than unbelief), that it excommunicates entire groups, that it does not await *proof* (hujja) or acknowledges that there may be legitimate *doubt* (shubha).

57. Wagemakers, *Salafism in Jordan: Political Islam in a Quietist Community*, 46–50.
58. Muhammad al-Qurashi, 'Al-Murji'ah Sect, Its History and Beliefs,' *Nida'ul Islam*, no. 17 (1997). The Khawarij and Murji'a agreed on the inflexibility of faith (iman) arguing that faith can not increase or decrease but only disappear.
59. Labelling someone khawarij has historically been used to legitimise fighting them. This was done by Ibn Taymiyya and Faraj, see Aaron Y. Zelin, 'Al-Farida al-Gha'iba and al-Sadat's Assassination, a 30 Year Retrospective,' *International Journal for Arab Studies* 3, no. 2 (2012): 15–16.
60. Al-Tartusi, 'A Declaration Regarding the Fighting Between the ISIS and the Mujahedeen of Al-Sham.'
61. Abu Basir al-Tartusi, 'The Validity of the Victorious Emirate,' March 15, 2014.
62. Tariq Abdelhaleem and Hani al-Sibai, 'A Declaration of Disownment and Divergence From the Ideology and Actions of ISIS,' *Al Maqreze Centre for Historical Studies* (London, 2014). A similar argument was elaborated in their booklet Hani Al-Sibai and Tariq Abdelhaleem, 'Statement on the Reality of the Islamic State,' August 25, 2014.
63. Abdelhaleem and al-Sibai, 'A Declaration of Disownment and Divergence From the Ideology and Actions of ISIS.'
64. Al-Filastini, 'Cloak of the Khalifah.' In fact Abu Qatada argues that the Islamic State is between al-khawarij and al-rafidha, the latter meaning 'rejectionists' and it is a derogatory title referring to the Shia.
65. In October 2015 Abdullah al-Muhaysini would publish a piece where he lists 25 characteristics of the Khawarij that he finds present in the Islamic State today.
66. Abu Muhammad al-Maqdisi, 'Why Did I Not Name Them Khawarij Even until Now?,' 2015.
67. After that statement, the Majlis Shura Ahl al-Ilm fi al-Sham came out with a critique of Maqdisi arguing his stance was too confusing and in fact helped the Islamic State. Also, Hani al-Sibai published a statement on Facebook claiming it was necessary to fight an offensive war against the Islamic State, which can only be interpreted as an implicit criticism of al-Maqdisi's position, see: https://www.facebook.com/mohibidrhani/photos/a.297278376999540.67815.297266940334017/884039081656797/
68. Abu Muhammad al-Maqdisi, 'The Killing of 'Ad and Eradication Fight Between International Desires and Sheikh Al-Islam Ibn Taymiyah,' *Minbar Al-Tawhid Wa-l-Jihad*, March 2016.
69. Abu al-Izz al-Najdi, 'Is the Islamic State Organization Khawarij – question number 8540', Minbar al-Tawhid wa-l-Jihad. For translated version see www.justpaste.it/lm9p
70. For a discussion of faith, unbelief and takfir see Wagemakers, *Salafism in Jordan: Political Islam in a Quietist Community*, 46–50.
71. Hussein Ibn Mahmoud, 'Study on Al-Khawarij,' *Ansar Al-Khilafah*, August 13, 2014.
72. Al-Binali, 'tabsir al-mahajij bi-l-farq bayn rijal al-dawla al-islamiyya wa-l-khawarij [Enlightening Arguments on the Differences between the Men of the Islamic State and the Khawarij).'

73. Turki al-Binali, 'Between the Ghulat Al-Mukaffira and the Ghulat Al-Murji'a,' n.d.
74. Michels, *Political Parties: A Sociological Study of the Oligarchical Tendencies of Modern Democracy*.
75. Martin Marty and Scott Appleby noted this as a persistent trend in extremist breakups where Islamist movements stall and then become challenged by younger upstarts, see Scott Appleby and Martin Marty, *Accounting for Fundamentalisms: The Dynamic Character of Movements* (Chicago: University of Chicago Press, 2004).
76. Hamid and Farrall, *The Arabs at War in Afghanistan*.
77. Hamming, 'Polemical and Fratricidal Jihadists: A Historical Examination of Debates, Contestation and Infighting Within the Sunni Jihadi Movement.'
78. The Islamic State has been described as particularly good at addressing popular youth culture making it likely that it has a younger 'membership' than other Jihadi groups. For this argument, see Olivier Roy, *Jihad and Death: The Global Appeal of Islamic State* (London: Hurst & Company, 2017). See also Charlie Winter, 'The Virtual 'Caliphate': Understanding Islamic State's Propaganda Strategy,' *Quilliam*, 2015; Christina Schori Liang, 'Cyber Jihad: Understanding and Countering Islamic State Propaganda,' *GCSP Policy Paper* 2 (2015); Jan Christoffer Andersen and Sveinung Sandberg, 'Islamic State Propaganda: Between Social Movement Framing and Subcultural Provocation,' *Terrorism and Political Violence*, 2018.
79. Brian Fishman and Joseph Felter, 'Al-Qa'ida's Foreign Fighters in Iraq: A First Look at the Sinjar Records', Combating Terrorism Center at West Point,' *Combating Terrorism Center at West Point*, December 2007.
80. Brian Dodwell, Daniel Milton, and Don Rassler, 'The Caliphate's Global Workforce: An Inside Look at the Islamic State's Foreign Fighter Paper Trail,' *Combating Terrorism Center at West Point*, April 2016; Nate Rosenblatt, 'All Jihad Is Local: What ISIS' Files Tell Us about Its Fighters,' *New America*, July 2016.
81. Cole Bunzel has covered this topic in several articles on Jihadica. See Cole Bunzel, 'Caliphate Now: Jihadis Debate the Islamic State,' *Jihadica*, November 25, 2013; Bunzel, 'The Islamic State of Disunity: Jihadism Divided.'
82. In mid-February 2014, a group of scholars issued a statement in support of the Islamic State. While the age of all the scholars is not known, none of them are among the most senior figures within the SJM. See Turki al-Binali, 'bayan al-ukhuwwa al-imaniyya fi nusrat al-dawla al-islamiyya [The Statement of the Brothers in Supporting the Islamic State],' *Al-Ghuraba Media*, February 18, 2014.
83. Umar Mahdi Zaydan's audio can be found here: https://archive.org/details/Jbha.Islmia.Syrai/Cmnts_012_Omdat_010_Cmnts_shyokh.mp3. In early November 2013, Umar Mahdi Zaydan responded to Abu Qatada's first criticism of the Islamic State in which he compared it to Shia theology, see Umar Mahdi Zaydan, 'al-naqd li-qawl man ja'ala al-khilafa al-islamiyya min din al-rafd [Denounce the Saying That Made the Caliphate from the Religion of Refusal],' November 5, 2013. Before his death Zaydan rose to head the Islamic State's Ministry of Education.
84. See for instance al-Binali's response to Abu Muhammad al-Julani's reconciliation initiative, Al-Binali, 'al-thamar al-dani fi-l-radd 'ala khitab al-julani [the Low Hanging Fruit in Responding to the Speech of Al-Julani].' Another example is directed against al-Nusra's most senior ideological figure Abu Abdullah al-Shami, see Turki al-Binali, 'mukhtasir kalami fi-l-radd 'ala abu abdullah al-shami [Brief Comment to the Response of Abu Abdullah al-Shami],' March 16, 2014. In the statement, al-Binali writes that al-Shami's criticism of the Islamic State is in matters of *ijtihad*

(interpretation), while the Islamic State's criticism of Jabhat al-Nusra is much more serious as it concerns the principles (usul) and constants (thawabit) of religion. Binali also authored a letter to al-Zawahiri complaining about al-Julani writing that it was al-Julani that rebelled against authority, but it is al-Zawahiri's responsibility to handle him.

85. See for example Turki al-Binali, 'la-qad sadaqa al-zawahiri [Al-Zawahiri Was Right],' May 1, 2014. In the article, al-Binali argues that al-Julani's pledge of allegiance to al-Zawahiri was simply a defence mechanism to protect himself and his group, but that the Jihadi masses will see through his tricks.
86. Al-Binali, 'tabsir al-mahajij bi-l-farq bayn rijal al-dawla al-islamiyya wa-l-khawarij [Enlightening Arguments on the Differences between the Men of the Islamic State and the Khawarij).'
87. Al-Binali, 'khatt al-midad fi-l-radd ʿala al-duktur iyad [Sufficient Answer to Respond to Doctor Iyad].' Al-Binali's criticism of Qunaybi's proposal to submit to a third party to arbitrate in the conflict is based on four arguments: The Islamic State is a state and not cannot arbitrate on the level of groups. The Islamic State's own judiciary follows the rules of God and not any organisational interests and is thus perfectly capable of arbitrating in the conflict. Any such third-party tribunal will not be entirely independent and it will have no power to enforce its decision.
88. Turki al-Binali, 'risala ila al-ʿulama wa-l-duʿat li-nusrat al-mujahidin al-ubat [Message to the 'ulama and Preachers in Support of the Proud Mujahideen],' audio statement, n.d.
89. Turki al-Binali, 'al-ifada fi-l-radd ʿala abi qatada [a Response to the Reply of Abu Qatada],' April 29, 2014.
90. Turki al-Binali, 'shaykhi al-asbaq [My Former Sheikh],' June 7, 2014.
91. Turki al-Binali, 'al-maqdisi: suqut fi-l-tin wa ansilakh ʿan al-deen [Al-Maqdisi: The Fall in the Mud and the Separation from Religion],' February 15, 2015.
92. Turki al-Binali, 'kullukum raʿin: risala ila shaykhina ayman al-zawahiri [You Are All Shepherd: A Letter to Our Sheikh Ayman Al-Zawahiri],' March 24, 2014.
93. Al-Binali, 'al-ifada fi-l-radd ʿala abi qatada [A Response to the Reply of Abu Qatada].'
94. Shane Drennan, 'Constructing Takfir,' *CTC Sentinel* 1, no. 7 (2008).
95. Between 2010–11 Turki al-Binali allegedly wrote some emails to Hani al-Sibai asking him for advice. Later, al-Sibai published the content of these email to chastise al-Binali. The video showing the emails used to be available on: https://www.youtube.com/watch?v=kEwAvhv6E2g [accessed on 5 June 2017]
96. Al-Maqdisi, 'bayan sadir fi bayan hal 'al-dawla al-islamiyya fi-l-iraq wa-l-sham' wa-l-mawqif al-wajib tujahaha [A Comdemning Statement on the Status of the Islamic State in Iraq and Sham and the Necessary Position against It].'
97. Al-Filastini, 'risala li-ahl al-jihad bi-sham [Message to the People of Jihad in Sham).'
98. Wagemakers, 'Reclaiming Scholarly Authority: Abu Muhammad al-Maqdisi's Critique of Jihadi Practices.'
99. Abu Muhammad al-Maqdisi, 'sada siham al-liam 'an al-akabir al-'alam [Resist the Arrows of the Depraved from the Greatest Dignitaries],' May 6, 2014.
100. For a thorough discussion of the importance of the Internet as a medium, see Moghadam, *Nexus of Global Jihad : Understanding Cooperation among Terrorist Actors*, 75–93.
101. The Islamic State video *Inside the Caliphate 8* published on October 30, 2018 shows the importance of the group's munasirun networks.

102. Al-Baghdadi tells munasirun to only use material that has been disseminated by the media diwan in Abu Bakr Al-Baghdadi, 'Give Glad Tidings to the Patient,' *Al-Furqan Media Foundation*, August 22, 2018.
103. Author's talk with the administrator of Abd al-Faqir numasir network verifies the close relationship between official media diwan and munasirun. The administrator told this author how it was instructed by the media diwan to take down a video, a cartoon that told the story of Abu Muhammed al-Adnani, as it overstepped the rules of showing facial features.
104. Hussein ibn Mahmoud remains a mysterious figure. He used to be supportive of al-Qaida but shifted side in 2014. Despite being active on Jihadi fora for many years, nobody appears to know details about who he is.
105. Lahoud and al-'Ubaydi, 'The War of Jihadists against Jihadists in Syria.'
106. An archive of al-Ghuraba material can be accessed here: http://web.archive.org/web/20160307213149/http://justpaste.it:80/archivealghuraba
107. Al-Batter used the twitter handle https://twitter.com/me_bttar
108. Al-Wafa used the twitter handle https://twitter.com/alwaf_aa
109. The website is now defunct but used to be on https://ansarukhilafah.wordpress.com
110. The website is now defunct but used to be on https://ahlutawheed.wordpress.com
111. Author's interview with Ahmad al-Hamdan, September 13, 2016.

## CHAPTER 7. EXPANDING THE CALIPHATE AND AL-QAIDA'S RESPONSE

1. Crone, *God's Rule: Government and Islam*, 24.
2. Abu Khalil Al-Madani, 'Advice to All the Fighting Groups in the Cause of Allah,' *As-Sahab Media Productions*, April 2014.
3. Donatella Della Porta, *Clandestine Political Violence* (New York: Cambridge University Press, 2013), 172.
4. Lahoud, *The Jihadis' Path to Self-Destruction*, 75.
5. For a convincing analysis of the Islamic State's attractiveness in the West, see Roy, *Jihad and Death: The Global Appeal of Islamic State*.
6. Drevon, 'The Jihadi Social Movement (JSM): Between Factional Hegemonic Drive, National Realities and Transnational Ambitions,' 58.
7. Barak Mendelsohn, *The Al-Qaeda Franchise :The Expansion of Al-Qaeda and Its Consequences* (New York: Oxford University Press, 2016).
8. This was similar to the tone in addresses to previous AQI leaders such as al-Zarqawi and Abu Umar al-Baghdadi, see chapter 4.
9. The same day, the Taliban issued its own statement on the caliphate declaration. While it does not mention the Islamic State by name, it warns Jihadis to refrain from extremism.
10. Cole Bunzel, 'Al-Qaeda's Quasi-Caliph: The Recasting of Mullah "Umar," *Jihadica*, July 23, 2014; Anne Stenersen and Phillipp Holtmann, 'The Three Functions of UBL's 'Greater Pledge' to Mullah Omar (2001–2006–2014),' *Jihadology*, January 8, 2015. The Islamic State was quick to respond to the video. A senior media operative Abu Maysara al-Shami issued a refutation on 15 July in which he explains that Bin Laden's words were ambiguous and that he in fact says that his 'supreme bay'a' is a step to the greater goal of establishing the caliphate.

11. Al-Qaida, 'Al-Nafir No. 1: ya ummat al-nasr infari wa jahadi wa istabshari [Al-Nafir No. 1: Oh Victorious Ummah, Carry Your Arms, Wage Jihad and Rejoice],' *As-Sahab Media*, July 19, 2014.
12. The video was released by as-Sahab Media Foundation on September 3, 2014 and featured Ayman al-Zawahiri and voice recordings by AQIS new amir Asim Umar and its spokesperson Usama Mahmoud.
13. The Taliban announced on July 30, 2015 that Mullah Umar had died two years prior on April 23, 2013.
14. Stenersen, *Al-Qaida in Afghanistan*.
15. Al-Qaida supporters are generally well aware of this instrumentalist relationship and acknowledge that Bin Laden pledged allegiance to Mullah Umar due to practical concerns. Author's interview with al-Qaida members in the period 2015–18.
16. Abu Muhammed al-Adnani, 'The State of Islam Will Remain Safe,' *Al Furqan Media*, August 7, 2011.
17. Abu al-Mundhir al-Shinqiti, 'i'lan al-khilafa fi-l-mizan al-shar'i [The Caliphate Announcement in the Balance of the Shari'a],' July 18, 2014.
18. Al-Adnani, 'This Is the Promise of Allah.'
19. Abu Ubaydah Abd al-Hakim, 'Untitled Letter to Abdelmalik Droukdal,' December 4, 2014.
20. Islamic State, 'Wilayat Khurasan and the Bay'at from Qawqaz,' *Dabiq* 7, February 2015.
21. Abu Bakr al-Baghdadi, 'Even If the Disbelievers Despise Such,' *Al Furqan Media Foundation*, November 13, 2014.
22. Accepted in Abu Muhammed al-Adnani, 'Say, "Die in Your Rage!,"' *Al Hayat Media Center*, January 26, 2015.
23. On March 7 Boko Haram issued a video through its al-Urwa al-Wuthqa Media Foundation in which its amir Abu Bakr Shekau pledged allegiance to Abu Bakr al-Baghdadi. The pledge was accepted later by al-Adnani.
24. Several pledges from Islamic State sympathisers in the Caucasus were reported in 2014 and early 2015. This was also reported by the group in Dabiq magazine in February 2015. But, likely because it did not fulfill the criteria for a wilaya, the group did not accept its establishment before 23 June in Abu Muhammed al-Adnani, 'Oh Our People Respond to the Caller of Allah,' June 23, 2015.
25. Although it took the Islamic State until December 2017 to formally accept the Somali wilaya.
26. For example al-Binali gave a khutbah in Sirte in early 2013, see Turki al-Binali, 'khutbah juma'ah gharbat al-deen [Friday prayer on the foreignness of religion]', 2013: https://archive.org/details/h_475
27. There were also rumors that Abu Ali al-Anbari and Abu Ayman al-Iraqi visited Libya but none of this appear to be true.
28. Al-Anbari, 'al-waqfu al-dari fi tarjamati al-sheikh al-anbari [Knowledgeable Study on the Biography of Sheikh Al-Anbari].'
29. For instance, al-Qaida never demanded bay'a from senior figures like Abu Khalid al-Suri and Muhammed Islambouli, author's interview with Abu Sulayman al-Muhajir, June 2017.
30. Al-Libi, 'Untitled Letter to Al-Zarqawi.'
31. Moghadam, *Nexus of Global Jihad : Understanding Cooperation among Terrorist Actors*, 27.

32. The three groups were Liwa Shuhada' al-Yarmouk, Jaysh al-Jihad and Harakat al-Muthanna al-Islamiya.
33. Jabhat al-Nusra, 'Statement Regarding the Ongoing Fighting with the State,' *Al-Manara Al-Bayda Media Foundation*, May 4, 2014.
34. The hadith that Jihadis typically rely on to legitimise attacks against khawarij can be accessed here: http://www.aljamaat.org/islam/articles/a35.htm
35. 'What Is the Khorasan Group?,' *BBC*, September 24, 2014.
36. For instance the biography for David Drugeon (Abu Hamza al-Jaza'iri, Salman al-Faransi), a French fighter with al-Qaida, issued by al-Fursan on August 21, 2017. See also Moussa and Doornbos, 'The Greatest Divorce in the Jihadi World.'
37. Will McCants, 'The Polarizing Effect of Islamic State Aggression on the Global Jihadist Movement,' *CTC Sentinel* 9, no. 7 (2016): 20–23.
38. Bakke, Cunningham, and Seymour, 'A Plague of Initials: Fragmentation, Cohesion, and Infighting in Civil Wars.'
39. Jihadi ideologies Abu Basir al-Tartusi and Abu Muhammad al-Maqdisi were out in February and July 2014, respectively, to warn about movement fragmentation.
40. Marco Giugni, Doug McAdam, and Charles Tilly, eds., *How Social Movements Matter* (Minneapolis: University of Minnesota Press, 1999).
41. Bakke, Cunningham, and Seymour, 'A Plague of Initials: Fragmentation, Cohesion, and Infighting in Civil Wars,' 276.
42. Islamic State, 'The Extinction of the Grayzone,' *Dabiq No.* 7, February 2015.
43. This was especially the case after the death of senior al-Qaida figures like Abu Yahya al-Libi and Atiyyatullah al-Libi. Their death implied that al-Qaida needed to rely increasingly on 'external' ideologues.
44. Anwar al-Awlaki, 'The New Mardin Declaration: An Attempt at Justifying the New World Order,' *Inspire No. 2*, October 2010.
45. Islamic State material also began to portray Abu Musab al-Suri, an al-Qaida linked strategist likely imprisoned in Syria, as an apostate.
46. Abu Abd al-Rahman al-Shami al-Zarqawi, 'ta'riat al-thiyat 'an al-sawab [Stripping the Attire from the Truth],' 2015.
47. While neither Abu Qatada nor al-Maqdisi were imprisoned at the time of al-Faisal's comment, the Jamaican suggests that simply being in Jordan robbed the two sheikhs of their ability to speak freely. As it is a condition for the legitimacy of a fatwa that the author is considered free, such 'imprisonment' should render their fatwas invalid, al-Faisal claims. See Abdullah al-Faisal, 'In the new caliphate valid?', July 21, 2014.
48. Author's interview with Ahmad al-Hamdan, May 2016.
49. Abu Basir al-Tartusi, 'mulhazat 'ala risala ila sadiqin mimman nafaru ila ard al-jihad fi souriya l-Abi Muhammad al-Maqdisi [Comment to Abu Muhammad al-Maqdisi's "Letter to the Honest Ones Who Travelled to the Land of Jihad,"'] August 23, 2014.
50. Abu Muhammad al-Maqdisi, 'malhuzat 'ala malhuzat al-sheikh abu basir [Comments on the Comments of Sheikh Abu Basir],' *Minbar Al-Tawhid Wa-l-Jihad*, August 2014.
51. Reading al-Shinqiti's statements in the period 2013–16 is illustrative of the polarised environment. He changes from referring to al-Baghdadi's group as 'the caliphate' (al-khilafa) to denounce it as 'lying-stan' (kadhdhabastan). He even compares the Islamic State's attacks against other Jihadi groups to Israel's assaults on Palestine writing that 'when they [other Jihad groups] try to defend themselves, they [the Islamic State] accuse them of terrorism', see Abu al-Mundhir al-Shinqiti, 'sheikh ayman al-zawahiri rajul umma [Sheikh Ayman al-Zawahiri: Man of the Umma],' *Minbar Al-Tawhid Wa-l-*

*Jihad*, January 20, 2015; Al-Shinqiti, 'yuriduna da'ishnat al-jihad [We Want Daish's Jihad]'; Al-Shinqiti, 'i'lan al-khilafa fi-l-mizan al-shar'i [The Caliphate Announcement in the Balance of the Shari'a].'

52. An example is that early on the Islamic State taught al-Maqdisi's books to its students, but when al-Maqdisi refused to join the Islamic State and escalated his critique, the group prohibited his books entirely.
53. One example of this 'delay' is the cooperation between the Kouachi brothers and Amedy Coulibaly in the January 2015 attacks. While the Kouachi brothers carried out their attack in the name of al-Qaida, Coulibaly swore allegiance to the Islamic State. A year later, a similar cooperation would have been unimaginable.
54. Sam Heller, 'Ahrar Al-Sham's Revisionist Jihadism,' *War on the Rocks*, September 30, 2015.
55. Perhaps the most obvious example of Ahrar al-Sham's moderate wing is Labib al-Nahhas' op-ed in the *Washington Post*, see Labib Nahhas, 'The deadly consequences of mislabeling Syria's revolutionaries', *Washington Post*, July 10, 2015.
56. The explosion hit a meeting of the group's shura council in the village of Ram Hamdan in Idlib. More than 20 senior figures were killed including its leader Hassan Abboud, its military commander Abu Talha al-Ghab, and its ideologues Abu Abdelmalik al-Shar'i and Abu Sariya al-Shami. While the perpetrator remains unknown, the Islamic State is the most likely suspect although the group never took responsibility.
57. Sam Heller, 'Ahrar Al-Sham's Revisionist Jihadism,' *War on the Rocks*, September 2015.
58. Author's interview with Labib Nahhas, April 15, 2018 (London).
59. See Abboud's tweet: https://twitter.com/HassanAbboud_Ah/status/380449693018238977
60. Sam Heller, 'How Ahrar Al-Sham Has Come to Define the Kaleidoscope of the Syrian Civil War,' *War on the Rocks*, June 6, 2016.
61. Drevon, 'The Jihadi Social Movement (JSM): Between Factional Hegemonic Drive, National Realities and Transnational Ambitions,' 59.
62. Hegghammer, 'The Hybridization of Jihadi Groups.'
63. Anthony Celso, *The Islamic State: A Comparative History of Jihadist Warfare* (New York: Lexington Books, 2018).
64. Al-Baghdadi, 'wa allah ya'lam wa antum la ta'lamun [God Knows and You Do Not Know].'
65. Hamming, 'Jihadi Competition and Political Preferences.'
66. These are Abu Ubaidah al Masri (dead December 2007), Abu Sulayman Jazairi (dead May 2008), Osama al-Kini (dead January 2009), and Saleh al-Somali (dead December 2009).
67. Most importantly Saif al-Adl and Abu Muhammad al-Masri who were both imprisoned in Iran until 2015 when their status shifted to 'house arrest'.

## CHAPTER 8. OUTSIDE THE LEVANT

1. Harith bin Ghazi al-Nadhari and Ibrahim Al-Rubeish, 'Responsibility of the Word,' *Al-Malahem Media Foundation*, July 2014.
2. Harith bin Ghazi al-Nadhari, 'A Statement about What Was Contained in the Speech of Sheikh Abu Bakr Al-Baghdadi "Even If the Disbelievers Despise Such",' *Al-Malahem Media Foundation*, November 2014. AQAP ideologues also signed a statement in

January 2015 together with independent ideologues and senior Jabhat al-Nusra members instructing Jihadis in the Caucasus not to defect from the al-Qaida sympathetic Islamic Emirate of Caucasus to join the Islamic State.

3. Harith bin Ghazi al-Nadhari, 'Civility of the Dispute Between the Mujahideen,' *Al-Malahem Media Foundation*, December 2014.
4. Abu Maysara al-Shami, 'The Qa'idah of Adh-Dhawahiri, Al-Harari, and An-Nadhari, and the Absent Yemeni Wisdom,' *Dabiq No. 6*, January 2015.
5. Islamic State, 'The Allies of Al-Qa'idah in Yemen,' *Dabiq No. 12*, November 2015.
6. Islamic State, 'Soldiers of the Caliphate in the Land of Yemen,' Wilayat Sana'a, April 24, 2015 [video].
7. Elisabeth Kendall, 'Contemporary Jihadi Militancy in Yemen,' *Middle East Institute Policy Paper*, July 2018.
8. Author's discussion with Wassim Nasr, November 2018.
9. An example is this audio: https://archive.org/details/baqia_201505, date unknown. Also see his tweets https://web.archive.org/web/20141113091742/https://twitter.com/mamoonhatem7
10. Author's discussion with Wassim Nasr, November 2018 and July 2019.
11. Antonio Giustozzi, *The Islamic State in Khorasan: Afghanistan, Pakistan and the New Central Asian Jihad* (London: Hurst & Company, 2018).
12. It is interesting that around the same time as the Islamic State emerged, the Taliban began to focus more on symbols like its flag as a unifying factor, see Borhan Osman, 'Rallying Around the White Flag: Taleban Embrace an Assertive Identity,' *Afghanistan Analysts Network*, February 1, 2017.
13. Initially, the main opposition to ISKP within Taliban came from its governing Quetta shura who saw the Islamic State's expansion to Afghanistan as a threat to its authority. It is being reported that the Miran Shah (haqqani) and Peshawar shuras initially managed to establish somehow cordial relations but that this ended when ISKP sought to recruit their fighters, see Giustozzi, *The Islamic State in Khorasan: Afghanistan, Pakistan and the New Central Asian Jihad*.
14. Al-Adnani, 'Say, "Die in Your Rage!"'
15. It is a discussion whether Mullah Mansour Dadullah actually joined ISKP or simply sided it with because of his opposition of Mullah Mansour as new Taliban amir after the announcement of Mullah Umar's death.
16. Giustozzi, *The Islamic State in Khorasan: Afghanistan, Pakistan and the New Central Asian Jihad*.
17. Increasing this doubt, in March 2013 the TTP published a new magazine, *Azan*, and the first issue contained an article titled 'On the Road to the Khilafah'. The article reads 'The Muslim Umma has awakened! From the land of the brave Khorasaani Mujahideen to the embattled soldiers of Syria – the Umma is experiencing a great revival. The road to the promised Khilafah, on the path of prophethood is nigh.' In the last edition of the magazine published in summer 2014, around the time of the Islamic State's caliphate declaration, another article on the topic was included. But this time it dealt with the fundamentals of the caliphate possibly to position TTP in relation to the new caliphate. Author's interview with TTP Media Official, June 2018 and December 2019.
18. There are reports that Jama'at ul-Ahrar (JuA) was negotiating with the Islamic State to join it, but JuA's condition was that a 'Wilayat al-Hind' (India Province) would be announced and that JuA would be its main component.

19. The IMU has longstanding relations to the Taliban as the group has operated in Afghanistan for many years as the Taliban's guest and they have previously given bay'a to Mullah Umar. And more recently, at least since 2009, they have been operating in Waziristan, allowed by the TTP.
20. Already in September 2014, Uthman Ghazi had shown support for the Islamic State, but the pledge of allegiance nonetheless came as a surprise.
21. A notable exemption is former IMU ideologue Abu Dhar Azzam. Azzam was initially supportive of the pledge of allegiance to the Islamic State but when it made takfir on the Taliban, he left and has since only featured in TIP material and is preaching under the banner of the Imam Bukhari Brigade, a Syrian based offshoot of the IMU which remains loyal to al-Qaeda–Taliban nexus.
22. Amira Jadoon, 'Allied and Lethal: Islamic State Khorasan's Network and Organizational Capacity in Afghanistan and Pakistan,' *Combating Terrorism Center at West Point*, December 2018.
23. In Pakistan ISKP similarly showed its ability to target urban centers like Quetta and Karachi.
24. Giustozzi, *The Islamic State in Khorasan: Afghanistan, Pakistan and the New Central Asian Jihad*.
25. Casey Garret Johnson, 'The Rise and Stall of the Islamic State in Afghanistan,' *United States Institute of Peace, Special Report 395*, November 2016.
26. Borhan Osman, 'The Islamic State in "Khorasan": How It Began and Where It Stands Now in Nangarhar,' *Afghanistan Analysts Network*, July 27, 2016.
27. Ibid.: 5.
28. Estimates vary greatly going from a high of 4,000 in June 2015 to 1,000 in early 2018. In October 2017 ISKP itself claimed to command as many as 20,000 fighters but that appears to be a gross exaggeration.
29. There are diverging reports about when the fatwa was given. Giustozzi, *The Islamic State in Khorasan: Afghanistan, Pakistan and the New Central Asian Jihad*, 176 claims it came in June 2015 while Osman argues it was in early January 2016, see Borhan Osman, 'The Islamic State in "Khorasan": How it began and where it stands now in Nangarhar'.
30. Borhan Osman, 'The Battle for Mamand: ISKP under Strain, but Not yet Defeated,' *Afghanistan Analysts Network*, May 23, 2017.
31. Hafidh Muaaz Badr, 'Tale of the War against Daesh,' *Nawai Ghazwa Hind Magazine* 13, no. 4 (2020): 103–05. I would like to thank Abdul Sayid for making me aware of the article and providing a translation from Pashto.
32. Matthew Dupée, 'Red on Red: Analyzing Afghanistan's Intra-Insurgency Violence,' *CTC Sentinel* 11, no. 1 (2018).
33. Jadoon, 'Allied and Lethal: Islamic State Khorasan's Network and Organizational Capacity in Afghanistan and Pakistan.'
34. In reality, the number is likely substantially higher since the Taliban generally has avoided communicating on military confrontations with ISKP.
35. Author's discussion with a local Taliban observer, April 5, 2019.
36. Mullah Mansour, 'Untitled Letter to Abu Bakr Al-Baghdadi,' June 16, 2015.
37. The author would like to thank Felix Kuhn for bringing Qari Saeed's booklet to my attention. A Pashto version of the booklet can be accessed here: https://drive.google.com/file/d/0B1WnHjI6IQjXanJjSGZBdUJ3Tm8yYkx3aEVvem1RdHJZYjVV/view. The document was most likely issued in late 2017 or early 2018. In

addition, in the month prior to Mansour's letter, a TTP figure, Abu Unman Salarzai, had issued a 60-page booklet exposing errors in al-Baghdadi's claim to be the new caliph, see Abdul Basit, 'IS Penetration in Afghanistan–Pakistan: Assessment, Impact and Implications,' *Perspectives on Terrorism* 11, no. 3 (2017): 19–39.

38. Al-Adnani, 'Oh Our People Respond to the Caller of Allah.'
39. See the foreword in the Islamic State's *Dabiq* no. 11.
40. See the article 'A fatwa for Khorasa,' in the Islamic State's *Dabiq* no. 10, July 2015.
41. The article states that Mullah Umar never identified his imamate as a *caliphate* and that he does not posses the necessary characteristics to be considered caliph.
42. An exception is a video titled 'cleansing Da'esh from Darzab' that portrays the Taliban's victory in Jowzjan Province. The video was issued August 19, 2018.
43. Borhan Osman, 'With an Active Cell in Kabul, ISKP Tries to Bring Sectarianism to the Afghan War,' *Afghanistan Analysts Network*, October 19, 2016; Jadoon, 'Allied and Lethal: Islamic State Khorasan's Network and Organizational Capacity in Afghanistan and Pakistan'; Basit, 'IS Penetration in Afghanistan–Pakistan: Assessment, Impact and Implications.'
44. 'Jund Al-Khalifa: The IS-Linked Group That Shot into the Spotlight,' *France 24*, September 23, 2014.
45. Abd-al-Hakim, 'Untitled Letter to Abdelmalik Droukdal.' The following quotes are from the letter.
46. For al-Maqdisi and Abu Qatada, he argues that they have long been critical of ISIS, suggesting they would be too biased to rule on its legitimacy. Flattering Droukdal, he writes, 'We deem you [AQIM] far above to be saying the same as Abu Qatada al-Filistini, who did not only describe us as Khawarij [a historical extreme Islamic sect], he asserted that we are the dogs of hellfire, and that the state – that was built on shreds, blood, and honor of believers in Tawhid [monotheism] and that has dazzled and giddied the unbelievers East to South – is a bubble state.' On al-Maqdisi he adds that one cannot trust a person who has never fired a weapon in the name of Allah. On al-Alwan he argues that the fact the Saudi scholar is in prison implies he has no free will, while on al-Ghazi he says that ISIS is not really familiar with him aside from a few online writings. This is either a show of ignorance or a provocation because al-Ghazi has been a top-tier jihadi scholar for many years, spending his early days in London as a protégée of Abu Qatada, before relocating to the AfPak area to become al-Qaeda's in-house scholar. At some point he was imprisoned by the Pakistanis, but in 2017 he was released and re-settled in Turkey. Mullah Omar of the Taliban, Abd al-Hakim claims, has not been seen alive for more than 11 years, while according to ISIS al-Zawahri is the main protagonist of the intra-jihadi conflict and cannot be trusted to decide on a caliph.
47. Al-Sahrawi used to be spokesperson in MUJAO before it merged with Belmokhtar's group to found al-Murabitoun. Some accounts state that al-Sahrawi was in fact Belmokhtar's deputy.
48. Djallil Lounnas, 'Jihadist Groups in North Africa and the Sahel: Between Disintegration, Reconfiguration and Resilience,' *MENARA Working Papers* 16 (2018). While it has been argued that the Islamic State accepted the pledge of allegiance in October 2016, it appears more correct that it was in fact al-Baghdadi's speech in April 2019 which officially recognised the pledge.
49. In July 2015, Al-Murabitoun officially announced that Belmokhtar was chosen as the new amir, but it is likely that he in fact had been amir since December 2014 when the

previous amir, Ahmed al-Tilemsi, was killed. See Al-Murabitoun, 'bayan haul tawdih ba'd al-masa'il wa takiduha' [Statement on the Clarification of Some Matters and Confirming Them],' *Al Ribat Media Foundation*, July 21, 2015.

50. Al-Murabitoun, 'Untitled Statement,' *Al Ribat Media Foundation*, December 4, 2015.
51. 'Interview with Yahya Abu Hummam,' *Al-Akhbar*, January 10, 2016.
52. Jacob Zenn, 'Boko Haram's Conquest for the Caliphate: How Al Qaeda Helped Islamic State Acquire Territory,' *Studies in Conflict & Terrorism*, 2018, 1–34.
53. Jacob Zenn, 'The Islamic State's Provinces on the Peripheries: Juxtaposing the Pledges from Boko Haram in Nigeria and Abu Sayyaf and Maute Group in the Philippines,' *Perspectives on Terrorism* 13, no. 1 (2019).
54. Aymenn Jawad al-Tamimi, 'Islamic State Sinai Province vs. Jama'at Jund Al-Islam: Report from Al-Naba',' July 2, 2020.
55. Cameron Glenn, 'Libya's Islamists: Who They Are – And What They Want,' *Wilson Centre*, August 2017; Aaron Y. Zelin, 'The Islamic State's First Colony in Libya,' *Washington Institute for Near East Studies*, October 2014.
56. Besides infighting, the groups were also competing for fighters. A substantial number of Jihadis from ASL had abandoned their group to join ISL, thus putting real pressure on ASL's survival. There were also reports suggesting that Mukhtar Belmokhtar's group al-Murabitoun participated in the fight against ISL, see Lounnas, 'Jihadist Groups in North Africa and the Sahel: Between Disintegration, Reconfiguration and Resilience.'
57. Henrik Gråtrud and Vidar Benjamin Skretting, 'Ansar Al-Sharia in Libya: An Enduring Threat,' *Perspectives on Terrorism* 11, no. 1 (2017): 40–53; Aaron Y. Zelin, 'The Rise and Decline of Ansar Al-Sharia in Libya,' *Hudson Institute's Current Trends in Islamist Ideology*, April 2015.
58. See Islamic State, *'Dabiq no. 11'*, September 2015.
59. Abu Qatada al-Filastini, 'fatwa fi daf'i siyal al-khawarij hin qasf al-kuffar aw al-murtaddin lihum [Fatwa in Deterrence of the Predators of the Khawarij When the Unbelievers or Apostates Attack Them],' *Al-Bushrayat*, June 2015.
60. The strength of the Islamic State in Somalia is typically estimated to approximately 150 fighters while al-Shabab controls approximately 7,000–9,000 fighters.
61. Maruf and Joseph, *Inside Al-Shabaab: The Secret History of Al-Qaeda's Most Powerful Ally*, 256.
62. Hamil al-Bushra, 'risalah ila ahlina fi al-somal [A Message to Our Brothers in Somalia],' *Al-Jabha Al-'Ilamiyyah Li-Nusrat Al-Dawla Al-Islamiyyah*, February 2015.
63. Jason Warner and Caleb Weiss, 'A Legitimate Challenger? Assessing the Rivalry between Al-Shabaab and the Islamic State in Somalia,' *CTC Sentinel* 10, no. 10 (2017).
64. The five videos are: Islamic State, 'ima' minna ayuha al-mujahid fi ard al-somal [O Mujahid in the Land of Somalia, Hear from Us],' Wilayat Ninawa, October 1, 2015; Islamic State, 'risalah lil-mujahidin fi ard al-somal [A Message to the Mujahidin in the Land of Somalia],' Wilayat Homs, October 1, 2015; Islamic State, 'min sina' ila al-somal [From Sinai to Somalia],' Wilayat Sinai, October 1, 2015; Islamic State, 'ilhaq bil-qafilah [Join the Caravan],' Wilayat al-Raqqa, October 2, 2015; Islamic State, 'min ard al-sham ila al-mujahidin fi al-somal [From the Land of the Levant to the Mujahidin in Somalia],' Wilayat al-Baraka, October 2, 2015. All five videos can be found on www.jihadology.com
65. Maruf and Joseph, *Inside Al-Shabaab: The Secret History of Al-Qaeda's Most Powerful Ally*, 258.

66. Adan's critique mainly concerns that al-Qaida's rejection of the caliphate, which is elaborated in al-Zawahiri's *Islamic Spring* series, is based on historical events and not legal disqualifications. For more on Adan, see Ibid.
67. Ibid.: 259.
68. Ibid.: 260.
69. This was not al-Shabab's first experience with internal dissent. In 2010–14 the group witnessed several episodes of opposition to its authoritarian leadership, which saw several high-ranking figures assassinated by the organisation's security service.
70. Christopher Anzalone, 'Black Banners in Somalia: The State of Al-Shabaab's Territorial Insurgency and the Specter of the Islamic State,' *CTC Sentinel* 11, no. 3 (2018). Even after December 24, 2017, the use of 'Wilayat Somal' would be irregular and not before summer 2018 would it be used regularly to refer to its province in Somalia.
71. Abu Maysara al-Shami, 'Behold, This Is the Treachery of the Leaders of Harakat Ash-Shabab!,' *Al Hayat Media Center*, n.d.

## CHAPTER 9. FIGHTING OVER THE PROPHETIC METHODOLOGY

1. I am aware of the various meanings of the word 'taghut'. I translate taghut as 'tyrant', which in the parlance of Jihadis is referring to political rulers in the Islamic world who claim adherence to Islam but in the eyes of Jihadis fail to govern in accordance to Islamic principles.
2. Gharib al-Sururiyya, 'ayat wa 'ibar fi taraka jabhat al-julani li-tanzim al-qa'ida [Verses and Morals in Leaving the Front of Al-Julani to the Organisation of Al-Qaida],' *Al Battar Media Foundation*, June 30, 2016.
3. Cited in Sami al-Uraydi, 'Advice for the Mujahedeen in the Time of Fitna,' *As-Sahab Media*, March 2017.
4. Maher, *Salafi–Jihadism: The History of an Idea*, 207.
5. Quintan Wiktorowicz, 'Anatomy of the Salafi Movement,' *Studies in Conflict & Terrorism* 29, no. 3 (May 2006): 207–39.
6. Lav, *Radical Islam and the Revival of Medieval Theology*.
7. Henri Lauzière, *The Making of Salafism: Islamic Reform in the Twentieth Century* (New York: Columbia University Press, 2016).
8. Al-Adnani, 'Apologies, Amir of Al-Qaida.'
9. This separation appears mainly connected to the dispute between various strands of Salafism. As the rivalling actors shared a common creed, they focused on differences in methodology as a way to criticise and delegitimise one another. For more see Stephane Lacroix, *Awakening Islam: The Politics of Religious Dissent in Contemporary Saudi Arabia* (Cambridge, MA: Harvard University Press, 2011).
10. According to Lauzière, Mustafa Hilmi, an Egyptian philosophy scholar, defined manhaj both as a 'method of investigation' to discover irrefutable knowledge (that is as an epistemology) and as a methodology to transform 'knowledge into practice.' Lauzière, *The Making of Salafism: Islamic Reform in the Twentieth Century*.
11. Wagemakers, *A Quietist Jihadi: The Ideology and Influence of Abu Muhammad al-Maqdisi*, 8.
12. Hamming, 'Polemical and Fratricidal Jihadists: A Historical Examination of Debates, Contestation and Infighting Within the Sunni Jihadi Movement.' For a discussion of Jihadis' view of the Taliban see Lahoud, *The Jihadis' Path to Self-Destruction*, 224–30.
13. Existing research on contestation between various trends of Salafism disagrees about the extent creed ('aqida) is the main source. Wiktorowicz argues that all trends

of Salafism 'share a common creed' but differ in how they view the reality of the contemporary context and as a result differ in their methodology by proposing 'different solutions,' see Wiktorowicz, 'Anatomy of the Salafi Movement,' 208. In contrast Lav and Wagemakers argue that the intra-Salafi differences are in fact also founded in differences in faith, see Wagemakers, *A Quietist Jihadi: The Ideology and Influence of Abu Muhammad Al-Maqdisi*; Lav, *Radical Islam and the Revival of Medieval Theology*.

14. Author's interview with Abu Qatada al-Filastini, December 7, 2016 (Zarqa).
15. Author's interview with Abu Qatada al-Filastini, August 23, 2018 (Zarqa).
16. Author's interview with Abu Mahmoud al-Filastini, July 18, 2016 (London).
17. For this argument see Wagemakers, 'Revisiting Wiktorowicz.'
18. Sherman A. Jackson, *Initiative to Stop the Violence (mubadarat waqf al-'unf): Sadat's Assassins and the Renunciation of Political Violence* (New Haven: Yale University Press, 2015).
19. Lacroix, *Awakening Islam: The Politics of Religious Dissent in Contemporary Saudi Arabia*. In a Q&A, Salih al-Fawzan, a member of the Saudi Arabian Council of Senior Scholars provides a typical regime-loyal quietist approach to fiqh al-waqi', see Salih al-Fawzan, 'The Methodology of the Salaf Concerning Politics: The Meaning of Fiqh ul-Waqi': http://www.spubs.com/sps/sp.cfm?subsecID=MNJ08&articleID=MNJ080003&articlePages=1. Wagemakers notes, however, that quietists are not opposed to fiqh al-waqi' and consider it helpful to support their own methodology of da'wa, while they oppose politics as an end, see Wagemakers, *Salafism in Jordan: Political Islam in a Quietist Community*, 84–85.
20. This is a difference between takfir al-mutlaq (general takfir) and takfir al-mu'ayyan (individual takfir) which have diverging requisites.
21. See Abd-al-Hakim, 'Untitled Letter to Abdelmalik Droukdal.'
22. A similar debate is the implementation of hudud. For the Islamic State this was a central feature of its governance project but for al-Qaida it could wait till after the war, when a stable Islamic political entity is established and people have been educated in Islam.
23. Sam Heller writes that 'Salafi–jihadism is still defined in terms of a single 'manhaj''. See Heller, 'Ahrar Al-Sham's Revisionist Jihadism,' September 2015.
24. Author's interview with Abu Sulayman al-Muhajir, June 2017. Abu Qatada insinuates the same when telling me that 'the manhaj of al-Qaida is not just Abu Abdullah [Bin Laden], but has developed as a product of the different parties within in. And it will continue to develop.' Author's interview with Abu Qatada al-Filastini, December 7, 2016 (Zarqa).
25. See for instance the videos 'Upon the Prophetic Methodology,' July 2014; 'kasr al-hudud' [The Breaking of the Borders], June 29, 2014; 'End of Sykes–Picot,' June 29, 2014; 'The Rise of the Caliphate and the Return of the Gold Dinar,' August 29, 2015; 'The Dark Rise of Banknotes and the Return of the Gold Dinar,' October 11, 2015. Especially Islamic State supporter Hussein ibn Mahmoud has issued a lot of publiations on the topic.
26. Abu Muhammed al-Adnani, 'That They Live by Proof,' *Al Hayat*, May 2016.
27. See for instance Abdullah al-Muhaysini, 'We Want It on the Manhaj of Prophethood Regarding the Declaration of "Khilafah",' July 2014.
28. Heller, 'How Ahrar Al-Sham Has Come to Define the Kaleidoscope of the Syrian Civil War.'

29. Michels, *Political Parties: A Sociological Study of the Oligarchical Tendencies of Modern Democracy*, 166.
30. Al-Shinqiti, 'sheikh ayman al-zawahiri rajul umma [Sheikh Ayman Al-Zawahiri: Man of the Umma].'
31. Michels, *Political Parties: A Sociological Study of the Oligarchical Tendencies of Modern Democracy*, 165.
32. Ayman al-Zawahiri, 'Support Your Prophet,' December 2015.
33. Al-Qaida, 'The False Dawn episode 1', *Al Fajr Media Centre*, April 2015; Al-Qaida, 'The False Dawn episode 2', *Al Fajr Media Centre*, May 2015
34. Al-Zawahiri, 'Islamic Spring Part 1.'
35. Abu Hajjaj was Governor of Iraq in the Umayyad dynasty and became known for his ruthlessness and the ordering of several massacres.
36. Abu Muslim al-Khorasani was an important Abbasid general that led the Abbasid struggle to overcome the Umayyad dynasty and who became the governor of Khorasan.
37. Al-Zawahiri, 'Islamic Spring Part 1.'
38. Al-Zawahiri, 'Islamic Spring Part 2.'
39. Ibid.
40. Al-Zawahiri, 'Islamic Spring Part 1.'In episode two he reiterates that 'we do not acknowledge the claim of al-Baghdadi for the Caliphate, and that we see that it is not a Caliphate on the prophetic method.'
41. Ibid.
42. Al-Zawahiri, 'Islamic Spring Part 2.'
43. Ibid.
44. Ibid.
45. Ayman al-Zawahiri, 'Islamic Spring Part 9: Turkistan: Patience and Then Victory,' *As-Sahab Media*, July 2016; Ayman Al-Zawahiri, 'Islamic Spring Part 8: The Sun of Victory Shines From Nusantara,' *As-Sahab Media*, January 13, 2016; Ayman al-Zawahiri, 'Islamic Spring Part 7: Yemen of Wisdom and Faith Between the Servants of Iran and the Slaves of America,' *As-Sahab Media*, May 2016.
46. Ayman Al-Zawahiri, 'Islamic Spring Part 6,' *As-Sahab Media*, October 2015.
47. Al-Zawahiri, 'Islamic Spring Part 3: A Talk on the Khilafa That Follows the Prophetic Path.'
48. Al-Zawahiri, 'Islamic Spring Part 5.'
49. Ayman Al-Zawahiri, 'Islamic Spring Part 4: Answering the Doubts Regarding the Khalifa Who Takes Authority by Force,' *As-Sahab Media*, April 2015.
50. Al-Hakim would respond to Droukdal's points of criticism. One by one he explained why the figures suggested by Droukdal to be part of the 'people of authority' (al-Maqdisi, Abu Qatada, Sulayman al-Alwan, Abu al-Waleed al-Ghazi al-Ansari, al-Zawahiri and Mullah Umar) were not included by the Islamic State. He rejects Droukdal's claim that the Islamic State does not have tamkin and on the issue of the pledge of allegiance, this is only valid in contexts where there is no caliphate. For more see Tore Refslund Hamming, 'ISIS's Charm Offensive toward Al-Qaeda in the Islamic Maghreb,' *Middle East Institute*, December 13, 2018.
51. Besides the productions of al-Binali and al-Shami, see also the Islamic State, 'Rumiyah no. 7: Establishing the Islamic State - Between the Prophetic Methodology and the Path of Deviants', March 2017; Abu Abdur Rahmah Raed al-Libi, 'Beautiful Pearls in The Fiqh of The Islamic Khilafah', *Ansar Al Khilafah Media*, 24 April 2015 (English

version 25 March 2016). Al-Libi's book covers the topics of the obligation of choosing a khalifa, the people of authority, the process of choosing a khalifa, the necessity of controlling all land to represent a legitimate caliphate and to what extent it is mandatory for Muslims to join the caliphate.

52. For some prominent primary literature on the topic by al-Qaida(-aligned) figures see Al-Filastini, 'Cloak of the Khalifah'; Abu Ahmad Abd al-Karim al-Jaza'iri, 'al-ta'liqat al-bahiyyah 'ala al-mubarrirat al-shar'iyyah wa-l-waqi'yyah li-bay'a al-dawla al-islamiyya [Glorious Comments on the Legitimate and Realistic Justifications for Allegiance to the Islamic State],' June 2015; Al-Muhajir, 'Conclusion in the Caliphate Declaration Discussion.'
53. Crone, *God's Rule: Government and Islam*; Mohammad Hashim Kamali, 'Caliphate and Political Jurisprudence in Islam: Historical and Contemporary Perspectives,' *The Muslim World* 106 (2016): 384–403.
54. Hugh Kennedy, *The Caliphate* (London: Penguin Books, 2016).
55. Kamali, 'Caliphate and Political Jurisprudence in Islam: Historical and Contemporary Perspectives.'
56. In the post-2013 era, the Islamic State has played on symbolic actions to illustrate adherence to prophetic methodology. One example is al-Baghdadi echoing the first two caliphs Abu Bakr and Umar when he from the pulpit of the al-Nuri mosque declared that while not being the best of people, he has been entrusted with authority and if people see him sin, he should be stopped.

## CHAPTER 10. STRUGGLING FOR AUTHORITY

1. Quintan Wiktorowicz, *Radical Islam Rising: Muslim Extremism in the West* (Oxford: Rowman & Littlefield Publishers, Inc, 2005), 135.
2. Nathan J. Brown, 'Official Islam in the Arab World: The Contest for Religious Authority,' *Carnegie Endownment for International Peace*, May 2017.
3. Lacroix, *Awakening Islam: The Politics of Religious Dissent in Contemporary Saudi Arabia*; Wagemakers, 'Contesting Religious Authority in Jordanian Salafi Networks.'
4. Wiktorowicz, 'Framing Jihad: Intramovement Framing Contests and Al-Qaeda's Struggle for Sacred Authority.'
5. Crone, *God's Rule: Government and Islam*.
6. See for instance Faisal Devji, *Landscapes of the Jihad: Militancy, Morality, Modernity* (London: Hurst & Company, 2005); Eickelman and Piscatori, *Muslim Politics*; Olivier Roy, *The Failure of Political Islam* (Cambridge: Harvard University Press, 1994); Muhammad Qasim Zaman, *Modern Islamic Thought in a Radical Age: Religious Authority and Internal Criticism* (New York: Cambridge University Press, 2012); Muhammad Qasim Zaman, *The Ulama in Contemporary Islam: Custodians of Change* (Princeton: Princeton University Press, 2007).
7. Lahoud, *The Jihadis' Path to Self-Destruction*, 105.
8. Zaman, Modern Islamic Thought in a Radical Age: Religious Authority and Internal Criticism, 181–82.
9. Zaman, Muhammad Qasim. Modern Islamic Thought in a Radical Age: Religious Authority and Internal Criticism. New York: Cambridge University Press, 2012: 1. It should be noted that in some domains more formalised structures of religious authorities remain dominant. For instance, in Hallaq's work on authority in relation to Islamic jurisprudence (fiqh), he highlights the formalised structure of authority

founded on knowledge of religious sciences, the discipline of ijtihad (interpretation) and the role of the mujtahid (the person exercising interpretation). See Wael B. Hallaq, *Authority, Continuity and Change in Islamic Law* (Cambridge: Cambridge University Press, 2001).

10. Peter Mandaville, 'Globalization and the Politics of Religious Knowledge: Pluralizing Authority in the Muslim World,' *Theory, Culture & Society* 24, no. 2 (2007): 2.
11. Roy, *The Failure of Political Islam*.
12. Alshech, 'The Doctrinal Crisis within the Salafi–Jihadi Ranks and the Emergence of Neo-Takfirism'; Olivier Roy, 'The Transformation of the Arab World,' *Journal of Democracy* 23, no. 3 (2012): 5–18.
13. Lahoud, *The Jihadis' Path to Self-Destruction*, 98.
14. Lav, *Radical Islam and the Revival of Medieval Theology*.
15. Uthman ibn 'Abd al-Rahman al-Tamimi, 'i'lam al-anam bi-milad dawlat al-islam [Informing the People of the Birth of the Islamic State],' *Al Furqan Media Foundation*, 2007.
16. Another exception is Abdullah al-Muhaysini. Al-Muhaysini enjoyed a religious upbringing in Saudi Arabia with a father who was a relatively known imam. At the age of 12, he was sent on 'vacation' to different villages to study Arabic and to memorise the Quran, which he succeeded at the age of 14 or 15. Between the age of 15 and 19, he memorised several collections of Hadith at the al-Haram Academy in Mecca. After this his father sent him to Mauritania to study Arabic and usul al-fiqh (foundations of jurisprudence) under sheikh Muhammad al-Dedew. He then returned to Riyadh to study under known scholars like Abd al-Aziz al Tarifi and Muhammad ibn al-Uthaymin and he studied 'aqida (creed) under sheikh Abdullah al-Ghunayman and tawhid (monotheism) under sheikh Abdul-Rahman al-Barrak. He eventually finished a master degree in Riyadh at the High Institute for Judges. After that he studied under sheikh Sulayman al-Ulwan from whom he received ijaza in 'aqida. Before migrating to Syria, he continued his studying finishing a doctorate in Mecca. The subject of the degree, which took two and a half years to complete, was 'the ruling of war refugees in Islamic jurisprudence' through a comparison of the four legal schools.
17. Alshech, 'The Doctrinal Crisis within the Salafi–Jihadi Ranks and the Emergence of Neo-Takfirism'; Wagemakers, 'Reclaiming Scholarly Authority: Abu Muhammad Al-Maqdisi's Critique of Jihadi Practices.'
18. Mark Juergensmeyer, *Terror in the Mind of God: The Global Rise of Religious Violence* (Berkeley: University of California Press, 2003).
19. Nelly Lahoud describes the story of Fadil Harun, the late secretary of al-Qaida and senior figure in the group's activities in East Africa. See Lahoud, 'Beware of the Imitator: Al-Qa'ida Through the Lens of Its Confidential Secretary.'
20. See for instance the 'Paths to Victory' series in the Islamic State's *Rumiyah* magazine no. 2, 3, 5, and 6.
21. For an example of al-Qaida criticising Salafi 'ulama see Al-Zawahiri, 'Support Your Prophet.'
22. Author's interview with Abu Mahmoud al-Filastini, July 15, 2016 (London).
23. Author's interview with Abu Qatada al-Filastini, December 7, 2016 (Zarqa).
24. Hamming, 'Polemical and Fratricidal Jihadists: A Historical Examination of Debates, Contestation and Infighting Within the Sunni Jihadi Movement.'
25. See for instance Zaydan, 'al-naqd li-qawl man ja'ala al-khilafa al-Islamiyya min din al-rafd [Denounce the Saying That Made the Caliphate from the Religion of Refusal].'

26. The first mention of rival Jihadi scholars in its official magazines is in *Dabiq* no. 6 which includes a photo of al-Maqdisi and Abu Qatada with the title 'Misleading Scholars.' In *Dabiq* no. 11, an article titled 'The Evil of Division and Taqlid' with a picture of al-Maqdisi discusses the mistakes of scholars. And in *Dabiq* no. 14, an article titled 'Kill the Imams of Kufr in the West' discusses Sufi and Salafi scholars who are considered apostates. There is an ending note on Abu Basir al-Tartusi and his apostasy. Islamic State supporters also joined the efforts to vilify Jihadi 'ulama. An example is Abu Khabab al-Iraqi, 'Refuting the Doubt: Who is With you from the "Ulama"?', date unknown.
27. Islamic State, 'The Wicked Scholars Are Cursed,' *Rumiyah No. 1*, September 2016.
28. Abu Hafs al-Shami, 'Traits of the Evil Scholars,' *Rumiyah No. 5*, January 2017.
29. Islamic State, 'The Obligation of Exposing Wicked Scholars,' *Rumiyah No. 3*, November 2016.
30. This argument is among other places introduced in Abu Hamza Al-Rumi, 'Who from the Scholars Support You,' April 11, 2017.
31. In Rumiyah issue 8, published in April 2017, the words to refer to al-Qaida and aligned figures had also changed dramatically from previous issues of the magazine. They were now described as *murtaddin* (apostates) or *scholars of taghut* (tyrant).
32. Islamic State, 'al-zilal fi-l-mawqifi al-shar'iyy min 'ulama al-haqqi wa al-dalal [In the Shadow of the Legitimate Position on the 'ulama of Truth and of Misguidance],' *Maktab Al-Buhouth Wal-Dirasat*, April 1, 2017.
33. Abu al-Hassan al-Muhajir, 'You Will Remember What I Have Told You,' *Al Furqan Media Foundation*, December 5, 2016.
34. AQAP, 'tanzim al-dawla yada'u 'ansaruhu fi-l-'alam ila qatala al-du'a wa 'ulama al-salatin [the Islamic State Calls on Its Supporters around the World to Kill the Preachers and the Scholars of the Sultan],' *Al Masra No. 40*, 2017.
35. Examples include two video series of al-Qaida, one entitled *Carrying the Weapons of Martyrs* and the other entitled *The Three Scholars of Jihad*.
36. AQAP, 'Responsibility of the Word,' *Al-Malahem Media Foundation*, July 5, 2014.
37. Al-Zawahiri, 'Islamic Spring Part 2.' That said, al-Qaida has also spent considerable efforts discrediting non-Jihadi 'ulama.
38. Al-Zawahiri, 'Support Your Prophet.'
39. Lahoud, 'Beware of the Imitator: Al-Qa'ida through the Lens of Its Confidential Secretary,' 51.
40. This is quite remarkable in the extremely polarised environment post-2013. A few other figures like Anwar al-Awlaki is also revered by both al-Qaida and the Islamic State.
41. The series was launched prior to the intra-Jihadi conflict but continued to run until 2019.
42. For instance Hamza Bin Laden's November 2017 speech was a homage to his father, see Hamza Bin Laden, 'Usama… The Fighter Against Invaders And The Inciter of Rebellion Against Tyrants,' *As-Sahab Media*, November 7, 2017.
43. In his letter exchange with Atiyyatullah prior to his death, Bin Laden stressed the importance of winning public support. A similar approach is evident is al-Zawahiri's book *Knights Under the Prophet's Banner* and has informed al-Qaida's strategy during the last period of Bin Laden's rule and during the era of his successor.
44. Like Bin Laden, al-Zawahiri define Shia as unbelievers, but they nevertheless caution against opening a conflict with the Shia from a strategic point of view. Furthermore,

both agree that excommunication of Shias as a group is in violation of the conditions of takfir as it must occur on an individual basis.

45. Al-Zawahiri, 'Support Your Prophet.'.
46. Al-Zawahiri, 'Islamic Spring Part 5.'
47. Al-Shami, 'Untitled Statement,' March 2014.
48. Author's interview with Abu Sulayman al-Muhajir, June 2017.
49. Author's interview with Abu Qatada al-Filastini, December 7, 2016 (Zarqa).
50. Al-Maqdisi, 'bayan sadir fi bayan hal 'al-dawla al-islamiyya fi-l-iraq wa-l-sham' wa-l-mawqif al-wajib tujahaha [A Comdemning Statement on the Status of 'the Islamic State in Iraq and Sham and the Necessary Position against It].'
51. Author's correspondence with Abu Muhammad al-Maqdisi, December 4, 2018.
52. Author's interview with Abu Sulayman al-Muhajir, June 2017.
53. Turki al-Binali, 'tanzim al-qa'ida al-shar'i wa tanzim al-qa'ida al-sha'bi [the Legitimate Al-Qaida Group and the Popular Al-Qaida Group],' April 5, 2014.
54. Abu Maysara Al-Shami, 'It Is from the Strangest Matters of History for Adh-Dhawahiri to Produce Three Abnormal Messages Contradicting the Manhaj That Shaykh Usamah Was Martyred upon, Almost Immediately after the Martyrdom of Shaykh Usamah,' n.d.
55. Author's interview with Danish foreign fighter with the Islamic State, April 16, 2019.
56. Christia, *Alliance Formation in Civil Wars*, 7.
57. Joas Wagemakers, 'The Transformation of a Radical Concept: Al-Wala' Wa-l-Bara' in the Ideology of Abu Muhammad Al-Maqdisi,' in *Global Salafism: Islam's New Religious Movement* (London: Hurst & Company, 2009), 81–106.
58. In fact, Islamic extremists usually consider al-wala' wa-l-bara' a 'protective tool' to defend Islam from deviation. Illustrative of its relevance in modern Jihadi tradition, it was key in the Taliban's refusal to handover Usama Bin Laden to the US after 9/11.
59. According to Shiraz Maher, Hamad ibn 'Atiq wrote that 'anyone who befriends a mushrik [polytheist] is a mushrik; anyone who befriends a kafir is a kafir, whether they are som the Ahl al-kitab [people of the book; monotheistic Jews and Christians], see Maher, *Salafi-Jihadism: The History of an Idea*, 118.
60. Wagemakers, 'The Transformation of a Radical Concept: Al-Wala' Wa-l-Bara' in the Ideology of Abu Muhammad Al-Maqdisi.'
61. 'Ulama loyal to the Saudi regime helped legitimise the royal family's call for assistance through the notion of akhaff al-dararayn (choosing between the lesser of two evils).
62. Maher, *Salafi-Jihadism: The History of an Idea*; Wagemakers, *A Quietist Jihadi: The Ideology and Influence of Abu Muhammad Al-Maqdisi*.
63. Wagemakers, 'The Transformation of a Radical Concept: Al-Wala' Wa-l-Bara' in the Ideology of Abu Muhammad Al-Maqdisi.'
64. Ali al-Khudair, a follower of Hamoud Uqla al-Shuaybi, makes a distinction between *tawalli* and *muwalat*. Tawalli is when a believer is emotionally attached to an unbeliever and in this case it constitutes kufr (unbelief) no matter the person's beliefs. Muwalat includes actions towards an unbeliever that are cordial but not empowering. Al-Khudair considers these actions major sins but not unbelief.
65. For explanation of al-Maqdisi's, see Wagemakers, 'The Transformation of a Radical Concept: Al-Wala' Wa-l-Bara' in the Ideology of Abu Muhammad Al-Maqdisi.'
66. Lahoud, *The Jihadis' Path to Self-Destruction*, 204.
67. Ibid.: 204.

68. Ayman Al-Zawahiri, 'Al-Wala' Wa-l-Bara': Changing an Article of Faith and Losing Sight of Reality,' 2002.
69. Even in academic circles takfir is a controversial topic with some academics engaging in assessments of the correctness of Jihadis' method of applying takfir. For an example Mohamed Badar, Masaki Nagata, and Tiphane Tueni, 'The Radical Application of the Islamist Concept of Takfir,' *Arab Law Quarterly* 31 (2017): 134–62.
70. Sahih Bukhari, Volume 8, Book 73, Number 125.
71. In 1998 he authored his caution against takfir, entitled 'al-risala al-thalathiniyya fi tahdhir min al-ghallu fi-l-takfir'. Of a more recent date, he touched upon the issue of takfir in relation to Turkey where he mentioned three points: takfir cannot be applied of a larger group, a person is a Muslim until he commits a known nullifier which is clear and not suspicious and the conditions of takfir must be present and there should be no preventions of takfir and no doubt, and hujjah (proof) must be presented to the person. See precise answers on the Turkish Questions. Other Jihadis like al-Tartusi, Abu Hamza al-Masri and Umar Abdel Rahman have authored books of caution on the use of takfir.
72. In 2009, al-Maqdisi issued an answer to a question about the infidelity of Hamas. Al-Maqdisi is not saying explicitly that Hamas should be considered unbelievers but limits his answer to concluding that some within the group have committed acts of unbelief. He also warns against fighting Hamas.
73. This studied period is not the first time al-wala' wa-l-bara' has been used in this way. There are historical examples of how some Jihadis in Afghanistan made takfir on the Taliban and in Algeria, GIA similarly proclaimed takfir on rival groups.
74. For how the Islamic State connects al-wala' wa-l-bara' to prophetic methodology, see Islamic State, 'Disavowal of the Mushrikin in the Lives of the Prophet and the Sahabah,' *Rumiyah No.* 7, March 7, 2017.
75. Al-Anbari, 'al-waqfu al-dari fi tarjamati al-sheikh al-anbari [Knowledgeable Study on the Biography of Sheikh Al-Anbari].'
76. Aymenn Jawad al-Tamimi, 'Specimen 7W: Conditions of Repentance, Al-Bab, Aleppo Province (January 2014),' *2015*, January.
77. Al-Baghdadi, 'wa allah ya'lam wa antum la ta'lamun [God Knows and You Do Not Know].'
78. Faraj, 'al-farida al-gha'iba [The Neglected Duty],' para. 136.
79. Abu Muhammed al-Adnani, 'Say to Those Who Disbelieve "You Will Be Overcome,"' *Al Hayat*, October 2015.
80. The al-Qaida-Taliban relationship have been heavily criticised in several leadership speeches, but also among supporters. For examples see Gharib Al-Sururiyya, 'tawaghit al-qa'ida [Tyrants of Al-Qaida],' *Al Battar Media Foundation*, July 16, 2017; Gharib Al-Sururiyya, 'An Elderly Rogue al-Qa'ida,' *Al Battar Media Foundation*, January 7, 2017.
81. Aymenn Jawad Al-Tamimi, 'Specimen 1B: Invitation to Repentance: Euphrates Province,' January 27, 2015.
82. Islamic State, 'The Allies of Al-Qa'idah in Sham,' *Dabiq No. 8*, March 2015.
83. Islamic State, 'The Allies of Al-Qa'idah in Sham: The End,' *Dabiq No. 12*, November 2015.
84. Ibid.: 16
85. Islamic State, 'The Allies of Al-Qa'idah in Sham: Part 4,' *Dabiq No. 11*, September 2015.

86. Islamic State, 'The Allies of Al-Qa'idah in Yemen.'
87. Islamic State, 'Document no. 175', *al-maktab al-markazi*, June 1, 2016.
88. In an article in *Dabiq* no. 7, the Islamic State claims that dozens of Ahrar al-Sham and Jabhat al-Nusra fighters have repented and joined the caliphate.
89. Islamic State, 'hatta tu'minu bi-allahi wahdahu [Until You Believe in Allah Alone],' *Al-Naba No. 129*, April 27, 2018. In a May 2019 al-Naba editorial, the Islamic State summed up its view of al-Qaida's different branches. Referring to them as murtaddin (apostates) the editorial explains how the various branches is allying with other murtaddin while fighting the Islamic State in violation of al-wala' wa-l-bara'.
90. Jaysh al-Islam responds on July 1, 2015 with a video showing Islamic State fighters being beheaded.
91. Muhaysini bounty poster was published on December 11, 2016.
92. In Knights under the Prophet's Banner, al-Zawahiri talks at length about seizing territory and jihadi coalitions.
93. Khalid Al-Batarfi, 'Message to the Muhajireen and Ansar in the Beloved Sham,' *GIMF*, October 28, 2016.
94. The issue of how to relate to Turkey is another example. While the Islamic State in its al-Naba newsletter no. 53 justified fighting Turkey, al-Qaida has on several occasions expressed its opposition because of the strategic downside.
95. Lahoud, *The Jihadis' Path to Self-Destruction*, 196.
96. From Leon Trotsky's '*Our Political Tasks*,' published in 1904.
97. In an interview with Abu Qatada, he similarly noted to this author how the Islamic State instrumentalise takfir.
98. Author's interview with Islamic State supporter, January 11, 2016.
99. Abu Sa'd al-Najdi, 'fath al-malik al-kabir muta'al fi tandim al-haqq 'ala ara' al-rijal (al-radd 'ala al-sheikh al-zawahiri) [Opening of the Exalted Great King In Providing the Truth Upon the Opinions of the Men (Reply To Shaykh Al-Zawahiri)],' *Al-Battar Media Foundation*, n.d.
100. Aymenn Jawad al-Tamimi, 'An Internal Report on Extremism in the Islamic State,' November 1, 2018. While the report was authored in November 2015, it was not made public before 2018.
101. Back in 2014 al-Adnani called on al-Zawahiri to proclaim takfir on the Egyptian Muslim Brotherhood leader Muhammad Morsi, see Al-'Adnani, ''udhran amir al-qai'da [Apologies, Amir of Al-Qaida].'
102. Abu Jarir al-Shamali, 'We Disassociated Ourselves from Tanzim al-Qa'ida and from the Shar'i Lapses of al-Zawahiri,' *Ahl Al-Tawhid*, December 17, 2016.
103. Al-Sururiyya, 'ayat wa 'ibar fi taraka jabhat al-julani li-tanzim al-qa'ida [Verses and Morals in Leaving the Front of Al-Julani to the Organization of Al-Qaida].'
104. Ahlam al-Nasr, 'al-zawahiri al-kurra al-'ajuz! [Al-Zawahiri: The Old Ball!],' *Al-Sumud Media Foundation*, August 2016.
105. Locally in Syria, Jihadis' early variance in their stance towards the Islamic State was partly a question of how close they were ideologically to the group and partly the result of diverging rationales, author's interview with Danish foreign fighter, March 14, 2018 (Copenhagen).
106. Abdelhaleem and al-Sibai, 'A Declaration of Disownment and Divergence From the Ideology and Actions of ISIS'; Al-Tartusi, 'A Declaration Regarding the Fighting Between the ISIS and the Mujahedeen of Al-Sham.'

107. Abu Muhammad al-Maqdisi, 'awradaha sa'ad wa sa'ad moshtamelo ma hakatha ya sa'ado towradi al-ibelo [Sa'ad Took the Camels to the Spring for Some Water While Wearing a Wool Garment with Nothing underneath, Oh Sa'ad Ths Is Not How Camels Are Handled],' *Minbar Al-Tawhid Wa-l-Jihad*, September 2014.
108. Abu Mariya al-Qahtani, 'My Advice to All Those Who Are Soft towards the Khawarij,' *Al-Muwahideen Media*, January 2015. Another Jabhat al-Nusra member, Abu Hassan al-Kuwaiti, also issued several statements in this period labelling the Islamic State as khawarij.
109. Group of scholars, 'Fatwa,' June 2015.
110. See the Facebook postings here: www.facebook.com/mohibidrhani/photos/a.297278376999540.67815.297266940334017/884039081656797/ and www.facebook.com/DTariqHaleem/posts/1012701202081959 [both accessed November 14, 2018].
111. Author's interview with Abu Qatada al-Filastini, December 2016 (Zarqa).
112. Al-Filastini, 'fatwa fi daf'i siyal al-khawarij hin qasf al-kuffar aw al-murtaddin lihum [Fatwa in Deterrence of the Predators of the Khawarij When the Unbelievers or Apostates Attack Them].'
113. Al-Maqdisi, 'Why Did I Not Name Them Khawarij Even until Now?'
114. Abu Muhammad al-Maqdisi, 'Repelling the Aggression of the Islamic State from Afar,' June 2015.
115. Sahih Muslim: Book 005, Number 2316
116. Sahih Muslim: Book 005, Number 2318
117. The hadith can be accessed here: https://islamqa.info/en/answers/182237/the-khawaarij-kharijites.
118. This is particularly interesting since al-Zawahiri is no stranger to applying the khawarij label. In his 2002 treatise on al-wala' wa-l-bara' he discusses people, including scholars, assisting the apostate rulers and says they have adopted the khariji method by assisting in the killing of Muslims.
119. Ayman al-Zawahiri, 'Sham: A Trust Upon Your Necks,' *As-Sahab Media*, January 14, 2016.
120. Ayman al-Zawahiri, 'infuru li-l-sham [Prepaing to Fight for Al-Sham],' *As-Sahab Media*, May 2016.
121. See al-Nafir no. 3–6 published between April 19 and July 22, 2016.

## CHAPTER 11. THE ISLAMIC STATE

1. Al-Uraydi, 'Advice for the Mujahedeen in the Time of Fitna.'
2. Abu Mahmoud al-Filastini, 'An Indispensable Though Imperfect Unity,' *Telegram Channel*, April 2017.
3. Turki al-Bin'ali's tweeted through the account @turky_albinali on May 22, 2014.
4. For an examination of this early period of the rise of the Hazimis within the Islamic State, see Tore Refslund Hamming, 'The Extremist Wing of the Islamic State,' *Jihadica*, June 9, 2016.
5. Omar Ashour, *The De-Radicalization of Jihadists* (New York: Routledge, 2009); Aaron Y. Zelin, 'Ultra Extremism Among Tunisian Jihadis Within The Islamic State,' *Jihadica*, February 2020.
6. 'Udhr bi-l-jahl is not an entirely new concept of disagreement within the SJM. Wagemakers have showed how the three ideologues Sayyid Imam, al-Maqdisi and

al-Tartusi previously debated the acceptance of ignorance. This, however, was mainly in the context of nominal Muslim rulers and democracy. See Joas Wagemakers, 'An Inquiry into Ignorance: A Jihadi Salafi Debate on Jahl as an Obstacle to Takfir,' in *The Transmission and Dynamics of the Textual Sources of Islam*, ed. Nicolet Boekhoff-van der Voort, Kees Versteegh, and Joas Wagemakers (Leiden: Brill, 2011).

7. Cole Bunzel, 'Manifest Enmity: The Origins, Development, and Persistence of Classical Wahhabism (1153–1351/1741–1932),' *Princeton University, Department of Near Eastern Studies* PhD Dissertation (2018).
8. See for example Ahmad al-Hazimi, 'Takfir is not a boogeyman,' [Youtube video], 2016, Available at: https://www.youtube.com/watch?v=NuJkKXeivps [Accessed May 11, 2016].
9. Cole Bunzel, 'Ideological Infighting in the Islamic State,' *Perspectives on Terrorism* 13, no. 1 (2019): 13–22.
10. Zelin, 'Ultra Extremism Among Tunisian Jihadis Within The Islamic State.'
11. Cole Bunzel, 'Caliphate in Disarray: Theological Turmoil in the Islamic State,' *Jihadica*, October 3, 2017. Discussing the factionalism with Ahmad al-Hamdan, a Jihadi observer who is close to al-Qaida and a childhood friend of Turki al-Binali—a protagonist in one of the competing factions—it was explained like this: 'I will try to explain that to you. A person went to a grave and stood by the grave of one of his deceased ones and said "Oh deceased one, help me and assist me to solve some matter". This action is termed in the Islamic Shareeah [shari'a] as 'Shirk', i.e. polytheism because instead of asking Allah, he asked from the dead for matters that only Allah alone can do. And he thought that these people can cause benefits and harms and not Allah. This action is considered by the both the movements [the Binalis and the Hazimis] as Shirk and the one who does this looses faith and becomes a disbeliever. But the point of the dispute is.... Will the one who does not make Takfeer on this person (i.e does not consider him to be a disbeliever) be a disbeliever himself or not? Bin'ali says no, rather the matter must be discussed and explained to him, and if he still insists after that, he will be a Kaafir (disbeliever). Al Hazimi says there is no need for a discussion or explanation in his case, rather is a Kaafir if he does not consider that person to be a Kaafir.'
12. The issue of takfir al-adhir was already a problem within the Russian speaking militant environment prior to 2014, but it migrated into the Islamic State when large numbers of Russian speaking Jihadis joined the group.
13. Abu Ja'far al-Shami, 'al-qawl al-naddi fi kufr dawlat al-baghdadi [the Moist Words on the Unbelief of the State of Al-Baghdadi],' April 2015. The piece is most likely authored in late August or early September 2014 as the deaths of Abu Musab al-Tunisi and others are mentioned (killed in August), but not the death of Abu Umar al-Kuwaiti (killed in September).
14. The forerunner to the Delegated Committee.
15. See Mansoor Jassem Alshamsi, *Islam and Political Reform in Saudi Arabia: The Quest for Political Change and Reform* (New York: Routledge, 2010).
16. Ahmad al-Hazimi did go to both Egypt and Tunisia to give lectures showing his ability to leave the Saudi kingdom.
17. Abu Maysara Al-Shami, 'al-hazimi been kabira al-qu'ud wa dalal al-jamiyyah [Al-Hazimi between the Great Sin of Abstention and the Error of the Jamiah],' 2014.
18. In its *Dabiq* magazine no. 6, the Islamic State had a brief notice on the dismantling of a 'khariji cell' which was working on recruiting others. Later a video was published showing the four men that had been arrested.

19. Aymenn Jawad al-Tamimi, 'Dissent in the Islamic State: Abu Al-Faruq Al-Masri's 'Message on the Manhaj',' *Combating Terrorism Center at West Point*, October 2016.
20. For a full overview of all the letters used in the part below on the dissent within the Islamic State in Yemen, see Aymenn Jawad al-Tamimi, 'Dissent in the Islamic State's Yemen Affiliates: Documents, Translation & Analysis,' February 29, 2016.
21. For the original booklet and a translation, see Al-Tamimi, 'Dissent in the Islamic State: Abu Al-Faruq Al-Masri's "Message on the Manhaj".' Al-Masri dates the booklet to 1437 corresponding to the period October 2015–September 2016.
22. Brynjar Lia and Thomas Hegghammer, 'Jihadi Strategic Studies: The Alleged Al Qaida Policy Study Preceding the Madrid Bombings,' *Studies in Conflict & Terrorism* 27, no. 5 (September 2004): 355–75.
23. Morrison, *Origins and Rise of Dissident Irish Republicanism: The Role and Impact of Organizational Splits*, 18.
24. Sons of Abu Yusuf al-Barnawi, 'khadh' al-waram min al-khawarij al-shikawiyya bi-bay'a ahl al-karam [Cutting Out the Tumor of Shekau's Khawarij Through Pledging Allegiance to the People of Benevolence],' *Al-Haqa'iq Dawlat Al-Khilafa Al-Islamiyya*, June 2018.
25. Aymenn Jawad al-Tamimi, 'AQIM Advice to 'Boko Haram' Dissidents: Full Translation and Analysis,' September 2018.
26. After 2013, most Ansaru members appear to have reintegrated into Boko Haram.
27. Al-Chadi was a senior military commander in charge of allegedly 80% of Shekau's 2014 territorial expansion and al-Hajj was his deputy. Both were killed in November-December 2014.
28. Abu Anisa replaced al-Chadi but was himself killed in April–May 2015.
29. An outspoken critic of Shekau who was killed in September–October 2015.
30. A deputy of Abu Hanifa. Malim Umar was killed in October–November 2015.
31. Al-Turath al-Ilm published the *Nigerian Questions* on March 1, 2018. Abu Malik al-Tamimi's rulings dealt with the following issues: Is a person an unbeliever simply by living in the abode of unbelief? Is it permissible to target the tyrant in public places where there is a threat of Muslim casualties? Does having a Nigerian ID card automatically qualify as unbelief? At this stage of the Jihad is it eligible to target apostate schools?
32. This point is corroborated by Shekau and Man Chari, a senior commander, who say that Abu Musab al-Barnawi was in charge of contact with the Islamic State, see Man Chari and Abu Bakr Shekau, 'Message from the Soldiers,' August 7, 2016.
33. Islamic State, 'Governor of West Africa Sheikh Abu Musab Al-Barnawi: We Will Come out of Our Plight with a More Solid Body and a Stronger Hand,' *Al-Naba No. 41*, August 2, 2016.
34. Jacob Zenn, 'Boko Haram's Factional Feuds: Internal Extremism and External Interventions,' *Terrorism and Political Violence*, 2019, 1–33.
35. Abu Bakr Shekau, 'Untitled audio statement,' *Media Foundation of Jama'at Ahl Al-Sunnah Li-l-Dawa Wa-l-Jihad*, August 3, 2016.
36. It is interesting to notice how this compares to the situation in Syria, where the control of media departments and communication channels have been extremely important to manage internal conflict. It is likely that al-Barnawi prevented Shekau's messages reaching al-Baghdadi while himself communicating his criticism of Shekau to the Islamic State amir.
37. In a speech from 16 August 2017 Shekau gives the impression that his group represents the true Islamic state in Nigeria, but that it is independent from al-

Baghdadi's group. Boko Haram videos from 2017–18 would, however, feature the same flag as al-Baghdadi's group and show executions resembling the ones from Syria and Iraq. In a video the day after Shekau's initial reaction to his demotion, a group of his supporter raised some of the same points of criticism as Shekau against al-Barnawi while concluding that their loyalty remained with Shekau, see Boko Haram, 'Message From the Soldiers', August 7, 2016.

38. Zenn, 'Boko Haram's Factional Feuds: Internal Extremism and External Interventions.'
39. Fulan Nasrullah, 'Strategic Thinking Behind Ongoing Insurgent Offensive Operations in Northeast Nigeria: An Analysis,' *Conflict Studies and Analysis Project*, August 2018.
40. Sons of Abu Yusuf al-Barnawi, 'khadh' al-waram min al-khawarij al-shikawiyya bi-bay'a ahl al-karam [Cutting Out the Tumor of Shekau's Khawarij Through Pledging Allegiance to the People of Benevolence].' See also the video from ISWA titled 'tribulations and blessings' from July 11, 2018. The video can be accessed here: https://jihadology.net/2018/07/11/new-video-message-from-the-islamic-state-tribulations-and-blessings-wilayat-gharb-ifriqiyyah/
41. Zenn, 'Boko Haram's Factional Feuds: Internal Extremism and External Interventions.'
42. 'Factional Boko Haram Leader Mamman Nur Killed by Own Fighters,' *Daily Trust*, September 14, 2018; Zenn, 'The Islamic State's Provinces on the Peripheries: Juxtaposing the Pledges from Boko Haram in Nigeria and Abu Sayyaf and Maute Group in the Philippines.'
43. 'Deposed Boko Haram Leader Detained Not Killed,' *Vanguard*, March 15, 2019. It was being reported that ISWA detained Abu Musab al-Barnawi but that the new leadership would not execute him because it feared a rebellion within the group due to al-Barnawi's special standing as the son of Muhammad Yusuf.
44. Jacob Zenn, 'Is Boko Haram's Notorious Leader about to Return from the Dead Again?,' *African Arguments*, December 10, 2018.
45. Turki al-Binali, 'Untitled Letter to the Delegated Committee,' *The Islamic State's Department of Research and Studies*, February 2016.
46. Author's interview with Islamic State supporter, May 2016. The recent resurgence of the dispute did not go unnoticed in Islamic State supporter networks. On May 12, 2016 an Islamic State affiliated Telegram channel (re-)published several pieces on the issue of takfir as a critique of the Hazimi trend. Firstly, it re-published an explanation titled 'Details regarding the questions of takfir on al 'adhir' by the Saudi sheikh 'Ali Al Khudayr, originally from March 2016, in which he gives his interpretation of the third nullifier of Islam. This was followed by a piece on the Ansaru Khilafah website on the same topic but attached with the Islamic State's official interpretation of the third nullifier as it is taught at their military camps. From this document it is clear that the Islamic State's position on takfir follows the interpretation of Turki al-Bin'ali rather than the Hazimis.
47. The circular containing a picture of Muhammad Yahya Qirtas was issued July 27, 2016 to all Islamic State provinces.
48. MEMRI, 'Losing Faith In Al-Baghdadi – Part 2: 'Extremists' Explain Why They Left ISIS,' April 15, 2019.
49. Daniel Milton, 'Down, but Not Out: An Updated Examination of the Islamic State's Visual Propaganda,' *Combating Terrorism Center at West Point*, July 2018.

50. Al-Binali's letter can be accessed here: http://www.jihadica.com/wp-content/uploads/2018/06/masalat-al-istitaba.pdf [Accessed 21 October 2019].
51. Al-Binali, 'Untitled Letter to the Delegated Committee.'
52. From another internal document, showing the final part of al-Binali's input to al-Furqan, he mentions that document 155 can be misinterpreted and needs clarification. For instance, he mentions that followers of the Islamic State can perceive it to state that those not proclaiming takfir on figures like Abdallah Azzam, al-Zawahiri, al-Maqdisi and Abu Qatada are themselves apostates.
53. Islamic State, 'Document no. 155', *Central Office for Overseeing the Shari'a Departments*, May 29, 2016. The document was circulated internally, but a summary was included in *Rumiyah* magazine no. 2 and later it was published in al-Naba no. 76.
54. Aymenn Jawad al-Tamimi, 'Turki Binali's Critique of The 'Theory of Balance': Translation and Analysis,' January 8, 2019.
55. The Central Office for Overseeing appears to have been established in February 2016 by Abu Muhammad al-Furqan, Abu Maysara al-Shami and Abu Khabbab al-Masri with the blessing of Abu Muhammad al-Adnani. Already before its establishment, al-Furqan functioned as an 'advisor' to al-Binali's office of scholars.
56. A French national who lived in Saudi Arabia and studied at the Islamic University in Medina. He once tried to join AQI in Iraq but was arrested in Syria and handed over to France, where he was imprisoned until 2009.
57. It has also been rumoured that the head of the Office for Methodological Inquiry was an Abu Zeid al-Iraqi (Ismail Alwaan al-Ithawi).
58. A separate committee was formed to work on a report on the issue of the Hazimis and was comprised of senior representatives from various Islamic State institutions. Almost nothing is known about this committee's work and conclusion, but in the Central Office's status report the challenge from extremism is considered under control.
59. This most likely explains why al-Furqan is describes in ambiguous terms by the Binaliyyah faction. He was generally seen as centrist who eventually gave in to the extremists.
60. See Turki al-Binali's letter to the Delegated Committee in February 2017.
61. Cole Bunzel, 'A House Divided: Origins and Persistence of the Islamic State's Ideological Divide,' *Jihadica*, June 5, 2018.
62. Bunzel, 'Caliphate in Disarray: Theological Turmoil in the Islamic State.'
63. The Department of Research and Fatwas (Diwan al-Buhuth wa-l-Ifta') was first demoted to a Committee (Hay'at al-Buhuth wa-l-Ifta') and finally an office (Maktab al-Buhuth wa-l-Dirasat).
64. Aymenn Jawad al-Tamimi, 'Dissent in the Islamic State: 'Hashimi Advice' to Abu Bakr Al-Baghdadi,' January 4, 2019.
65. Turki al-Binali, 'Letter to Delegated Committee,' May 2017.
66. Al-Tamimi, 'Dissent in the Islamic State: 'Hashimi Advice' to Abu Bakr Al-Baghdadi.'
67. Some accounts state that Abu Maryam al-Jaza'iri was also imprisoned or successfully fled to Turkey like many other Hazimis.
68. An Arabic version of the Silsila can be accessed here: http://www.jihadica.com/wp-content/uploads/2018/09/silsila-ilmiyya.pdf; For an English version, access here: http://www.jihadica.com/wp-content/uploads/2018/09/Knowledge-Series.pdf
69. It has been alleged that the actual narrator was Abu Muhammad al-Masri.

70. Aymenn Jawad al-Tamimi, 'The Killing of Abu Hafs Al-Jazrawi by the Islamic State,' January 2019.
71. Aymenn Jawad al-Tamimi, 'Opposition to Abu Bakr Al-Baghdadi: Sheikh Abu Eisa Al-Masri's Critique of Islamic State Media,' May 2019. It has even been asserted that Abu Hakim al-Urduni, the head of the Central Media Department at the time, was running the Telegram channel Wa Harridh al-Mu'mineen. Al-Urduni was later replaced by Abu Abdullah al-Australi.
72. Isa ibn Abi Abdillah, 'Refutation of Al-Hazimi and the Misconceptions of Al-Ghulah Al-Hazimiyyah,' *Ahl Al-Tawhid*, August 27, 2018.
73. Aymenn Jawad al-Tamimi, 'Dissent in the Islamic State: Secret Advice Sent to Islamic State Leaders,' September 2019.
74. The office was later replaced by the Council of 'Ilm, which then ceased to exist.
75. Aymenn Jawad al-Tamimi, 'Abu Ya'qub Al-Maqdisi's Reform Plan: Translation and Analysis,' January 22, 2019.
76. Imprisoned on December 8, 2017 and released on December 15, 2017. Al-Masri was imprisoned for another two weeks in February 2018. In the following year, other Binalis such as Abu Eisa al-Masri, Aws al-Najdi, Abu al-Hassan al-Jarrah, Abu Marwan al-Masri, Abu Musab al-Sahrawi, Abu Abdul Rahman al-Gharib, Abu Saif al-Urduni and Abu Hafs al-Hamdani were also arrested.
77. Despite being released after approximately three weeks, al-Shami would be arrested again just two months later.
78. He was accused of 13 different transgression which involved cooperation with the US think tank *Rand* and that he had been in dialogue with Abu Muhammad al-Maqdisi, although Abu Yaqub in fact had proclaimed takfir on Abu Muhammad al-Maqdisi.
79. Aymenn Jawad al-Tamimi, 'Dissent in the Islamic State: The Controversy Over Abu Ya'qub Al-Maqdisi,' September 27, 2018. On June 25, 2018, an internal security document authored by the head of security in Wilayat al-Sham and addressed to the head of security in Wilayat al-Baraka asked about the status and work of a list of Binalis including Abu Yaqub and Abu Muhammad.
80. As noted by Cole Bunzel, there are doubts concerning the death of Abu Yaqub. The Hazimis claim that he died in a coalition bombing while in prison, but the Binalis argue that in fact Abu Yaqub had already been killed at the time of the airstrike (April 28, 2018). See Cole Bunzel, 'Death of a Mufti: The Execution of the Islamic State's Abu Ya'qub Al-Maqdisi,' *Jihadica*, January 4, 2019.
81. Other senior Binalis like al-Hashimi were luckier as he managed to escape in 2018.
82. See for instance Abu Mu'adh al-Assimi, 'bayan taghutiyya al-baghdadi [Statement of the Tyrannical Baghdadi],' February 28, 2017.
83. For these examples, see Moaz al-Fatih, 'fasadu 'aqida abu muhammad al-'adnani, al-mutahaddith al-sabiq bi-lism dawlat al-asnam fi-l-iraq wa-l-sham [Corruption of the Creed of Abu Muhammad Al-Adnani, Former Speaker of the State of Idols in Iraq and Sham],' April 2017; 'al-qawl al-nadiyy fi kufr dawlat al-baghdadi [the Dewy Remark on the Unbelief of Al-Baghdadi's State],' April 2017.
84. Christia, *Alliance Formation in Civil Wars*, 42–44.
85. Feras Kilani, 'A Caliph Without a Caliphate: The Biography of ISIS's New Leader,' *Newlines Magazine*, April 15, 2021.

## CHAPTER 12. AL-QAIDA AND THE SYRIAN JIHAD

1. Abu Mariya al-Qahtani made his tweets on March 5, 2015.
2. Abu al-Khayr's audio was issued just hours before the announcement through al-Nusra's media centre. While Abu al-Khayr did give his permission for the break, it was conditioned on al-Zawahiri's approval. Hence, if al-Zawahiri at some point rejected the fakk al-irtibat, so would Abu al-Khayr and, implicitly, so should al-Nusra. Abdullah al-Muhaysini also issued a video speech prior to the announcement discussing the conditions allowed for a break of allegiance.
3. Ahrar al-Sham issued a fatwa on September 20, 2016 legitimising collaboration with Turkey.
4. The infighting between Ahrar al-Sham and Jund al-Aqsa erupted in September and lasted three separate rounds. After the first round of infighting September–October, Jund al-Aqsa accepts to merge into JFS based on four conditions of the latter: 1. Accepting a shari'a court, 2. Handing over all wanted persons, 3. Entirely integrating into JFS ranks and 4. Submitting to the views of JFS. In December a second round of infighting erupted, mainly in Hama, and in January a third round takes place. This leads to JFS announcing that Jund al-Aqsa is no longer part of its group. Afterwards Jund al-Aqsa splits into three factions: one joining JFS, another joining TIP and a third faction staying independent. This third faction later became Liwa al-Aqsa which allied closely with the Islamic State.
5. Ahmad Al-Hamdan, 'Current Situation of the Jihadi Movement: Answers to a Number of Questions,' April 1, 2017.
6. Author's interview with Abu Mahmoud al-Filastini, April 15, 2018 (London).
7. Ibid.
8. Aymenn Jawad al-Tamimi, 'The Hay'at Tahrir Al-Sham-Al-Qaeda Dispute: Primary Texts (II),' December 10, 2017.
9. As reported by Cole Bunzel, Bilal Khuraysat later wrote in a letter to HTS saying 'I have remained steadfast upon [my bay'a]. You are the ones who changed and altered. I have kept my bay'a to the Qaidat al-Jihad Organization from the first day I entered Syria. I don't know you, while I know al-Qaida,' see Cole Bunzel, 'Abandoning Al-Qaida: Tahrir Al-Sham and the Concerns of Sami Al-'Uraydi,' *Jihadica*, May 12, 2017.
10. Tore Refslund Hamming, 'What We Learned from Sami Al-Uraydi's Testimony Concerning Abu Abdullah Al-Shami',' *Jihadica*, October 24, 2017.
11. Author's interview with Abu Sulayman al-Muhajir, June 2017.
12. Al-Uraydi and al-Hajar defected on February 8, 2017. In a meeting in mid-February 2017, al-Qaida loyalists including Abu al-Khayr, al-Uraydi, Abu Julaybib, Abu al-Qassam, and Abu Hummam discussed how to respond to HTS's fakk al-irtibat. It is unknown if future organisational arrangements were discussed at this meeting.
13. Some elements within the al-Qaida loyalist faction believe that Abu al-Faraj and Abu al-Khayr's deaths were the result of JFS/HTS collaborating with the Americans because they opposed the break from al-Qaida.
14. Al-Hamdan, 'Current Situation of the Jihadi Movement: Answers to a Number of Questions.'
15. Al-Tamimi, 'The Hay'at Tahrir Al-Sham-Al-Qaeda Dispute: Primary Texts (II).'
16. Ayman al-Zawahiri, 'We Shall Fight You Until There Is No More Persecution,' *As-Sahab Media*, October 2017.
17. Ibid.

18. Ibid.
19. Ayman al-Zawahiri, 'Let Us Fight Them As A Solid Structure,' *As-Sahab Media*, November 28, 2017.
20. Kalyvas, 'The Ontology of "Political Violence": Action and Identity in Civil Wars.'
21. Abu Abdullah al-Shami, 'To the esteemed Sheikh... Abu Muhammad al-Maqdisi,' February 10, 2017.
22. See episode 6 of the show *Daimeh* hosted by Abdullah al-Muhaysini.
23. Cole Bunzel, 'Diluting Jihad: Tahrir Al-Sham and the Concerns of Abu Muhammad Al-Maqdisi,' *Jihadica*, March 29, 2017.
24. Like al-Maqdisi, al-Uraydi has a history of engaging in controversial debates. An example is how he once debated al-Albani over issues of takfir, see Lav, *Radical Islam and the Revival of Medieval Theology*.
25. Sami al-Uraydi and Abu Muhammad al-Maqdisi, 'Methodology: Between Praise and Contempt, the Sunnah and Heresy,' September 10, 2017.
26. Wagemakers, 'Protecting Jihad: The Sharia Council of the Minbar Al-Tawhid Wa-l-Jihad.'
27. Lav, *Radical Islam and the Revival of Medieval Theology*.
28. Adnan Hadid, an al-Qaida commentator, in August 2018 issued an article examining a letter by Abu Firas al-Suri to Jabhat al-Nusra's shura council dated 20 May 2015. In the letter, al-Suri allegedly warns about the role of Turkey and aligning with it. See Adnan Hadid, 'Commenting the Letter of Sheikh Abu Firas to the Shura Council of Jabhat Al-Nusra,' *Telegram Channel*, August 24, 2018.
29. Sami al-Uraydi, 'Answering the Questioners about the Faithfulness of the Allegiance to the Jihadi Groups to Rule the Shari'a of the Lord of the Worlds,' *Telegram Channel*, April 2017.
30. Sami al-Uraydi, 'Untitled statement,' *Telegram Channel*, October 2018.
31. Abu Muhammad al-Maqdisi, 'risala al-mu'ataba wa munasaha li-l-duktur abdullah al-muhaysini [Letter of Reprimand and Advice to Doctor Abdullah Al-Muhaysini],' June 2017.
32. In a fatwa from March 2017, Abu Qatada denounced fighting under the banner of Turkey, but in a Q&A from October the same year he leaves it open to HTS to decide on cooperation with Turkey, see Abu Qatada al-Filastini, 'Meeting of the Khayr Umma Media with Abu Qatada al-Filastini,' *Khayr Umma Media*, October 2017.
33. Anas Hassan Khattab, 'Wrong Terms between the Mujahideen,' July 22, 2017.
34. Abu Muhammad al-Maqdisi, 'al-thamarat al-shani'a li-naqd al-tawhid aw tamiyy'hu [The Terrible Fruits to Invalidate or Dilute Monotheism],' *Minbar Al-Tawhid Wa-l-Jihad*, December 2017.
35. Sami al-Uraydi, 'kalimat hamasat 'ala kalimat al-sheikh abu qatada al-filastini [Words of Whisper to the Words of Sheikh Abu Qatada al-Filastini],' October 2018.
36. Al-Filastini, 'al-tahawwulat al-mutawaqqaah an tahaadatha fi-l-tayyar al-jihadiyya [The Expected Transformations to Happen in the Jihadi Movement].'
37. Sami al-Uraydi, 'What Is the Shami Jihad but a Jewel in a Decade and a Stage of History?,' *Telegram Channel*, April 2017.
38. Sami al-Uraydi and Abu Muhammad al-Maqdisi, 'jihad al-umma wa jama'at al-umma [Jihad of the Umma and Groups of the Umma],' *Maktab Khayr Umma Al-Islamiyya*, July 2017.
39. Sami al-Uraydi, 'jihad al-umma wa manhaj al-harakat al-jihadiyya [Jihad of the Nation and the Methodology of the Jihadi Movement],' *Telegram Channel*, August 2017.

40. Sami al-Uraydi, 'The Fighting Movements between Two Calls: O People of Samura and O People of Yathreb,' *Telegram Channel*, August 2018.
41. Sami al-Uraydi, 'It Is a Jurisprudence of Attraction and Not a Jurisprudence of Gradual Advance,' October 2018.
42. Abu Mahmoud is originally from Lebanon but moved to the UK in 1997 where he first completed an undergraduate in engineering and later a master's degree in telecommunication from the University of Westminster. Over the years, he developed close bonds with Hani al-Sibai and especially with Abu Qatada al-Filastini whom he studied under for several years.
43. Author's interview with Abu Mahmoud al-Filastini, April 15, 2018 (London).
44. Abu Mahmoud al-Filastini, 'The Umma before Organisations,' *Telegram Channel*, October 2017.
45. Abu Mahmoud al-Filastini, 'The Jihadi Movement Between the Jurisprudence of Balances and the Jurisprudence of Comparisons,' *Telegram Channel*, 2017.
46. Abu Mahmoud al-Filastini, 'Jihad of the Ummah or Puritanical Narrow,' *Telegram Channel*, January 2017.
47. Al-Filastini, 'An Indispensable Though Imperfect Unity.'
48. On the Turkey issue, it was especially the Egyptian ideologue Abu Fath al-Farghali who defended HTS. Referring to Abu Qatada's March 2017 fatwa to defend the legitimacy of Turkey's incursion into Idlib, al-Farghali noted three conditions for the incursion, namely (1) that in the liberated areas (under HTS or rebel control) the Turkey's army would serve the mujahideen's interests, (2) that Turkey was prohibited interfering in the administration of the liberated areas, and (3) that Turkey would have no control over HTS's battlefield engagement. On 2 February 2018, al-Farghali also held a lecture in Idlib defending HTS's engagement with Turkey.
49. Bailey Ulbricht, 'Justifying Relations with an Apostate Suring a Jihad: A Salafi-Jihadist Group's Reltions with Turkey in Syria,' *Middle East Institute*, March 2019.
50. Abu Muhammad al-Maqdisi, 'shar'iyyun kidhba [the Jurists Are a Lie],' *Telegram Channel*, November 2017.
51. HTS also engaged Jaysh al-Islam militarily in East Ghouta in late April–early May 2017. HTS's Abu Mariya al-Qahtani came out with a strong critique of Jaysh al-Islam and said they were extremist murji'a, but also khawarij in their manhaj of killing Muslims.
52. Abu Sulayman al-Muhajir published his analysis on Telegram July 20, 2017 in a series of messages.
53. See the tweet from Abu Sulayman al-Muhajir from July 20, 2017: https://twitter.com/AbuSulaymanMM3/status/888033431128604672
54. Sam Heller, '"Frogs" and "Geckos": Syri'a Jihadists Speak the Language of Rebellion,' *War on the Rocks*, October 22, 2018.
55. Hayat Tahrir al-Sham, 'wa 'ala al-baghi tadour al-dawai'r [Life of the Rebel Will Turn Back on Him],' February 2018.
56. 'What next for Syria's Idlib?,' *France 24*, January 11, 2019.
57. Hayat Tahrir al-Sham, 'Jihad and Shari'a Politics between Constants and Alternations,' June 8, 2018.
58. Author's discussion with scholar (anonymised) who had just visited Idlib to interview HTS officials, July 2, 2019.
59. Haid Haid, 'HTS's Offline Propaganda: Infrastructure, Engagement and Monopoly,' *International Centre for the Study of Radicalisation*, 2019.

60. The prohibition for preachers was issued on June 19, 2017; the prohibition for rank and file was issued on July 12, 2017.
61. HTS issued the fatwa on July 20, 2017.
62. Author's communication with Abu Muhammad al-Maqdisi and Abu Qatada al-Filastini, October 28, 2017.
63. Sami al-Uraydi, 'The Lord of the Prison Loved Me to Keep Silent about Injustice Part 1,' *Telegram Channel*, December 2017.
64. Al-Zubayr al-Ghazi, 'Untitled Statement,' *Telegram Channel*, November 2017.
65. Hani al-Sibai, 'About the Decision to Arrest Some of the Elders in Syria,' *Telegram Channel*, November 2017.
66. The other members were Abu Malik al-Shami, Abu Qatada al-Albani, Mukhtar al-Turki, Abu Muhammad al-Turkistani and Mus'ab al-Shami.
67. Hayat Tahrir al-Sham, 'tatawa'a wa la takhtalefa [Agree with Each Other and Do Not Disagree],' December 2017.
68. Hayat Tahrir al-Sham, 'Why Did "Hayat Tahrir Al-Sham" Lately Arrest Some of the Brothers and Why Is It Demanding Their Trial?,' *Internal Document*, December 2, 2017.
69. Abu Muhammad Al-Maqdisi, 'Repelling the Attacker and Jihad of the Umma Is Wide Issues, so Do Not Restrict It Based on Your Standards,' *Telegram Channel*, December 26, 2017.
70. Author's interview with Hassan Abu Hanieh, June 18, 2018 (Amman); author's interview with Labib Nahhas, April 15, 2018 (London).
71. Abu Qatada al-Filastini, 'Untitled Statement,' *Telegram Channel*, December 11, 2017.
72. Author's interview with HTS media official, September 22, 2017.

## CHAPTER 13. RENEWED COHESION OR CONTINUED POLARISATION?

1. Examples include the scholarly initiative in October 2017 to solve the tensions between al-Qaida-loyalists and HTS, the Unified Popular Initiative led by Abdullah al-Muhaysini in April 2018 to stop the conflict between JTS and HTS, and the call by senior scholars (Muhaysini, al-Mahdi, al-Sadeq, al-Ulayni) for a ceasefire between HTS and Nour al-Deen al-Zinki and to settle things in court.
2. Hani al-Sibai, 'miftah shakhsiyya al-sheikh al-duktur ayman [Key of the Personality of the Sheikh Dr. Ayman],' *Telegram Channel*, May 2017. Hani al-Sibai gives a fatwa saying no matter how much you disagree with the leadership of HTS, it is not permissible to refuse fighting as some AQ loyalists did. But he stresses that one does not need to pledge to HTS, but can simply fight alongside it. He mentions TIP as an example of a group that did not pledge to HTS, but fights alongside it and says that HTS should accept this model, see Hani al-Sibai, 'Is It Permissible for Young People in Syria to Sit in Their Homes Because of Their Disagreement with the Leaders of the Committee,' *Telegram Channel*, January 2018.
3. Author's interview with Abu Qatada al-Filastini, June 17, 2018 (Zarqa). This is perhaps not as surprising as it may seem. Wagemakers has shown how Abu Qatada has always been less rigid that Maqdisi, for instance in his view on al-Albani, while Lav explains how Abu Qatada already in a response to Sayyid Imam challenged the idea that allegiance to unbelievers always equalled unbelief (kufr), instead considered different levels of allegiance. See Wagemakers, *Salafism in Jordan: Political Islam in a Quietist Community*; Lav, *Radical Islam and the Revival of Medieval Theology*.

4. Al-Filastini, 'Untitled Statement,' December 11, 2017.
5. Abu Qatada al-Filastini, 'hal al-Kkilaf been jama'at al-jihad khususan huwa khilaf tanawwu am tadadd? [Is the Conflict between Jihadi Groups a Conflict of Diversity or of Contradiction?],' *2018*, August.
6. Abu Qatada al-Filastini, 'Untitled Statement,' *Telegram Channel*, October 4, 2018.
7. This situation was summed up by an al-Qaida sympathiser, Abu Hamza, in an article titled neo-Jihadis (al-jihadiyyun al-judud). He describes HTS and the Islamic State as Neo-Jihadis because both of them have deviated from the correct Jihadi methodology albeit in different directions.
8. Aby Yahya al-Libi, 'al-mawrid al-'adub li-bayyab hukm al-ista'anah bi-l-kuffar fi-l-harb [Fresh resource to explain the rule of recourse to infidels in war]', re-issued in February 2018.
9. Abu Yahya al-Libi, 'A Message from Sheikh Abu Yahya to One of the Groups' Emirs,' February 16, 2011 (re-issued March 2018 by al-Sahab).
10. Al-Zawahiri, 'We Shall Fight You Until There Is No More Persecution.'
11. Abu al-Harith al-Masri, 'al-amir al-musardib [The Hidden Amir],' December 2017.
12. Al-Filastini, 'Untitled Statement,' December 11, 2017.
13. Ayman al-Zawahiri, 'How to Confront America,' *As-Sahab Media*, September 2018.
14. Awwab bin Hassan al-Hasan, 'Lapses of the Islamic Pens: An Open Letter of Advice to Jihadi Youths,' *As-Sahab Media*, February 2018.
15. Ayman al-Zawahiri, 'Editorial,' *One Umma*, April 2019.
16. Ayman al-Zawahiri, 'The Shari'a Ruling on Governance without Shari'a,' *As-Sahab Media*, October 2018.
17. Ayman al-Zawahiri, 'The Way of Salvation,' *As-Sahab Media*, February 2019.
18. Al-Qaida, 'sayha nafir wa sarkha tahdhir [A Call to Mobilize and a Cry of Warning],' *As-Sahab Media*, August 2019.
19. Author's discussion with various HTS members and al-Qaida loyalists.
20. Statement made by *Shaybat Hukuma*, an al-Qaida supporter, on Telegram, November 30, 2017.
21. Jaysh al-Badiyya was formed in 2015 by senior Jabhat al-Nusra official Abu Turab al-Hamawi, but later Bilal al-Sanani took over as leader until his death in June 2020. After the arrests, Jaysh al-Badiyya sided with al-Qaeda. Its leaders threatened al-Julani that they would defect if he did not release al-Qaida loyalists. On December 11, 2017 it announced: 'We are an entity that is independent of HTS, and we are cooperating with everyone against the aggressive forces in the desert, until the clerics who are working on the reconciliation initiative announce their decision.'
22. Jaysh al-Malahim was led by Abu Abd al-Rahman al-Makki, a Saudi cleric that was previously with Jund al-Aqsa but who left to join HTS.
23. Jaysh al-Badiyya created a Telegram channel on December 5 using hashtags such as #Qaedat_al-Jihad and #al-Qaeda_in_the_land_of_Syria and in a photoset released on January 12 from its fighting in southern Idlib an al-Qaida flag was seen flying from a Jaysh al-Badiyya tank. Both factions were also promoted by senior al-Qaida loyalists like al-Uraydi on Telegram.
24. Established in 2014, Jabhat Ansar al-Deen mainly operated as an independent group in Idlib.
25. The six groups and factions were identified the following day as Jaysh al-Malahim, Jaysh al-Sahel, Jaysh al-Badiyya, Saraya al-Sahel, Saraya Kabul and Jund al-Shari'a.

On March 4, 2018 these different groups and factions officially pledged to be part of Hurras ad-Deen.

26. At the time, it was reported that its shura council was composed of Abu Julaybib, Abu Khadija al-Urduni (Bilal Khuraysat), Sami al-Uraydi, Abu al-Qassam and Abu Abd al-Rahman al-Makki.
27. Author's interview with Hurras al-Deen member on Telegram, March 25, 2020.
28. Eric Schmitt, 'U.S. Sees Rising Threat in the West From Qaeda Branch in Syria,' *New York Times*, September 29, 2019.
29. On March 10, 2018 it was reported that Jund al-Aqsa was resurgent under the name of Ansar al-Tawhid. In February 2017 Jund al-Aqsa had ceased to exist and split into four factions. One joined HTS, another joined TIP, a third re-structured under the name of Liwa al-Aqsa and allied with the Islamic State and a fourth opted to remain neutral.
30. Islamic State, 'hatta tu'minu bi-allahi wahdahu [Until You Believe in Allah Alone],' *al-Naba no. 129*, April 27, 2018.
31. Abu al-Hassan al-Muhajir, 'So Follow Their Guidance,' *Al-Furqan Media Foundation*, April 2018.
32. Al-Shami said to HTS's Ebaa News Agency that a car did not stop when it was asked to stop at the checkpoint and thus the HTS guard fired his gun at the car. Only afterwards did they realise the person in the car was from Hurras al-Deen. On February 7, 2019, Hurras al-Deen and HTS once again clashed which led to the death of an HTS fighter named Abu Ibrahim Huwair. Again, a court was established to resolve the issue and Hurras al-Deen published their condolences.
33. On July 12 HTS arrested Abu Miqdad al-Urduni. Al-Urduni was not officially member of Hurras al-Deen but he was very close to its high-ranking figures. Showing this on July 29 Abu Khadijah and Abu Julaybib issued a statement calling for his release. On August 7 HTS also arrested the two Hurras al-Deen members Abu Samir and Abu Qatada. Finally, on October 2 HTS arrested two Egyptians close to Hurras al-Deen, Abu Anas al-Masri and Abu Hud al-Iglami, and on November 26 it arrested Abu al-Yaman al-Wazzani, the leader of Jama'at Ansar al-Haqq, an HTS break-away faction that had joined Hurras al-Deen.
34. On June 8 Abu Talha al-Hadede, HTS's amir in western Aleppo defected from the group in reaction to its clashes with other Jihadi groups and its assistance to Turkey. In August several factions joined Hurras al-Deen. On August 2, Ansar al-Haqq and Abna al-Sharia announced joining the group. On August 20 they were followed by Jund al-Sham Battalion and Fursan al-Iman Brigades. And finally, in late August, the Abdullah Azzam Brigade originally from Damascus but relocated to Idlib and Quwat Nukhba in Daraa also joined Hurras al-Deen. Omar Omsen's group Firqatul Ghuraba sided with Hurras al-Deen, while the Turkistan Islamic Party sided with HTS despite its long running relationship with al-Qaida (likely because of the social bonds established in the previous years and because it knew that it would have a hard time operating without the support of HTS).
35. Hurras al-Deen also claims that HTS obstructed several of the group's planned attacks against the Assad regime.
36. Author's interview with Abu Mahmoud al-Filastini, July 7, 2019 (London). During the interview, he gives the example how he instructed HTS to teach Shafi'i maddhab in fiqh because that is the dominant maddhab in Syria.
37. Farghali was previously a member of Ahrar al-Sham. After he arrived in Syria in 2012 he was part of the group's hardliners that would later join HTS. In HTS he

has become one of the most prominent ideological figures and is much used in its media output.

38. In October 2017 Abu Qatada also issued a statement saying that he considers Erdogan an apostate, but he is open to different opinions if people are more familiar with Erdogan's policies.
39. Al-Filastini, 'Meeting of the Khayr Umma Media with Abu Qatada Al-Filastini.'
40. Author's interview with Abu Mahmoud al-Filastini, October 16, 2018 (London).
41. Above quotations are from Telegram messages publicised from June 4 to 6, 2018 on Abu Mahmoud al-Filastini's Telegram channel. The author has screenshots of all the statements.
42. The operation room was created on October 15, 2018 but officially announced on November 17. It has mainly been active on the fronts in Lattakia, southern Idlib and northern Hama.
43. Other ideologues such as Tariq Abdelhaleem and Hani al-Sibai also issued criticism of HTS. This came just a year after that Al-Maqdisi and Abdelhaleem were attacking one another on their respective Telegram channels.
44. Abu Muhammad al-Maqdisi, 'nasaih li-l-mutaqaribin [Advices to Those Who Are Related],' *Telegram Channel*, April 10, 2018.
45. This schism became evident in three specific events: Erdogan's election victory in June 2018 and Jamal Khashoggi and Muhammad Morsi's deaths. For further information on the reactions to Khashoggi and Morsi's deaths, see Cole Bunzel, 'Mourning Morsi: The Death of an Islamist and Jihadi Divisions,' *Jihadica*, September 27, 2019; Cole Bunzel, 'Abu Qatada al-Filastini: 'I Am Not a Jihadi, or a Salafi,'' *Jihadica*, October 26, 2018.
46. Cole Bunzel, 'Rehabilitating the Bin'aliyya: Al-Maqdisi and the Scholarly Remnant of the Islamic State,' *Jihadica*, December 11, 2019.
47. Abu Mahmoud al-Filastini, 'Maqdisi and the Free Fall,' *Telegram Channel*, January 20, 2018.
48. Al-Filastini, 'Untitled Statement,' December 11, 2017.
49. Abu Qatada al-Filastini, 'hal al-khilaf been jama'at al-jihad khususan huwa khilaf tanawwu am tadadd? [Is the Conflict between Jihadi Groups a Conflict of Diversity or of Contradiction?]'
50. Al-Filastini, 'Untitled Statement,' October 4, 2018.
51. Cole Bunzel, 'Abu Qatada al-Filastini: 'I Am Not a Jihadi, or a Salafi,'' *Jihadica*, October 26, 2018.
52. Al-Uraydi, 'kalimat hamasat 'ala kalimat al-sheikh abu qatada al-filastini [Words of Whisper to the Words of Sheikh Abu Qatada al-Filastini].'
53. Hani al-Sibai, 'Is It Permissible for Young People in Syria to Sit in Their Homes Because of Their Disagreement with the Leaders of HTS,' January 7, 2018. It first came as an audio on 19 December 2017 but was later released as a report.
54. For a detailed account of the events, see Tore Refslund Hamming, 'Hayat Tahrir Al-Sham's Internal Conflict and Renewed Tensions with Hurras Al-Deen,' *Jihadica*, February 15, 2019.
55. Abu al-Yaqzan al-Masri, 'Ruling on Participating in the Battle of East Euphrates,' *Mu'assasat 'ilamiyya Min Ard Al-Sham*, December 30, 2018 [video].
56. Abu al-Abd Ashida, 'So as Not to Sink the Ship,' [Video], September 9, 2019.
57. Abu Fath al-Farghali, 'So That the Ship Isn't Hampered,' *Telegram Channel*, September 10, 2019.

58. Author's discussion with Abu Muhammad al-Maqdisi, 29 January 2019.
59. Author's discussion with Abu Qatada, 29 January 2019.
60. While the ideologues nominated by Hurras al-Deen to judge appear overwhelmingly in favour of Abu Hummam and al-Uraydi, HTS has the support of the most important factions of foreign fighters in Syria. The fact that the Turkistani Islamic Party (TIP) continued to side with HTS was particularly important as there were doubts if it would switch sides due to its historic relationship with al-Qaida.
61. Abu al-Qassam al-Urduni, 'Untitled Statement,' February 7, 2019.
62. Later in 2019, the issue of the weapons had still not been solved, however. In August 2019, al-Uraydi announced a proposal to create common storehouses in northwestern Syria for weapons that all factions can use instead of limiting it to specific factions.
63. Bunzel, 'Rehabilitating the Bin'aliyya: Al-Maqdisi and the Scholarly Remnant of the Islamic State.'
64. See for example Islamic State newsletter *al-Naba* no. 30 published 10 May 2016 and Islamic State magazine *Dabiq* no. 12 published November 2015.
65. AQAP, 'hurras al-shari'a [Guardians of the Shari'a],' *Al-Malahim media*, December 2015 [video].
66. See for example AQAP newsletter *al-Masra* no. 28 published November 2, 2016.
67. Islamic State, 'jaysh al-madad [The Army of Reinforcement],' Wilayat Bayda, 14 April 2017 [video].
68. For a detailed accounting of the evolving relationship, see Tore Refslund Hamming, 'Why Did the Jihadi Cold War in Yemen End?,' *War on the Rocks*, November 7, 2018.
69. Although infighting began in early July and the incidents were reported in unofficial media, it was not until October 7 that the Islamic State issued its first formal communique acknowledging an attack against AQAP.
70. Islamic State, 'And The Initiator is the Aggressor,' Wilayat Bayda, August 1, 2018 [video].
71. An example from the Islamic State is its Amaq News Agency release of a video testimony of an alleged former AQAP fighter, Abu Muslim al-Hashimi, who defected to ISY and then criticised AQAP for cooperating with the Yemeni army (issued August 6 2018). AQAP examples include its video series 'Prisons of the Kharijites in Yemen' released in the period May–July 2019 showing how ISY treated its own members, imprisoning and killing them; another series issued by AQAP is titled 'Hollywood Realities of al-Baghdadi [haqiqah hollywood al-baghdadi]' and was released in August 2019. The second episode uses 'bloopers' from captured video material from ISY productions to ridicule the intelligence of its fighters; a third example is the nasheed published by AQAP's al-Basha'ir Foundation on August 14, 2019 titled 'Foolish State [ya dawn sufaha']' that de-legitimises the Islamic State's claim to be a state.
72. Elisebeth Kendall, 'The Failing Islamic State Within The Failed State of Yemen,' *Perspectives on Terrorism* 13, no. 1 (2019): 78–87. See also the interview with the ISY commander of al-Bayda in the Islamic State newsletter al-Naba no. 197 published on August 29, 2019.
73. Caleb Weiss, 'Reigniting the Rivalry: The Islamic State in Somalia vs. Al-Shabaab,' *CTC Sentinel* 12, no. 4 (2019).
74. Weiss; Abdi Guled, 'Bloody Rivalry Erupts between Al-Shabab, IS Group in Somalia,' *AP*, December 6, 2018.
75. See Islamic State newsletter al-Naba no. 156 published November 16, 2018. In the article, the Islamic State states that al-Shabab courts punish possession of Islamic State videos with between 6 months and 2 years in prison.

76. The Islamic State attack took place on December 15, but the claim came on December 16, 2018 through the Islamic State's Amaq News Agency. Later, a video of the clashes was also published by Amaq.
77. Mohamed Olad Hassan, 'Somalia's Al-Shabab Declares War on Pro-Islamic State Group,' *VOA News*, December 21, 2018.
78. Al-Zawahiri, 'Islamic Spring Part 1.'
79. See the database managed by the Long War Journal tracking ISS attacks: https://public.tableau.com/profile/fddmaps#!/vizhome/SomaliaClaims/Dashboard1

EPILOGUE

1. Asim Umar, 'And On That Day the Believers Will Rejoice,' June 13, 2019.
2. Lahoud and al-'Ubaydi , 'The War of Jihadists against Jihadists in Syria.'
3. Nasr, 'ISIS in Africa: The End of the "Sahel Exception".'
4. Military confrontations likely occurred earlier with the first unconfirmed case reported in July 2019 in the town of Ariel in Burkina Faso; Caleb Weiss and Héni Nsaibia, 'The End of the Sahelian Anomaly: How the Global Conflict between the Islamic State and Al-Qa`ida Finally Came to West Africa,' *CTC Sentinel* 13, no. 7 (2020).
5. Islamic State, 'al-hamla al-salibiyya 'ala gharb 'ifriqiyya. khasa'ir mutawasila fi sufuf al-quwwat al-faransiyya wa-l-qa'ida tusharik fi-l-harb didda al-mujahidin [The Crusader Campaign on West Africa. Continuous Losses in the Ranks of the French Force, and al-Qaeda Participates in the War Against the Mujahideen,' *Al-Naba No. 233*, May 7, 2020.
6. Abu Hamza Al-Qurayshi, 'And the Disbelievers Will Know Who Gets the Good End,' *Al-Furqan Media Foundation*, May 2020.
7. Al-Muraqib, 'Striving for Hegemony: The HTS Crackdown on Al-Qaida and Friends in Northwest Syria.'
8. Hamid and Farrall, *The Arabs at War in Afghanistan*, 170.
9. Bard E. O'Neill, *Insurgency & Terrorism: Inside Modern Revolutionary Warfare* (Virginia: Potomac Books, 1990); Wendy Pearlman and Kathleen Gallagher Cunningham, 'Nonstate Actors, Fragmentation, and Conflict Processes,' *Journal of Conflict Resolution* 56, no. 1 (2012): 3–15; Krause, *Rebel Power: Why National Movements Compete, Fight, and Win*; Paul Staniland, 'Explaining Cohesion, Fragmentation, and Control in Insurgent Groups' (Massachusetts Institute of Technology, 2010).
10. In his book on the Islamist insurrection in Hama in 1982, Abu Musab al-Suri notes that the failure to create a broad Islamist project and win the public's support were the main reasons behind the failed insurrection. On the contemporary context, Abu al-Mundhir al-Shinqiti, an ideologue that first supported al-Qaida, then shifted to the Islamic State before going back again, lists five results of the Islamic State's aggression: (1) the weakening of the Taliban and al-Qaeda, distorting their reputation and eliminating the symbols and leaders of Jihad, (2) shattering the image of Jihad, (3) weakening the Syrian factions fighting the Syrian regime, (4) transforming Iraq and Syria into a holocaust, and (5) giving the West an argument to interfere in the region under the pretext of fighting the Islamic State, see al-Shinqiti, 'yuriduna da'ishnat al-jihad [We Want Daish's Jihad].'
11. Watts, 'Deciphering Competition Between Al-Qa'ida and the Islamic State.'
12. Della Porta, *Clandestine Political Violence*, 70.

13. Ibid.: 72.
14. See for example Bennett Clifford and Seamus Hughes, 'United States v. Aws Mohammed Younis Al-Jayab: A Case Study on Transnational Prosecutions of Jihadi Foreign Fighter Networks,' *CTC Sentinel* 11, no. 11 (2018).
15. Hegghammer, 'Violent Islamism in Saudi Arabia, 1979–2006: The Power and Perils of Pan-Islamic Nationalism,' 75.
16. Morrison, *Origins and Rise of Dissident Irish Republicanism: The Role and Impact of Organizational Splits*, 29.
17. Lahoud, *The Jihadis' Path to Self-Destruction*, 47.
18. See for instance Audrey Kurth Cronin, 'How Al-Qaida Ends,' *International Security* 31, no. 1 (2006): 7–48.
19. Christian Davenport, *How Social Movements Die : Repression and Demobilization of the Republic of New Africa* (New York: Cambridge University Press, 2015).
20. Al-Qaida, 'sayha nafir wa sarkha tahdhir [A Call to Mobilize and a Cry of Warning].'
21. Al-Zawahiri, 'Islamic Spring Part 2.'
22. 'Al Qaeda's "Re-Radicalisation" Schools Lure ISIL Fighters in Syria,' *The National*, January 20, 2018.
23. Sultan Al Kanj, 'Reviewing the Turkey-HTS Relationship,' *Chatham House*, May 2019; Raúl Redondo, 'Growing Tension in Idlib among Jihadist Factions,' *Atalayar*, June 26, 2020; Jacob Zenn, 'Negotiating With Jihadists in the Sahel and Nigeria,' *Lawfare*, June 14, 2020.
24. Al-Muraqib, 'Striving for Hegemony: The HTS Crackdown on Al-Qaida and Friends in Northwest Syria,' *Jihadica*, September 15, 2020.
25. Wassim Nasr, 'ISIS in Africa: The End of the "Sahel Exception",' *Center for Global Policy*, June 2020.
26. Author's interview with Abu Qatada al-Filastini, December 7, 2016 (Zarqa).

# BIBLIOGRAPHY AND SOURCES


*Jihadi Magazines and Newsletters*

Inspire (AQAP)
Resurgence (AQ)
Al-Nafir (AQ)
Al Risalah (AQ in Syria)
Al-Falah (AQ)
Al Masra (AQAP)
Al-Haqiqa (AQ in Syria)
One Ummah (AQ)
Azan (TTP)
Ihyae Khilafat (Jama'at ul-Ahrar)
Dabiq (IS)
Rumiyah (IS)
Dar al-Islam (IS)
Al-Naba (IS)
From Dabiq to Rome (IS)
Al Risalah (ISJK)
Sana al-Sham (IS)
ISR (IS)
Sawt al-Sham (IS)

*Jihadi Websites*

AQ and affiliate material: https://emaad.net
AQ: https://alsahabmedia.net/
Al-Shabab: http://shahadanews.com
AQ supporter network: https://almuwahideenmedia.wordpress.com
HTS Ebaa: https://ebaa.news
Taliban: https://alemarahenglish.com
TTP: http://shahamat-english.com/
Al-Ghuraba archive (IS supporter network): http://web.archive.org/web/20160307213149/http://justpaste.it:80/archivealghuraba
Al Wafa: http://wfmdxyu.blogspot.com/p/blog-page_23.html
Al-Turath al-Ilmi: http://turath3elmy.blogspot.com
Tahaddi: http://www.atahadii.com/vb/
IS video archive: https://isdarat.xyz
Ahl ul-Tawheed (IS supporter network): https://ahlutawheed.wordpress.com
Ansaru Khilafa (IS supporter network): https://ansarukhilafah.wordpress.com
Abu Muhammad al-Maqdisi's Minbar al-Tawhid wa-l-Jihad: http://www.ilmway.com/site/maqdis/index.html

Abu Basir al-Tartusi: http://www.abubaseer.bizland.com/articles.htm

### *Other Databases*

Jihadology: www.jihadology.com
Aymenn Jawad al-Tamimi: http://www.aymennjawad.org
University of Oslo's Jihadi repository: https://www.hf.uio.no/ikos/english/research/jihadi-document-repository/index.html
Pieter van Ostaeyen: https://pietervanostaeyen.wordpress.com
Harmony Program: https://ctc.usma.edu/harmony-program/
UBL bookshelf: https://www.dni.gov/index.php/features/bin-laden-s-bookshelf?start=1
Captured Document Index: http://www.docexdocs.com/docindex.html#SOCOM
Jihadi Document Repository: https://www.hf.uio.no/ikos/english/research/jihadi-document-repository/
Haverford Global Terrorism Research Project: https://scholarship.tricolib.brynmawr.edu/handle/10066/4022/browse?order=ASC&rpp=20&sort_by=1&etal=-1&offset=20&type=title

### *Telegram Channels*

Abdullah al-Muhaysini
Abu Muhammad al-Maqdisi
Abu Qatada al-Filastini
Umar al-Haddoushi
Abu Mahmoud al-Filastini
Iyad al-Qunaybi
Dr. Abdullah al-Shami
Abu Fath al-Farghali
Abu Hafs al-Mauritani
Abu Sulayman al-Muhajir
Islamic Emirate of Afghanistan
Ebaa News
Al-Zubayr al-Ghazi
Al-Jabhat al-Wataniyya lil-Tahrir
Jaysh al-Islam
Al-Jaysh al-Watani al-Suri
Xhemati Alban
Katibat al-Imam al-Bukhari
Markaz Da'at al-Tawhid
Ahrar al-Sham
Umar Khattab
Various supporter networks (see appendix 4)
Info an-Nur
Nashir News Agency
Al-Nadhir al-Uryan
Umar Media
Al Malahim

GIMF
Al Haqiqa
Bilad al-Sham Media
Jabhat Tahrir Suriyya
Amaq Agency

## *References*


'A Message from the Umma to the Wise Man of the Umma,' April 11, 2014.

Abbas, Hassan. *The Taliban Revival*. New Haven: Yale University Press, 2014.

Abbas, Yasir. 'Al-Nusra's Quest to Establish an Islamic Emirate in the Levant.' *Current Trends in Islamist Ideology* 20 (2016).

Abbottabad letter. 'Dear Honorable Brother Shaykh Azmaray.' *Batch 2*, March 5, 2008.

———. 'Give the Tribes More than They Can Handle.' *Batch 2*, n.d.

———. 'In the Name of God, the Merciful.' *Batch 2*, 2010.

———. 'Jihad and Reform Front.' *Batch 1*, May 22, 2007.

———. 'Letter about the Matter of the Islamic Maghreb.' *Batch 2*, March 5, 2010.

———. 'Letter Dtd 07 August 2010.' *Batch 1*, August 7, 2010.

———. 'Letter to Abu Basir.' *Batch 2*, n.d.

———. 'Letter to Shaykh Abu Muhammad.' *Batch 2*, August 17, 2007.

———. 'Letter to the Generous Brother Shaykh Abu Muhammad.' *Batch 2*, n.d.

———. 'SOCOM-2012-0000003,' August 27, 2010.

———. 'SOCOM-2012-0000004,' January 2011.

———. 'SOCOM-2012-0000005,' July 8, 2010.

———. 'SOCOM-2012-0000007,' December 3, 2010.

———. 'SOCOM-2012-0000009,' n.d.

———. 'SOCOM-2012-0000010,' April 26, 2011.

———. 'SOCOM-2012-0000016,' 2010.

———. 'SOCOM-2012-0000019,' May 2010.

———. 'Three Stages Letter.' *Batch 3*, n.d.

———. 'To Our Honorable Emir the Emir of All Believers.' *Batch 2*, 2011.

Abboud, Hassan. 'kalimat sawtiyya li-l-sheikh abu abdullah al-hamawi 'an ahdath al-sham al-akhira [Audio Message from Sheikh Abu Abdullah Al-Hamawi on the Recent Events in Sham],' January 27, 2014. https://www.youtube.com/watch?v=RYa7MnqeqsI&feature=youtu.be.

Abd-al-Hakim, Abu Ubaydah. 'Untitled Letter to Abdelmalik Droukdel,' December 4, 2014.

Abdelhaleem, Tariq, and Hani Al-Sibai. 'A Declaration of Disownment and Divergence From the Ideology and Actions of ISIS.' *Al Maqreze Centre for Historical Studies*. London, 2014.

Abdillah, Isa ibn Abi. 'Refutation of Al-Hazimi and the Misconceptions of Al-Ghulah Al-Hazimiyyah.' *Ahl Al-Tawhid*, August 27, 2018.

Abdullah, Azzam. 'al-qaida al-sulba [The Solid Base].' *Al Jihad* 41 (1988).

Abou El Fadl, Khaled. *Rebellion and Violence in Islamic Law*. New York: Cambridge University Press, 2001.

Abrams, Philip. *Historical Sociology*. Ithaca: Cornell University Press, 1982.

Abu Hanieh, Hassan, and Mohammad Abu Rumman. *The 'Islamic State' Organization: The Sunni Crisis and the Struggle of Global Jihadism*. Amman: Friedrich-Ebert-Stiftung, 2015.

———. *The Jihadi Salafist Movement in Jordan after Zarqawi: Identity, Leadership Crisis and Obscured Vision*. Amman: Friedrich-Ebert-Stiftung, 2009.

Ahrar al-Sham. 'No Title,' May 4, 2013. https://justpaste.it/hcg0.

Akhundzada, Haibatullah. 'Guidance to the Mujahideen.' *Taliban's Commission for Cultural Affairs*, May 2017.

Al-'Adnani, Abu Muhammed. 'This Is the Promise of Allah.' *Al-Itisaam Media Foundation*, June 29, 2014.

Al-'Ubaydi, Muhammad. 'Khattab - Jihadi Bios Project.' *Combating Terrorism Center at West Point*, 2015.

Al-Adl, Saif. 'al-khamsa al-shidadd: maqalat jadida min abir sabil [the Five Tough Ones: New Articles from the Wayfarer],' March 23, 2011.

———. 'Jihadist Biography of the Slaughtering Leader Abu Mus'ab Al-Zarqawi.' *Global Islamic Media Front*, 2005.

———. 'Untitled Letter to Mukhtar.' *Combating Terrorism Center*, n.d. https://www.ctc.usma.edu/harmony-program/al-adl-letter-original-language-2/.

Al-Adnani, Abu Muhammed. 'Apologies, Amir of Al-Qaida.' *Al-Furqan Media Foundation*, May 11, 2014.

———. 'May Allah Be With You, O Oppressed State.' *Al-Furqan Media Foundation*, September 30, 2013.

———. 'Oh Our People Respond to the Caller of Allah,' June 23, 2015.

———. 'Say, "Die in Your Rage!"' *Al Hayat Media Center*, January 26, 2015.

———. 'Say to Those Who Disbelieve "You Will Be Overcome."' *Al Hayat*, October 2015.

———. 'So Leave Them Alone with Their Fabrications,' June 18, 2013.

———. 'That They Live by Proof.' *Al Hayat*, May 2016.

———. 'The State of Islam Will Remain Safe.' *Al-Furqan Media Foundation*, August 7, 2011.

———. 'They Will Do You No Harm, Barring a Trifling Annoyance.' *Al-Furqan Media Foundation*, July 2013.

———. 'This Was Not Our Methodology, and It Will Not Be.' *Chabab Tawhid Media*, April 17, 2014.

Al-Afghani, Abd-al-Hakim. 'Our Honorable Shaykh.' *Abbottabad Documents Batch 2*, February 12, 2008.

Al-Anbari, Abu Abdullah. 'al-waqfu al-dari fi tarjamati al-sheikh al-anbari [Knowledgeable Study on the Biography of Sheikh Al-Anbari].' *Mu'assasat Al-Turath Al-'Ilmi*, 2018.

Al-Ansari, Abu al-Walid. 'risala nasiha l-abu umar al-baghdadi min al-sheikh abu al-walid al-ansari [Letter of Advice to Abu Umar Al-Baghdadi from the Sheikh Abu Al-Walid Al-Ansari],' 2007.

Al-Assimi, Abu Mu'adh. 'bayan taghutiyyah al-baghdadi [Statement of the Tyrannical Baghdadi],' February 28, 2017.

Al-Awlaki, Anwar. 'The New Mardin Declaration: An Attempt at Justifying the New World Order.' *Inspire No. 2*, October 2010.

Al-Baghdadi, Abu Bakr. 'Even If the Disbelievers Despise Such.' *Al-Furqan Media Foundation*, November 13, 2014.

———. 'Give Glad Tidings to the Believers.' *Al-Furqan Media Foundation*, April 8, 2013.

———. 'Give Glad Tidings to the Patient.' *Al-Furqan Media Foundation*, August 22, 2018.

———. 'Remaining in Iraq and the Levant.' *Al-Furqan Media Foundation*, June 14, 2013.

———. 'wa allah ya'lam wa antum la ta'lamun [God Knows and You Do Not Know].' *Al-Furqan Media Foundation*, January 19, 2014.

Al-Baghdadi, Abu Umar. 'fa amma al-zabad fa yathhab jafaa [As for the Foam It Passes Away as Scum].' *Al-Furqan Media Foundation*, December 3, 2007.

———. 'Say: I Am Aware of My God.' *Al-Furqan Media Foundation*, March 13, 2007.

———. 'wa qul ja'a al-haqqu wa zahaqa al-batil [Truth Has Come and Falsehood Has Vanished].' *Al-Furqan Media Foundation*, December 22, 2006.

Al-Basha, Abu Dujana. 'This Is Our Message,' September 26, 2014.

Al-Batarfi, Khalid. 'Message to the Muhajireen and Ansar in the Beloved Sham.' *GIMF*, October 28, 2016.

Al-Binali, Turki. 'al-ifada fi al-radd 'ala abi qatada [a Response to the Reply of Abu Qatada],' April 29, 2014.

———. 'al-lafz al-sani fi tarjamat al-adnani [Clear Words in the Understanding of Al-Adnani],' May 26, 2014.

———. 'al-maqdisi: suqut fi al-tin wa ansilakh 'an al-deen [Al-Maqdisi: The Fall in the Mud and the Separation from Religion],' February 15, 2015.

———. 'al-qiyafa fi 'adam ishtirat al-tamkin al-kamil li-l-khilafa [the Pursuit of the Caliphate Does Not Depend on Full Consolidation],' April 30, 2014.

———. 'al-thamar al-dani fi 'l-radd 'ala khitab al-julani [the Low Hanging Fruit in Responding to the Speech of Al-Julani],' January 8, 2014.

———. 'bayan al-ukhuwwa al-imaniyya fi nusrat al-dawla al-islamiyya [The Statement of the Brothers in Supporting the Islamic State].' *Al-Ghuraba Media*, February 18, 2014.

———. 'Between the Ghulat Al-Mukaffira and the Ghulat Al-Murji'a,' n.d.

———. 'khatt al-midad fi al-radd 'ala al-duktur iyad [Sufficient Answer to Respond to Doctor Iyad],' December 15, 2013.

———. 'kullukum ra'in: risala ila shaykhina ayman al-zawahiri [You Are All Shepherd: A Letter to Our Sheikh Ayman Al-Zawahiri],' March 24, 2014.

———. 'la-qad sadaqa al-zawahiri [Al-Zawahiri Was Right],' May 1, 2014.

———. 'Letter to Delegated Committee,' May 19, 2017.

———. 'mudd al-ayadi li-bay'at al-baghdadi [Extend Your Hands to Give Bay'a to Al-Baghdadi],' August 5, 2013.

———. 'mukhtasir kalami fi al-radd 'ala abu abdullah al-shami [Brief Comment to the Response of Abu Abdullah Al-Shami],' March 16, 2014.

———. 'risala ila 'l-'ulama wa-l-du'at li-nusrat al-mujahidin al-ubat [Message to the 'ulama and Preachers in Support of the Proud Mujahideen].' Audio Statement, n.d.

———. 'shaykhi al-asbaq [My Former Sheikh],' June 7, 2014.

———. 'tabsir al-mahajij bi-l-farq bayn rijal al-dawla al-islamiyya wa-l-khawarij [Enlightening Arguments on the Differences between the Men of the Islamic State and the Khawarij).' *Al-Ghuraba Media*, January 19, 2014.

———. 'tanzim al-qa'ida al-shar'i wa-tanzim al-qa'ida al-sha'bi [the Legitimate Al-Qaida Group and the Popular Al-Qaida Group],' April 5, 2014.

———. 'Untitled Letter to the Delegated Committee.' *The Islamic State's Department of Research and Studies*, February 13, 2016.

Al-Bushra, Hamil. 'risalah ila ahlina fi al-somal [A Message to Our Brothers in Somalia].' *Al-Jabha Al-'Ilamiyyah Li-Nusrat Al-Dawla Al-Islamiyyah*, February 24, 2015.

Al-Fadhli, Muhsin. 'Untitled Letter to Nasir Al-Wuhayshi,' January 1, 2015.

Al-Farghali, Abu Fath. 'So That the Ship Isn't Hampered.' *Telegram Channel*, September 10, 2019.

Al-Fatih, Moaz. 'fasadu 'aqida abu muhammad al-'adnani, al-mutahaddith al-sabiq bi-lism dawlat al-asnam fi-l-iraq wa-l-sham [Corruption of the Creed of Abu Muhammad Al-Adnani, Former Speaker of the State of Idols in Iraq and Sham],' April 13, 2017.

Al-Filastini, Abu Mahmoud. 'An Indispensable Though Imperfect Unity.' *Telegram Channel*, April 2017.

———. 'Jihad of the Ummah or Puritanical Narrow.' *Telegram Channel*, January 17, 2017.

———. 'Maqdisi and the Free Fall.' *Telegram Channel*, January 20, 2018.

———. 'The Jihadi Movement Between the Jurisprudence of Balances and the Jurisprudence of Comparisons.' *Telegram Channel*. 2017.

———. 'The Umma before Organisations.' *Telegram Channel*, October 14, 2017.

Al-Filastini, Abu Qatada. 'A Message from the Sheikh Abu Qatada to the Mujahideen Brothers,' January 2014.

———. 'al-tahawwulat al-mutawaqqa'a an tahadatha fi al-tayyar al-jihadi [the Expected Transformations to Happen in the Jihadi Movement],' March 3, 2017.

———. 'Cloak of the Khalifah.' *Al Muwahideen Media*, 2014.

———. 'fatwa fi daf'i siyal al-khawarij hin qasf al-kuffar aw al-murtaddin lihum [Fatwa in Deterrence of the Predators of the Khawarij When the Unbelievers or Apostates Attack Them].' *Al-Bushrayat*, June 2015.

———. 'hal al-khilaf been jama'at al-jihad khususan huwa khilaf tanawwu am tadadd? [Is the Conflict between Jihadi Groups a Conflict of Diversity or of Contradiction?].' 2018, August.

———. 'Meeting of the Khayr Umma Media with Abu Qatada Al-Filasini.' *Khayr Umma Media*, October 2017.

———. 'risala l-ahl al-jihad b-sham [Message to the People of Jihad in Sham),' November 2013.

———. 'Untitled Statement.' *Telegram Channel*, December 11, 2017.

———. 'Untitled Statement.' *Telegram Channel*, October 4, 2018.

Al-Ghazi, Al-Zubayr. 'Untitled Statement.' *Telegram Channel*, November 29, 2017.

Al-Hamdan, Ahmad. 'Current Situation of the Jihadi Movement: Answers to a Number of Questions,' April 1, 2017. justpaste.it/1532x.

Al-Hasan, Awwab bin Hassan. 'Lapses of the Islamic Pens: An Open Letter of Advice to Jihadi Youths.' *As-Sahab Media*, February 20, 2018.

Al-Iraqi, Abd al-Hadi. 'Notes from 'Abd Al-Hadi.' *Document ID AFGP-2002-000091*, 1999.

Al-Jaza'iri, Abu Ahmad Abd al-Karim. 'al-ta'liqat al-bahiyyah 'ala al-mubarrirat al-shar'iyyah wa-l-waqi'yyah li-bay'a al-dawla al-islamiyya [Glorious Comments on the Legitimate and Realistic Justifications for Allegiance to the Islamic State],' June 2015.

Al-Julani, Abu Muhammad. 'A Message of Support and Acceptance for the "Initiative of the Umma,"' January 24, 2014.

———. 'About the Fields of Al-Sham.' *Al-Manara Al-Bayda Media Foundation*, April 10, 2013.

———. 'Allah, Allah, in the Field of Al-Sham.' *Al-Manara Al-Bayda Media Foundation*, January 7, 2014.

Al-Libi, Abu Yahya. 'A Letter to Mujahid Commander Abu Musab Al-Zarqawi from Abu Yahya Yunes Al-Sahrawi,' November 23, 2005.

———. 'A Message from Sheikh Abu Yahya to One of the Groups' Emirs,' February 16, 2011.

———. 'risala khassa min fadila al-sheikh al-mujahid abu yahya al-libi ila sheikh al-mujahid abu umar al-baghdadi [Private Letter from the Virtous Mujahid Sheikh Abu Yahya Al-Libi to the Mujahid Sheikh Abu Umar Al-Baghdadi],' April 4, 2007.

Al-Libi, Atiyyatullah. 'Ila ikhwanana al-mujahideen fi al-'iraq: tahiya wa nasah [to the Mujahideen Brothers in Iraq: Greeting and Advice,' August 24, 2005.

———. 'The Importance of the Sanctity of Muslim Blood,' 2011.

———. 'Untitled Article,' January 5, 2007.

———. 'Untitled Letter to Al-Zarqawi,' December 11, 2005.

Al-Madani, Abu Khalil. 'Advice to All the Fighting Groups in the Cause of Allah.' *As-Sahab Media Productions*, April 2014.

Al-Maqdisi, Abu Muhammad. 'A Call to the Umma and Mujahideen,' May 2014.

———. 'al-risala al-thalathiniyya fi al-tahdhir min al-ghulu fi al-takfir [Thirteen Messages of Warning of Extremism in Takfir],' 1998.

———. 'al-thamarat al-shani'a li-naqd al-tawhid aw tamiyy'hu [The Terrible Fruits to Invalidate or Dilute Monotheism].' *Minbar Al-Tawhid Wa-l-Jihad*, December 15, 2017.

———. 'al-zarqawi: munasaha wa munasara (Al-Zarqawi: Advice and Support),' July 2004.

———. 'And Be Not Like Her Who Undoes the Thread Which She Has Spun, After It Has Become Strong.' *Minbar Al-Tawhid Wa-l-Jihad*, July 10, 2014.

———. 'awradaha sa'ad wa sa'ad moshtamelo. ma hakatha ya sa'ado towradi al-ibelo [Sa'ad Took the Camels to the Spring for Some Water While Wearing a Wool Garment with Nothing underneath, Oh Sa'ad Ths Is Not How Camels Are Handled].' *Minbar Al-Tawhid Wa-l-Jihad*, September 2014.

———. 'bayan sadir fi bayan hal ' al-dawla al-islamiyya fi al-iraq wa-l-sham' wa-l-mawqif al-wajib tujahaha [a Comdemning Statement on the Status of 'the Islamic State in Iraq and Sham and the Necessary Position against It].' *Minbar Al-Tawhid Wa-l-Jihad*, May 26, 2014.

———. *hadhihi aqidatuna [This Is Our Aqida]*, 1997.

———. 'malhuzat 'ala malhuzat al-sheikh abu basir [Comments on the Comments of Sheikh Abu Basir].' *Minbar Al-Tawhid Wa-l-Jihad*, August 2014.

———. 'nasaih li-l-mutaqaribin [Advices to Those Who Are Related].' *Telegram Channel*, April 10, 2018.

———. 'Repelling the Aggression of the Islamic State from Afar,' June 2015.

———. 'Repelling the Attacker and Jihad of the Umma Is Wide Issues, so Do Not Restrict It Based on Your Standards.' *Telegram Channel*, December 26, 2017.

———. 'risala al-mu'ataba wa munasaha li-l-duktur abdullah al-muhaysini [Letter of Reprimand and Advice to Doctor Abdullah Al-Muhaysini],' June 2017.

———. 'sada siham al-liam 'an al-akabir al-'alam [Resist the Arrows of the Depraved from the Greatest Dignitaries],' May 6, 2014.

———. 'shar'iyyun kidhba [the Jurists Are a Lie].' *Telegram Channel*, November 25, 2017.

———. 'The Killing of 'Ad and Eradication Fight Between International Desires and Sheikh Al-Islam Ibn Taymiyah.' *Minbar Al-Tawhid Wa-l-Jihad*, March 2016.

———. 'Untitled Statement,' July 5, 2005.

———. 'Why Did I Not Name Them Khawarij Even until Now?,' 2015.

'al-maqdisi wa al-tahawi yud'aman mubadarat al-umma li-da'iyyat sa'udi [Al-Maqdisi and Al-Tahawi Support the Initiative of the Umma by a Saudi Preacher].' *Al-Quds Al-Arabi*, January 26, 2014.

Al-Masri, Abu al-Harith. 'al-amir al-musardib [the Hidden Amir],' December 9, 2017.

Al-Masri, Abu al-Yaqzan. 'Ruling on Participating in the Battle of East Euphrates.' *Mu'assasat 'ilamiyya Min Ard Al-Sham*, December 30, 2018.

Al-Muhajir, Abu al-Hassan. 'So Follow Their Guidance.' *Al-Furqan Media Foundation*, April 23, 2018.

———. 'You Will Remember What I Have Told You.' *Al-Furqan Media Foundation*, December 5, 2016.

Al-Muhajir, Abu Hamza. 'inna al-hukm illa illaha [the Judgement Is for None but Allah],' November 12, 2006.

———. 'sa-yuhzamu al-jam'u wa-yuwalluna al-dubra' [All Will Be Defeated and Flee],' June 13, 2006.

Al-Muhajir, Muhammad ibn Saleh. 'Conclusion in the Caliphate Declaration Discussion.' *Minbar Al-Tawhid Wa-l-Jihad*, September 2014.

Al-Muhaysini, Abdullah. 'mubadarat al-umma [Initiative of the Umma].' *Telegram Channel*, January 22, 2014.

———. 'We Want It on the Manhaj of Prophethood Regarding the Declaration of "Khilafah,"' July 2014.

Al-Muqaddam, Muhammad Ismail. *basair fi fitna [Insights into Fitna]*. Alexandria: Dar al-Tawhid, 2009.

Al-Murabitoun. 'bayan haul tawdih ba'd al-masa'il wa takiduha' [Statement on the Clarification of Some Matters and Confirming Them].' *Al Ribat Media Foundation*, July 21, 2015.

———. 'Untitled Statement.' *Al Ribat Media Foundation*, December 4, 2015.

Al-Muraqib. 'Striving for Hegemony: The HTS Crackdown on Al-Qaida and Friends in Northwest Syria.' *Jihadica*, September 15, 2020.

Al-Nadhari, Harith bin Ghazi. 'A Statement about What Was Contained in the Speech of Sheikh Abu Bakr Al-Baghdadi "Even If the Disbelievers Despise Such."' *Al-Malahem Media Foundation*, November 21, 2014.

———. 'Civility of the Dispute Between the Mujahideen.' *Al-Malahem Media Foundation*, December 10, 2014.

Al-Nadhari, Harith bin Ghazi, and Ibrahim Al-Rubeish. 'Responsibility of the Word.' *Al-Malahem Media Foundation*, July 5, 2014.

Al-Najdi, Abu Sa'd. 'fath al-malik al-kabir muta'al fi tandim al-haqq 'ala ara' al-rijal (al-radd 'ala al-sheikh al-zawahiri) [Opening of the Exalted Great King In Providing the Truth Upon the Opinions of the Men (Reply To Shaykh Al-Zawahiri].' *Al-Battar Media Foundation*, n.d.

Al-Nasr, Ahlam. 'al-zawahiri al-kurra al-'ajuz! [Zawahiri: The Old Ball!].' *Al-Sumud Media Foundation*, August 2016.

Al-Qahtani, Abu Mariya. 'Humiliating Proofs Regarding The Ignorance Of The Extremists.' *Al Muwahideen*, February 24, 2014.

———. 'My Advice to All Those Who Are Soft towards the Khawarij.' *Al-Muwahideen Media*, January 2015.

———. 'risala ila ahluna fi al-sharqiyya [Message to Our People in Al-Sharqiyya],' August 3, 2014.

———. 'risala jadida min al-sheikh abu mariya al-qahtani li-l-sheikh al-zawahiri yakshifu fiha haqaiq jadida [Message from Sheikh Abu Mariya Al-Qahtani to Sheikh Al-Zawahiri Revealing New Truth],' August 17, 2014.

Al-Qaida. 'al-nafir no. 1: ya ummat al-nasr infari wa jahadi wa istabshari [Al-Nafir No. 1: Oh Victorious Ummah, Carry Your Arms, Wage Jihad and Rejoice].' *As-Sahab Media*, July 19, 2014.

———. 'bayan bishan 'alaqa jama'a qa'idat al-jihad bi-jama'a al-dawla al-islamiyya fi al-'iraq wa-l-sham [Statement about the Relations of Al-Qaida with the Islamic State in Iraq and Sham],' February 3, 2014.

———. 'sayha nafir wa sarkha tahdhir [a Call to Mobilize and a Cry of Warning].' *As-Sahab Media*, August 15, 2019.

'al-qawl al-nadiyy fi kufr dawlat al-baghdadi [the Dewy Remark on the Unbelief of Al-Baghdadi's State],' April 13, 2017.

Al-Qunaybi, Iyad. 'al-waquf ma 'al-dawla' ala muftaraq turuq [Standing with 'the Islamic State' at a Crossroad],' 2013.

———. 'munaqasha li-radd al-dawla ala mubadarat al-umma [Discussion of the State's Response to the Initiative of the Umma],' February 3, 2014.

Al-Qurashi, Muhammad. 'Al-Murji'ah Sect, Its History and Beliefs.' *Nida'ul Islam*, no. 17 (1997).

Al-Qurayshi, Abu Hamza. 'And the Disbelievers Will Know Who Gets the Good End.' *Al-Furqan Media Foundation*, May 2020.

Al-Rumi, Abu Hamza. 'Who from the Scholars Support You', April 11, 2017.

Al-Shamali, Abu Jarir. 'We Disassociated Ourselves from Tanzim Al-Qa'ida and from the Shar'i Lapses of Al-Zawahiri.' *Ahl Al-Tawhid*, December 17, 2016.

Al-Shami, Abu Abdullah. 'The Establishment of Jabhat Al-Nusra and the Events of Al Sham from the Beginning of the Disagreement to the Announcement of Dawlah.' *Bilad Al-Sham Media*, November 20, 2016.

———. 'Untitled Statement,' June 30, 2014.

Al-Shami, Abu Hafs. 'Traits of the Evil Scholars.' *Rumiyah No. 5*, January 2017.

Al-Shami, Abu Ja'far. 'al-qawl al-naddi fi kufr dawlat al-baghdadi [the Moist Words on the Unbelief of the State of Al-Baghdadi],' April 28, 2015.

Al-Shami, Abu Maysara. 'al-hazimi been kabira al-qu'ud wa dalal al-jamiyyah [Al-Hazimi between the Great Sin of Abstention and the Error of the Jamiah],' 2014.

———. 'Behold, This Is the Treachery of the Leaders of Harakat Ash-Shabab!' *Al Hayat Media Center*, n.d.

———. 'It Is from the Strangest Matters of History for Adh-Dhawahiri to Produce Three Abnormal Messages Contradicting the Manhaj That Shaykh Usamah Was Martyred Upon, Almost Immediately after the Martyrdom of Shaykh Usamah,' n.d.

———. 'The Qa'idah of Adh-Dhawahiri, Al-Harari, and an-Nadhari, and the Absent Yemeni Wisdom.' *Dabiq No. 6*, January 2015.

Al-Shinqiti, Abu al-Mundhir. 'i'lan al-khilafa fi al-mizan al-shar'i [The Caliphate Announcement in the Balance of the Shari'a],' July 18, 2014.

———. 'sheikh ayman al-zawahiri rajul umma [Sheikh Ayman Al-Zawahiri: Man of the Umma].' *Minbar Al-Tawhid Wa-l-Jihad*, January 20, 2015.

———. 'yuriduna da'ishnat al-jihad [We Want Daish's Jihad],' December 5, 2015.

Al-Sibai, Hani. 'About the Decision to Arrest Some of the Elders in Syria.' *Telegram Channel*, November 28, 2017.

———. 'Is It Permissible for Young People in Syria to Sit in Their Homes Because of Their Disagreement with the Leaders of HTS,' January 7, 2018.

———. 'Is It Permissible for Young People in Syria to Sit in Their Homes Because of Their Disagreement with the Leaders of the Committee.' *Telegram Channel*, January 7, 2018.

———. 'miftah shakhsiyya al-sheikh al-duktur ayman [Key of the Personality of the Sheikh Dr. Ayman].' *Telegram Channel*, May 5, 2017.

———. *Qissah Jama'at Al-Jihad [The Story of Al Jihad Group]*. Minbar al-Tawhid wa-l-Jihad, 2002.

Al-Sibai, Hani, and Tariq Abdelhaleem. 'da'wa li-l-sulh wa-l-safh been al-mujahideen fi al-sham li-l-dawla wa jabhat al-nusra wa ahrar al-sham wa ghayruhum min kata'ib.' *Minbar Al-TawhidWa-l-Jihad*, January 21, 2014.

———. 'Statement on the Reality of the Islamic State,' August 25, 2014.

Al-Suri, Abu Firas. 'shahadat qabil intiha' muhlat al-mubahala: shahada al-sheikh abu firas al-suri [Testimonies before the Ending of the Mubahala: Testimony of Sheikh Abu Firas Al-Suri].' *Al Basira Media*, March 18, 2014.

Al-Suri, Abu Khalid. 'Untitled Statement,' January 16, 2014.

Al-Suri, Abu Musab. 'The Global Islamic Resistance Call,' December 2004.

Al-Sururiyya, Gharib. 'An Elderly Rogue Al-Qa'ida.' *Al Battar Media Foundation*, January 7, 2017.

———. 'Ayat wa 'ibar fi taraka jabhat al-julani li-tanzim al-qa'ida [Verses and Morals in Leaving the Front of Al-Julani to the Organization of Al-Qaida].' *Al Battar Media Foundation*, June 30, 2016.

———. 'tawaghit al-qa'ida [Tyrants of Al-Qaida].' *Al Battar Media Foundation*, July 16, 2017.

Al-Suwailem, Samir Saleh. 'Memories of Amir Khattab: The Experience of the Arab Ansar in Chechnya, Afghanistan and Tajikistan,' n.d.

Al-Tabari, Abu Jafar Muhammed bin Jarir. *The History of Al-Tabari: The First Civil War*. Annotated translation by G.R. Hawting. Volume XVI, 1996.

Al-Tamimi, Aymenn Jawad. 'A Complete History of Jamaat Ansar Al-Islam,' December 15, 2015.

———. 'Abu Ya'qub Al-Maqdisi's Reform Plan: Translation and Analysis,' January 22, 2019.

———. 'An Internal Report on Extremism in the Islamic State,' November 1, 2018.

———. 'AQIM Advice to 'Boko Haram' Dissidents: Full Translation and Analysis,' September 15, 2018.

———. 'Dissent in the Islamic State: Abu Al-Faruq Al-Masri's "Message on the Manhaj"'. *Combating Terrorism Center at West Point*, October 31, 2016.

———. 'Dissent in the Islamic State: 'Hashimi Advice' to Abu Bakr Al-Baghdadi,' January 4, 2019.

———. 'Dissent in the Islamic State: Secret Advice Sent to Islamic State Leaders,' September 12, 2019.

———. 'Dissent in the Islamic State: The Controversy Over Abu Ya'qub Al-Maqdisi,' September 27, 2018.

———. 'Dissent in the Islamic State's Yemen Affiliates: Documents, Translation & Analysis,' February 29, 2016.

———. 'Islamic State Sinai Province vs. Jama'at Jund Al-Islam: Report from Al-Naba', July 2, 2020.

———. 'Jabhat Al-Nusra and the Islamic State of Iraq and Ash-Sham: Aleppo Area,' June 13, 2013.

———. 'Opposition to Abu Bakr Al-Baghdadi: Sheikh Abu Eisa Al-Masri's Critique of Islamic State Media,' May 27, 2019.

———. 'Specimen 1B: Invitation to Repentance: Euphrates Province,' January 27, 2015.

———. 'Specimen 7W: Conditions of Repentance, Al-Bab, Aleppo Province (January 2014).' 2015, January.

———. 'The Evolution in Islamic State Administration: The Documentary Evidence.' *Perspectives on Terrorism* 9, no. 4 (2015): 117–29.

———. 'The Hay'at Tahrir Al-Sham-Al-Qaeda Dispute: Primary Texts (II),' December 10, 2017.

———. 'The Killing of Abu Hafs Al-Jazrawi by the Islamic State,' January 19, 2019.

———. 'The Life of Abu Muhammad al-Furqan: Head of the Media Department of the Islamic State (Part Two),' May 20, 2021.

———. 'Turki Binali's Critique of The "Theory of Balance": Translation and Analysis,' January 8, 2019.

Al-Tartusi, Abu Basir. 'A Declaration Regarding the Fighting Between the ISIS and the Mujahedeen of Al-Sham,' January 14, 2014.

———. 'mulhazat 'ala 'risala ila sadiqin mimman nafaru ila ard al-jihad fi souriya' l-abi muhammad al-maqdisi [Comment to Abu Muhammad Al-Maqdisi's "Letter to the Honest Ones Who Travelled to the Land of Jihad,"' August 23, 2014.

———. 'Stance on the Words of Sheikh Ayman Al-Zawahiri "Testimony to Preserve the Blood of Al-Mujahedeen in Al-Sham",' March 3, 2014.

———. 'The Validity of the Victorious Emirate,' March 15, 2014.

Al-Tunisi, Abu Iyadh. 'Untitled Letter to Al-Zawahiri,' 2014.

Al-Uraydi, Sami. 'Advice for the Mujahedeen in the Time of Fitna.' *As-Sahab Media*, March 2017.

———. 'Answering the Questioners about the Faithfulness of the Allegiance to the Jihadi Groups to Rule the Shari'a of the Lord of the Worlds.' *Telegram Channel*, April 2017.

———. 'Gamblers of Jihad.' *Telegram Channel*, October 2018.

———. 'It Is a Jurisprudence of Attraction and Not a Jurisprudence of Gradual Advance.' *2018*, October.

———. 'jihad al-umma wa manhaj al-harakat al-jihadiyya [Jihad of the Nation and the Methodology of the Jihadi Movement].' *Telegram Channel*, August 15, 2017.

———. 'kalimat hamasat 'ala kalimat al-sheikh abu qatada al-filastini [Words of Whisper to the Words of Sheikh Abu Qatada Al-Filastini],' October 14, 2018.

———. 'rasail manhajiyya min al-thughur al-shamiyya [Methodological Messages from the Syrian Front],' May 2017.

———. 'The Fighting Movements between Two Calls: O People of Samura and O People of Yathreb.' *Telegram Channel*, August 20, 2018.

———. 'The Lord of the Prison Loved Me to Keep Silent about Injustice Part 1.' *Telegram Channel*, December 30, 2017.

———. 'What Is the Shami Jihad but a Jewel in a Decade and a Stage of History?' *Telegram Channel*, April 4, 2017.

Al-Uraydi, Sami, and Abu Muhammad Al-Maqdisi. 'jihad al-umma wa jama'at al-umma [Jihad of the Umma and Groups of the Umma].' *Maktab Khayr Umma Al-Islamiyya*, July 2017.

———. 'Methodology: Between Praise and Contempt, the Sunnah and Heresy,' September 10, 2017.

Al-Urduni, Abu al-Qassam. 'Untitled Statement,' February 7, 2019.

Al-Utaybi, Abu Sulayman. 'risala al-sheikh abu sulaiman al-utaybi li-qiyada fi khorasan [Letter from Sheikh Abu Sulaiman Al-Utaybi to the Leadership in Khorasan],' 2007.

Al-Zarqawi, Abu Abd al-Rahman al-Shami. 'ta'riat al-thiyat 'an al-sawab [Stripping the Attire from the Truth],' 2015.

Al-Zarqawi, Abu Musab. 'risala min abu musab al-zarqawi ila al-sheikh usama bin laden [Letter from Abu Musab Al-Zarqawi to Sheikh Usama Bin Laden],' February 15, 2004.

———. 'risala min jundi ila amirihi [Letter from a Soldier to His Prince],' May 30, 2005.

———. 'Untitled Letter,' January 2004. https://2001-2009.state.gov/p/nea/rls/31694.htm.

Al-Zawahiri, Ayman. 'Al-Wala' Wa-l-Bara': Changing an Article of Faith and Losing Sight of Reality,' 2002.

———. 'And the Noble Knights Dismount,' June 8, 2011.

———. 'Answers to the Esteemed Shaykhs.' *As-Sahab Media*, May 2, 2014.

———. 'Editorial.' *One Umma*, April 5, 2019.

———. 'General Guidelines for Jihad.' *As-Sahab Media*, September 2013.

———. 'How to Confront America.' *As-Sahab Media*, September 11, 2018.

———. 'infuru li-l-sham [Prepaing to Fight for Al-Sham].' *As-Sahab Media*, May 7, 2016.

———. 'Interview: A Review of Events.' *As-Sahab Media*, December 16, 2007.

———. 'Islamic Spring Part 1.' *As-Sahab Media*, March 2015.

———. 'Islamic Spring Part 2.' *As-Sahab Media*, April 2015.

———. 'Islamic Spring Part 3: A Talk on the Khilafa That Follows the Prophetic Path.' *As-Sahab Media*, April 2015.

———. 'Islamic Spring Part 4: Answering the Doubts Regarding the Khalifa Who Takes Authority by Force.' *As-Sahab Media*, April 2015.

———. 'Islamic Spring Part 5.' *As-Sahab Media*, October 2015.

———. 'Islamic Spring Part 6.' *As-Sahab Media*, October 2015.

———. 'Islamic Spring Part 7: Yemen of Wisdom and Faith Between the Servants of Iran and the Slaves of America.' *As-Sahab Media*, May 2016.

———. 'Islamic Spring Part 8: The Sun of Victory Shines From Nusantara.' *As-Sahab Media*, January 13, 2016.

———. 'Islamic Spring Part 9: Turkistan: Patience and Then Victory.' *As-Sahab Media*, July 2016.

———. *Knights Under the Prophet's Banner*. Translation by Laura Mansfield, 2006.

———. 'Let Us Fight Them As A Solid Structure.' *As-Sahab Media*, November 28, 2017.

———. 'nida' 'ajilun li-ahluna fi al-sham [an Urgent Call to Our People in Al-Sham].' *As-Sahab Media*, January 15, 2014.

———. 'Sham: A Trust Upon Your Necks.' *As-Sahab Media*, January 14, 2016.

———. 'Support Your Prophet,' December 2015.

———. 'Testimony to Preserve the Blood of the Mujahideen in Sham.' *As-Sahab Media*, May 2, 2014.

———. 'The Exoneration: A Letter Exonerating the Umma of the Pen and Sword from the Unjust Allegation of Feebleness and Weakness.' *English Translation*, 2008.

———. 'The Reality Between the Pain and the Hope.' *As-Sahab Media*, April 18, 2014.

———. 'The Shari'a Ruling on Governance without Shari'a.' *As-Sahab Media*, October 11, 2018.

———. 'The Way of Salvation.' *As-Sahab Media*, February 5, 2019.

———. 'Untitled Letter to Al-Julani and Al-Baghdadi,' May 23, 2013.

———. 'Untitled Letter to Al-Zarqawi,' July 9, 2005.

———. 'We Shall Fight You Until There Is No More Persecution.' *As-Sahab Media*, April 23, 2017.

'Al Qaeda's 'Re-Radicalisation' Schools Lure ISIL Fighters in Syria.' *The National*, January 20, 2018.

Ali, Abdallah Suleiman. 'IS Disciplines Some Emirs to Avoid Losing Base.' *Al Monitor*, September 2, 2014.

Alimi, Eitan Y. 'Relational Dynamics in Factional Adoption of Terrorist Tactics: A Comparative Perspective.' *Theory and Society* 40, no. 1 (2011): 95–118.

Alimi, Eitan Y., Lorenzo Bosi, and Chares Demetriou. *The Dynamics of Radicalization: A Relational and Comparative Perspective*. Oxford: Oxford University Press, 2015.

Almohammad, Asaad. 'Seven Years of Terror: Jihadi Organisations' Strategies and Future Directions.' *ICCT*, August 2019.

Alshamsi, Mansoor Jassem. *Islam and Political Reform in Saudi Arabia: The Quest for Political Change and Reform*. New York: Routledge, 2010.

Alshech, Eli. 'The Doctrinal Crisis within the Salafi–Jihadi Ranks and the Emergence of Neo-Takfirism.' *Islamic Law and Society* 21 (2014): 419–52.

Amarasingam, Amarnath. *Pain, Pride, and Politics : Social Movement Activism and the Sri Lankan Tamil Diaspora in Canada*. London: University of Georgia Press, 2015.

Anas, Abdullah, and Tam Hussein. *To the Mountains: My Life in Jihad, from Algeria to Afghanistan*. London: Hurst Publishers, 2019.

Andersen, Jan Christoffer, and Sveinung Sandberg. 'Islamic State Propaganda: Between Social Movement Framing and Subcultural Provocation.' *Terrorism and Political Violence*, 2018.

Ansar al-Islam. 'Untitled Statement,' June 30, 2014. https://justpaste.it/h2a4.

Anzalone, Christopher. 'Black Banners in Somalia: The State of Al-Shabaab's Territorial Insurgency and the Specter of the Islamic State.' *CTC Sentinel* 11, no. 3 (2018).

———. 'Revisiting Shaykh Atiyyatullah's Works on Takfir and Mass Violence.' *CTC Sentinel* 5, no. 4 (2012).

———. 'The Life and Death of Al-Shabab Leader Ahmed Godane.' *CTC Sentinel* 7, no. 9 (2014).

Appleby, Scott, and Martin Marty. *Accounting for Fundamentalisms: The Dynamic Character of Movements*. Chicago: University of Chicago Press, 2004.

AQAP. 'Responsibility of the Word.' *Al-Malahem Media Foundation*, July 5, 2014.

———. 'risala ila al-mujahideen fi-l-sham [Message to the Mujahideen in Sham].' *Al-Malahem Media Foundation*, February 27, 2014.

———. 'tanzim al-dawla yada'u 'ansaruhu fi al-'alam ila qatala al-du'a wa 'ulama al-salatin [the Islamic State Calls on Its Supporters around the World to Kill the Preachers and the Scholars of the Sultan].' *Al Masra No. 40*, 2017.

AQIM. 'Year of the Group... Hope of the Umma.' *Al-Andalus Media Foundation*, July 4, 2014.

AQIS. 'Code of Conduct.' *As-Sahab Media*, June 2017.

Arab Liaison Committee of the Islamic Emirate. 'Untitled.' *AFGP-2002-0001000-0003*, n.d.

Ashida, Abu al-Abd. 'So as Not to Sink the Ship.' [Video], September 9, 2019.

Ashour, Omar. *The De-Radicalization of Jihadists*. New York: Routledge, 2009.

Bacon, Tricia. 'Alliance Hubs: Focal Points in the International Terrorist Landscape.' *Perspectives on Terrorism* 8, no. 4 (2014): 4–26.

Bacon, Tricia, and Elizabeth Grimm Arsenault. 'Al Qaeda and the Islamic State's Break: Strategic Strife or Lackluster Leadership?' *Studies in Conflict and Terrorism* 42, no. 3 (2019): 229–63.

Badar, Mohamed, Masaki Nagata, and Tiphane Tueni. 'The Radical Application of the Islamist Concept of Takfir.' *Arab Law Quarterly* 31 (2017): 134–62.

Bakke, Kristin M., Kathleen Gallagher Cunningham, and Lee J.M. Seymour. 'A Plague of Initials: Fragmentation, Cohesion, and Infighting in Civil Wars.' *Perspectives on Politics* 10, no. 2 (2012): 265–83.

Basit, Abdul. 'IS Penetration in Afghanistan–Pakistan: Assessment, Impact and Implications.' *Perspectives on Terrorism* 11, no. 3 (2017): 19–39.

Berger, J.M. 'The Islamic State vs. Al Qaeda.' *Foreign Policy*, September 2, 2014.

Biddle, Stephen, Jeffrey A Friedman, Eli Berman, Richard Betts, Daniel Byman, Luke Condra, Dan Reiter, et al. 'Testing the Surge' 37, no. 1 (2012): 7–40.

Bloom, Mia. *Dying to Kill :The Allure of Suicide Terror*. New York: Columbia University Press, 2005.

Bloom, Mia, and John Horgan. *Small Arms: Children and Terrorism*. London: Cornell University Press, 2019.

Bourdieu, Pierre. 'Genesis and Structure of the Religious Field.' *Comparative Social Research* Vol. 13 (1991): 1–44.

———. *Outline of a Theory of Practice*. Cambridge: Cambridge University Press, 1977.

———. 'The Forms of Capital.' In *Knowledge Vol. 3*, edited by Nico Stehr and Reiner Grundmann, 93–111. London: Taylor and Francis, 2005.

Bowering, Gerhard, Patricia Crone, Wadad Kadi, Devin Stewart, Muhammad Qasim Zaman, and Mahan Mirza, eds. *The Princeton Encyclopedia of Islamic Political Thought*. Princeton: Princeton University Press, 2013.

'BREAKING: Mujahideen Shura Council Has Been Formed in Deir Ez-Zor,' May 25, 2014. https://www.reddit.com/r/syriancivilwar/comments/26gnfk/breaking_mujahideen_shura_council_has_been_formed/.

Brooke, Steven. 'Jihadist Strategic Debates before 9/11.' *Studies in Conflict & Terrorism* 31, no. 3 (2008): 201–26.

Brown, Nathan J. 'Official Islam in the Arab World: The Contest for Religious Authority.' *Carnegie Endownment for International Peace*, May 2017.

Brown, Vahid, and Don Rassler. *Fountainhead of Jihad: The Haqqani Nexus, 1973-2010*. London: Hurst & Company, 2013.

Bunzel, Cole. 'A House Divided: Origins and Persistence of the Islamic State's Ideological Divide.' *Jihadica*, June 5, 2018.

———. 'A Jihadi Civil War of Words: The Ghuraba' Media Foundation and Minbar Al-Tawhid Wa'l-Jihad.' *Jihadica*, October 21, 2014.

———. 'Abandoning Al-Qaida: Tahrir Al-Sham and the Concerns of Sami Al-'Uraydi.' *Jihadica*, May 12, 2017.

———. 'Abu Qatada Al-Filastini: "I Am Not a Jihadi, or a Salafi."' *Jihadica*, October 26, 2018.

———. 'Al-Qaeda's Quasi-Caliph: The Recasting of Mullah 'Umar.' *Jihadica*, July 23, 2014.

———. 'Caliphate in Disarray: Theological Turmoil in the Islamic State.' *Jihadica*, October 3, 2017.

———. 'Caliphate Now: Jihadis Debate the Islamic State.' *Jihadica*, November 25, 2013.

———. 'Death of a Mufti: The Execution of the Islamic State's Abu Ya'qub Al-Maqdisi.' *Jihadica*, January 4, 2019.

———. 'Diluting Jihad: Tahrir Al-Sham and the Concerns of Abu Muhammad Al-Maqdisi.' *Jihadica*, March 29, 2017.

———. 'Ideological Infighting in the Islamic State.' *Perspectives on Terrorism* 13, no. 1 (2019): 13–22.

———. 'Jihadism on Its Own Terms.' Hoover Institution, 2017.

———. 'Manifest Enmity: The Origins, Development, and Persistence of Classical Wahhabism (1153–1351/1741–1932).' *Princeton University, Department of Near Eastern Studies* PhD Disser (2018).

———. 'Mourning Morsi: The Death of an Islamist and Jihadi Divisions.' *Jihadica*, September 27, 2019.

———. 'Rehabilitating the Bin'aliyya: Al-Maqdisi and the Scholarly Remnant of the Islamic State.' *Jihadica*, December 11, 2019.

———. 'The Islamic State of Disobedience: Al-Baghdadi Triumphant.' *Jihadica*, October 5, 2015.

———. 'The Islamic State of Disunity: Jihadism Divided.' *Jihadica*, January 2014.

Callimachi, Rukmini, and Andrew Higgins. 'Video Shows a Paris Gunman Declaring His Loyalty to the Islamic State.' *New York Times*, January 11, 2015.

Captured Document. 'Status of Jihad.' *AFGP-2002-601693*, July 26, 2002.

Celso, Anthony. *The Islamic State: A Comparative History of Jihadist Warfare*. New York: Lexington Books, 2018.

Checkel, Jeffrey T. 'Socialization and Violence: Introduction and Framework.' *Journal of Peace Research* 54, no. 5 (2017): 592–605.

Christia, Fotini. *Alliance Formation in Civil Wars*. Cambridge: Cambridge University Press, 2012.

Clifford, Bennett, and Seamus Hughes. 'United States v. Aws Mohammed Younis Al-Jayab: A Case Study on Transnational Prosecutions of Jihadi Foreign Fighter Networks.' *CTC Sentinel* 11, no. 11 (2018).

Coll, Steve. *Ghost Wars: The Secret History of the CIA, Afghanistan, and Bin Laden, from the Soviet Invasion to September 10, 2001*. New York: Penguin Press, 2005.

Cook, David. *Understanding Jihad*. London, England: University of California Press, 2005.

Cozzens, Jeffrey B. 'Al-Takfir Wa'l Hijra: Unpacking an Enigma.' *Studies in Conflict & Terrorism* 32, no. 6 (2009): 489–510.

Crenshaw, Martha. 'The Causes of Terrorism.' *Comparative Politics* 13, no. 4 (1981): 379–99.

———. 'There Is No Global Jihadist "Movement."' *The Atlantic*, March 10, 2015.

Crone, Patricia. *God's Rule: Government and Islam*. New York: Columbia University Press, 2004.

Cronin, Audrey Kurth. 'How Al-Qaida Ends.' *International Security* 31, no. 1 (2006): 7–48.

Cruickshank, Paul. 'Al-Qaeda's New Course Examining Ayman Al-Zawahiri's Strategic Direction.' *IHS Defense, Risk and Security Consulting* May (2012).

CTC Harmony Project. 'Cracks in the Foundation: Leadership Schisms in Al-Qaida from 1989-2006 Combating Terrorism Center at West Point,' 2007.

Daumas, Cécile. 'Gilles Kepel: "Il Faut Écouter Les Prêches Du Vendredi".' *Libération*, April 14, 2016.

Davenport, Christian. *How Social Movements Die : Repression and Demobilization of the Republic of New Africa*. New York: Cambridge University Press, 2015.

Dean, Aimen, Paul Cruickshank, and Tim Lister. *Nine Lives: My Time as MI6's Top Spy inside Al-Qaeda*. London: Oneworld Publications, 2018.

Deol, Jeevan, and Zaheer Kazmi, eds. *Contextualising Jihadi Thought*. London, England: C. Hurst & Co., 2012.

'Deposed Boko Haram Leader Detained Not Killed.' *Vanguard*, March 15, 2019.

Devji, Faisal. *Landscapes of the Jihad: Militancy, Morality, Modernity*. London: Hurst & Company, 2005.

Dodwell, Brian, Daniel Milton, and Don Rassler. 'The Caliphate's Global Workforce: An Inside Look at the Islamic State's Foreign Fighter Paper Trail.' *Combating Terrorism Center at West Point*, April 2016.

Drennan, Shane. 'Constructing Takfir.' *CTC Sentinel* 1, no. 7 (2008).

Drevon, Jerome. 'The Jihadi Social Movement (JSM): Between Factional Hegemonic Drive, National Realities and Transnational Ambitions.' *Perspectives on Terrorism* 11, no. 6 (2017): 55–62.

Drevon, Jérôme. 'Assessing Islamist Armed Groups' De-Radicalization in Egypt.' *Peace Review: A Journal of Social Justice* 27, no. 3 (2015): 296–303.

Drevon, Jerome Nicolas. 'Theorising Militant Groups' Meso-Level Evolution: A Comparative Study of the Egyptian Islamic and Jihad Groups.' PhD dissertation, Durham University, 2015.

Dupée, Matthew. 'Red on Red: Analyzing Afghanistan's Intra-Insurgency Violence.' *CTC Sentinel* 11, no. 1 (2018).

Eickelman, Dale F., and James Piscatori. *Muslim Politics*. Princeton: Princeton University Press, 1996.

English, Richard. *Does Terrorism Work?* Oxford: Oxford University Press, 2016.

'Factional Boko Haram Leader Mamman Nur Killed by Own Fighters.' *Daily Trust*, September 14, 2018.

Falleti, Tulia G., and Julia F. Lynch. 'Context and Causal Mechanisms in Political Analysis.' *Comparative Political Studies* 42, no. 9 (2009): 1143–66.

Faraj, Muhammad Abd al-Salam. 'al-farida al-gha'iba [The Neglected Duty].' Translated by Johannes J. G. Jansen, n.d.

Felshtinsky, Yuri. 'Lenin, Trotsky, Stalin and the Left Opposition in the USSR, 1918–1928.' *Cahiers Du Monde Russe* 31, no. 4 (1990): 569–78.

Filastini, Abu Qatada Al. 'A Letter to the People of Jihad and Those Who Love It,' April 28, 2014.

Fineman, Mark, and Steven Braun. 'Life inside Al Qaeda: A Destructive Devotion.' *Los Angeles Times*, September 24, 2001. http://articles.latimes.com/2001/sep/24/news/mn-49201.

Fishman, Brian. 'Ansar Al-Sunnah Threatens Al-Qa'ida in Iraq.' *Combating Terrorism Center*, February 26, 2007.

———. 'Dysfunction and Decline : Lessons Learned from Inside Al Qa'ida in Iraq.' *Combating Terrorism Center*, 2009.

———. 'Revising the History of Al-Qa`ida's Original Meeting with Abu Musab Al-Zarqawi.' *CTC Sentinel* 9, no. 10 (2016).

———. 'The First Defector: Abu Sulayman Al-Utaybi, the Islamic State, and Al-Qa`ida.' *CTC Sentinel* 8, no. 10 (2015).

———. 'The Man Who Could Have Stopped the Islamic State.' *Foreign Policy*, November 23, 2016.

Fishman, Brian, and Joseph Felter. 'Al-Qa'ida's Foreign Fighters in Iraq: A First Look at the Sinjar Records', Combating Terrorism Center at West Point.' *Combating Terrorism Center at West Point*, December 2007.

Fjelde, Hanne, and Desirée Nilsson. 'Rebels against Rebels: Explaining Violence between Rebel Groups.' *Journal of Conflict Resolution* 56, no. 4 (2012): 604–28.

Foucault, Michel. *Discipline and Punish: The Birth of the Prison*. Harmondsworth: Penguin Books, 1991.

Francis, Matthew D. M. 'Why the 'Sacred' Is a Better Resource Than 'Religion' for Understanding Terrorism.' *Terrorism and Political Violence* 28, no. 5 (2016): 912–27.

Gartenstein-Ross, Daveed, and Bridget Moreng. 'Al Qaeda Is Beating the Islamic State.' *Politico*, April 2015.

Gerges, Fawaz. *ISIS: A History*. Princeton: Princeton University Press, 2016.

Gerges, Fawaz A. *Journey of the Jihadist: Inside Muslim Militancy*. Orlando, Florida: Harcourt Inc., 2007.

———. *The Far Enemy: Why Jihad Went Global*. Cambridge: Cambridge University Press, 2005.

Girard, René. *Violence and the Sacred*. Baltimore: John Hopkins University Press, 1977.

Giugni, Marco, Doug McAdam, and Charles Tilly, eds. *How Social Movements Matter*. Minneapolis: University of Minnesota Pres, 1999.

Giustozzi, Antonio. *The Islamic State in Khorasan: Afghanistan, Pakistan and the New Central Asian Jihad*. London: Hurst & Company, 2018.

Glenn, Cameron. 'Libya's Islamists: Who They Are—And What They Want.' Wilson Centre, August 2017.

Gråtrud, Henrik, and Vidar Benjamin Skretting. 'Ansar Al-Sharia in Libya: An Enduring Threat.' *Perspectives on Terrorism* 11, no. 1 (2017): 40–53.

Group of scholars. 'Fatwa,' June 2015.

———. 'Statement of the Brotherhood of Iman for the Support of the State of Islam: Statement of Scholars, Students of Knowledge and Shuyukh to Support the Joined Firmly Structure.' *Al-Ghuraba Media*, September 30, 2014.

Guidère, Mathieu. 'The Timbuktu Letters: New Insights about AQIM.' *Res Militaris*, 2014.

Guled, Abdi. 'Bloody Rivalry Erupts between Al-Shabab, IS Group in Somalia.' *AP*, December 6, 2018.

Günther, Christoph, and Tom Kaden. 'The Authority of the Islamic State.' *Max Planck Institute for Social Anthropology Working Paper no. 169* (2016).

Habib, Kamal. 'Another Wave of Jihadist Adjustment: Internal Debates of the Movement.' *Arab Insights* 2, no. 6 (2009).

Hadid, Adnan. 'Commenting the Letter of Sheikh Abu Firas to the Shura Council of Jabhat Al-Nusra.' *Telegram Channel*, August 24, 2018.

Hafez, Mohammed M. 'Fratricidal Rebels: Ideological Extremity and Warring Factionalism in Civil Wars.' *Terrorism and Political Violence*, 2017.

Hafez, Muhammed. 'Tactics, Takfir, and Anti-Muslim Violence.' In *Self Inflicted Wounds: Debates and Divisions within Al Qa'ida and Its Periphery*, edited by Assaf Moghadam and Brian Fishman, 19–44. West Point: CTC Harmony Project, 2010.

Hafidh Muaaz Badr. 'Tale of the War against Daesh.' *Nawai Ghazwa Hind Magazine* 13, no. 4 (2020): 103–5.

Haid, Haid. 'HTS's Offline Propaganda: Infrastructure, Engagement and Monopoly.' *International Centre for the Study of Radicalisation*, 2019.

Hallaq, Wael B. *Authority, Continuity and Change in Islamic Law*. Cambridge: Cambridge University Press, 2001.

Hamid, Mustafa. 'The Airport 1990.' *Document ID AFGP-2002-600090*, n.d.

Hamid, Mustafa, and Leah Farrall. *The Arabs at War in Afghanistan*. London: Hurst & Company, 2015.

Hamming, Tore Refslund. 'Hayat Tahrir Al-Sham's Internal Conflict and Renewed Tensions with Hurras Al-Deen.' *Jihadica*, February 15, 2019.

———. 'ISIS's Charm Offensive toward Al-Qaeda in the Islamic Maghreb.' *Middle East Institute*, December 13, 2018.

———. 'Jihadi Competition and Political Preferences.' *Perspectives on Terrorism* 11, no. 6 (2017): 63–88.

———. 'Polemical and Fratricidal Jihadists: A Historical Examination of Debates, Contestation and Infighting Within the Sunni Jihadi Movement.' *International Centre for the Study of Radicalisation*, August 2019.

———. 'The Al Qaeda–Islamic State Rivalry: Competition Yes, but No Competitive Escalation.' *Terrorism and Political Violence*, 2017, 1–18.

———. 'The Extremist Wing of the Islamic State.' *Jihadica*, June 9, 2016. http://www.jihadica.com/the-extremist-wing-of-the-islamic-state/.

———. 'The Hardline Stream of Global Jihad: Revisiting the Ideological Origin of the Islamic State.' *CTC Sentinel* 12, no. 1 (2019).

———. 'What We Learned from Sami Al-Uraydi's Testimony Concerning Abu Abdullah Al-Shami'. *Jihadica*, October 24, 2017.

———. 'Why Did the Jihadi Cold War in Yemen End?' *War on the Rocks*, November 7, 2018.

Hamming, Tore Refslund, and Olivier Roy. 'Al-Zawahiri's Bay'a to Mullah Mansoor: A Bitter Pill but a Bountiful Harvest.' *CTC Sentinel* 9, no. 5 (2016).

Hamzawy, Amr, and Sarah Grebowski. 'From Violence to Moderation: Al-Jama' Al-Islamiya and Al-Jihad.' *Carnegie Middle East Center*, 2010.

Hansen, Stig Jarle. 'An In-Depth Look at Al-Shabab's Internal Divisions.' *CTC Sentinel* 7, no. 2 (2014).

Hassan, Hassan. 'Two Houses Divided: How Conflict in Syria Shaped the Future of Jihadism.' *CTC Sentinel* 11, no. 9 (2018).

Hassan, Mohamed Olad. 'Somalia's Al-Shabab Declares War on Pro-Islamic State Group.' *VOA News*, December 21, 2018.

Hayat Tahrir al-Sham. 'Jihad and Shari'a Politics between Constants and Alternations,' June 8, 2018.

———. 'tatawa'a wa la takhtalefa [Agree with Each Other and Do Not Disagree],' December 2, 2017.

———. 'wa 'ala al-baghi tadour al-dawai'r [Life of the Rebel Will Turn Back on Him],' February 12, 2018.

———. 'Why Did 'Hayat Tahrir Al-Sham' Lately Arrest Some of the Brothers and Why Is It Demanding Their Trial?' *Internal Document*, December 2, 2017.

Hegghammer, Thomas. *Jihad in Saudi Arabia: Violence and Pan-Islamism since 1979*. Cambridge: Cambridge University Press, 2010.

———. 'The Hybridization of Jihadi Groups.' *Current Trends in Islamist Ideology* 9 (2009): 26–45.

———. 'Violent Islamism in Saudi Arabia, 1979-2006: The Power and Perils of Pan-Islamic Nationalism.' PhD thesis, Institut d'Etudes Politiques de Paris, Ecole Doctorale de Sciences Po, 2007.

Helfont, Samuel, and Michael Brill. 'Saddam's ISIS?' *Foreign Affairs*, January 12, 2016.

Heller, Sam. 'Ahrar Al-Sham's Revisionist Jihadism.' *War on the Rocks*, September 2015.

———. 'Ahrar Al-Sham's Revisionist Jihadism.' *War on the Rocks*, September 30, 2015.

———. '"Frogs" and "Geckos": Syri'a Jihadists Speak the Language of Rebellion.' *War on* the Rocks', October 22, 2018.

———. 'How Ahrar Al-Sham Has Come to Define the Kaleidoscope of the Syrian Civil War.' *War on the Rocks*, June 6, 2016.

Hoffman, Bruce. 'ISIL Is Winning.' *Politico Magazine*, September 10, 2015.

Husayn, Fu'ad. 'Al-Zarqawi: The Second Generation of Al-Qa'ida,' June 2006.

Ibn Mahmoud, Hussein. 'A Message to Emir Al-Zawahiri,' June 16, 2011.

———. 'Study on Al-Khawarij.' *Ansar Al-Khilafah*, August 13, 2014.

Ibrahimi, Niamatullah, and Shahram Akbarzadeh. 'Intra-Jihadist Conflict and Cooperation: Islamic State–Khorasan Province and the Taliban in Afghanistan.' *Studies in Conflict & Terrorism*, 2019.

Imam, Sayyid. 'tarshid al-'amal al-jihadi fi misr wa al-'alam' [Advice Regarding the Conduct of Jihadist Action in Egypt and the World],' November 2007.

Ingram, Haroro J. 'How ISIS Survives Defeat: Propaganda and Decisive Minorities.' *Oxford Research Group*, September 26, 2016.

International Crisis Group. 'Iraq after the Surge I: The New Sunni Landscape.' *Middle East Report No. 74*, April 30, 2008.

'Interview with Yahya Abu Hummam.' *Al-Akhbar*, January 10, 2016.

Islamic State. 'al-hamla al-salibiyya 'ala gharb 'ifriqiyya. khasa'ir mutawasila fi sufuf al-quwwat al-faransiyya wa-l-qa'ida tusharik fi-l-harb didda al-mujahidin [The Crusader Campaign on West Africa. Continuous Losses in the Ranks of the French Force and al-Qaida Participates in the War Against the Mujahideen.' *Al-Naba No. 233*, May 2020.

———. 'al-zilal fi al-mawqifi al-shar'iyy min 'ulama al-haqqi wa al-dalal [In the Shadow of the Legitimate Position on the 'ulama of Truth and of Misguidance].' *Maktab Al-Buhouth Wal-Dirasat*, April 1, 2017.

———. 'bayan mauqif al-dawlat al-islamiyyah min maqalat al-muftirin [Statement on the Position of the Islamic State to the Article of the Slanderers].' *Al-Itisam Media Foundation*, March 1, 2014.

———. 'Disavowal of the Mushrikin in the Lives of the Prophet and the Sahabah.' *Rumiyah No.* 7, March 7, 2017.

———. 'Editorial.' *Al-Naba No. 182*, May 15, 2019.

———. 'Governor of West Africa Sheikh Abu Musab Al-Barnawi: We Will Come out of Our Plight with a More Solid Body and a Stronger Hand.' *Al-Naba No. 41*, August 2, 2016.

———. 'hatta tu'minu bi-allahi wahdahu [until you believe in allah alone].' *Al-Naba No. 129*, April 27, 2018.

———. 'Irja' – The Most Dangerous Bid'ah.' *Dabiq 8*, March 2015.

———. 'The Allies of Al-Qa'idah in Sham: Part 4.' *Dabiq No. 11*, September 2015.

———. 'The Allies of Al-Qa'idah in Sham: The End.' *Dabiq No. 12*, November 2015.

———. 'The Allies of Al-Qa'idah in Sham.' *Dabiq No. 8*, March 2015.

———. 'The Allies of Al-Qa'idah in Yemen.' *Dabiq No. 12*, November 2015.

———. 'The Extinction of the Grayzone.' *Dabiq No.* 7, February 2015.

———. 'The Obligation of Exposing Wicked Scholars.' *Rumiyah No. 3*, November 2016.

———. 'The Wicked Scholars Are Cursed.' *Rumiyah No. 1*, September 2016.

———. 'Wilayat Khurasan and the Bay'at from Qawqaz.' *Dabiq* 7, February 2015.

Jabhat al-Nusra. 'Interview with Abu Sulayman Al-Muhajir.' *Al Basira Media*, April 2014.

———. 'manhajina wa aqidatuna: muqabila ma' al-duktur sami al-uraydi [Our Methodology and Creed: Interview with Doctor Sami Al-Uraydi].' *Al-Manara Al-Bayda Media Foundation*, October 21, 2013.

———. 'Statement Regarding the Ongoing Fighting with the State.' *Al-Manara Al-Bayda Media Foundation*, May 4, 2014.

———. 'wa qad a'thara man anthar [He Who Issues a Warning Is Relieved of Responsibility].' *Al-Manara Al-Bayda Media Foundation*, February 7, 2014.

Jackson, Kévin. 'Abu Mus'ab Al Zarqawi under Influence: One Mentor?,' May 15, 2012.

Jackson, Sherman A. *Initiative to Stop the Violence (Mubadarat Waqf Al-'unf): Sadat's Assassins and the Renunciation of Political Violence*. New Haven: Yale University Press, 2015.

Jadoon, Amira. 'Allied and Lethal: Islamic State Khorasan's Network and Organizational Capacity in Afghanistan and Pakistan.' *Combating Terrorism Center at West Point*, December 2018.

Johnson, Casey Garret. 'The Rise and Stall of the Islamic State in Afghanistan.' *United States Institute of Peace, Special Report 395*, November 2016.

Juergensmeyer, Mark. *Terror in the Mind of God: The Global Rise of Religious Violence*. Berkeley: University of California Press, 2003.

'Jund Al-Khalifa: The IS-Linked Group That Shot into the Spotlight.' *France 24*, September 23, 2014.

Kalyvas, Stathis N. 'The Ontology of 'Political Violence': Action and Identity in Civil Wars.' *Perspectives on Politics* 1, no. 3 (2003): 475–94.

Kamali, Mohammad Hashim. 'Caliphate and Political Jurisprudence in Islam: Historical and Contemporary Perspectives.' *The Muslim World* 106 (2016): 384–403.

Kamolnick, Paul. 'The Egyptian Islamic Group's Critique of Al-Qaeda's Interpretation of Jihad.' *Perspectives on Terrorism* 7, no. 5 (2013): 93–110.

Kanj, Sultan Al. 'Reviewing the Turkey–HTS Relationship.' *Chatham House*, May 2019.

Kazimi, Nibras. 'A Virulent Ideology in Mutation: Zarqawi Upstages Maqdisi.' *Current Trends in Islamist Ideology* 2 (2005): 59–73.

Kendall, Elisabeth. 'Contemporary Jihadi Militancy in Yemen.' *Middle East Institute Policy Paper*, July 2018.

Kendall, Elisebeth. 'The Failing Islamic State Within The Failed State of Yemen.' *Perspectives on Terrorism* 13, no. 1 (2019): 78–87.

Kennedy, Hugh. *The Caliphate*. Penguin Books, 2016.

Kenney, Jeffrey, T. *Muslim Rebels: Kharijites and the Politics of Extremism in Egypt*. Oxford: Oxford University Press, 2006.

Kepel, Gilles. *Fitna: Guerre Au Cœur de l'islam*. Paris: Gallimard, 2004.

———. *Jihad: The Trail of Political Islam*. London: I.B. Tauris, 2006.

———. *Muslim Extremism in Egypt: The Prophet and Pharaoh*. Berkeley: University of California Press, 1985.

Kepel, Gilles, and Jean-Pierre Milelli, eds. *Al Qaeda in Its Own Words*. Boston: Harvard University Press, 2008.

Khaled al-Saud, Abdullah bin. 'The Spiritual Teacher and His Truants: The Influence and Relevance of Abu Mohammad Al-Maqdisi.' *Studies in Conflict and Terrorism* 41, no. 9 (2018): 736–54.

Khattab, Anas Hassan. 'Wrong Terms between the Mujahideen,' July 22, 2017.

Kilani, Feras. 'A Caliph Without a Caliphate: The Biography of ISIS's New Leader,' *Newlines Magazine*, April 15, 2021.

Kozinets, Robert V. *Netnography: Doing Ethnographic Research Online*. London: Sage Publications, 2010.

Krause, Peter. *Rebel Power: Why National Movements Compete, Fight, and Win*. New York: Cornell University Press, 2017.

Kydd, Andrew H., and Barbara F. Walter. 'The Strategies of Terrorism.' *International Security* 31, no. 1 (2006): 49–80.

Lacroix, Stephane. *Awakening Islam: The Politics of Religious Dissent in Contemporary Saudi Arabia*. Cambridge, MA: Harvard University Press, 2011.

Laden, Hamza Bin. 'Usama… The Fighter Against Invaders And The Inciter of Rebellion Against Tyrants.' *As-Sahab Media*, November 7, 2017.

Lahoud, Nelly. 'Beware of the Imitator: Al-Qa'ida through the Lens of Its Confidential Secretary.' *Combating Terrorism Center*, 2012.

———. 'The 'Islamic State' and Al-Qaeda.' In *Jihadism Transformed : Al-Qaeda and Islamic State's Global Battle of Ideas*, edited by Simon Staffell and Akil N. Awan, 21–34. London: Hurst & Company, 2016.

———. *The Jihadis' Path to Self-Destruction*. New York: Columbia University Press, 2010.

Lahoud, Nelly, and Muhammad Al-'Ubaydi. 'The War of Jihadists against Jihadists In Syria.' *CTC Sentinel* 7, no. 3 (2014): 1–6.

Lane, D. S. 'Social and Organizational Differences between the Bolsheviks and Mensheviks, 1903 to 1907.' *Discussion Paper* May (1964): 1–14.

Lauzière, Henri. *The Making of Salafism: Islamic Reform in the Twentieth Century*. New York: Columbia University Press, 2016.

Lav, Daniel. *Radical Islam and the Revival of Medieval Theology*. Cambridge: Cambridge University Press, 2012.

Law, Daniel J. 'Jihadists and Jurispredents: The 'Revisions' Literature of Sayyid Imam and Al-Gama'a Al-Islamiyya.' In *Political Islam from Muhammad to Ahmadinejad: Defenders, Detractors, and Definitions*, edited by Joseph Morrison Skelly, 105–46. Santa Barbara: Praeger, 2009.

Lia, Brynjar. *Architect of Global Jihad: The Life of Al Qaeda Strategist Abu Musab Al-Suri*. London: Hurst & Company, 2008.

———. 'Jihadi Strategists and Doctrinarians.' In *Self Inflicted Wounds: Debates and Divisions within Al Qa'ida and Its Periphery*, edited by Assaf Moghadam and Brian Fishman, 100–31. Combating Terrorism Center at West Point, 2010.

Lia, Brynjar, and Thomas Hegghammer. 'Jihadi Strategic Studies: The Alleged Al Qaida Policy Study Preceding the Madrid Bombings.' *Studies in Conflict & Terrorism* 27, no. 5 (September 2004): 355–75.

Liang, Christina Schori. 'Cyber Jihad: Understanding and Countering Islamic State Propaganda.' *GCSP Policy Paper* 2 (2015).

'limadha qatala al-sheikh abu abd al-aziz al-qatari/al-iraqi/al-urduni/al-filastini [Why Did the Sheikh Abu Abd Al-Azaz Al-Qatari/Al-Iraqi/Al-Urduni/Al-Filastini Die],' March 26, 2014.

Lister, Charles. 'Al-Qa'ida Plays a Long Game in Syria.' *CTC Sentinel* 8, no. 9 (2015).

———. 'Al-Qaeda versus ISIS: Competing Jihadist Brands in the Middle East.' *Middle East Institute*, November 2017.

———. 'Jihadi Rivalry: The Islamic State Challenges Al-Qaida.' Brookings Doha Center, 2016.

———. 'The Dawn of Mass Jihad: Success in Syria Fuels Al-Qai'da's Evolution.' *CTC Sentinel* 9, no. 9 (2016).

———. *The Syrian Jihad: Al-Qaeda, the Islamic State and the Evolution of an Insurgency*. London: Hurst Publishers, 2015.

Lounnas, Djallil. 'Jihadist Groups in North Africa and the Sahel: Between Disintegration, Reconfiguration and Resilience.' *MENARA Working Papers* 16 (2018).

Lund, Aron. 'Pushing Back Against the Islamic State of Iraq and the Levant: The Islamic Front.' *Carnegie Middle East Center*, January 8, 2014.

Macklin, Graham, and Joel Busher. 'The Missing Spirals of Violence: Four Waves of Movement – Countermovement Contest in Post-War Britain.' *Behavioral Sciences of Terrorism and Political Aggression* 7, no. 1 (2015): 1–16.

Maher, Shiraz. *Salafi–Jihadism: The History of an Idea*. London: Hurst & Company, 2016.

Mandaville, Peter. 'Globalization and the Politics of Religious Knowledge: Pluralizing Authority in the Muslim World.' *Theory, Culture & Society* 24, no. 2 (2007): 101–15.

Mansour, Mullah. 'Untitled Letter to Abu Bakr Al-Baghdadi,' June 16, 2015.

Martinez, Luis. *The Algerian Civil War*. New York: Columbia University Press, 2000.

Maruf, Harun. 'In Somalia, Businesses Face 'Taxation' by Militants.' *VOA News*, December 3, 2018.

Maruf, Harun, and Dan Joseph. *Inside Al-Shabaab: The Secret History of Al-Qaeda's Most Powerful Ally*. Bloomington: Indiana University Press, 2018.

McCants, Will. 'How Zawahiri Lost Al Qaeda.' *Foreign Affairs*, November 19, 2013.

———. 'The Polarizing Effect of Islamic State Aggression on the Global Jihadist Movement.' *CTC Sentinel* 9, no. 7 (2016): 20–23.

McCants, William. *The ISIS Apocalypse: The History, Strategy, and Doomsday Vision of the Islamic State*. New York: St. Martin's Press, 2015.

McCants, William F. *The ISIS Apocalypse: The History, Strategy, and Doomsday Vision of the Islamic State*. New York: St. Martin's Press, 2015.

MEMRI. 'Losing Faith In Al-Baghdadi – Part 2: 'Extremists' Explain Why They Left ISIS,' April 15, 2019.

Mendelsohn, Barak. *Jihadism Constrained: The Limits of Transnational Jihadism and What It Means for Counterterrorism*. London: Rowman & Littlefield Publishers, Inc, 2018.

———. *The Al-Qaeda Franchise : The Expansion of Al-Qaeda and Its Consequences*. New York: Oxford University Press, 2016.

———. 'The Battle for Algeria: Explaining Fratricide among Armed Nonstate Actors.' *Studies in Conflict and Terrorism*, 2019.

Michels, Robert. *Political Parties: A Sociological Study of the Oligarchical Tendencies of Modern Democracy*. New York: Hearst's International Library Co, 1915.

Milton, Daniel. 'Down, but Not Out: An Updated Examination of the Islamic State's Visual Propaganda.' *Combating Terrorism Center at West Point*, July 2018.

Moghadam, Assaf. *Nexus of Global Jihad : Understanding Cooperation among Terrorist Actors*. New York: Columbia University Press, 2017.

Moghadam, Assaf, and Brian Fishman, eds. *Self Inflicted Wounds: Debates and Divisions within Al Qa'ida and Its Periphery*. West Point: CTC Harmony Project, 2010.

Morrison, John. *Origins and Rise of Dissident Irish Republicanism: The Role and Impact of Organizational Splits*. London: Bloomsbury, 2013.

Moussa, Jenan, and Harald Doornbos. 'Present at the Creation.' *Foreign Policy*, August 16, 2016.

———. 'The Greatest Divorce in the Jihadi World.' *Foreign Policy*, August 18, 2016.

Muhammad, Abdullah bin. 'The Reality of the Penetration of the Islamic State of Iraq's Leadership,' February 17, 2013.

Naji, Abu Bakr. *The Management of Savagery*. [Translation by Will McCants 2006], 2004.

Nasr, Wassim. 'ISIS in Africa: The End of the "Sahel Exception."' *Center for Global Policy*, June 2020.

Nasrullah, Fulan. 'Strategic Thinking Behind Ongoing Insurgent Offensive Operations in Northeast Nigeria: An Analysis.' *Conflict Studies and Analysis Project*, August 2018.

Novenario, Celine Marie I. 'Differentiating Al Qaeda and the Islamic State Through Strategies Publicized in Jihadist Magazines.' *Studies in Conflict & Terrorism* 39, no. 11 (2016): 953–67.

O'Neill, Bard E. *Insurgency & Terrorism: Inside Modern Revolutionary Warfare*. Virginia: Potomac Books, 1990.

Orton, Kyle. 'How Saddam Hussein Gave Us ISIS.' *The New York Times*, December 23, 2015.

Osman, Borhan. 'Rallying Around the White Flag: Taleban Embrace an Assertive Identity.' *Afghanistan Analysts Network*, February 1, 2017.

———. 'The Battle for Mamand: ISKP under Strain, but Not yet Defeated.' *Afghanistan Analysts Network*, May 23, 2017.

———. 'The Islamic State in 'Khorasan': How It Began and Where It Stands Now in Nangarhar.' *Afghanistan Analysts Network*, July 27, 2016.

———. 'With an Active Cell in Kabul, ISKP Tries to Bring Sectarianism to the Afghan War.' *Afghanistan Analysts Network*, October 19, 2016.

Ostaeyen, PIeter Van, and Guy Van Vlierden. 'The Role of Belgian Fighters in the Jihadification of the Syrian War: From Plotting Early in 2011 to the Paris and Brussels Attacks,' 2017.

Pantucci, Raffaello, and A.R. Sayyid. 'Foreign Fighters in Somalia and Al-Shabaab's Internal Purge.' *Terrorism Monitor* 11, no. 22 (2013).

Pearlman, Wendy, and Kathleen Gallagher Cunningham. 'Nonstate Actors, Fragmentation, and Conflict Processes.' *Journal of Conflict Resolution* 56, no. 1 (2012): 3–15.

Peters, Rudolph. *Jihad: A History in Documents*. Princeton: Markus Wiener Publishers, 2016.

Phillips, Andrew. 'How Al Qaeda Lost Iraq.' *Australian Journal of International Affairs* 63, no. 1 (2009): 64–84.

Pool, Jeffrey. 'Zarqawi's Pledge of Allegiance to Al-Qaeda: From Mu'askar Al-Battar, Issue 21.' *Jamestown Terrorism Monitor* 2, no. 24 (December 16, 2004).

Porta, Donatella Della. *Clandestine Political Violence*. New York: Cambridge University Press, 2013.

———. *Social Movements, Political Violence, and the State: A Comparative Analysis of Italy and Germany*. Cambridge: Cambridge University Press, 1995.

Porta, Donatella Della, and Mario Diani. *Social Movements: An Introduction*. 2. edition. Oxford: Blackwell Publishing, 2006.

Porter, Geoff. 'Terrorist Outbidding: The In Amenas Attack.' *CTC Sentinel* 8, no. 5 (2015): 14–17.

Prucha, Nico. 'IS and the Jihadist Information Highway – Projecting Influence and Religious Identity via Telegram.' *Perspectives on Terrorism* 10, no. 6 (2016): 48–58.

Qutb, Sayyid. *Milestones*, 1964.

Rashwan, Diaa. 'Struggle within the Ranks.' *Al Ahram Weekly*, November 1998. http://weekly.ahram.org.eg/Archive/1998/402/op5.htm.

Redondo, Raúl. 'Growing Tension in Idlib among Jihadist Factions.' *Atalayar*, June 26, 2020.

Reuter, Christoph. 'The Terror Strategist: Secret Files Reveal the Structure of Islamic State.' *Der Spiegel*, April 18, 2015. http://www.spiegel.de/international/world/islamic-state-files-show-structure-of-islamist-terror-group-a-1029274.html.

Rodgers, Dennis. 'Bróderes in Arms: Gangs and the Socialization of Violence in Nicaragua.' *Journal of Peace Research* 54, no. 5 (2017): 648–60.

Roggio, Bill. 'Omar Hammami's Personal Dispute with Shabaab.' *Long War Journal*, January 6, 2013.

Roggio, Bill, Daveed Gartenstein-Ross, and Tony Badran. 'Intercepted Letters from Al-Qaeda Leaders Shed Light on State of Network in Iraq.' *Long War Journal*, September 12, 2008.

Rosenblatt, Nate. 'All Jihad Is Local: What ISIS' Files Tell Us about Its Fighters.' *New America*, July 2016.

Ross, Daveed Gartenstein, Jason Fritz, and Bridget Moreng. 'Islamic State vs. Al-Qaeda: Strategic Dimensions of a Patricidal Conflict,' 2015.

Roy, Olivier. *Globalized Islam: The Search for a New Ummah*. New York: Columbia University Press, 2004.

———. *Jihad and Death: The Global Appeal of Islamic State*. London: Hurst & Company, 2017.

———. *The Failure of Political Islam*. Cambridge: Harvard University Press, 1994.

———. 'The Transformation of the Arab World.' *Journal of Democracy* 23, no. 3 (2012): 5–18.

Sassoon, Joseph. *Saddam Hussein's Ba'th Party: Inside an Authoritarian Regime*. New York: Cambridge University Press, 2012.

Scahill, Jeremy. 'The Purge: How Somalia's Al Shabaab Turned Against Its Own Foreign Fighters.' *The Intercept*, May 19, 2015.

Schmitt, Eric. 'U.S. Sees Rising Threat in the West From Qaeda Branch in Syria.' *New York Times*, September 29, 2019.

Scott-Clark, Cathy, and Adrian Levy. *The Exile: The Stunning Inside Story of Osama Bin Laden and Al Qaeda in Flight*. New York: Bloomsbury, 2017.

Senate Select Committee on Intelligence. 'Committee Study of the Central Intelligence Agency's Detention and Interrogation Program.' *United States Senate*, December 13, 2012.

———. 'Committee Study of the Central Intelligence Agency's Detention and Interrogation Program,' 2014.

Shehada, Marwan. 'Weakening Al-Qaeda: Literature Review Challenges Its Authority.' *Arab Insights* 2, no. 6 (2009).

Shekau, Abu Bakr. 'Untitled audio statement.' *Media Foundation of Jama'at Ahl Al-Sunnah Li-l-Dawa Wa-l-Jihad*, August 3, 2016.

Simpson, Adam. 'The 'Islamic State' Challenges Al-Qaeda in Yemen.' *International Institute for Middle East and Balkan Studies*, December 18, 2016.

Sly, Liz. 'The Hidden Hand behind the Islamic State Militants? Saddam Hussein's.' *The Washington Post*, April 5, 2015.

Smith, Dennis. *The Rise of Historical Sociology*. Philadelphia: Temple University Press, 1991.

Sons of Abu Yusuf al-Barnawi. 'Khadh' Al-Waram Min Al-Khawarij Al-Shikawiyya Bi-Bay'a Ahl Al-Karam [Cutting Out the Tumor of Shekau's Khawarij Through Pledging Allegiance to the People of Benevolence].' *Al-Haqa'iq Dawlat Al-Khilafa Al-Islamiyya*, June 2018.

Soufan, Ali. 'Next in Line to Lead Al-Qa'ida: A Profile of Abu Muhammad Al-Masri.' *CTC Sentinel* 12, no. 10 (2019).

Speckhard, Anne, and Ahmet S. Yayla. 'The ISIS Emni: Origins and Inner Workings of ISIS's Intelligence Apparatus.' *Perspectives on Terrorism* 11, no. 1 (2017).

Staffell, Simon, and Akil N. Awan, eds. *Jihadism Transformed : Al-Qaeda and Islamic State's Global Battle of Ideas*. London: Hurst & Company, 2016.

Staniland, Paul. 'Between a Rock and a Hard Place: Insurgent Fratricide, Ethnic Defection, and the Rise of pro-State Paramilitaries.' *Journal of Conflict Resolution* 56, no. 1 (2012): 16–40.

———. 'Explaining Cohesion, Fragmentation, and Control in Insurgent Groups.' Massachusetts Institute of Technology, 2010.

'Statement of Noor Uthman Muhammed.' *Military Commissions Trial Judiciary Guantanamo Bay*, February 17, 2011.

Steinberg, Guido. 'Ahrar Al-Sham: The "Syrian Taliban."' *SWP Comments*, May 27, 2016.

Stenersen, Anne. *Al-Qaida in Afghanistan*. Cambridge: Cambridge University Press, 2018.

———. 'Jihadism after the ' Caliphate ': Towards a New Typology.' *British Journal of Middle Eastern Studies*, 2018, 1–20.

Stenersen, Anne, and Phillipp Holtmann. 'The Three Functions of UBL's 'Greater Pledge' to Mullah Omar (2001–2006–2014).' *Jihadology*, January 8, 2015.

Stern, Jessica, and J.M. Berger. *ISIS: The State of Terror*. London: William Collins, 2015.

Tawil, Camille. *Brothers in Arms. The Story of Al-Qaida and the Arab Jihadists*. London, England: SAQI, 2010.

Tehreek-e-Taliban. 'Operation Manual for Mujahideen of Tehreek-e-Taliban Pakistan.' *Umar Media*, September 2018.

'The 9/11 Commission Report,' 2004. https://www.9-11commission.gov/report/911 Report.pdf.

Tilly, Charles. *As Sociology Meets History*. New York: Academic Press, 1981.

———. 'Mechanisms in Political Processes.' *Annual Review of Political Science* 4 (2001): 21–41.

Tonnessen, Truls Hallberg. 'Heirs of Zarqawi or Saddam ? The Relationship between Al-Qaida in Iraq and the Islamic State.' *Perspectives on Terrorism* 9, no. 4 (2015): 48–60.

Turner, John. 'Strategic Differences: Al Qaeda's Split with the Islamic State of Iraq and Al-Sham.' *Small Wars and Insurgencies*. Taylor & Francis, 2015.

Ulbricht, Bailey. 'Justifying Relations with an Apostate Suring a Jihad: A Salafi–Jihadist Group's Reltions with Turkey in Syria.' *Middle East Institute*, March 2019.

Umar, Asim. 'And On That Day the Believers Will Rejoice,' June 13, 2019.

Uthman ibn 'Abd al-Rahman al-Tamimi. 'i'lam al-anam bi-milad dawlat al-islam [Informing the People of the Birth of the Islamic State].' *Al-Furqan Media Foundation*, 2007.

'Various Admin Documents and Questions.' *AFGP-2002-801138*, 2000.

Wagemakers, J. 'Protecting Jihad: The Sharia Council of the Minbar Al-Tawhid Wa-l-Jihad.' *Middle East Policy* CVIII, no. 2 (2011): 148–62.

Wagemakers, Joas. *A Quietist Jihadi: The Ideology and Influence of Abu Muhammad Al-Maqdisi*. Cambridge: Cambridge University Press, 2012.

———. 'An Inquiry into Ignorance: A Jihadi–Salafi Debate on Jahl as an Obstacle to Takfir.' In *The Transmission and Dynamics of the Textual Sources of Islam*, edited by Nicolet Boekhoff-van der Voort, Kees Versteegh, and Joas Wagemakers. Brill, 2011.

———. 'Between Purity and Pragmatism? Abu Basir Al-Tartusi's Nuanced Radicalism.' In *Jihadism and Terrorism: Jihadi Thought and Ideology*, edited by Rüdiger Lohlker and Tamara Abu-Hamdeh, 16–36. Logos Verlag, 2014.

———. 'Contesting Religious Authority in Jordanian Salafi Networks.' *Perseverance of Terrorism: Focus on Leaders* 117 (2014): 111–25.

———. 'Jihadi–Salafism in Jordan and the Syrian Conflict: Divisions Overcome Unity.' *Studies in Conflict & Terrorism*, 2017, 1–22.

———. 'Reclaiming Scholarly Authority: Abu Muhammad Al-Maqdisi's Critique of Jihadi Practices.' *Studies in Conflict & Terrorism* 34, no. 7 (2011): 523–39.

———. 'Revisiting Wiktorowicz.' In *Salafism After the Arab Awakening*, edited by Francesco Cavatorta and Fabio Merone, 7–24. London: Oxford University Press, 2017.

———. *Salafism in Jordan: Political Islam in a Quietist Community*. New York: Cambridge University Press, 2016.

———. '"Seceders" and "Postponers"? An Analysis of the 'Khawarij' and 'Murji'a' Labels in Polemical Debates between Quietist and Jihadi–Salafis.' In *Contextualising Jihadi Thought*, edited by Deol Jeevan and Zaheer Kazmi, 145–64. London: Hurst & Company, 2012.

———. 'The Transformation of a Radical Concept: Al-Wala' Wa-l-Bara' in the Ideology of Abu Muhammad Al-Maqdisi.' In *Global Salafism: Islam's New Religious Movement*, 81–106. London: Hurst & Company, 2009.

———. 'What Should an Islamic State Look Like? Jihadi-Salafi Debates on the War in Syria.' *The Muslim World* 106, no. July (2016): 501–22.

Warner, Jason, and Caleb Weiss. 'A Legitimate Challenger? Assessing the Rivalry between Al-Shabaab and the Islamic State in Somalia.' *CTC Sentinel* 10, no. 10 (2017).

Watts, Clint. 'Deciphering Competition Between Al-Qa'ida and the Islamic State.' *CTC Sentinel* 9, no. 7 (2016): 1–6.

Weisfuse, Ari. 'Negotiating Oblivion. Sayf Al 'Adl: Al Qaeda's Top Operative.' Brandeis University, 2014.

Weiss, Caleb. 'Reigniting the Rivalry: The Islamic State in Somalia vs. Al-Shabaab.' *CTC Sentinel* 12, no. 4 (2019).

Weiss, Caleb, and Héni Nsaibia. 'The End of the Sahelian Anomaly: How the Global Conflict between the Islamic State and Al-Qa'ida Finally Came to West Africa.' *CTC Sentinel* 13, no. 7 (2020).

Weiss, Michael, and Hassan Hassan. *ISIS: Inside the Army of Terror*. New York: Regan Arts., 2015.

'What Is the Khorasan Group?' *BBC*, September 24, 2014.

'What next for Syria's Idlib?' *France 24*, January 11, 2019.

Whiteside, Craig. 'A Pedigree of Terror: The Myth of the Ba'athist Influence in the Islamic State Movement.' *Perspectives on Terrorism* 11, no. 3 (2017).

———. 'Nine Bullets for the Traitors, One for the Enemy: The Slogans and Strategy behind the Islamic State's Campaign to Defeat the Sunni Awakening (2006–2017).' *ICCT Research Paper*, September 2018.

Wiktorowicz, Quintan. 'Anatomy of the Salafi Movement.' *Studies in Conflict & Terrorism* 29, no. 3 (May 2006): 207–39.

———. 'Framing Jihad: Intramovement Framing Contests and Al-Qaeda's Struggle for Sacred Authority.' *International Review of Social History* 49, no. S12 (December 2004): 159–77.

———. *Radical Islam Rising: Muslim Extremism in the West*. Oxford: Rowman & Littlefield Publishers, Inc, 2005.

Winter, Charlie. 'The Virtual "Caliphate": Understanding Islamic State's Propaganda Strategy.' *Quilliam*, 2015.

Wood, Elisabeth Jean. 'Rape as a Practice of War: Toward a Typology of Political Violence.' *Politics & Society*, 2018, 1–25.

Wright, Lawrence. *The Looming Tower : Al Qaeda and the Road to 9/11*. New York: Vintage Books, 2006.

———. 'The Rebellion Within.' *The New Yorker*, May 23, 2008.

Zald, Mayer N, and John D. McCarthy. 'Social Movement Industries: Competition and Cooperation Among Movement Organizations.' *CRSO Working Paper 201*, 1979, 1–32.

Zald, Mayer N, and Bert Useem. 'Movement and Countermovement: Loosely Coupled Conflict.' *CRSO Working Paper 302*, 1983, 1–31.

Zaman, Muhammad Qasim. *Modern Islamic Thought in a Radical Age: Religious Authority and Internal Criticism*. New York: Cambridge University Press, 2012.

———. *The Ulama in Contemporary Islam: Custodians of Change*. Princeton: Princeton University Press, 2007.

Zaydan, Umar Mahdi. 'al-naqd li-qawl man ja'ala l-khilafa al-islamiyya min din al-rafd [Denounce the Saying That Made the Caliphate from the Religion of Refusal],' November 5, 2013.

Zelin, Aaron Y. 'Al-Farida Al-Gha'iba and Al-Sadat's Assassination, a 30 Year Retrospective.' *International Journal for Arab Studies* 3, no. 2 (2012).

———. 'The Islamic State's First Colony in Libya.' *Washington Institute for Near East Studies*, October 2014.

———. 'The Islamic State's Territorial Methodology.' *The Washington Institute for Near East Policy, Research Note No. 29*, January 2016.

———. 'The Rise and Decline of Ansar Al-Sharia in Libya.' *Hudson Institute's Current Trends in Islamist Ideology*, April 2015.

———. 'The War between ISIS and Al-Qaeda for Supremacy of the Global Jihadist Movement.' *Washington Institute for Near East Policy*, June 2014.

———. 'Ultra Extremism Among Tunisian Jihadis Within The Islamic State.' *Jihadica*, February 2020.

Zenn, Jacob. 'Boko Haram's Conquest for the Caliphate: How Al Qaeda Helped Islamic State Acquire Territory.' *Studies in Conflict & Terrorism*, 2018, 1–34.

———. 'Boko Haram's Factional Feuds: Internal Extremism and External Interventions.' *Terrorism and Political Violence*, 2019, 1–33.

———. 'Is Boko Haram's Notorious Leader about to Return from the Dead Again?' *African Arguments*, December 10, 2018.

———. 'Negotiating With Jihadists in the Sahel and Nigeria.' *Lawfare*, June 14, 2020.

———. 'The Islamic State's Provinces on the Peripheries: Juxtaposing the Pledges from Boko Haram in Nigeria and Abu Sayyaf and Maute Group in the Philippines.' *Perspectives on Terrorism* 13, no. 1 (2019).

Zirakzadeh, Cyrus Ernesto. 'From Revolutionary Dreams to Organizational Fragmentation: Disputes over Violence within ETA and Sendero Luminoso.' *Terrorism and Political Violence* 14, no. 4 (2002): 66–92.

# INDEX

Note: Page numbers followed by '*n*' refer to notes, '*t*' refer to tables, '*f*' refer to figures